Roasting meat

As all cuts of meat can vary, these times are intended as a general guide. When calculating timings, add an extra 450g (1lb) of weight to your joint if it weighs less than 1.35kg (3lb). Be sure to preheat the oven before cooking your meat, use a meat thermometer (inserted into the thickest part of the cut, away from any bones) for an accurate internal temperature, and always allow the meat to rest for 15-30 minutes before carving.

MEAT		OVEN TEMPERATURE	COOKING TIME	INTERNAL TEMPERATURE
Beef	Rare	180°C (350°F/Gas 4)	15 mins per 450g (1lb)	60°C (140°F)
	Medium	180°C (350°F/Gas 4)	20 mins per 450g (1lb)	70°C (160°F)
	Well-done	180°C (350°F/Gas 4)	25 mins per 450g (1lb)	80°C (175°F)
Pork	Well-done	180°C (350°F/Gas 4)	25 mins per 450g (1lb)	80°C (175°F)
Lamb	Medium	180°C (350°F/Gas 4)	20 mins per 450g (1lb)	70°C (160°F)
	Well-done	180°C (350°F/Gas 4)	25 mins per 450g (1lb)	80°C (175°F)

Roasting poultry

Use these times as a guide, bearing in mind the size and weight of each bird vary. Be sure to preheat the oven before cooking your bird(s), and always check that the bird is fully cooked before serving.

MEAT		OVEN TEMPERATURE	COOKING TIME
Poussin		190°C (375°F/Gas 5)	12 mins per 450g (1lb) plus 12 mins
Chicken		200°C (400°F/Gas 6)	20 mins per 450g (1lb) plus 20 mins
Duck		180°C (350°F/Gas 4)	20 mins per 450g (1lb) plus 20 mins
Goose		180°C (350°F/Gas 4)	20 mins per 450g (1lb) plus 20 mins
Pheasant		200°C (400°F/Gas 6)	50 mins total cooking
Turkey	3.5-4.5kg (7-9lb)	190°C (375°F/Gas 5)	2½-3 hrs total cooking
	5-6kg (10-12lb)	190°C (375°F/Gas 5)	3½-4 hrs total cooking
	6.5-8.5kg (13-17lb)	190°C (375°F/Gas 5)	4½-5 hrs total cooking

cook express

cook express

Editor-in-Chief **Heather Whinney**

LONDON, NEW YORK, MELBOURNE,
MUNICH, AND DELHI

Written by Heather Whinney

Additional recipe contributors
Guy Mirabella
Kate Titford

Photography William Reavell,
William Shaw, Jon Whitaker

Project Editor Laura Nickoll
Art Editor Anne Fisher
Managing Editor Dawn Henderson
Managing Art Editor Christine Keilty
Senior Jacket Creative Nicola Powling
Production Editor Ben Marcus
Production Controller Alice Holloway
CTS Sonia Charbonnier

Dorling Kindersley (India)
Editor Alicia Ingty
Designer Neha Ahuja
Design Manager Romi Chakraborty
Editorial Manager Glenda Fernandes
DTP Designer Tarun Sharma
DTP Coordinator Balwant Singh
Head of Publishing Aparna Sharma

This edition published in
Great Britain in 2009
by Dorling Kindersley Limited
80 Strand, London, WC2R 0RL

A Penguin Company

2 4 6 8 10 9 7 5 3 1

A CIP catalogue record for this book is
available from the British Library.

ISBN 978-1-4053-4132-5

Printed in China by Toppan

See our complete catalogue at
www.dk.com

CONTENTS

INTRODUCTION

My obsession started many years ago – cookery books by the side of bed, and stacked high on heaving shelves. I constantly daydreamed about the next meal, and the need to be stirring a big pot of something on the hob. I'm not sure this constitutes being a "foodie" or whether it just means I am plain greedy! However, it certainly filled me with enough enthusiasm, 20 years ago, to embark upon a career in food.

I have always enjoyed cooking from scratch. Making something to eat just seems a more natural process than opening a packet of food that someone else has made, and waiting for the microwave to "ping". That said, I have never enjoyed cooking complicated or time-consuming meals, so I am certainly not about to start writing about them. All my culinary training has come from bringing up two children and being a home economist, not a chef, so complicated techniques and long ingredient lists are not really my thing. I love eating at restaurants, but consider myself a home cook. If I were to describe my cooking, I would say it is "no frills". My food is simple but hearty, and the recipes in the book reflect this.

I worked for many years on women's magazines as a food editor, which has given me precious insight into what people really want from recipes. Above all, they want simple and straightforward steps, and familiar ingredients. Confident and adventerous cooks want new ideas and inspiration, and beginners want clear and concise recipes to boost their confidence in the kitchen. This book is for the inexperienced cook to learn from, and the experienced cook to learn more from, and for both to enjoy!

This book was an ambitious undertaking, as it had to be many things – practical and inspirational, simple but instructive, easy yet creative and, most importantly, full of quick meals. It certainly delivers this, and more. It guides you effortlessly through hundreds of recipes that are easy to make, and all take 30 minutes or less of your full attention. Using familiar ingredients, it covers all bases, from Speedy Suppers – meals you can cook when you come home from work – to All-in-One Roasts, perfect for the weekend cook. For those of us who don't like the heat of the kitchen, the No Cook chapter has delicious flavours running through it, and for those of you who crave pudding, Cakes and Bakes, and Indulgent Puddings, will more than satisfy your sweet tooth.

The Everyday section has hundreds of recipes to feed the family, and for entertaining, there is the second section, Food for Friends. I hope you will dip in and out of chapters in both sections, and mix and match – the Recipe Choosers at the start will help you choose, as will the Menu Planners. Each chapter is full of time-saving tips and shortcuts, all of which aim to minimize stress and time in the kitchen.

Making time to cook isn't all about time spent in the kitchen. It's also about shopping and planning. The way we shop affects the way we eat, and the secret is in the planning. This needn't be anything more than a scribbled note of meals for the week, and having a budget.

I have learnt the art of efficient shopping over the years. Making the right choice at the butcher's, greengrocer's, farmers' market, and supermarket all helps to ease the pressure of providing meals from scratch every day. Buying organic vegetables and good-quality fish and meat might be expensive, but you can cancel out this extra cost by shopping seasonally, and buying cheaper (often tastier) cuts of meat. In my experience, an hour spent at the market on a Saturday morning is far more enjoyable and useful than a late night trolley-dash at the supermarket. That said, supermarket food and storecupboard goods are invaluable for busy people, so keep your storecupboard well stocked at all times. You can then concentrate on buying fresh foods; the main ingredients of most of the recipes in this book. If your fridge is bare, however, a well-stocked cupboard can be a lifesaver. The storecupboard chapter makes good use of all those packets, cans, and jars, offering meal solutions for when there simply isn't time to shop.

I hope this book becomes a trusty and reliable cookery book in your kitchen – one that you will turn to again and again, whether to check the quantities for a pancake, whip up a quick supper, or revisit a favourite chocolate cake. With over 700 foolproof tried-and-tested recipes, this book is a bumper selection of quick and easy meals that cater for any palate and any occasion. Most importantly, it's the food that my family, friends and I really love to eat!

Heather Whinney

USEFUL INFORMATION

These charts and guidelines are here to help you in the kitchen, with measurements, ingredients information, and equipment tips, and guide to the symbols that accompany every recipe in the book. All the recipes have been tested on a gas ring hob and an electric oven – (for a fan oven, reduce the temperature by at least 10°C). If in doubt about how accurate your oven is, it may be wise to invest in an oven thermometer.

Linear measures

3mm (⅛in)	2.5cm (1in)	10cm (4in)	20cm (8in)	30cm (12in)
5mm (¼in)	5cm (2in)	12cm (5in)	23cm (9in)	46cm (18in)
1cm (½in)	6cm (2½in)	15cm (6in)	25cm (10in)	50cm (20in)
2cm (¾in)	7.5cm (3in)	18cm (7in)	28cm (11in)	61cm (24in)
				77cm (30in)

Weights

10g (¼oz)	85g (3oz)	250g (9oz)	750g (1lb 10oz)	2kg (4½lb)
15g (½oz)	100g (3½oz)	300g (10oz)	800g (1¾lb)	2.25kg (5lb)
20g (¾oz)	115g (4oz)	350g (12oz)	900g (2lb)	2.5kg (5½lb)
25g (scant 1oz)	125g (4½oz)	400g (14oz)	1kg (2¼lb)	2.7kg (6lb)
30g (1oz)	140g (5oz)	450g (1lb)	1.1kg (2½lb)	3kg (6½lb)
45g (1½oz)	150g (5½oz)	500g (1lb 2oz)	1.25kg (2¾lb)	
50g (1¾oz)	175g (6oz)	550g (1¼lb)	1.35kg (3lb)	
60g (2oz)	200g (7oz)	600g (1lb 5oz)	1.5kg (3lb 3oz)	
75g (2½oz)	225g (8oz)	675g (1½lb)	1.8kg (4lb)	

Volume measures

1 tsp	75ml (2½fl oz)	240ml (8fl oz)	500ml (16fl oz)	1.4 litres (2½ pints)
2 tsp	90ml (3fl oz)	250ml (9fl oz)	600ml (1 pint)	1.5 litres (2¾ pints)
1 tbsp (which is	100ml (3½ fl oz)	300ml (10fl oz)	750ml (1¼ pints)	1.7 litres (3 pints)
equivalent to 3 tsp)	120ml (4fl oz)	350ml (12fl oz)	900ml (1½ pints)	2 litres (3½ pints)
2 tbsp	150ml (5fl oz)	400ml (14fl oz)	1 litre (1¾ pints)	3 litres (5¼ pints)
3 tbsp	200ml (7fl oz)	450ml (15fl oz)	1.2 litres (2 pints)	
4 tbsp or 60ml (2fl oz)				

Oven temperatures

130°C (250°F/Gas ½)	190°C (375°F/Gas 5)	Gas mark ¼–½ – very cool oven
140°C (275°F/Gas 1)	200°C (400°F/Gas 6)	Gas mark 3 – low oven
150°C (300°F/Gas 2)	220°C (425°F/Gas 7)	Gas mark 1–2 – very low oven
160°C (325°F/Gas 3)	230°C (450°F/Gas 8)	Gas mark 4–5 – moderate oven
180°C (350°F/Gas 4)	240°C (475°F/Gas 9)	Gas mark 6–7 – hot oven
		Gas mark 8–9 – very hot oven

Measurements

- Always use the measurements stated, especially when baking – a few extra pinches of spice, herbs, or seasoning in a stew is down to personal taste, but a few extra pinches of something in a cake could end up in failure.
- Always use measuring spoons. The recipes refer to a level spoon, unless otherwise stated.
- Use a measuring jug for liquids, and take the measurement looking at it from eye level.
- Never mix metric and imperial.
- A good old fashioned pair of balancing scales with weights are the most accurate, will last for ever, and won't suddenly run out of battery!
- There are so many variables in cooking, from the intensity of the heat to the type of pan used, so certain recipes may take less time or longer. All recipes have been tested, and the cooking times given are as accurate as possible, but learn to rely on your instincts for doneness, and check as you go.

Ingredients

Eggs
Use large eggs, which weigh 65–75g (2¼–2½oz) unless otherwise stated, and choose free-range where possible. If preparing a recipe using raw eggs, make sure they are really fresh. It is advisable not to serve raw eggs to children or the elderly.

Ingredients
Use humanely reared free-range meats if you can and always use free-range chicken – the finished dish will taste far better and you will have made an ethical decision about the life of an animal or bird. Use unrefined sugars if you can as these have not been chemically treated.

Seasoning
This brings out the flavour of the food and is an important part of cooking. Use sea salt if you can as this is more natural and tastes so much better. Season at the beginning of cooking, then taste at the end and correct the seasoning. You must keep tasting as you cook, so you can adjust and perfect the flavour of your food.

Equipment

A small selection of good-quality basic equipment makes life so much easier, and cooking so much more pleasurable.

Pots and pans
- A few heavy-based pans, which conduct heat well.
- A non-stick frying pan, a small one for omelettes, and a large one for pan-frying.
- A heavy cast-iron pan for cooking casseroles and stews. They need to retain heat well.

Knives
- A large cook's knife.
- A small vegetable knife.
- A sharp vegetable peeler, such as the swivel-head style, will reduce preparation time by half.

Thick wooden chopping board
For fruit and vegetable food preparation.

Plastic board for meat and fish.

Hygiene in the kitchen
Food poisoning occurs when food has been contaminated by bacteria. This can be easily avoided by taking a little care in the kitchen. Wash your hands before and after handling foods, and thoroughly clean boards, knives, and utensils used in the preparation of raw meat and fish before using them again.

A guide to symbols

Special equipment and essential marinating or chilling times are listed at the top of the recipe, so you start a recipe armed with all the information you need.

 Prep time – this is an average time, as some people chop and peel far quicker than others, but it's a pretty good guide.

 Cook time – this is as accurate as possible, but many variable factors are involved, so check your food just before the cook time is up.

 Indicates a dish, or part of a dish, can be frozen.

 Indicates a dish is "healthy" – either low in fat and saturated fat, or low GI. Healthy recipes are not high in salt, sugar, or saturated fat.

RECIPE CHOOSERS

An instant visual reference to a selection of super-fast recipes for meat, fish, vegetarian dishes, and desserts – 15 minutes from start to finish, or 30 minutes from start to finish, including both preparation and cooking time.

MEAT IN UNDER 15 MINUTES

Beef with beetroot and spinach
p241

PREP 15 MINS

Smoked chicken salad with papaya fruit salsa p45

PREP 15 MINS

The perfect steak
p124

PREP 2 MINS COOK 10 MINS

Quesadilla with ham, gherkin, and smoked cheese p191

PREP 5 MINS COOK 5 MINS

Caesar salad
p47

PREP 15 MINS

Sliced beef and rocket salad with green olive and raisin salsa p41

PREP 15 MINS

Chicken salad with carrot and apple relish p225

PREP 15 MINS

Chicken with aduki beans and herbs p53

PREP 10 MINS

Thai-style beef salad
p240

PREP 15 MINS

MEAT IN UNDER 30 MINUTES: STARTERS

Chargrilled asparagus and pancetta
p356

PREP 15 MINS COOK 5 MINS

Lemon and soy skewered chicken with hot dipping sauce p114

PREP 15 MINS COOK 10 MINS

Lamb and mint burgers
p60

PREP 10 MINS COOK 20 MINS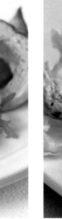

Chicken satay
p361

PREP 15 MINS COOK 10 MINS

Smoked chicken with basil mayonnaise on cucumber rounds p320

PREP 20 MINS

Chorizo with peppers p335

PREP 10 MINS COOK 10 MINS

Ham with pears p337

PREP 10 MINS COOK 15 MINS

MEAT IN UNDER 30 MINUTES: MAIN MEALS

Pasta carbonara with pancetta and cream p173

PREP 10 MINS COOK 15 MINS

Fillet steaks with horseradish cream p442

PREP 10 MINS COOK 10 MINS

Pad Thai p381

PREP 15 MINS COOK 15 MINS

Beef tacos p64

PREP 15 MINS COOK 15 MINS

Pork escalopes with breadcrumb and parsley crust p69

PREP 15 MINS COOK 15 MINS

Seared duck with five-spice and noodles p70

PREP 10 MINS COOK 20 MINS

Pork and spring greens p233

PREP 10 MINS COOK 10 MINS

Chicken escalopes with chilli and parsley p117

PREP 10 MINS COOK 10 MINS

MEAT IN UNDER 30 MINUTES: MAIN MEALS CONTINUED

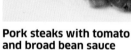

Pan-fried gammon with pineapple salsa p68   PREP 5 MINS   COOK 20 MINS

Quesadilla with spiced beef and tomato p188   PREP 5 MINS   COOK 20 MINS

Thai-style minced pork with noodles p66   PREP 10 MINS   COOK 15 MINS   ♥

Pork steaks with tomato and broad bean sauce p66   PREP 5 MINS   COOK 25 MINS   ♥

Beef escalopes with anchovies, capers, and olives p64   PREP 10 MINS   COOK 20 MINS

Wasabi beef and pak choi p443   PREP 10 MINS   COOK 10 MINS

Turkey burgers p71   PREP 15 MINS   COOK 15 MINS

Turkey and noodles p244   PREP 15 MINS   COOK 15 MINS

Caramelized pork tenderloin with pecan nuts and apricots p70

PREP 10 MINS · COOK 15 MINS

Pizza bianca with Parma ham, rocket, and mozzarella p185

PREP 10 MINS · COOK 10 MINS

Corned beef hash with horseradish p65

PREP 10 MINS · COOK 20 MINS

Beef with soy and lime, and a grapefruit and ginger salsa p63

PREP 10 MINS · COOK 15 MINS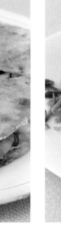

Quesadilla with chicken and sweet onion p191

PREP 5 MINS · COOK 15 MINS

Chicken stir-fried with spring onion, basil, and lemongrass p110

PREP 10 MINS · COOK 15 MINS

Steak and oyster mushroom salad p126

PREP 5 MINS · COOK 15 MINS

Hot and sour beef stir-fry with green beans p63

PREP 10 MINS · COOK 20 MINS

Chicken with noodles and basil p108

PREP 5 MINS · COOK 15 MINS

FISH IN UNDER 15 MINUTES: STARTERS

Smoked trout with beetroot, apple, and dill relish
p40

PREP **15** MINS

Smoked mackerel pâté
p363

PREP **5** MINS

Smoked salmon with radishes and a spiced yogurt dressing p52

PREP **15** MINS

Chilli prawns with coriander and lime p45

PREP **15** MINS

Smoked trout with chilli and lime dressing p366

PREP **10** MINS

Smoked salmon with mustard and dill dressing p365

PREP **5** MINS

Smoked trout with pickled cucumber and minted yogurt p42

PREP **15** MINS

FISH IN UNDER 15 MINUTES: MAIN MEALS

Niçoise-style salad
p47

PREP 15 MINS

Crab salad with grapefruit and coriander p360

PREP 10 MINS

Baked salmon with salsa verde and cucumber p236

PREP 15 MINS

Pasta with crab and lemon p166

PREP 5 MINS COOK 10 MINS

Crayfish and crisp lettuce panini with herbed mayonnaise p319
PREP 15 MINS

Smoked fish, fennel, and mango salad p52

PREP 15 MINS

Tuna and white beans with olives p277

PREP 10 MINS

Seafood and fennel salad with anchovy dressing p49

PREP 15 MINS

17

FISH IN UNDER 30 MINUTES: STARTERS

Salt and pepper prawns
p362
| PREP 10 MINS | COOK 10 MINS |

Mixed tikka fish kebabs with mango salsa and lime raita p84
| PREP 15 MINS | COOK 15 MINS |

Scallops skewered with Parma ham p327
| PREP 10 MINS | COOK 8 MINS |

Battered fish with lemon mayonnaise p338
| PREP 20 MINS | COOK 10 MINS |

Skewered swordfish with caperberries p344
| PREP 15 MINS | COOK 10 MINS |

Thai fish cakes
p361
| PREP 15 MINS | COOK 15 MINS |

Minced crab balls
p363
| PREP 10 MINS | COOK 15 MINS |

Smoked salmon and cream cheese roulades p360
| PREP 30 MINS |

Sesame prawn toasts p326

Prawn cocktail-style wraps with avocado and red pepper mayonnaise p42

PREP 15 MINS COOK 10 MINS

PREP 20 MINS

Griddled prawns with hot pepper sauce p74

PREP 10 MINS COOK 10 MINS

Chargrilled squid and rocket salad p434

PREP 15 MINS COOK 2 MINS

Sautéed scallops with pancetta and wilted spinach p77

PREP 5 MINS COOK 15 MINS

Tuna, tomato, and courgette skewers p81

PREP 10 MINS COOK 10 MINS

Fish fingers with chunky tartar sauce p80

PREP 15 MINS COOK 10 MINS

19

FISH IN UNDER 30 MINUTES: MAIN MEALS

White fish with spinach and pine nuts p81

PREP 10 MINS · COOK 15 MINS

Sweet and sour stir-fried fish with ginger p80

PREP 10 MINS · COOK 20 MINS

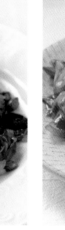

Pasta with clams and parsley p175

PREP 10 MINS · COOK 15 MINS

Teriyaki fish with noodles p83

PREP 10 MINS · COOK 15 MINS

Butterflied sardines stuffed with tomatoes and capers p73

PREP 15 MINS · COOK 10 MINS

Mussels in fennel broth p76

PREP 10 MINS · COOK 20 MINS

Pan-fried prawns, olives, and tomatoes p79

PREP 5 MINS · COOK 15 MINS

Olive and anchovy open tart p206

PREP 15 MINS · COOK 15 MINS ❄

Baked white fish in wine and herbs p73

PREP 5 MINS · COOK 20 MINS

Pasta with seafood and tomatoes
p169

PREP **5** MINS COOK **12** MINS

Pan-fried clams with parsley and garlic
p83

PREP **10** MINS COOK **20** MINS

Spiced haddock with coconut, chilli, and lime p82

PREP **10** MINS COOK **20** MINS

Roasted squid and potato with spiced coriander pesto p76

PREP **10** MINS COOK **20** MINS

Tuna with sweet shallots p74

PREP **10** MINS COOK **20** MINS

Pasta with tuna and roasted onion p172

PREP **10** MINS COOK **20** MINS

Lemon sole with herbs p78

PREP **10** MINS COOK **20** MINS

VEGETARIAN IN UNDER 15 MINUTES: STARTERS

Bruschetta with tomato and basil
p324

PREP
10
MINS

Hummus p323

PREP
10
MINS

Mini topped rye breads
p327

PREP
15
MINS

Rocket, ricotta cheese, and black olive dip p317

PREP
15
MINS

Quesadilla with cheese and chilli p189

PREP
5
MINS

COOK
5
MINS

Baby Gem lettuce with blue cheese and beetroot p339

PREP
15
MINS

Chilled tomato and red pepper soup p41

PREP
15
MINS

22

Grilled goat's cheese with honey p335
PREP 10 MINS COOK 5 MINS

Quesadilla with avocado, spring onion, and chilli p189
PREP 10 MINS COOK 5 MINS

Pea and mint soup p48
PREP 10 MINS ♥

Mixed mushrooms, spinach, and orange salad p44
PREP 15 MINS ♥

Feta and pea salad with watercress mayonnaise p49
PREP 15 MINS ♥

Artichoke and fennel dip p316
PREP 15 MINS ♥

Quesadilla with mushrooms and Gruyère cheese p190
PREP 5 MINS COOK 10 MINS

VEGETARIAN IN UNDER 15 MINUTES: SIDE DISHES

Tomato, red onion, and mozzarella salad
p48

PREP 10 MINS

Spinach with pine nuts and raisins p338

PREP 5 MINS | COOK 10 MINS

Chickpeas in olive oil and lemon p342

PREP 10 MINS | COOK 5 MINS

Asparagus with lemony dressing p364

PREP 5 MINS | COOK 6 MINS

Green beans with toasted hazelnuts
p427

PREP 5 MINS | COOK 5 MINS

Bread salad p51

PREP 15 MINS

VEGETARIAN IN UNDER 15 MINUTES: MAIN MEALS

Pasta with no-cook tomato sauce p160

PREP 5 MINS COOK 10 MINS

Lentil, broad bean, and feta salad p40

PREP 15 MINS

Carrot and shredded cabbage with peanuts p50

PREP 15 MINS

Goat's cheese, beetroot, and pistachios p46

PREP 15 MINS

Bulgur wheat with mixed peppers, mint, and goat's cheese p43

PREP 15 MINS

The perfect omelette p144

PREP 2 MINS COOK 1 MINS

VEGETARIAN IN UNDER 30 MINUTES: STARTERS

Pancakes witb peppers and basil p195 · PREP 10 MINS · COOK 20 MINS

Mushrooms in garlic sauce p340 · PREP 10 MINS · COOK 15 MINS

Fresh tomatoes stuffed with fruity couscous p46 · PREP 30 MINS

Vegetable tempura with chilli dipping sauce p362 · PREP 15 MINS · COOK 15 MINS

Butterbeans with fresh tomato and lime p50 · PREP 20 MINS

Courgettes stuffed with sultanas, red onion, and pine nuts p91 · PREP 10 MINS · COOK 20 MINS

Mushrooms on toast with Manchego cheese p336 · PREP 10 MINS · COOK 20 MINS

Chargrilled asparagus and Gorgonzola p454 · PREP 20 MINS · COOK 10 MINS

Baked eggs with tomatoes p146 · PREP 5 MINS · COOK 15 MINS

VEGETARIAN IN UNDER 30 MINUTES: MAIN MEALS

Chargrilled pepper and leek couscous p453

PREP 15 MINS COOK 15 MINS

Asparagus, broccoli, ginger, and mint stir-fry p92

PREP 15 MINS COOK 15 MINS

Bean burgers p280

PREP 15 MINS COOK 10 MINS

Halloumi with garlic, chilli, and coriander p341

PREP 10 MINS COOK 15 MINS

Pasta with mushroom sauce p167

PREP 10 MINS COOK 20 MINS

Rice and beans p95

PREP 5 MINS COOK 25 MINS

Tomato and harissa tart p210

PREP 10 MINS COOK 15 MINS

Spicy garlic green vegetable medley p93

PREP 15 MINS COOK 15 MINS

Tomato bulgur wheat with capers and olives p277

PREP 15 MINS COOK 15 MINS

Baked eggs with tomato and peppers p95

PREP 10 MINS COOK 20 MINS

DESSERTS IN UNDER 15 MINUTES

Peaches with meringue and raspberry sauce p470

PREP 15 MINS

Apricots with Amaretti biscuits and mascarpone p471

PREP 15 MINS

Mixed berry flan p472

PREP 10 MINS

Middle Eastern oranges p466

PREP 15 MINS

Fresh figs with cassis cream p469

PREP 15 MINS

Mixed berries with white chocolate sauce p500

PREP 5 MINS

COOK 5 MINS

Bannoffee pie p466

PREP 15 MINS

Knickerbocker glory p467

PREP 15 MINS

Vanilla ice cream with coffee drizzle p468

PREP 10 MINS

Chocolate biscuit cake p487

PREP 10 MINS

DESSERTS IN UNDER 30 MINUTES

Mini summer puddings
p482

PREP 30 MINS

Mocha pots
p480

PREP 30 MINS

Black cherry cheesecake
p497

PREP 30 MINS

Melon with vodka, orange, and mint p467

PREP 15 MINS

Melting-middle chocolate fudge puddings p495

PREP 15 MINS COOK 12 MINS

SAVOURY

Quick techniques and shortcuts

Assemble a no-cook meal p37

Make your own pasta p159

Make perfect quesadillas p182

Make beef stock p220

Make mayonnaise p313

Stir-fry p58

SWEET

Quick techniques and shortcuts

Prepare passion fruit p459

Make fruit fool p460

Make cheesecake p461

Make easy ice cream without a machine p478

Make fruit sorbet p479

Make basic sponge cake p506

Make basic biscuit dough p508

EVERYDAY

NO COOK

Instant food – no heat required.

NO COOK

When time is short, there are plenty of ingredients around that can be eaten as they are, with no cooking necessary. With a little imagination and clever shopping, meals can be whipped up in minutes, saving not just time, but washing up and fuel bills, too.

Psst...

To pep up smoked fish, add a handful of fresh basil leaves and flat-leaf parsley to a mortar and pestle, and grind with a clove of garlic, drizzle of olive oil, and a splash of vinegar. Refrigerate until ready to use. Drizzle over fish just before serving.

Best fresh no-cook ingredients Grab a meal from the deli or salad counter.

CHOOSE	USE		STORE

COOKED AND CURED MEAT
Choose cooked meats that are whole and sliced to order at the deli counter, as these will be fresher than ready-sliced and packaged cooked meats. Cured meats are raw meats that have been salted, dried, or smoked, and usually sliced paper-thin.

Ham is fabulous served with chutneys and pickles, or chopped and stirred into a salad of beetroot and sweetcorn.
Cured ham pairs well with delicate sweet flavours such as melon or figs, or mozzarella and rocket.
Beef slices make a tasty sandwich: beef, watercress, and mustard is a great combination; or, try it sliced and tossed with spinach and an oriental dressing (see p38).

Chicken can be mixed with mayonnaise, a pinch of curry powder, and cayenne pepper for the timeless classic, coronation chicken.
Salami makes a hearty salad: combine with sliced mushrooms and spring onions, and a fruity dressing.
Chorizo can be eaten raw or cooked. Toss with nutty chickpeas and chopped red pepper, or served as part of a meat platter with rustic bread.

• Ready-cooked and cured meats in the refrigerator for 3–5 days. Keep them well away from any raw meats.

SMOKED AND PICKLED FISH
Hot or cold smoking is an old preserving method, and imparts a delicious woody flavour to fish such as salmon, trout, and mackerel. Try pickled herring (rollmops) cured in brine, or succulent cured anchovies in olive oil, a tasty alternative to the jarred, salted variety.

Smoked salmon is fairly rich and fatty, so it needs foods to cut through this, such as beetroot, horseradish, or citrus fruit. Serve as part of a seafood salad with chopped gherkins, or with a soy and lime juice dressing.
Mackerel is the ultimate no-cook superfood. Whiz with Greek yogurt or cream cheese and lemon juice for an instant pâté, or flake and stir into rice or couscous.
Trout can be bought hot or cold smoked.

It makes a great inexpensive alternative to smoked salmon. It has a more delicate taste and texture, and is lower in calories. Serve with peppery salad leaves, such as chicory or rocket, as part of a salad.
Pickled herring is most often served with brown or rye bread, and a simple potato salad.
Anchovies, salty or oily, add a real punch to a crisp green salad, tossed with a light creamy dressing.

• In the refrigerator. If vacuum-packed, eat within 2 days of opening. If bought loose, eat within 4 days of purchase.
• Smoked salmon and trout can be frozen for up to 3 months.
• Pickled fish will keep for up to 6 months, unopened.

CHEESE
Choose traditionally-made cheeses, and keep the cheaper packaged cheese for cooking. Buying cheese from the deli is perfect as you can buy as little or as much as required, and you can try different varieties. For the perfect cheeseboard, serve a hard cheese, a soft cheese, and a blue cheese.

Hard and semi-hard cheese such as Cheddar, Cheshire, Wensleydale, Gruyère, and emmental, are all good sliced or grated. Cheddar teams perfectly with seasonal fruits such as apple or pears, and nutty cheeses like Gruyère are better suited to chutneys and earthy spinach leaves.
Soft cheese such as Brie or Camembert, works well with sharp fruits such as redcurrants or cranberries, or sweet fruits such as figs or pears. Enjoy as part of a salad, or blend with walnuts into a pâté.

Goat's cheese can be paired with some bitter leaves, sweet beetroot and apple, with a drizzle of balsamic vinegar.
Blue cheese comes in three types: mild and creamy (eg. Gorgonzola), mature (eg. Stilton) or super-sharp (eg. Roquefort or Danish blue). Try crumbling your favourite type into a dressing, and drizzle it over bitter leaves, or whiz with some Greek yogurt for a dip, and serve with crisp raw red pepper strips.

• Wrap hard cheese, goat's cheese, and blue cheese in greaseproof paper or foil. Don't wrap in cling film, or it will sweat. Keep cool. If refrigerating, allow to come to room temperature, before serving.
• Store soft cheese in the refrigerator. Eat within 3–4 days.

SALAD AND HERBS
Buy salad leaves and lettuce loose rather than packaged if possible, as they will last longer and taste better. Herbs are best bought in the pot or – better still – home-grown. Choose blemish-free leaves.

Cos lettuce is the perfect ingredient for the classic Caesar salad.
Iceberg is good for shredding and tucking into pitta pockets with barbecued lamb and mint yogurt, or used in the classic prawn cocktail.
Rocket or **wild rocket** is hot and peppery, and ideal for adding to a mixed salad, or serving with cured meats, carpaccio, or a strong cheese.
Chicory or **endive** are bitter leaves, best paired with sweet or salty foods such as ham, orange, and beetroot.

Watercress has a clean peppery taste. Use instead of, or alongside, salad leaves. It goes particularly well with smoked fish or salty cheeses such as Parmesan or Pecorino.
Spring onions are perfect for slicing and stirring into a leafy salad, or tossing with dressed cucumber before serving with smoked fish.
Soft leafy herbs, such as coriander, basil, mint, and dill can be added to a mixture of salad leaves, a fresh tomato salad, or a platter of smoked fish.

• All (except basil – place this on your windowsill) keep well in the bottom of the refrigerator, which is the coldest part. They will keep for longer if wrapped in damp kitchen paper. Give them plenty of room, and remove any plastic to prevent them from sweating.

VEGETABLES
When using vegetables raw they need to be very fresh. Baby varieties of vegetables, such as courgettes, carrots, or leeks, are often sweeter, and can be easier to digest.

Fennel has a unique aniseed flavour that will perk up any salad, and works as a good digestive aid when eaten raw between meals. Reserve the feathery fronds to use as a garnish. Add to coleslaw, toss with grated raw carrot, apple, and mayonnaise, or serve with a simple drizzle of lemon juice.
Red, **yellow**, and **orange peppers** are deliciously sweet – finely dice or slice, to add colour and texture to a salad of leaves, olives, capers, anchovies, tomatoes, and avocado.

Avocado can be tossed with cooked prawns and crayfish, and a hot wasabi dressing, or try mashing the flesh for an instant dip, with lime or lemon juice, chilli, Tabasco, and coriander.
Spinach leaves make great salads, and team well with smoked fish, ham, cheese, and nuts.
Carrots add sweetness and vitamins to any salad. Try grated carrot with plump raisins, tossed in a poppy seed dressing, or spiced up with a pinch of paprika and cinnamon, and fresh mint and parsley.

• In the refrigerator. Eat as soon as possible. If storing in plastic, make sure it is perforated so the vegetables don't sweat, or store in a paper bag.
• Avocado has a short shelf life. Refrigerate ripe ones and eat within 2 days. Store unripe ones at room temperature, out of sunlight.

Assemble a no-cook meal These quick and simple "1, 2, 3" preparation steps will turn your raw ingredients into a delicious meal. Experiment with your own combination of ingredients listed in the chart opposite.

1 Slice 3 baby courgettes, or the vegetable of your choice, thinly using a vegetable peeler, and add them to a bowl. Season with salt.

2 Mix together 3 tbsp extra virgin olive oil, 1 tbsp cider vinegar, ½ a red chilli, deseeded and finely chopped, and 1 tbsp freshly chopped mint leaves. Add to the courgettes, and gently toss together using your hands.

3 Serve Season the mixture with salt and freshly ground black pepper, and pile it onto a serving plate. Sprinkle with some shaved Parmesan cheese, and a few torn fresh mint leaves.

EVERYDAY

Perfect pairings
A mixture of classic and the more unusual – the key to marrying flavours is to experiment!

- Combine **fresh peaches** or **apricots** with **Parma ham**.
- Crumble some **feta cheese** over **fresh figs**.
- Dish up juicy **strawberries** with a drizzle of **balsamic vinegar**.
- Serve **cured meats** with **melon**.
- Team **smoked salmon** with **horseradish**.
- Toss **cooked prawns** with **lemongrass** and freshly **grated root ginger**.
- Try **smoked mackerel** with **beetroot** and **fresh dill** or **fresh tarragon**.
- Try **raw shredded red cabbage** with freshly **grated root ginger** and **fresh dill** or a **blue cheese dressing**.

- Enjoy **goat's cheese** with **honey**.
- Serve **raw fennel** with **sliced oranges** and finely chopped **rosemary leaves**.
- Pair **radicchio** with **blue cheese** and **walnuts**.
- Toss **spinach** with **pomegranate seeds** and **pine nuts**.
- Drizzle **soy sauce**, **chilli** and **lime juice** over **smoked salmon**.

the raw facts
Lots of precious nutrients are lost in the cooking process, so eating raw foods such as fruit and vegetables, nuts, seeds, grains, pulses, and dried fruits is extremely good for your health. Raw foods are packed with antioxidants: eating them increases energy levels, helps with digestion, and the high levels of vitamins B, C, and E are beneficial to both skin and hair. A good rule of thumb when preparing a raw dish is to use as many different coloured fruits and vegetables as possible, for optimum health benefits.

Deli salad A fresh and filling salad can be made up in minutes with salad and deli ingredients.

Storecupboard ingredients
A few lifesavers in the cupboard will help perk up meals in minutes (see also pp270–71).

Scatter **mixed olives** over salad leaves. Serve **caper berries** with cooked meats and pâtés. **Pickles** and **chutneys** enhance cheese. **Horseradish sauce** goes well with smoked meats and fish. **Mustards, honey,** sweet and hot **chilli sauces,** and **soy sauce,** all make great dressing ingredients. A jar of **mayonnaise** is a must. **Canned cooked pulses** and **beans, tuna, crab** or **sardines** make an instant meal, as do **canned sweetcorn, bulgur wheat,** or **easy-soak noodles. Dried fruits, nuts,** and **seeds** enhance salads.

EVERYDAY

Dressings
Making your own dressing is easy and quick and, once mastered, you can customize it to suit your dish, and can experiment with flavoured oils and vinegars. Double up the quantities if using for large salads or a number of meals, and store in the refrigerator.

Basic technique
From a classic French or Italian dressing, to a blue cheese one, the preparation method remains the same. Remember to taste as you go, tweaking it by adding a little more vinegar, or a little more oil.

1 Measure out your basic ingredients – 3 parts oil to 1 part vinegar.

2 Combine the vinegar and oil, together with other ingredients, if using.

3 Whisk or shake to emulsify.

French
Good for: drizzling over green salads, avocados, or shredded vegetables.

2 tbsp white wine vinegar
2 tsp Dijon mustard
6 tbsp extra virgin olive oil
Salt and freshly ground black pepper

1 Add the vinegar and mustard to a small bowl, or screw-top jar with lid, and mix or shake together until well combined.

2 Add the oil, and either whisk until combined, or put the lid on the jar and shake well.

3 Taste, and add more vinegar, mustard, or oil if needed. Season to taste with salt and black pepper, and whisk or shake again.

Oriental
Good for: drizzling over noodles, seafood, and Thai-style salads.

2 tbsp white wine vinegar
Juice of ½ lime
Pinch of caster sugar
6 tbsp extra virgin olive oil
1 red chilli, deseeded and finely diced
2.5cm (1in) of fresh ginger, peeled and grated
2 garlic cloves, peeled and grated
2 lemongrass stalks, topped and tailed, and outer hard leaves removed
Salt and freshly ground black pepper

1 Add the vinegar, lime juice, and sugar to a small bowl, or screw-top jar with lid. Whisk.

2 Add the oil and either whisk until combined, or put the lid on the jar and shake well. Add the remaining ingredients, whisk or shake, and season to taste with salt and black pepper.

Blue cheese
Good for: drizzling over crisp leaves, or a chicory and pear salad.

2 tbsp white wine or cider vinegar
Juice of ½ lemon
2 tsp mayonnaise
6 tbsp extra virgin olive oil
75g (2½oz) Gorgonzola cheese, crumbled
Salt and freshly ground black pepper

1 Add the vinegar, lemon juice, and mayonnaise to a small bowl, or screw-top jar with lid, and mix or shake together until well combined.

2 Add the oil, and either whisk until combined, or put the lid on the jar and shake well, until it has emulsified. Add the cheese, and whisk or shake again. Season to taste with salt and black pepper.

Marinate fish

Marinating raw fish, such as finely sliced salmon, trout, sea bass, or tuna in an acidic marinade, such as lemon or lime, will basically "cook" the fish (known as ceviche). Uncooked vegetables also benefit from being marinated. You can also use raw marinades as a base for salad dressings. Make sure your fish is very fresh.

Marinating technique

This step-by-step method will suit most firm fresh fish.

1 Place all the ingredients for the marinade in a shallow bowl.

2 Slice your fish fillet paper-thin, making sure all the bones have been removed.

3 Add the fish to the marinade of your choice, making sure it is well covered.

4 Stir it occasionally to make sure all the fish is marinating. Leave for 30 minutes to 1 hour in the refrigerator, until the fish has turned opaque.

5 Remove with a slotted spoon, and transfer to a serving plate. Serve with a squeeze of lemon or lime, and a fresh leaf salad.

TIP: Put the fish in the freezer for 10 minutes before slicing it paper-thin. This will firm it up, and make slicing much easier.

storing marinades and dressings

Marinades: Keep covered in the refrigerator for a couple of days. If using for fish, discard after use.

Dressings: Can be stored, covered in the refrigerator, for about 3 days. Remember to remove from the refrigerator at least one hour before using, to bring to room temperature, and shake or stir before use.

Lemon marinade

Great with: Tuna, sea bass, and salmon.

Juice of 4 large lemons, plus 1 lemon quartered, and finely sliced

2 garlic cloves, peeled and finely sliced

Pinch of sea salt

Lime and coriander

Great with: Swordfish, tuna, and sea bass.

Juice of 4 limes, plus 1 lime finely sliced and quartered

Handful of fresh coriander, leaves only, finely chopped

2 garlic cloves, peeled and finely sliced

Pinch of sea salt

Lime and chilli

Great with: Swordfish, scallops, sea bass, and tuna.

Juice of 4 limes, plus 1 lime finely sliced and quartered

1 red chilli, deseeded and finely sliced

2 garlic cloves, peeled and finely sliced

2.5cm (1in) piece of fresh root ginger, peeled and finely sliced

Pinch of sea salt

More marinade ideas

There are many variations that can be used, as long as the base is citrus. Try these with scallops, sea bass, trout, or turbot:

• Juice of 3 limes and 2 lemons with finely sliced **spring onions**, a pinch of **paprika**, and a pinch of sugar.

• Juice of 1 lime, with torn **fresh basil** leaves, and a pinch of salt.

• Juice of 2 limes, 2 lemons, and 1 orange, with a handful of **fresh thyme** leaves.

• Juice of 2 lemons with 1 teaspoon of **capers** and 1 tablespoon of **fresh dill**, finely chopped.

• Juice of 2 lemons, with a handful of **spring onions** and 1 clove of **garlic**, crushed.

Smoked trout with beetroot, apple, and dill relish

PREP 15 MINS

SERVES 4

3–4 tsp creamed horseradish

½ red onion, finely diced

1–2 heads chicory, leaves separated
   and rinsed

2 large cold-smoked trout fillets,
   about 225g (8oz) each, flaked

drizzle of olive oil

juice of ½ lemon

salt and freshly ground black pepper

2–3 eating apples

2 whole cooked beetroot, diced

handful of fresh dill, finely chopped

1 In a small bowl, mix together the
horseradish and half of the onion.
Set aside.

2 Arrange the chicory and flaked
trout on a serving plate, and drizzle
the oil and lemon juice over it.
Sprinkle over a pinch of salt and
some black pepper.

3 Peel, core, and chop the apple into
bite-sized pieces. Put in a separate
bowl with the beetroot and dill, and
mix together to make the relish.

4 To serve, spoon the relish over
the leaves and fish. Sprinkle over the
remaining red onion, and serve with
the creamed horseradish on the side.

VARIATION

If you can't get hold of
chicory, use crisp lettuce
leaves such as Cos instead.

Lentil, broad bean, and feta salad

PREP 15 MINS

SERVES 4

85g (3oz) frozen broad beans

400g can green or brown lentils
   in water, drained and rinsed

salt and freshly ground black pepper

1 bunch of spring onions,
   finely chopped

1 fresh green chilli, deseeded and
   finely chopped

175g (6oz) feta cheese, cut into cubes

handful of fresh flat-leaf parsley,
   finely chopped

For the dressing

3 tbsp olive oil

1 tbsp white wine vinegar

2.5cm (1in) piece of fresh root ginger,
   peeled and grated

pinch of caster sugar (optional)

1 Soak the broad beans in boiling
water for 5 minutes, then drain.

2 Put the lentils in a serving bowl,
and season with a pinch of salt and
some black pepper. Add the spring
onions, chilli, and drained broad
beans, and stir well.

3 To make the dressing, put the oil,
vinegar, and ginger in a jug or small
bowl. Season with salt and pepper,
and a pinch of sugar (if using), and
whisk until well combined. Drizzle
over the salad and leave to stand
for 10 minutes, to allow the flavours
to develop. When ready to serve, stir
through the feta and parsley.

VARIATION

This works equally well with
a goat's, smoked, or blue
cheese instead of the feta.
For an added twist, add some
peeled orange segments to
the salad.

COOK'S NOTES

Do rinse the lentils, as they often
tend to be salty when canned.
Canned lentils are an excellent
storecupboard standby and will
keep for 6–12 months.

EVERYDAY

Chilled tomato and red pepper soup

PREP 15 MINS

Special equipment • blender

SERVES 4
3 slices white bread, crusts removed
1 garlic clove, roughly chopped
1 tbsp sherry vinegar or red
   wine vinegar
1 tbsp olive oil
6 very ripe tomatoes,
   roughly chopped
2 red peppers, halved, deseeded,
   and roughly chopped
1 fresh red chilli, deseeded and
   roughly chopped
salt and freshly ground
   black pepper

For the garnish
1 tomato, finely diced
¼ cucumber, finely diced
1 spring onion, finely diced

1 Using a blender, purée the bread, garlic, and vinegar until smooth. With the motor running, gradually pour in the oil, and continue to purée until incorporated. Add the tomatoes, peppers, and chilli, and blend until well combined.

2 Keep the motor running, and slowly add about 500ml (16fl oz) iced water, checking the consistency of the soup as you go – it should be like a gazpacho. Taste, and season with a pinch of salt and some black pepper. Add a splash more vinegar if the soup needs it. Chill until required.

3 Make the garnish just before serving. Put the tomato, cucumber, and spring onion in a small bowl, and stir to combine. Serve the soup chilled, topped with the tomato and cucumber garnish.

VARIATION
To give the soup a real fiery kick, add a splash of Tabasco or smoked chilli sauce, or even a little vodka, and serve chilled in shot glasses.

COOK'S NOTES
If you prefer to skin the tomatoes, make a cross on the bottom of each, then immerse them in a bowl of boiling water. Count to 10, drain, return the tomatoes to the bowl, and cover with cold water. The skins should come away effortlessly.

Sliced beef and rocket salad with green olive and raisin salsa

PREP 15 MINS

SERVES 2
handful of fresh wild rocket leaves
175g (6oz) sliced pastrami or
   other cooked sliced beef from
   the deli counter

For the salsa
8–10 green olives, pitted and sliced
handful of plump raisins
2 tsp capers, rinsed and gently
   squeezed dry
drizzle of olive oil
small handful of fresh flat-leaf
   parsley, finely chopped
salt and freshly ground
   black pepper

1 First, make the salsa. In a bowl, mix together the olives, raisins, capers, oil, and parsley. Taste, and season with a pinch of salt and some black pepper.

2 Arrange the rocket and pastrami or other sliced beef in a shallow serving bowl. Spoon over the salsa, and serve at room temperature.

VARIATION
Top the salad with some fresh Parmesan shavings if you wish.

EVERYDAY

Smoked trout with pickled cucumber and minted yogurt

PREP
15
MINS

SERVES 4

1 avocado, halved, stoned, and peeled
juice of 1 lemon
2 tbsp white wine vinegar
2 tsp caster sugar
1 fresh red chilli, deseeded and
    finely chopped
½ large cucumber, peeled and halved
    lengthways, deseeded, and sliced
4 tbsp Greek-style yogurt
handful of fresh mint leaves, chopped
2 large handfuls of mixed salad leaves
12 green olives, pitted
2 x 200g (7oz) cold-smoked trout
    fillets, flaked
salt and freshly ground black pepper

1 Cut the avocado flesh into slices lengthways, then sprinkle with the lemon juice to prevent discolouration. Set aside.

2 To make the pickled cucumber, whisk the vinegar, sugar, and chilli in a jug or small bowl until combined. Add the cucumber, and toss it all together. In a separate small bowl, stir together the yogurt and mint until well mixed.

3 Arrange the salad leaves and olives in a large salad bowl or on 4 individual plates. Top with the flaked trout and avocado. Season with a pinch of salt and some black pepper. Spoon over some of the cucumber mixture, and keep the rest in a bowl for serving on the side with the minted yogurt.

COOK'S NOTES

Slightly bitter leaves such as curly endive are perfect for this salad. Try to buy salad leaves loose, rather than already packaged in bags, as they will keep for far longer.

Prawn cocktail–style wraps with avocado and red pepper mayonnaise

PREP
20
MINS

Freeze • mayonnaise and prawn mixture
Special equipment • food processor

SERVES 4

2 red peppers, deseeded and roughly
    chopped, plus 1 extra, deseeded
    and diced (see Cook's Notes)
4 tbsp mayonnaise
pinch of mild paprika
salt and freshly ground
    black pepper
4 flour tortillas
12 cooked prawns, peeled
    and deveined
1 avocado, halved, stoned, peeled,
    and diced (toss in a little lemon
    juice to prevent discolouration)
handful of crisp lettuce leaves, such
    as romaine or cos, shredded

1 Put the 2 chopped peppers in a food processor, and whiz until smooth. Add the mayonnaise, and whiz again until everything is combined. Sprinkle in a pinch of paprika, and season with salt and black pepper; pulse to mix. Taste, and adjust the seasoning as needed.

2 Roughly chop 4 of the prawns, and stir into the mayonnaise. Lay the tortillas flat on a clean work surface. Slice in half horizontally, then roll to make a cone, folding the bottom up to enclose one end.

3 To fill the wraps, divide half of the shredded lettuce between each of the tortilla "cones". Layer with the prawn and mayonnaise mixture, avocado, diced extra pepper, and remaining lettuce. Top each wrap with a whole prawn. Allow two wraps per person, and serve immediately.

VARIATION Add some chopped fresh mango to jazz things up a little.

COOK'S NOTES

To cut up a pepper with minimum effort, slice the top and bottom off, then cut a lengthways slit in one side — you can now "unroll" the pepper, and simply slice away the seeds and membrane. Cut the flesh into fine slices, then dice.

Parma ham with pear, nectarine, and endive

PREP 15 MINS

SERVES 4

2–3 heads chicory, leaves separated
  and rinsed
3 sweet, ripe pears
3 sweet, ripe nectarines
12 slices Parma ham
handful of almonds (skins on)

For the dressing
90ml (3fl oz) extra virgin olive oil
2 tbsp apple juice
1 tbsp good-quality balsamic vinegar
salt and freshly ground black pepper

1 First, make the dressing. Put the oil, apple juice, and balsamic vinegar in a jug or small bowl, and whisk together. Season well with salt and black pepper. Arrange the chicory leaves in a single layer on a large serving platter, and drizzle over a little of the dressing.

2 Core and slice the pears, and halve, stone, and slice the nectarines. Arrange over the chicory leaves with the Parma ham, and toss together gently. Scatter over the almonds, then drizzle with a little more dressing. Season again, if you wish. Serve immediately with some fresh crusty bread.

VARIATION Use red chicory instead of the white – it adds an amazing colour to the salad – or perhaps use a combination of the two.

Bulgur wheat with mixed peppers, mint, and goat's cheese

PREP 15 MINS

SERVES 4

250g (9oz) fine bulgur wheat
300ml (10fl oz) hot good-quality light
  or low-salt vegetable stock
salt and freshly ground black pepper
1 bunch of spring onions,
  finely chopped
1 orange pepper, deseeded and diced
1 yellow pepper, deseeded and diced
pinch of mild paprika
handful of fresh mint leaves,
  finely chopped
juice of 1 lemon
125g (4½oz) soft goat's
  cheese, crumbled
extra virgin olive oil, for drizzling

1 Put the bulgur wheat in a large bowl, and pour over the stock – it should just cover the bulgur. Leave to stand for 10 minutes, then stir with a fork to fluff up the grains. Season well with a pinch of salt and black pepper.

2 Add the spring onions, orange and yellow peppers, paprika, mint, and lemon juice, and stir well. Taste, and season again if needed. To serve, top with the goat's cheese and a generous drizzle of olive oil.

VARIATION Use skinned, chopped tomatoes, instead of the peppers.

EVERYDAY

Mixed mushrooms, spinach, and orange salad

PREP 15 MINS

SERVES 4

250g (9oz) mixed mushrooms, such as chestnut and shiitake, sliced
pinch of red chilli flakes
1 bunch of spring onions, sliced
1–2 oranges, depending on size, segmented, and any pith removed (reserve the juice for the dressing)
2 handfuls of fresh spinach leaves
handful of fresh basil leaves, shredded (see Cook's Notes)

For the dressing
90ml (3fl oz) extra virgin olive oil
3 tbsp cider vinegar
pinch of caster sugar
1 tsp grainy mustard
salt and freshly ground black pepper

1 First, make the dressing. Put the olive oil and vinegar in a jug or small bowl, and whisk until combined. Add a little of the juice reserved from segmenting the oranges for the salad, together with the caster sugar and mustard. Season with salt and black pepper, whisk again, and taste. Add a little more of the orange juice if needed. Leave the dressing to stand for a while, to allow the flavours to infuse.

2 To make the salad, put the mushrooms in a large bowl. Add the chilli flakes, and drizzle over a little of the dressing. Toss together. Leave to stand for 10 minutes, then add the spring onions and orange segments, and gently toss to combine.

3 When ready to serve, add the spinach and basil leaves, and more of the dressing. Taste, and season again if needed. Serve immediately.

COOK'S NOTES

Basil leaves are best torn, rather than chopped, as they tend to bruise; however, if you roll a few leaves together like a cigar, then shred them finely using a sharp knife, they will be fine.

Flageolet bean and smoked cheese salad

PREP 15 MINS

SERVES 4

400g can flageolet beans, drained and rinsed
1 tsp Dijon mustard
handful of fresh flat-leaf parsley, finely chopped
salt and freshly ground black pepper
½ red onion, finely chopped
2 handfuls of watercress, rinsed, drained, and roughly chopped
1 lemon, halved
125g (4½oz) lightly smoked cheese such as applewood, cubed

1 Put the beans in a large bowl. Add the mustard and parsley, and stir through. Season with salt and black pepper. Tip in half of the chopped onion and stir through well.

2 Arrange the watercress on a large serving platter or 4 individual plates.

Squeeze over the juice from the lemon, and sprinkle over a pinch of salt. Spoon over the bean mixture, then scatter over the remaining onion. Top with the smoked cheese, and serve.

VARIATION

Slices of ready-cooked boiled or smoked ham, or some sweet Parma ham, would be fabulous with this. If you can't find a smoked cheese, try the salad with pecorino instead.

COOK'S NOTES

Make sure that you use really fresh watercress. To help prevent the cress going limp, keep it in the refrigerator, upside down in a bowl of water.

Smoked chicken salad with papaya fruit salsa

PREP
15
MINS

SERVES 4
1 ripe fresh papaya
1 fresh red chilli, deseeded and
   finely chopped
juice of 1 lime
pinch of caster sugar
salt and freshly ground
   black pepper
2 large handfuls of fresh
   spinach leaves
handful of fresh basil leaves
450g (1lb) smoked chicken, sliced

For the dressing
3 tbsp extra virgin olive oil
1 tbsp white wine vinegar
1 tbsp mango juice

1 First, make the dressing. Whisk together the oil, vinegar, and mango juice in a jug or small bowl. Season well with salt and black pepper, and set aside.

2 Now make the salsa. Halve the papaya, and remove the seeds. Peel then chop the flesh. Put the papaya in a bowl with the chilli, lime juice, and sugar. Season well with salt and black pepper, then taste and adjust the seasoning if needed.

3 Toss the spinach and basil in a large bowl with the dressing, then divide among 4 individual plates. Arrange the smoked chicken over the top. Serve with the salsa spooned over the top or on the side.

VARIATION
If you can't get hold of a fresh papaya, use a fresh mango instead.

EVERYDAY

Chilli prawns with coriander and lime

PREP
15
MINS

SERVES 4
16 cooked prawns, peeled and
   deveined, but with tails left on
handful of fresh coriander,
   finely chopped
1-2 fresh red chillies, deseeded and
   finely chopped
400g can butterbeans, drained
   and rinsed
2 handfuls of wild rocket leaves
juice of 1 lime
salt and freshly ground
   black pepper
splash of sweet chilli sauce

1 Put the prawns in a large bowl. Add half of the coriander and the fresh chillies, and mix well. Tip in the butterbeans, and toss again.

2 Arrange the rocket leaves in a large serving bowl or on 4 individual plates. Sprinkle over a little of the lime juice, a pinch of salt, and some black pepper. Add the remaining lime juice to the prawns, stir through, then taste and adjust the seasoning as needed.

3 Spoon the prawn mixture over the rocket leaves, then drizzle the sweet chilli sauce over it, and sprinkle over the remaining coriander. Serve immediately.

VARIATION
Use finely chopped fresh flat-leaf parsley instead of coriander if you wish.

COOK'S NOTES

If you would like to soften the butterbeans a little before using, put them in a bowl, and cover with hot water. Leave to stand for 10 minutes, then drain well.

 EVERYDAY

Fresh tomatoes stuffed with fruity couscous

PREP 30 MINS

SERVES 4
4 large beef tomatoes
150ml (5fl oz) tomato juice
125g (4½oz) couscous
50g (1¾oz) sultanas
handful of fresh basil leaves, chopped
handful of fresh flat-leaf
   parsley, chopped
salt and freshly ground black pepper

1 Slice the tops off the tomatoes, and reserve. Scoop out the seeds and flesh from the tomatoes, so that you are left with a "shell", and put in a large bowl with the tomato juice. Set the tomato shells aside.

2 Put the couscous in a separate bowl, pour over 150ml (5fl oz) of hot water so that it just covers the couscous, and leave to stand for 10 minutes. Use a fork to fluff up the grains, then tip in the tomato mixture. Mix together, and leave to stand for a further 10 minutes.

3 Stir the couscous well, breaking up any bits of tomato. Add the sultanas, basil, and parsley, and mix again. Taste, and season with salt and black pepper as needed. Spoon the mixture into the reserved tomato shells, and put the tops on to serve. Any leftover couscous can be served on the side.

VARIATION
Use pine nuts instead of sultanas if you are not a fan of dried fruits.

COOK'S NOTES
When preparing couscous, it can be a little tricky working out how much water you need. It is best to add the water slowly, and stop as soon as it sits just on top of the grains.

Goat's cheese, beetroot, and pistachios

PREP 15 MINS

SERVES 4
2 handfuls of wild rocket leaves
4–6 large ready-cooked beetroots
   (not in vinegar), roughly chopped
175g (6oz) goat's cheese, sliced
handful of shelled pistachio nuts,
   roughly chopped

For the dressing
3 tbsp extra virgin olive oil
1 tbsp white wine vinegar
2 shallots, finely chopped
1 tsp grainy mustard
pinch of sugar
salt and freshly ground
   black pepper

1 First, make the dressing. Put the oil, vinegar, and shallots in a jug or small bowl, and whisk together thoroughly. Add the mustard and sugar, and season well with salt and black pepper. Whisk again, then taste. Season again as needed – but remember to let the dressing stand for a while first, to allow the flavours to develop.

2 Arrange the rocket leaves on a large serving platter or 4 individual plates, then top with the beetroot and goat's cheese. Drizzle over a little of the dressing, then sprinkle over the pistachio nuts. Add more dressing, if you wish. Serve with crusty bread.

Cheat...
If you don't have the time to make a dressing, use a drizzle of balsamic vinegar instead.

Caesar salad

PREP 15 MINS

SERVES 4

2 handfuls of crisp lettuce leaves, such as Cos
150g (5½oz) ready-made croutons
50g (1¾oz) Parmesan cheese, freshly grated
350g (12oz) ready-cooked chicken, sliced
10 salted brown anchovy fillets

For the dressing
2 egg yolks
2 tbsp lemon juice
pinch of English mustard powder
½ tbsp Worcestershire sauce
½ tbsp Tabasco sauce
150ml (5fl oz) sunflower oil
50ml (2fl oz) olive oil

1 First, make the dressing. In a bowl, whisk together the egg yolks, lemon juice, mustard powder, Worcestershire sauce, and Tabasco sauce. As you are whisking, add a tiny amount of the sunflower oil; keep whisking and adding the sunflower oil, then the olive oil, a little at a time, until the dressing forms an emulsion. If it is too thick, add a little cold water.

2 Put a little of the dressing in a bowl, then add the lettuce leaves, croutons, and half of the Parmesan. Toss together gently, making sure the leaves are coated. Lay out the leaves on 4 individual serving plates or a serving dish, and top with the chicken and anchovies. Sprinkle with the remaining Parmesan, drizzle over some more dressing, and serve.

VARIATION Instead of chicken, use large, ready-cooked peeled prawns with tails on.

Cheat... If you don't have time to make your own Caesar dressing, some good varieties can be found on supermarket shelves.

EVERYDAY

Niçoise-style salad

PREP 15 MINS

SERVES 4

125g (4½oz) frozen broad beans
400g can tuna in olive oil, drained
10 cherry tomatoes, halved
handful of fresh flat-leaf parsley, finely chopped
bunch of fresh chives, finely chopped
salt and freshly ground black pepper
12 black olives, pitted
12 salted anchovies
1 crisp lettuce such as Cos, leaves separated
2–3 spring onions, finely sliced

For the dressing
6 tbsp extra virgin olive oil
2 tbsp white wine vinegar
2 garlic cloves, grated or finely chopped
1–2 tsp Dijon mustard

1 Soak the broad beans in hot water for 5 minutes, then drain.

2 To make the dressing, put all the dressing ingredients in a screw-top jar, season well with salt and black pepper, cover with the lid, and shake to combine.

3 Put the tuna and tomatoes in a bowl, and drizzle over half of the dressing. Sprinkle in half of the fresh herbs, and season generously with salt and black pepper. Toss together. Now add the drained broad beans, olives, and anchovies, and mix gently.

4 Line a shallow serving bowl with the lettuce leaves, and arrange the tuna mixture on top. Drizzle with the remaining dressing, and sprinkle over the remaining herbs. Top with the spring onion, and serve.

VARIATION Throw in some cooked fine green beans if you have them, some boiled new potatoes, and a few hard-boiled eggs, shelled and quartered.

Pea and mint soup

PREP 10 MINS

Special equipment • blender

SERVES 4

250g (9oz) frozen peas, such as
   petit pois
450ml (15fl oz) hot vegetable stock
handful of fresh mint leaves,
   roughly chopped
a few fresh thyme stalks,
   leaves picked
salt and freshly ground black pepper
1–2 tbsp crème fraîche (optional)
pinch of freshly grated nutmeg

1 Put the peas in a bowl, then pour over boiling water and leave to stand for about 5 minutes. Drain.

2 Using a blender, whiz the peas, stock, and herbs until smooth and combined. You may have to do this in batches. Add more stock if the soup is too thick. Season well with salt and black pepper, and whiz again.

3 To serve, stir through the crème fraîche (if using), and top with a pinch of nutmeg. Serve hot or cold with crusty bread.

VARIATION You could also make this using frozen broad beans in place of the peas, or a mixture of the two if you wish.

Tomato, red onion, and mozzarella salad

PREP 10 MINS

SERVES 4

8 ripe plum tomatoes, sliced
6 cherry tomatoes, halved
1 small red onion, peeled and sliced
handful of fresh basil leaves, torn
extra virgin olive oil, for drizzling
salt and freshly ground black pepper
2 handfuls of wild rocket leaves
balsamic vinegar, for drizzling
2 balls of mozzarella, torn

1 Put the tomatoes, red onion, and half of the basil leaves in a bowl. Drizzle over plenty of olive oil, season well with salt and black pepper, and toss through.

2 Arrange the rocket leaves on a serving platter, and drizzle over a little olive oil and some balsamic vinegar. Season with salt and black pepper, and spoon over the tomato and basil mixture. Add the torn mozzarella. Scatter over the remaining basil leaves, and drizzle again with a little olive oil and balsamic vinegar. Serve immediately.

COOK'S NOTES

It's well worth investing in a good-quality balsamic vinegar, one that is deliciously sweet and thick, and a good-quality fruity extra virgin olive oil.

Feta and pea salad with watercress mayonnaise

PREP 15 MINS

Special equipment • food processor

SERVES 4

handful of fresh watercress,
    roughly chopped
3–4 tbsp good-quality mayonnaise
1 tsp creamed horseradish
salt and freshly ground black pepper
175g (6oz) feta cheese, cubed
125g (4½oz) fresh peas
2 handfuls of baby spinach leaves
small handful of fresh mint leaves
lemon wedges, to serve

1 Using a food processor, whiz the watercress, mayonnaise, and horseradish sauce until well combined. Taste, and season with salt and black pepper.

2 Put the feta, peas, spinach, and mint leaves in a bowl, and gently mix through. Season with a little black pepper if you wish. Transfer to a serving bowl, and serve with the mayonnaise and lemon wedges on the side.

VARIATION

You could use a good-quality fresh ricotta instead of the feta; if you do, omit the mayonnaise mixture.

COOK'S NOTES

If it's not the season for fresh peas, frozen ones make an ideal substitute. Leave them to defrost in a bowl, then pour over boiling water and leave for about 5 minutes. Drain and refresh with fresh cold water.

Seafood and fennel salad with anchovy dressing

PREP 15 MINS

SERVES 4

handful of mixed crisp lettuce leaves,
    such as Cos
1 fennel bulb, finely sliced
450g (1lb) ready-cooked mixed
    seafood, such as prawns, mussels,
    or squid rings, rinsed and dried
6 whole anchovies in oil, drained
1 fresh hot green chilli, deseeded
    and finely chopped
handful of fresh coriander,
    roughly chopped
lemon wedges, to serve
rice noodles, to serve

For the dressing
3 tbsp extra virgin olive oil
1 tbsp white wine vinegar
6 whole anchovies in oil, drained
    and finely chopped
pinch of sugar
handful of fresh flat-leaf parsley,
    finely chopped
salt and freshly ground black pepper

1 First, make the dressing. In a jug, whisk together the oil and vinegar. Add the anchovies, sugar, and parsley, season well with salt and black pepper, and whisk again.

2 In a bowl, toss together the salad leaves, fennel, seafood, anchovies, chilli, and coriander. Pour over the dressing, and carefully mix together. Pile up in a shallow serving bowl, and serve with lemon wedges for squeezing over, and some rice noodles.

COOK'S NOTES

Rice noodles are so easy to prepare – just soak them in hot water for about 10 minutes, then drain and serve.

Butterbeans with fresh tomato and lime

 PREP 20 MINS

SERVES 4

400g can butterbeans, drained
 and rinsed
8 tomatoes, skinned and
 roughly chopped
2 limes, segmented and chopped
 (see Cook's Notes)
extra virgin olive oil, for drizzling
salt and freshly ground black pepper

1 Put the beans, tomatoes, and lime in a bowl, and gently toss together. Season well with salt and black pepper. Drizzle over the olive oil. Serve with crusty bread and a selection of sliced cooked meats.

COOK'S NOTES

To segment a lime, chop off the top and bottom. Using a sharp knife, carefully cut around the whole lime to remove the skin. Remove any pith. Next, use a small serrated knife to slice a segment at a time, leaving the thin membrane behind that separates each one.

Carrot and shredded cabbage with peanuts

PREP 15 MINS

SERVES 4

2 eating apples
4 carrots, peeled and grated
1 small white cabbage, shredded
handful of sunflower seeds
handful of salted or
 dry-roasted peanuts

For the dressing
1 tbsp light soy sauce
1 tbsp Thai fish sauce, such as nam pla
1 fresh green chilli, deseeded
 and finely chopped
1 garlic clove, grated or
 finely chopped
juice of 2 limes
1–2 tsp caster sugar
handful of fresh coriander,
 finely chopped
salt and freshly ground black pepper

1 First, make the dressing. Put all the dressing ingredients in a small bowl, and mix thoroughly until the sugar has dissolved. Taste, and season with salt and black pepper as needed, then check the seasoning again. If it needs sweetening, add more sugar; if it needs saltiness, add a little more fish sauce.

2 Quarter and core the apples, then chop into bite-sized pieces. Put in a bowl with the carrot, cabbage, and sunflower seeds. Toss well. Drizzle over the dressing, and toss together so that everything is well mixed. Transfer to a serving dish, and scatter over the peanuts.

VARIATION

Use fine rice noodles instead of the cabbage if you prefer.

Curried chickpeas with mango

 PREP 20 MINS

SERVES 4

400g can chickpeas, drained
  and rinsed
1 mango, cut into cubes
  (see Cook's Notes)
1 red onion, finely chopped
handful of whole almonds, halved
handful of fresh mint leaves,
  finely chopped

For the dressing
3 tbsp extra virgin olive oil
1 tbsp cider vinegar
pinch of caster sugar
pinch of mild curry powder
salt and freshly ground
  black pepper

1 First, make the dressing. In a jug, whisk together the oil and vinegar, then add the sugar and curry powder. Season with salt and black pepper.

2 Put the chickpeas, mango, red onion, and almonds in a bowl, and mix through. Pour over the dressing, and stir together. Just before serving, stir in the fresh mint leaves.

 VARIATION
Add some ready-cooked chicken slices for a more substantial dish.

COOK'S NOTES

To cut up a mango, lay it down on its side, and slice it lengthways along one side as near to the stone as possible. Turn the sliced piece over, slice a crisscross pattern in the flesh, and turn the pieces out. Repeat with the other side (see p459).

Bread salad

PREP 15 MINS

SERVES 4

3 slices ciabatta or other rustic
  country-style bread, toasted and
  cut into chunky bite-sized cubes
2–3 tbsp olive oil
handful of fresh basil leaves, torn
salt and freshly ground black pepper
½ 190g jar ready-cooked roasted
  peppers, drained and sliced
4 tomatoes, roughly chopped
handful of toasted pine nuts
125g (4½oz) Dolcelatte or other
  mild blue cheese, cut into
  bite-sized cubes

1 Put the bread cubes in a large bowl, and drizzle over the olive oil. Add the basil, and season with salt and black pepper. Toss together, and leave to stand for about 10 minutes, to allow the flavours to develop.

2 Add the peppers, tomatoes, pine nuts, and cheese, and toss gently until everything is evenly mixed. Serve with cold cooked meats.

EVERYDAY

51

Smoked fish, fennel, and mango salad

PREP 15 MINS

SERVES 4

300g (10oz) smoked mackerel
150g (5½oz) smoked trout
1 fennel bulb, trimmed
  and finely shredded
1 mango, stoned, peeled, and sliced
1 pomegranate, halved and
  seeds removed (see p459)

For the dressing
90ml (3fl oz) extra virgin olive oil
3 tbsp red wine vinegar
2 garlic cloves, grated or finely chopped
pinch of caster sugar
handful of fresh dill, finely chopped
salt and freshly ground black pepper

1 First, make the dressing. Put all the ingredients in a small bowl or jug, and whisk together until well combined. Season with salt and black pepper.

2 Flake the mackerel into chunky pieces, and slice the trout into chunky strips. Arrange the fish on a platter, top with the fennel and mango slices, and scatter over the pomegranate seeds.

3 When ready to serve, drizzle over the dressing, and serve with slices of fresh wholemeal or other brown bread.

VARIATION Use raspberry vinegar in place of the red wine vinegar.

Smoked salmon with radishes and a spiced yogurt dressing

PREP 15 MINS

SERVES 4

3 tomatoes, skinned, deseeded, and
  diced (see Cook's Notes)
1 tbsp capers, rinsed, gently squeezed
  dry, and chopped
handful of radishes, diced
1 orange pepper, deseeded and diced
4 spring onions, finely chopped
1 fresh red chilli, deseeded and
  finely chopped
juice of 1 large orange
juice of 1 lime
salt and freshly ground black pepper
250g (9oz) smoked salmon, chopped
  into bite-sized pieces

For the spiced yogurt dressing
4–6 tbsp Greek-style yogurt
juice of 1 lemon
pinch of five-spice powder

1 In a bowl, mix together the tomatoes, capers, radish, pepper, spring onions, and chilli. Tip over

the orange and lime juice, and season with salt and black pepper. Toss together, and leave to stand for about 10 minutes, to allow the flavours to develop.

2 To make the spiced yogurt dressing, mix together the yogurt, lemon juice, and five-spice powder in a small bowl. Season to taste.

3 When ready to serve, add the smoked salmon pieces to the salad mixture, and stir through well. Serve with the yogurt dip on the side.

VARIATION Use fresh white cooked crabmeat instead of the smoked salmon – it won't be as rich.

COOK'S NOTES

Make a cross in the skin, immerse in boiling water for 10 seconds, drain, cover with cold water, and skin.

Chicken with aduki beans and herbs

 PREP 10 MINS

SERVES 4

½ large red onion, very finely diced
400g can aduki beans,
    drained and rinsed
1 tsp wholegrain mustard
splash of white wine vinegar
drizzle of extra virgin olive oil
salt and freshly ground black pepper
handful of fresh flat-leaf parsley,
    finely chopped
350g (12oz) ready-cooked skinless
    chicken, shredded

1 Mix together the onion (reserve a little to garnish the salad), beans, and mustard in a bowl. Add a splash of vinegar and a drizzle of olive oil, and season with salt and black pepper. Stir through the parsley.

2 Spoon the bean mixture into a shallow serving bowl, then top with the shredded chicken. Sprinkle over the remaining red onion, and serve with some fresh crusty bread and wild rocket leaves.

VARIATION
Use cooked brown or green lentils instead of aduki beans, and you could always use smoked chicken if you can find it.

EVERYDAY

Lentils with artichokes and peppers

PREP 15 MINS

SERVES 4

400g can Puy lentils, drained
    and rinsed
400g can artichoke hearts, drained
    and sliced
4 or 5 ready-roasted peppers from
    a jar or the deli counter
1–2 fresh thyme sprigs,
    leaves only
handful of fresh flat-leaf parsley,
    finely chopped
4 spring onions, finely chopped
2–3 tbsp walnut oil
1 tbsp cider vinegar
salt and freshly ground black pepper
4 or 5 Parma ham slices, chopped
handful of wild rocket leaves

1 Put the lentils, artichokes, peppers, herbs, and spring onions in a large bowl. Drizzle over the oil and vinegar, season with salt and black pepper, and stir well to combine.

2 Add the Parma ham and rocket, and toss gently. Transfer to a serving dish, and serve with a green salad.

SPEEDY SUPPERS

30 minutes or less, from start to finish.

SPEEDY SUPPERS

Time is everything, especially when you are home late from work, or cooking for a family. Preparing something quick needn't mean it's not tasty, good food – simply choose cuts of meat and fish that require little attention and minimal cooking. Along with some quick-prep vegetables, you can have a meal made from scratch in minutes.

Psst...

To speed things up in the kitchen, marinate your meat the night before cooking. Even a simple combination of olive oil and lemon juice will add that extra edge to your dish. Always remember to season your meat, too.

Quick-cook meat cuts The best quick-cook cuts for meals in minutes.

CHOOSE	USE	COOK

STEAKS

Beef – rump, sirloin, minute, rib-eye, fillet

Pork – tenderloin, escalope, fillet

Lamb – leg, loin, shoulder, fillet

Turkey – steak

These cuts come from the middle fleshy part of the animal, which produces the most succulent quick-cook cuts. As these muscles are used infrequently, the meat is very tender.

Although steaks can cost more than more muscly cuts, there is very little wastage. They are best suited to dry cooking methods, such as frying, griddling, or grilling. Beef steaks should be at least 2.5cm (1in) thick; pork, lamb, and turkey steaks about 2cm (¾in) thick, and escalopes about 1cm (½in) thick. Brush with oil before adding to the pan or grill, and turn them once during cooking.

	Fry/griddle/grill	Rest
Rare	beef 1–2 mins per side	6 mins
Medium	beef 3 mins per side	4 mins
	lamb 6–8 mins per side	
Well done	beef 4–5 mins per side	1 min
	pork (escalopes) 2–4 mins per side	1 min
	pork (tenderloin/fillet) 3–5 mins per side	1 min
	turkey steaks 6–8 mins per side	1 min

CUTLETS

Lamb

Veal

Cutlets are cut from a rib of lamb (sometimes veal). They are thinner than a chop, with only one rib bone. The meat has an intense flavour, and they suit quick cooking.

Cutlets benefit from being marinated and seasoned well with salt and black pepper, or a pinch of herbs. Cutlets are usually 2–3cm (¾–1¼in) thick, and are best eaten when they are still a little pink in the middle. Brush with a little oil before adding to the pan or grill.

	Fry/griddle/grill	Rest
Rare	lamb 3–4 mins per side	2–3 mins
	veal 1–2 mins per side	
Medium	lamb 4–5 mins per side	1–2 mins
	veal 3–4 mins per side	
Well done	lamb 6–8 mins per side	2–3 mins
	veal 5 mins per side	

CHOPS

Lamb – blade, rib, loin

Pork – rib, loin, tenderloin, chump

Chops are cut from the loin of an animal, usually lamb or pig. You can buy them with or without the bone.

Chops are tender and succulent, and great for a quick meal. Pork chops need to be cooked right through, but it is important not to overcook them, or the meat will dry out. An oil-based marinade will help to both tenderize and add flavour. The thickness of a chop varies but they are usually about 2.5cm (1in) thick. Cook for longer if using thicker cuts.

	Fry/griddle/grill	Rest
Rare	lamb 5 mins per side	3 mins
Medium	lamb 8 mins per side	2 mins
Well done	lamb 10 mins per side	1 min
	pork 8–10 mins per side	

BREAST FILLETS

Chicken

Duck

This boneless cut is ideal for fast cooking with little effort, and is both versatile and economical.

Chicken and duck breasts are about the same size, and are both well suited to high heat and quick, dry cooking methods. Chicken breasts can be pounded to an even thickness, which speeds up the cooking process. Pound them thin for escalopes. Another way to speed up cooking is to slash the breast a few times on the diagonal. Duck, which has a richer meat, can be cooked with no added fat, as it produces a lot of its own.

	Fry/griddle/grill	Rest
Rare	duck 3–4 mins per side	2 mins
Medium	duck 5–6 mins per side	1 min
Well done	chicken 4–5 mins per side	2 mins
	escalope 2–3 mins per side	2 mins
	duck 4–5 mins per side	2 mins

keeping meat fresh

Look at the colour of the flesh, as this is the best indication of freshness. It should be bright, and have no odour at all. It's important to take care when storing raw meat, in order to avoid food poisoning. Keep it well sealed so that it doesn't drip, either securely wrapped in cling film or in a sealed container, and store it in the bottom of the refrigerator, away from other foods, particularly cooked meats. Use before the use-by date.

Quick-cook fish
Fish requires very little cooking; in fact the less you do to it, the better it will taste. It is the ultimate fast food.

CHOOSE

WHOLE FISH
To cook whole fish quickly, choose fish that aren't too large, and make sure the fish is cleaned, gutted, and trimmed before you start cooking. Whole cooked fish are moist and succulent, and the skin will crisp up beautifully. For added flavour, slash the fish a few times, and rub over some seasoned oil or herbs. The fish will fall away from the bone easily when ready.

STEAKS
This is a fleshy cut, ideally suited to fast cooking methods. It is meaty, rich, and delicious, particularly if marinated before cooking. Cooking time really depends on thickness; the time guidelines here are for steaks about 2.5cm (1in) thick. As a rule, allow about 10 minutes cooking time per extra inch.

FILLETS
This fish portion is probably the most widely used for quick cooking, as it is the easiest to handle, and will cook in minutes. Cook with the skin on, as it will protect the delicate flesh from the heat. The time guidelines here are for fillets about 1–2cm (½–¾in) thick. Delicate fish tends to break up when griddled, so it is better suited to frying and grilling.

SHELLFISH
For an instant satisfying meal, shellfish can't be beaten. It can be bought ready-prepared, and makes a nutritious low-fat supper dish. You can cook prawns with or without their shells, but they remain meatier and far more succulent if cooked in the shell. Both prawns and scallops will turn rubbery if overcooked.

COOK

	Fry/griddle/grill
Mackerel	1–2 mins each side
Sardine	1–2 mins each side
Trout	4–5 mins each side
Sea bass	4–5 mins each side

	Fry/griddle/grill
Salmon	4–5 mins each side
Halibut	4–5 mins each side
Tuna	3–5 mins each side

	Fry/grill
Sea bass	2–3 mins each side
Mackerel	2–3 mins each side
Trout	2–3 mins each side
Salmon	2–3 mins each side
Cod/haddock	2–3 mins each side

	Fry/griddle/grill
Prawns	2–3 mins each side
Scallops	3–4 mins each side

keeping fish fresh
Look for fish that is ultra fresh. The flesh should be firm, and it should have no "fishy" smell. Ideally use fish on the day of purchase, but it will store in the refrigerator for 1–2 days, depending on its sell-by date. Wrap in foil or waxed paper, and keep away from other foods in the refrigerator.

Quick-cook veg
Low maintenance vegetables, like the ones listed below, add flavour, colour, and texture.

PEAS
Cook fresh from the pod, or cook from frozen, for about 3 minutes. Mix with fresh mint, tarragon, or chives before serving. Fresh peas are also great raw, in salads.

SPINACH
Baby or young spinach can be eaten raw, tossed with other vegetables such as spring onions and radishes. Older spinach should be cooked for a minute or two in a pan, with a little water, or steamed. Try seasoning with nutmeg, or stir-frying with garlic.

BROCCOLI
Versatile, and available all year round, broccoli responds well to high heat and quick cooking such as stir-frying, or it can be cooked for a few minutes in boiling salted water, or steamed. Try purple sprouting broccoli when it's in season.

MUSHROOMS
Available in several varieties, from the button mushroom to the earthy chestnut mushroom, which adds depth of flavour to a dish. Slice, dice, or grate, and serve raw, or cook in a little melted butter.

CARROTS
Extremely good value, and full of vitamins. Can be eaten raw, if peeled and sliced or grated, in a salad. To cook, sauté in a little melted butter, or steam.

ASPARAGUS
A delicious spring vegetable that will liven up any dish. It's delicate, however, and can easily be overcooked. Trim, oil, and season the stems, and cook on a hot grill pan, or steam (unoiled) for 4 minutes.

BEANS
All beans, from French to broad beans, can be cooked quickly in a pan of boiling salted water (or steamed) for 3–4 minutes. Delicious served alone, or tossed with a piquant dressing.

COURGETTES
These require no peeling. Just top and tail, and slice or dice. They are best pan-fried in a little olive oil, salt and black pepper, and cooked until they soften and turn golden.

LEEKS
A member of the onion family, with a more subtle taste. Top and tail, and wash well (see p404). To cook, slice finely and pan-fry in a little olive oil or butter, until soft.

FENNEL
This vegetable has a slight aniseed taste that complements fish well. It can be shredded and eaten raw, or sliced/quartered, tossed in olive oil, and cooked on a hot griddle, or under a hot grill.

EVERYDAY

STEP-BY-STEP

EVERYDAY

Speedy cooking Four essential quick cooking methods.

Pan-fry
This quick cooking method is best suited to lean cuts of meat, fish, or tender vegetables. We've used a fish fillet here because it best illustrates the technique. With meat and vegetables, follow the same basic steps. Use a shallow frying pan, preferably non-stick, and a little oil or fat.

1 Pat two fish fillets dry with kitchen paper, and season with salt and freshly ground black pepper. Heat ½ a tablespoon of olive oil or sunflower oil in a non-stick frying pan until hot (but not spitting). Carefully add the fish, skin-side down and leave to cook for 2–3 minutes, depending on thickness (see chart on p57).

2 Turn the fish over using a fish slice or spatula, and cook the other side for a further 2–3 minutes, or longer if the fish fillet is thick. Keep the heat at medium-high.

3 Turn the fish over again, to serve. It should be an even golden colour. To check if the fish is cooked, use a round-ended knife to gently move the flesh away from the bone down the middle at the thickest part; if cooked, it will come away with ease.

Stir-fry
Stir-frying is a quick and healthy cooking method, and can be used to cook meat and fish, as well as vegetables (demonstrated here): in all cases, chop your ingredients to the same size, keep the heat high, stir constantly, and use very little oil. Use a large frying pan, if you don't have a wok.

1 When stir-frying, you need to prepare everything ahead of time, so it can be added to the pan in an instant. If you prepare as you go, the time between adding ingredients will mean those already cooking in the pan will cook for too long. Slice or dice your vegetables to a similar size, and finely slice the chilli, fresh root ginger, and garlic (if using).

2 Heat the wok over medium-hot heat, then add ½ a tablespoon of vegetable or sunflower oil. Heat until hot and sizzling. Add the spices first, and stir-fry vigorously for a minute, making sure they don't brown. If you want to add meat or seafood to your stir-fry, add it to the pan now.

3 Add the vegetables in order of firmness (firmest first), adding the garlic last, as it burns easily. Continue stirring all the time so the vegetables don't catch in the wok, and burn. Stir-fry for 4–5 minutes, until the vegetables are cooked. Season well, and serve immediately.

Griddle

Griddle Use a heavy ridged cast-iron pan. This is a fast and low fat cooking method: the pan gets very hot, and oil is added to the ingredient, not the pan. Griddle vegetables and meaty fish using this technique (demonstrated below with pork), brushing with oil *before* adding to the pan.

1 Brush 2–3 pork steaks with a little olive oil, and season well with salt and freshly ground black pepper. Retain the fat on the meat, as this will add flavour when cooking. You can always remove it before eating.

2 Heat the griddle pan on a high heat until it's very hot and begins to smoke. Add the oiled pork steaks, leaving room between them in the pan, and cook undisturbed for 2–3 minutes, depending on thickness (see chart on p57).

3 Once the underside is cooked it will move freely when you try to turn it over. Turn it, and cook the other side for 2–3 minutes, depending on thickness, until it is golden and cooked through. Pierce with a sharp knife, and if no pink is visible, it is cooked through. Let it rest for a couple of minutes before serving.

Grill

Grill The fierce direct heat of the grill is a fast way of cooking, and is particularly healthy, as there is no addition of oil, unless it is added to the ingredient. For meat and fish, follow steps 1 and 2, and check they are cooked through before removing from the grill.

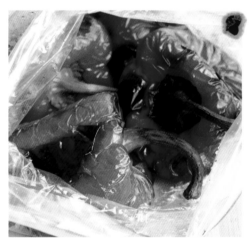

1 Line the grill pan with kitchen foil, then replace the wire rack. Turn the grill to high. Brush the peppers evenly with olive oil, and sit them on the rack.

2 Cook the peppers under the hot grill for 5–8 minutes, until they begin to blacken slightly, and the skin starts to blister. Carefully turn, and cook for a further 5–8 minutes, until blistered all over.

3 Remove the peppers from the heat and put them in a plastic bag. Seal, and leave to cool. The steam will help the removal of the skins. To prepare, remove the peppers from the bag, pull away the stem, deseed, and peel away the skin.

EVERYDAY

59

Pan-fried lamb with green chillies

PREP 5 MINS · COOK 30 MINS

SERVES 4

1 tbsp olive oil
1 onion, finely chopped
1 bay leaf
pinch of cumin seeds
salt
2 garlic cloves, grated or finely chopped
1 fresh medium-hot green chilli, deseeded and finely chopped
900g (2lb) lean lamb, cut into bite-sized pieces
1 tbsp plain flour
600ml (1 pint) hot vegetable or chicken stock
3–4 green bird's-eye chillies, left whole
juice of ½ lemon

1 Heat the oil in a large deep-sided frying pan. Add the onion, bay leaf, cumin seeds, and a pinch of salt, and sauté gently until soft. Stir through the garlic and chopped chilli, and sauté for a few seconds more.

2 Add the lamb, and brown on all sides, then stir through the flour. Pour in a little of the stock, increase the heat, and keep stirring.

3 Bring to the boil, then add the remaining stock and the whole bird's-eye chillies. Simmer for about 20 minutes until the lamb is cooked and the sauce has thickened. Stir in the lemon juice, and serve.

COOK'S NOTES

This is a good dish to prepare in advance, as the flavours will only get better. To reheat and eat, cook in the microwave on High for 3 minutes, or reheat in a pan until piping hot.

Lamb and mint burgers

PREP 10 MINS · COOK 20 MINS

SERVES 4

1 tbsp olive oil
knob of butter
1 onion, finely chopped
2 garlic cloves, grated or finely chopped
2.5cm (1in) piece of fresh root ginger, grated
salt and freshly ground black pepper
675g (1½lb) lamb mince
handful of fresh mint leaves, finely chopped
vegetable oil for frying

1 In a large frying pan, heat the oil and butter over a low heat. Add the onion, and sweat for about 5 minutes until soft. Add the garlic, ginger, and some salt and black pepper. Remove from the heat, and allow to cool.

2 Put the lamb mince in a large bowl, then tip in the cooled onion mixture and the mint. Season again, then mix together until well combined – this is best done using your hands. Roll large balls of the mixture together, and flatten to make burgers. Sit the burgers on a plate, and chill in the refrigerator to firm, if time permits.

3 Shallow-fry the burgers, a few at a time, in a little hot vegetable oil. Fry for 5–6 minutes on each side until cooked through and no longer pink. Alternatively, grill on a hot griddle, ridged cast-iron grill pan, or barbecue. Serve hot. These are delicious with some roasted butternut squash and wild rocket leaves.

EVERYDAY

Marinated lamb chops with crushed lemon and chilli broccoli

PREP 5 MINS · COOK 30 MINS

Marinating • 5 minutes

SERVES 4

4 lean lamb loin chops, fat removed
salt and freshly ground black pepper
handful of fresh rosemary stalks
1 head broccoli, about 300g (10oz), florets and stalks chopped fairly small
juice of 1 lemon
pinch of chilli flakes
mint jelly, to serve

For the marinade
2 tbsp sherry vinegar, cider vinegar, or white wine vinegar
pinch of sugar
splash of dark soy sauce

1 Preheat the oven to 200°C (400°F/ Gas 6). First, prepare the marinade. Mix together the vinegar, sugar, and soy sauce, then pour over the lamb. Leave to marinate for 5 minutes, or longer if time permits.

2 Sit the lamb chops in a roasting tin, season well with salt and black pepper, and throw in the rosemary stalks. Roast in the oven for 20–30 minutes until cooked to your liking.

3 While the lamb is cooking, put the broccoli in a pan of boiling salted water, and cook for about 10 minutes until just soft. Drain, keeping the broccoli in the pan, then mash very gently with a fork. Squeeze over the lemon juice, and add the chilli, a pinch of salt, and some black pepper. Put a lid on the pan, and give it a shake. Serve immediately with the roasted lamb chops and a dollop of mint jelly on the side.

Cheat... Use a ready-made paste to coat the lamb, such as a pesto or a tapenade.

Skewered lamb with crispy rosemary potatoes

PREP 15 MINS · COOK 30 MINS

Special equipment • wooden skewers

SERVES 4

675g (1½lb) potatoes, peeled and cut into small cubes
1–2 tbsp olive oil, plus extra for coating the lamb
handful of fresh rosemary stalks
salt and freshly ground black pepper
900g (2lb) lean lamb, cut into bite-sized pieces
juice of 1 lemon
2 tsp paprika

1 Preheat the oven to 200°C (400°F/Gas 6). Soak the skewers in cold water for at least 30 minutes before using. Put the potatoes, ½ tablespoon olive oil, rosemary, and some salt in a roasting tin. Using your hands, mix everything together so that the potatoes are evenly coated. Roast in the oven for 20–25 minutes until golden and crispy.

2 Meanwhile, put the lamb in a bowl, and toss with the remaining olive oil, the lemon juice, paprika, some salt, and plenty of black pepper. Thread the pieces of lamb onto small skewers until they are tightly packed.

3 Add the lamb skewers to the roasting tin with the potatoes, turning them after 5–8 minutes, and roast until they are cooked through. Serve with the potatoes and a green salad.

Devilled lamb cutlets with crushed potato and mustard seed salad

PREP 10 MINS **COOK 30 MINS**

SERVES 4
250g (9oz) new potatoes
1 tbsp olive oil
1 tbsp mustard seeds
1 bunch of spring onions, finely chopped
8 lamb cutlets
salt and freshly ground black pepper

For the coating
2 tbsp English mustard
2 tbsp tomato ketchup
1 tbsp cayenne pepper
2 tbsp onion, finely chopped
1 tbsp olive oil

1 Preheat the oven to 200°C (400°F/Gas 6). Cook the potatoes in a large pan of boiling salted water for about 15 minutes until soft, then drain. Add the olive oil, and crush the potatoes gently with a fork. Throw in the mustard seeds and spring onions, and season with salt and black pepper. Set aside.

2 While the potatoes are cooking, make the coating for the lamb. In a bowl, mix together all the ingredients, and season well with salt and black pepper. Coat the lamb cutlets evenly, put in a roasting tin, and roast for 20–30 minutes until cooked to your liking. Serve hot with the potato salad.

Lamb with chickpeas, green peppers, and couscous

PREP 10 MINS **COOK 30 MINS**

SERVES 4
1 tbsp olive oil
1 onion, finely chopped
2 garlic cloves, grated or finely chopped
900g (2lb) lean lamb, cut into bite-sized pieces
1 tsp ground cinnamon
1 tsp paprika
salt and freshly ground black pepper
2–3 green peppers, deseeded and roughly chopped
400g can chickpeas, drained and rinsed
900ml (1½ pints) hot vegetable stock
175g (6oz) couscous
50g (1¾oz) pine nuts, toasted
handful of fresh flat-leaf parsley, finely chopped

1 Heat the olive oil in a large frying pan over a low heat. Add the onion, and sweat for about 5 minutes until soft. Add the garlic, lamb, cinnamon, and paprika, and season.

2 Tip in the peppers and chickpeas, and cook, stirring occasionally, until the meat is browned on all sides. Pour over 600ml (1 pint) of the hot stock, cover the pan, and simmer gently for 20 minutes. Top up with a little hot water if the mixture starts to dry out.

3 Meanwhile, prepare the couscous. Tip the couscous into a bowl, then pour over enough of the remaining stock just to cover. Leave for about 5 minutes, then use a fork to fluff up and separate the grains. Season with plenty of salt and black pepper.

4 To serve, sprinkle the lamb mixture with the pine nuts and parsley, and serve immediately with the couscous.

 VARIATION You could sprinkle over toasted sesame seeds instead of pine nuts.

Beef with soy and lime, and a grapefruit and ginger salsa

PREP 10 MINS COOK 15 MINS

Special equipment • wok

SERVES 4

1 tbsp groundnut or sunflower oil
1 red onion, cut into 8 wedges
675g (1½lb) rump steak, cut
 into strips
1 fresh medium-hot red chilli,
 deseeded and finely sliced
 into strips
splash of dark soy sauce
juice of 1 lime
1 tbsp clear honey
200g (7oz) chestnut mushrooms,
 cleaned and sliced
handful of fresh coriander
rice or noodles, to serve

For the grapefruit and ginger salsa
2 grapefruit, segmented, and chopped
 (see Cook's Notes)
2.5cm (1in) piece of fresh root
 ginger, grated
1 fresh medium-hot red chilli,
 deseeded and finely chopped
pinch of sugar (optional)

1 First, make the salsa. Put all the ingredients in a bowl, stir, and taste. Add a little black pepper, if you wish. Set aside.

2 Heat the oil in a wok over a high heat until hot. Add the onion, and stir-fry for about 5 minutes until soft, before adding the beef strips and chilli. Continue to stir-fry for another 5 minutes or so, keeping everything moving in the wok. Add the soy, lime juice, and honey, and keep stir-frying.

3 Throw in the mushrooms, and stir-fry for a few minutes until they are soft and begin to release their juices.

4 To serve, pile the coriander on top of the beef, and serve immediately with rice or noodles, and the grapefruit salsa.

COOK'S NOTES

To segment a grapefruit, cut a slice from each end, then cut away all the peel and pith, following the shape of the fruit. Now cut away each segment, leaving the thin layer of membrane in between each one.

Hot and sour beef stir-fry with green beans

PREP 10 MINS COOK 20 MINS

SERVES 4

1 tbsp clear honey
splash of Thai fish sauce
675g (1½lb) rump steak, cut into
 thin strips
handful of fine green beans, trimmed
1 tbsp sesame oil
rice or noodles, to serve

For the hot and sour sauce
2 garlic cloves, grated or
 finely chopped
1 tsp soft dark brown sugar
6 salted brown anchovy
 fillets, chopped
3 fresh medium-hot red chillies,
 deseeded and finely chopped
splash of Chinese rice wine
juice of 1 lime
salt

1 First, make the hot and sour sauce. Using a mortar and pestle, pound all the ingredients, except the rice wine and lime juice, into a smooth paste. Add the lime juice slowly, tasting as you go, and season with salt. Set aside.

2 Put the honey and fish sauce in a bowl, add the steak, and combine well. Blanch the beans in a pan of boiling salted water for a few minutes, then drain and refresh in cold water.

3 Heat the oil in a wok or large frying pan over a medium-high heat. Add the steak, and stir-fry, tossing the meat constantly, for 3–5 minutes until it is sealed and cooked. Remove with a slotted spoon, and set aside.

4 Add the hot and sour sauce to the wok or frying pan, and stir for a couple of minutes. Return the meat to the pan, and throw in the beans. Increase the heat to high, add the rice wine, and let boil for a minute or two. Serve immediately with rice or noodles.

Cheat...
Use a ready-made hot and sour sauce, or sweet and sour sauce, and toss it with the meat and vegetables.

COOK'S NOTES

Refreshing the beans in cold water will stop the cooking process and help the beans keep their vibrant green colour.

Beef escalopes with anchovies, capers, and olives

  PREP 10 MINS **COOK 20 MINS**

SERVES 4

2 rump or sirloin steaks, 175–225g
   (6–8oz) each, cut in half
6 salted brown anchovies,
   roughly chopped
2 tsp capers, rinsed and drained
handful of black olives, pitted
3 tbsp olive oil
2 handfuls of wild rocket leaves
juice of ½–1 lemon
sea salt
small handful of fresh basil
   leaves, torn

1 First, prepare the escalopes. Working with one piece of steak at a time, sandwich them between two sheets of cling film, and bash with a meat hammer or the side of a rolling pin until thin and an even thickness.

2 In a bowl, pound together the anchovies, capers, and half of the olives to form a rough paste – it shouldn't need seasoning, as the anchovies will be salty enough. Now smother the paste evenly over each escalope.

3 Heat 1 tablespoon of the oil in a non-stick frying pan over a high heat. Cook the escalopes two at a time, adding another tablespoon of the oil for the second batch. Cook for 3–4 minutes on each side.

4 Dress the rocket leaves with the remaining 1 tablespoon of olive oil, the lemon juice, and a pinch of salt. Toss with the remaining olives. To serve, top the steak with the torn basil leaves, and serve alongside the salad.

Use veal instead of beef, if you wish.

COOK'S NOTES

Bashing the meat like this will tenderise it; as it becomes so thin, it cooks in no time. You can do this with other meats, such as pork, chicken, or turkey.

Beef tacos

  PREP 15 MINS **COOK 15 MINS**

SERVES 4

1 tbsp olive oil
1 onion, finely chopped
salt
2 garlic cloves, grated or
   finely chopped
1 fresh hot green chilli, deseeded
   and finely chopped
675g (1½lb) lean beef mince
300ml (10fl oz) hot vegetable stock
4 tomatoes, skinned and chopped
handful of fresh coriander,
   finely chopped
8 taco shells
75g (2½oz) strong Cheddar
   cheese, grated

1 Preheat the grill to hot. Heat the oil in a frying pan over a medium heat. Add the onion and a pinch of salt, and sauté for a couple of minutes until soft and translucent. Add the garlic and chilli, and sauté for a few seconds before adding the beef mince. Cook, stirring, until no longer pink, adding just enough of the stock to prevent the meat sticking, but not so much that it gets too wet.

2 When the beef is cooked, stir in the tomatoes and coriander. Spoon the mixture into the tacos, and top each one with grated cheese. Sit the tacos upright in an ovenproof dish, and put under the grill until the cheese has melted. Serve hot.

Indian spiced beef curry

 PREP 15 MINS **COOK 30 MINS**

Special equipment • food processor

SERVES 4

900g (2lb) lean beef, cut into
  bite-sized pieces
1 tsp ground coriander
1 tsp ground cumin
1 tsp ground turmeric
1 tsp garam masala
1 tbsp sunflower oil
1 onion, roughly chopped
2 garlic cloves, peeled
2.5cm (1in) piece of fresh root
  ginger, peeled
4 tomatoes, skinned and
  roughly chopped
2 fresh hot red chillies, deseeded
  and finely chopped
150ml (5fl oz) double cream
handful of fresh coriander, finely
  chopped (optional)

1 Put the beef, ground coriander, cumin, turmeric, garam masala, and oil in a bowl, and mix thoroughly. Heat a large frying pan over a medium heat. Add the spiced beef, and sauté for about 10 minutes until cooked through. Remove from the pan, and set aside.

2 In a food processor, whiz the onion, garlic, ginger, tomatoes, and chillies until minced. Add to the same frying pan as used for the beef, and cook for about 5 minutes over a medium heat. Stir in the cream, add 150ml (5fl oz) water, and bring to the boil. Return the meat to the pan, reduce the heat slightly, and simmer for 15–20 minutes.

3 Stir through the chopped coriander (if using), and serve immediately.

> ### COOK'S NOTES
>
> If you want to watch the calories, swap the double cream for Greek-style yogurt. To reheat and eat, heat in the microwave on High for 3 minutes, or reheat in a pan until piping hot.

EVERYDAY

Corned beef hash with horseradish

 PREP 10 MINS **COOK 20 MINS**

SERVES 4

1 tbsp olive oil
1 onion, finely chopped
salt
1 garlic clove, grated or finely chopped
675g (1½lb) potatoes, peeled,
  quartered, and boiled
3 large carrots, peeled and finely diced
450ml (15fl oz) hot beef stock
250g can corned beef,
  roughly chopped
2–3 tsp creamed horseradish
splash of Worcestershire
  sauce (optional)
pickled red cabbage, to serve

1 Heat the oil in a large frying pan over a low heat. Add the onion and a pinch of salt, and sweat for about 5 minutes until soft and translucent. Next, add the garlic, potato, and carrot, and sweat for about 5 minutes. Pour in a little of the stock, and bring to the boil. Stir through the corned beef and horseradish sauce, and mix well.

2 Add the remaining stock, reduce the heat slightly, and simmer gently for about 15 minutes, stirring occasionally so that it doesn't stick, and to break up the chunks of corned beef, until the potatoes and carrots are cooked. Taste, and season if needed. Stir through the Worcestershire sauce (if using). Serve hot with pickled red cabbage.

VARIATION Use hot horseradish if you like it with more of a kick.

Pork steaks with tomato and broad bean sauce

PREP 5 MINS COOK 25 MINS

SERVES 4

4 pork steaks, about 150g (5½oz)
    each, trimmed
2 tbsp olive oil
pinch of dried oregano
salt and freshly ground black pepper
1 onion, finely chopped
2 garlic cloves, grated or
    finely chopped
400g can whole peeled plum
    tomatoes, chopped
125g (4½oz) frozen broad beans,
    or use fresh if in season
handful of fresh flat-leaf parsley,
    very finely chopped

1 Preheat the oven to 200°C (400°F/ Gas 6). Brush the chops with 1 tablespoon of the oil, and sprinkle over the oregano. Season well with salt and black pepper. Sit the chops in a roasting tin, and roast in the oven for 15 minutes until golden and cooked through.

2 Meanwhile, heat the remaining oil in a frying pan over a low heat, and add the onion and a pinch of salt.

Sweat for 5 minutes until soft and translucent, then add the garlic and stir for a couple of seconds.

3 Tip in the tomatoes, including any juices, and bring to the boil. Reduce the heat slightly, and simmer for about 15 minutes. Add the broad beans, and cook for a further 10 minutes, adding a little water if the mixture dries out.

4 When ready to serve, taste the sauce, and season some more if needed. Stir through the parsley, sit the chops on the sauce, and serve hot.

VARIATION
Use fresh or frozen peas instead of broad beans.

Cheat...
If time is limited, use a ready-made tomato sauce, and simmer gently before adding the beans.

Thai-style minced pork with noodles

PREP 10 MINS COOK 15 MINS

SERVES 4

1 tbsp vegetable oil
675g (1½lb) pork mince
4 garlic cloves, grated or
    finely chopped
salt
2 fresh hot red chillies, deseeded
    and finely chopped
juice of 1 lime
splash of Thai fish sauce
splash of dark soy sauce
handful of fresh coriander,
    finely chopped
medium rice noodles or rice, to serve

1 Heat the oil in a wok or large frying pan over a medium-high heat.

Add the pork, garlic, and a pinch of salt. Stir-fry until no longer pink, tossing continuously.

2 Add the chillies, lime juice, fish sauce, and soy sauce, and stir-fry for a further 5 minutes.

3 When ready to serve, sprinkle over the coriander, and stir well. Serve hot with noodles or rice.

VARIATION
Add some finely chopped vegetables to the pork if you wish.

EVERYDAY

Sticky pork ribs

PREP 10 MINS | COOK 30 MINS

SERVES 4
900g (2lb) meaty pork spare ribs

For the sauce
1 tbsp clear honey
1 tbsp Dijon mustard
1 tbsp tomato ketchup
splash of dark soy sauce
1 tsp paprika
drizzle of olive oil
salt and freshly ground black pepper

1 Preheat the oven to 200°C (400°F/ Gas 6). To make the sauce, put the honey, mustard, tomato ketchup, soy sauce, paprika, and olive oil in a bowl. Season generously with salt and black pepper, and mix well.

2 Smother the ribs with the sauce, then sit them in a roasting tin and cook for 25–30 minutes until well charred. Serve with pitta bread and a crisp green salad.

Pork fillet stuffed with olives and jalapeño peppers, wrapped in bacon

PREP 15 MINS | COOK 30 MINS

SERVES 4
675g (1½lb) pork tenderloin, trimmed (see Cook's Notes)
50g (1¾oz) black olives, finely chopped
50g (1¾oz) jalapeño peppers, finely chopped
handful of fresh flat-leaf parsley, finely chopped
150g (5oz) streaky bacon
1 tbsp olive oil

1 Preheat the oven to 200°C (400°F/ Gas 6). Slice the pork lengthways so that it opens up; don't slice all the way through. In a bowl, mix together the olives, jalapeños, and parsley, then spoon onto one half of the pork, and fold the top piece over.

2 Now wrap the bacon around the pork, tightly and evenly, then sit the wrapped pork in a roasting tin and smother with the oil. Roast in the oven for 20–25 minutes until the pork is cooked through. Leave to rest for a few minutes.

3 To serve, cut the pork into slices, and serve hot with a salad of baby spinach leaves and cherry tomatoes.

COOK'S NOTES

To prepare the pork tenderloin, trim the thin membrane from the meat using a small sharp knife.

EVERYDAY

Pan-fried gammon with pineapple salsa

 PREP 5 MINS COOK 20 MINS

SERVES 4
1 tbsp olive oil
4 gammon steaks
1 tbsp honey
250g can pineapple rings, drained
 and juice reserved
knob of butter
3 tomatoes, skinned and chopped
½ red onion, finely diced

1 Heat the oil in a large non-stick frying pan over a high heat. Add the pieces of gammon, and cook for 3–4 minutes on each side, depending on thickness, until golden and cooked through. Remove from the pan, and set aside to keep warm.

2 Smother the pineapple rings in honey. Melt a knob of butter in the same frying pan. Add the pineapple rings, and cook for a couple of minutes until golden and lightly charred. Remove from the pan, cool slightly, and chop into small pieces.

3 To make the salsa, put the pineapple, tomato, and red onion in a bowl, and mix until combined.

4 To serve, tip the reserved pineapple juice into the same pan as used for cooking the pineapple, and let it simmer over a high heat for a few seconds. Pour over the warm gammon steaks, and serve with the salsa and perhaps some chunky chips or a salad.

Pork and butterbeans

 PREP 10 MINS COOK 25 MINS

SERVES 4
1 tbsp olive oil
1 onion, finely chopped
handful of fresh rosemary stalks,
 leaves finely chopped
salt and freshly ground black pepper
2 garlic cloves, grated or
 finely chopped
675g (1½lb) diced pork, such
 as pork tenderloin
1 small glass of dry white wine
2 x 400g cans butterbeans,
 drained and rinsed
500ml (16fl oz) hot chicken stock
handful of fresh mint leaves

1 Heat the oil in a large deep frying pan over a low heat. Add the onion, rosemary, and a pinch of salt. Sweat for about 5 minutes until soft and translucent, then add the garlic and pork pieces. Continue cooking for

a few minutes, stirring from time to time, until the pork is no longer pink. Increase the heat to high, add the wine, and cook for a couple of minutes until the alcohol evaporates.

2 Tip in the butterbeans, pour over the stock, and allow to simmer for about 20 minutes. Add a little more stock if needed, but be careful not to make the mixture too wet.

3 Crush some of the beans with a fork, taste, and season the dish with salt and black pepper if needed. Stir through the mint, and serve hot.

> **COOK'S NOTES**
>
> *Pork tenderloin is reasonably priced and is well suited to high-heat cooking. If you buy it whole, cut the tenderloin into bite-sized pieces or into slices.*

Pork escalopes with breadcrumb and parsley crust

  PREP 15 MINS COOK 15 MINS

SERVES 4
75g (2½oz) breadcrumbs, toasted
handful of fresh flat-leaf parsley,
   finely chopped
salt and freshly ground black pepper
2 large pork steak fillets, 175–225g
   (6–8oz) each
1–2 eggs, beaten
1–2 tbsp plain flour
1–2 tbsp olive oil
1 small glass of dry white wine

1 In a bowl, mix the breadcrumbs and parsley, and season well with salt and black pepper. Halve each piece of pork, then sandwich each one between two sheets of cling film. Bash with a meat hammer or the side of a rolling pin until thin and an even thickness. Season well with salt and black pepper.

2 Put the egg, flour, and breadcrumbs each on separate plates. Coat each piece of pork first in the flour, then the egg, and lastly the breadcrumbs. Heat half of the oil in a large non-stick frying pan over a high heat. Add 2 of the pork escalopes, and cook for 3–4 minutes on each side until golden and cooked through. Remove from the pan, sit on kitchen paper, and set aside to keep warm while you cook the remaining 2 escalopes. Keep warm while making the sauce.

3 To make the sauce, tip the wine into the same frying pan, and scrape up all the crispy bits from the bottom with a wooden spoon. Let simmer until the alcohol has evaporated, then pour over the pork. Serve immediately with a spinach and tomato salad, or rocket drizzled with a little lemon juice.

EVERYDAY

Pilaf with chorizo, pancetta, and cranberries

  PREP 10 MINS COOK 25 MINS

SERVES 4
1 tbsp olive oil
knob of butter
1 onion, finely chopped
2 garlic cloves, grated or
   finely chopped
3 celery stalks, finely chopped
125g (4½oz) chorizo, sliced
125g (4½oz) pancetta, cubed
350g (12oz) basmati rice
600ml (1 pint) hot vegetable stock
25g (scant 1oz) dried cranberries
handful of fresh flat-leaf parsley,
   finely chopped
salt and freshly ground black pepper

1 In a large non-stick frying pan, heat the oil and add the butter over a low heat. Add the onion and sweat for about 5 minutes until soft and

translucent. Add the garlic and celery, and sweat for a few seconds more. Now add the chorizo and pancetta, and cook for a further 5 minutes. in the rice, and stir well.

2 Pour in half of the stock, and bring to the boil. Next, pour in the remaining stock, reduce the heat slightly, and simmer gently for about 15 minutes. Add the cranberries, and stir through.

3 Cook until the liquid has been absorbed and the rice is cooked through, adding a little more stock if it needs it. Taste, and season with salt and black pepper if required. Stir through the chopped parsley, and serve.

 VARIATION
If you can't get hold of cranberries, use dried apricots instead.

Seared duck with five-spice and noodles

PREP 10 MINS   COOK 20 MINS

SERVES 4

4 duck breasts, about 150g
   (5½oz each), skin on and scored
   in a crisscross pattern
2–3 tsp five-spice paste
knob of butter
2 tbsp freshly squeezed orange juice
1 tsp soft brown sugar
250g packet ready-to-wok noodles
handful of fresh coriander,
   finely chopped

1 Rub the duck breasts in the five-spice paste. Melt the butter in a frying pan over a high heat. Add the duck breasts, skin-side down, and cook for about 10 minutes until the skin is golden and crisp. Carefully pour the fat away from the pan, then turn the breasts over and cook on the other side for a further 8 minutes.

2 Remove the meat from the pan, cut into slices, and arrange on a warm plate. Pour away any remaining fat, then add the orange juice to the pan along with the sugar. Let it simmer for a minute or two, scraping up any bits from the bottom of the pan with a wooden spoon.

3 Add the noodles, and toss them in the sauce for a couple of minutes. Remove from the heat, and stir through the coriander. Serve immediately with the warm duck breasts.

Caramelized pork tenderloin with pecan nut and apricots

PREP 10 MINS   COOK 15 MINS

SERVES 4

1–2 tsp brown sugar
675g (1½lb) pork tenderloin
   (in one piece)
1 tbsp olive oil
knob of butter
handful of pecan nuts
handful of dried apricots, halved
splash of whisky (optional)
300ml (10fl oz) double cream

1 Preheat the oven to 200°C (400°F/ Gas 6). Rub the brown sugar over the pork, then slice the pork horizontally into medallions.

2 Heat the oil and butter in a frying pan over a medium-high heat. Brown the pork medallions for 3–4 minutes on each side until golden. Add the pecans and apricots, and cook for a few more minutes.

3 Increase the heat to high, and add the whisky (if using). Let it simmer for a couple of minutes until the alcohol has evaporated. Reduce the heat to medium, pour over the cream, and let it simmer for a few minutes more. Serve hot with mashed potato.

COOK'S NOTES

This recipe would work just as well with turkey or chicken breast. Cook in 1 tablespoon of olive oil for 8 minutes until golden, then cook as per recipe above.

Turkey burgers

PREP 15 MINS · COOK 15 MINS

SERVES 4
675g (1½lb) turkey mince
handful of fresh thyme, leaves only, finely chopped
grated zest and juice of 1 lemon
1 fresh medium-hot red chilli, deseeded and finely chopped
salt and freshly ground black pepper
knob of butter, melted
2 tbsp plain flour, to dust
olive oil or vegetable oil for frying
4 hamburger or other bread buns, to serve
crisp lettuce leaves such as Iceberg, to serve
tomato slices, to serve
good-quality mayonnaise, to serve

1 Put the turkey mince, thyme, lemon zest and juice, and chilli in a bowl. Season well with salt and black pepper. Mix together until well combined.

2 Now add the melted butter and, using your hands, work the mixture until it all sticks together. Divide the mixture into four, then scoop up each portion and form into a ball. Press flat with your hands to form a burger. Dust with the flour, then chill in the refrigerator for 5–10 minutes to firm up.

3 Heat a little olive or vegetable oil in a non-stick frying pan over a medium-high heat. Fry the burgers for about 4 minutes on each side until golden and cooked through. Serve in a bun with crisp lettuce, slices of tomato, and a dollop of mayonnaise.

COOK'S NOTES
The melted butter helps to bind everything together, much like eggs and flour do.

EVERYDAY

Duck with pink grapefruit and chicory salad

PREP 10 MINS · COOK 25 MINS

SERVES 4
knob of butter
4 duck breasts, about 150g (5½oz each), skin on and scored in a crisscross pattern
handful of fresh rosemary stalks
2 tbsp balsamic vinegar
1 head chicory, leaves separated
1 fennel bulb, trimmed and finely sliced
2 pink grapefruits, peeled and segmented
salt and freshly ground black pepper

1 Preheat the oven to 200°C (400°F/Gas 6). Melt the butter in a large non-stick frying pan over a high heat, then add the duck breasts, skin-side down, and the rosemary. Cook the breasts for 2–3 minutes on each side until golden all over. Increase the heat, add half of the balsamic vinegar, and let it simmer for a few minutes, scraping up any bits from the bottom of the pan with a wooden spoon.

2 Transfer everything to a roasting tin, and roast in the oven for 15–20 minutes until cooked to your liking.

3 Meanwhile, prepare the salad. Mix together the chicory and fennel, add the grapefruit segments, and toss gently. Drizzle over the remaining balsamic vinegar, and season with salt and black pepper.

4 To serve, slice each duck breast in two, and serve with the salad.

Poached turkey with sticky noodles and chilli cashew nuts

 PREP 15 MINS COOK 30 MINS

Special equipment • wok

SERVES 4

2 large skinless turkey breasts, about 150g (5½oz) each
3 tbsp dark soy sauce
125g (4½oz) cashew nuts
salt
pinch of chilli powder
1 tbsp sesame oil
1 bunch of spring onions, roughly chopped
1 tbsp honey
2 garlic cloves, grated or finely chopped
2.5cm (1in) piece of fresh root ginger, grated
juice of 1 lemon
250g packet ready-to-wok noodles

1 Put the turkey breasts and 1 tablespoon of the soy sauce in a large pan, and cover with water. Bring to the boil, then reduce the heat slightly and simmer gently for 15–20 minutes until the turkey is cooked. Remove with a slotted spoon and, when cool enough to handle, shred the meat and set aside.

2 In a small dry frying pan, toss together the cashew nuts, chilli, and some salt. Toast for a few minutes over a medium-high heat until the nuts are well coated and golden. Set aside.

3 While the turkey is cooking, heat the sesame oil in a wok over a high heat. Add the spring onions, and toss for a couple of minutes. Add the remaining 2 tablespoons of soy sauce, honey, garlic, ginger, and lemon juice, and cook for a minute or two.

4 Add the noodles, and toss until they separate, stirring all the time so that they soak up the sauce. Pile the noodles into a serving bowl, then top with the turkey and the chilli cashew nuts, and drizzle over any excess sauce. Serve immediately.

 VARIATION
Omit the turkey to serve up a vegetarian version.

Chicken livers with shallots and rocket

 PREP 15 MINS COOK 20 MINS

SERVES 4

75g (2½oz) hazelnuts
1 tbsp olive oil
9 shallots, peeled but left whole
salt
1–2 tbsp demerara sugar
knob of butter
250g (9oz) chicken livers, tossed in a little seasoned flour
2 handfuls of wild rocket leaves
drizzle of good-quality balsamic vinegar

1 Spread the hazelnuts over a baking tray. Toast under a hot grill until golden brown, turning them frequently. Put the hazelnuts in a clean tea towel, and rub off the skins. Roughly chop, and set aside.

2 Heat the oil in a large frying pan over a medium heat. Add the shallots, and sweat for about 5 minutes until they start to colour slightly, then sprinkle over some salt and the sugar. Move the shallots around the pan, and cook for a further 10–15 minutes until they soften and begin to caramelize.

3 In a separate frying pan, heat a knob of butter over a medium-high heat. When melted and foaming, add the chicken livers. Cook for 3–5 minutes, turning halfway through the cooking time, until sealed and cooked through.

4 Cut the cooked shallots in half, and arrange with the liver on a bed of rocket leaves. Sprinkle over the toasted hazelnuts, and drizzle over the balsamic vinegar. Serve immediately with chunky slices of wholemeal toast.

COOK'S NOTES
Liver can easily be overcooked and become tough. Be careful to cook only until just cooked through.

EVERYDAY

Butterflied sardines stuffed with tomatoes and capers

PREP 15 MINS | COOK 10 MINS

SERVES 4

4–6 tomatoes, skinned and
 finely chopped
2 tsp capers, rinsed and gently
 squeezed dry
handful of fresh flat-leaf parsley, finely
 chopped, plus extra, to garnish
2 garlic cloves, grated or finely chopped
salt and freshly ground black pepper
12 fresh sardines, butterflied
a little olive oil
juice of 1 lemon

1 Preheat the oven to 200°C (400°F/
Gas 6). Put the tomatoes, capers,
parsley, and garlic in a bowl. Season
well with salt and black pepper, and
stir well until everything is combined.

2 Lay the sardines out flat, skin-side
down, and spoon on the tomato
mixture. Either roll up the sardines
lengthways or just fold them over,
then sit them all in a baking tray.

Drizzle with the olive oil and
lemon juice.

3 Bake in the oven for 10–15 minutes
until the sardines are cooked through.
Garnish with extra parsley, if you wish,
and serve with a crisp green salad.

You could use mackerel
in place of the sardines.

> **COOK'S NOTES**
> Ask your fishmonger to butterfly
> the sardines for you. To do this,
> they need to be scaled and
> the backbone removed, before
> being flattened.

Baked white fish in wine and herbs

PREP 5 MINS | COOK 20 MINS

SERVES 4

675g (1½lb) white fish, such as
 haddock, skinned and cut into
 4 pieces
salt
1 large glass of white wine
12 cherry tomatoes
handful of fresh flat-leaf parsley,
 finely chopped

1 Preheat the oven to 190°C (375°F/
Gas 5). Sprinkle the fish with salt, then
lay in an ovenproof dish. Pour over
the wine, and add the tomatoes
and herbs.

2 Cover the dish tightly with
foil, then bake in the oven for

15–20 minutes, until the fish is
cooked through and the alcohol has
evaporated. Serve with salad and
fresh crusty bread for a summery
dish, or creamy mashed potato
in winter.

Use any white fish for this,
such as pollack, turbot, or
sustainable cod.

> **COOK'S NOTES**
> Use really fresh fish. It should
> have no fishy odour at all, and
> should have firm, moist flesh.

EVERYDAY

Tuna with sweet shallots

PREP 10 MINS · COOK 20 MINS

Special equipment • food processor
• ridged cast-iron grill pan

SERVES 4
6 shallots, peeled
2 garlic cloves, peeled
a few sprigs of fresh thyme,
    leaves only, plus extra sprigs,
    to garnish (optional)
salt and freshly ground black pepper
3 tbsp olive oil
3 tbsp balsamic vinegar
4 tuna steaks, about 150g (5½oz) each

1 Whiz the shallots, garlic, and half of the thyme in a food processor until chopped, making sure that the mixture doesn't become mushy. Season with salt and black pepper.

2 Heat 1 tablespoon of the olive oil in a non-stick frying pan over a low heat. Add the shallot mixture, and gently sweat until soft and translucent, but not coloured at all.

Increase the heat slightly, add the balsamic vinegar, and continue cooking for about 15 minutes.

3 Meanwhile, heat a ridged cast-iron grill pan until hot. Drizzle the remaining olive oil over the tuna steaks, and smother to cover using your hands. Season with salt and black pepper, and sprinkle over the remaining thyme leaves. Add the steaks to the hot pan, two at a time, and cook for 3–5 minutes on each side, depending on the thickness and your preference.

4 To serve, divide the shallot mixture among 4 serving plates. Sit a tuna steak on top of each pile, and garnish with extra thyme stalks (if using). Serve with fine green beans or a rocket salad.

VARIATION Red onions can be used instead of the shallots.

Griddled prawns with hot pepper sauce

PREP 10 MINS · COOK 10 MINS

SERVES 4
250g (9oz) large raw
    prawns, unpeeled
2 tbsp olive oil
1 fresh hot red chilli, deseeded
    and finely chopped

For the hot pepper sauce
1 garlic clove, grated or
    finely chopped
1 tsp hot chilli powder
1 tsp paprika
pinch of ground cumin
juice of 1 lime
4–5 tbsp mayonnaise
salt and freshly ground
    black pepper

1 Put the prawns in a bowl, and combine with 1 tablespoon of the olive oil and the chilli. Toss well, and set aside.

2 To make the hot pepper sauce, in another bowl, stir together the remaining olive oil, garlic, chilli powder, paprika, cumin, lime, and mayonnaise until well combined. Taste, and season accordingly.

3 Heat a large heavy frying pan or ridged cast-iron grill pan over a high heat. Tip in the prawns, cook them for about 2 minutes on each side until they turn pink. Serve with the hot pepper sauce, salad, and fresh crusty bread.

VARIATION To speed things up, use a pinch of chilli flakes instead of fresh chilli.

COOK'S NOTES
You could thread the prawns onto skewers if you wish, and serve two or three per person.

Smoked fish and anchovy gratin

SERVES 4
125g (4½oz) smoked mackerel
125g (4½oz) smoked salmon
8–12 whole anchovies in oil, drained
4 waxy potatoes, peeled, boiled,
    and sliced
knob of butter

For the sauce
knob of butter
1 onion, finely chopped
1 garlic clove, grated or finely chopped
1 tbsp plain flour
300ml (10fl oz) milk
salt and freshly ground black pepper
handful of fresh curly parsley,
    finely chopped

1 Preheat the oven to 200°C (400°F/Gas 6). To make the sauce, melt the butter in a pan over a low heat. Add the onion, and sweat gently for about 5 minutes until soft and translucent, then add the garlic and cook for a few seconds more. Remove from the heat, and stir through the flour using a wooden spoon, then add a little milk and beat until smooth.

2 Return the pan to the heat, and slowly add the rest of the milk, stirring until the sauce has thickened. Season well with salt and black pepper, and stir through the parsley.

3 Layer the smoked fish and anchovies in an ovenproof dish, then spoon over the sauce and gently combine. Top with a layer of potatoes, brush with melted butter, and bake in the oven for 15–20 minutes until golden, crispy, and heated through. Serve with a crisp green salad.

> ## COOK'S NOTES
> For lump-free sauce every time, once you've beaten in the first amount of milk with a wooden spoon, switch to a balloon whisk while adding the remaining milk.

EVERYDAY

Salmon fish cakes

SERVES 4
900g (2lb) potatoes, peeled and
    cut into chunks
knob of butter
900g (2lb) salmon, skinned
handful of fresh curly parsley,
    finely chopped
flour for dusting
salt and freshly ground black pepper
vegetable oil for frying
tartar sauce, to serve
lemon wedges, to serve

1 First, prepare the mashed potato. Boil the potatoes in a pan of salted water for about 15 minutes until soft, then drain well and mash. Add the knob of butter, and mash again until smooth. Set aside.

2 Put the salmon in a large frying pan, and cover with water. Simmer for 5–8 minutes until the fish turns opaque. Remove with a fish slice, and put on a plate. Leave to cool for a minute or two. Using your fingers, flake the fish into pieces.

3 Gently mix the fish with the mashed potato. Add the parsley, and season well with salt and black pepper. Take a small handful of the mixture, roll into a ball, and flatten into a cake. Continue until all the mixture has been used – there should be enough for 2 fish cakes per person. Dust the fish cakes with a little flour.

4 Heat just enough vegetable oil for shallow-frying in a non-stick frying pan over a medium heat. Cooking a few at a time, fry the fish cakes for about 5 minutes on each side until golden. Serve hot with tartar sauce and lemon wedges.

VARIATION
You could, of course, use white fish for this recipe.

Mussels in fennel broth

SERVES 4
1 tbsp olive oil
1 onion, finely chopped
1 fennel bulb, trimmed and
    finely chopped
salt and freshly ground black pepper
2 garlic cloves, grated or finely chopped
2 waxy potatoes, peeled and
    finely diced
300ml (10fl oz) hot vegetable stock
    or light fish stock
400g can coconut milk
1.35kg (3lb) fresh mussels, cleaned
    (see Cook's Notes)
handful of fresh basil leaves, torn

1 Heat the oil in a large pan over
a low heat. Add the onion, fennel,
and a pinch of salt, then sweat for
about 5 minutes until softened. Add
the garlic and potatoes, and cook for
a few minutes more, being careful not
to allow it to brown at all.

2 Pour in the stock, and bring to the
boil. Add the coconut milk, reduce
the heat slightly, and simmer gently
for about 10 minutes, or until the
potatoes are cooked. Bring back to
the boil, add the mussels, and put a lid
on the pan. Cook for about 5 minutes,
until all the mussels are open (discard
any that do not).

3 To serve, stir through the basil,
taste the broth, and season if needed.
Serve immediately.

COOK'S NOTES

To clean the mussels, tip them into
the sink and cover with plenty of
cold water. Scrape them one by one,
to remove any barnacles or hairy
"beards", and scrub. Throw away
any that are open or badly cracked.
Cook them straight away.

Roasted squid and potato with spiced coriander pesto

Special equipment • food processor

SERVES 4
1.1kg (2½lb) waxy potatoes, peeled
    and cubed
2 tbsp olive oil
salt and freshly ground black pepper
350g (12oz) squid, prepared, cleaned,
    and scored (ask your fishmonger
    to do this)
pinch of chilli flakes (optional)

For the pesto
large handful of fresh coriander
large handful of fresh basil leaves
2 garlic cloves, chopped
large handful of pine nuts
60g (2oz) Parmesan cheese,
    freshly grated
pinch of chilli flakes
150ml (5fl oz) extra virgin olive oil
    (use more or less as required)

1 Preheat the oven to 200°C
(400°F/Gas 6). To make the pesto,
put the coriander, basil, garlic,
and pine nuts in a food processor,
and whiz until the nuts are ground.
Add most of the Parmesan and chilli
flakes, and whiz again. Now slowly
add the olive oil in a gradual stream,
and pulse until the pesto forms

a smooth paste and reaches the
right consistency. Stir through
the remaining Parmesan, taste,
and season with salt and black
pepper if it needs it. Set aside.

2 Put the potatoes in a roasting tin.
Drizzle over 1 tablespoon of the olive
oil, and toss through. Season with salt
and black pepper. Roast in the oven
for 15–20 minutes until golden.

3 Meanwhile, in a bowl, mix together
the squid with the remaining olive oil
and the chilli flakes (if using). Add to
the potatoes for the last 10 minutes
or so of cooking. Cook until the squid
is slightly charred. Toss everything
together, and serve hot with the
coriander pesto.

Cheat...
Instead of making the
pesto use a ready-made
pesto, either a green
or a red one.

Roasted salmon with Swiss chard and herb butter

PREP 10 MINS **COOK 30 MINS**

SERVES 4
4 salmon fillets, about 150g
  (5½oz) each
1 tbsp olive oil
salt and freshly ground black pepper
2 handfuls of Swiss chard, trimmed

For the herb butter
125g (4½oz) butter
handful of fresh curly parsley,
  finely chopped
handful of fresh dill, finely chopped
juice of 1 lemon
pinch of chilli flakes

1 First, make the herb butter. Put the butter and herbs in a mixing bowl, and beat well until everything is combined. Spoon the butter onto a piece of greaseproof paper, then roll into a log shape. Twist the edges of the paper, and put the roll in the refrigerator.

2 Preheat the oven to 200°C (400°F/ Gas 6). Sit the salmon fillets in a non-stick roasting tin, drizzle with the olive oil, and season with salt and black pepper. Bake in the oven for 15-20 minutes until the salmon is cooked through.

3 Meanwhile, cook the Swiss chard in a large pan of boiling salted water for 5-8 minutes until it still has a bite to it. Drain well, and transfer to a serving dish. Squeeze over the lemon juice, and add a pinch of chilli flakes.

4 Place the roasted salmon on top of the Swiss chard, with a slice of the herb butter on each piece, and serve immediately.

Serve up curly kale or spinach instead of chard.

Sautéed scallops with pancetta and wilted spinach

PREP 5 MINS **COOK 15 MINS**

SERVES 4
12 fresh scallops, with or without
  coral (depending on preference)
salt and freshly ground black pepper
1-2 tbsp olive oil
115g (4oz) pancetta, cubed
splash of good-quality thick
  balsamic vinegar
2 handfuls of fresh spinach, rinsed
  and drained
juice of 1 lemon

1 Pat dry the scallops with kitchen paper, and season with salt and black pepper. Heat the oil in a non-stick frying pan over a medium-high heat. When hot, add the scallops, positioning them around the edge of the pan. Sear for 1-2 minutes on one side, then turn them over, starting with the first one you put in the pan. Once you have completed the circle, remove the scallops from the pan (again starting with the first one), and set aside to keep warm.

2 Add the pancetta to the same pan, and cook for a couple of minutes until crispy. Splash in a generous amount of balsamic vinegar, increase the heat to high, and let boil for a couple of minutes, stirring to deglaze the pan. Drizzle over the reserved scallops.

3 Still using the same pan, tip in the spinach. Keep moving it around the pan, and cook for 2-3 minutes until just wilted. Squeeze over the lemon juice, and serve immediately with the scallops.

White fish, green beans, and artichoke paella

PREP 15 MINS | COOK 30 MINS

SERVES 4-6
1 tbsp olive oil
1 onion, finely chopped
salt and freshly ground black pepper
pinch of ground turmeric
2 garlic cloves, grated or
    finely chopped
200g (7oz) fresh green
    beans, trimmed
280g jar artichoke hearts, drained
    and rinsed
4 tomatoes, skinned and chopped
pinch of hot or regular paprika
400g (14oz) basmati rice
1.4 litres (2½ pints) hot
    vegetable stock
675g (1½lb) skinned white fish,
    such as haddock or sustainable
    cod, cut into chunky pieces
handful of fresh dill or flat-leaf
    parsley, finely chopped
juice of 1 lemon

1 Heat the oil in a large heavy frying pan over a medium heat. Add the onion and a pinch of salt, and sauté for about 5 minutes until soft and translucent. Stir through the turmeric, then add the garlic, beans, and artichokes. Cook gently for about 5 minutes until the beans begin to wilt, adding a little more oil if needed.

2 Now add the tomatoes and paprika, and cook for 5 minutes. Tip in the rice, and stir through. Pour in half of the hot stock. Bring to the boil, then reduce the heat slightly and simmer for about 15 minutes. Add the remaining stock and the fish, cover the pan, and cook over a low heat until the rice and fish are cooked through.

3 Keep the lid on the pan until ready to serve, then stir through the fresh herbs and lemon juice. Taste, and season with salt and black pepper.

Cheat...
Use quick-cook rice instead of the basmati rice – it will speed things up.

Lemon sole with herbs

PREP 10 MINS | COOK 20 MINS

SERVES 4
3 tbsp extra virgin olive oil
1 tbsp white wine vinegar
1 tsp Dijon mustard
small handful of fresh mixed herbs,
    such as parsley, thyme, and dill
salt and freshly ground black pepper
4 lemon sole fillets or other flat fish
    fillets such as plaice or brill, about
    175g (6oz) each

1 Preheat the oven to 200°C (400°F/Gas 6). To make the dressing, whisk together the oil and vinegar in a jug. Add the mustard and herbs, and mix well. Season well with salt and black pepper, and mix again.

2 Lay out the fish in a roasting tin, then cover with about 5mm (¼in) water. Season well with salt and black pepper. Bake in the oven for 15–20 minutes, until the fish is cooked through and the water has almost evaporated.

3 Using a fish slice or spatula, carefully lift the fish onto a serving dish or individual plates. Spoon over some of the herb dressing. Serve hot with sautéed potatoes and broccoli.

VARIATION

For a special occasion choose Dover sole – it is far superior in taste and can be served as either fillets or a whole fish. It is, however, more costly.

COOK'S NOTES

To check whether the fish is cooked, poke it to make sure that the flesh lifts away from the bone easily. The flesh should be white with no traces of pink.

Quick fish pie with peas

PREP 15 MINS · COOK 20 MINS

SERVES 4

900g (2lb) floury potatoes, peeled and quartered

knob of butter

675g (1½lb) white fish, such as haddock, hake, sustainable cod, or pollack (or even salmon), cut into chunky pieces (see Cook's Notes)

salt and freshly ground black pepper

150ml (5fl oz) milk

175g (6oz) frozen peas

4 hard-boiled eggs, peeled and chopped (optional)

For the sauce

30g (1oz) butter

30g (1oz) plain flour

300ml (10fl oz) milk

1 tbsp Dijon mustard

1 Preheat the oven to 200°C (400°F/ Gas 6), or the grill to high. Boil the potatoes in a pan of salted water for about 15 minutes until soft. Drain well, and mash. Add the butter, and mash again. Set aside.

2 Put the fish in a shallow frying pan. Season well with salt and black pepper. Pour over just enough of the milk to cover, and poach over a medium heat for 3–4 minutes. Remove the fish with a slotted spoon, and transfer to an ovenproof dish.

3 To make the sauce, melt the butter in a pan over a low heat. Remove from the heat, and stir in the flour with a wooden spoon until smooth. Return the pan to the heat, and add the milk little by little, stirring constantly. Keep cooking and stirring for 5–10 minutes until the sauce has thickened. Add more milk if needed. Stir through the mustard, and season with salt and black pepper. Add the peas and eggs (if using), and stir gently.

4 Spoon the sauce on top of the fish, and stir gently. Top with the reserved mashed potato, and fork the top so that the potato forms peaks. Dot with a little extra butter if you wish, then cook in the oven or under a hot grill for about 10 minutes until the top is crisp and golden.

COOK'S NOTES

If the fish needs skinning, lay it skin-side down on a work surface, and slice crossways along the tip of the tail. Now hold on to the end of the tail, and use a filleting knife to slice under the skin until it comes away easily.

Pan-fried prawns, olives, and tomatoes

PREP 5 MINS · COOK 15 MINS

SERVES 4

1 tbsp olive oil

1 onion, finely chopped

2 garlic cloves, grated or finely chopped

12 large raw prawns, peeled and deveined, but with tail left intact

splash of dry sherry

6 tomatoes, skinned

large handful of mixed olives, pitted

handful of fresh basil and flat-leaf parsley, chopped

salt and freshly ground black pepper

1 Heat the oil in a large frying pan over a medium heat. Add the onion, and sauté for about 5 minutes until soft and translucent. Add the garlic, and cook for a few seconds, then tip in the prawns and cook over a high heat until the prawns are just turning pink.

2 Add the sherry, and continue cooking for 5 minutes, stirring, until the alcohol has evaporated. Add the tomatoes and olives and cook for a further couple of minutes, stirring occasionally, until the tomatoes start to break down. Season well with salt and black pepper, and stir through the herbs. Serve immediately with fresh crusty bread.

VARIATION

Use a splash of white wine instead of the sherry if you like.

EVERYDAY

EVERYDAY

Fish fingers with chunky tartar sauce

 PREP 15 MINS COOK 10 MINS ❄

Special equipment • food processor

SERVES 4
675g (1½lb) thick white fish fillets (loin works best), such as haddock, sustainable cod, or pollack, skinned
1–2 tbsp plain flour
1 egg, lightly beaten
115g (4oz) fresh breadcrumbs, toasted (see Cook's Notes)
60g (2oz) Parmesan cheese, finely grated
salt and freshly ground black pepper
3 tbsp tartar sauce
1 tsp capers, rinsed, drained, and chopped
3 gherkins, drained and finely chopped

1 Preheat the oven to 200°C (400°F/Gas 6). Cut the fish fillets into thick even strips about 2.5cm (1in) wide – you should end up with about 20 "fingers".

2 Tip the flour and egg onto separate plates. Mix the breadcrumbs with the Parmesan, and season with salt and black pepper. Dredge the fish in the flour, then dip in the egg to coat. Use the breadcrumb mixture to coat each of the fish fingers. Make sure that you coat them well, as it protects the fish while it's cooking.

3 Sit the fish fingers on a lightly oiled baking tray, and bake in the oven for 5–8 minutes on each side until golden and cooked through. (Alternatively, you can shallow-fry them in a little sunflower oil if you prefer.)

4 Tip the tartar sauce into a bowl, and stir through the capers and gherkins. Serve with the hot fish fingers.

COOK'S NOTES
To make fine crispy golden breadcrumbs, whiz stale slices of bread in a food processor to coarse crumbs. Spread out the crumbs on a baking tray, and toast in a preheated 200°C (400°F/Gas 6) oven for about 5 minutes until golden. Tip them back into the processor, and whiz again until fine. Either use immediately, or freeze in a plastic bag until needed.

Sweet and sour stir-fried fish with ginger

 PREP 10 MINS COOK 20 MINS ♥

Special equipment • wok

SERVES 4
1–2 tbsp cornflour
salt and freshly ground black pepper
675g (1½lb) thick white fish fillets, such as haddock, cut into strips
1–2 tbsp vegetable or sunflower oil
1 onion, roughly chopped
2 garlic cloves, grated or finely chopped
2.5cm (1in) piece of fresh root ginger, finely sliced
large handful mangetout or sugarsnap peas, sliced into strips
rice, to serve

For the sweet and sour sauce
1 tbsp white wine vinegar
1 tbsp tomato purée
1 tbsp sugar
1 tsp cornflour
2 tsp light soy sauce
2 tbsp pineapple juice

1 First, make the sauce. Mix together the vinegar, tomato purée, sugar, cornflour, soy sauce, and pineapple juice in a jug, and set aside.

2 Put the cornflour on a plate, and season with salt and black pepper. Toss the fish in the seasoned flour to coat.

3 In a wok, heat about half of the oil until hot, then add the fish. Stir-fry for about 5 minutes until golden. Remove with a slotted spoon, and set aside to keep warm. Carefully wipe out the wok with kitchen paper, and add a little more oil. When hot, add the onion and stir-fry until it begins to soften, then add the garlic and ginger, and stir-fry for a few minutes more.

4 Pour in the sweet and sour sauce, and let boil for a few minutes, stirring constantly. Reduce the heat to medium, add the mangetout or sugarsnap peas, and stir-fry for 1 minute. Return the fish to the wok, quickly toss together to combine, and serve hot with rice.

White fish with spinach and pine nuts

PREP 10 MINS · COOK 15 MINS

SERVES 4

4 turbot fillets or other white
   fish fillets, such as haddock,
   sustainable cod, or pollack,
   about 150g (5½oz) each
salt and freshly ground black pepper
2 tbsp olive oil
1 onion, finely chopped
handful of plump raisins
handful of pine nuts, toasted
1–2 tsp capers, rinsed and gently
   squeezed dry
2 large handfuls of fresh spinach,
   rinsed and drained

1 Season the fish with salt and black pepper. Heat 1 tablespoon of the olive oil in a large non-stick frying pan over a medium heat. Add the fish, and cook gently for 5–6 minutes on one side. Turn over, and cook on the other side until cooked through – this will depend on the thickness of the fish, but be careful not to overcook. Remove from the pan, and set aside to keep warm.

2 Carefully wipe out the pan with kitchen paper, then add the remaining olive oil. Sauté the onion for about 5 minutes until soft and translucent. Add the raisins, pine nuts, and capers, and cook for a few minutes more, breaking up the capers with the back of a fork. Add the spinach, and cook until just wilted. Taste, and season if needed. Serve the fish on a bed of the wilted spinach mixture.

COOK'S NOTES

Salting the fish, ideally with sea salt, before cooking firms the flesh by removing excess moisture.

EVERYDAY

Tuna, tomato, and courgette skewers

PREP 10 MINS · COOK 10 MINS

Special equipment • 8 wooden skewers
• ridged cast-iron grill pan

SERVES 4

2 large tuna steaks, 115–150g (4–5½oz)
   each, cut into chunky cubes
juice of 1 lemon
1 tsp five-spice powder
splash of olive oil
salt and freshly ground black pepper
1 red onion, quartered and separated
12 cherry tomatoes
2 small courgettes, sliced
handful of fresh coriander,
   finely chopped

1 Soak the skewers in cold water for 30 minutes before using. Put the tuna, lemon juice, five-spice, and oil in a bowl, and mix well to coat. Season with salt and black pepper.

2 Thread the tuna, onion, tomatoes, and courgettes onto the skewers. Cook in a ridged cast-iron grill pan for 3–5 minutes on each side, until the tuna is seared. Sprinkle with the coriander, and serve immediately.

EVERYDAY

Spiced haddock with coconut, chilli, and lime

PREP 10 MINS · COOK 20 MINS

SERVES 4

4 haddock fillets, about 675g (1½lb) in total

salt and freshly ground black pepper

400ml can coconut milk

1 fresh medium-hot red chilli, deseeded and finely chopped

juice of 1 lime

splash of Thai fish sauce

pinch of sugar (optional)

150g (5½oz) fresh green beans, trimmed

1 tbsp groundnut or sunflower oil

For the spice mixture

1–2 tsp cayenne pepper, to taste

1 tsp paprika

1 tsp ground cinnamon

1 tsp ground coriander

1 tbsp cornflour

1 To make the spice mixture, mix together the spices and the cornflour in a bowl. Season the haddock fillets with salt and black pepper, then coat well with the spice mixture. Set aside.

2 Pour the coconut milk into a wide pan, add the chilli, and bring to the boil. Reduce the heat to a simmer, and add the lime juice, fish sauce, and a pinch of sugar (if using). Throw in the green beans, and simmer for about 5 minutes.

3 Meanwhile, heat the oil in a non-stick frying pan over a high heat. Add the fish, and fry for about 5 minutes on each side until golden.

4 To serve, add the fish to the sauce, and serve hot. Alternatively, serve the sauce on the side.

VARIATION

Try salmon fillets instead of haddock.

COOK'S NOTES

You can use a low-fat coconut milk if you like; however, as with any lower-fat ingredient, heat gently to avoid it splitting.

Mackerel with garlic and tomatoes

PREP 10 MINS · COOK 25 MINS

SERVES 4

24 cherry tomatoes on the vine, snipped with a little of the stem left

4 garlic cloves, peeled

few sprigs of fresh thyme

grated zest of 1 lemon

pinch of chilli flakes

1–2 tbsp olive oil

salt and freshly ground black pepper

4 mackerel fillets, 115–150g (4–5½oz) each

1 Preheat the oven to 200°C (400°F/Gas 6). Put the tomatoes, garlic, and thyme sprigs in a roasting tin. Sprinkle over the lemon zest and chilli flakes. Drizzle with the oil, and season with salt and black pepper. Roast in the oven for about 10 minutes until the tomatoes are beginning to soften and shrivel.

2 Remove from the oven, sit the mackerel on top of the tomatoes, then cover the roasting tin with foil. Return to the oven, and cook for a further 10–15 minutes, until the fish is cooked through. Serve hot with salad and fresh crusty bread.

VARIATION

Use sardines in place of the mackerel, if they are in season.

Teriyaki fish with noodles

PREP 10 MINS **COOK** 15 MINS

SERVES 4
4 cod loins, about 150g (5½oz)
 each (use sustainable cod)
250g (9oz) thick or medium
 udon noodles
4 spring onions, sliced
handful of fresh coriander,
 leaves only
lime quarters, to serve

For the teriyaki sauce
1–2 tbsp dark soy sauce
1 tbsp runny honey
2.5cm (1in) piece of fresh
 root ginger, grated
pinch of sugar
1 tbsp mirin or dry sherry

1 Preheat the oven to 200°C (400°F/
Gas 6). To make the teriyaki sauce, put
all the ingredients in a bowl, and mix
well. Pour all over the fish, and leave
to marinate for about 10 minutes.

2 Sit the fish pieces with the sauce
in a roasting tin, and bake in the
oven for about 15 minutes, until
the fish is cooked through.

3 Meanwhile, put the noodles in
a bowl, and pour over boiling water.
Leave for few minutes, then drain
and toss with the spring onions and
coriander. Serve with the fish and
a squeeze of lime.

VARIATION Thin rice noodles can be used
instead of the udon noodles.

Cheat...
Use some ready-made
teriyaki sauce – you'll
find it with other
Asian ingredients in
most supermarkets.

Pan-fried clams with parsley and garlic

PREP 10 MINS **COOK** 20 MINS

SERVES 4
1 tbsp olive oil
1 onion, finely chopped
salt
2 garlic cloves, grated and
 finely chopped
1–2 green peppers, deseeded and
 finely chopped
1 large glass of dry white wine
450g (1lb) fresh clams, rinsed well
 (discard any that have cracked or
 broken shells)
handful of fresh flat-leaf parsley,
 finely chopped
lemon wedges, to serve (optional)

1 Heat the oil in a large frying pan
over a medium heat. Add the onion
and a pinch of salt, and sweat for
about 5 minutes until soft and

translucent. Add the garlic and peppers,
and gently sweat until the peppers
begin to soften. Increase the heat
to high, and add the wine. Cook for
a couple of minutes until the wine
begins to evaporate.

2 Add the clams, shaking the pan
occasionally, and cook for 5–6 minutes
until the clams open (discard any that
do not). Add the parsley, and stir to
combine. Serve piping hot with fresh
crusty bread to mop up the juices and
some lemon wedges for squeezing
over (if using).

VARIATION Meat is often paired with
seafood in Portuguese and
Spanish cooking. Try adding
cubes of pork or chorizo to
this dish, cooking it just
before you add the clams.

EVERYDAY

EVERYDAY

Mixed tikka fish kebabs with mango salsa and lime raita

 PREP 15 MINS COOK 15 MINS

Special equipment • 8 skewers

SERVES 4

1–2 tbsp medium-hot tikka
   curry paste
4 tbsp Greek-style yogurt
salt
1.1kg (2½lb) mixed filleted fish, such
   as swordfish and salmon, skinned
   and cut into bite-sized pieces
handful of fresh mint leaves,
   finely chopped
½ cucumber, deseeded and diced
juice of 1 lime

For the salsa

1 fresh mango, stoned and diced
1 fresh hot red chilli, deseeded and
   finely chopped
1 cucumber, halved lengthways,
   peeled, deseeded, and
   finely chopped
½ red onion, finely chopped
2.5cm (1in) piece of fresh root
   ginger, grated

1 If using wooden or bamboo skewers, soak in cold water for 30 minutes to prevent them from burning. Preheat the oven to 200°C (400°F/Gas 6), or the grill to high.

2 To make the mango salsa, mix together the mango, chilli, cucumber, onion, and ginger in a bowl. Set aside to allow the flavours to develop. In another bowl, mix together the tikka paste and 2 tablespoons of the yogurt. Season with salt. Smother the fish with the paste, making sure that each piece is well coated. Leave to marinate for a few minutes while you prepare the raita dip.

3 Mix together the remaining yogurt with the mint, cucumber, and lime juice, taste, and season with salt.

4 Thread the fish onto skewers to make kebabs. Line a baking tray with foil, then sit the kebabs on it. Put in the oven or under the grill, and cook for 5–8 minutes until slightly charred, turning during cooking. Serve hot with the salsa and raita.

COOK'S NOTES

Use full-fat yogurt, as it is far more stable than the low-fat versions, which can sometimes curdle when heated.

Quick fish stew

 PREP 10 MINS COOK 30 MINS

Special equipment • blender

SERVES 4

1 tbsp olive oil
1 onion, finely chopped
3 garlic cloves, grated or
   finely chopped
5 celery sticks, chopped
2 carrots, chopped
salt
sprig of fresh thyme, leaves only
squirt of tomato purée
1 glass of dry white wine
4 tomatoes, skinned
900ml (1½ pints) light fish stock
2 haddock fillets, about 675g (1½lb)
   in total, cut into chunky pieces
200g (7oz) raw prawns, peeled
   and deveined
handful of fresh flat-leaf parsley,
   finely chopped

1 Heat the oil in a pan over a low heat, and add the onion, garlic, celery, and carrots, along with a pinch of salt and the thyme. Sweat gently for about 10 minutes.

2 Now stir through the tomato purée, increase the heat to high, and add the wine. Let it simmer for a couple of minutes, then add the tomatoes (squashing them with a fork) and a little of the stock, and simmer a little more. Pour in almost all of the remaining stock, and bring to the boil. Reduce the heat slightly, and simmer for 10 minutes. At this point, you can blend the sauce with a hand-held blender until smooth, or leave it as it is. Top up with the remaining stock if it needs it.

3 Add the fish and prawns, cover the pan, and cook for 5–10 minutes until the fish is cooked through. Serve hot with fresh crusty bread.

Cheat...
Use a ready-cooked pack of seafood to add to the soup instead of the fresh fish. Simply stir through to heat.

Pan-fried scallops with chilli, ginger, and an anchovy dressing

 PREP 10 MINS   COOK 30 MINS

SERVES 4

2–3 tbsp olive oil
675g (1½lb) waxy potatoes, peeled
  and thinly sliced
12 fresh scallops, with or without
  coral (depending on
  your preference)
salt and freshly ground black pepper
1 fresh hot red chilli, deseeded and
  finely chopped
2.5cm (1in) piece of fresh root
  ginger, grated
1 lemon, halved
handful of fresh flat-leaf parsley,
  finely chopped

For the anchovy dressing
3 tbsp extra virgin olive oil
1 tbsp white wine vinegar
8 anchovies in oil, drained and
  finely chopped
pinch of sugar (optional)

1 Heat 1–2 tablespoons of the olive oil in a large non-stick frying pan over a medium-high heat. Add the potatoes, and sauté for 15–20 minutes until the potatoes are golden and cooked through. Drain on kitchen paper, and set aside to keep warm.

2 Meanwhile, make the anchovy dressing. In a jug, whisk together the extra virgin olive oil, vinegar, and anchovies until well combined. Taste, and add a pinch of sugar if it needs it. Season with black pepper.

3 Next, pat dry the scallops with kitchen paper, and season with salt and black pepper. Put the remaining olive oil in the frying pan over a high heat. When hot, add the scallops. Sear for about 1 minute on one side, then turn them over. Add the chilli and ginger, and squeeze over the lemon juice, being careful as it may spit. Remove the pan from the heat, and sprinkle over the parsley.

4 Serve immediately with the sautéed potatoes and a drizzle of the anchovy dressing.

Roasted monkfish with chilli, tomatoes, anchovies, and capers

  PREP 20 MINS   COOK 30 MINS

SERVES 4

1kg (2¼lb) monkfish tail fillets,
  (see Cook's Notes)
drizzle of olive oil
salt and freshly ground black pepper
2 fresh mild to medium red chillies,
  deseeded and very finely chopped
6–8 salted anchovies, finely chopped
2–3 tsp capers, rinsed, gently
  squeezed dry, and chopped
12 cherry tomatoes

1 Preheat the oven to 200°C (400°F/ Gas 6). Sit the monkfish fillets in a roasting tin, and drizzle over a little olive oil. Season well with salt and black pepper, and set aside.

2 Using a mortar and pestle, pound together the chillies, anchovies, and capers until they become a paste. Alternatively, squash into a paste with a fork. Using your hands, smother the monkfish with the paste.

3 Put the fish in a roasting tin, and cook in the oven for about 10 minutes. Throw in the tomatoes, and roast for a further 5–10 minutes until the fish is cooked through.

4 Leave to rest for 5 minutes, then slice and serve immediately with either a green salad or baby roast potatoes.

VARIATION
Use chilli flakes instead of fresh chillies if you prefer.

COOK'S NOTES
To prepare the monkfish, rinse under cold water and remove the thin membrane.

Tomato and tarragon pilaf

 PREP 10 MINS **COOK** 25 MINS

SERVES 4

1 tbsp olive oil
knob of butter
1 onion, finely chopped
salt and freshly ground black pepper
2 garlic cloves, grated or
    finely chopped
250g (9oz) easy-cook rice
900ml (1½ pints) hot vegetable stock
450g (1lb) tomatoes, quartered
2 or 3 stalks of fresh tarragon, leaves
    picked and torn

1 Heat the oil and butter in a large frying pan over a low heat. Add the onion and a pinch of salt, and sweat gently for about 5 minutes until soft and translucent. Stir in the garlic and rice, making sure that the rice is well coated and soaks up the butter.

2 Pour over the hot stock, and stir again. Leave to simmer gently until the rice has cooked, and the stock has all been absorbed. If the pilaf starts to dry out, add a little more hot water.

3 Season well with salt and black pepper, then stir through the tomatoes and tarragon. Serve hot with a crisp green salad.

 VARIATION
Tarragon isn't everyone's favourite herb – swap for thyme or rosemary if you wish.

Cheesy potato and mushroom gratin

 PREP 10 MINS **COOK** 30 MINS

SERVES 4

knob of butter
125g (4½oz) chestnut or button
    mushrooms, sliced
2 garlic cloves, grated or
    finely chopped
a few sprigs of fresh thyme,
    leaves picked
900g (2lb) potatoes, peeled and
    thinly sliced
125g (4½oz) Gruyère cheese, grated
salt and freshly ground black pepper

1 Preheat the oven to 200°C (400°F/Gas 6). Melt the butter in a pan, then add the mushrooms and cook for a few minutes until soft. Add the garlic and thyme, and cook for a minute more.

2 Arrange a layer of potatoes in the bottom of an ovenproof dish, then layer with some of the cheese and mushrooms. Keep layering until you have used all of the ingredients, finishing with a layer of potato and a sprinkling of cheese on top. Season with a pinch of salt and black pepper as you go.

3 Bake in the oven for 25 minutes until golden and simmering. Serve with a crisp green salad.

 VARIATION
Use a smoked cheese, or strong Cheddar if preferred.

COOK'S NOTES

If you are cooking for strict vegetarians, check that the cheese is made with vegetarian rennet. Many are now, and the packaging should specify this.

Chickpea and vegetable stew

SERVES 4
1 tbsp olive oil
1 onion, finely chopped
salt and freshly ground black pepper
2 garlic cloves, grated or
   finely chopped
3 celery sticks, finely chopped
3 carrots, finely chopped
1 small glass of white wine
400g can chopped plum tomatoes
150ml (5fl oz) hot vegetable stock
400g can chickpeas, drained
   and rinsed
handful of fresh runner or green
   beans, sliced diagonally

1 Heat the oil in a large wide pan over a low heat. Add the onion and a pinch of salt, and sweat gently for about 5 minutes until soft and translucent. Stir in the garlic, celery, and carrots, and cook gently for a further 5 minutes.

2 Increase the heat, add the wine, and let boil until the alcohol has evaporated. Tip in the tomatoes, bring to the boil, and pour in the stock. Add the chickpeas, reduce the heat slightly, and simmer gently for 15 minutes.

3 Add the beans to the stew, and cook for 10 minutes more until soft. Season well with salt and black pepper. Serve hot with crusty bread.

VARIATION
Swap the chickpeas for butterbeans or haricot beans.

COOK'S NOTES
This dish tastes even better the next day, as the flavours mature. Simply reheat in a pan.

EVERYDAY

Gnocchi with Gorgonzola and walnut sauce

SERVES 4
knob of butter
1 onion, finely chopped
75g (2½oz) walnuts, roughly chopped
1 tbsp plain flour
450ml (15fl oz) milk
125g (4½oz) Gorgonzola cheese
salt and freshly ground
   black pepper
500g packet ready-made gnocchi
handful of fresh basil leaves,
   to garnish (optional)

1 In a pan, melt the butter over a low heat. Add the onion, and sweat gently for about 5 minutes until soft and translucent. Now add the walnuts, and cook for another couple of minutes. Remove from the heat, and stir in the flour, then add a little milk. Return to the heat, and add the remaining milk, stirring constantly for 4–6 minutes until the sauce thickens.

2 Remove from the heat again, and stir through the Gorgonzola. Season with salt and black pepper.

3 In a separate pan, cook the gnocchi in plenty of boiling salted water for a few minutes, or according to the packet instructions. Drain well. Add to the sauce, and stir through well. Garnish with the basil leaves (if using), and serve immediately with a tomato and rocket salad.

Cheat...
Use a carton of ready-made blue cheese sauce, instead of making your own.

87

EVERYDAY

Spinach, squash, and horseradish bake

 PREP 10 MINS COOK 30 MINS

SERVES 4

2 handfuls of fresh spinach leaves, rinsed and drained

1 small to medium butternut squash, halved, deseeded, peeled, and thinly sliced

2 garlic cloves, grated or finely chopped

300ml (10fl oz) double cream

3–4 tsp creamed horseradish

salt and freshly ground black pepper

1 Preheat the oven to 200°C (400°F/Gas 6). Put the spinach in a pan with a little water (the water clinging to the leaves should be enough), and cook for a few minutes until just wilted. Alternatively, put in a microwave-proof bowl, cover loosely, and wilt in the microwave. Drain, and squeeze out the excess water. Set aside.

2 Put the squash and garlic in a wide pan, pour over the cream, and simmer gently over a low heat for 10 minutes. Using a slotted spoon, remove the squash, and layer it in an ovenproof dish with the wilted spinach.

3 Stir the creamed horseradish into the cream in the pan, then pour the mixture over the squash. Season with salt and lots of black pepper. Cover with foil, and roast in the oven for 20 minutes.

 VARIATION If it's the season for pumpkins, use instead of the butternut squash.

> **COOK'S NOTES**
> Make sure that you use double cream for this dish; it is very stable and won't split.

Spiced beans and herb hash

 PREP 10 MINS COOK 30 MINS

SERVES 4

1 tsp olive oil

knob of butter

1 red onion, roughly chopped

salt and freshly ground black pepper

handful of fresh thyme sprigs, leaves picked

450g (1lb) floury potatoes, peeled and cubed

400g can chilli mixed beans

150ml (5fl oz) hot vegetable stock

handful of fresh flat-leaf parsley, finely chopped

1 Heat the oil and butter in a non-stick frying pan over a low heat. Add the onion, a pinch of salt, and the thyme leaves, and sweat for about 5 minutes until the onion is soft.

2 Add the potatoes, and sauté until beginning to turn golden – you may need to add more olive oil.

3 When the potatoes are nearly cooked – about 15 minutes – tip in the mixed beans, and stir together. Pour in the hot stock, and simmer for 10 minutes. Stir through the parsley, and season well with salt and black pepper. Serve hot.

Potato and pea curry

SERVES 4

1 tbsp sunflower oil
2.5cm (1in) piece of fresh root ginger,
    finely chopped
2-3 fresh hot green chillies, deseeded
    and finely chopped
1 tsp cumin seeds
1 tsp mustard seeds
small handful of curry leaves
6 tomatoes, skinned and chopped
675g (1½lb) waxy potatoes, peeled
    and cubed
1 tsp ground turmeric
300ml (10fl oz) hot vegetable stock
75g (2½oz) frozen peas
salt and freshly ground black pepper
handful of fresh coriander,
    finely chopped

1 Heat the oil in a large frying pan over a medium heat. Add the ginger, chillies, cumin seeds, and mustard seeds, and crumble in the curry leaves. Cook for a couple of minutes until the mustard seeds start to pop. Add the tomatoes, stir through, and cook for a few more minutes.

2 Add the potatoes and turmeric, and pour in the stock. Bring to the boil, reduce the heat slightly, cover, and simmer for about 15 minutes.

3 Tip in the peas, stir through, and cook for a further 5-10 minutes. Season well with salt and black pepper, and stir through the coriander. Serve hot with rice or naan bread.

Cheat...
Use a couple of teaspoons of ready-made curry paste instead of the dried spices.

COOK'S NOTES

This is a fairly dry curry; if you want a wetter consistency, simply add more stock.

Shepherdless pie

PREP 15 MINS   **COOK** 30 MINS

Special equipment • food processor

SERVES 4

675g (1½lb) floury potatoes, peeled
    and quartered
2 knobs of butter
1 tbsp olive oil
1 onion, finely chopped
1 bay leaf
3 celery sticks, finely chopped
3 carrots, finely chopped
200g (7oz) chestnut mushrooms,
    roughly chopped
handful of fresh thyme sprigs,
    leaves picked
splash of dark soy sauce
400g can aduki beans, drained
    and rinsed
salt and freshly ground black pepper
150ml (5fl oz) hot vegetable stock

1 Preheat the oven to 200°C (400°F/ Gas 6). To make the mash topping, boil the potatoes in a pan of salted water for 15-20 minutes until soft. Drain, then mash. Add a knob of butter, and mash again. Set aside.

2 Meanwhile, heat the oil in a large frying pan over a low heat. Add the onion, bay leaf, and a pinch of salt, and sweat for about 5 minutes until the onion is soft. Now add the celery and carrot, and continue to sweat gently for a further 5 minutes.

3 Pulse the mushrooms in a food processor until broken down - you want them shredded, but not mushy. Add these to the pan, along with the thyme leaves and soy sauce, and cook for a further 5-10 minutes until the mushrooms begin to release their juices. Add the aduki beans, and season well with salt and black pepper. Pour over the stock, bring to the boil, reduce the heat slightly, and simmer gently for 5 minutes.

4 Tip into an ovenproof dish, and top with the reserved mashed potato. Dot with butter, and bake in the oven until the top is starting to become crisp and golden. Serve hot.

VARIATION

If you can't find aduki beans, use drained canned lentils or red kidney beans instead.

Chunky ratatouille

PREP 15 MINS COOK 30 MINS

SERVES 4
1 tbsp olive oil
1 onion, finely chopped
salt and freshly ground black pepper
1 bay leaf
2 garlic cloves, thinly sliced
1–2 tsp dried oregano
pinch of fennel seeds
1 aubergine, cut into chunky pieces
1 small glass of red wine
150ml (5fl oz) tomato juice
2 small courgettes, cut into
   chunky pieces
3 tomatoes, roughly chopped
large handful of Swiss chard leaves
freshly chopped flat-leaf parsley,
   to garnish

1 Heat the oil in a large pan over a low heat. Add the onion, a pinch of salt, and the bay leaf, and sweat for 5 minutes until the onion is soft and translucent.

2 Add the garlic, oregano, fennel seeds, aubergine, and wine. Let simmer for a minute, then add the tomato juice. Cook for about 10 minutes until the aubergine is soft.

3 Now add the courgettes and tomatoes, and cook for a further 5–10 minutes. Stir through the Swiss chard, and cook for another couple of minutes until all the vegetables are tender. Taste, and season if needed.

4 Garnish with the chopped parsley, and serve hot with fluffy rice or some fresh crusty bread.

VARIATION
Swap the Swiss chard for spinach or even Savoy cabbage.

COOK'S NOTES
Chop the vegetables smaller if you prefer; the ratatouille will stew down a little quicker.

Haricot bean and cauliflower gratin

PREP 10 MINS COOK 30 MINS

SERVES 4
knob of butter
1 tbsp plain flour
300ml (10fl oz) milk
pinch of paprika
salt and freshly ground
   black pepper
125g (4½oz) strong Cheddar
   cheese, grated
2 tsp Dijon mustard
1 head cauliflower, broken into florets
400g can haricot beans, drained
   and rinsed

1 Preheat the oven to 200°C (400°F/ Gas 6). To make the cheese sauce, melt the butter in a pan over a low heat. Remove from the heat, and stir in the flour with a wooden spoon until smooth. Add a little of the milk, and stir until smooth. Return to the heat, and slowly add the remaining milk, stirring continuously. Keep stirring for 5–10 minutes until the sauce has thickened.

2 Remove from the heat, sprinkle in the paprika, and season well with salt and black pepper. Stir in 75g (2½oz) of the cheese and the mustard, and set aside.

3 Cook the cauliflower in a pan of boiling salted water for about 10 minutes until soft. Drain.

4 Put the cauliflower in an ovenproof dish with the beans, and toss together. Pour over the sauce, and top with the remaining cheese. Cook in the oven for 10–15 minutes until golden and simmering. Serve hot.

Lemony dahl

PREP 10 MINS · COOK 30 MINS

SERVES 4

1 tbsp olive oil
1 onion, finely chopped
salt and freshly ground black pepper
2 garlic cloves, grated or finely chopped
5cm (2in) piece of fresh root
    ginger, grated
pinch of ground turmeric
pinch of garam masala
300g (10oz) red lentils
grated zest and juice of 1 lemon
900ml (1½ pints) hot vegetable stock
2 tomatoes, skinned and chopped
handful of fresh coriander,
    finely chopped

1 Heat the oil in a frying pan over a low heat. Add the onion and a pinch of salt, and sweat for 5 minutes until soft and translucent. Stir in the garlic, ginger, turmeric, and garam masala, and cook for a minute.

2 Stir in the lentils and lemon zest, pour over the stock, and simmer for about 20 minutes until the lentils are cooked.

3 Season well with salt and black pepper, and stir through the lemon juice, tomatoes, and coriander. Serve hot with naan bread or chapattis.

Courgettes stuffed with sultanas, red onion, and pine nuts

PREP 10 MINS · COOK 20 MINS

SERVES 4

8 courgettes
1 tbsp olive oil
1 red onion, finely chopped
salt
pinch of chilli flakes
handful of pine nuts, toasted
handful of sultanas
75g (2½oz) feta cheese, crumbled

1 Preheat the oven to 200°C (400°F/ Gas 6). First, prepare the courgettes. Cut in half lengthways. Scoop out the flesh, roughly chop, and set aside with the courgette shells.

2 Heat the oil in a large frying pan over a low heat. Add the onion and a pinch of salt. Sweat for 5 minutes until soft and translucent, then stir in the courgette flesh and chilli flakes, and cook for a couple more minutes.

3 Stir through half of the pine nuts and the sultanas, then remove from the heat. Spoon the mixture into the courgette shells, and top with the feta. Sit on a baking tray, and roast in the oven for 10-15 minutes until golden.

4 Sprinkle over the remaining pine nuts, and serve hot with a simple salad of mixed leaves and tomatoes.

EVERYDAY

Sweet potato and butterbean stew

PREP 10 MINS   COOK 30 MINS

SERVES 4

450g (1lb) sweet potatoes, peeled
 and cut into thick slices
2 tbsp maple syrup
1 tbsp olive oil
1 red onion, finely chopped
1 tsp cumin seeds
400g can peeled whole plum
 tomatoes, chopped
splash of balsamic vinegar
salt and freshly ground black pepper
400g can butterbeans, drained
 and rinsed
handful of Swiss chard
 or spinach leaves
150ml (5fl oz) Greek-style yogurt
handful of fresh mint leaves,
 to garnish

1 Cook the sweet potatoes and maple syrup in a large wide pan of boiling salted water for 10 minutes until tender, but not too soft. Drain well, and set aside to keep warm.

2 Meanwhile, heat the oil in a large wide pan or deep frying pan over a low heat. Add the onion, cumin seeds, and a pinch of salt, and sweat for about 5 minutes until the onion is soft and translucent. Tip in the tomatoes, including any juices, and the balsamic vinegar, and cook for about 10 minutes. Taste, and season with salt and black pepper.

3 Add the butterbeans, and simmer for a further 5 minutes, then stir through the Swiss chard or spinach. Cook for a couple of minutes more until the leaves just wilt. Remove from the heat, and top with the sweet potatoes. Preheat the grill to hot.

4 Transfer to an ovenproof dish, top with yogurt, and grill until golden. Garnish with mint leaves.

COOK'S NOTES

Canned whole peeled plum tomatoes are often far juicer and cheaper than ready-chopped ones. Just snip them in the can, using a pair of scissors.

Asparagus, broccoli, ginger, and mint stir-fry

PREP 15 MINS   COOK 15 MINS

Special equipment • wok

SERVES 4

1 tbsp sesame oil or vegetable oil
2 fresh red chillies, deseeded and
 finely chopped
5cm (2in) piece of fresh root ginger,
 sliced into fine strips
1 bunch of spring onions, cut into
 5cm (2in) lengths
2 garlic cloves, grated or
 finely chopped
1 red pepper, deseeded and sliced into
 fine strips
1 head broccoli, about 300g (10oz),
 cut into florets
1 bunch of fine asparagus spears,
 trimmed and halved
1 tbsp caster sugar
salt and freshly ground black pepper
handful of fresh mint leaves

1 Heat the oil in a wok over a medium-high heat, and swirl to coat the surface. Add the chillies and ginger and toss for a few seconds, then add the spring onions and a few seconds later add the garlic. Stir-fry for 5 minutes until soft.

2 Add the pepper, and stir-fry for a few minutes. Add the broccoli, and stir-fry for a few minutes more, before adding the asparagus. Continue stir-frying for another minute or two.

3 Sprinkle over the sugar, and season well with salt and black pepper. Stir-fry for a few seconds until the sugar has dissolved. Remove from the heat, and stir through the mint leaves. Serve immediately either on its own, or with some fluffy rice.

Cheat...
Tip in a bag of
ready-prepared and
chopped vegetables,
either frozen
or fresh.

COOK'S NOTES

Stir-fries require quick work; have all ingredients ready-prepared, chopped, or sliced. You can use your own selection of vegetables – just remember to add them in the right order, with the ones that require longer cooking going in first.

Thai red vegetable curry

PREP 15 MINS · COOK 20 MINS

SERVES 4
1–2 tbsp good-quality Thai red
    curry paste
400g can coconut milk
2 aubergines, cut into chunks
6 kaffir lime leaves, torn in
    half lengthways
300ml (10fl oz) hot vegetable stock
1 tbsp palm sugar or demerara
splash of dark soy sauce
salt
1 red pepper, deseeded and cut
    into strips
1 green pepper, deseeded and cut
    into strips
juice of 1 lime
handful of fresh coriander

1 Heat the curry paste in a large
frying pan or wok over a medium-high
heat for a few seconds, stirring around
the pan. Shake the coconut milk, then
pour into the pan or wok. Bring to
a gentle boil, stirring occasionally,
and cook for 2–3 minutes until the
sauce releases its aroma.

2 Add the aubergine, lime leaves,
stock, sugar, and soy sauce. Season
with salt, and bring to the boil again.
Reduce the heat slightly, and simmer
gently for about 15 minutes until the
aubergines are soft.

3 Now add the peppers and lime
juice, and stir well. Taste, and adjust
the seasoning accordingly, adding
more sugar (sweetness), lime juice
(sourness), or salt as needed. Stir
through the coriander, and serve
immediately with some jasmine
or sticky rice.

> **COOK'S NOTES**
>
> You could add firm tofu to this
> curry; it's best bought from
> a specialist Asian supermarket
> because it is often home-made
> and tastes wonderful.

EVERYDAY

Spicy garlic green vegetable medley

PREP 15 MINS · COOK 15 MINS

Special equipment • wok

SERVES 4
handful of hazelnuts
1 tbsp sesame oil or vegetable oil
2 fresh medium-hot green chillies,
    deseeded and finely chopped
3 garlic cloves, thinly sliced
1 tbsp dark soy sauce
1 tbsp Chinese rice wine
1–2 heads pak choi,
    quartered lengthways
handful of spinach or
    Swiss chard
2 handfuls of sugarsnap peas or
    mangetout, sliced into strips
salt and freshly ground black pepper

1 Spread the hazelnuts over
a baking tray. Toast under a hot
grill until golden brown, turning
them frequently. Put the hazelnuts
in a clean tea towel, and rub off the
skins. Roughly chop, and set aside.

2 Heat the oil in a wok over
a medium-high heat, and swirl
it around to coat the surface. Add
the chillies and garlic, and cook for
10 seconds, then add the soy sauce
and Chinese rice wine, and cook for
a few seconds more.

3 Throw in the pak choi and spinach
or Swiss chard, and stir-fry for a
minute. Add the sugarsnap peas or
mangetout, and stir-fry for a minute
more. Toss, and season with salt and
black pepper. Serve immediately with
the hazelnuts scattered over the top,
and some fluffy rice.

VARIATION
Throw in some whole oyster
mushrooms along with the
green vegetables.

Cheat...
For an instant meal,
just stir-fry the
vegetables simply
with a splash of
soy sauce.

Lentils with mushrooms and leeks

PREP 10 MINS **COOK 25 MINS**

SERVES 4
1 tbsp olive oil
1 onion, finely chopped
1 bay leaf
salt and freshly ground black pepper
2 garlic cloves, grated or
    finely chopped
3 leeks, sliced
2 tsp Marmite or Vegemite, or
    a splash of light soy sauce
225g (8oz) chestnut mushrooms,
    halved, or quartered if large
400g can green or Puy lentils, drained
    and rinsed
300ml (10fl oz) hot vegetable stock
handful of fresh curly parsley, stalks
    removed, finely chopped

1 Heat the oil in a large frying
pan over a low heat. Add the onion,
bay leaf, and a pinch of salt, and
sweat for 5 minutes until the onion
is soft and translucent.

2 Add the garlic and leek, and stir
through the Marmite, Vegemite, or soy
sauce. Sweat for a further 5 minutes
until the leeks begin to soften.

3 Now add the mushrooms, and cook
until they release their juices – you
may need to add a little more oil.
Season well with salt and black
pepper, then stir through the lentils
and hot stock. Bring to the boil,
reduce the heat slightly, and simmer
gently for 15 minutes.

4 Remove from the heat, and stir in
the parsley. Taste, and season again
if needed. Serve with some roasted
tomatoes and fresh crusty bread.

> **COOK'S NOTES**
>
> If cooking for vegetarians, this
> dish is good served with some
> vegetarian sausages. Roast them
> first in a preheated 200°C
> (400°F/Gas 6) oven for 15–20
> minutes, then add with the lentils
> in step 3, and simmer gently.

Grated courgette and goat's cheese omelette

PREP 10 MINS **COOK 15 MINS**

SERVES 1
3 eggs, lightly beaten
1 small courgette, grated
salt and freshly ground black pepper
knob of butter
50g (1¾oz) soft goat's cheese,
    crumbled
small handful of fresh thyme, leaves
    picked, to garnish (optional)

1 Put the beaten egg and grated
courgette in a jug. Season with salt
and some black pepper.

2 Melt the butter in a small non-stick
frying pan over a medium-high heat
until foaming, then pour in the egg
mixture, swirling it around the pan to
cover the base. Gently slide a knife
under the edges of the omelette.

3 When the omelette is beginning
to cook around the edges, scatter over
the goat's cheese, so that it is covered
evenly. Continue cooking until the
centre is almost cooked, but still just
a little wet. Remove from the heat,
and leave for a couple of minutes to
set – the retained heat will continue
to cook the omelette.

4 Sprinkle over a little black pepper,
and garnish with thyme leaves (if
using). Carefully slide out of the pan,
and serve immediately.

VARIATION
Many cheeses work well in an
omelette: feta, smoked, or even
creamed cheese can be tasty.

Baked eggs with tomatoes and peppers

PREP 10 MINS | COOK 20 MINS

SERVES 4

1 tbsp olive oil

1 red onion, sliced

salt and freshly ground black pepper

2 red peppers, deseeded and sliced

2 yellow or orange peppers, deseeded and sliced

2 fresh medium-hot red chillies, deseeded and finely chopped

3 tomatoes, skinned and roughly chopped

2 handfuls of fresh spinach leaves

pinch of paprika

4 eggs

1 Preheat the oven to 200°C (400°F/ Gas 6). Heat the oil in a large flameproof frying pan over a low heat. Add the onion and a pinch of salt. Sweat for 5 minutes until the onion is soft, then add the peppers and chillies. Cook for a further 5 minutes until the peppers soften.

2 Stir through the tomatoes, and cook until the tomatoes begin to soften, stirring well. Add the spinach and paprika, and cook for a few minutes more until the spinach is just beginning to wilt.

3 Make a little pocket in the mixture for each of the eggs, then carefully break an egg into each one. Slide the pan into the oven, and cook for about 5 minutes until the eggs are baked. Be careful not to let them overcook – the residual heat will keep cooking them after you have removed them from the oven. Sprinkle with black pepper, and serve immediately.

Rice and beans

PREP 5 MINS | COOK 25 MINS

SERVES 4

1 tbsp olive oil

1 onion, finely chopped

2 garlic cloves, grated or finely chopped

2–3 fresh hot chillies, deseeded and finely chopped

450g (1lb) basmati rice, rinsed

400g can black-eye beans, drained and rinsed

400g can coconut milk

500ml (16fl oz) hot vegetable stock

salt and freshly ground black pepper

1 Heat the oil in a large lidded pan over a low heat, and sweat the onion for 5 minutes until soft and translucent. Add the garlic and chillies, and cook for a few seconds more.

2 Stir through the rice, making sure that the grains are well coated, then tip in the beans, coconut milk, and most of the stock. Cover the pan, and gently cook over a low heat for about 20 minutes until all the liquid has been absorbed and the rice is cooked; if you need to add more stock, do so.

3 Season to taste with salt and black pepper, and serve hot with some chunky roasted vegetables and chillies.

VARIATION

Use red kidney beans instead of black-eye beans if you wish.

COOK'S NOTES

Do rinse the rice before you use it; this will help to remove some of the starch.

Pea and mint risotto

PREP 10 MINS | **COOK 25 MINS**

SERVES 4

1.1 litres (2 pints) light
   vegetable stock
1 tbsp olive oil
knob of butter
1 onion, finely chopped
salt and freshly ground black pepper
350g (12oz) risotto rice, such
   as Arborio
1 large glass of dry white wine
150g (5½oz) frozen or fresh peas
   (if using frozen, cover with boiling
   water for 3 minutes, then drain)
50g (1¾oz) Parmesan cheese,
   freshly grated
handful of fresh mint leaves
handful of fresh basil leaves

1 First, pour the stock into a large pan, and heat to a gentle simmer.

2 Heat the oil and butter in a large non-stick frying pan over a low heat. Add the onion and a pinch of salt. Sweat for about 5 minutes until soft and translucent, then stir through the rice, making sure that the grains are completely coated. Increase the heat

to medium-high, pour in the wine, and let it simmer for a couple of minutes until the alcohol has evaporated.

3 Reduce the heat slightly, and add the simmering stock a ladleful or two at a time, stirring frequently with a wooden spoon; when each addition of stock has been absorbed, add some more. Continue like this for about 20 minutes until the rice is cooked; it should still have a bite to it. Use more or less stock as required – every risotto is different.

4 Stir through the peas, Parmesan, mint, and basil. Season well with salt and black pepper, and serve hot.

VARIATION
Fresh asparagus tips also taste wonderful in a risotto.

COOK'S NOTES

For extra creaminess, stir through a knob of butter at the end of the cooking time.

Squash, sage, and blue cheese risotto

PREP 15 MINS | **COOK 30 MINS**

SERVES 4

1 butternut squash, halved,
   deseeded, peeled, and cut into
   bite-sized pieces
pinch of chilli flakes
2 tbsp olive oil
1.1 litres (2 pints) light
   vegetable stock
knob of butter
1 onion, finely chopped
salt and freshly ground black pepper
2 garlic cloves, grated or finely chopped
4 fresh sage leaves, torn (optional)
350g (12oz) risotto rice, such
   as Arborio
1 large glass of dry white wine
75g (2½oz) Gorgonzola or similar
   blue cheese

1 Preheat the oven to 200°C (400°F/Gas 6). Put the squash in a roasting tin, sprinkle over the chilli flakes, and drizzle over 1 tablespoon of the oil. Mix together, using your hands. Roast in the oven for about 15 minutes until golden and beginning to soften.

2 Meanwhile, pour the stock into a large pan, and heat to a gentle simmer. Heat the remaining oil and

a knob of butter in a large non-stick frying pan over a low heat. Add the onion and a pinch of salt, and sweat for 5 minutes until the onions are soft and translucent. Stir through the garlic and sage leaves (if using), and cook for a few seconds more.

3 Next, stir through the rice, making sure that the grains are completely coated. Increase the heat to medium-high, pour in the wine, and let it simmer for a couple of minutes until the alcohol has evaporated.

4 Reduce the heat slightly, and add the simmering stock a ladleful at a time, stirring frequently with a wooden spoon; when each addition of stock has been absorbed, add some more. Continue like this for about 20 minutes until the rice is cooked; it should still have a bite to it. Use more or less stock as required. Stir through the roasted squash and the Gorgonzola, season with black pepper, and serve hot.

VARIATION
If you're not a fan of blue cheese, simply omit, and stir through freshly grated Parmesan or pecorino cheese instead.

EVERYDAY

Aubergines stuffed with tomato rice

PREP 10 MINS • COOK 30 MINS

SERVES 4
4 aubergines, halved lengthways
1 tbsp olive oil
200g (7oz) long-grain rice, rinsed
300ml (10fl oz) tomato juice
1 tsp sugar
salt and freshly ground black pepper
1 tbsp olive oil
1 onion, finely chopped
small handful of fresh dill,
    finely chopped

1 Preheat the oven to 200°C (400°F/Gas 6). Scoop out the flesh from the aubergines, chop into bite-sized chunks, and set aside. Sit the shells in a roasting tin, and brush with the oil. Cover with foil, and roast in the oven for 10–15 minutes while you cook the rice.

2 Put the rice in a pan and cover with water. Simmer for 10–15 minutes, or according to the packet instructions, until cooked. Drain if needed, then pour over the tomato juice. Sprinkle over the sugar, and season well with salt and black pepper. Stir until the tomato juice is absorbed.

3 Heat 1 tablespoon of the oil in a large frying pan over a low heat. Add the onion, dill, and a pinch of salt. Sweat until the onion is soft and translucent, then add the reserved aubergine flesh, and cook for a further 5 minutes. Season with black pepper, add the tomato rice mixture, and stir well.

4 Remove the aubergine shells from the oven, and carefully spoon the mixture into them. Drizzle over the remaining olive oil, and return to the oven for a further 5 minutes. Serve hot with a crisp green salad.

Veggie Pad Thai

PREP 15 MINS • COOK 15 MINS

Special equipment • wok

SERVES 4
250g (9oz) wide or medium
    rice noodles
3–4 tbsp vegetable oil
200g (7oz) firm tofu, cut into cubes
2 garlic cloves, grated or
    finely chopped
1 egg, lightly beaten
150ml (5fl oz) hot vegetable stock
juice of 1 lime
1 tsp Thai fish sauce, such as nam
    pla (optional)
2 tsp tamarind paste
2 tsp demerara sugar
1 tbsp dark soy sauce
1 fresh hot red chilli, deseeded
    and finely chopped
75g (2½oz) dry-roasted peanuts,
    roughly chopped
1 bunch of spring onions,
    finely chopped
75g (2½oz) beansprouts (optional)
small handful of fresh coriander

1 Soak the rice noodles in boiling water for 10 minutes, then drain. Meanwhile, heat 1 tablespoon of the vegetable oil in a wok over a medium-high heat, and swirl it around to coat the surface. Add the tofu, and cook for about 10 minutes until golden – you may need to use more oil. Remove with a slotted spoon, and set aside.

2 Add another tablespoon of oil to the pan. When hot, add the garlic and cook for 10 seconds, then tip in the egg and cook, stirring and breaking it up with a wooden spoon, until scrambled. Remove from the pan, and set aside.

3 Now add another tablespoon of the oil. Again, when hot, add the drained noodles, and stir gently to coat with the oil. Pour over the stock, lime juice, fish sauce, tamarind paste, sugar, and soy sauce; toss to combine. Let it simmer for a few minutes, sprinkle over the chilli, and stir through.

4 Add half of the peanuts, the spring onions, and the beansprouts (if using), and stir-fry for a minute. Now add the reserved scrambled egg, stir to combine, and transfer to a serving plate. Scatter over the remaining peanuts and a sprinkling of coriander to serve.

Cheat... Buy a ready-prepared pad thai sauce, and toss with the noodles for a quick home-from-work dish.

EVERYDAY

Potato cakes

 PREP 10 MINS **COOK 25 MINS**

SERVES 4
450g (1lb) floury potatoes, peeled
1 onion, peeled and grated
handful of fresh chives,
    finely chopped
125g (4½oz) feta cheese, grated
1 egg, lightly beaten, to bind
salt and freshly ground black pepper
1 tbsp olive oil

1 Boil the potatoes in a pan of salted water for 15-20 minutes until soft. Drain, then mash. Mix the mashed potatoes with the onion, chives, feta cheese, and egg. Season with plenty of salt and black pepper.

2 Heat the olive oil in a non-stick frying pan over a medium heat. Using floured hands, scoop up large balls of the potato mixture, roll, and flatten slightly. Carefully add to the hot oil, and fry for 2-3 minutes on each side until golden, topping up the pan with more oil, if needed. Serve hot.

Potato gnocchi

 PREP 20 MINS **COOK 25 MINS**

SERVES 4
450g (1lb) floury potatoes, peeled
1 egg
1-2 tbsp plain flour
tomato or Gorgonzola sauce, or
    a drizzle of extra virgin olive oil,
    to serve
pesto, to serve

1 Boil the potatoes in a pan of salted water for 15-20 minutes until soft. Drain, then mash. Put the mashed potato in a bowl. Crack in the egg, and mix gently until combined. Add the flour, and stir until it forms a soft dough.

2 Transfer the dough to a floured work surface, and knead gently for a couple of minutes - don't overwork the dough, or it will become tough.

Divide the mixture into four, and roll each portion into a sausage shape. Cut each one into pieces about 3cm (1¼in) long. Use the back of a fork to mark each piece of gnocchi with a ridge pattern.

3 Cook in a large pan of boiling salted water for 2-3 minutes - when the gnocchi float to the surface they are ready. Scoop out using a slotted spoon, and divide among 4 pasta bowls or plates. Serve immediately with a tomato or Gorgonzola sauce, or a drizzle of olive oil and some pesto.

COOK'S NOTES

It's important that the potatoes aren't too wet. You could boil them in their skins, which will help, but remember to peel them before mashing.

Potato and leek soup

PREP 5 MINS **COOK 30 MINS**

SERVES 4
450g (1lb) floury potatoes, peeled
1 tbsp olive oil
1 onion, finely chopped
4 leeks, cleaned and sliced
salt and freshly ground black pepper
900ml (1½ pints) hot vegetable stock
small handful of fresh thyme leaves

1 Boil the potatoes in a pan of salted water for 15–20 minutes until soft. Drain, then cut into bite-sized pieces.

2 Heat the olive oil in a large pan over a low heat. Add the onion, and sweat gently for about 5 minutes until soft and translucent. Add the leeks,

and cook for a further 5 minutes. Season well with salt and black pepper. Pour in the hot vegetable stock, and bring to the boil. Reduce the heat slightly, and simmer for about 10 minutes. Add the potatoes, and sprinkle in the thyme leaves. Continue cooking the soup until the potatoes are heated through, then serve hot with some fresh crusty bread.

 VARIATION Add some chopped ready-cooked bacon or ham to the soup.

EVERYDAY

Potato and horseradish mash

PREP 15 MINS **COOK 30 MINS**

SERVES 4
450g (1lb) floury potatoes, peeled
1 tbsp olive oil
knob of butter
200g (7oz) bacon rashers, chopped
3 tsp creamed horseradish
salt and freshly ground black pepper
250g (9oz) curly kale, cooked
    and chopped

1 Boil the potatoes in a pan of salted water for 15–20 minutes until soft. Drain, then cut into bite-sized pieces, or mash, if you like.

2 Heat the olive oil and butter in a large non-stick frying pan over a medium heat. When the butter has melted, add the bacon rashers. Fry for 5–6 minutes until golden and crispy. Tip in the potatoes and stir through. Add the horseradish cream, and season with salt and black pepper. Stir through the curly kale until everything is combined. Cook for a few minutes until lightly golden and a little crispy. Serve hot with some red cabbage on the side.

EVERYDAY CHICKEN

Grilled, poached, steamed, baked, fried
– and always easy.

EVERYDAY CHICKEN

Chicken is not only one of the most versatile foods you can cook with, it is also good value. Every part of it can be used in a different way: it can be roasted whole and unadorned (see p222), used as cuts, seasoned with exotic spices, and cooked on a grill or barbecue, or slowly until meltingly soft. However chicken is cooked, it's always a favourite.

Chicken doner kebab.
For recipe, see page 120.

Free-range or organic?

Buying chicken can sometimes be confusing, with labelling varying from "free-range" and "organic", to "corn-fed" and "farm-fresh".

Free-range birds have been provided with access to open-air runs. "Traditional free-range" has to keep to stricter rules – the birds have more freedom and space. Free-range birds must have continuous daytime access to the open air, for at least half their life.

Organic birds have been fed on a completely organic diet, given no meat by-products, and won't have been given antibiotics. They usually have outdoor access, and are reared for up to 12 weeks, twice as long as intensively-farmed chickens. They are often the most expensive choice, but you can taste the difference in the meat. Choose chickens that have a recognized "organic" certification.

Corn-fed simply means that the birds have been fed on a diet of corn or maize, resulting in a yellow, golden skin. It doesn't mean that they are free-range or organic.

Farm-fresh is a misleading label, and can still mean that the bird has been intensively reared.

chicken nutrition
Chicken is packed with protein, and is low in saturated fat. Most of the fat is in the skin, but this can easily be avoided by removing it before or after cooking. A 100g (3½oz) piece of skinless chicken breast is around 100 calories and 2g (¹⁄₁₆oz) of fat, and with skin on around 200 calories and 12g (½oz) of fat. It's a good low-cholesterol meat choice, and provides all the essential amino acids, along with vitamins B6 and B12, needed for a healthy diet.

Quick-cook cuts A jointed chicken provides many different cuts, each one suiting various quick cooking methods.

CHOOSE	USE	COOK
 **BREAST** The breast is available on the bone (the most succulent), or as a fillet. It is the leanest and most popular part of the chicken, and is quick to cook. Breasts are usually around 175-200g (6-7oz) in weight, and are the most expensive cut of chicken.	Breast meat is more delicate than leg or thigh: if overcooked, it can become very dry. It can be dry-cooked (under the grill, or on the barbecue), roasted, poached, pan-fried, or added to a casserole.	**Grill or barbecue** 4-5 mins each side, over a low-medium heat **Roast** 15-20 mins at 200°C (400°F/Gas 6) **Poach** 15-20 mins **Steam** 20-30 mins **Pan-fry** 6-8 mins each side, over a high heat
LEG The leg contains the drumstick, which is the lower end of the leg. The leg can also be bought attached to the thigh – a quarter joint. As the leg does all the work, there is more muscle, which turns the meat darker, and makes it more flavoursome. Legs are a cheaper alternative to breast meat.	Chicken legs are easy to cook. They can be dry-cooked (under the grill, or on the barbecue), oven-cooked, poached, or added to a casserole. To check they are cooked, insert a skewer into the thickest part of the leg. If the juices run clear, they are cooked through; if not, cook for longer.	**Grill or barbecue** 15-20 mins each side, over a low heat **Roast** 35-40 mins at 200°C (400°F/Gas 6) **Poach** 20-25 mins **Barbecue** 30-40 mins over a low-medium heat
 **THIGHS** They are available on or off the bone, skin on, and skinless. As with the leg, the meat is darker, but thigh meat is more tender than leg meat. They are cheaper but smaller than the breast portions, so you should allow two per person.	Thighs with the bone in are a good choice for slow cooking. Boned thighs can be stuffed with a variety of flavours, from mushrooms, to nuts and spices, and then pan-fried or roasted until cooked through. The meat from boneless thighs can be skinned and chopped for casseroles or stews, or for skewering onto kebabs.	**Roast (bone in)** 35-40 mins at 200°C (400°F/Gas 6) **(bone out)** 25-30 mins at 200°C (400°F/Gas 6) **Grill or barbecue (bone out)** 25-30 mins, over a high heat **Pan-fry (bone in)** 8-10 mins each side, over a medium-high heat **(bone out)** 6-8 mins each side, over a medium-high heat
 **WINGS** Bony wing sections have dark meat, and are delicious when cooked until the skin is crispy. There is not much meat on them, so allow 4-5 per person, although they do contain around 100 calories per wing so they are not a low-fat option.	To get the best from chicken wings, they need to be marinated for a few hours in something hot and spicy (such as cayenne pepper, olive oil, and garlic), or sticky and sweet (such as honey, soy sauce, and Worcestershire sauce). They need a hot, dry heat, so are best oven-roasted or barbecued.	**Roast** 30-40 mins at 200°C (400°F/Gas 6) **Grill or barbecue** 30-40 mins over a low-medium heat

STEP-BY-STEP

Time-saving techniques Six quick and simple ways to prepare and cook chicken – each technique results in a different flavour and texture. The first three are preparation techniques, and the last three are cooking techniques.

Flatten Bashing a chicken breast so it is thin and even will speed up the cooking time.

1 Place a skinless chicken breast fillet between two sheets of cling film on a clean board.

2 Pound evenly with a meat hammer, or the side of a rolling pin, until it is an even thickness, about 5mm (¼in).

3 Remove the cling film, and season. Flattened (escalope) chicken breast fillet needs only 2–3 minutes of pan-frying or grilling on each side.

Stuff Stuffing a chicken breast adds extra flavour, and keeps the chicken moist.

1 Lay a skinned chicken breast on a clean board, and bash briefly with a meat hammer or the side of a rolling pin to flatten it a little.

2 Working out from the middle, slash each side with a knife, making sure you don't cut all the way through, to form a pocket for the filling.

3 Fill, and pull together tightly. Wrap with pancetta or streaky bacon, or sit open-side down and fry in a little olive oil for 6-8 minutes each side, or until cooked through.

Skewer Threading small pieces of chicken onto skewers will speed up the cooking time.

1 Soak wooden skewers for 30 minutes in cold water, so they don't burn. Use 2 chicken breast fillets or 2 thigh fillets for 6 skewers.

2 Cut 1 portion into bite-sized pieces, then thread onto the skewers, about 6 per stick. Cut the other portion into strips, and thread onto the skewers. Marinate (see overleaf for suggestions).

3 Sit the skewers on a hot ridged cast-iron pan or over a barbecue, and cook for 3-4 minutes each side, or until cooked through and charred.

Roast Oven-roasting suits most cuts (see left), as well as a whole bird.

1 Preheat the oven to 200°C (400°F/Gas 6). Sit the chicken, about 1.35kg (3lb), in a roasting tin and smother with butter (using your hands).

2 Season, and sprinkle over a handful of fresh thyme leaves. Stuff two lemon halves into the cavity to help it stay moist, then put in the oven.

3 Cook for 30 minutes, remove and spoon the juices in the tin all over the bird (basting), then cook for a further hour, until golden and cooked. To test, pierce the thigh with a skewer: if the juices run clear, it's ready.

Steam Steaming keeps the chicken moist. A healthy way to cook skinless chicken breasts.

1 Preheat the oven to 200°C (400°F/Gas 6). Lay out a large square of foil, then sit a chicken breast, plump side up, in it.

2 Season well, throw in a handful of fresh herbs and a few lemon pieces, and pour over a tablespoon of dry white wine, then close the foil, leaving plenty of room for the chicken, sealing the edges together tightly.

3 Sit on a baking tray, and put in the oven to cook for 20-30 minutes, or until cooked through. Be careful when opening the parcel as it will be hot, and full of steam.

Poach Cooking in liquid keeps the chicken moist. Suits breasts and legs.

1 Put 2 breasts or legs, plump side up, in a deep-sided frying pan, add some lemon slices, a handful of fresh parsley (or fresh herb of your choice), a pinch of salt, and a teaspoon of black peppercorns.

2 Pour in enough cold water to cover, then bring to the boil. Simmer gently, sitting a lid loosely on top, and cook for 15-20 minutes for breasts, or 20-25 minutes for legs.

3 Turn off the heat, and leave the chicken in the pan for about 5 minutes. Remove with a slotted spoon and serve immediately.

EVERYDAY

5 quick flavour mixes for chicken
Transform chicken from simple to special with these fresh, hot, and aromatic spice and herb combinations. Use as rubs or marinades before grilling, roasting, or barbecuing.

Thai spice
A wonderful assortment of colourful, aromatic, and pungent spices.

Mix together a couple of finely shredded **lemongrass stalks**, 6 finely chopped and deseeded **red** and **green chillies**, a thumb-sized piece of grated **fresh root ginger**, 1 tbsp **lime juice**, a handful of **fresh coriander**, and 1 tbsp **dark soy sauce**. Will keep, chilled, for 3–4 days.

Use to marinate chicken portions (preferably overnight), before pan-frying, or roasting in the oven.

Caribbean spice
A diverse fusion of hot and peppery tropical spices.

Whiz a handful of **fresh thyme** leaves, 2–3 **Scotch Bonnet chillies**, 1 tbsp **black peppercorns**, 1 tsp **sea salt**, and 2 tsp **allspice** in a food processor, or pound in a mortar and pestle until finely ground. Will keep, chilled, for 3–4 days.

Smother chicken portions in olive oil, add to a plastic bag with the spice mix, and shake. Leave to marinate (preferably overnight). Grill or barbecue for 30–40 minutes, turning once, until cooked through.

Indian spice
A delicious warm and fragrant mix of dry spices, fiery chillies, and cooling yogurt.

Crush 1 tsp **cardamom pods** and 1 tsp **coriander seeds**, and deseed and chop 2 **fresh medium-hot green chillies**. Measure out 3 tsp each of **garam masala** and **turmeric**. Will keep, chilled, for 3–4 days.

Put the crushed spices in a hot pan with a little oil or ghee. Cook for a minute, then add the chillies. Mix Greek yogurt with the ground spices, and smother over chicken thighs. Cook for 8–10 minutes each side.

Mediterranean herbs
A classic mix: light, sweet, and woody herbs with the sharp tang of lemon.

Combine 2 tsp **dried oregano** in a bowl with 3 **crushed garlic cloves**, a few **fresh rosemary** and **thyme stalks**, 1 tbsp **black pitted olives** (optional), and 2 **lemon wedges**. Will keep, chilled, for 3–4 days.

Rub chicken thighs or legs with olive oil, season, and sit in a roasting tin. Smother the chicken pieces with the mix, and cook in the oven at 200°C (400°F/Gas 6) for 35–40 minutes.

Storing chicken

Chill Cooked and uncooked chicken should be kept in the refrigerator at all times, and used within a couple of days of purchase (or by the use-by date on the packaging). Keep uncooked chicken tightly wrapped in cling film at the bottom of the refrigerator, and keep it away from other foods, particularly cooked meats. Don't let it sit at room temperature, as this is when germs can breed.

Freeze Freeze uncooked chicken straight away, and make sure it is well wrapped in cling film, so it doesn't suffer from freezer burn. It will freeze for up to 6 months. Never freeze uncooked chicken ready-stuffed. Cooked chicken is best frozen in a freezer-proof plastic container with a sealable lid. Only freeze it if it is covered in a sauce, otherwise it will be dry and tasteless. Freeze for up to 3 months. Defrost in the refrigerator overnight (never cook chicken from frozen).

Reheating chicken

Chicken can be reheated only once. Don't reheat it if it's still warm – it needs to be cooled quickly and completely chilled in the refrigerator. Reheat it until it is piping hot, as bacteria is killed at high heat (above 75°C, to be precise). Put your dish in the microwave, cover with a plate to retain moisture, and cook on High for 3–4 minutes.

Tools of the trade

For pan-frying, a **heavy-based frying pan** is essential. A **pair of metal tongs** are also good to have on hand, for turning the chicken while it's cooking. A **heavy-duty roasting tin** and **baking sheet** are preferable, as they don't buckle under high heat. A **cast-iron ridged grill pan** is excellent for cooking chicken, and a combination of **wooden and metal skewers** is essential for kebabs.

EVERYDAY

Moroccan spice A blend of sweet and tangy flavours, scented and perfumed to add a distinctive taste and aroma.

Combine 1 tbsp each of **smoked paprika** and **harissa paste** with 2 tbsp **lemon juice**, 2 **cinnamon sticks**, and a handful of **preserved lemons**, chopped.

Fry chicken thighs in a large casserole dish with a little olive oil, then add the spice mix, together with some tomato passata, and cook – covered – over a medium heat for 30–40 minutes. At the end of cooking, stir in some chopped **fresh flat-leaf parsley**.

Psst...

To save on time and money spent on shop-bought mixes, get creative. Go through your cupboards and whiz up your own blend of herbs and spices in the food processor. Keep in a sealed jar until needed (no longer than 6 months). Turmeric and cumin seeds, below, can be blended with other Indian spices.

Tools for cooking everyday chicken dishes.

EVERYDAY

Spanish-style chicken with pine nuts

PREP 10 MINS · COOK 1 HR

SERVES 4

2 tbsp olive oil
8 chicken thighs
1 onion, finely chopped
salt and freshly ground black pepper
3 garlic cloves, grated or
    finely chopped
6 ripe tomatoes, skinned and chopped
1 small glass of red wine
900ml (1½ pints) hot chicken stock
handful of pine nuts, toasted
handful of sultanas (optional)

1 In a large pan, heat 1 tablespoon of the olive oil over a medium heat. Add the chicken pieces, and brown for 5–8 minutes on each side until they are golden all over. Remove from the pan, and set aside.

2 Reduce the heat to medium. Add the remaining oil, the onion, and a pinch of salt to the same pan, and sweat for about 5 minutes until soft.

3 Tip in the garlic and fresh tomatoes, and season with black pepper. Cook for a few minutes until the tomatoes are starting to break down. Add the red wine, increase the heat slightly, and simmer for a few minutes.

4 Pour in the hot stock, and bring to the boil. Reduce the heat to low, and return the chicken to the pan along with the pine nuts and sultanas (if using). Gently simmer for 30–40 minutes. Top up with a little hot water if it gets too dry. Serve hot with rice or boiled new potatoes.

COOK'S NOTES

A large, roomy cast-iron pan, if you have one to hand, is ideal for this sort of dish. It can be used on the hob or in the oven, and you can cook the dish as fast or slow as you wish.

Garlic and chilli chicken with honey sweet potato

PREP 15 MINS · COOK 1¼ HRS

SERVES 4

8 chicken pieces (a mixture of thighs
    and drumsticks), skin on
salt and freshly ground black pepper
4 sweet potatoes, peeled and
    roughly chopped
1–2 tbsp clear honey
2 tbsp olive oil
2 fresh medium-hot red chillies,
    deseeded and sliced
a few sprigs of fresh thyme
½ garlic bulb, cloves separated,
    peeled, and squashed
1 small glass of dry white wine
300ml (10fl oz) hot light chicken stock

1 Preheat the oven to 200°C (400°F/Gas 6). Season the chicken liberally with salt and black pepper, and coat the sweet potato in the honey.

2 In a heavy flameproof casserole, preferably a cast-iron one, heat 1 tablespoon of the oil over a medium heat. Add the sweet potato, and cook for about 5 minutes until beginning to colour, then remove from the pan and set aside.

3 Increase the heat to medium-high, and heat the remaining oil in the same pan. Brown the chicken for about 5 minutes on each side until nicely golden all over. Add the chillies, thyme, and garlic. Return the sweet potato to the pan, and season well.

4 Pour in the wine and stock, cover the pan, and transfer to the oven to cook for 1 hour. Check the casserole a few times during cooking; give it a stir if needed, or add a small amount of stock if it is too dry. Serve hot with chunks of fresh crusty bread.

VARIATION

Substitute the sweet potato with your favourite winter squash, if it is in season.

Chicken thighs stuffed with pistachio nuts and chillies

PREP 15 MINS **COOK** 35 MINS

Special equipment • food processor

SERVES 4
4 large skinless and boneless chicken
   thigh fillets
8 slices Parma ham
1 tbsp olive oil

For the stuffing
125g (4½oz) skinned pistachio nuts,
   ground in a food processor
handful of fresh flat-leaf parsley,
   finely chopped
2–3 fresh medium-hot red chillies,
   deseeded and finely chopped
drizzle of olive oil
salt and freshly ground black pepper

1 Preheat the oven to 200°C (400°F/ Gas 6). To make the stuffing, mix together the nuts, parsley, chillies, and olive oil in a bowl. Season well with salt and black pepper, and set aside.

2 Using a sharp knife, cut diagonal slashes across the chicken pieces, but without slicing all the way through. Carefully spoon the stuffing mixture into the gaps, dividing it evenly among the pieces. You may have some stuffing left over.

3 Lay out 4 slices of the Parma ham on a flat work surface, and place a chicken thigh on top of each one. Roll up each thigh in the ham so that you have 4 parcels. Use the remaining ham slices to wrap around each thigh the other way, so that everything is covered.

4 Sit the parcels in a roasting tin, drizzle with the olive oil, and roast in the oven for about 35 minutes until cooked through. Serve with a salad and bread.

VARIATION
If you can't find large thigh fillets, you can use skinless chicken breast fillets instead.

COOK'S NOTES
If you have any stuffing mixture left over, sprinkle it over the wrapped chicken pieces when they go into the oven.

Chicken poached in coconut milk

PREP 5 MINS **COOK** 15 MINS

SERVES 4
8 chicken breast fillets, skin on, about
   200g (7oz) each
500ml (16fl oz) hot light
   vegetable stock
400ml can coconut milk
3 bay leaves
3 garlic cloves, peeled but left whole
salt and freshly ground black pepper

1 To poach the chicken, put the chicken breasts in a large lidded pan over a medium heat, then pour over the hot stock and the coconut milk. Add the bay leaves, garlic cloves, and salt and black pepper. Bring to the boil, then cover the pan, reduce the heat slightly, and simmer for 10–15 minutes until the chicken is cooked. Poke a sharp knife into the thickest part of the flesh to check – the juices should run clear.

2 Using a slotted spoon, remove the chicken from the pan, and leave to cool for a minute or two. When cool enough to handle, either slice the chicken or shred using two forks, and serve with fluffy rice and a little of the juices.

VARIATION
You could poach the chicken in boiling water and 2–3 tablespoons of dark soy sauce if you have no coconut milk.

COOK'S NOTES
Use any rice you wish to serve with this, but basmati is certainly the best. If you wait until the chicken is cooked before cooking the rice, you can then use the coconut milk liquid to cook the rice – it'll be really tasty.

EVERYDAY (side tab)

Chicken with cider and cream

PREP 10 MINS · COOK 1 HR

SERVES 4
1 tbsp olive oil
2 onions, cut into 8 wedges
salt and freshly ground black pepper
2 garlic cloves, grated or finely chopped
8 chicken thighs
300ml (10fl oz) cider
300ml (10fl oz) double cream
a few sprigs of fresh rosemary

1 Preheat the oven to 200°C (400°F/Gas 6). Heat the olive oil in a large flameproof casserole over a low-medium heat. Add the onion and a pinch of salt, and sweat for 5 minutes until soft and translucent. Now add the garlic, and cook for 10 seconds.

2 Push the onions to one side of the casserole, and increase the heat to medium-high. Add a little more oil if needed, and put the chicken thighs in the casserole skin-side down. Brown for about 5 minutes on each side until golden.

3 Increase the heat slightly, and pour in the cider. Let boil for a few minutes, then reduce the heat to a simmer, and add the cream. Throw in the rosemary sprigs, and season well with salt and black pepper.

4 Cover with a lid, and transfer to the oven to cook for about 40 minutes. If it is becoming too dry, add a little hot water or hot chicken or vegetable stock. Serve hot with mashed potato and chunks of fresh crusty bread, to mop up all the juices.

Chicken with noodles and basil

PREP 5 MINS · COOK 15 MINS

Special equipment · wok

SERVES 4
1 tbsp sesame oil
2 large skinless chicken breast fillets, sliced
1 tbsp dark soy sauce
1 tbsp clear honey
300g (10oz) thick or medium ready-to-wok udon noodles
handful of fresh basil leaves, torn

1 Heat the sesame oil in a large wok or frying pan over a medium-high heat. When hot, swirl around the wok or pan, and add the chicken. Stir-fry quickly for a few minutes until beginning to turn golden. Remove from the pan, and set aside to keep warm.

2 Add the soy sauce and honey to the wok or frying pan, and let simmer for a few minutes. Return the chicken to the pan along with the noodles, and stir so that everything is well coated.

3 When ready to serve, stir through the basil. Serve immediately.

Chicken with broad beans

PREP 10 MINS · **COOK 1 HR**

SERVES 4

8 chicken thighs
salt and freshly ground black pepper
2 tbsp olive oil
1 onion, finely chopped
2 celery sticks, finely chopped
2 garlic cloves, grated
   or finely chopped
a few sprigs of fresh rosemary, leaves
   picked and finely chopped
1 large glass of dry white wine
200g (7oz) frozen broad beans, or
   fresh if in season (see Cheat)
500ml (16fl oz) hot chicken stock

1 Preheat the oven to 200°C (400°F/ Gas 6). Season the chicken pieces well with salt and black pepper. Heat 1 tablespoon of the oil in a large flameproof casserole over a medium-high heat. Add the chicken, skin-side down, and brown for 5–6 minutes on each side until golden all over. Remove from the pan, and set aside.

2 Reduce the heat to low, and add the remaining oil to the casserole. Add the onion and a pinch of salt, and sweat for 5 minutes until soft. Now add the celery, garlic, and rosemary, and sweat for a further 5 minutes. Increase the heat, pour in the wine, and let simmer for about 5 minutes.

3 Stir through the broad beans, and return the chicken to the pan, tucking the pieces in and around the beans. Pour over the stock, cover, and cook in the oven for 45 minutes to 1 hour. Check halfway through the cooking time, topping up with a little hot water if too dry. Serve with oven-roasted tomatoes and fresh crusty bread.

VARIATION

You could make this dish using good-quality pork sausages instead of chicken.

Cheat...
Frozen broad beans are a fantastic stand-in for fresh; always keep a bag on hand in the freezer.

Chicken with chicory and bacon

PREP 5 MINS · **COOK 40 MINS**

SERVES 4

knob of butter
pinch of demerara sugar
3 large heads chicory, halved
   lengthways
1 tbsp olive oil
4 large chicken breast fillets, skin on
12 streaky bacon rashers

1 Preheat the oven to 200°C (400°F/ Gas 6). Put the butter and the sugar in a large frying pan over a low heat. Cook until the sugar has dissolved and the butter has melted. Add the chicory, and cook for 5–8 minutes until golden, then set aside.

2 Increase the heat to medium-high, and add the olive oil to the same pan. When hot, add the chicken, skin-side down, and brown for 3–5 minutes on each side until golden all over. Transfer the chicken to a roasting tin.

3 Wrap the bacon around the reserved chicory, and tuck it into the roasting tin so that it all sits snugly. You want everything tightly packed, so that the dish will produce plenty of juice. Roast in the oven for about 25 minutes until golden. Serve hot with baby roast potatoes.

VARIATION

Use pancetta or Parma ham instead of bacon.

COOK'S NOTES
Sprinkle Parmesan or Gruyère cheese over the chicory once you have put it in the roasting tin, if you like.

Chicken stir-fried with spring onion, basil, and lemongrass

PREP 10 MINS   COOK 15 MINS

Special equipment • wok

SERVES 4

2–3 skinless chicken breast fillets,
   sliced into strips
salt and freshly ground black pepper
1 tbsp cornflour
2 tbsp sesame oil or vegetable oil
bunch of spring onions,
   sliced diagonally
3 garlic cloves, sliced
1 stalk lemongrass, tough outer leaves
   removed, chopped
2 fresh mild red chillies, deseeded
   and sliced
1 tbsp Chinese rice wine
handful of fresh basil leaves

1 Season the chicken with salt and
black pepper. Put the cornflour on
a plate, and toss the chicken strips
in it until very well coated.

2 Heat 1 tablespoon of the oil in
a wok over a high heat. Swirl around
the wok, then add the chicken and
stir-fry quickly, moving the chicken
around the wok for 3–5 minutes until
golden and cooked through. Remove

with a slotted spoon, and set aside
to keep warm.

3 Carefully wipe out the wok with
kitchen paper, reduce the heat to
medium-high, and add the remaining
oil. When hot, add the spring onions,
garlic, lemongrass, and chillies.
Stir-fry for a couple of minutes, then
increase the heat to high once again,
and add the rice wine. Let boil for
a few minutes.

4 Return the chicken to the wok to just
heat through, stir in the basil, and serve
immediately with some fluffy rice.

VARIATION

This is just as tasty
made with prawns
instead of chicken.

COOK'S NOTES

*Tossing the chicken in cornflour
is key; it gives it a light almost
tempura-like coating, and makes
the chicken a little crispy.*

Five-spice and honey chicken with chilli greens

PREP 10 MINS   COOK 45 MINS

SERVES 4

2 handfuls of Chinese greens, such as
   pak choi, sliced
splash of light soy sauce
2.5cm (1in) piece of fresh root
   ginger, grated
pinch of chilli flakes
salt and freshly ground black pepper
1–2 tbsp runny honey
juice of 2 limes
3 tbsp olive oil
2 tbsp five-spice paste
8 chicken pieces (a mixture of thighs
   and drumsticks), skin on

1 Preheat the oven to 200°C (400°F/
Gas 6). Put the greens in a large bowl.
Add the soy sauce, ginger, and chilli
flakes, and season well with salt and
black pepper. Set aside.

2 In another bowl, mix together the
honey, lime juice, 1 tablespoon of

the oil, and the five-spice paste until
well combined. Spread over the
chicken, and season well. Leave to
marinate in the refrigerator for at
least 20 minutes, if you have time.

3 Heat another tablespoon of
the oil in a large frying pan over
a medium-high heat. Add the chicken
pieces, skin-side down – cook a few
pieces at a time if the pan is not big
enough. Cook for 5–8 minutes on each
side until golden and crispy, then
transfer to a roasting tin. Roast in
the oven for about 40 minutes until
beginning to char.

4 Meanwhile, wipe out the frying pan
with kitchen paper, reduce the heat
slightly, and add the greens. Drizzle
over the remaining tablespoon of oil,
and stir-fry for about 5 minutes until
beginning to wilt. Serve hot with the
crispy-skinned chicken.

Pan-fried chicken stuffed with spinach and Gruyère cheese

 PREP 10 MINS **COOK 25 MINS**

SERVES 4

200g (7oz) fresh spinach leaves
75g (2½oz) Gruyère cheese, grated
pinch of ground nutmeg
salt and freshly ground
   black pepper
4 large skinless chicken breast
   or thigh fillets
1 tbsp olive oil
8–12 cherry tomatoes

1 First, prepare the spinach. Put in a pan with a sprinkling of water, and cook for a few minutes until just wilted. Alternatively, put in a microwave-proof bowl, cover loosely, and wilt in the microwave on Medium for about 2 minutes. Drain, and squeeze out the excess water. Mix the spinach with the Gruyère cheese and nutmeg, and season well with salt and black pepper.

2 Slice each of the chicken fillets lengthways to form a pocket – be careful not to cut all the way through. Stuff each one with some of the spinach mixture, then fold over to seal.

3 Heat the olive oil in a frying pan over a medium-high heat. Carefully add the chicken breasts, pocket-side down, and leave to cook undisturbed for 6–8 minutes. Carefully turn over, and cook the other side for about the same time until golden and cooked all the way through.

4 Meanwhile, add the tomatoes to the pan towards the end of the cooking time. Leave them to sit undisturbed for 5 minutes until they begin to split. Remove the chicken from the pan when it is cooked, and set aside to keep warm. Stir the tomatoes around for a couple of minutes to break them up a little, then serve with the warm chicken.

COOK'S NOTES

Add a splash of good-quality balsamic vinegar to the tomatoes while they are cooking – for that little something extra.

Chicken stuffed with wild mushrooms and thyme

 PREP 10 MINS **COOK 25 MINS**

Soaking • 30 minutes

SERVES 4

25g (scant 1oz) mixed
   dried mushrooms
4 large skinless chicken breast fillets
salt and freshly ground black pepper
handful of fresh thyme sprigs,
   leaves picked
splash of chilli oil (optional)
1 tbsp olive oil

1 Put the dried mushrooms in a small bowl. Just cover with boiling water, and leave to soften for 30 minutes. Drain through a sieve, reserving the soaking liquid.

2 Slice the chicken breasts lengthways to form a pocket – be careful not to cut all the way through. Season well with salt and black pepper, and scatter with half of the thyme leaves. Put the soaked mushrooms, remaining thyme, and chilli oil (if using), in a bowl and season well. Mix together, then stuff each chicken breast with the mixture, and fold over the top to seal.

3 Heat the oil in a large frying pan over a medium-high heat. Carefully add the chicken, pocket-side down. Leave to cook undisturbed for 6–8 minutes, then turn over and cook the other side for about the same time until cooked through. Remove from the pan, and set aside to keep warm.

4 Pass the reserved soaking liquid from the mushrooms through a fine sieve, then add to the pan. Increase the heat, and let boil and reduce by half. To serve, spoon a little of the reduced mushroom stock over the chicken, and serve with creamy mashed potato.

COOK'S NOTES

Do pass the reserved liquid from the mushrooms through a fine sieve before using, as it can be very gritty.

Chicken escalopes in wine

PREP 10 MINS · COOK 20 MINS

SERVES 4

4 skinless chicken breast fillets
1 tbsp plain flour
1-2 tbsp olive oil
150ml (5fl oz) dry white wine
150ml (5fl oz) hot light chicken stock
handful of salted capers, rinsed,
    gently squeezed dry, and large
    ones chopped
salt and freshly ground black pepper
handful of fresh flat-leaf parsley,
    finely chopped

1 Sandwich each of the chicken fillets between 2 large sheets of cling film, and pound with a meat hammer or the side of a rolling pin until thin and an even thickness. Lightly dust each one with flour.

2 Heat the oil in a large heavy-based frying pan over a high heat. Add the chicken escalopes – two at a time if there isn't enough room in the pan – and cook for 3-4 minutes on each side until cooked through and golden. Remove from the pan, and set aside on a plate to keep warm.

3 Pour the wine into the pan, and increase the heat. Let boil for a few minutes, scraping up any bits from the bottom of the pan with a wooden spoon, until the alcohol has evaporated. Now pour in the stock, and boil for about 5 minutes until the sauce has reduced and slightly thickened. Add the capers, taste, and season if needed.

4 Return the chicken to the pan, heat through for a few seconds, then sprinkle with the parsley. Serve immediately with chunks of fresh crusty bread.

Chicken flattened and breaded with lemon and sage

PREP 10 MINS · COOK 15 MINS

SERVES 4

4 large skinless chicken breast fillets
salt and freshly ground black pepper
125g (4½oz) toasted
    fresh breadcrumbs
grated zest and juice of 1 lemon
1 tbsp plain flour
1 egg, lightly beaten
1 tbsp olive oil
4-6 fresh sage leaves, finely chopped

1 Sandwich the chicken fillets between 2 large sheets of cling film, and pound with a meat hammer or the side of a rolling pin until thin and an even thickness. Season with salt and black pepper.

2 Put the breadcrumbs and lemon zest in a bowl, and season well. Mix together, then tip out onto a plate. Now tip the flour onto another plate and the beaten egg onto another one.

Coat the chicken in the flour, then the egg, and lastly the breadcrumbs.

3 Heat the olive oil in a large heavy frying pan over a high heat. Add the chicken two pieces at a time – you may need to add more oil in between. Cook the chicken for about 5 minutes on each side until cooked through and golden. Squeeze the lemon juice into the pan for the last few seconds of cooking, and sprinkle over the sage. Serve hot with a mixed salad and fresh crusty bread.

Cheat...
If you don't want to make your own, you can buy ready-made dried breadcrumbs, and store them until required.

Chinese-style salt and pepper chicken drumsticks

 PREP 10 MINS **COOK** 25 MINS

Special equipment • bamboo steamer

SERVES 4

8 chicken drumsticks
2 tbsp plain flour
1 tbsp salt
1 tbsp cracked black pepper
2 tbsp vegetable oil
3 fresh hot red chillies, deseeded
    and sliced into strips lengthways
bunch of spring onions, sliced
    on the diagonal
lemon wedges, to serve

1 Preheat the oven to 200°C (400°F/ Gas 6). Lay the chicken drumsticks in a bamboo steamer basket (or use a colander if you don't have a steamer basket). Position over a pan of boiling water, cover, and steam for 10–15 minutes. Remove the chicken from the pan, and leave to cool slightly.

2 In a bowl, mix together the flour, salt, and cracked black pepper. Use to coat the chicken. Sit the drumsticks in a roasting tin with a little of the vegetable oil, and cook for 10–15 minutes until completely crispy and golden.

3 Meanwhile, heat 1 tablespoon of vegetable oil in a wok or frying pan over a high heat. Add the chillies and spring onions, and cook for about 5 minutes, or until they begin to crisp. Remove with a slotted spoon, and set aside on a piece of kitchen paper. Serve sprinkled over the piping-hot drumsticks, with lemon wedges for squeezing over.

 VARIATION Use chicken wings instead of drumsticks – they will need a little less cooking time for both steaming and roasting.

Flattened chicken with tomato sauce

 PREP 10 MINS **COOK** 20 MINS

SERVES 4

4 skinless chicken breast fillets
salt and freshly ground black pepper
1 tbsp plain flour
2 tbsp olive oil
1 onion, very finely diced
2 garlic cloves, grated or finely chopped
400g can peeled whole plum
    tomatoes, chopped

1 Sandwich each chicken fillet between 2 large sheets of cling film, and pound with a meat hammer or the side of a rolling pin until thin and an even thickness and about 6mm (¼in) thick. Season well with salt and black pepper, dust with the flour, and set aside.

2 Heat 1 tablespoon of the olive oil in a large frying pan over a low heat. Add the onion, and sweat for 5 minutes until soft. Add the garlic, and cook, stirring, for about 10 seconds.

3 Stir in the tomatoes and any juices, and bring to the boil. Reduce the heat to a low simmer, and cook for about 20 minutes. Stir occasionally, and keep crushing the tomatoes. Season well with salt and black pepper.

4 Meanwhile, heat the remaining oil in another frying pan over a high heat. Add the chicken pieces, and cook for 5–8 minutes on each side until cooked through and golden. Remove from the pan, and serve immediately with the rich tomato sauce spooned over the top.

COOK'S NOTES

A couple of teaspoons of pesto stirred into the sauce really pep up the flavours, or try stirring through a pinch of chilli flakes.

Hot and sour chicken soup

PREP 10 MINS COOK 20 MINS

SERVES 4

500ml (16fl oz) hot light
   vegetable stock
splash of light soy sauce
2 skinless chicken breast fillets
2–4 tbsp tom yum paste (depending
   on how hot you like it)
1 bunch of spring onions, sliced
200g (7oz) button mushrooms
6 tomatoes, skinned and quartered
splash of Thai fish sauce, such as
   nam pla
salt and freshly ground black pepper

1 To poach the chicken, bring the
stock and soy sauce to the boil in
a large pan. Add the chicken, reduce
the heat slightly, and simmer for
10–15 minutes until the chicken
is cooked. Remove with a slotted
spoon, and set aside. Slice or shred
when cool enough to handle.

2 Stir the tom yum paste into the
stock until it dissolves, then throw
in the spring onions, mushrooms,
and tomatoes, and simmer for
5–8 minutes. Return the chicken
to the pan.

3 Add a splash of fish sauce, taste,
and season accordingly with salt and
black pepper – or add more fish sauce.
Top up with a little more stock if
needed. Serve hot.

Cheat...
If you use cherry
tomatoes, you don't
have to skin
them first.

COOK'S NOTES
Tom yum paste is available in
most large supermarkets, and
specialist Asian food stores.

Lemon and soy skewered chicken with hot dipping sauce

PREP 15 MINS COOK 10 MINS

Special equipment • 8 skewers

SERVES 4

1 stalk lemongrass, tough outer leaves
   removed, finely chopped
juice of 1 lemon
1 tbsp light soy sauce
1 tsp caster sugar
salt and freshly ground black pepper
4 skinless chicken breast
   or thigh fillets
150g (5½oz) fine rice noodles

For the dipping sauce
4 garlic cloves, grated or
   finely chopped
4 fresh hot red chillies, deseeded and
   finely chopped
1 tbsp rice wine vinegar
pinch of caster sugar
juice of 1 lemon

1 If using wooden or bamboo
skewers, soak them in cold water
for at least 30 minutes before using.
Put the lemongrass, lemon juice, soy
sauce, and sugar in a bowl. Season
with salt and black pepper. Cut each
chicken fillet in half lengthways, add
to the lemongrass mixture, and leave
to marinate while you prepare the
noodles and dipping sauce.

2 Prepare the rice noodles according
to the packet instructions, drain, and
keep warm.

3 To make the dipping sauce, put all
the ingredients, except the lemon juice,
in a small pan. Add 2 tablespoons of
water, and heat gently until the sugar
has dissolved – do not boil. Allow to
cool, then stir in the lemon juice.

4 Thread the chicken lengthways
onto 8 medium skewers, allowing two
for each person. Heat a ridged cast-
iron grill pan or frying pan until hot.
Grill the chicken for 3–4 minutes on
each side until cooked through and
lightly charred. Serve with the dipping
sauce and the rice noodles.

VARIATION
This dish is equally
good made with pork
instead of chicken.

Piri piri chicken

PREP 10 MINS **COOK 1 HR**

Marinating • 30 minutes
Special equipment • food processor

SERVES 4
1 whole chicken, spatchcocked
(see Cook's Notes)

For the piri piri
2–3 fresh hot red chillies, deseeded
and finely chopped
2 garlic cloves, peeled
handful of fresh coriander,
finely chopped
handful of fresh flat-leaf parsley,
finely chopped
2–3 tbsp olive oil
1 tbsp tomato purée
juice of 1 lemon
salt and freshly ground black pepper

1 To make the piri piri, put the chillies, garlic, coriander, and parsley in a food processor. Add a little of the oil, and whiz until it begins to form a paste. Add the remaining oil, tomato purée, and lemon juice, season with salt and black pepper, and whiz again.

2 Put the chicken in a shallow glass or ceramic dish, and season with salt and black pepper. Smother all over with the piri piri paste so that the entire chicken is evenly covered. Cover with cling film, and leave to marinate in the refrigerator for at least 30 minutes, or preferably overnight.

3 Preheat the oven to 200°C (400°F/Gas 6). Sit the chicken in a roasting tin, and roast in the oven for about 50 minutes until cooked through, golden, and crispy. Quarter to serve, and dish up with rice and a green salad.

COOK'S NOTES
"Spatchcocked" means that the chicken has been flattened and the backbone removed. Buy one ready-prepared, ask the butcher to do it, or do it yourself (see p432). It cooks far quicker this way.

Minced chicken with exotic mushrooms, soy, and lime

PREP 10 MINS **COOK 20 MINS**

Special equipment • food processor

SERVES 4
2 or 3 skinless chicken breast fillets,
roughly sliced
1 tbsp olive oil
1 onion, finely chopped
salt and freshly ground black pepper
1 garlic clove, grated or finely chopped
1 fresh medium-hot red chilli,
deseeded and finely chopped
300g (10oz) mixed fresh exotic
mushrooms (such as oyster,
shiitake, and enoki) or chestnut
mushrooms, finely chopped
3 tbsp dark soy sauce
juice of 2 limes
handful of fresh coriander,
finely chopped
handful of fresh basil leaves,
finely chopped
hot cooked rice, to serve

1 Whiz the sliced chicken in a food processor until minced. Set aside.

2 Heat the oil in a large frying pan over a medium heat. Add the onion and a pinch of salt, and sauté for 5 minutes until soft. Tip in the garlic and chilli, and cook for a few seconds more.

3 Add the chicken mince to the pan, season well with salt and black pepper, and cook, stirring occasionally, for a few minutes until the chicken is no longer pink. Add the mushrooms, and cook for about 5 minutes more.

4 Stir through the soy sauce and lime juice, and cook for a further 2 minutes. Taste, and season again if needed. Just before serving, stir through the coriander and basil. Serve immediately with the hot rice, either on the side or mixed together.

VARIATION
For a lower fat version, use minced turkey instead of chicken.

COOK'S NOTES
A splash of Thai fish sauce, such as nam pla, would perk up this dish.

Jerk chicken with roasted pineapple

PREP 10 MINS   COOK 40 MINS

Marinating • 30 minutes
Special equipment • food processor

SERVES 4

1 whole chicken, jointed (ask your
   butcher to do this)
432g can pineapple
   pieces, drained

For the jerk marinade
2 fresh hot red chillies, deseeded
2 fresh hot green chillies, deseeded
pinch of ground cinnamon
pinch of ground nutmeg
salt
1 tsp cracked black pepper
grated zest and juice of 2 limes
3 tbsp soft brown sugar
2 tbsp vegetable oil
handful of fresh flat-leaf parsley
handful of fresh coriander
few sprigs of fresh thyme,
   leaves picked

1 First, make the marinade. Put all
the ingredients in a food processor.
Whiz to a paste, and add a little more
oil if needed.

2 Deeply slash all the chicken
joints, then put in a large plastic
freezer bag. Add the jerk marinade,
and squish everything together
until the chicken is well coated.
Leave to marinate in the refrigerator
for at least 30 minutes, or
preferably overnight.

3 Preheat the oven to 200°C (400°F/
Gas 6). Arrange the chicken pieces in
a large roasting tin, making sure that
there is plenty of room. Roast in the
oven for 35–40 minutes until golden
and crisp. Add the pineapple pieces
for the last 10 minutes of cooking
time. Serve hot with fluffy rice.

Cheat...
Feel free to
use a ready-made
jerk seasoning instead
of making your own.

Baked chicken with onion, garlic, and tomatoes

PREP 5 MINS   COOK 1½ HRS

SERVES 4

8 chicken pieces, skin on
salt and freshly ground black pepper
1 tbsp plain flour
2 tbsp olive oil
6 streaky bacon rashers, chopped
1 onion, finely chopped
2 garlic cloves, grated or finely chopped
3 celery sticks, finely chopped
3 carrots, finely chopped
1 small glass of dry white wine
400g can peeled whole plum
   tomatoes, chopped
300ml (10fl oz) hot vegetable stock

1 Preheat the oven to 200°C (400°F/
Gas 6). Season the chicken well with
salt and black pepper, then dust with
the flour.

2 Heat 1 tablespoon of the oil in a
large flameproof casserole (preferably
a cast-iron one) over a high heat. Add
the chicken pieces, skin-side down,
together with the bacon, and cook the
chicken for 5–8 minutes on each side
until everything is golden. Remove
from the pan, and set aside.

3 Reduce the heat to low, and add
the remaining oil to the casserole
with the onion and a pinch of salt.
Sweat for about 5 minutes until
soft, then add the garlic, celery,
and carrots. Sweat for a further
5–6 minutes until soft.

4 Increase the heat to high once
again, and add the wine. Let boil
for a few minutes until the alcohol
has evaporated. Tip in the tomatoes
and their juices, and pour in the stock.
Gently boil for a few minutes more.
Reduce the heat to a simmer, and
return the chicken and bacon to the
casserole. Stir through, cover, and
transfer to the oven to cook for about
1 hour. Top up with more stock or hot
water if it begins to dry out. Serve
with creamy mashed potato.

Griddled chicken with satay sauce

 PREP 10 MINS COOK 30 MINS

SERVES 4
4 large skinless chicken breast fillets
splash of olive oil
cucumber slices, to serve
a little white wine vinegar, to serve
pinch of sugar, to serve
small handful of fresh coriander,
    chopped, to serve

For the satay sauce
400ml can coconut milk
1 tsp Thai red curry paste
300ml (10fl oz) hot vegetable stock
2 tbsp demerara sugar
4 tbsp crunchy peanut butter
salt and freshly ground black pepper
juice of 1 lime

1 First, make the satay sauce. Pour the coconut milk into a heavy-based pan, and warm until it comes to a gentle boil. Reduce the heat slightly, and simmer until it releases its sweet fragrance. Now stir through the curry paste, add the stock and sugar, and simmer for a further 5 minutes. Add the peanut butter, and stir for a few more minutes until well blended. Remove from the heat, and season with some salt and the lime juice. Taste, and add more salt or lime if needed. Set aside to keep warm.

2 Slash the chicken breasts diagonally, making sure that you don't slice all the way through. Rub over with a little olive oil, and season well with salt and black pepper. Heat a griddle pan or grill until hot, and cook the chicken for 8–10 minutes on each side until cooked through and nicely charred.

3 Meanwhile, prepare the cucumber. Sprinkle the cucumber slices with a little vinegar and a pinch of sugar. Scatter over the chopped coriander. Serve the chicken breasts with the satay sauce and the cucumber mixture.

EVERYDAY

Cheat...
Serve up the chicken with some ready-made peanut satay sauce.

Chicken escalopes with chilli and parsley

 PREP 10 MINS COOK 10 MINS

SERVES 4
4 skinless chicken breast fillets
salt and freshly ground black pepper
1 tbsp plain flour
125g (4½oz) lightly toasted
    fresh breadcrumbs
handful of fresh flat-leaf parsley,
    finely chopped
2 fresh medium-hot red chillies,
    deseeded and finely chopped
1 egg, lightly beaten
1–2 tbsp olive oil
300g (10oz) fresh spinach leaves
juice of 1 lemon
chilli oil (optional)

1 Sandwich each of the chicken breasts between 2 large sheets of cling film. Pound with a meat hammer or the side of rolling pin until thin and an even thickness. Season well with salt and black pepper, and dust with flour.

2 In a bowl, mix together the breadcrumbs, parsley, and chilli. Dip the chicken in the beaten egg, then coat with the breadcrumbs.

3 In a large frying pan, heat the oil over a high heat. Add the chicken pieces, two at a time, and cook for 3–4 minutes on each side until golden and cooked through. Remove from the pan, and set aside to keep warm.

4 Reduce the heat slightly, and add the spinach to the same pan with a sprinkling of water. Cook for a few minutes until just wilted. Sprinkle over some of the lemon juice, and serve on warm plates with the chicken. Squeeze over the remaining lemon juice and a drizzle of chilli oil (if using), and serve immediately.

COOK'S NOTES
You could easily prepare this dish a day ahead. Coat the chicken pieces with the breadcrumbs, and leave in the refrigerator until ready to use.

EVERYDAY CHICKEN

EVERYDAY

Chicken with cayenne, lemon, and oregano

PREP 10 MINS COOK 40 MINS

SERVES 4
8 chicken thighs
1–2 tbsp olive oil
1 tbsp cayenne pepper
juice of 1 lemon
1 tbsp dried oregano
salt and freshly ground
   black pepper
bunch of spring onions, chopped
200g (7oz) wild rocket leaves
good-quality thick balsamic vinegar
small handful of fresh Parmesan
   cheese shavings, to serve

1 Preheat the oven to 200°C (400°F/ Gas 6). Put the chicken, olive oil, cayenne, lemon juice, and oregano in a large bowl. Season well with salt and black pepper. Rub everything together using your hands until the chicken is well coated. Leave to marinate in the refrigerator for

30 minutes if you have time; if not, cook straight away.

2 Tip the chicken into a large roasting tin, and roast for about 40 minutes until beginning to char slightly. Meanwhile, in a bowl, mix together the spring onion and rocket leaves.

3 When ready to serve, drizzle a little balsamic vinegar and sprinkle a pinch of salt over the rocket mixture. Top with the Parmesan shavings, and serve alongside the chicken.

> **COOK'S NOTES**
>
> *Make sure that you use a big enough roasting tin with plenty of room. This way the chicken will roast, rather than steam – which it will do if it is too tightly packed.*

Chicken cooked in coriander yogurt

PREP 10 MINS COOK 30 MINS

SERVES 4
200g (7oz) Greek-style yogurt
handful of fresh coriander,
   finely chopped, plus extra
   to garnish
2 tbsp medium-hot curry powder
salt and freshly ground black pepper
4 large skinless chicken breast fillets
250g (9oz) baby new potatoes
1 tbsp olive oil
1 lemon, cut into wedges, to serve

1 Preheat the oven to 200°C (400°F/ Gas 6). Put the yogurt, coriander, and 1 tablespoon of the curry powder in a large bowl. Season with salt and black pepper, and mix well. Add the chicken pieces, and leave to marinate for a few minutes.

2 Sit the coated chicken pieces in a roasting tin, and roast in the oven for about 30 minutes until cooked through and lightly charred.

3 Meanwhile, tip the potatoes into a separate roasting tin. Drizzle over the olive oil, and add the remaining curry powder. Mix together using your hands, then roast in the oven for about 20 minutes until golden.

4 Serve the chicken and potatoes together with a sprinkling of extra coriander and the lemon wedges. Serve a crisp green salad on the side, if you wish.

Baked chicken with apricots and almonds

PREP 10 MINS
COOK 1 HR

SERVES 4
8 chicken pieces, skin on
salt and freshly ground black pepper
2 tsp ground cinnamon
2 tbsp olive oil
1 onion, finely chopped
3 garlic cloves, grated or finely chopped
pinch of ground ginger
1 cinnamon stick
400g can chickpeas, drained
    and rinsed
900ml (1½ pints) hot chicken stock

handful of whole blanched almonds
handful of ready-to-eat dried apricots
handful of fresh coriander,
    finely chopped
juice of 1 lemon
couscous, to serve
harissa, to serve

1 Preheat the oven to 200°C (400°F/ Gas 6). Season the chicken well with salt and black pepper, and sprinkle over the cinnamon. Heat 1 tablespoon of the olive oil in a large flameproof casserole over a medium-high heat. Add the chicken pieces, skin-side down, and cook for 5-10 minutes until golden all over. Remove and set aside.

2 Reduce the heat to medium, and add the remaining oil, onion, and a pinch of salt to the casserole. Sauté for 5 minutes until soft. Add the garlic, ginger, and cinnamon stick, and cook for a few seconds.

3 Return the chicken pieces to the casserole, stir through the chickpeas, and pour in the stock. Bring to the boil, tip in the almonds and apricots, and stir through. Cover, and bake in the oven for about 1 hour until beginning to thicken.

4 Stir through the coriander, and squeeze over the lemon juice. Serve hot with fluffy couscous and a spoonful of harissa.

VARIATION
Use turkey instead of chicken for a slightly lower-fat version.

EVERYDAY

Chicken fajitas with tomato and avocado salsa

PREP 15 MINS COOK 15 MINS

SERVES 4

1 tbsp olive oil
2 onions, sliced into strips
2 red peppers, deseeded and cut into strips
2 green peppers, deseeded and cut into strips
2 fresh medium-hot red chillies, deseeded and finely chopped
2 garlic cloves, sliced
4 skinless chicken breast fillets, cut into strips
1 small glass of dry white wine
handful of fresh coriander, finely chopped
12 corn tortillas

For the salsa
1 ripe avocado
handful of cherry tomatoes, chopped
1 bunch of spring onions, finely chopped
handful of fresh flat-leaf parsley, finely chopped
1 tbsp olive oil
1 tbsp white wine vinegar
salt and freshly ground black pepper

1 First, make the salsa. Halve, stone, peel, and chop the avocado. Put in a bowl with the tomatoes, spring onions, and parsley. Drizzle over the olive oil and vinegar. Season with salt and black pepper.

2 To make the chicken fajitas, heat the oil in a large frying pan over a low heat. Add the onions and red and green peppers, and sauté for 5 minutes until starting to soften. Stir through the chilli and garlic, and cook for a few seconds.

3 Increase the heat to medium-high, and add the chicken. Keep the mixture moving around the pan, so that it doesn't burn and the chicken is evenly cooked. Stir-fry for 3-5 minutes until the chicken is no longer pink. Pour in the wine, and cook fiercely for 5 minutes. Stir through the coriander.

4 To serve, spoon the mixture onto the tortillas. Top with the salsa, and roll into wraps. Serve any extra mixture on the side.

Chicken doner kebab

 PREP 15 MINS COOK 15 MINS

Marinating • 1 hour

SERVES 4

1 tsp cayenne pepper
1 tbsp olive oil
juice of 1 lemon
4 skinless chicken breast fillets, cut into fine strips
4 pitta breads
1 crispy lettuce, such as Cos or Little Gem, shredded
2 onions, sliced
¼ red cabbage, shredded
hot chilli sauce, to taste
garlic mayonnaise, to taste
1 ripe tomato, sliced
¼ cucumber, sliced
4 whole pickled green chillies

1 In a bowl, mix together the cayenne pepper, olive oil, and a quarter of the lemon juice. Add the chicken strips, and leave to marinate in the refrigerator for 1 hour.

2 Heat the grill until hot. Arrange the chicken strips in a shallow baking tin, and cook under the hot grill for about 10 minutes, turning occasionally.

3 Lightly toast the pitta breads, and cut open along one edge to form a pocket.

4 Stuff each pitta pocket with a handful of lettuce, onion, and red cabbage, then the chicken pieces. Dress with the remaining lemon juice, and some chilli sauce and garlic mayonnaise to taste. Garnish with the tomato slices, cucumber, and a pickled chilli. Serve immediately.

Use wholemeal pitta bread for an even healthier dish.

Chicken with pancetta, peas, and mint

PREP 15 MINS   COOK 1¾ HRS

Special equipment • large flameproof casserole

SERVES 4

2 tbsp olive oil

4 large or 8 smaller chicken pieces, such as thighs and breasts, skin on

2 onions, finely chopped

200g (7oz) pancetta, cubed, or bacon lardons

2 garlic cloves, grated or finely chopped

2 glasses of dry white wine

600ml (1 pint) hot chicken stock

salt and freshly ground black pepper

225g (8oz) frozen peas

handful of fresh flat-leaf parsley, finely chopped

handful of fresh mint leaves, finely chopped

1 Preheat the oven to 150°C (300°F/Gas 2). Heat 1 tablespoon of the oil in a large flameproof casserole (preferably cast-iron) over a medium heat. Add the chicken pieces, and cook for about 8 minutes until golden all over. Remove from the casserole, and set aside.

2 Reduce the heat to low, and add the remaining oil and onions to the casserole. Sweat gently for about 5 minutes until soft and translucent, then add the pancetta or bacon. Increase the heat a little, and cook for a further 5 minutes until the pancetta or bacon is golden. Stir in the garlic, then pour in the wine. Increase the heat to high, and simmer for a few minutes until the alcohol has evaporated.

3 Add the stock, and bring to the boil once again. Season with salt and black pepper, tip in the peas, and stir through. Return the chicken pieces to the casserole. Stir through the parsley and mint, cover with a lid, and transfer to the oven to cook for 1½ hours. Check the level of liquid occasionally while cooking – it needs to be fairly dry, but if it does need topping up, just add a little hot water. Serve hot with fresh crusty bread or sautéed potatoes.

Marsala chicken with pine nuts and sultanas

PREP 15 MINS   COOK 45 MINS

Special equipment • large cast-iron pan or flameproof casserole

SERVES 4

2 tbsp olive oil

8 chicken pieces, such as thighs and breasts, skin on

1 onion, finely chopped

2 carrots, finely chopped

2 celery sticks, finely chopped

3 glasses of Marsala, about 300ml (10fl oz)

salt and freshly ground black pepper

50g (1¾oz) pine nuts, toasted

50g (1¾oz) sultanas

handful of fresh flat-leaf parsley, finely chopped

1 Heat the oil in a large cast-iron pan or casserole over a medium heat. Add the chicken pieces, and cook for about 8 minutes until golden all over. Remove from the pan, and set aside.

2 Reduce the heat to low. Add the onion, carrots, and celery to the pan, and sweat gently for a few minutes until soft. Pour in the Marsala, season with salt and black pepper, and simmer gently for about 30 minutes, topping up with water a little at a time if it begins to dry out – but don't add too much because it should be fairly dry and the water will dilute the flavour.

3 Stir through the pine nuts and sultanas, and cook for a few minutes more. Just before serving, stir through the parsley. Serve with a dressed green salad and fresh crusty bread.

10
WAYS WITH...

A favourite ingredient, and 10 ways to cook it.

10 WAYS WITH...
STEAK

EVERYDAY

1 Griddled steak with peppery crust

PREP 10 MINS **COOK** 15 MINS

Special equipment • food processor • ridged cast-iron grill pan or griddle

SERVES 4

Whiz 1 teaspoon of **black peppercorns**, 1 teaspoon of **red peppercorns**, 1 teaspoon of **green peppercorns**, 1 teaspoon of **mustard seeds**, 1 teaspoon of **caraway seeds**, 1 teaspoon of **salt**, 2 teaspoons of **soft brown sugar**, and 2 deseeded **red chillies** to a paste. Tip onto a plate, and roll a 350g (12oz) piece of **fillet steak** in the mixture; kneading it into the meat. Heat the grill pan or griddle, and cook the steak to your preference.

2 Steak sandwich with horseradish and watercress

PREP 5 MINS **COOK** 10 MINS

Special equipment • ridged cast-iron grill pan or griddle

SERVES 1

Cook a 150g (5½oz) **rump steak** on a grill pan or griddle, and leave to rest. Cut 2 slices of fresh crusty **bread**, or halve and lightly toast half a **ciabatta**. Smother one slice of the bread or a ciabatta half with a dollop of **creamed horseradish**, then top with the steak and **watercress**, and some sliced fresh **tomatoes**. Season generously. Sit the other slice of bread or ciabatta half on top to make a sandwich, and serve immediately.

3 Oriental steak salad

PREP 15 MINS **COOK** 5 MINS

SERVES 4

Slice 300g (10oz) **sirloin steak** into fine strips, and put in a bowl. Mix together 1 tablespoon of **vegetable oil**, 1 tablespoon of light **soy sauce**, the juice of 1 **lime**, a 2.5cm (1in) piece of fresh root **ginger**, shredded, 2 crushed **garlic cloves**, and 1 teaspoon of **granulated sugar**. Pour over the steak, and leave to marinate. Spread 200g (7oz) **beansprouts** over a platter. Quarter 1 head **pak choi** lengthways, and braise with a little oil in a frying pan over a medium heat for 3–4 minutes. Remove from the pan, and arrange on top of the beansprouts. Add the marinated steak to the same pan, increase the heat, and stir-fry for a few minutes, until cooked. Tip in the remaining marinade mixture along with 1 tablespoon of **rice wine vinegar**, and cook vigorously for 1 minute. Tip the steak strips over the beansprouts and pak choi, and gently toss through.

4 The perfect steak

PREP 2 MINS **COOK** 10 MINS

Special equipment • ridged cast-iron grill pan or griddle

SERVES 1

Season a 225g (8oz) **rump** or **T-bone steak**, and drizzle with a little **olive oil**. Heat the grill pan or griddle until hot, add the steak, and cook for 3–4 minutes on each side, depending on thickness, and how you like your steak cooked. Remove from the pan, sit on a plate, and allow the steak to rest for 5 minutes before serving.

The perfect steak

EVERYDAY

5 Seared steak salad

PREP 5 MINS COOK 5 MINS

Special equipment • ridged cast-iron grill pan or griddle

SERVES 4

Season two 175g (6oz) **sirloin steaks**. Heat the grill pan or griddle, and cook the steaks, one at a time, for a minute on each side. Remove and rest. Arrange 200g (7oz) **rocket** on a serving plate, sprinkle over freshly shaved **Parmesan cheese** and some **cherry tomatoes**, halved. Slice the steak diagonally and lay on top of the salad. Dress with an **olive oil** and **balsamic vinegar** dressing.

6 Breaded steak with black olives

PREP 15 MINS COOK 20 MINS

SERVES 4

Sandwich four 125g (4½oz) pieces of **sirloin steak** between two pieces of cling film. Pound with a meat hammer or rolling pin until thin, and set aside. Blend, or finely slice 125g (4½oz) **black olives**, a handful of fresh **flat-leaf parsley**, and 6 **sun-dried tomatoes**. Combine to form a rough paste. Spread most of the paste on the steaks, and roll tightly. Mix the remaining paste with 125g (4½oz) seasoned toasted **fresh breadcrumbs**. Dip the rolled steaks in a little **plain flour**, then the beaten **egg**, and then roll in the breadcrumbs. Roast in a preheated 220°C (425°F/Gas 7) oven for 15–20 minutes until the coating is crisp. Slice the steaks diagonally, and serve with **garlic** and **chilli spinach**.

7 Steak and oyster mushroom salad

PREP 5 MINS COOK 15 MINS

Special equipment • ridged cast-iron grill pan or griddle

SERVES 4

Cook two 125g (4½oz) **sirloin steaks** on a hot grill pan or griddle. Leave to rest for 5 minutes, then slice into chunky strips. Heat 1 tablespoon of **olive oil** in a frying pan over a medium heat. Add 175g (6oz) **oyster mushrooms**, and sauté for 5 minutes. Toss with the steak. Whisk together 3 tablespoons of olive oil, 1 tablespoon of **white wine vinegar**, and 1 teaspoon of **wholegrain mustard**. Drizzle the dressing over the salad, and stir in a handful of chopped fresh **parsley**. Season, and serve with fresh crusty **bread**.

8 Steak and vegetable parcels

PREP 15 MINS COOK 30 MINS

SERVES 4

In a hot frying pan, sear 225g (8oz) cubed **sirloin** or **rump steak** with a little **olive oil** for 5 minutes. Pour in 150ml (5fl oz) hot **beef stock**, and simmer for a few minutes, then stir in 3 cooked **potatoes**, cut into cubes, and 3 diced cooked **carrots**. Season. Roll out 350g (12oz) **ready-made shortcrust pastry** to about 5mm (¼in) thick, then cut into 4 squares. Spoon the steak mixture into the middle of the pastry squares. Sprinkle a handful of grated **Cheddar cheese** over the top. Brush the edges of the pastry with a little water, then pull each corner up to the middle to make a parcel. Pinch the edges of the pastry together to seal. Brush each parcel with beaten **egg yolk**, and bake in a preheated 200°C (400°F/Gas 6) oven for 20 minutes until golden.

Steak and oyster mushroom salad

Paprika steak skewers

9 Paprika steak skewers

PREP 10 MINS **COOK 10** MINS

Marinating • 1 hour
Special equipment • skewers • ridged cast-iron grill pan or griddle

SERVES 4

If using wooden or bamboo skewers, soak in cold water for at least 30 minutes before using. Slice 350g (12oz) **rump steak** into 2.5cm (1in) cubes, and mix together in a bowl with 2 teaspoons of **paprika**, the juice of 1 **lemon**, a small handful of finely chopped fresh **flat-leaf parsley**, 1 tablespoon of **olive oil**. Season. Thread the steak cubes onto the skewers and marinate in the refrigerator for 1 hour. Heat a grill pan or griddle until hot, then cook the skewers for 1–2 minutes on each side, turning. Allow to rest for a couple of minutes, before serving with a drizzle of olive oil and **mashed potato** with fresh flat-leaf parsley.

10 Swedish-style steak

PREP 20 MINS **COOK 20** MINS

SERVES 4

Peel and boil 1kg (2¼lb) waxy **potatoes** for about 15 minutes, or until nearly soft. Drain, put in a bowl, and cover with cold water. Cut 300g (10oz) **sirloin steak** into large chunks, then seal in a hot frying pan with a little **olive oil**. Set aside. Blend 250g (9oz) **butter** with 5 crushed **garlic cloves**, and a handful of finely chopped fresh **flat-leaf parsley**. Season. Cut the potatoes into thick slices, and layer in the bottom of a baking dish. Sit the steak on top, and cover with the garlic butter. Roast in a preheated 200°C (400°F/Gas 6) oven for 20 minutes.

10 WAYS WITH...
CHEESE

1 Cheesy leeks on toast

PREP
10
MINS

COOK
10
MINS

SERVES 2

Heat 1 tablespoon of **olive oil** in a pan over a low heat. Add 1 chopped **leek**, and sweat gently until soft. Remove, and set aside. Put 25g (scant 1oz) **butter**, 150ml (5fl oz) **brown ale**, and 175g (6oz) grated **mature Cheddar cheese** in the same pan, and cook gently, stirring, until melted and smooth. Remove from the heat, and stir in 1 tablespoon of **plain flour** until smooth, then return to the heat, stirring continuously. Remove from the heat, stir in 2 teaspoons of **English mustard**, a splash of **Worcestershire sauce**, and the reserved leeks. Season. Leave to cool, then stir in 2 **egg yolks** until combined. Toast 4 slices of **bread** on one side, turn, then arrange on a grill tray or baking tray, and smother with the cheesy leeks. Cook under a hot grill until simmering and golden.

2 Baked Camembert

PREP
5
MINS

COOK
10
MINS

SERVES 4

Take a whole **Camembert cheese** still packaged in its wooden box. Remove all plastic packaging, and return the cheese round to the box. Cut a series of small crosses in the top of the Camembert, and stick a small sprig of fresh **rosemary** into each one. Bake the Camembert in the box, without the lid, in a preheated 180°C (350°F/Gas 4) oven for about 10 minutes until starting to simmer and melt. Serve immediately with fresh crusty **bread**, a farmhouse-style **apple chutney**, and fresh **apple slices** and **celery sticks**.

3 Seared halloumi cheese with figs

PREP
10
MINS

COOK
20
MINS

SERVES 4

Take 8 large ripe **figs**, and cut into quarters lengthways. Cut 300g (10oz) **halloumi cheese** into 5mm (¼in) slices. Put the halloumi and figs in a large non-stick frying pan over a medium heat, and cook for 2–3 minutes on each side until starting to brown. Once cooked, add to a platter of **mixed salad leaves**. Now pour 60ml (2fl oz) **red wine vinegar** into the same pan, and increase the heat slightly. Add a small handful of finely chopped fresh **coriander**, 1 deseeded and finely chopped fresh **red chilli**, and 1 crushed **garlic clove**. Simmer over a medium-high heat until reduced in volume by three-quarters, and tip sparingly over the figs and cheese. Splash the salad with a little **olive oil**, and serve immediately.

4 Cheese fondue

PREP
10
MINS

COOK
15
MINS

SERVES 4

Pour 250ml (8fl oz) **dry white wine** into a pan, and bring to the boil. Add 200g (7oz) grated **Emmental cheese**, and stir until melted. Now add 200g (7oz) grated **Gruyère cheese**, and stir again until melted and smooth. Once thickened, pour the sauce into a warm bowl, and serve with fresh crusty **bread** on skewers for dipping into the cheesy fondue.

Seared halloumi cheese with figs

5 Feta and watermelon salad with pumpkin seeds

PREP 5 MINS COOK 2 MINS

SERVES 4

Halve 1 small ripe **watermelon**, and cut the flesh into chunky pieces. Put in a bowl, and crumble in 150g (5½oz) **feta cheese** along with ½ teaspoon of freshly ground **black pepper**, 1 tablespoon of **chilli oil**, and a handful of finely chopped fresh **mint leaves**. Toss gently to combine. In a small dry frying pan, toast 50g (1¾oz) **pumpkin seeds** with a little **salt** for a few minutes, and sprinkle liberally over the top of individual portions and serve.

6 Dauphinoise with emmental and pancetta

PREP 20 MINS COOK 45 MINS

SERVES 4

In a frying pan, over a medium heat, cook 200g (7oz) cubed **pancetta** until starting to crisp. Remove, and drain on kitchen paper. Simmer 1½kg (3lb 3oz) peeled and thinly sliced **potatoes** in 300ml (10fl oz) **milk** and 300ml (10fl oz) **double cream** for 10–15 minutes, then remove with a slotted spoon (reserve the milk and cream mixture). Layer the potatoes in a baking dish with 150g (5½oz) sliced **emmental** and the pancetta. Season. Pour over the milk and cream, cover with foil, and cook in a preheated 200°C (400°F/Gas 6) oven for 45 minutes. Remove the foil for the last 15 minutes of cooking time to brown the top.

7 Easy cheese soufflé

PREP 30 MINS COOK 15 MINS

Special equipment • ramekins

SERVES 4

Melt 25g (scant 1oz) **butter** in a pan over a low heat. Sprinkle in 1 teaspoon of **plain flour**. Cook, stirring, for a couple of minutes, then add 300ml (10fl oz) **milk**, a little at a time, stirring constantly. Add 50g (1¾oz) grated **Gruyère cheese**, 25g (scant 1oz) grated **Parmesan cheese**, and 1 teaspoon of **wholegrain mustard**. Continue stirring until the cheese has melted. Season. Once tepid, beat in 4 **egg yolks**. Whisk 4 **egg whites** to soft peaks. Gently fold the whites into the cheese mixture, a little at a time, until combined. Divide the mixture between 4 ramekins, leaving space at the top, and bake in a preheated 200°C (400°F/Gas 6) oven for 12–15 minutes until risen.

8 Tandoori paneer

PREP 20 MINS COOK 10 MINS

Marinating • 30 minutes

Special equipment • food processor or blender • skewers • ridged cast-iron grill pan or barbecue

SERVES 4

If using wooden or bamboo skewers, soak them in cold water for at least 30 minutes before using. In a blender or food processor, whiz 3 **garlic cloves**, 2 deseeded fresh **green chillies**, a 2.5cm (1in) piece of fresh **root ginger**, the grated zest and juice of ½ a **lemon**, and 3 tablespoons of **Greek-style yogurt** until smooth. Add 1 tablespoon of **garam masala** and 1 teaspoon of **ground cumin**, and whiz again. Season. Cut 250g (9oz) **paneer cheese** into chunky cubes, and marinate in the tandoori mixture for 30 minutes. Thread the cubes onto skewers, and grill on a hot ridged cast-iron grill pan, on a barbecue, or grill for 5–8 minutes, turning halfway through cooking, until golden. Serve hot and sizzling on a bed of shredded **lettuce**, sliced **red onions**, and sliced ripe **tomatoes**.

Easy cheese soufflé

Rice balls filled with cheese

9 Shredded red cabbage with blue cheese dressing

PREP 10 MINS

Special equipment • food processor

SERVES 4

Combine 125g (4½oz) **blue cheese** such as Danish blue or cambozola with 225g (8oz) **Greek-style yogurt**, a small handful of chopped **tarragon leaves**, and plenty of freshly ground **black pepper**. Blend or process until smooth. Finely shred 1 **red cabbage**, and mix with 25g (scant 1oz) **raisins** and 25g (scant 1oz) **toasted pine nuts**. Combine with the blue cheese dressing, and serve with fresh crusty **wholemeal** or **rye bread**.

10 Rice balls filled with cheese

 PREP 30 MINS **COOK 5 MINS**

SERVES 4

Generously season 225g (8oz) cold cooked **Arborio** or other **risotto rice**, then roll into 12 even-sized balls. Push a cube of **mozzarella cheese** into the centre of each ball, then cover so that the cheese is enclosed. Roll each ball in some beaten egg, then in some toasted fresh **breadcrumbs**. Fry in a little **olive oil** over a medium heat for 2–5 minutes, until golden. Serve hot.

131

10 WAYS WITH...
SALMON

1 Chinese salmon with black bean sauce

PREP 10 MINS • COOK 15 MINS

Marinating • 30 minutes

Special equipment • ridged cast-iron grill pan or griddle

SERVES 4

Mix 4 tablespoons of **black bean sauce** with a 2.5cm (1in) grated piece of fresh **root ginger**, 3 grated **garlic cloves**, and 1 deseeded and finely chopped fresh hot **red chilli**. Spread the mixture over 4 **salmon fillets**, about 150g (5½oz) each, and season. Leave to marinate in the refrigerator for 30 minutes. Heat a ridged cast-iron grill pan or griddle until hot. Add the salmon fillets, two at a time and skin-side down, and cook for about 4 minutes until opaque and lightly charred. Turn over, and cook on the other side for the same time. Serve hot with **rice** or **noodles**.

2 Salmon patties

PREP 15 MINS • COOK 20 MINS

SERVES 4

Mix 300g (10oz) cooked **fresh salmon** and 150g (5½oz) chopped **smoked salmon** in a bowl. Add 1 finely chopped **onion**, 2 crushed **garlic cloves**, 1 deseeded and finely chopped fresh hot **red chilli**, 300g (10oz) cooked **mashed potato**, 1 tablespoon of chopped **tarragon**, 1 tablespoon of chopped **dill**, and 2 beaten **eggs**. Season, and use your hands to combine and mould into 5cm (2in) balls. Flatten into patties. Roll in toasted fresh breadcrumbs and put in a roasting tin with a little vegetable oil. Roast in a preheated 200°C (400°F/Gas 6) oven for 20 minutes until golden, turning once. Serve with **salad** and buttered **brown bread**.

3 Salmon with dill and Madeira

PREP 10 MINS • COOK 20 MINS

SERVES 4

Place four 150g (5½oz) **salmon fillets** skin-side down on a baking tray, and season. Add a sprinkle of fresh **dill**. Loosely cover with foil, and bake in a preheated 200°C (400°F/Gas 6) oven for 15 minutes until cooked. In a shallow pan, heat 2 tablespoons of **olive oil** over a low heat, and sweat 2 finely chopped **shallots** and 2 crushed **garlic cloves** for about 5 minutes. Add a drizzle of **Madeira wine**, increase the heat, and let boil until reduced by half. Stir through a handful of chopped **dill**. Serve the salmon with the **potatoes** and **green beans**, with the dressing drizzled over the top.

4 Poached salmon with coriander and lime

PREP 5 MINS • COOK 25 MINS

SERVES 4

Cut a side of **salmon** – about 600g (1lb 5oz) – in half lengthways so that it opens up, but don't slice all the way through. Roughly chop a large handful of fresh **coriander**, mix with 2 peeled, segmented, and roughly chopped **limes**, and season. Spread the mixture on the opened salmon, season well once again, then fold closed. Place the salmon on a large sheet of foil, and pour over ½ small glass of **dry white wine**. Loosely seal the foil to make a parcel. Place on a baking tray, and bake in a preheated 200°C (400°F/Gas 6 oven) for 25 minutes. Serve hot with boiled **new potatoes**.

Poached salmon with coriander and lime

Salmon with soy

PREP 5 MINS   COOK 15 MINS

Marinating • 1 hour

SERVES 4

Mix together 4 tablespoons of light **soy sauce**, 2 crushed **garlic cloves**, and the grated zest and juice of ½ a **lemon**. Pour the mixture over 4 **salmon steaks**, and leave to marinate in the refrigerator for 1 hour, if you can. Transfer the salmon steaks to a baking tray, and sprinkle with **sesame seeds**. Bake in a preheated 200°C (400°F/Gas 6) oven for 15 minutes until the salmon is opaque and cooked. Serve hot with a **spinach salad**.

Salmon kedgeree

PREP 10 MINS   COOK 20 MINS

SERVES 4

Melt 50g (1¾oz) **butter** in a pan over a low heat, add 1 finely chopped **onion**, and sweat gently for a few minutes until soft. Add 350g (12oz) **long-grain rice**, such as basmati, and stir until the grains are well coated. Gradually add 750ml (1¼ pints) hot **vegetable stock**, cover the pan (tilt the lid to allow steam to escape), and simmer gently for 15–20 minutes until all the liquid has been absorbed and the rice is cooked. Add 500g (1lb 2oz) sliced cooked **salmon**, 1 teaspoon of mild **curry powder**, and 1 teaspoon of **cayenne pepper**. Season and serve hot with fresh **mango** slices.

Salmon, horseradish, and kale bake

PREP 10 MINS   COOK 25 MINS

SERVES 4

Sit 4 skinned **salmon fillets**, about 150g (5½oz) each, in a frying pan, and cover with **milk**. Poach gently over a low heat for about 10 minutes until opaque and cooked, then transfer the salmon to an ovenproof dish using a slotted spoon or fish slice. Discard the poaching liquid. Trim the tough stalks from 2 handfuls of **kale**, and roughly chop the leaves. Boil or steam for about 5 minutes until nearly soft, then drain and add to the salmon. Combine gently. Pour over a **cheese sauce** (see p251) with 1–2 tablespoons of **creamed horseradish**, and bake in a 200°C (400°F/Gas 6) oven for about 15 minutes until golden.

EVERYDAY

Salmon jungle curry

PREP 10 MINS   COOK 20 MINS

SERVES 4

In a large frying pan, heat 2 tablespoons of **vegetable oil** until hot. Add 2 tablespoons of **Thai green curry paste**, and stir around the pan to combine. Throw in 3 crushed **garlic cloves**, a 5cm (2in) piece of fresh **root ginger**, cut into fine strips, and 2 fresh hot **red chillies**, deseeded and cut into fine strips. Keep stirring for 2–3 minutes, then pour in 400ml (14fl oz) **coconut milk**. Bring to the boil, then add a good splash of **Thai fish sauce**, 200g (7oz) drained **bamboo shoots**, 2 heaped tablespoons of **pea aubergines** (only if you can get them), and 75g (2½oz) **baby corn**, sliced lengthways. Reduce the heat slightly, and simmer for 5 minutes. Add 400g (14oz) skinned fresh **salmon**, cut into 4cm (1½in) chunks, and a small handful of fresh **Thai basil leaves**. Simmer for a further 5–10 minutes until the salmon is opaque and cooked. Season and serve hot with sticky **Thai jasmine rice**.

Salmon jungle curry

Salmon salad with mint yogurt dressing

9 Salmon salad with mint yogurt dressing

PREP 15 MINS · COOK 25 MINS

SERVES 4

Put 2 tablespoons of **red wine vinegar**, 2 tablespoons of finely chopped fresh **mint**, and 4 tablespoons of **Greek-style yogurt** in a bowl, season, and whisk. Set aside. Lay a side of **salmon** – about 550g (1¼lb) – on a large piece of foil. Sprinkle with a handful of chopped fresh **dill**, and overlap a few slices of **lemon** on top. Season, and loosely seal the foil to make a parcel. Place on a baking tray, and bake in a preheated 200°C (400°F/Gas 6) oven for 20-25 minutes. Allow to cool. Transfer the salmon to a plate, drizzle over the dressing, and scatter with fresh **mint leaves**. Serve with a cucumber salad.

10 Smoked salmon sushi

PREP 20 MINS · COOK 35 MINS

SERVES 4

Make up 300g (10oz) **short-grain sushi rice** as per packet instructions so that it is sticky. Spread out over a baking tray or similar, cover with a clean tea towel, and leave to cool. Once the rice has cooled completely, arrange a double layer of cling film in a square or rectangular shallow tin, then spoon in the rice. Smooth out evenly so that the rice is about 5cm (2in) deep. Layer pieces of **smoked salmon**, about 300g (10oz) in total, all over the rice to cover, and press it down firmly. Using a sharp knife dipped in hot water, slice into neat rectangles or squares, and serve.

10 WAYS WITH...
MINCE

EVERYDAY

1 Beef mince fruity curry

PREP 10 MINS | COOK 30 MINS

SERVES 4

In a large frying pan, sweat 1 finely chopped **onion** in a little **olive oil**. Season. When translucent, add 2 deseeded and finely chopped fresh medium-hot **red chillies**, a 2.5cm (1in) piece of fresh root **ginger**, grated, and 2 grated **garlic cloves**. Stir through, and add 2 tablespoons of medium **curry powder**. Tip in 675g (1½lb) **beef mince**, and cook, stirring, until the meat is no longer pink. Pour in 150ml (5fl oz) hot **vegetable stock**, and bring to the boil. Add 2 peeled, cored, and diced **eating apples**, and a handful of **raisins**, and simmer for 10 minutes until thickened. Season, and serve hot with **rice**.

2 Stuffed squash with mince

PREP 15 MINS | COOK 40 MINS

SERVES 4

Halve a **butternut squash**, and scoop out the seeds to make a good-sized "bowl" for the mince. Put in a roasting tin, drizzle with **olive oil**, and roast in a preheated 200°C (400°F/Gas 6) oven for 10–15 minutes, until softened. Meanwhile, in a frying pan over a low heat, sweat 1 finely chopped **onion** in a little **olive oil** until soft. Add 675g (1½lb) **beef mince**, and cook, stirring, until beginning to colour. Season, and stir through a handful of finely chopped fresh **flat-leaf parsley**. Remove the squash from the oven, spoon the mince into the "bowl". Cover with foil, and roast for 30 minutes. Remove the foil, and grate over some **Gruyère cheese**. Return to the oven until the cheese has melted.

3 Nachos topped with minced beef and cheese

PREP 5 MINS | COOK 20 MINS

SERVES 4

In a large frying pan over a medium-high heat, cook 500g (1lb 2oz) **beef mince** in a drizzle of **olive oil** for about 10 minutes, until no longer pink. Add a splash of **chilli sauce**, and season. Lay 2 or 3 large handfuls of **plain** or **chilli tortilla chips** on a large platter. Spoon the mince beef over the top, and sprinkle over 125g (4½oz) grated **Cheddar cheese**. Sit the platter under a hot grill until the cheese has melted, then serve with **guacamole**, **salsa**, and **soured cream**.

4 Greek stuffed tomatoes

PREP 10 MINS | COOK 1½ HRS

SERVES 4

Slice the tops off 4 large **beefsteak tomatoes**, and scoop out the flesh. Roughly chop the flesh, and reserve the tomatoes shells and their "lids". Heat ½ tablespoon of **olive oil** in a large frying pan over a medium heat. Add 400g (14oz) **lamb mince**, and cook, stirring to break up lumps, until the meat is no longer pink. Add the reserved flesh (including juices and seeds) and a pinch each of **paprika**, **ground cumin**, and **ground cinnamon**. Cook, stirring, for a couple of minutes. Add 2 deseeded and finely chopped fresh **green chillies**, 1 tablespoon of **tomato purée**, 1 tablespoon of **harissa**, and a handful of chopped fresh **mint leaves**. Pour in 150ml (5fl oz) hot **vegetable stock**, and bring to the boil. Simmer for 15 minutes until thickened. Season. Spoon the mixture into the reserved tomato shells, put their lids on, and sit in a roasting tin. Cover with foil, and bake in a preheated 200°C (400°F/Gas 6) oven for 1 hour.

Greek stuffed tomatoes

5 Meatballs with butternut squash

PREP 15 MINS | **COOK** 30 MINS

SERVES 4

In a bowl, mix together 500g (1lb 2oz) **beef mince**, 1 finely chopped **onion**, and 2 finely chopped **garlic cloves**. Season. Add 1 **egg**, and combine. Form into 12 balls, and chill. Halve, deseed, and peel a **butternut squash**, and cut into bite-sized pieces. Tip into a roasting tin, drizzle over a little **olive oil**, and sprinkle over some **chilli flakes** and **salt**. Roast in a preheated 200°C (400°F/Gas 6) oven for 15–20 minutes. Meanwhile, shallow-fry the meatballs in **olive oil** over a medium-high heat; cook for 5–10 minutes until golden, then transfer to the roasting tin with the squash, and roast for 10 minutes.

6 Turkish pizza with mince and shredded salad

PREP 5 MINS | **COOK** 20 MINS

SERVES 4

In a large frying pan over a low heat, sauté 1 finely chopped **onion** in a little **olive oil** until soft, then add 2 finely chopped **garlic cloves** and 450g (1lb) lamb mince. Cook, stirring to break up lumps, until the meat is browned, then add a pinch of **chilli powder** and the juice of 1 **lemon**. Season, and stir through. Spoon the beef mixture onto four **flatbreads**, such as pitta or naan, and add a handful of **pine nuts** and a sprinkling of mild **paprika**. Cook in a preheated 200°C (400°F/Gas 6) oven for 5–10 minutes until golden. Garnish with fresh **coriander**, and serve with **hummus**.

7 Mince and chickpeas cooked with orange and cinnamon

PREP 10 MINS | **COOK** 20 MINS

SERVES 4

In a large pan over a low heat, sweat 1 finely chopped **red onion** in a little **olive oil** for 5 minutes, until soft. Add 2 grated **garlic cloves**, a 2.5cm (1in) piece of **ginger**, grated, and a pinch of **ground cinnamon**. Season, stir in 675g (1½lb) **beef mince**, and cook for a few minutes until the meat is no longer pink. Add the grated zest and juice of 1 **orange**, and a 400g can of drained and rinsed **chickpeas**. Pour in 150ml (5fl oz) hot **vegetable stock**, and bring to the boil. Reduce the heat and simmer gently, stirring occasionally, for about 15 minutes.

8 Mediterranean burgers

PREP 10 MINS | **COOK** 15 MINS

SERVES 4

Combine 500g (1lb 2oz) **beef mince** with 1 finely chopped **onion**, 2 finely chopped **garlic cloves**, 1 tablespoon of **dried oregano**, 2 deseeded and finely diced **red peppers**, a handful of finely chopped fresh **basil leaves**, and a handful of fresh **flat-leaf parsley**, finely chopped. Season, and add a drop of **red wine**. Using your hands, mix until well combined. Divide the mixture into 4 large balls, and flatten into burgers. Melt a knob of **butter** in a frying pan over a medium-high heat, and fry the burgers for 3–5 minutes on each side until browned and cooked through. Serve sandwiched in a fresh **bun or roll**, with fresh **salad leaves** and **tomato**.

Mediterranean burgers

EVERYDAY

Mince and chickpeas cooked with orange and cinnamon

Mince and aubergine bake

PREP 10 MINS COOK 30 MINS

SERVES 4

Heat 1 tablespoon of **olive oil** in a large frying pan over a medium-high heat. Fry 1 sliced **aubergine** until golden on both sides. Remove from the pan, and drain on kitchen paper. In the same pan, sauté 1 finely chopped **onion** in a little olive oil until soft. Add 2 finely chopped **garlic cloves** and a pinch of **dried oregano**. Cook for a minute, then stir through a pinch of **ground allspice** and **ground cinnamon**. Season. Add 675g (1½lb) **lamb mince**, and cook, stirring to break up lumps, until no longer pink. Layer the mince with the aubergine in an ovenproof dish, starting with a layer of mince and finishing with a layer of aubergine. Mix 150ml (5fl oz) **Greek-style yogurt** and 1 **egg**. Season. Spoon the mixture over the top of the aubergine, and bake in a preheated 200°C (400°F/Gas 6) oven for 20–30 minutes until set and golden.

Minced beef with noodles

PREP 5 MINS COOK 20 MINS

SERVES 4

In a large frying pan over a medium heat, cook 500g (1lb 2oz) **beef mince** in a little **olive oil** for about 10 minutes until no longer pink, stirring with a wooden spoon to break up lumps. Add 75ml (2½fl oz) **passata** or **tomato juice**, and simmer for about 10 minutes. Stir through a handful of fresh **thyme leaves**, and season. Meanwhile, melt a knob of **butter** in another frying pan over a medium heat, and sauté 200g (7oz) halved **button mushrooms** for 5–10 minutes until golden. Tip into the mince, and stir through. Serve with **egg noodles** tossed in butter, and a little grating of **Cheddar** or **Gruyère cheese**.

10 WAYS WITH...
SAUSAGES

EVERYDAY

1 Hot dogs with sweet red onions

PREP 10 MINS
COOK 30 MINS

SERVES 4

Add 3 peeled and sliced **onions** to a large frying pan with a drizzle of **olive oil**. Sweat over a very low heat for about 5 minutes until soft, then sprinkle in 1 tablespoon of **demerara sugar**. Continue to cook over a very low heat for about 20 minutes until beginning to caramelize. Meanwhile, tip 8 good-quality **sausages** into a roasting tin. Drizzle with a little olive oil, and cook in a preheated 200°C (400°F/Gas 6) oven for 20–25 minutes, turning occasionally, until golden all over and the juices run clear. Serve with the **sweet onions** in split white **finger rolls** with a squirt of your favourite **mustard**.

2 Sausage rolls

PREP 15 MINS
COOK 20 MINS

SERVES 4

Remove the skin from 8 good-quality **pork sausages**. Crumble the peeled sausages into a bowl, and add 2 peeled, cored, and chopped **eating apples** and a few chopped **sage leaves**. Mix well. Roll out 500g (1lb 2oz) ready-prepared **puff pastry** into an oblong shape about 15 x 30cm (6 x 12in) and 5mm (¼in) thick. Mould the sausagemeat into a large sausage shape about as long as the pastry on its widest side, and lay along one long edge of the pastry. Brush the edges of the pastry with a little water, then fold one side over so that the edges meet and cover the meat; seal using the back of a fork or by pinching together with your finger and thumb. Cut into 8 sausage rolls, brush with a little beaten **egg yolk**, and cook in a preheated 200°C (400°F/Gas 6) oven for about 20 minutes until golden. Serve hot.

3 Toad in the hole

PREP 15 MINS
COOK 40 MINS

SERVES 4

Sift 125g (4½oz) **plain flour** into a bowl with a pinch of **salt**. Make a well in the centre, crack in 2 **eggs**, pour in a little **milk**, from 300ml (10fl oz), and stir with a wooden spoon. Add the remaining milk a little at a time, and use a whisk to mix the batter. Season and stir in a few chopped **sage leaves**. Leave the batter in the refrigerator to rest. Meanwhile, put 8 **spicy sausages**, halved if large, into an ovenproof dish. Drizzle with a little **olive oil**, and cook in a preheated 200°C (400°F/Gas 6) oven for 15–20 minutes until the sausages are golden. Remove the dish from the oven, and carefully pour over the prepared batter. Return to the oven, and cook for about 15 minutes more until the batter is risen and golden. Serve with mashed potato and gravy.

4 Spicy sausage, onion, and potato tray bake

PREP 10 MINS
COOK 40 MINS

SERVES 4

Tip 8–12 **spicy sausages** into a large roasting tin, along with 250g (9oz) **baby new potatoes** and 2 **red onions**, peeled and cut into eight wedges. Mix together 4 tablespoons of **wholegrain mustard**, 1 tablespoon of **cranberry** or **redcurrant jelly**, and 1 tablespoon of **olive oil**. Add to the sausage mix, and combine well using your hands. Scatter over a few sprigs of fresh **rosemary**, and season. Roast in a preheated 200°C (400°F/Gas 6) oven for 30–40 minutes until golden. Serve immediately.

Toad in the hole

5 Sausages in cider with lentils

PREP 10 MINS **COOK 50 MINS**

SERVES 4

In a large heavy frying pan over a medium-high heat, lightly brown 8 good-quality **sausages** in a little **olive oil** for 8–10 minutes. Remove from the pan, and set aside. Reduce the heat to low and, in the same pan, gently sweat 1 chopped **onion** in a little olive oil for 5 minutes until soft. Add 2 chopped **garlic cloves**, a few sprigs of **rosemary**, leaves picked and finely chopped, and season. Stir through 200g (7oz) **dried brown** or **Puy lentils**. Increase the heat, and pour over 300ml (10fl oz) **dry cider**. Boil for a few minutes, then add 500ml (16fl oz) hot **vegetable stock**. Return the sausages to the pan, and simmer gently for about 40 minutes, or until the lentils are cooked. Season to taste and serve.

6 Sausage and chestnut stuffing

PREP 10 MINS **COOK 20 MINS**

SERVES 4

In a frying pan over a low heat, sweat 1 chopped **onion** in a little **olive oil** for about 5 minutes until soft. Season, and set aside to cool. Peel the skin from 6 good-quality **pork sausages**, and add the meat to a bowl. Chop 250g (9oz) ready-cooked **chestnuts**, and add to the sausagemeat, along with a handful of fresh **flat-leaf parsley** and the cooled onions. Mix together, and season. Use to stuff the neck of a **turkey**, or under the skin of a whole **chicken**. Alternatively, roll the mixture into balls, and roast in a preheated 200°C (400°F/Gas 6) oven for about 20 minutes, or fry in a little olive oil until cooked through and golden.

7 Spicy sausage and tomato skewers

PREP 15 MINS **COOK 20 MINS**

Special equipment • skewers • ridged cast-iron grill pan

SERVES 4

If using wooden or bamboo skewers, soak in cold water for 30 minutes. Cut 12 **spicy sausages** into chunky pieces, and alternately thread onto skewers with 12 **cherry tomatoes** and a few **bay leaves**. Brush with **olive oil**, sprinkle over chopped **rosemary leaves** and season. Heat a ridged cast-iron grill pan or griddle until hot. Add the skewers, and grill for 5–8 minutes on each side until the sausages are well cooked and lightly charred.

8 Sausagemeat, courgette, and bulgur wheat

PREP 10 MINS **COOK 20 MINS**

SERVES 4

Put 125g (4½oz) **bulgur wheat** in a bowl, and just cover with boiling water. Let stand for 10 minutes, then stir well with a fork to fluff up the grains. Season. In a heavy frying pan over a low heat, sauté 1 finely chopped **onion** with a pinch of **salt** and mild **paprika** in a little **olive oil** for about 5 minutes until soft. Increase the heat to medium, and add 225g (8oz) good-quality **sausagemeat** to the pan. Cook, stirring to break up any lumps, until no longer pink. Reduce the heat slightly, and add 2 grated **courgettes**. Cook slowly, stirring from time to time, for a further 10–15 minutes. Remove from the heat, and stir through the bulgur wheat. Sprinkle with a handful of finely chopped fresh **flat-leaf parsley**, and serve immediately.

Spicy sausage and tomato skewers

Chorizo and baby onion casserole

9 Courgettes stuffed with sausagemeat and red onion

 PREP 15 MINS **COOK 40 MINS**

SERVES 4

Halve 4 large **courgettes** lengthways. Scoop out the flesh, roughly chop, and set aside with the courgette "shells". In a frying pan, sauté 1 chopped large **red onion** in a little **olive oil** over a low-medium heat for a few minutes until soft. Add 2 chopped **garlic cloves**, and the chopped courgette flesh. Season and sauté for few minutes more. Next, add 225g (8oz) good-quality **sausagemeat** and a pinch of **ground cinnamon**. Cook, stirring to break up any lumps, until the meat is no longer pink. Brush the courgette shells with a little olive oil, season, and sit upright in a roasting tin. Tightly fill each courgette shell with the sausagemeat mixture. Any leftover mixture can be rolled into balls and cooked alongside the stuffed courgettes. Roast in a preheated 200°C (400°F/Gas 6) oven for 30–40 minutes until the courgettes are soft and beginning to char, and the meat is cooked through. Serve hot, either whole or cut into slices, with the extra meatballs alongside.

10 Chorizo and baby onion casserole

 PREP 15 MINS **COOK 45 MINS**

Special equipment • flameproof casserole

SERVES 4

Fry a handful of peeled whole **baby onions** in a flameproof casserole until golden, then sprinkle in a pinch of **fennel seeds**, 2 chopped **garlic cloves**, and 1 deseeded and finely chopped fresh **red chilli**. Throw in 225g (8oz) sliced or cubed **chorizo**, and cook for a couple of minutes, then tip in the contents of a 400g can chopped **tomatoes**. Fill the can with hot water, and tip this in too. Stir through, and season. Cook, covered, in a preheated 200°C (400°F/Gas 6) oven for about 40 minutes. Top up with hot water if needed. Serve hot with creamy mashed potato.

10 WAYS WITH...
EGGS

EVERYDAY

1 The perfect omelette

PREP 2 MINS · COOK 1 MIN

SERVES 1

Lightly whisk 2 **eggs** with a tiny drop of **milk**, and season. Heat a small frying pan until hot, and add a knob of **butter**. Once the butter is melted and foaming, pour in the egg mixture, and pull the edges away from the side of the pan towards the centre using a spatula or fish slice; keep doing this so that any uncooked mixture runs to the edge. After about 30 seconds, most of the egg will be set. It will still be soft and uncooked in the middle, but residual heat will continue cooking the omelette after you have taken it out of the pan. Sprinkle a handful of grated **cheese** down the centre of the omelette, then fold one half of the omelette over the top of the other. Slide onto a plate, and serve immediately.

2 French toast

PREP 5 MINS · COOK 10 MINS

SERVES 1

Cut 1 medium slice of **bread** from a white loaf. Lightly whisk together 2 **eggs**, and season. Pour into a bowl, then sit the bread in the beaten egg mixture so that it is completely covered and soaks up all the liquid. Heat a non-stick frying pan over a medium-high heat. Add a drop of **olive oil** and, when hot, sit the slice of bread in the pan. Cook for 2–3 minutes on each side until golden. Serve immediately.

3 Indian spiced scrambled eggs

PREP 5 MINS · COOK 5 MINS

SERVES 2

Whisk together 4 **eggs** and 4 tablespoons of **milk**, and season. Melt a knob of **butter** in a deep-sided frying pan. Once the butter is foaming, tip in the egg mixture, and stir with a wooden spoon or spatula over a low heat until the eggs begin to scramble very lightly. Add a pinch of ground **turmeric** and **garam masala**, and stir. The eggs will continue to cook after being removed from the heat, so make sure to take them off when they are still creamy. Serve immediately.

4 Egg-fried rice

PREP 5 MINS · COOK 8 MINS

Special equipment • wok

SERVES 4

Whisk together 2 **eggs** and season. Heat 1 tablespoon of **sesame oil** in a wok over a medium-high heat. Swirl, then add 300g (10oz) completely cold cooked **basmati rice** (use rice cooked the day before and refrigerated overnight for the best results). Stir-fry for a few minutes, then add the beaten egg. Continue stir-frying for a few more minutes while the egg begins to set. Stir through a handful of ready-cooked or fresh **garden peas** and a bunch of finely chopped **spring onions**. Season, and serve straight away.

The perfect omelette

5 Baked eggs with tomatoes

PREP 5 MINS · COOK 15 MINS

Special equipment • 4 ramekins

SERVES 4

Spoon 1 tablespoon of **double cream** into each ramekin, then break an **egg** into each one, taking care not to break the yolks. Season, then top each egg with another tablespoon of double cream and 1 tablespoon each of chopped skinned **tomatoes**. Sit the ramekins in a roasting tin, and pour in hot water to come just halfway up their sides. Cover the roasting tin with foil, then carefully slide into a preheated 180°C (350°F/Gas 4) oven. Cook for about 15 minutes, and serve immediately.

6 Peppered tuna with eggs

PREP 10 MINS · COOK 10 MINS

SERVES 4

Roll a 250g (9oz) fresh **tuna loin** in some cracked **black pepper**, then sear in a pan, over a medium heat, with a little hot **olive oil** for 3-4 minutes on each side. Remove from the pan, and leave to rest while preparing the eggs. Soft-boil 4 **eggs** for 4 minutes. Slice the tuna, and serve with a handful of pitted and sliced **black olives**, 10 **anchovies** in oil, drained, and the peeled and quartered eggs. Arrange on a plate with wild **rocket leaves**, squeeze over the juice of ½ a **lemon**, add a drizzle of **extra virgin olive oil**, and season to taste.

7 Egg curry with turmeric

PREP 10 MINS · COOK 25 MINS

SERVES 4

Heat a little **olive oil** in a heavy frying pan over a low heat. Add 1 finely chopped **onion**, 1 deseeded and finely chopped fresh hot **green chilli**, and a 2.5cm (1in) piece of grated fresh **root ginger**. Sweat for about 5 minutes until soft, then stir through 1-2 tablespoons of **ground turmeric** and 2 tablespoons of good-quality Indian **curry paste**. Pour in 300ml (10fl oz) **tomato juice** and 150ml (5fl oz) **double cream**. Season, and simmer gently for 15-20 minutes. Meanwhile, boil 4 **eggs** for 6 minutes. When cool enough to handle, shell and quarter the eggs, and add to the sauce to just heat through. Serve with fluffy **rice**, and fresh **coriander** sprinkled over the top.

Baked eggs with tomatoes

8 Blue cheese and herb baked omelette

PREP 5 MINS · COOK 30 MINS

SERVES 4

Whisk together 8 **eggs** and 150ml (5fl oz) **double cream**. Season and stir in a bunch of finely chopped fresh **chives** and fresh **flat-leaf parsley**. In a large ovenproof non-stick frying pan over a low-medium heat, sauté 2 sliced **red onions** in a little **olive oil** and **butter** for 5-8 minutes until soft. Season. Pour the egg mixture into the frying pan over the top of the onions, and cook for 2-3 minutes, pulling the mixture away from the edge of the pan towards the centre. Scatter over 125g (4½oz) **blue cheese** such as **Stilton**, and transfer to a 200°C (400°F/Gas 6) oven. Bake for 10-15 minutes until the egg is set and golden. Remove from the oven, and leave for a few minutes before turning out and slicing.

9 Cheese and herb frittata

PREP 15 MINS · COOK 15 MINS

SERVES 4

Preheat the grill to its highest setting. Whisk together 8 **eggs** in a large bowl and season. Stir through a handful of finely chopped fresh **flat-leaf parsley**, and a few finely chopped fresh **tarragon leaves**. Add 125g (4½oz) grated **Gruyère cheese**, and combine well. Transfer to a jug for easy pouring. Melt 50g (1¾oz) **butter** in a non-stick frying pan about 20cm (8in) in diameter. When the butter begins to foam, pour in the egg mixture, and reduce the heat to low. Swirl the egg mixture around the pan so that it runs towards the edges, and leave to cook for 10–12 minutes until the bottom is set and slightly brown; the top will still be runny. Now sit the pan under the hot grill, and grill the top of the frittata for a couple of minutes until just set. Leave to stand for a few minutes, then run a knife around the edge, and slide the frittata onto a plate. Serve immediately.

10 Egg and fennel potato salad

PREP 10 MINS · COOK 15 MINS

SERVES 4

Boil 4 **eggs** for 6 minutes – less if you prefer a runnier yolk. Cook 250g (9oz) **new potatoes** in lightly salted boiling water for 15–20 minutes until soft; drain. Drizzle over some **olive oil** while the potatoes are still hot, and season. Mix in a handful of finely chopped fresh **flat-leaf parsley**, and 1 trimmed and finely chopped **fennel bulb**. Shell and quarter the hard-boiled eggs, and add to the potato salad. Serve immediately.

EVERYDAY

Egg and fennel potato salad

10 WAYS WITH...
BACON AND HAM

1 Crispy bacon and avocado wraps

  PREP 5 MINS **COOK** 10 MINS

SERVES 4

Fry 225g (8oz) thick **back bacon rashers** over a medium-high heat until golden and crispy. Use to fill 4 **flour tortillas**, along with a handful of shredded **Cos lettuce**, and 1 ripe **avocado**, peeled, stoned, and cut into slices. Squeeze the juice of 1 **lemon** and lots of freshly ground **black pepper** into 3-4 tablespoons of **mayonnaise**, stir well, and use to top the bacon mix. Roll up the tortillas, and serve immediately.

2 Savoury cheese and bacon muffins

  PREP 15 MINS **COOK** 25 MINS

Special equipment • 4 x 150ml (5fl oz) metal pudding moulds or ramekins

SERVES 4

Fry 150g (5½oz) **back bacon rashers**, over a medium-high heat, until cooked but not too crispy, then cut into bite-sized pieces. Mix together 200g (7oz) **Cheddar cheese**, cut up into small pieces, with 125g (4½oz) fresh **breadcrumbs**, ½ bunch of finely chopped **spring onions**, 3 **eggs**, and 100ml (3½fl oz) **milk**. Stir through the **bacon** and a handful of chopped fresh **chives**. Season, then spoon into the buttered pudding moulds or ramekins. Bake in the oven at 190°C (375°F/Gas 5) for about 25 minutes until risen and golden.

3 Parma ham, grape, and walnut salad

  PREP 10 MINS **COOK** 2 MINS

SERVES 4

Whisk together 3 tablespoons of **extra virgin olive oil** with 1 tablespoon of freshly squeezed **lemon juice** and 1 teaspoon of **runny honey**. Season and set aside. Melt a knob of **butter** with a pinch of **demerara sugar** in a small frying pan over a medium heat. Once the sugar has dissolved, add a handful of halved **walnuts**, and stir until well coated. Remove from the pan, and set aside on a plate. Put 2 large handfuls of mixed **salad leaves** in a large shallow serving bowl. Add a handful of seedless black grapes, the caramelized walnuts, and 1 peeled, stoned, and sliced ripe **avocado**. Drizzle over a little of the dressing, and toss gently. Top with 225g (8oz) sweet **Parma ham**.

4 White fish wrapped in bacon

  PREP 5 MINS **COOK** 20 MINS

SERVES 4

Wrap 225g (8oz) **streaky bacon rashers** around 4 chunky **haddock loins**, about 150g (5½oz) each. Sit the wrapped fish in a roasting tin, drizzle with a little **olive oil**, and throw in some sprigs of fresh **rosemary**. Cook in a preheated 200°C (400°F/Gas 6) oven for 15-20 minutes, until the fish is cooked and the bacon is golden and crispy. Serve immediately.

Savoury cheese and bacon muffins

5

Pancetta and potatoes with red cabbage

PREP 10 MINS **COOK 15 MINS**

SERVES 4

Heat a large frying pan over a medium-high heat. Add a knob of **butter** and 1 tablespoon of **olive oil**, tip in 3 cubed cooked **potatoes**, and sauté for 5–10 minutes until golden and crispy, adding more oil if needed. Season. Push the potatoes to one side of the pan, add 175g (6oz) cubed **pancetta**, and cook until crispy. Stir through 200g (7oz) lightly cooked shredded red cabbage and 2 chopped eating apples. Cook until well combined and the apple is golden. Season again if needed.

6

Bacon, pear, and blue cheese salad

PREP 10 MINS **COOK 10 MINS**

SERVES 4

Whisk together 3 tablespoons of **extra virgin olive oil**, 1 tablespoon of **white wine vinegar**, and a pinch of **sugar**, and season. Add 50g (1¾oz) crumbled **blue cheese,** such as Stilton, and whisk together well until the dressing thickens. Set aside. In a small frying pan, cook 225g (8oz) thick **back bacon rashers**, over a medium-high heat, for 5–9 minutes until crispy, then cut into small pieces. Core and slice 3 ripe **eating pears**, and add to a shallow bowl with 2 handfuls of mixed **salad leaves** and the bacon pieces, then crumble over 50g (1¾oz) blue cheese. Drizzle over the dressing and serve.

7

Ham with minted peas and broad beans

PREP 10 MINS **COOK 20 MINS**

SERVES 4

In a large frying pan over a low heat, sweat 1 finely chopped **onion** in a little **olive oil** for about 5 minutes until soft. Add 2 finely chopped **garlic cloves**, and stir in 150g (5½oz) frozen **broad beans** and 75g (2½oz) frozen **peas**. Pour in 150ml (5fl oz) hot **chicken stock**, and bring to the boil. Reduce the heat slightly, and simmer for 15 minutes. Stir through a handful of fresh **mint leaves**, chopped, and 175g (6oz) good-quality cooked **ham**, cut into cubes. Serve immediately.

8

Pancetta and artichoke risotto

PREP 10 MINS **COOK 30 MINS**

SERVES 4

In a large frying pan over a medium heat, cook 150g (5½oz) cubed **pancetta** in a little **olive oil** until crispy. Remove with a slotted spoon, and set aside. Add a knob of **butter** and 1 tablespoon of **olive oil** to the same pan, reduce the heat to low, and sweat 1 finely chopped **onion** for about 5 minutes until soft. Stir through 250g (9oz) **Arborio** or other **risotto rice** until well coated, then tip in a glass of **dry white wine**. Increase the heat, and let it boil for a few minutes, then pour in some hot **vegetable stock** taken from 900ml (1½ pints) simmering in a separate pan. Keep stirring and adding stock until the rice has absorbed all the liquid and is creamy but still has a bit of bite to it. Use more or less stock as required. Tip the pancetta back into the pan, and stir through. Add a 400g jar of drained halved **artichoke hearts**, and gently stir again until heated through. Serve hot with some freshly grated **Parmesan cheese**.

Ham with minted peas and broad beans

Pancetta with scallops

9 Bacon and tomato sauce with gnocchi

PREP 10 MINS · COOK 20 MINS

SERVES 4

In a heavy pan over a medium-high heat, cook 150g (5½oz) diced **back bacon** or cubed **pancetta** for 5–8 minutes until crispy, then set aside. In the same pan, bring 300ml (10fl oz) **passata** to the boil. Stir through a heaped teaspoon of ready-made **red** or **green pesto**, and return the bacon to the sauce. Reduce the heat, and simmer gently for about 15 minutes. In a separate large pan, cook 300g (10oz) **gnocchi** in plenty of boiling salted water according to the packet instructions, then drain and serve with the sauce. Top with freshly grated **Parmesan cheese** and torn fresh **basil leaves**, and serve immediately.

10 Pancetta with scallops

PREP 5 MINS · COOK 10 MINS

SERVES 4

Heat a non-stick frying pan over a medium-high heat. Add a knob of **butter** and 1 tablespoon of **olive oil**. Season 12 fresh **scallops** and add to the pan. Sear for 2 minutes on one side (or longer, depending on thickness), then turn over and cook on the other side for a couple of minutes more, turning the first scallop that went into the pan first and quickly working your way to the last one. Remove from the pan with a slotted spoon, and set aside to keep warm. Add a drizzle of olive oil to the same pan, tip in 150g (5½oz) cubed **pancetta**, and cook for 5–8 minutes until crispy. When cooked, tip over the scallops to serve, along with any juices from the pan. Serve immediately.

10 WAYS WITH...
TURKEY

EVERYDAY

1 Turkey and tarragon broth

PREP 10 MINS | COOK 20 MINS

SERVES 4

In a large pan over a low heat, sweat 1 finely chopped **onion** in a little **olive oil** for 5 minutes until soft. Add 2 finely chopped **garlic cloves**, and season. Add 3 peeled and sliced **carrots**, together with a few chopped fresh **tarragon leaves**, and cook for 10 minutes until the carrots begin to soften. Pour in 900ml (1½ pints) hot **chicken stock**, and bring to the boil. Reduce the heat to a simmer, and add 3 cubed cooked **potatoes**, 225g (8oz) shredded or sliced cooked **turkey**, and a few more fresh tarragon leaves. Simmer gently until everything is heated through, and serve.

2 Turkey curry

PREP 10 MINS | COOK 30 MINS

SERVES 4

In a large frying pan over a low heat, sweat 1 finely chopped **onion** in 1 tablespoon of **olive oil** for 5 minutes until soft. Stir through 3 finely chopped **garlic cloves**, and season. Add 1 teaspoon of crushed **coriander seeds**, 4 **cardamom pods**, a handful of crushed **curry leaves**, a 2.5cm (1in) piece of fresh **root ginger**, grated, and 2–3 deseeded and finely chopped fresh medium-hot **red chillies**. Cook for few minutes, then tip in a 400g can of whole peeled **plum tomatoes**, chopped, including any juices. Bring to the boil, reduce the heat slightly, and simmer for 15 minutes. Add 200g (7oz) shredded or sliced cooked **turkey**. Tip in 150ml (5fl oz) **double cream**, and stir well. Simmer for 10 more minutes. Season. Stir through some chopped fresh **coriander** and serve.

3 Turkey escalopes stuffed with prunes and pecans

PREP 15 MINS | COOK 30 MINS

Special equipment • cocktail sticks or skewers

SERVES 4

Cut 2 skinless **turkey breast fillets** in half, about 400g (14oz) each, and sandwich between sheets of cling film. Pound with a meat hammer or the edge of a rolling pin until they are an even thickness of about 5mm (¼in). Slice the breasts in half so that you have 8 escalopes. Chop a large handful of pitted **prunes**, and mix with a handful of finely chopped roasted **pecan nuts** and fresh **flat-leaf parsley**. Spoon the mixture into the middle of each turkey escalope, then roll up and secure with a cocktail stick. Sit the turkey rolls in a roasting tin, drizzle with **olive oil**, and roast in a preheated 200°C (400°F/ Gas 6) oven for 15–20 minutes, until cooked through.

4 Shredded turkey, mint, and pomegranate salad

PREP 15 MINS

SERVES 4

Arrange 2 large handfuls of **wild rocket leaves** on a serving plate, and top with 300g (10oz) sliced cooked **turkey breast**. Scatter over a bunch of sliced **spring onions**, a handful of fresh **mint leaves**, and the seeds of 1 **pomegranate**. Whisk together 3 tablespoons of **extra virgin olive oil**, 1 tablespoon of freshly squeezed **lemon juice**, 1 tablespoon of **pomegranate molasses**, and a pinch of **ground cinnamon**. Season. Taste the dressing, and add some **sugar**, if needed. Drizzle over the salad, and serve.

Turkey escalopes stuffed with prunes and pecans

5 Turkey and mixed rice salad

PREP 10 MINS

SERVES 4

Mix together 200g (7oz) cold cooked long-grain **rice** with a 400g can of drained and rinsed **chickpeas**. Season. Stir through 400g (14oz) sliced cooked **turkey breast**, 50g (1¾oz) dried **cranberries**, and a handful of toasted **pine nuts**. Whisk together 3 tablespoons of **extra virgin olive oil**, 1 tablespoon of **white wine vinegar**, 1 teaspoon of **wholegrain mustard**, and 1 teaspoon of **honey**. Season. To serve, drizzle the dressing over the rice, and stir through some finely chopped fresh **flat-leaf parsley**.

6 Turkey, chilli, and cashew stir-fry

PREP 5 MINS | COOK 15 MINS

Special equipment • wok

SERVES 4

In a wok, over a medium heat, stir-fry a bunch of sliced **spring onions** in a drizzle of **sesame oil** for 5 minutes. Slice 2 large skinless **turkey breast fillets**, 400g (14oz) each. Toss in the oil with the spring onions until no longer pink. Throw in 3 sliced **garlic cloves** and 2 **red** and 1 **green** deseeded and shredded fresh hot **chillies**. Continue to stir-fry for a further 10 minutes, then add a handful of **cashew nuts** and a splash of **soy sauce**, and toss the **turkey** well. Serve immediately with a splash of **sweet chilli sauce** and some **fluffy rice**.

7 Turkey breasts with honey and roasted hazelnuts

PREP 15 MINS | COOK 40 MINS

Special equipment • food processor

SERVES 4

Gently heat 2 tablespoons of **runny honey** in a small pan, then brush it over 4 **turkey breasts**, about 400g (14oz) each, skin on. Season. Whiz a handful of toasted **hazelnuts** in a food processor until ground, then tip onto a plate. Roll each of the turkey breasts in the ground nuts until evenly coated. Sit in a roasting tin skin-side up, and roast in a preheated 200°C (400°F/Gas 6) oven for 25–40 minutes, until the turkey is cooked through. Pierce with a knife to check – the juices should run clear. Leave the turkey to rest for a few minutes, then slice and serve with cooked **broccoli** tossed in **lemon juice**, a little **chilli oil**, and some **sautéed potatoes**.

8 Marinated turkey breasts with harissa and lemon

PREP 10 MINS | COOK 45 MINS

Marinating • 30 minutes

SERVES 4

Mix 3 tablespoons of **harissa** with the juice of 1 **lemon** and a handful of finely chopped fresh **mint leaves**. Take 4 large **turkey breast fillets**, 400g (14oz) each, skin on, and slash 3 or 4 times on the diagonal, slicing through the skin and into the flesh. Sit in a roasting tin, and smother with the harissa mixture, making sure that it gets into the slashes. Season and leave to marinate in the refrigerator for at least 30 minutes, or preferably overnight. Roast in a preheated 200°C (400°F/Gas 6) oven for 20–30 minutes until the turkey is cooked through and the skin is golden and crispy. Leave to rest for 5 minutes, then slice and serve with **salad leaves**, a squeeze of **lemon**, and a **potato salad** made with **olive oil**, instead of **mayonnaise**.

Marinated turkey breasts with harissa and lemon

Asian turkey and noodle soup

9 Asian turkey and noodle soup

 PREP 10 MINS COOK 30 MINS

SERVES 4

Pour 900ml (1½ pints) hot **vegetable stock** into a large pan. Add a generous splash of **soy sauce**, 1 stalk of **lemongrass**, a 2.5cm (1in) piece of fresh **root ginger**, sliced, and 2 large skinless **turkey breast fillets**, about 400g (14oz) each. Bring to the boil, reduce the heat slightly, and simmer for 15–20 minutes, until the turkey is fully poached and cooked through. Remove from the pan using a slotted spoon, and shred when cool. To cook the noodles, top up the poaching liquid with boiling water if needed. Add 300g (10oz) fine **rice noodles** and 1 fresh hot **red chilli**, deseeded and sliced, and simmer for 1 minute. Return the shredded turkey to the pan with a handful of fresh **coriander** to heat through. Season, and serve immediately.

10 Turkey and sweetcorn balls

 PREP 15 MINS COOK 10 MINS

Special equipment • food processor

SERVES 4

Process 2 large skinless **turkey breast fillets**, about 400g (14oz) each, until minced – be careful not to turn into a paste. Add a 400g can of drained **sweetcorn kernels** and a bunch of chopped **spring onions**. Pulse until well combined. Transfer the mixture to a bowl, add a handful of finely chopped fresh **flat-leaf parsley**, and season. Add 1 **egg**, and use your hands to mix everything together until well combined. Shape into balls a little larger than a walnut, and roll until tightly formed; you should end up with 12 balls. Roll each ball in a little **plain flour**. Shallow-fry a few at a time in a little **olive oil** in a large non-stick frying pan over a medium-high heat; cook for 5–8 minutes until golden. Serve hot with **potato wedges** or **chips**.

FASTER PASTA

Simple sauces and easy bakes, many ready
in under 20 minutes.

FASTER PASTA

If there is pasta in your storecupboard, a quick and easy meal is just minutes away. Pasta can taste delicious on its own, simply seasoned and drizzled with olive oil, or it can be the vehicle for a variety of sauces. Convenient and versatile, there are dozens of shapes to choose from, and each has sauces it works best with.

Types of pasta
Here are the most widely available shapes, and how to use them.

dried versus fresh

This is one occasion when fresh is not always best. If making your own pasta or buying it fresh from the deli then fresh is superior. However, if buying pasta from the supermarket, dried pasta is usually the best option, because the fresh pasta is often too wet. Choose a good brand, preferably one made in Italy, where it is made with durum wheat.

LONG	RIBBON	SHORT	TUBULAR	STUFFED
			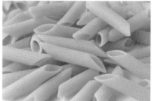	

LONG

SPAGHETTI ("strings")
Long, thin, round, and rigid. Probably the most common of all shapes, and extremely versatile.

LINGUINE ("small tongues")
Similar to spaghetti in appearance, but flat rather than round. Can be used whenever a recipe calls for spaghetti.

CAPELLI D'ANGELO ("angel hair")
Very fine strands. Not sturdy enough for sauce, so best added to soups and broths.

BUCATINI (buco = "hole")
A fat, long, and hollow spaghetti.

OTHER TYPES
Fusilli lunghi (long fusilli), spaghettini (thin spaghetti)

BEST WITH...
Oil-based or tomato sauces are ideal, as each strand of pasta gets well coated. Perfect tossed with seafood, especially linguine, which is wonderful paired with clams.

RIBBON

TAGLIATELLE (to "cut")
This wide, flat pasta is the most well-known of the ribbon pastas. It is often flavoured with spinach to produce a green pasta, or tomato to produce a red one.

PAPPARDELLE (pappare = "to stuff oneself")
The widest of the ribbon pastas. As a rule of thumb, big pasta needs a big sauce.

FETTUCCINI ("little ribbons")
Long and flat, similar to tagliatelle, but a little wider.

OTHER TYPES
Lasagne

BEST WITH...
Best served with a robust chunky sauce. Meat- or tomato-based sauces – such as ragù – work well, as do thick, cream-based sauces, which are heavy, and cling well to the wide ribbons.

SHORT

FARFALLE ("butterflies")
Look like little butterflies, or bows, and have a ridged edge. They are quite delicate, and go well with light sauces.

FUSILLI ("little spindles")
Look like short springs. A good choice to serve in a salad, as they holds their shape well. They often come in a variety of colours.

CONCHIGLIE ("shells")
These are available in a variety of sizes, either very small (which are added to soups), or really large ones that look like sea shells.

OTHER TYPES
Orecchiette, trofie, strozzapreti,

BEST WITH...
Short pasta is fairly dense, so it can take chunky sauces, and works particularly well with rich meat sauces, and oily sauces. If serving with a vegetable sauce, cut the vegetables to match the size of the pasta shapes.

TUBULAR

PENNE ("quills")
The most well-known tubular pasta. They have a pointed end, and are either smooth or ridged. A versatile pasta shape, it can be combined with numerous sauces.

RIGATONI ("ridged")
Very similar to penne, but ridged, and without the pointed "pen" end.

MACARONI ("dumpling")
Hollow pasta tubes that can be small or large. Very sturdy, they go well with a cheese sauce.

OTHER TYPES
Ziti, cavatappi, gigantoni

BEST WITH...
These shapes are ideal for trapping and holding thick and chunky rich sauces. Serve with a heavy meat ragù, or a chunky arrabbiata sauce.

STUFFED

RAVIOLI (to "wrap")
Widely known, and usually bought fresh. Delicious flat parcels of egg pasta, they can be filled with meat, cheese, vegetables, or seafood, depending on the region in which they're made.

TORTELLINI (torta = "cake")
Ring-shaped pasta, filled and pinched in the middle. They can be bought dried or fresh, and are often filled with classic combinations, such as ricotta cheese and spinach.

OTHER TYPES
Cannelloni, tortelloni

BEST WITH...
This depends on what the pasta is stuffed with. Ravioli stuffed with pumpkin and ricotta cheese is delicious with melted butter and sage, for instance. Make sure the sauce complements and doesn't drown the flavour of the filling.

How to cook pasta

Use lots of water. Pasta needs room to move around while it is cooking, otherwise it will stick together. Use a large pan with plenty of water. As a rule, 100g (3½oz) of pasta needs about 1 litre (1¾ pints) of water. Don't cook too much at one time.

Don't add oil to the water while it cooks. If anything, this prevents the sauce from clinging to it.

Bring the water to a rolling boil, and add a pinch of salt just before adding the pasta. Keep at a rolling ball while cooking.

Watch the clock. Fresh pasta will cook much quicker than dried. Some will cook in a couple of minutes, so always have your sauce prepared.

Cook until "al dente", meaning it still has a bit of bite to it. You can remove a piece while it's cooking to test it.

Drain and return to the pan with a little of its cooking water, which will prevent it from sticking.

Go easy on the sauce. The sauce is supposed to coat the pasta, not drench it. Remember the pasta is the main ingredient, and the correct way is to add the sauce to the pasta, not the pasta to the sauce.

Serve instantly, as pasta doesn't take kindly to being reheated.

STEP-BY-STEP

Make your own pasta
It's far easier than you think, satisfying, and tastes wonderful. This method makes enough pasta for 4 people.

1 Make the dough Tip 450g (1lb) of "00" flour, or strong flour, onto a large clean surface, and make a well in the centre. Add a pinch of salt, then 3 large eggs, plus 2 egg yolks, to the well. Using a fork, gradually stir the egg, and bring the flour in from the sides so it begins to turns into a paste. Keep adding the flour, a little at a time, until it is all incorporated.

2 Knead Using your hands, bring the mixture together, then begin kneading the dough using the heel of your hand. Knead for about 10 minutes, or until the dough is still springy, but has a smooth texture. Wrap in cling film, and rest in the refrigerator for about 30 minutes.

3 Roll On a floured (or semolina-sprinkled) surface, roll the pasta out to an oval shape about 2.5cm (1in) thick. Set the machine to its widest setting, and feed through the dough a couple of times, turning the wheel as you go. Continue, changing the roller settings as you go so the pasta becomes thinner. As it gets longer, use your hands to guide it through. Now it is ready to cut to your preferred shape. Leave to dry in bundles for 10 minutes before cooking.

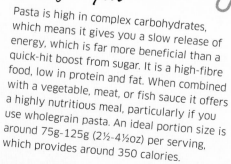

good for you
Pasta is high in complex carbohydrates, which means it gives you a slow release of energy, which is far more beneficial than a quick-hit boost from sugar. It is a high-fibre food, low in protein and fat. When combined with a vegetable, meat, or fish sauce it offers a highly nutritious meal, particularly if you use wholegrain pasta. An ideal portion size is around 75g–125g (2½–4½oz) per serving, which provides around 350 calories.

How to store

Dried A cool dark storecupboard, for up to 1 year. If opened, keep in a sealed jar, or in its pack, well-wrapped with cling film.

Fresh In the refrigerator for 2–3 days. Can be frozen for up to 1 month.

Cooked In the refrigerator, in a sealed container, for 2–3 days. Not suitable for freezing.

Psst...
Did you know that in Italy pasta is always served as a first course? Traditionally this was done in order to fill you up before the more expensive main course of meat or fish was served.

3 easy lunchbox recipes
A simple way to try some of the pasta shapes in the chart opposite. Or, you can use cold leftover pasta instead.

Pasta with vegetables Cook 225g (8oz) of pasta shells until "al dente". Drain, and return to the pan with a little of the pasta water. Toss with 2 tbsp olive oil, 2 finely chopped garlic cloves, and season. Leave to cool, then add 2 chopped tomatoes, a handful of basil leaves, torn, 3 finely chopped spring onions, 1 deseeded and finely sliced yellow pepper, and ¼ cucumber, cut into chunks. Toss together.

Pasta with beans Cook 225g (8oz) of pasta bows until "al dente". Drain, and return to the pan with a little of the pasta water. Toss with 2 tbsp of olive oil, and ½ a drained and rinsed can of flageolet beans. Leave to cool, then add a handful of fresh flat-leaf parsley, finely chopped, and season.

Pasta with tuna Cook 225g (8oz) of pasta twists until "al dente". Drain and return to the pan with a little of the pasta water. Toss with 2 tbsp of olive oil, the juice of 1 lemon, 1 deseeded and finely chopped red chilli, and a 200g can of drained tuna steaks. Season, and leave to cool.

EVERYDAY

Pasta with courgettes and saffron

PREP 10 MINS   COOK 15 MINS

SERVES 4

1 tbsp olive oil
1 onion, finely chopped
3 garlic cloves, grated or finely chopped
pinch of saffron strands
3–4 courgettes (depending on size),
    cut in half and diced
salt and freshly ground black pepper
200ml (7fl oz) double cream
pinch of chilli flakes (optional)
225g (8oz) tagliatelle
handful of fresh flat-leaf parsley,
    finely chopped (optional)
50g (1¾oz) Parmesan cheese, grated

1 Heat the oil in a large frying pan, add the onion, and cook on a medium heat for 5 minutes or until soft and translucent. Add the garlic and saffron, cook for a few seconds more, then add the courgettes. Season well with salt and pepper. Stir in the cream and chilli flakes (if using), and gently simmer for about 4 minutes.

2 Meanwhile, cook the pasta in a pan of boiling salted water for 6 minutes or until it is cooked but still has a bit of bite to it. Drain, keeping back a tiny amount of the cooking water. Return the pasta to the pan and toss together.

3 Add the sauce, then toss again. Add the parsley, if using, and toss once more. Sprinkle with Parmesan and serve.

VARIATION Swap the courgettes for asparagus when in season.

Pasta with no-cook tomato sauce

PREP 5 MINS   COOK 10 MINS

SERVES 4

6 tomatoes, deseeded and
    roughly chopped
2 garlic cloves, grated or finely chopped
handful of fresh basil leaves, torn
3 tbsp extra virgin olive oil
salt and freshly ground black pepper
350g (12oz) farfalle

1 Put the tomatoes, garlic, basil, and olive oil in a large bowl and season well with salt and black pepper. Stir well to combine, then leave to sit while you cook the pasta – the flavours will develop.

2 Cook the pasta in a large pan of boiling salted water for 10 minutes or until it is cooked but still has a bit of bite to it. Drain well, then toss with the tomato sauce and serve.

COOK'S NOTES

A pinch of chilli flakes works well in this dish. The longer you leave the tomato mixture to sit, the tastier it gets.

Pasta with hot pepper sauce

SERVES 4

1 tbsp olive oil

1 onion, finely chopped

salt and freshly ground black pepper

2 garlic cloves, grated or
   finely chopped

2 fresh hot red chillies, deseeded and
   finely chopped

2 red peppers and 1 yellow pepper,
   deseeded and roughly chopped

350g (12oz) penne or large
   pasta shells

handful of fresh basil leaves, torn

25g (scant 1oz) Parmesan
   cheese, grated

good-quality thick balsamic
   vinegar (optional)

1 Heat the oil in a large frying pan, add the onion, and cook on a low heat for 5 minutes, or until soft and translucent. Season well with salt and black pepper. Add the garlic and chillies and cook for a few seconds more. Add the peppers and cook, stirring occasionally, on a low heat for 5 minutes, or until soft.

2 Meanwhile, cook the pasta in a pan of boiling salted water for 8 minutes, or until it is cooked but still has a bit of bite. Drain, keeping back a tiny amount of the cooking water. Return the pasta to the pan and toss together. Add the pepper mixture and the basil and toss well. Sprinkle with Parmesan and balsamic vinegar (if using), and serve.

Cheat...
To speed things up, use a 300g jar of roasted peppers and toss it with hot pasta.

EVERYDAY

Pasta with beef and mushroom sauce

Freeze • the sauce can be frozen

SERVES 4

1 tbsp olive oil

1 onion, finely chopped

salt and freshly ground black pepper

500g (1lb 2oz) good-quality
   beef mince

200g (7oz) mushrooms,
   finely chopped

2 garlic cloves, grated or finely chopped

pinch of dried oregano

400g can plum tomatoes, chopped

1 tsp pesto

350g (12oz) tortiglioni

1 Heat the oil in a large frying pan, add the onion, and cook on a low heat for 5 minutes, or until soft and translucent. Season well with salt and black pepper, then stir in the beef mince and cook, stirring, for about 5 minutes, or until no longer pink.

2 Add the mushrooms, garlic, oregano, and tomatoes, and stir well. Simmer for 10 minutes, then stir through the pesto, taste, and season again, if needed.

3 Meanwhile, cook the pasta in a large pan of boiling salted water for 10–12 minutes, or until it is cooked but still has a bit of bite to it. Drain, keeping back a tiny amount of the cooking water. Return the pasta to the pan and toss together. Toss with the meat sauce and serve.

Cheat...
Chop canned tomatoes while they are still in the can, with a pair of scissors or a knife.

COOK'S NOTES

Tossing pasta with a little of the water it was cooked in helps the sauce cling to it better.

Pasta with sun-dried tomato pesto

Special equipment • food processor

SERVES 4

½ 270g jar sun-dried tomatoes
   in oil, drained
handful of pine nuts
2 garlic cloves, roughly chopped
handful of fresh basil leaves
50g (1¾oz) Parmesan cheese, grated
   (more if required)
salt and freshly ground black pepper
extra virgin olive oil
350g (12oz) fusilli
fresh basil leaves, to
   garnish (optional)

1 Place the first five ingredients
in a food processor and whiz until
blended. Season with salt and black
pepper and whiz again. Taste and
add more Parmesan and/or some
extra virgin olive oil, if required.

2 Cook the pasta in a large pan of
boiling salted water for 10 minutes,
or until it is cooked but still has a bit
of bite to it. Drain, keeping back a tiny
amount of the cooking water. Return
the pasta to the pan and toss together.
Toss with the sauce, drizzle with extra
virgin olive oil, garnish with basil
leaves (if using), and serve.

VARIATION

Use a handful of blanched
almonds instead of the pine nuts.

Cheat...
For a quick sauce,
combine the sun-dried
tomatoes with
2 tablespoons ready-
made pesto from
a jar.

Pasta with tomato sauce

Freeze • the sauce can be frozen

SERVES 4

2 x 400g cans whole plum
   tomatoes, chopped
1 tbsp tomato purée
2 tbsp olive oil
salt and freshly ground black pepper
350g (12oz) penne
Parmesan cheese, grated, to serve

1 Place the tomatoes, tomato purée,
and olive oil in a pan, season well
with salt and black pepper, then bring
to the boil. Reduce the sauce to a
simmer and cook, uncovered, for
20 minutes.

2 Meanwhile, cook the pasta in
a large pan of boiling salted water
for 10 minutes, or until it is cooked
but still has a bit of bite to it. Drain,
keeping back a tiny amount of the
cooking water. Return the pasta

to the pan and toss together. Toss
with the tomato sauce, sprinkle with
Parmesan, season with more black
pepper, and serve.

VARIATION

Use rigatoni instead of penne.

Cheat...
Use a 300g jar tomato
sauce for pasta. Perk it
up with a drizzle of some
good-quality olive oil,
then serve with
the pasta.

Pasta with pecorino and peas

PREP 10 MINS **COOK 20 MINS**

SERVES 4

1 tbsp olive oil
1 onion, finely chopped
salt and freshly ground black pepper
1 garlic clove, grated or finely chopped
1 fresh red chilli, deseeded and
    finely chopped
2 tsp plain flour
½ small glass of dry white wine
150ml (5fl oz) milk
150g (5½oz) frozen peas
125g (4½oz) pecorino cheese, grated,
    plus extra to serve
350g (12oz) farfalle

1 Heat the oil in a large frying pan, add the onion and a pinch of salt, and cook over a low heat for 5 minutes, or until soft and translucent. Stir in the garlic and chilli and cook for a few seconds more. Stir in the flour, then add the wine, and simmer for a couple of minutes. Add the milk and stir.

2 Stir in the peas, then add the pecorino and cook at a low simmer – do not allow to boil – for 10 minutes or until the sauce has thickened slightly. Season well with salt and black pepper.

3 Meanwhile, cook the pasta in a pan of boiling salted water for 10 minutes, or until it is cooked but still has a bit of bite to it. Drain, keeping back a tiny amount of the cooking water. Return the pasta to the pan and toss together. Toss with the sauce, top with extra pecorino, and serve.

VARIATION Use Parmesan if you don't have pecorino, but reduce the amount a little, as Parmesan is stronger.

EVERYDAY

Pasta with spicy sausagemeat

PREP 15 MINS **COOK 25 MINS**

SERVES 4

1 tbsp olive oil
1 large red onion, very finely chopped
6–8 good-quality pork sausages,
    skins removed
1 fresh medium-hot red chilli,
    deseeded and finely chopped
1 tsp cayenne pepper
1 small glass of dry white wine
2 garlic cloves, grated or finely chopped
pinch of dried oregano
salt and freshly ground black pepper
150ml (5fl oz) hot vegetable stock or
    mushroom stock
300ml (10fl oz) double cream
350g (12oz) penne rigate
small handful of fresh flat-leaf
    parsley, finely chopped

1 Heat the oil in a large frying pan, add the onion, and cook over a low heat for 5 minutes or until soft and translucent. Chop up the sausagemeat and add to the pan, using the back of a fork to break it up. Cook until they are no longer pink, about 5 minutes, then add the chilli and cayenne and stir.

2 Raise the heat, add the wine, and simmer for a few minutes. Add the garlic and oregano, and season well with salt and black pepper. Pour in the stock and cream, bring to the boil, then simmer for 10 minutes.

3 Meanwhile, cook the pasta in a pan of boiling salted water for 10 minutes, or until it is cooked but still has a bit of bite to it. Drain, keeping back a tiny amount of the cooking water. Return the pasta to the pan and toss together. Toss with the sausage sauce, garnish with parsley, and serve.

COOK'S NOTES

For a fresh tomato flavour, stir a couple of chopped tomatoes into the sauce, just before serving.

Pasta with butternut squash, cream, and sage

  PREP 15 MINS COOK 20 MINS

SERVES 4

1 butternut squash, peeled, cut in half, deseeded, and cubed
pinch of chilli flakes
2 tbsp olive oil
1 red onion, finely chopped
2 garlic cloves, grated or finely chopped
6 fresh sage leaves, roughly chopped
150ml (5fl oz) double cream
salt and freshly ground black pepper
350g (12oz) conchiglie
Parmesan cheese, grated, to serve

1 Preheat the oven to 200°C (400°F/Gas 6). Place the squash in a large roasting tin, sprinkle with chilli flakes, and drizzle with 1 tablespoon of the oil. Combine well and roast for 10–15 minutes, or until the squash starts to soften.

2 Heat the remaining oil in a large frying pan, add the onion, and cook over a low heat for 5 minutes, or until soft and translucent. Add the almost-cooked squash, the garlic, and the sage leaves, and stir together. Pour in the cream and simmer gently for 5 minutes. Season well with salt and lots of black pepper.

3 Meanwhile, cook the pasta in a large pan of boiling salted water for 10 minutes, or until it is cooked but still has a bit of bite to it. Drain, keeping back a tiny amount of the cooking water. Return the pasta to the pan and toss together. Toss with the sauce, sprinkle with Parmesan, and serve.

Pasta with fennel and olives

   PREP 10 MINS COOK 20 MINS

SERVES 4

2 fennel bulbs, trimmed and roughly chopped
1 tbsp olive oil
1 red onion, finely chopped
salt and freshly ground black pepper
1 small glass of dry white wine
2 garlic cloves, grated or finely chopped
handful of pitted black olives
350g (12oz) linguine
Parmesan cheese, grated, to serve

1 Put the fennel in a pan, pour over enough boiling water to cover, and simmer for a couple of minutes. Drain, reserving a little of the cooking liquid.

2 Heat the oil in a large frying pan, add the onion and a pinch of salt, and cook on a low heat for 5 minutes, or until soft and translucent. Raise the heat, add the wine, and simmer for 3–5 minutes. Add the garlic, the fennel, and reserved liquid. Stir in the olives, and cook gently over a low heat for 5 minutes. Season well with salt and black pepper.

3 Meanwhile, cook the pasta in a large pan of boiling salted water for 6 minutes, or until it is cooked but still has a bit of bite to it. Drain, keeping back a tiny amount of the cooking water. Return the pasta to the pan and toss together. Combine with the fennel and olive mixture, then sprinkle with Parmesan and serve.

 VARIATION Use spaghetti instead of linguine.

Pasta with pancetta and rocket

  PREP 5 MINS · COOK 15 MINS

SERVES 4

1 tbsp olive oil
1 onion, finely chopped
1 fresh red chilli, deseeded and
  finely chopped
250g (9oz) pancetta, cubed
2 garlic cloves, grated or finely chopped
350g (12oz) spaghetti
200g (7oz) wild rocket leaves
salt and freshly ground black pepper
Parmesan cheese, grated, to serve

1 Heat the oil in a large frying pan, add the onion, and cook over a low for 5 minutes, or until soft and translucent. Add the chilli and cook for a few minutes more. Add the pancetta and cook for 5 minutes, or until crisp and golden, then stir in the garlic and cook for a few more seconds.

2 Meanwhile, cook the pasta in a large pan of boiling salted water for 6–8 minutes, or until it is cooked but still has a bit of bite to it. Drain, keeping back a tiny amount of the cooking water. Return the pasta to the pan and toss together. Toss with the pancetta mixture, add the rocket, season to taste with salt and black pepper, and toss gently. Sprinkle with Parmesan and serve.

 VARIATION
Serve with mozzarella torn into pieces instead of Parmesan.

COOK'S NOTES

Don't add the rocket leaves until the very last minute or the leaves will begin to cook and wilt, and lose their precious peppery flavour.

Pasta with anchovies, chilli, and lemon

  PREP 10 MINS · COOK 10 MINS

SERVES 4

1 tbsp olive oil
2 red onions, finely chopped
salt
2 garlic cloves, grated or finely chopped
1 fresh red chilli, deseeded and
  finely chopped
1 green chilli, deseeded and
  finely chopped
zest of 1 lemon
350g (12oz) linguine or spaghetti
12 white anchovies in oil, drained
handful of finely chopped fresh
  flat-leaf parsley
juice of 1 lemon, to serve

1 Heat the oil in a large frying pan, add the onions and a pinch of salt, and cook over a low heat for 5 minutes, or until soft. Add the garlic, chillies, and lemon zest, and cook for

a few minutes more, stirring to make sure the mixture does not brown.

2 Meanwhile, cook the pasta in a large pan of boiling salted water for 6–8 minutes, or until it is cooked but still has a bit of bite to it. Drain, keeping back a tiny amount of the cooking water. Return the pasta to the pan and toss together.

3 Stir the anchovies into the onion mixture, then toss with the pasta, add the parsley, and toss again. Serve with a squeeze of lemon.

COOK'S NOTES

You should find white anchovies in oil at the deli counter of the supermarket.

EVERYDAY

Pasta with spinach and ricotta cheese

PREP 10 MINS   COOK 15 MINS

SERVES 4

2 tbsp olive oil
2 garlic cloves, finely sliced
½ small glass of dry white wine
250g (9oz) fresh spinach, rinsed
    and drained
3 tomatoes, diced
salt and freshly ground black pepper
350g (12oz) farfalle
200g (7oz) ricotta cheese
extra virgin olive oil, to serve

1 Heat the oil in a large frying pan, add the garlic, and cook gently over a low heat for a few seconds. Add the wine, raise the heat, and allow to boil for a few minutes.

2 Stir in the spinach and cook until wilted, for 3–5 minutes. Stir through the tomatoes and cook for a few seconds. Season with salt and black pepper.

3 Meanwhile, cook the pasta in a large pan of boiling salted water for 10 minutes, or until it is cooked but still has a bit of bite to it. Drain, keeping back a tiny amount of the cooking water. Return the pasta to the pan and toss together. Stir three-quarters of the ricotta cheese into the spinach mixture, taste, and season, if needed. Toss the sauce with the pasta and serve with a scattering of the remaining ricotta cheese and a splash of extra virgin olive oil.

COOK'S NOTES

Shop around for good ricotta cheese – the fresher the better for this dish.

Pasta with crab and lemon

PREP 5 MINS   COOK 10 MINS

SERVES 4

1 tbsp olive oil
1 large onion, cut into quarters, then
    finely sliced
salt and freshly ground black pepper
2 garlic cloves, finely sliced
grated zest and juice of 1 lemon
handful of fresh flat-leaf parsley,
    finely chopped
200g (7oz) fresh or canned
    white crabmeat
350g (12oz) linguine or spaghetti
chilli oil, to serve (optional)

1 Heat the oil in a large frying pan, add the onion and a pinch of salt, and cook over a low heat for 5 minutes, or until soft and translucent. Stir in the garlic and lemon zest and cook for a few seconds more.

2 Stir through the parsley and crabmeat, then season well with salt and lots of black pepper. Add lemon juice to taste.

3 Meanwhile, cook the pasta in a large pan of boiling salted water for 6–8 minutes, or until it is cooked but still has a bit of bite to it. Drain, keeping back a tiny amount of the cooking water. Return the pasta to the pan and toss together. Add the crab sauce, toss again, drizzle with chilli oil (if using), and serve.

VARIATION   Add 1 teaspoon of capers or a chopped green pepper to the crabmeat.

COOK'S NOTES

Fresh crabmeat has a far superior taste to canned. If you are using canned crabmeat, make sure you drain it well.

Pasta with aubergine sauce

PREP 10 MINS   COOK 25 MINS

SERVES 4

1 large aubergine, cut into cubes
salt and freshly ground black pepper
2–3 tbsp olive oil
½ small glass of red wine
1 onion, finely diced
2 garlic cloves, grated or
    finely chopped
400g can chopped tomatoes
pinch of dried oregano
1 tsp red pesto
350g (12oz) large pasta shells
Parmesan cheese, grated,
    to serve (optional)

1 Place the aubergine cubes in a colander, and sprinkle well with salt. Cover with a plate, then place a heavy weight on top for 10 minutes to extract the bitter juices.

2 Heat the oil in a large frying pan, add the aubergine cubes, and cook over a medium heat for 4-6 minutes, or until they turn golden. Add the wine, raise the heat, and allow to boil for a couple of minutes. Stir in the onion and garlic and cook for a few seconds, then add the tomatoes and stir. Add the oregano and pesto, and simmer gently for 15 minutes.

3 Meanwhile, cook the pasta in a large pan of boiling salted water for 10 minutes, or until it is cooked but still has a bit of bite to it. Drain, keeping back a tiny amount of the cooking water. Return the pasta to the pan and toss together. Taste the sauce, and season with salt and black pepper. Toss with the pasta, sprinkle with grated Parmesan cheese (if using), and serve.

Pasta with mushroom sauce

PREP 10 MINS   COOK 20 MINS

SERVES 4

4 tbsp olive oil
150g (5½oz) baby button mushrooms
200g (7oz) chestnut mushrooms,
    finely chopped
125g (4½oz) field mushrooms, grated
1 small glass of dry white wine
3 garlic cloves, grated or
    finely chopped
salt and freshly ground black pepper
handful of fresh flat-leaf parsley,
    finely chopped
pinch of mild paprika
300ml (10fl oz) double cream
350g (12oz) pappardelle or tagliatelle

1 Gently heat the oil in a large frying pan, add all the mushrooms, and cook on a low heat for 5 minutes, or until they begin to release their juices. Add the wine, raise the heat, and boil for a couple of minutes. Add the garlic and lots of black pepper.

2 Reduce the heat, stir through the parsley and paprika, then pour in the cream and cook, stirring occasionally, on a low heat for 5 minutes.

3 Meanwhile, cook the pasta in a pan of boiling salted water for 10 minutes, or until it is cooked but still has a bit of bite to it. Drain, keeping back a tiny amount of the cooking water. Return the pasta to the pan and toss together. Taste the sauce and season if needed, then toss with the pasta and serve.

FASTER PASTA

Pasta with lamb sauce

PREP 5 MINS · **COOK 30 MINS** · ❄

Freeze • the sauce can be frozen

SERVES 4
1 tbsp olive oil
1 onion, finely diced
salt
500g (1lb 2oz) diced lamb
1 large glass of red wine
zest of 1 lemon
pinch of paprika
few stalks of fresh thyme,
   leaves only
3 garlic cloves, grated or
   finely chopped
400g can chopped tomatoes
350g (12oz) pappardelle
Parmesan cheese, grated, to serve

1 Heat the oil in a large frying pan, add the onion and a pinch of salt, and cook over a low heat for 5 minutes, or until soft and translucent. Add the lamb and cook, stirring, until browned all over, for about 5 minutes. Turn the heat up, add the wine, and allow to boil for 2 minutes.

2 Add the lemon zest, paprika, and thyme. Stir in the garlic, cook for a few seconds, then add the tomatoes. Bring to the boil, then simmer gently for about 15 minutes.

3 Meanwhile, cook the pasta in a large pan of boiling salted water for 6–8 minutes, or until it is cooked but still has a bit of bite to it. Drain, keeping back a tiny amount of the cooking water. Return the pasta to the pan and toss together. Toss with the sauce, sprinkle with Parmesan, and serve.

> **COOK'S NOTES**
>
> *If you have the time, the lamb sauce will benefit from cooking for longer. Simmer with a lid on, over a very low heat, for an hour. Or transfer to a cast-iron pan and cook in an oven preheated to 200°C (400°F/Gas 6) for an hour or so.*

Pasta with sausage and artichoke

PREP 10 MINS · **COOK 20 MINS**

SERVES 4
1 tbsp olive oil
1 onion, finely diced
salt and freshly ground black pepper
1 fresh medium-hot red chilli,
   deseeded and finely chopped
6 good-quality pork sausages,
   skinned and chopped
pinch of dried oregano
400g jar or can artichoke hearts,
   drained and roughly chopped
3 tomatoes, skinned and diced
handful of pitted black olives
350g (12oz) penne

1 Heat the oil in a large frying pan, add the onion and a pinch of salt, and cook over a low heat for 5 minutes, or until soft and translucent. Add the chilli and cook for a few seconds more, then add the sausages, breaking them up with the back of a fork until they are roughly mashed. Cook until they are no longer pink, about 10 minutes, stirring occasionally, then add the oregano and artichokes and cook for a few minutes more. Stir in the tomatoes and olives, then season well with salt and black pepper.

2 Meanwhile, cook the pasta in a large pan of boiling salted water for 10 minutes, or until it is cooked but still has a bit of bite to it. Drain, keeping back a tiny amount of the cooking water. Return the pasta to the pan and toss together. Combine with the sausage mixture and serve.

VARIATION Try sun-dried tomatoes and capers instead of the tomatoes and olives.

> **COOK'S NOTES**
>
> *Using good-quality pork sausages will make all the difference to the finished dish.*

Pasta with asparagus and courgettes

PREP 10 MINS · **COOK 20 MINS**

SERVES 4

1 tbsp olive oil
1 onion, finely chopped
salt
4 small courgettes, 2 diced and 2 grated
3 garlic cloves, grated or finely chopped
1 bunch fine asparagus spears, trimmed and stalks cut into 3
1 small glass of white wine
1-2 tsp capers, rinsed and chopped
zest of 1 lemon
350g (12oz) penne
handful of fresh flat-leaf parsley, finely chopped
Parmesan cheese, grated, to serve

1 Heat the oil in a large frying pan, add the onion and a pinch of salt, and cook over a low heat for 5 minutes or until soft and translucent. Add all the courgettes, and cook for 10 minutes or until they have cooked down and softened. Don't allow them to brown.

2 Stir in the garlic and asparagus. Add the wine, raise the heat, and allow to boil for 2-3 minutes, then return to a simmer. Cook for 2-3 minutes, or until the asparagus has softened, then stir in the capers and lemon zest.

3 Meanwhile, cook the pasta in a large pan of boiling salted water for 10 minutes or until it is cooked but still has a bit of bite to it. Drain, keeping back a tiny amount of the cooking water. Return the pasta to the pan and toss together. Add the courgette mixture and parsley, then toss again. Sprinkle with Parmesan and serve.

VARIATION
Use pecorino instead of Parmesan.

Pasta with seafood and tomatoes

PREP 5 MINS · **COOK 12 MINS**

SERVES 4

1 tbsp olive oil
1 onion, finely chopped
salt and freshly ground black pepper
3 garlic cloves, grated or finely chopped
400g can chopped tomatoes
350g (12oz) linguine or spaghetti
350g (12oz) cooked mixed seafood (such as prawns, squid, and mussels)
handful of fresh flat-leaf parsley, finely chopped

1 Heat the oil in a large frying pan, add the onion and a pinch of salt, and cook over a low heat for 5 minutes or until soft and translucent. Stir in the garlic and cook for a few seconds more. Add the tomatoes, bring to the boil, then simmer gently for 10-12 minutes.

2 Meanwhile, cook the pasta in a large pan of boiling salted water for 8 minutes, or until it is cooked but still has a bit of bite to it. Drain, keeping back a tiny amount of the cooking water. Return the pasta to the pan and toss together.

3 Stir the seafood into the tomato mixture for the last few minutes of cooking. Season well with salt and black pepper, stir in the parsley, then toss with the pasta.

VARIATION
Uncooked seafood can also be used, but add it to the sauce in plenty of time for it to cook through.

COOK'S NOTES
Use good-quality canned tomatoes – the finished dish will be all the better for it.

Pasta with broccoli and lemon

PREP 10 MINS   COOK 25 MINS

SERVES 4

1 head broccoli, about 300g (10oz), broken into florets with stalks
1 tbsp olive oil
1 red onion, finely chopped
salt and freshly ground black pepper
1 fresh medium-hot red chilli, deseeded and finely chopped
½ small glass of dry white wine
zest of 1 lemon
2 garlic cloves, grated or finely chopped
350g (12oz) penne
1 lemon, halved
Parmesan cheese, grated, to serve (optional)

1 Cook the broccoli florets in a pan of boiling salted water for 10–15 minutes or until soft and slightly overcooked. Drain and dice. Heat the oil in a large frying pan, add the onion and a pinch of salt, and cook over a low heat for 5 minutes or until soft and translucent. Stir in the chilli, then add the wine. Raise the heat and simmer for a couple of minutes.

2 Lower the heat, add the lemon zest and garlic, then season well with salt and black pepper. Add the broccoli, stir, and put to one side.

3 Meanwhile, cook the pasta in a large pan of boiling salted water for 10 minutes or until it is cooked but still has a bit of bite to it. Drain, keeping back a tiny amount of the cooking water. Return the pasta to the pan and toss together. Toss with the broccoli mixture, then squeeze over the lemon juice. Sprinkle with Parmesan (if using), and serve.

VARIATION Add some cubed pancetta to the frying onion. Or add cooked ham to the broccoli mixture.

Cheat... For ease and convenience, use frozen broccoli florets instead of the fresh broccoli.

Pasta with flageolet beans, parsley, and lemon

PREP 10 MINS   COOK 10 MINS

SERVES 4

1 red onion, finely diced
400g can flageolet beans, drained and rinsed
handful of fresh flat-leaf parsley, roughly chopped
1 garlic clove, grated or finely chopped
2 tbsp good-quality balsamic vinegar
zest of 1 lemon and juice of ½ lemon
salt and freshly ground black pepper
350g (12oz) orecchiette or other small pasta shells

1 Place the first six ingredients in a large bowl and stir well to combine. Season well with salt and black pepper. Leave to sit while you cook the pasta – the flavours will develop.

2 Cook the pasta in a large pan of boiling salted water for 10 minutes, or until it is cooked but still has a bit of bite to it. Drain, keeping back a tiny amount of the cooking water. Return the pasta to the pan and toss together. Add the sauce, toss to combine, and serve.

VARIATION Add a few chopped anchovies, some torn mozzarella, or a handful of wild rocket leaves to the sauce.

COOK'S NOTES
The sauce will keep in the refrigerator for up to 24 hours. Before using, stir in a little olive oil to bring it back to life.

Pasta with pork, roasted garlic, and balsamic vinegar

 PREP 10 MINS COOK 30 MINS

SERVES 4

1 bulb garlic, left whole with the top
   sliced off
1 tbsp olive oil
1 onion, sliced
300g (10oz) pork tenderloin, cubed
1–2 tbsp good-quality
   balsamic vinegar
squeeze of tomato purée
1 tbsp plain flour
300ml (10fl oz) hot vegetable stock
salt and freshly ground black pepper
small handful of fresh flat-leaf
   parsley, finely chopped
350g (12oz) pappardelle

1 Preheat the oven to 200°C (400°F/
Gas 6). Roast the garlic in the oven
for 20 minutes, then set to one side
to cool. Meanwhile, heat the oil in
a large frying pan, add the onion,
and cook over a medium heat for 5
minutes, or until lightly golden. Add
the pork and cook, stirring, until
golden, about 5 minutes. Add the
balsamic vinegar, raise the heat, and
cook for a few more minutes.

2 Stir in the tomato purée, followed
by the flour and then the stock. Stir

well to get rid of any lumps. Bring
to the boil, then cook on a fairly high
simmer for 10 minutes, or until the
sauce has thickened and reduced.
Top up with boiling water if it begins
to look a little dry. Season well with
salt and black pepper. Squeeze the
cooled garlic out of its skin, roughly
chop, then stir into the sauce along
with half the parsley.

3 Meanwhile, cook the pasta
in a large pan of boiling water for
6 minutes or until it is cooked but still
has a bit of bite to it. Drain, keeping
back a tiny amount of the cooking
water. Return the pasta to the pan
and toss together. Toss with the sauce,
sprinkle with the remaining parsley,
and serve.

COOK'S NOTES

*If you have the time once you
have added the stock, let the sauce
simmer over a very low heat for
a further 20 minutes. The flavour
will improve greatly. If it starts to
look a little dry, add some more
hot vegetable stock or water.*

Pasta with black olives

 PREP 10 MINS COOK 10 MINS

Special equipment • food processor

SERVES 4

200g (7oz) pitted black olives
2 garlic cloves
zest and juice of 1 lemon
2 tbsp extra virgin olive oil
salt and freshly ground black pepper
350g (12oz) linguine or spaghetti
handful of fresh flat-leaf parsley,
   finely chopped
handful of fresh basil leaves, torn
25g (scant 1oz) Parmesan cheese,
   shaved with a vegetable peeler

1 Place the olives, garlic, lemon
zest, and lemon juice in a food
processor and whiz until chopped.
With the motor still running, slowly
add the oil until the mixture forms
a smooth paste. Transfer to a bowl.
Taste and season with salt and black
pepper, if needed.

2 Cook the pasta in a large pan of
boiling salted water for 6 minutes, or
until it is cooked but still has a bit of
bite to it. Drain, keeping back a tiny
amount of the cooking water. Return
the pasta to the pan, and toss together.

3 Toss the pasta with the flat-leaf
parsley and basil, then either toss
with the olive paste, or spoon the
paste over the top. Sprinkle with
the Parmesan shavings, and serve.

Cheat...

*For a quick fix meal,
toss the hot pasta with
2 tablespoons of
ready-made
tapenade.*

EVERYDAY

Pasta with porcini and Parmesan

PREP 10 MINS **COOK 20 MINS**

SERVES 4

1 tbsp olive oil

1 red onion, finely chopped

½ small glass of red wine

50g (1¾oz) dried porcini mushrooms, soaked in 300ml (10fl oz) boiling water for 15 minutes (soaking liquid reserved)

50g (1¾oz) chunk Parmesan cheese or Parmesan rind

350g (12oz) tagliatelle

handful of fresh flat-leaf parsley, finely chopped

few stalks of fresh thyme, leaves only

2 tomatoes, skinned and diced

salt and freshly ground black pepper

Parmesan cheese, grated, to serve

1 Heat the oil in a large frying pan, add the onion, and cook over a low heat for 5 minutes or until soft and translucent. Turn up the heat, add the wine, and allow to boil for a couple of minutes. Drain the mushrooms (reserving the liquid) and add to the pan. Add the Parmesan.

2 Strain the reserved mushroom liquid through a sieve, then pour into the pan. Bring to the boil, then simmer gently for 10 minutes, stirring occasionally.

3 Meanwhile, cook the pasta in a large pan of boiling salted water for 6 minutes or until it is cooked but still has a bit of bite to it. Drain, keeping back a tiny amount of the cooking water. Return the pasta to the pan and toss together.

4 Remove the Parmesan chunk or rind from the sauce, stir in the parsley, thyme, and tomatoes, then taste and season. Toss with the pasta, then serve with lots of grated Parmesan and black pepper.

VARIATION
Use a mix of dried wild mushrooms instead of the porcini.

Pasta with tuna and roasted onion

PREP 10 MINS **COOK 20 MINS**

Special equipment • ridged cast-iron grill pan or griddle

SERVES 4

3 red onions, each cut into eight wedges

handful of cherry tomatoes

few stalks of fresh thyme

3 tbsp olive oil

salt and freshly ground black pepper

2 x 175g (6oz) fresh tuna steaks

350g (12oz) penne

zest of ½ lemon

pinch of chilli flakes

drizzle of good-quality balsamic vinegar, to serve (optional)

1 Preheat the oven to 200°C (400°F/Gas 6). Place the onions, tomatoes, and thyme in a large roasting tin, drizzle with 2 tablespoons olive oil, season with salt, then mix well with your hands. Roast for 15 minutes, or until soft and lightly charred.

2 Meanwhile, heat a grill pan or griddle until hot. Rub the tuna steaks with the remaining oil and season with salt and black pepper. Fry for 3–4 minutes on each side (depending on thickness and how you like it), remove, and put to one side to rest.

3 Cook the pasta in a pan of boiling salted water for 10 minutes or until it is cooked but still has a bit of bite to it. Drain, keeping back a tiny amount of the cooking water. Return the pasta to the pan and toss together. Toss with the roasted onions and tomatoes. Slice the tuna into chunks, add to the pan along with the lemon zest and chilli flakes, and toss gently. Season to taste, then drizzle with balsamic vinegar (if using), and serve.

Cheat...
Use a 170g can, good-quality tuna, preferably in olive oil, and add it to the cooked pasta without cooking.

Pasta with pesto and pine nuts

PREP 5 MINS **COOK 12 MINS**

Special equipment • food processor

SERVES 4
handful of fresh basil
2 garlic cloves, chopped
50g (1¾oz) Parmesan cheese, grated
3 tbsp pine nuts, 1 tbsp toasted
4 tbsp olive oil
salt and freshly ground black pepper
350g (12oz) spaghetti

1 Place the basil, garlic, Parmesan, and the 2 tablespoon of untoasted pine nuts in a food processor and whiz for a few seconds until combined. Scrape the paste away from the sides, put the lid back on and, with the motor running, gently pour in the olive oil until you have a smooth paste. Season with salt and black pepper.

2 Cook the pasta in a large pan of boiling salted water for 6 minutes or until it is cooked but still has a bit of bite to it. Drain, keeping back a tiny amount of the cooking water. Return the pasta to the pan and toss together. Gently toss with the pesto, then top with the toasted pine nuts and serve.

VARIATION
Use small pasta shells or bows in place of the spaghetti.

COOK'S NOTES
Make double the quantity of the pesto, spoon half into a jar, and top with a little olive oil – it will keep in the refrigerator for up to a week.

EVERYDAY

Pasta carbonara with pancetta and cream

PREP 10 MINS **COOK 15 MINS**

SERVES 4
1 tbsp olive oil
150g (5½oz) pancetta
    or bacon, cubed
2 sage leaves, finely sliced
6 eggs
150ml (5fl oz) double cream
125g (4½oz) Parmesan cheese,
    finely grated
pinch of freshly grated nutmeg
salt and freshly ground black pepper
350g (12oz) linguine or spaghetti
handful of fresh flat-leaf parsley,
    finely chopped, to serve

1 Heat the oil in a large frying pan. Add the pancetta or bacon, and sage, and toss together. Cook over a medium heat for 5 minutes or until golden. Put to one side.

2 Place the eggs, cream, Parmesan, and nutmeg in a bowl, season well with salt and black pepper, then stir with a fork until well combined. Set to one side while you cook the pasta.

3 Cook the pasta in a large pan of boiling salted water for 6 minutes or until it is cooked but still has a bit of bite to it. Drain, keeping back a tiny amount of the cooking water. Return the pasta to the pan and toss together. Give the egg mixture one final stir, then add to the hot pasta and stir really well to combine. Put the lid on, leave to sit for 1 minute, then stir again. Add the pancetta or bacon and sage and toss together. Sprinkle with parsley and serve.

VARIATION
You could add some cooked peas to the final dish. For a vegetarian version, leave out the pancetta.

Cheat...
Use a 200g carton of carbonara sauce (but it won't be as good as the real thing!).

Pasta with roasted peppers

PREP 10 MINS COOK 25 MINS

SERVES 4

6 red peppers
2–3 tbsp olive oil
2 garlic cloves, grated or
   finely chopped
1 fresh red chilli, deseeded
   and finely chopped
1 fresh green chilli, deseeded
   and finely chopped
pinch of dried oregano
few stalks of fresh thyme, leaves only
salt
350g (12oz) penne
25g (scant 1oz) pecorino, grated
chilli oil, to serve

1 Preheat the oven to 200°C (400°F/
Gas 6). Smother the peppers with
the oil, leaving a little to cook
the garlic and chillies. Sit them
in a roasting tin and roast for
15 minutes or until soft. Remove
from the oven, and leave to cool.

2 Meanwhile, place the remaining
oil in a frying pan, add the garlic and
chillies, and cook for a few minutes
on a gentle heat, taking care not
to let them brown. Stir through
the oregano and thyme.

3 Remove the skins from the peppers
and deseed them. Cut the flesh into
strips, then add to the pan. Season
well and leave to stand.

4 Meanwhile, cook the pasta in a pan
of boiling salted water for 10 minutes,
or until it is cooked but still has a bit
of bite to it. Drain, keeping back a tiny
amount of the cooking water. Return
the pasta to the pan and toss together.
Add the pepper mixture and the
pecorino, toss well, then drizzle with
chilli oil and serve.

VARIATION
Use roasted pumpkin or
a mix of roasted vegetables,
in place of the peppers.

COOK'S NOTES

*Pop the roasted peppers in a plastic
bag – as they cool down, the
steam will help loosen the skins.*

Macaroni cheese with red onion

PREP 5 MINS COOK 20 MINS

SERVES 4
knob of butter
1 tbsp plain flour
300ml (10fl oz) milk
150g (5½oz) strong Cheddar cheese
salt and freshly ground black pepper
300g (10oz) macaroni
1 small red onion, very finely diced

1 Preheat the oven to 200°C (400°F/
Gas 6). Melt the butter in a small pan,
then remove from the heat and stir
in the flour with a wooden spoon.
Return to the heat and gradually
add the milk, a little at a time, stirring
continuously. Switch to a whisk
(to avoid any lumps) and stir until
the sauce begins to thicken. Remove
from the heat and add 125g (4½oz) of
the cheese. Season well with salt and
black pepper.

2 Cook the pasta in a large pan of
boiling salted water for 10–12 minutes,
or until it is cooked but still has a bit
of bite to it. Drain, keeping back a tiny
amount of the cooking water. Return
the pasta to the pan and toss together.
Mix with the cheese sauce, add the
onion, and stir well.

3 Spoon into an ovenproof dish,
top with the remaining cheese, and
bake for 5–10 minutes, or until golden
and simmering.

VARIATION
You could use penne for
this dish. Or add some
cooked peas to the sauce
along with the red onion.

Cheat...
Use a 250g carton of
ready-made cheese sauce.
Stir in 1 tsp wholegrain
mustard to liven it
up and enhance
the flavour.

Pasta with clams and parsley

SERVES 4

1 tbsp olive oil
1 onion, finely diced
3 garlic cloves, finely diced
handful of fresh flat-leaf parsley,
   finely chopped
1 small glass of dry white wine
450g (1lb) fresh clams, cleaned
350g (12oz) linguine or spaghetti
splash of olive oil
salt and freshly ground black pepper

1 Heat the oil in a large frying pan, add the onion, and cook over a low heat for a couple of minutes or until it begins to soften. Add the garlic and parsley, and stir for a few seconds.

2 Add the wine, raise the heat, then add the clams and stir. Allow to boil for 5 minutes or until the shells start to open, shaking the pan from time to time. Turn the heat off and put a lid on the pan.

3 Meanwhile, cook the pasta in a large pan of boiling salted water for 6 minutes or until it is cooked but still has a bit of bite to it. Drain, keeping back a tiny amount of the cooking water. Return the pasta to the pan and toss together. Add a splash of olive oil, season with salt and black pepper, then toss with the clams and serve.

COOK'S NOTES

Discard any clams that are open before you cook them, then discard any that are not open after you've cooked them. They are inedible.

EVERYDAY

Pasta with meatballs and olives

SERVES 4

1 onion, very finely diced
2 garlic cloves, grated or
   finely chopped
450g (1lb) good-quality lamb mince
salt and freshly ground black pepper
1 tbsp olive oil
400g can plum tomatoes, chopped
handful of pitted black olives
350g (12oz) spaghetti
handful of fresh flat-leaf parsley,
   finely chopped
Parmesan cheese, finely grated,
   to serve

1 Place the onion, garlic, and lamb mince in a bowl, and combine with your hands until the mixture comes together. Season with salt and black pepper then roll into balls a bit larger than a walnut.

2 Heat the oil in a large frying pan, add the meatballs, and cook for about 5 minutes or until they begin to brown. Add the tomatoes and olives, bring to the boil, then reduce to a simmer for 20 minutes.

3 Meanwhile, cook the spaghetti in a large pan of boiling salted water for 10–12 minutes, or until it is cooked but still has a bit of bite to it. Drain, keeping back a tiny amount of the cooking water. Return the pasta to the pan and toss together. Stir the parsley into the sauce, then toss together with the pasta. Sprinkle with Parmesan and serve.

COOK'S NOTES

Don't worry if the meatballs break up – they will make the sauce even more delicious. To enrich the sauce, add a few finely chopped anchovies along with the tomatoes and olives.

EVERYDAY

Pasta and aubergine bake

PREP 15 MINS   COOK 40 MINS

SERVES 4

250g (9oz) pasta
3 tbsp olive oil
1 onion, finely chopped
2 garlic cloves, grated or
 finely chopped
pinch of dried oregano
pinch of mild paprika
750g jar passata
2 aubergines, sliced
handful of Parmesan cheese,
 freshly grated

1 Preheat the oven to 200°C (400°F/ Gas 6). Put the aubergines in a colander, sprinkle with salt, and weigh down with a plate. Leave to drain for 15 minutes, rinse, and pat dry with kitchen paper. Cook the pasta in a large pan of boiling salted water for 10 minutes, or until it is cooked but still has a bit of bite to it. Drain and set aside.

2 Heat 1 tablespoon of olive oil in a large heavy pan over a low heat. Add the onion, and sweat gently for 5 minutes, or until soft and translucent. Stir through the garlic, oregano, paprika, and the passata.

Bring to the boil, reduce the heat slightly, and simmer gently for about 15 minutes.

3 Meanwhile, heat the remaining olive oil in a large frying pan over a medium heat. Cooking in batches, fry the aubergine slices for about 3 minutes on each side until golden, adding more oil as needed. Drain on kitchen paper.

4 Layer the bottom of an ovenproof dish with half of the aubergine slices. Spoon over some of the tomato sauce, then add a layer of the pasta. Repeat the layers, ending with a final layer of tomato sauce. Top with the Parmesan cheese, and bake in the oven for about 20 minutes until simmering and golden. Serve with a crisp green salad with a vinaigrette-style dressing.

Cheat...
Use a 250g jar of ready-made tomato sauce, instead of making your own.

Minestrone soup

PREP 10 MINS   COOK 40 MINS

SERVES 4

1 tbsp olive oil
1 onion, finely chopped
salt and freshly ground
 black pepper
1 tsp dried oregano
4 carrots, finely diced
4 celery sticks, finely diced
3 garlic cloves, grated or
 finely chopped
1 small glass of red wine
1 tbsp tomato purée
400g can whole peeled plum
 tomatoes, chopped in the can
600ml (1 pint) hot vegetable stock
200g (7oz) pasta, such as macaroni
 or vermicelli
handful of fresh flat-leaf parsley,
 finely chopped
Parmesan cheese, freshly grated,
 for sprinkling

1 Heat the oil in a large pan over a low heat. Add the onion, and sweat gently for 5 minutes, or until soft and translucent. Add a pinch of salt, the oregano, and stir through the carrot and celery. Sweat gently for about 10 minutes until softened.

2 Now stir through the garlic and cook for a few seconds more. Pour in the wine, increase the heat, and let it boil for a couple of minutes until the alcohol has evaporated. Stir through the tomato purée, and season well with salt and black pepper. Pour in the canned tomatoes and vegetable stock. Bring to the boil, reduce the heat slightly, and simmer for about 20 minutes, topping up with hot water if the minestrone gets too thick (but don't make it too thin).

3 Meanwhile, cook the pasta in a large pan of boiling salted water for 10 minutes, or until it is cooked but still has a bit of bite to it. Drain, and chop if large. Add the pasta to the minestrone. Sprinkle over the parsley, and serve hot with a bowl of Parmesan cheese for sprinkling over the top.

COOK'S NOTES

Always keep any leftover rind from Parmesan cheese – you can add it to your minestrone while it's cooking, for extra flavour.

Pasta salad

PREP 15 MINS   COOK 10 MINS

SERVES 4

225g (8oz) pasta, such as penne,
   fusilli, or farfalle
2 tbsp mayonnaise
handful of wild rocket leaves
125g (4½oz) fresh or cooked
   garden peas
6 cherry tomatoes, finely chopped
salt and freshly ground black pepper

1 Cook the pasta in a large pan of
boiling salted water for 10 minutes,
or until it is cooked but still has a bit
of bite to it. Drain, keeping back a tiny
amount of the cooking water, return
the pasta to the pan, and toss through.

2 Mix the pasta with the
mayonnaise, rocket leaves, peas,
and tomatoes. Season well with
salt and black pepper, cover with cling
film, and keep in the refrigerator.
Serve at room temperature.

EVERYDAY

Pasta with meat sauce

PREP 15 MINS   COOK 30 MINS

SERVES 4

250g (9oz) pasta
1 tbsp olive oil
1 onion, finely chopped
2 garlic cloves, grated or
   finely chopped
300g (10oz) beef, such as rump steak,
   cut into chunks
1 beef stock cube
salt and freshly ground black pepper
handful of Parmesan cheese, freshly
   grated, to serve
fresh flat-leaf parsley, finely chopped,
   to sprinkle

1 Heat the olive oil in a large frying
pan over a low heat. Add the onion,
and sweat gently for 5 minutes, or
until soft and translucent. Stir
through the garlic, and cook for
a few seconds more.

2 Add the beef, and sauté over a high
heat for a few minutes until browned
all over. Sprinkle in the beef stock
cube, and stir through. Pour in 600ml
(1 pint) hot water and bring to the
boil. Reduce the heat slightly, and
leave to simmer for 20 minutes.
Season well with salt and black pepper.

3 Cook the pasta in a large pan of
boiling salted water for 10 minutes,
or until it is cooked but still has a bit
of bite to it. Drain, keeping back a tiny
amount of the cooking water, add the
meat sauce, and toss together. Serve
hot with the Parmesan cheese and
some parsley sprinkled over the top.

PIZZAS, QUESADILLAS, AND PANCAKES

Quick ways to top, stuff, or roll.

PIZZAS, QUESADILLAS, AND PANCAKES

Fast meal solutions couldn't be simpler. Top ready-made pizza dough with your favourite foods, serve up a quick quesadilla with whatever happens to be in the refrigerator, or fill a pancake with sweet or savoury treats – the variations are endless. Making pizzas, quesadillas, and pancakes is fun, and they can all be prepared ahead, ready for last-minute toppings – ideal for busy households when everyone eats at different times.

Pizzas

A meal in itself, this Italian bread crust is topped with a variety of ingredients, the most classic being simply tomato and mozzarella. The bread-base dough needs to be cooked at an extremely high heat to become firm and crisp. The traditional Italian-style pizza has a thin, crisp, and delicate base, lightly smeared with a tomato sauce, and topped with 2–3 toppings. American-style pizza has a thicker doughy base, with more toppings.

Tips and tricks

A hot oven High heat is essential. Traditionally, pizzas are made in a wood-burning oven at about 400°C (750°F), so the top melts and the base turns crispy in minutes. As conventional ovens don't get this hot, preheat the oven and a flat baking sheet or pizza stone at least 1 hour before cooking.

"00" flour This is a super-fine Italian flour, and is the best flour to use for making pizza, as it produces a soft, stretchy dough. It can be found in supermarkets or good delicatessens. Alternatively, use strong plain white flour.

Rising The longer the dough takes to rise, the better the flavour of the crust will be.

Kneading Do take the time to knead the dough for at least 10 minutes, so the gluten develops in the dough and becomes firm when cooked.

Topping Keep it simple, and don't overcrowd the pizza. Overcrowding it with toppings will stop it cooking quickly. You don't need to use cheese, but if you do, use mozzarella, mild Cheddar, Parmesan cheese, or feta cheese.

reheat and eat

Pizza is best eaten fresh, but if you have leftovers, and want to reheat it, sit it on a plate and put it in the microwave for 1 minute on Medium to warm it through (any longer and it will go soggy), then sit it on a preheated baking tray and put in a hot oven for a couple of minutes to crisp up the base. Otherwise, it is good eaten cold or at room temperature.

How to freeze pizzas

Part-baked bases Roll out the dough, then bake in a hot oven for about 5 minutes, or until firm. Cool completely, then wrap in cling film and freeze for up to 3 months.

Dough Double up quantities and freeze some for later, or freeze leftover dough. Prepare the dough, let it rise, then knock the air out of it. Divide into four and put in a plastic bag, seal, and freeze for up to 3 months.

Pizza toppings

- Crumbled sausagemeat, artichoke, and mozzarella cheese
- Spicy tomato sauce, olives, capers, and chorizo
- Tomato sauce, mozzarella, ham, and spinach
- Tomato sauce, aubergine, olives, and mozzarella
- Tomato sauce, pine nuts, sultanas, and spinach

Psst...

Uncooked pizza dough can be kept in the refrigerator. Once the dough has risen, knock out the air, and leave to cool. Lightly oil a plastic bag, add the dough, seal, and keep in the refrigerator for up to 2 days before using.

Perfect pizza dough A quick dough mixture using dried yeast – the quantities given here make 4 thin-crust Italian-style pizzas.

1 Sift 500g (1lb 2oz) of "00" or strong white flour into a bowl, and add a pinch of salt, and a 7g sachet of dried yeast. Make a well in the centre of the flour, then slowly add 360ml (12fl oz) of warm water. Mix with a wooden spoon, or the dough beaters of a food mixer, until it comes together, then add 60ml (2fl oz) of olive oil, and continue to mix until it forms a soft dough.

2 Place the dough on a floured surface, and knead firmly, using the heel of your hand, folding the dough over as you go. Do this for about 10 minutes, until it becomes soft and spongy.

3 Put the dough in a bowl, cover with cling film or a tea towel, and leave in a warm place (you can preheat the oven and leave the bowl on top of the hob above) for 30–40 minutes, or until it has doubled in size.

4 Turn the dough out onto the floured surface again, and knead with your knuckles for a couple of minutes to knock out the air (known as "knocking back"). Divide the dough into four and roll each piece out as thinly as you can, rolling away from you, and turning it as you go. You may have to pull and stretch the dough a little as it tends to spring back. You need it to be about 25cm (10in) in diameter, although it doesn't have to be perfectly round. Transfer to a hot, lightly oiled baking tray, and top with your favourite topping (see previous page for some ideas).

Quesadillas

The ultimate fast food snack, quesadillas are essentially a toasted sandwich, using tortillas. You can use **wheat**, **wholewheat**, or **corn** tortillas, and fill them with cheese and your favourite ingredients. Corn tortillas are the wheat-free option, made with ground maize, giving them their distinctive yellow colour. "Queso" means "cheese" in Spanish, so this is the one ingredient that must be added.

How to freeze quesadillas

Freeze uncooked tortillas in a sealed plastic bag for up to 3 months. Cooked and filled tortillas don't freeze well.

Quesadilla fillings

- Brie, grated apple, and chutney
- Mozzarella, cooked butternut squash, and green chilli
- Gruyère cheese, grated courgette, and ham
- Cheddar cheese, tuna, and spring onion

Tips and tricks

Store Keep tortillas in cling film once open, as they go dry quickly. Keep for 1 week. Sprinkle with water to refresh.

Cheese Choose cheese that melts easily, such as mild Cheddar or mozzarella cheese.

Serve Eat straight away. To keep warm, if you are making a few, wrap them in foil and put in a moderate oven.

Leftovers Tear up leftover tortillas and add to soup.

STEP-BY-STEP

EVERYDAY

Perfect quesadillas A satisfying dish that's ready in minutes.

1 Have all your ingredients ready-prepared; 2 flour or corn tortillas, and your chosen fillings. Here we're using 25g (scant 1oz) Gruyère cheese, grated, and a handful of sliced jalapeño chillies from a jar.

2 Heat a small frying pan with a little olive oil (you can omit this if you prefer), then place one tortilla in the pan. Add the topping ingredients, leaving a little room around the edge so the cheese doesn't spill out.

3 Top with another tortilla, and press down with a spatula. Leave it to warm through for a couple of minutes.

4 Flip it over to cook the other side for a minute or two, then transfer to a plate, slice into half or quarters, and serve.

Pancakes

Crêpes, or pancakes, are made with a light batter mix, and are cooked as thin as possible so they are almost lacy in texture. They can be served hot or cold, and filled or topped with savoury or sweet fillings. The ingredients are staples (flour, milk, and egg), so pancakes are a perfect spur-of-the-moment dish. American-style pancakes are thicker and smaller, made with added baking powder. They are usually served with sweet toppings of cream or maple syrup for breakfast.

How to freeze pancakes

Cooked pancakes can be frozen for up to 1 month. Layer them between sheets of greaseproof paper (see right). Cool, seal in a plastic bag, and freeze.

Pancake fillings

- Sautéed leeks, goat's cheese, and thyme
- Mushrooms, spinach, tomatoes, and chilli
- Salmon and cream cheese
- Figs, honey, and mascarpone
- Banana, toffee sauce, and toasted almonds

STEP-BY-STEP

Perfect pancakes A simple batter mix and a good pan are all you need.

1 Sieve 125g (4½oz) plain flour into a bowl, and add a pinch of salt. Make a well in the centre and crack 1 egg into it. Gradually add 300ml (10fl oz) milk, stirring with a wooden spoon and incorporating the flour as you go. Continue stirring until all the milk is added, then whisk until smooth. Put in the refrigerator to rest for 30 minutes.

2 Heat a drizzle of oil in a non-stick crêpe pan, or frying pan, and swirl it around. Tip it out, so the pan isn't swimming in oil. Add a little of the batter, swirling it around so it coats the bottom of the pan.

3 Cook for 1–2 minutes, over a medium heat, until the edges start to look dry then, using a round-ended knife, loosen the edges and turn it using a spatula, or flip it, to cook the other side.

4 Check the second side, after a minute or two. When brown speckles appear, transfer to a plate to serve. Fill with your favourite filling, or serve flat, drizzled with lemon juice and sprinkled with sugar.

EVERYDAY

Pizza bianca with four cheeses

PREP 10 MINS COOK 15 MINS

MAKES 1
1 ball pizza dough (see p181)
plain flour, to dust
semolina, for sprinkling
75g (2½oz) mozzarella, torn
 into pieces
handful of freshly grated
 Parmesan cheese
25g (scant 1oz) Gorgonzola or other
 blue cheese, crumbled
25g (scant 1oz) Gruyère
 cheese, grated
pinch of dried oregano

1 Preheat the oven to its highest setting. Very lightly oil a baking tray and put it in the oven to get hot. They both need to be really hot before cooking the pizza.

2 Place the dough on a floured surface and use a rolling pin to roll it out as

thin as you can – about 25-30cm (10-12in) in diameter. Sprinkle the hot baking tray with semolina and transfer the dough onto it.

3 Cover each quarter segment of the pizza with a different cheese, using the 4 cheeses or more of the one you prefer. Sprinkle with the oregano, then bake for 10-15 minutes, or until the crust and base are crispy and the cheese is lightly golden and melted.

VARIATION
Sprinkle the pizza with toasted pine nuts and raisins before you put it in the oven.

COOK'S NOTES
If you are making more than one pizza, cook one at a time so the oven isn't overcrowded and remains as hot as it can be.

Pizza bianca with rosemary and garlic

PREP 10 MINS COOK 10 MINS

MAKES 1
1 ball pizza dough (see p181)
plain flour, to dust
semolina, for sprinkling
handful of rosemary sprigs
2 garlic cloves, grated or
 finely chopped
salt
olive oil, to drizzle

1 Preheat the oven to its highest setting. Very lightly oil a baking tray and put it in the oven to get hot. They both need to be really hot before cooking the pizza.

2 Place the dough on a floured surface and use a rolling pin to roll it out as thin as you can – about 25-30cm (10-12in) in diameter.

Sprinkle the hot baking tray with semolina and transfer the dough onto it.

3 Stab the pizza base all over with a fork, then scatter the rosemary, garlic, and plenty of salt over the top and pat flat. Drizzle with olive oil, then bake for 10 minutes, or until the top is melted.

VARIATION
Sprinkle with mozzarella, torn into pieces, or crumble blue cheese over the top.

COOK'S NOTES
If you make pizzas often, invest in a pizza stone – your bases will always be wonderfully crispy.

Pizza with tomatoes, olives, and capers

MAKES 1
1 ball pizza dough (see p181)
plain flour, to dust
semolina, for sprinkling
2-3 tbsp passata
3 tomatoes, sliced
handful of pitted black olives
1-2 tsp capers, rinsed
freshly ground black pepper

1 Preheat the oven to its highest setting. Very lightly oil a baking tray and put it in the oven to get hot. They both need to be really hot before cooking the pizza.

2 Place the dough on a floured surface and use a rolling pin to roll it out as thin as you can - about 25-30cm (10-12in) in diameter. Sprinkle the hot baking tray with semolina and transfer the dough onto it.

3 Spoon the passata onto the pizza base, using the back of the spoon to smooth it out evenly. Top with the tomato slices, then arrange the olives and capers on top. Bake for 10-15 minutes, or until the crust and base are crisp and golden. Season with black pepper and serve.

VARIATION
Instead of passata, use canned tomatoes, which are sometimes cheaper. Whiz them briefly with a stick blender beforehand.

Cheat...
Buy a jar of tomato-based pizza topping – there are plenty of varieties available.

Pizza bianca with Parma ham, rocket, and mozzarella

MAKES 1
1 ball pizza dough (see p181)
plain flour, to dust
semolina, for sprinkling
200g (7oz) mozzarella, torn into chunks
freshly ground black pepper
4 slices Parma ham
handful of wild rocket

1 Preheat the oven to its highest setting. Very lightly oil a baking tray and put it in the oven to get hot. They both need to be really hot before cooking the pizza.

2 Place the dough on a floured surface and use a rolling pin to roll it out as thin as you can - about 25-30cm (10-12in) in diameter. Sprinkle the hot baking tray with semolina and transfer the dough onto it.

3 Top the base with the mozzarella, season with lots of black pepper, then bake for 10 minutes, or until the crust and base are crispy, and the top is melted. Drape the Parma ham on top, scatter evenly with the rocket, season again with black pepper, and serve.

VARIATION
Add some diced tomato along with the rocket.

COOK'S NOTES
You might want to cut the Parma ham into pieces with a pair of scissors so that the pizza is easier to eat.

Pizza with sausagemeat

PREP 10 MINS | COOK 20 MINS

MAKES 1

3 good-quality pork sausages, skinned
  and chopped
25g (scant 1oz) freshly grated
  Parmesan cheese (optional)
salt and freshly ground black pepper
1 ball pizza dough (see p181)
plain flour, to dust
semolina, for sprinkling
3-4 tomatoes, finely sliced

1 Preheat the oven to its highest
setting. Very lightly oil a baking
tray and put it in the oven to get hot.

2 Put the sausagemeat in a dry
frying pan and cook over a medium
heat for 5 minutes, or until no longer
pink. While it is cooking, mash it
with the back of a fork or a wooden
spatula so it becomes crumbly. Stir
through the Parmesan cheese
(if using), and season with salt
and black pepper.

3 Place the dough on a floured
surface and use a rolling pin to roll
it out as thinly as you can – about
25-30cm (10-12in) in diameter.
Sprinkle the hot baking tray with
semolina and transfer the dough onto
it. Cover the pizza base with tomato
slices and bake for 5 minutes, or until
the tomatoes are soft, then remove
from the oven and spoon the sausage
mixture on top. Bake for a further
10 minutes, or until the crust and
base are golden and crispy.

COOK'S NOTES

*Get the children involved in
the pizza-making. Or, if that
sounds too messy, ask them to
choose their toppings and arrange
them on the pizza bases before
the pizzas are cooked.*

Pizza with mozzarella and mushrooms

PREP 10 MINS | COOK 15 MINS

MAKES 1

1 tbsp olive oil
125g (4½oz) chestnut
  mushrooms, sliced
salt and freshly ground black pepper
1 ball pizza dough (see p181)
plain flour, to dust
semolina, for sprinkling
2-3 tbsp passata
150g (5½oz) mozzarella, torn
  into pieces
chilli oil, to serve (optional)

1 Preheat the oven to its highest
setting. Very lightly oil a baking tray
and put it in the oven to get hot.

2 Heat the oil in a pan, add the
mushrooms, and cook over a low heat
for 5 minutes, or until they begin to
soften. Season well with salt and
black pepper.

3 Place the dough on a floured
surface and use a rolling pin to roll

it out as thinly as you can – about
25-30cm (10-12in) in diameter.
Sprinkle the hot baking tray with
semolina and transfer the dough
onto it.

4 Spoon the passata over the pizza
base, using the back of the spoon to
smooth it out evenly. Top with the
mozzarella and then the mushrooms.
Bake for 10 minutes, or until the crust
and base are golden and crispy, and the
cheese is beginning to bubble. Drizzle
with chilli oil (if using), and serve.

VARIATION For a special occasion,
use wild mushrooms and
buffalo mozzarella.

COOK'S NOTES

*You can freeze rolled-out, part-
baked pizza dough (untopped), so
you are ready to go when needed.*

Calzone with cheese, ham, and spinach

MAKES 1

1 ball pizza dough (see p181)
plain flour, to dust
semolina, for sprinkling
200g (7oz) fresh spinach, wilted
 and drained
125g (4½oz) cooked ham, chopped
125g (4½oz) mozzarella, torn
 into pieces
handful of torn basil leaves

1 Preheat the oven to its highest setting. Very lightly oil a baking tray and put it in the oven to get hot.

2 Place the dough on a floured surface and use a rolling pin to roll it out as thinly as you can – about 25-30cm (10-12in) in diameter. Sprinkle the hot baking tray with semolina and transfer the dough onto it.

3 Squeeze any remaining liquid from the spinach, and spread it over half the pizza base, leaving about 1cm (½in) around the edge. Top with the ham, mozzarella, and basil, then dampen all around the edge of the pizza with water. Fold one half of the pizza over the other, seal the edges together with your fingers, then sprinkle the top with a little water. Bake for 15-20 minutes, or until golden and crispy.

VARIATION
Add the cooked ingredients of your choice, but keep it simple – no more than three or four are really necessary.

COOK'S NOTES
Sprinkling the top of the calzone with a little water helps crisp up the dough.

EVERYDAY

Pizza with spinach and ricotta cheese

MAKES 1

1 ball pizza dough (see p181)
plain flour, to dust
semolina, for sprinkling
2-3 tbsp passata
200g (7oz) spinach, wilted
 and drained
2-3 tbsp ricotta cheese
freshly ground black pepper

1 Preheat the oven to its highest setting. Very lightly oil a baking tray and put it in the oven to get hot.

2 Place the dough on a floured surface and use a rolling pin to roll it out as thinly as you can – about 25-30cm (10-12in) in diameter. Sprinkle the hot baking tray with semolina and transfer the dough onto it.

3 Spoon the passata onto the pizza base, using the back of the spoon to smooth it out evenly. Squeeze any remaining liquid from the spinach, then spread it on top of the passata. Dot with spoonfuls of ricotta cheese, season with black pepper, then bake for 10 minutes, or until the crust and base are golden and crispy.

EVERYDAY

Quesadilla with spiced beef and tomato

PREP 5 MINS · COOK 20 MINS

MAKES 1

1½ tbsp olive oil
150g (5½oz) good-quality
    minced beef
pinch of hot cayenne pepper
salt and freshly ground black pepper
small handful fresh flat-leaf parsley,
    finely chopped
2 wheat or corn tortillas
2 tomatoes, diced
50g (1¾oz) Cheddar cheese

1 Heat 1 tablespoon of the oil in
a frying pan, then fry the beef with
the cayenne pepper on a medium heat
for 5 minutes, or until no longer pink.
Turn the heat down and loosen with
a little hot water. Season with a pinch
of salt and some black pepper. Cook
for a further 10 minutes, until the
beef is completely cooked through.
Stir in the parsley.

2 Heat the remaining oil in
a non-stick frying pan, then fry one
tortilla for 1 minute, or until lightly
golden. Spoon over the beef mixture,
leaving a little room around the edge.
Scatter over the tomato and the cheese,
then top with the other tortilla, pressing
it down with the back of a fish slice to
sandwich the two together. Scoop the
quesadilla up, carefully turn it over,
and cook the other side for another
minute, or until golden. Slice in half
or quarters, and serve.

VARIATION
Vary the cheese to your
liking: try grated Gruyère
or emmental cheese.

COOK'S NOTES

*If you are only using a couple
of tortillas from a packet, either
wrap the remaining tightly in
cling film and keep in the bread
bin, or wrap and freeze for up
to 1 month.*

Calzone with peppers, capers, and olives

PREP 15 MINS · COOK 20 MINS

MAKES 1

1 ball pizza dough (see p181)
plain flour, to dust
semolina, for sprinkling
3-4 ready-roasted peppers from a jar,
    drained and chopped
handful of pitted black olives,
    roughly chopped
1-2 tsp capers, rinsed
2-3 tbsp ricotta cheese or mozzarella,
    torn into pieces
salt and freshly ground black pepper

1 Preheat the oven to its highest
setting. Very lightly oil a baking tray
and put it in the oven to get hot. They
both need to be really hot before
cooking the calzone.

2 Place the dough on a floured surface
and use a rolling pin to roll it out as
thinly as you can – about 25-30cm
(10-12in) in diameter. Sprinkle the hot
baking tray with semolina and transfer
the dough onto it.

3 Spoon the peppers, olives, capers,
and ricotta cheese or mozzarella onto
half the pizza base, leaving about 1cm
(½in) around the edge. Season well
with salt and black pepper. Dampen
the edges of the pizza with a little
water, then fold one half of the pizza
over the other, and seal together with
your fingers. Sprinkle the top with a
little water, then bake for 15-20
minutes, or until golden and crispy.

Quesadilla with cheese and chilli

PREP 5 MINS   COOK 5 MINS

MAKES 1
½ tbsp olive oil
2 wheat or corn tortillas
50g (1¾oz) strong mature Cheddar cheese, grated
1 fresh mild green chilli, deseeded and finely chopped
1-2 tsp sliced green jalapeños from a jar
small handful of fresh coriander, chopped
freshly ground black pepper

1 Heat the olive oil in a non-stick frying pan, then fry one tortilla for a minute or until lightly golden.

2 Scatter over the cheese, leaving a little room around the edge, then add the chilli, jalapeños, coriander, and a pinch of black pepper.

3 Top with the other tortilla, pressing it down with the back of a fish slice to sandwich the two together, Scoop the quesadilla up, carefully turn it over, and cook the other side for another minute until golden and the cheese has melted. Slice in half or quarters and serve.

COOK'S NOTES
Leave an edge when adding the filling, and don't overfill, or the cheese will ooze out.

EVERYDAY

Quesadilla with avocado, spring onion, and chilli

PREP 10 MINS   COOK 5 MINS

MAKES 1
4 spring onions, finely chopped
1-2 fresh hot red chillies, deseeded and finely chopped
juice of ½ lime
salt and freshly ground black pepper
1½ tbsp olive oil
2 wheat or corn tortillas
½ avocado, sliced
50g (1¾oz) Cheddar cheese

1 Place the spring onions, chillies, and lime juice in a bowl, season well with salt and black pepper, and mix together. Leave to sit for a couple of minutes to let the flavours develop.

2 Heat the olive oil in a non-stick frying pan, then fry one tortilla for 1 minute, or until lightly golden. Scatter over the avocado, leaving a little space around the edge, and spoon on the spring onion mixture, and sprinkle with the cheese.

3 Top with the other tortilla, pressing it down with the back of a fish slice to sandwich the two together. Scoop the quesadilla up, carefully turn it over, and cook the other side for another minute, or until golden. Slice in half or quarters, and serve.

Quesadilla with mushrooms and Gruyère cheese

 PREP 5 MINS COOK 10 MINS

MAKES 1
2 tbsp olive oil
125g (4½oz) chestnut
   mushrooms, sliced
salt and freshly ground black pepper
pinch of chilli flakes
handful of fresh flat-leaf parsley,
   finely chopped
2 wheat or corn tortillas
50g (1¾oz) Gruyère cheese, grated

1 Heat 1 tablespoon of the oil in a frying pan, then cook the mushrooms with a pinch of salt on a low heat for 5 minutes, or until they begin to release their juices. Add the chilli flakes and stir through the parsley.

2 Heat the remaining oil in a non-stick frying pan and fry one tortilla for 1 minute, or until golden. Using a slotted spoon to drain them, spoon the mushrooms onto the tortilla, leaving a little room around the edge. Top with the cheese and season with salt and black pepper.

3 Top with the other tortilla, pressing it down with the back of a fish slice to sandwich the two together. Scoop the quesadilla up, carefully turn it over, and cook the other side for another minute, or until it is golden and the cheese melted. Slice in halves or quarters, and serve.

Quesadilla with feta cheese, green olives, and peppers

PREP 5 MINS COOK 15 MINS

MAKES 1
2 tbsp olive oil
2 red peppers, deseeded and
   roughly chopped
salt and freshly ground black pepper
2 wheat or corn tortillas
handful of pitted green olives, sliced
125g (4½oz) feta cheese, crumbled

1 Heat 1 tablespoon of the oil in a frying pan, add the peppers, and cook on a low heat for 10 minutes, or until soft. Season with salt and black pepper.

2 Heat the remaining oil in a non-stick frying pan, then fry one tortilla for 1 minute, or until golden. Spoon the peppers onto it, leaving a little room around the edge. Scatter with the olives and feta cheese.

3 Top with the other tortilla, pressing it down with the back of a fish slice to sandwich the two together. Scoop the quesadilla up, carefully turn it over, and cook the other side for another minute, or until golden. Slice in halves or quarters, and serve.

VARIATION

Use mozzarella instead of feta cheese.

Cheat...
Save on chopping and use ready-roasted peppers from a jar, instead of fresh red peppers.

Quesadilla with chicken and sweet onion

PREP 5 MINS   COOK 15 MINS

MAKES 1
2 tbsp olive oil
2 red onions, finely sliced
pinch of rosemary leaves,
   finely chopped
salt and freshly ground black pepper
2 wheat or corn tortillas
125g (4½oz) ready-cooked
   chicken, sliced
50g (1¾oz) Cheddar cheese, grated

1 Heat 1 tablespoon of the oil in large frying pan, add the onions, the rosemary, and a pinch of salt, and cook over a medium heat for 10 minutes, or until the onions begin to soften and sweeten.

2 Heat the remaining oil in a non-stick frying pan and fry one tortilla for 1 minute, or until golden. Spoon the onion mixture onto the tortilla, leaving a little room around the edge. Top with the chicken and cheese and sprinkle with black pepper.

3 Top with the other tortilla, pressing it down with the back of a fish slice to sandwich the two together. Scoop the quesadilla up, carefully turn it over, and cook the other side for another minute, or until it is golden. Slice in halves or quarters, and serve.

Quesadilla with ham, gherkin, and smoked cheese

PREP 5 MINS   COOK 5 MINS

MAKES 1
1 tbsp olive oil
2 wheat or corn tortillas
75g (2½oz) smoked cheese or strong
   mature Cheddar, grated
125g (4½oz) cooked ham, sliced
2 gherkins, sliced
salt and freshly ground black pepper

1 Heat the oil in a non-stick frying pan, then fry one tortilla for 1 minute or until golden.

2 Sprinkle over the cheese, leaving a little room around the edge. Top with the ham and gherkin, then season with salt and black pepper.

3 Top with the other tortilla, pressing it down with the back of a fish slice to sandwich the two together. Scoop the quesadilla up, carefully turn it over, and cook the other side for another minute, or until it is golden and the cheese melted. Slice in halves or quarters, and serve.

VARIATION
Use baby gherkins instead of big ones – they are much sweeter.

PIZZAS, QUESADILLAS, AND PANCAKES

EVERYDAY

Pancakes with asparagus, feta cheese, and dill

 PREP 5 MINS COOK 15 MINS

MAKES 2-4
125g (4½oz) plain flour
salt
1 egg
300ml (10fl oz) milk

For the filling
4-6 fine asparagus spears, trimmed and cut into 3 pieces
handful of finely chopped dill
125g (4½oz) feta cheese, crumbled
freshly ground black pepper
olive oil, for frying

1 Put the flour in a mixing bowl with a pinch of salt, stir, then make a well in the centre. Crack the egg into the well and add a tiny amount of the milk. Using a wooden spoon, stir the egg and milk, letting the flour gradually tumble in. Add the rest of the milk, little by little, stirring continuously, until all the flour has been incorporated and the mixture is lump-free. Put it in the refrigerator to rest for 30 minutes, if you have time.

2 Cook the asparagus in boiling salted water for 4 minutes, or until soft. Drain and refresh in cold water. Transfer to a bowl and mix with the dill, feta cheese, and some black pepper.

3 In a small flat frying pan or pancake pan, heat a drizzle of olive oil over a high heat, swirling it around the pan, then tipping it out again. Stir the batter mix, then spoon in 2 tablespoons of it, swirling it around the pan so it reaches the edges. Cook for a couple of minutes, then pull up the edges with a palette knife. Turn the pancake over and cook the other side for 1 minute. Slide it out onto a plate.

4 Spoon half the filling onto one half of the pancake and either roll or fold it up. Make and fill the other pancakes in the same way.

Cheat...
Instead of making the batter, use ready-bought pancakes or a batter mix.

COOK'S NOTES
Make a batch of pancakes ahead of time, and cool. Stack between sheets of greaseproof paper, wrap in cling film, and freeze (see p183).

Curried prawn pancakes

PREP 10 MINS COOK 20 MINS

MAKES 2-4
125g (4½oz) plain flour
salt
1 egg
300ml (10fl oz) milk

For the filling
1 tbsp olive oil, plus a little extra for frying
handful of small uncooked prawns
1-2 tbsp medium-hot curry paste
small handful of fresh coriander
1 lemon, halved

1 Put the flour in a mixing bowl with a pinch of salt, stir, and make a well in the centre. Crack the egg into the well and add a tiny amount of the milk. Using a wooden spoon, stir the egg and milk, letting the flour gradually tumble in. Add the rest of the milk, little by little, stirring continuously until all the flour has been incorporated and the mixture is lump-free. Put it in the refrigerator to rest for 30 minutes, if you have time.

2 Heat 1 tablespoon of the oil in a frying pan, add the prawns, and cook over a high heat for 2-4 minutes, or until pink. Stir in the curry paste, add

a little hot water, and simmer for 10 minutes, or until thickened. Stir through the coriander, and add a squeeze of lemon juice and a pinch of salt.

3 In a small flat frying pan or pancake pan, heat a drizzle of oil over a high heat, swirling it around the pan, then tipping it out again. Stir the batter mix, then spoon in 2 tablespoons of it, swirling it around the pan so it reaches the edges. Cook for a couple of minutes, then pull up the edges with a palette knife. Turn the pancake over and cook the other side for 1 minute. Slide it out onto a plate.

4 Spoon half the prawn mixture onto one half of the pancake, and either roll or fold into four. Make and fill the other pancakes in the same way, then serve with a squeeze of lemon.

COOK'S NOTES
The batter will keep in the refrigerator for up to 24 hours, so you could serve savoury pancakes one night and sweet ones the following day.

192

Moroccan-style pancakes

PREP 5 MINS   COOK 25 MINS

MAKES 2-4
125g (4½oz) plain flour
1 egg
300ml (10fl oz) milk

For the filling
1 tbsp olive oil, plus a little
    extra for frying
1 aubergine, diced
2 tomatoes, finely chopped
salt and freshly ground black pepper
pinch of ground cinnamon
small handful of fresh mint leaves,
    finely chopped
squeeze of lemon, to serve

1 Put the flour in a mixing bowl with a pinch of salt, stir, and make a well in the centre. Crack the egg into the well and add a tiny amount of the milk. Using a wooden spoon, stir the egg and milk, letting the flour gradually tumble in. Add the rest of the milk, little by little, stirring continuously until all the flour has been incorporated and the mixture is lump-free. Put it in the refrigerator to rest for 30 minutes, if you have time.

2 Heat 1 tablespoon of olive oil in a frying pan, add the aubergine, and cook over a medium heat for 5-8 minutes, or until golden. Add the tomatoes and cook for a further 5 minutes, or until they start to break down a little. Season well with salt and black pepper, then add the cinnamon and mint and stir well.

3 In a small flat frying pan or pancake pan, heat a drizzle of olive oil over a high heat, swirling it around the pan, then tipping it out again. Stir the batter mix, then spoon in 2 tablespoons of it, swirling it around the pan so it reaches the edges. Cook for a couple of minutes, then pull up the edges with a palette knife. Turn the pancake over and cook the other side for 1 minute. Slide it out onto a plate.

4 Spoon half the aubergine mixture on top of the pancake and either roll or fold it up, or simply serve the aubergine mixture on top. Make and fill the other pancakes in the same way then serve with a squeeze of lemon.

Pancakes with goat's cheese and chives

PREP 15 MINS   COOK 5 MINS

MAKES 2-4
125g (4½oz) plain flour
1 egg
300ml (10fl oz) milk

For the filling
125g (4½oz) goat's cheese
small handful of chives,
    finely chopped
salt and freshly ground black pepper
1 tomato, skinned
olive oil, for frying

1 Put the flour in a mixing bowl with a pinch of salt, stir, and make a well in the centre. Crack the egg into the well and add a tiny amount of the milk. Using a wooden spoon, stir the egg and milk, letting the flour gradually tumble in. Add the rest of the milk, little by little, stirring continuously until all the flour has been incorporated and the mixture is lump-free. Put it in the refrigerator to rest for 30 minutes, if you have time.

2 Mix the goat's cheese and chives together in a bowl, and season with a pinch of salt and some black pepper.

Cut the tomato in half, scoop out the seeds and discard, then dice the flesh and mix with the cheese mixture.

3 In a small flat frying pan or pancake pan, heat a drizzle of olive oil over a high heat, swirling it around the pan, then tipping it out again. Stir the batter mix, then spoon in 2 tablespoons of it, swirling it around the pan so it reaches the edges. Cook for a couple of minutes, then pull up the edges with a palette knife. Turn the pancake over and cook the other side for 1 minute. Slide it out onto a plate.

4 Spoon half the cheese mixture onto one half of the pancake and roll it up. Make and fill the other pancakes in the same way.

 VARIATION Use feta or cream cheese instead of goat's cheese.

COOK'S NOTES
For ease, snip the chives with scissors rather than chopping them with a knife.

EVERYDAY

Pancakes with courgettes and emmental

PREP 10 MINS **COOK 15 MINS**

MAKES 2–4
125g (4½oz) plain flour
salt and freshly ground black pepper
1 egg
300ml (10fl oz) milk

For the filling
1 tbsp olive oil, plus a little
  extra for frying
2 small courgettes, grated
125g (4½oz) emmental, grated

1 Put the flour in a mixing bowl with a pinch of salt, stir, and make a well in the centre. Crack the egg into the well and add a tiny amount of the milk. Using a wooden spoon, stir the egg and milk, letting the flour gradually tumble in. Add the rest of the milk, little by little, stirring continuously until all the flour has been incorporated and the mixture is lump-free. Put it in the refrigerator to rest for 30 minutes, if you have time.

2 Heat 1 tablespoon of olive oil in a frying pan, add the courgettes, and cook on a medium heat for 5–8 minutes, or until golden. Season well with salt and black pepper, then remove from the heat and stir in the emmental.

3 In a small flat frying pan or pancake pan, heat a drizzle of olive oil over a high heat, swirling it around the pan, then tipping it out again. Stir the batter mix, then spoon in 2 tablespoons of it, swirling it around the pan so it reaches the edges. Cook for a couple of minutes, then pull up the edges with a palette knife. Turn the pancake over and cook the other side for 1 minute. Slide it out onto a plate.

4 Spoon a quarter of the courgette mixture onto half the pancake, sprinkle with black pepper, then either roll it or fold it up. Make and fill three more pancakes in the same way.

VARIATION
Use 4 asparagus spears, boiled or steamed until tender, per pancake instead of courgettes.

Pancakes with blue cheese and bacon

PREP 5 MINS **COOK 10 MINS**

MAKES 2–4
125g (4½oz) plain flour
salt
1 egg
300ml (10fl oz) milk

For the filling
3 rashers bacon, chopped
olive oil, for frying
75g (2½oz) Gorgonzola or other
  blue cheese

1 Put the flour in a mixing bowl with a pinch of salt, stir, and make a well in the centre. Crack the egg into the well and add a tiny amount of the milk. Using a wooden spoon, stir the egg and milk, letting the flour gradually tumble in. Add the rest of the milk, little by little, stirring continuously until all the flour has been incorporated and the mixture is lump-free. Put it in the refrigerator to rest for 30 minutes, if you have time.

2 Place the bacon with a drizzle of olive oil in a hot frying pan and cook over a high heat for 5 minutes, or until golden. Remove and sit on kitchen paper to soak up any fat.

3 In a small flat frying pan or pancake pan, heat a drizzle of olive oil over a high heat, swirling it around the pan, then tipping it out again. Stir the batter mix, then spoon in 2 tablespoons of it, swirling it around the pan so it reaches the edges. Cook for a couple of minutes, then pull up the edges with a palette knife. Turn the pancake over and cook the other side for 1 minute.

4 Spoon half the bacon onto one half of the pancake and top with half the cheese. Fold the pancake over and cook for a further minute or so until the cheese begins to melt, then slide onto a plate. Make and fill the other pancakes in the same way. Serve immediately.

Pancakes with garlicky mushrooms

MAKES 2-4
125g (4½oz) plain flour
salt and freshly ground black pepper
1 egg
300ml (10fl oz) milk

For the filling
1 tbsp olive oil, plus a little
   extra for frying
125g (4½oz) chestnut
   mushrooms, sliced
2 garlic cloves, finely diced

1 Put the flour in a mixing bowl with a pinch of salt, stir, and make a well in the centre. Crack the egg into the well and add a tiny amount of the milk. Using a wooden spoon, stir the egg and milk, letting the flour gradually tumble in. Add the rest of the milk, little by little, stirring continuously until all the flour has been incorporated and the mixture is lump-free. Put it in the refrigerator to rest for 30 minutes, if you have time.

2 Heat 1 tablespoon of olive oil in a frying pan, add the mushrooms, and cook over a medium heat for 5 minutes, or until beginning to soften. Stir in the garlic and cook for a few minutes more, until the mushrooms have released their juices. Season well with salt and black pepper.

3 In a small flat frying pan or pancake pan, heat a drizzle of olive oil over a high heat, swirling it around the pan, then tipping it out again. Stir the batter mix, then spoon in 2 tablespoons of it, swirling it around the pan so it reaches the edges. Cook for a couple of minutes, then pull up the edges with a palette knife. Turn the pancake over and cook the other side for 1 minute. Slide it out onto a plate.

4 Spoon half the mushroom mixture onto one quarter of the pancake, then fold it in four. Make and fill the other pancakes in the same way.

Pancakes with peppers and basil

MAKES 2-4
125g (4½oz) plain flour
salt
1 egg
300ml (10fl oz) milk

For the filling
1 tbsp olive oil, plus a little
   extra for frying
2 red peppers, deseeded and cut
   into strips
pinch of caster sugar
handful of fresh basil leaves, torn

1 Put the flour in a mixing bowl with a pinch of salt, stir, and make a well in the centre. Crack the egg into the well and add a tiny amount of the milk. Using a wooden spoon, stir the egg and milk, letting the flour gradually tumble in. Add the rest of the milk, little by little, stirring continuously until all the flour has been incorporated and the mixture is lump-free. Put it in the refrigerator to rest for 30 minutes, if you have time.

2 Heat 1 tablespoon of olive oil in a frying pan, add the peppers, the sugar, and a pinch of salt, and cook over a low heat for 10-15 minutes, or until soft. Stir through the basil.

3 In a small flat frying pan or pancake pan, heat a drizzle of olive oil on a high heat, swirling it around the pan, then tipping it out again. Stir the batter mix, then spoon in 2 tablespoons of it, swirling it around the pan so it reaches the edges. Cook for a couple of minutes, then pull up the edges with a palette knife. Turn the pancake over and cook the other side for 1 minute. Slide it out onto a plate.

4 Spoon half the pepper mixture onto half the pancake, then fold it in two. Make and fill the other pancakes in the same way.

EASY TARTS AND PIES

Pastry bakes, with and without tops!

EASY TARTS AND PIES

Nothing beats a home-made tart or pie – it's real back-to-basics cooking. Whether you are making your own pastry, or taking a shortcut with ready-made, home baking is time well spent in the kitchen. Tarts are open, with a pastry base, whereas pies are often deeper, and almost always topped. Both can be made with either sweet or savoury fillings.

Onion Tart For recipe, see page 198.

Types of pastry Choose the right pastry for the right dish.

PASTRY		USE FOR
	**SHORTCRUST** The most widely used pastry, and the easiest to make. It's a half-fat-to-flour combination, and is made by rubbing the fat into the flour with the addition of a little water. For richer pastry, egg yolk is used instead of water. This pastry is usually used for savoury dishes.	Savoury tart base Pie crust
	**PUFF** Has a higher fat content than shortcrust, but the end result is lighter. Making puff pastry takes a long time, so – for quick-cook pastries – buy ready-made pastry, preferably made with butter.	French-style sweet pastry Savoury pie topping "En croute" - savoury dish encasing meat or fish
	**SWEET** This is a type of shortcrust pastry, made with added sugar. The sugar is added to the flour, and can be icing sugar or caster sugar.	Sweet dessert tart or tartlet
	**SUET** This is made with self-raising flour instead of plain, and the fat content is either a beef suet or, for vegetarians, a vegetable suet. It's a heavier pastry with a dough-like texture.	Steam pudding (sweet or savoury) Pasty
	**FILO** Also known as phylo, filo pastry is a paper-thin delicate mixture of flour and oil that has been beaten and stretched. It has the lowest fat content of all the pastries. It's not easy to make at home, so buy it fresh or frozen. It can be fragile to work with, as it gets brittle when dry, so keep it wrapped in cling film, and brush with melted butter when using.	Greek and Middle Eastern dishes Encasing a sweet or savoury filling

Dough know-how

Cool hands make good "short" and crisp pastry. Always use your fingertips, and don't overwork the pastry, otherwise it will become tough. Wash your hands in ice-cold water (then dry them) before starting to rub the fat in.

Keep all ingredients cool before starting, especially the butter. A good tip is to measure out all the ingredients, and cut the butter into cubes, then sit everything in refrigerator for 1 hour before starting.

Measure ingredients accurately, as baking is a science, and it won't work without the correct quantities.

The less liquid, the better the pastry. Be careful when adding water; do so a little at a time. Too much, and the pastry will be tough and may shrink from the edges of the tin when baked. Make sure the water is ice-cold.

Don't add too much flour when dusting the work surface or rolling pin, as it will dry out the pastry.

Chill the pastry dough, if time permits. It will make it easier to roll.

storing and freezing

Uncooked pastry can be kept in the refrigerator for 1–2 days. Wrap well in a plastic bag and seal, or wrap in cling film. If cooked pastry cases are kept in the refrigerator they will lose their crispness, but if filled with a custard mixture, such as a quiche, they will need refrigerating.

Uncooked pastry cases can be frozen for up to 3 months, and baked "blind" straight from the freezer. Wrap well in a plastic bag or cling film. Cooked pastry cases can be frozen for up to 6 months.

STEP-BY-STEP

Make perfect shortcrust pastry Shortcrust is the most versatile pastry, suitable for both tarts and pies.

1 Sieve 225g (8oz) of plain flour into a large bowl, and add a pinch of salt. Cut 125g (4½oz) of butter into cubes, and add to the flour.

2 Rub the butter lightly into the flour using your fingertips, lifting it as you go. For light pastry you want as much air in it as possible. Continue rubbing the mixture in until it resembles fine breadcrumbs.

3 Add about 2 tablespoons of cold water and, using a round-bladed knife, bring the pastry together.

4 Gather the pastry together, into a ball, using your fingertips. It should come away from the sides of the bowl easily. If it is too dry and crumbly, add a sprinkling of water until it comes together. Cover the pastry with cling film, and put it the refrigerator to rest for 30 minutes.

EVERYDAY

EASY TARTS AND PIES

Line a tart tin Use these simple steps to line any size and shape of tin.

Psst...

To work out the amount of pastry you need to line a tin, the rule of thumb is to subtract 2 from the diameter of the tart tin in inches, and this will be the amount of pastry, in ounces, you need. So a 20cm (8in) tin would need 175g (6oz) of pastry. This is useful if you are using a different size tin than the recipe states. The filling quantity will also need adjusting.

1 Roll out the pastry (see previous page for quantities and method) on a lightly floured surface, to a circle about 5cm (2in) wider than the tart tin. The pastry should be fairly thin.

2 Carefully drape the pastry over a rolling pin and gently lay it over the tart tin, so the pastry hangs over the edge.

3 Gently ease the pastry into the sides of the tin using your fingertips or knuckles, being careful not to tear it.

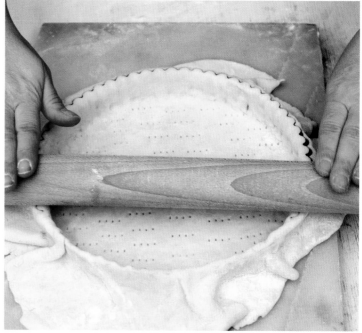

4 Once in place, prick the base all over with a fork, then roll a rolling pin over the top of the tin to remove the pastry that hangs over the edge. Put in the refrigerator to rest for 30 minutes.

Bake blind
Baking the pastry before filling will ensure your tart has a crisp base.

Line the uncooked pastry case with greaseproof paper, then tip in enough ceramic baking beans to cover the base. This will stop the pastry from rising up while it is cooking. The tart is now ready to bake blind in the oven at 200°C (400°F/Gas 6) for 15 minutes, or until the edges of the pastry are cooked.

Tools of the trade

A **selection of pie and tart tins**, of varying shapes and sizes (metal tins produce crispier pastry than glass or ceramic ones); a **rolling pin**, either wooden or marble; some **ceramic baking beans** to bake the pastry blind (dried beans or rice can be used instead); **greaseproof paper** for lining the pastry case; and a **pastry brush** for brushing butter or egg wash over the tops of pies, and brushing filo pastry layers.

Ready-made pastry

For convenience, ready-made pastry is a good substitute for home-made. Shortcrust and puff pastry can be bought fresh or frozen, ready-rolled or in blocks. There are low-fat versions, but all-butter pastry will taste more home-made. Blocks of pastry (that you roll out yourself) tend to produce better results than the ready-rolled, as the ready-rolled are often a little wetter in texture. The recipes in this chapter refer to the ready-bought blocks of pastry, unless otherwise stated.

Pastry block Ready-made pastry can be bought in a fresh or frozen block. Roll out on a floured surface as you would with home-made dough.

Ready-rolled This is ready-made pastry that has already been rolled. Available fresh or frozen, and a handy cheat when time is short.

201

EVERYDAY

Onion tart

PREP 15 MINS · COOK 55 MINS

Special equipment • 20cm (8in) round pie tin • ceramic baking beans

SERVES 6

1 tbsp olive oil
4 onions, sliced
1 tbsp plain flour
300ml (10fl oz) milk
2 tsp mild paprika
salt and freshly ground black pepper
300g (10oz) shortcrust pastry
1 egg, lightly beaten, for egg wash

1 Preheat the oven to 200°C (400°F/ Gas 6). Heat the oil in a large non-stick frying pan over a low heat. Add the onions, and sweat very gently for about 15 minutes until soft and translucent. Keep stirring throughout, so that they don't stick or brown at all.

2 Remove from the heat, and stir in the flour with a wooden spoon. Add a little of the milk, and stir until combined. Return the pan to the heat, and keep adding the milk, slowly and gradually, stirring continuously as the mixture thickens. Add 1 teaspoon of the paprika, and season well with salt and black pepper. Remove from the heat, and set aside.

3 Roll out the pastry on a floured work surface, and use to line the pie tin. Trim away any excess, line the pastry shell with greaseproof paper, and fill with the ceramic baking beans. Bake in the oven for 15–20 minutes until the edges of the pastry are golden. Remove the beans and paper, brush the bottom of the shell with a little of the egg wash, and return to the oven for a couple of minutes to crisp. Reduce the oven temperature to 180°C (350°F/Gas 4).

4 Carefully spoon the onion mixture into the pastry shell, and sprinkle with the remaining paprika. Return the pie to the oven, and bake for 15–20 minutes until lightly golden. Serve warm.

> **COOK'S NOTES**
>
> Do make sure that you cook the onions very slowly over a low heat – you want them to soften, but not colour.

Meat and potato pie

PREP 15 MINS · COOK 1½ HRS

Special equipment • 1.2-litre (2-pint) pie dish or 4 small individual pie dishes

SERVES 4

3 potatoes, peeled and cut into bite-sized pieces
675g (1½lb) braising steak, chopped into bite-sized pieces
1 tbsp olive oil
1 onion, finely chopped
salt and freshly ground black pepper
1 tbsp plain flour
1 tbsp Worcestershire sauce
450ml (15fl oz) hot beef stock
300g (10oz) ready-made puff pastry
1 egg, lightly beaten, for egg wash

1 Boil the potatoes in a pan of salted water for about 15 minutes until soft. Drain and set aside. Put the meat in a large frying pan with a drop of olive oil, and cook over a high heat for 5–8 minutes until browned all over. Remove with a slotted spoon, and set aside.

2 Using the same pan, heat 1 tablespoon of oil over a low heat. Add the onion and a pinch of salt, and sweat gently for about 5 minutes until soft and translucent. Stir in the flour, and continue to cook for a further 2 minutes. Increase the heat a little, and add the Worcestershire sauce and stock. Bring to the boil, reduce the heat slightly, and return the meat to the pan. Cover, and simmer gently over a low heat for about 30 minutes, stirring occasionally. Stir through the potato, and season well with salt and black pepper.

3 Meanwhile, preheat the oven to 200°C (400°F/Gas 6). Spoon the meat filling into a pie dish or 4 small individual dishes. On a floured work surface, roll out the pastry so that it is about 5cm (2in) larger all around than the top of the pie dish. Cut out a strip of pastry about 2.5cm (1in) in from the edge to make a collar. Wet the edge of the pie dish with a little water; fit the pastry strip all the way around, and press down firmly.

4 Brush the pastry collar with a little of the egg wash, then top with the pastry lid. Trim away the excess. Using your finger and thumb, pinch together the edges to seal. Brush the top of the pie all over with the egg wash, and make 2 slits in the top with a sharp knife to allow steam to escape. Bake in the oven for about 30 minutes until puffed and golden. Serve hot.

VARIATION
Top with shortcrust pastry if you prefer, using the same amount.

Sausage and tomato pie

PREP 15 MINS · COOK 40 MINS

Special equipment • 20cm (8in) square pie dish or fluted tart tin • ceramic baking beans

SERVES 4

225g (8oz) ready-made
   shortcrust pastry
1 egg, lightly beaten
½ tbsp olive oil
1 onion, finely chopped
salt and freshly ground black pepper
400g (14oz) good-quality pork
   sausages, skinned
1 tsp dried oregano
4 tomatoes, sliced

1 Preheat the oven to 200°C (400°F/ Gas 6). Roll out the pastry on a floured work surface, and use to line the pie dish or tart tin. Trim away any excess, line the pastry shell with greaseproof paper, and fill with ceramic baking beans. Bake in the oven for 15–20 minutes until the edges are golden. Remove the beans and paper, brush the bottom of the pastry with a little of the beaten egg, and return to the oven for 2–3 minutes to crisp. Remove from the oven, and set aside. Reduce the oven temperature to 180°C (350°F/Gas 4).

2 Meanwhile, heat the oil in a large frying pan over a low heat. Add the onion and a pinch of salt, and sweat gently for about 5 minutes until soft and translucent. Add the sausagemeat, breaking it up with a fork or the back of a spatula. Season well with salt and black pepper, and sprinkle over the oregano. Cook, stirring regularly, over a low-medium heat for about 10 minutes until no longer pink. Leave to cool, then mix in the remaining egg.

3 Spoon the sausage mixture into the pastry shell, then layer the tomatoes over the top. Bake in the oven for about 20 minutes until lightly golden. Leave to cool for about 10 minutes, then slice in the dish or tin. Serve with a crisp green salad.

VARIATION You could chop the tomatoes, and combine them with the sausage mixture, instead of layering them on top.

Chicken and sweetcorn pie

PREP 15 MINS · COOK 1 HR

Special equipment • 1.2-litre (2-pint) pie dish or 4 individual pie dishes

SERVES 4

2 tbsp olive oil
3 skinless chicken breast fillets, cut
   into chunks
salt and freshly ground black pepper
1 onion, finely chopped
1 tbsp plain flour
150ml (5fl oz) double cream
300ml (10fl oz) hot vegetable stock
340g (12oz) can sweetcorn
   kernels, drained
handful of fresh flat-leaf parsley,
   finely chopped
300g (10oz) ready-made puff pastry
1 egg, lightly beaten, for egg wash

1 Preheat the oven to 200°C (400°F/ Gas 6). Heat 1 tablespoon of the oil in a large frying pan over a medium-high heat. Season the chicken with salt and black pepper. Add to the pan, and cook, stirring, for about 10 minutes until golden brown all over. Remove from the pan, and set aside.

2 Heat the remaining oil in the same pan over a low heat, and add the onion and a pinch of salt. Sweat gently for about 5 minutes until soft and translucent. Remove from the heat, and stir in the flour and a little of the cream. Return the pan to a low heat, and add the remaining cream and the stock, stirring continuously for 5–8 minutes until the mixture thickens. Stir through the sweetcorn and parsley, and season well with salt and black pepper.

3 Spoon the mixture into a pie dish or dishes. Roll out the pastry on a floured work surface so that it is 5cm (2in) larger all around than the top of the pie dish. Cut out a strip of pastry about 2.5cm (1in) in from the edge to make a collar. Wet the edge of the dish with a little water; fit the pastry strip all the way around, and press down firmly. Brush the pastry collar with a little of the egg wash, then top with the pastry lid. Using your fingers or the back of a fork, pinch or press together the edges to seal.

4 Brush the top well with the egg wash. Make 2 slits in the top to allow steam to escape, and bake the pie or pies in the oven for 30–40 minutes until the pastry is puffed and golden. Serve hot.

VARIATION Add sliced mushrooms to the filling mixture when you add the onion.

Roasted red pepper tart

PREP 15 MINS · **COOK 1 HR**

Special equipment • 23cm (9in) square loose-bottomed fluted tart tin • ceramic baking beans • food processor

SERVES 6–8

4 large red peppers
1 tbsp olive oil
300g (10oz) ready-made
    shortcrust pastry
2 eggs, plus 1 extra, lightly beaten,
    for egg wash
1 tbsp mascarpone
handful of fresh basil leaves, plus
    extra to garnish
salt and freshly ground black pepper
1 tsp red pesto

1 Preheat the oven to 200°C (400°F/Gas 6). Put the peppers in a roasting tin. Using your hands, smear each one with the olive oil. Roast in the oven for about 20 minutes until lightly charred. Transfer to a plastic bag, and leave until cool enough to handle before skinning and deseeding.

2 Meanwhile, roll out the pastry on a floured work surface, and use to line the tart tin. Trim away the excess, line the pastry shell with greaseproof paper, and fill with ceramic baking beans. Bake in the oven for 15–20 minutes until the edges are golden. Remove the beans and paper, brush the bottom of the shell with the extra egg, and return to the oven for 2–3 minutes to crisp. Remove from the oven, and set aside. Reduce the oven temperature to 180°C (350°F/Gas 4).

3 Put the roasted peppers, the 2 eggs, mascarpone, and the basil leaves in a food processor, and whiz until combined. Season well with salt and black pepper. Spread the pesto evenly over the bottom of the pastry shell, then carefully pour in the pepper mixture. Bake in the oven for 25–35 minutes until set. Leave to cool for 10 minutes before releasing from the tin. Garnish with extra basil leaves, and serve with a wild rocket and fennel salad.

Artichoke, green olive, and feta tart

PREP 15 MINS · **COOK 1 HR**

Special equipment • 35 x 12.5cm (14 x 5in) loose-bottomed fluted tart tin • ceramic baking beans

SERVES 6

250g (9oz) ready-made
    shortcrust pastry
2 eggs, plus 1 extra, lightly beaten,
    for egg wash
1 tbsp olive oil
1 onion, finely chopped
2 garlic cloves, grated or
    finely chopped
400g can artichoke hearts, drained
12 green olives, pitted
175g (6oz) feta cheese, cubed
few sprigs of fresh thyme,
    leaves picked
200ml (7fl oz) double cream
salt and freshly ground black pepper

1 Preheat the oven to 200°C (400°F/Gas 6). Roll out the pastry on a floured work suface, and use to line the tart tin. Trim away the excess, line the pastry shell with greaseproof paper, and fill with ceramic baking beans. Bake in the oven for 15–20 minutes until the edges are golden. Remove the beans and paper, brush the bottom of the shell with a little of the egg wash, and return to the oven for 2–3 minutes to crisp. Remove from the oven, and set aside. Reduce the oven temperature to 180°C (350°F/Gas 4).

2 Heat the oil in a pan over a low heat. Add the onion, and sweat gently for about 5 minutes until soft and translucent. Add the garlic, and cook for a few seconds more. Spoon the onion mixture evenly over the bottom of the tart shell. Arrange the artichokes and olives over the top, and sprinkle with the feta and thyme leaves.

3 Mix together the cream and the 2 eggs, and season well with salt and black pepper. Carefully pour over the tart filling. Bake in the oven for 25–35 minutes until set, puffed, and golden. Leave to cool for about 10 minutes before releasing from the tin. Serve warm, or at room temperature, with a rocket and tomato salad.

Swiss chard and Gruyère cheese tart

PREP 15 MINS · COOK 1 HR

Special equipment • 23cm (9in) loose-bottomed fluted tart tin • ceramic baking beans

SERVES 6

300g (10oz) ready-made
  shortcrust pastry
2 eggs, plus 1 extra, lightly beaten,
  for egg wash
1 tbsp olive oil
1 onion, finely chopped
salt and freshly ground black pepper
2 garlic cloves, grated or
  finely chopped
few sprigs of fresh rosemary, leaves
  picked and finely chopped
250g (9oz) Swiss chard,
  stalks trimmed
125g (4½oz) Gruyère cheese, grated
125g (4½oz) feta cheese, cubed
200ml (7fl oz) double cream or
  whipping cream

1 Preheat the oven to 200°C (400°F/ Gas 6). Roll out the pastry on a floured work surface and use to line the tart tin. Trim away the excess, line the pastry shell with greaseproof paper, and fill with ceramic baking beans. Bake in the oven for 15–30 minutes until the edges are golden. Remove the beans and paper, and brush the bottom of the shell with a little of the egg wash. Return to the oven for 1–2 minutes to crisp. Remove from the oven, and set aside. Reduce the oven temperature to 180°C (350°F/Gas 4).

2 Heat the oil in a pan over a low heat. Add the onion and a pinch of salt, and sweat gently for about 5 minutes until soft and translucent. Add the garlic and rosemary, and cook for a few seconds, then roughly chop the Swiss chard and add to the pan. Stir for about 5 minutes until it wilts.

3 Spoon the onion and chard mixture into the pastry shell. Sprinkle over the Gruyère cheese, and scatter evenly with the feta. Season well with salt and black pepper. Mix together the cream and the 2 eggs until well combined, and carefully pour over the tart filling. Bake in the oven for 30–40 minutes until set and golden. Leave to cool for 10 minutes before releasing from the tin. Serve warm or at room temperature.

VARIATION
If you can't find Swiss chard, use the same amount of fresh spinach.

EVERYDAY

Cheese and onion pie

PREP 15 MINS · COOK 40 MINS

Special equipment • 18cm (7in) round pie tin

SERVES 4

1 tbsp olive oil
1 large onion, finely chopped
salt and freshly ground black pepper
2 eggs
200g (7oz) mature Cheddar
  cheese, grated
350g (12oz) ready-made
  shortcrust pastry

1 Preheat the oven to 200°C (400°F/ Gas 6). Heat the oil in a small pan over a low heat. Add the onion and a pinch of salt, and sweat for a couple of minutes until transparent and just starting to soften. Tip into a bowl, and leave to cool completely. Lightly beat one of the eggs, and stir into the cooled onion with the cheese. Season with salt and black pepper.

2 Halve the pastry, and roll out each piece on a floured work surface. Use one of the pastry circles to line the pie tin, overlapping the edges, and fill with the cheese and onion mixture. Wet the edge of the pastry with a little water, then top with the other round of pastry. Trim away the excess, then pinch the edges together with your finger and thumb to seal. Using a sharp knife, make two slits in the top of the pie to allow steam to escape.

3 Lightly beat the remaining egg to make an egg wash, and brush all over the top of the pie. Bake in the oven for 25–35 minutes until cooked and golden. Serve with a mixed salad and boiled or steamed new potatoes.

VARIATION
Use a mixture of cheese for the filling, if you like – half Cheddar with a crumbly light cheese such as Cheshire or Caerphilly is a good combination.

EVERYDAY

Olive and anchovy open tart

PREP 15 MINS · COOK 15 MINS

SERVES 6

375g (13oz) ready-made puff pastry
1 egg, lightly beaten, for egg wash
3 tbsp tomato passata
12 unsalted anchovies in oil, drained
12 black olives, pitted
freshly ground black pepper

1 Preheat the oven to 200°C (400°F/ Gas 6). Roll out the pastry, and lay on a baking tray. Using a sharp knife, score a line about 5cm (2in) in from the edges all the way around to form a border, but do not cut all the way through the pastry. Next, using the back of the knife, score the pastry all the way around the outer edges. This helps it to puff up when cooking.

2 Brush the border with the egg wash, then smooth the passata over the inside area right to the scored edges. Arrange the anchovies and olives over the tart so that everyone gets a taste of each, and sprinkle over a pinch of black pepper.

3 Bake in the oven for about 15 minutes, until the pastry is cooked and the edges are puffed and golden. Cut into 6 squares, and serve warm with a crisp green salad.

VARIATION
Top with green instead of black olives, or use a mixture of both.

COOK'S NOTES
If feeding fussy eaters, lay the anchovies at one end and the olives at the other.

Spicy beef pies

PREP 20 MINS · COOK 50 MINS

SERVES 2

2 tbsp olive oil
250g (9oz) rump steak
1 onion, finely chopped
salt
2 garlic cloves, grated or finely chopped
1–2 fresh medium-hot green chillies, deseeded and finely chopped
5cm (2in) piece of fresh root ginger, finely chopped
1 tsp coriander seeds, crushed
125g (4½oz) mushrooms, finely chopped
½ tsp cayenne pepper
300g (10oz) ready-made shortcrust pastry
1 egg, lightly beaten, for egg wash

1 Preheat the oven to 200°C (400°F/ Gas 6). Heat 1 tablespoon of the oil in a large frying pan over a medium-high heat. Add the steak, and brown for about 3 minutes on each side to seal. Remove from the pan, and set aside.

2 Heat the remaining oil in the same pan over a low heat. Add the onion and a pinch of salt, and sweat for about 5 minutes until soft and translucent. Add the garlic, chillies, ginger, and coriander seeds, and cook, stirring, for about 2 minutes until fragrant. Tip in the mushrooms, season with the cayenne, and continue cooking over a low heat for 5 minutes until the mushrooms soften and begin to release their juice.

3 Slice the reserved steak into strips, and return to the pan along with 1 tablespoon of water. Cook for about 2 minutes until the mixture is thick and moist, but not too runny.

4 Roll out the pastry on a floured work surface, and cut into 4 18cm (7in) squares. Wet each square around the edges with a little water. Divide the meat and onion filling into 4 equal portions, and spoon each one into the middle of a square. Bring together the opposite corners of each pastry square to form a parcel, pinching together to seal. Brush all over with the egg wash, and bake in the oven for 20–30 minutes until golden. Serve hot.

VARIATION
You could fold these into half-moon shapes to make pasties. Roll out the pastry, cut out 4 large circles, and fill with the spicy beef mixture.

COOK'S NOTES
These pies can be made a day ahead. Fill the pastry and make into parcels, then keep in the refrigerator until needed. Brush with the egg wash, and bake as above.

Lamb and pea pie

PREP 15 MINS | COOK 1¼ HRS

Special equipment • 1.2-litre (2-pint) pie dish

SERVES 4

1–2 tbsp olive oil
1 onion, finely chopped
salt and freshly ground black pepper
2 garlic cloves, grated or
    finely chopped
350g (12oz) lamb leg steaks, cut into
    bite-sized pieces
1 tsp ground turmeric
½ tsp ground allspice
2 tbsp plain flour
900ml (1½ pints) hot vegetable stock
2 waxy potatoes, peeled and cut into
    small cubes
125g (4½oz) frozen peas, thawed
300g (10oz) ready-made
    shortcrust pastry
1 egg, lightly beaten, for egg wash

1 Heat 1 tablespoon of the oil in a large pan over a low heat. Add the onion and a pinch of salt, and sweat gently for about 5 minutes until soft and translucent. Add the garlic then increase the heat to medium, and add a little extra oil if needed. Tip in the lamb, and sprinkle over the turmeric and allspice. Cook, stirring now and then, for 6–8 minutes until the lamb is browned all over.

2 Remove from the heat, and stir in the flour and a tablespoon of the stock. Return to the heat, and pour in the remaining stock. Bring to the boil, reduce the heat to low, and add the potatoes. Simmer gently, stirring occasionally so that the mixture doesn't stick, for about 20 minutes until the potatoes have cooked and the sauce has thickened. Add the peas, and season well with salt and black pepper.

3 Meanwhile, preheat the oven to 200°C (400°F/Gas 6). Spoon the meat filling into the pie dish. On a floured work surface, roll out the pastry so that it is about 5cm (2in) larger than the top of the pie dish. Cut out a strip of pastry about 2.5cm (1in) in from the edge to make a collar. Wet the edge of the pie dish with a little water; fit the pastry strip all the way around, and press down firmly. Brush the pastry collar with a little of the egg wash, then top with the pastry lid. Trim away the excess. Using your finger and thumb, pinch together the edges to seal, and decorate the top with any leftover pastry, if you wish.

4 Brush the top of the pie all over with the remaining egg wash. Using a sharp knife, make 2 slits in the top to allow steam to escape. Bake in the oven for 30–40 minutes until cooked and golden all over. Serve hot.

Sweetcorn and pepper filo triangles

PREP 20 MINS | COOK 20 MINS

SERVES 2

1 tbsp olive oil
1 onion, finely chopped
salt and freshly ground black pepper
3 red peppers, deseeded and diced
340g can sweetcorn kernels,
    drained
175g (6oz) feta cheese, cut into
    small cubes
200g (7oz) filo pastry
a little butter, melted, plus extra
    for glazing

1 Preheat the oven to 200°C (400°F/Gas 6). Heat the oil in a large frying pan over a low heat. Add the onion and a pinch of salt, and sweat gently for about 5 minutes until soft and translucent. Tip in the peppers, and continue cooking for a further 10 minutes until the peppers are soft. Stir through the sweetcorn and feta, and season well with black pepper.

2 Lay out the filo sheets into four piles of 3 or 4 layers about 30 x 10cm (12 x 4in), brushing each pile with a little melted butter. Divide the pepper mixture between each pile of pastry, spooning it onto the bottom right-hand corner of each one. Fold this corner so that it makes a triangle, then fold the top right-hand corner down. Repeat until you have made 5 folds in all for each one, and end up with 4 large triangles.

3 Brush the triangles all over with a little melted butter, and put them on an oiled baking tray. Bake in the oven for about 20 minutes until crisp and golden. Serve hot.

Squash, thyme, and goat's cheese tart

PREP 15 MINS · **COOK 50 MINS** · ❄

Special equipment • 20cm (8in) round loose-bottomed fluted tart tin • ceramic baking beans

SERVES 4-6

300g (10oz) ready-made shortcrust pastry
2 eggs, lightly beaten
1-2 tbsp olive oil
1 onion, finely chopped
salt and freshly ground black pepper
2 garlic cloves, grated or finely chopped
1 butternut squash, about 1kg (2¼lb), peeled, deseeded, and chopped into small cubes
few sprigs of fresh thyme, leaves picked
125g (4½oz) soft goat's cheese
200ml (7fl oz) double cream

1 Preheat the oven to 200°C (400°F/Gas 6). Roll out the pastry on a floured work surface, and use to line the tart tin. Trim away the excess, line the pastry shell with greaseproof paper, and fill with ceramic baking beans. Bake in the oven for 15-20 minutes until the edges of the pastry are golden. Remove the beans and paper, brush the bottom of the pastry shell with a little of the beaten egg, and return to the oven for 2-3 minutes to crisp. Remove from the oven, and set aside. Reduce the oven temperature to 180°C (350°F/Gas 4).

2 Meanwhile, heat 1 tablespoon of the oil in a large frying pan over a low heat. Add the onion and a pinch of salt, and sweat gently for about 5 minutes until soft and translucent. Add the garlic, squash, and half of the thyme leaves, and continue cooking over a low heat for 10-15 minutes until the squash softens and begins to turn golden. You may have to add a little more oil.

3 Spoon the squash and onion mixture into the pastry shell, then crumble over the goat's cheese. Mix the cream with the remaining beaten egg, and season well with salt and black pepper. Carefully pour the cream mixture over the tart filling, and sprinkle with the remaining thyme leaves. Bake in the oven for 20-25 minutes until the tart is puffed and set. Leave to cool for at least 10 minutes before releasing from the tin. Serve warm with a rocket salad.

VARIATION

If you want to make small individual tarts, use 6 round 10cm (4in) round loose-bottomed fluted tart tins. Cut the pastry into 6 rounds, and use to line each tin.

Pea and pancetta tart

PREP 10 MINS · **COOK 1¼ HRS** · ❄

Special equipment • 18cm (7in) round loose-bottomed straight-sided tart tin • ceramic baking beans

SERVES 4-6

300g (10oz) ready-made shortcrust pastry
2 eggs, plus 1 extra, lightly beaten, for egg wash
1 tbsp olive oil
1 onion, finely chopped
salt and freshly ground black pepper
125g (4½oz) pancetta, cubed
6 fresh sage leaves, roughly chopped
225g (8oz) frozen peas
150ml (5fl oz) double cream

1 Preheat the oven to 200°C (400°F/Gas 6). Roll out the pastry on a floured work surface, and use to line the tart tin. Trim away the excess, line the pastry shell with greaseproof paper, and fill with ceramic baking beans. Bake in the oven for 15-20 minutes until the edges of the pastry are golden. Remove the beans and paper, brush the bottom of the shell with a little of the egg wash, and return to the oven for 2-3 minutes to crisp. Remove from the oven, and set aside. Reduce the oven temperature to 180°C (350°F/Gas 4).

2 Meanwhile, heat the oil in a large frying pan over a low heat. Add the onion and a pinch of salt, and sweat gently for about 5 minutes, until soft and translucent. Add the pancetta and sage, increase the heat a little, and cook for 6-8 minutes until the pancetta is golden and crispy. Stir through the peas, and season well with salt and black pepper.

3 Spoon the onion and pancetta mixture into the pastry shell, and level the top. Mix together the cream and eggs, season, and carefully pour the mixture over the filling to cover. Bake in the oven for 20-30 minutes until set and golden. Leave to cool for 10 minutes before releasing from the tin. Serve warm with a tomato salad.

COOK'S NOTES

The tart will be much easier to slice if you leave it to cool for a while first – the residual heat means that it remains soft for a little while once you have taken it out of the oven.

Egg and ham pie

PREP 15 MINS · COOK 35 MINS

Special equipment • 25 x 15cm (10 x 6in) rectangular pie tin

SERVES 6

400g (14oz) ready-made shortcrust pastry

200g (7oz) cooked ham, chopped into bite-sized pieces

6 eggs, plus 1 extra, lightly beaten, for egg wash

90ml (3fl oz) double cream

salt and freshly ground black pepper

1 Preheat the oven to 200°C (400°F/Gas 6). Halve the pastry, then roll out both pieces on a floured work surface to fit the pie tin. Use one of the pieces to line the tin, making sure that the pastry fits neatly into the corners.

2 Scatter the ham evenly over the bottom of the pastry shell. Carefully break the 6 eggs into the shell, positioning them evenly and making sure that the yolks remain whole. Pour over the cream, and season well with salt and black pepper.

3 Wet the edges of the pastry shell with a little water, then cover with the other piece of pastry to make a lid. Trim away the excess, and press the edges of the pastry together with your finger and thumb to seal. Brush with a little of the egg wash, and bake in the oven for 25–35 minutes until golden brown. Leave to cool for at least 10 minutes before slicing. Serve warm or cold with a fresh tomato salad.

Curried vegetable pies

PREP 15 MINS · COOK 45 MINS

Special equipment • 15cm (6in) round biscuit cutter

SERVES 2

2 carrots, peeled and diced

2 potatoes, peeled and finely diced

450g (1lb) ready-made shortcrust pastry

1 egg, lightly beaten, for egg wash

1 tbsp curry paste

2 tbsp Greek-style yogurt

1 garlic clove, grated or finely chopped

2cm (1in) piece of fresh root ginger, finely chopped

2 spring onions, finely sliced

handful of fresh coriander, finely chopped

juice of ½ lemon

salt and freshly ground black pepper

1 Preheat the oven to 200°C (400°F/Gas 6). Cook the carrots and potato in a pan of salted water for about 15 minutes until soft; drain well.

2 Roll out the pastry on a floured work surface, then cut out 4 circles using the biscuit cutter. Put the pastry rounds on a baking tray, and brush the edges with a little of the egg wash.

3 Put the carrots and potatoes in a bowl, and gently mix with the curry paste and yogurt. Add the garlic, ginger, spring onions, coriander, and lemon juice, and season well with salt and black pepper. Stir through gently until well mixed.

4 Divide the vegetable mixture evenly among the pastry circles, spooning it into the centre of each one. Fold over the pastry to make a half-moon shape, and pinch the edges together to seal. Using a sharp knife, make 2 slashes in the top of each pie, then brush all over with the remaining egg wash. Bake in the oven for 20–30 minutes until golden. Serve hot or cold.

EVERYDAY

Spiced pork and chicken pie

PREP 20 MINS · **COOK 1¼ HRS**

Special equipment · 23cm (9in) round loose-bottomed straight-sided tart tin

SERVES 6-8
2 tbsp olive oil
2 skinless chicken breast fillets
1 onion, finely chopped
pinch of chilli flakes
½ tsp ground cinnamon
½ tsp ground allspice
4 good-quality pork sausages, skinned
salt and freshly ground black pepper
450g (1lb) ready-made
    shortcrust pastry
2 eggs, plus 1 extra, lightly beaten,
    for egg wash
½ tsp cayenne pepper (optional)

1 Preheat the oven to 200°C (400°F/ Gas 6). Heat 1 tablespoon of the oil in a large frying pan over a high heat. Add the chicken, and cook for 6-8 minutes on each side until lightly browned and cooked through. Remove from the pan, and leave to cool; shred into chunky pieces.

2 Add the remaining oil and the onion to the same pan, and reduce the heat to low. Sweat gently for about 5 minutes until soft and translucent. Stir in the chilli flakes, cinnamon, allspice, and sausagemeat, breaking up the meat with a fork or the back of a spatula until it is crumbly. Increase the heat slightly, and sauté for 10-15 minutes until the meat is no longer pink. Season well with salt and plenty of black pepper. Return the shredded chicken to the pan, and stir through until evenly mixed. Remove from the heat, and leave to cool.

3 Halve the pastry, then roll out each piece on a floured work surface to fit the tart tin. Use one of the pieces of pastry to line the tin, allowing the edges to hang over the side. Lightly beat the 2 eggs, then stir into the meat mixture to bind. Add the cayenne (if using). Spoon the mixture into the pastry shell. Wet the edge of the pastry shell, and top with the other piece of pastry to make a lid. Press the edges together to seal, and trim away the excess. Using a sharp knife, make a hole or a slit on the top to allow steam to escape.

4 Brush the top of the pie all over with the egg wash, and bake in the oven for 35-45 minutes until the pastry is cooked and golden. Leave to cool for 10 minutes before releasing from the tin. Serve hot with chips or potato wedges, or with some chutney.

COOK'S NOTES

If the pie is browning too quickly, reduce the oven temperature to 190°C (375°F/Gas 5), or place a sheet of foil on top of the pie.

Tomato and harissa tart

PREP 10 MINS · **COOK 15 MINS**

SERVES 6
400g (14oz) ready-made puff pastry
2 tbsp red pepper pesto
6 tomatoes, halved
2-3 tbsp harissa paste
1 tbsp olive oil
few sprigs of fresh thyme,
    leaves picked

1 Preheat the oven to 200°C (400°F/ Gas 6). Roll out the pastry on a floured work surface, into a large rectangle or square. Lay on a baking tray, then use a sharp knife to score a border about 5cm (2in) in from the edges all the way around, being careful not to cut all the way through the pastry. Next, using the back of the knife, score the pastry around the outer edges – this will help it to puff up.

2 Working inside the border, smother the pastry with the pesto. Arrange the tomatoes on top, cut-side up. Mix the harissa with the olive oil, and drizzle over the tomatoes. Scatter over the thyme leaves.

3 Bake in the oven for about 15 minutes until the pastry is cooked and golden. Serve hot.

Fish and leek pie

PREP 15 MINS | COOK 50 MINS | ❄

Special equipment • 1.2-litre (2-pint) pie dish

SERVES 4

1 tbsp olive oil
1 onion, finely chopped
salt and freshly ground black pepper
4 leeks, finely sliced
1 tsp plain flour
150ml (5fl oz) cider
handful of fresh flat-leaf parsley, finely chopped
150ml (5fl oz) double cream
675g (1½lb) raw white fish, such as haddock or pollack, cut into chunks
300g (10oz) ready-made puff pastry
1 egg, lightly beaten, for egg wash

1 Preheat the oven to 200°C (400°F/Gas 6). Heat the oil in a large frying pan over a low heat. Add the onion and a pinch of salt, and sweat gently for about 5 minutes until soft and translucent. Add the leeks, and continue to sweat gently for about 10 minutes until softened. Remove from the heat, stir in the flour, and add a little of the cider. Return to the heat, pour in the remaining cider, and cook for 5–8 minutes until thickened.

2 Stir through the parsley and cream, and spoon the mixture into the pie dish with the fish. Combine gently, and season well with salt and black pepper.

3 Roll out the pastry on a floured work surface so that it is about 5cm (2in) larger all around than the top of the pie dish. Cut out a strip of pastry about 2.5cm (1in) in from the edge to make a collar. Wet the edge of the pie dish with a little water; fit the pastry strip all the way around, and press down firmly. Brush the pastry collar with a little of the egg wash, then top with the pastry lid. Trim away the excess, and pinch together the edges to seal. Using a sharp knife, make 2 slits in the top to allow steam to escape.

4 Brush the top of the pie all over with the egg wash, and bake in the oven for 20–30 minutes until the pastry is puffed and golden. Serve hot.

Asparagus and herb tart

PREP 15 MINS | COOK 1 HR

Special equipment • 18 x 30cm (7 x 12in) loose-bottomed fluted rectangular tart tin • ceramic baking beans

SERVES 6–8

250g (9oz) ready-made shortcrust pastry
2 eggs, plus 1 extra, lightly beaten, for egg wash
350g (12oz) bunch of fresh asparagus, woody ends trimmed
1 tbsp olive oil
1 bunch of spring onions, finely chopped
handful of fresh mint leaves, finely chopped
salt and freshly ground black pepper
125g (4½oz) Cheddar cheese, grated
200ml (7fl oz) double cream
pinch of freshly grated nutmeg

1 Preheat the oven to 200°C (400°F/Gas 6). Roll out the pastry on a floured work surface, and use to line the tart tin. Trim away the excess, line the pastry shell with greaseproof paper, and fill with ceramic baking beans. Bake in the oven for 15–20 minutes until the edges are golden. Remove the beans and paper, and use a little of the egg wash to brush the bottom of the shell. Return to the oven for 2–3 minutes to crisp. Remove from the oven, and set aside. Reduce the oven temperature to 180°C (350°F/Gas 4).

2 Meanwhile, blanch the asparagus in a large pan of boiling salted water for 3–4 minutes until "al dente". Drain, and quickly refresh in cold water; drain again. Heat the oil in a small frying pan over a low heat. Add the spring onions, and sweat gently for a couple of minutes. Remove from the pan with a slotted spoon, and scatter over the bottom of the pastry shell. Neatly arrange the asparagus on top.

3 Scatter over the mint, and season well with salt and black pepper. Sprinkle the cheese evenly over the top. Mix together the cream and the 2 eggs, and stir in the nutmeg. Carefully pour the cream mixture over the tart filling, and bake in the oven for 30–40 minutes until set, puffed, and golden. Leave in the tin for at least 10 minutes before releasing from the tin. Serve with a tomato salad.

COOK'S NOTES

"Al dente" means "to the tooth". It's used to describe pasta, rice, and vegetables that are soft on the outside, but still have some resistance when bitten into. You don't want sloppy, overcooked asparagus.

EVERYDAY

Brie and bacon tart

 PREP 15 MINS · **COOK 1¼ HRS**

Special equipment • 18 x 30cm (7 x 12in) rectangular loose-bottomed fluted tart tin • ceramic baking beans

SERVES 6-8

300g (10oz) ready-made
 shortcrust pastry
2 eggs, plus 1 extra, lightly beaten,
 for egg wash
1 tbsp olive oil
1 onion, finely chopped
salt and freshly ground black pepper
125g (4½oz) thick bacon rashers,
 chopped into bite-sized pieces
8 sunblush or other
 semi-dried tomatoes
125g (4½oz) Brie cheese,
 sliced into long strips
small handful of fresh chives,
 finely chopped
200ml (7fl oz) double cream
2 garlic cloves, grated
 or finely chopped

1 Preheat the oven to 200°C (400°F/ Gas 6). Roll out the pastry on a floured work surface, and use to line the tart tin, letting the pastry hang over the edges. Trim away the excess, line the pastry shell with greaseproof paper, and fill with ceramic baking beans. Bake in the oven for about 20 minutes until the edges are golden.

Remove the beans and paper, brush the bottom of the shell with a little egg wash, and return to the oven for 1-2 minutes to crisp. Remove from the oven, and set aside. Reduce the oven temperature to 180°C (350°F/Gas 4).

2 Heat the oil in a large frying pan over a low heat. Add the onion and a pinch of salt, and sweat gently for about 5 minutes until soft and translucent. Increase the heat slightly, add the bacon, and cook for 5-8 minutes until crispy and golden. Remove from the heat, and stir through the sunblush or other semi-dried tomatoes.

3 Spoon the onion and bacon mixture into the pastry shell. Top evenly with the Brie strips, and sprinkle with the chives. Mix together the cream and the 2 eggs. Add the garlic, and season well with salt and black pepper. Carefully pour over the tart filling. Bake in the oven for 30-40 minutes until set, puffed, and lightly golden. Serve with a crisp green salad.

VARIATION Use soft goat's cheese instead of Brie.

Mixed mushroom and walnut tart

 PREP 15 MINS · **COOK 1 HR** · ❄

Special equipment • 12 x 35cm (5 x 14in) rectangular loose-bottomed fluted tart tin • ceramic baking beans

SERVES 6

250g (9oz) ready-made
 shortcrust pastry
2 eggs, plus 1 extra, lightly beaten,
 for egg wash
3-4 tbsp olive oil
140g (5oz) exotic mushrooms
 (such as porcini or shiitake),
 roughly chopped
200g (7oz) chestnut mushrooms,
 roughly chopped
3 garlic cloves, grated or
 finely chopped
50g (1¾oz) walnut halves,
 roughly chopped
salt and freshly ground black pepper
2 handfuls of fresh spinach leaves,
 roughly chopped
200ml (7fl oz) double cream

1 Preheat the oven to 200°C (400°F/ Gas 6). Roll out the pastry on a floured work surface, and use to line the tart tin. Trim away the excess, line the pastry shell with greaseproof paper, and fill with ceramic baking beans. Bake in the oven for 15-20 minutes

until the edges are golden. Remove the beans and paper, brush the bottom of the shell with a little of the egg wash, and return to the oven for 2-3 minutes to crisp. Remove from the oven, and set aside. Reduce the oven temperature to 180°C (350°F/Gas 4).

2 Heat the oil in a large deep-sided frying pan over a low heat. Add the mushrooms, garlic, and walnuts, and season well with salt and black pepper. Cook, stirring occasionally, for about 10 minutes until the mushrooms release their juices. Tip in the spinach, and cook, stirring, for a further 5 minutes until just wilted. Spoon the mixture into the pastry shell.

3 Mix together the cream and the 2 eggs. Season well with salt and black pepper. Carefully pour the cream mixture over the mushroom filling. Sprinkle with a pinch of black pepper, and bake in the oven for 15-20 minutes until set. Leave to cool for 10 minutes before releasing from the tin. Serve hot or cold.

EVERYDAY

Gruyère cheese, potato, and thyme tartlets

PREP 20 MINS · COOK 1 HR

Special equipment • 4 10cm (4in) tart tins • ceramic baking beans

SERVES 4
300g (10oz) ready-made shortcrust pastry
2 eggs, plus 1 extra, lightly beaten, for egg wash
2 potatoes, peeled and diced into 1cm (½in) pieces
2 tbsp olive oil
1 small onion, very finely diced
salt and freshly ground black pepper
few sprigs of fresh thyme, leaves picked
150g (5½oz) Gruyère cheese, grated
200ml (7fl oz) double cream

1 Preheat the oven to 200°C (400°F/Gas 6). Roll out the pastry on a floured work surface, and use to line the 4 tart tins. Trim away the excess, line the pastry shells with greaseproof paper, and fill with ceramic baking beans. Bake in the oven for 15–20 minutes until the edges are golden. Remove the beans and paper, brush the bottom of each pastry shell with a little of the egg wash, and return to the oven for 2–3 minutes to crisp. Remove from the oven, and set aside. Reduce the oven temperature to 180°C (350°F/Gas 4).

2 Parboil the potatoes in a small pan of water for about 5 minutes until just starting to soften; do not overcook. Drain.

3 Meanwhile, heat the oil in a large non-stick frying pan over a low heat. Add the onion and a pinch of salt, and sweat gently for about 5 minutes until soft and translucent. Add the parboiled potatoes and the thyme, and season with some black pepper. Cook, stirring occasionally, for about 10 minutes until the potatoes begin to brown.

4 Remove from the heat, and stir through the Gruyère cheese. Taste, and adjust the seasoning if necessary. Divide the mixture evenly among the pastry shells. Mix together the cream and the 2 eggs, then carefully pour equal amounts into each tart. Sit the tarts on a baking tray, and bake in the oven for 20–30 minutes until set and golden. Serve hot.

COOK'S NOTES

Always remember to reduce the oven temperature before cooking the custard mixture; if you don't, it may curdle.

Creamy spinach tart

PREP 15 MINS · COOK 1 HR

Special equipment • 20cm (8in) round loose-bottomed fluted tart tin • ceramic baking beans • food processor

SERVES 4-6
300g (10oz) ready-made shortcrust pastry
2 eggs, plus 1 extra, lightly beaten, for egg wash
1 tbsp olive oil
1 onion, finely chopped
salt and freshly ground black pepper
2 garlic cloves, grated or finely chopped
450g (1lb) fresh spinach
200g (7oz) watercress
200ml (7fl oz) double cream
pinch of freshly grated nutmeg

1 Preheat the oven to 200°C (400°F/Gas 6). Roll out the pastry on a floured work surface, and use to line the tart tin. Trim away the excess, line the pastry shell with greaseproof paper, and fill with ceramic baking beans. Bake in the oven for 15–20 minutes until the edges are golden. Remove the beans and paper, brush the bottom of the shell with a little of the egg wash, and return to the oven for 2–3 minutes to crisp. Remove from the oven, and set aside. Reduce the oven temperature to 180°C (350°F/Gas 4).

2 Heat the oil in a large frying pan over a low heat. Add the onion and a pinch of salt, and sweat gently for about 5 minutes until soft soft and translucent. Add the garlic, and cook for a few more seconds until the garlic turns white. Spoon the mixture into the pastry shell.

3 Put the spinach and watercress in a food processor, and pulse a couple of times until broken up but not mushy. Pour in the cream and the 2 eggs, and pulse again until everything is combined. Season well with salt and black pepper, and pulse once more. Carefully pour into the pastry shell, sprinkle over the nutmeg, and bake in the oven for 20–30 minutes until set. Leave to cool for 10 minutes before releasing from the tin. Serve with boiled or steamed new potatoes and a fresh tomato salad.

Cheat... If time is short, buy a ready-made tart shell.

EVERYDAY

Filo pie with Swiss chard, ricotta cheese, and tomatoes

 PREP 15 MINS COOK 30 MINS

Special equipment • 20cm (8in) round non-stick loose-bottomed cake tin

SERVES 4–6

200g (7oz) ricotta cheese
550g (1¼lb) Swiss chard,
    stems chopped
4–6 sun-dried tomatoes in oil, drained
    and chopped
4 fresh tomatoes, sliced
1 egg
salt and freshly ground black pepper
12 sheets filo pastry
25g (scant 1oz) butter, melted

1 Preheat the oven to 180°C (350°F/ Gas 4). In a bowl, mix together the ricotta, Swiss chard, sun-dried and fresh tomatoes, and egg. Season well with salt and black pepper.

2 Lay 2 sheets of filo pastry, one on top of the other, in the cake tin, letting them hang over the edge on two sides. Next, lay 2 more sheets of filo at right angles to the first layer. Continue in this way until you have 8 sheets for the base of the pie.

3 Spoon the ricotta mixture into the pie. Fold in the edges of the pastry, and top the pie with the remaining 4 sheets of filo pastry, tucking them in neatly. Brush all over with the melted butter, and bake in the oven for 20–30 minutes until golden and crisp. Serve hot with a crisp green salad and some sweet onion chutney.

COOK'S NOTES

Always work quickly with filo, and don't let it dry out because it becomes very brittle.

Smoked mackerel and spring onion tart

 PREP 15 MINS COOK 50 MINS

Special equipment • 18cm (7in) round loose-bottomed straight-sided tart tin • ceramic baking beans

SERVES 4

250g (9oz) ready-made
    shortcrust pastry
2 eggs, plus 1 extra, for egg wash
1 tbsp olive oil
1 bunch of spring onions,
    finely chopped
salt and freshly ground black pepper
2 smoked mackerel fillets, about 100g
    (3½oz) each, skinned and flaked
200ml (7fl oz) crème fraîche
handful of fresh flat-leaf parsley,
    finely chopped
1 bunch of fresh chives,
    finely chopped

1 Preheat the oven to 200°C (400°F/Gas 6). Roll out the pastry on a floured work surface, and use to line the tart tin. Trim away the excess, line the pastry shell with greaseproof paper, and fill with ceramic baking beans. Bake in the oven for 15–20 minutes until the edges are golden. Remove the beans and paper, brush the bottom of the shell with a little of the egg wash, and return to the oven for 2–3 minutes to crisp. Remove from the oven, and set aside. Reduce the oven temperature to 180°C (350°F/Gas 4).

2 Meanwhile, heat the oil in a small frying pan over a low heat. Add half of the spring onions and a pinch of salt, and sweat gently for about 5 minutes. Spoon evenly over the bottom of the pastry shell along with the remaining uncooked spring onion. Scatter over the mackerel, and season with plenty of black pepper.

3 Mix together the crème fraîche and the 2 eggs. Add the parsley and chives, and season with a little salt. Mix through. Carefully pour over the tart filling, then bake in the oven for 20–30 minutes until set and golden. Leave to cool for 10 minutes before releasing from the tin. Serve with a tomato and cucumber salad.

Filo pie with spinach, ricotta cheese, pine nuts, and raisins

 PREP 15 MINS COOK 35 MINS

Special equipment • 20cm (8in) round or square loose-bottomed cake tin

SERVES 4

1 tbsp olive oil
1 onion, finely chopped
salt and freshly ground black pepper
2 garlic cloves, grated or
   finely chopped
550g (1¼lb) fresh spinach leaves
handful of raisins
75g (2½oz) pine nuts, toasted
200g (7oz) ricotta cheese
1 egg, lightly beaten
12 sheets filo pastry
30g (1oz) butter, melted

1 Preheat the oven to 180°C (350°F/ Gas 4). Heat the oil in a frying pan over a low heat. Add the onion and a pinch of salt, and sweat gently for about 5 minutes until soft and translucent. Add the garlic, and cook for a few seconds more until the garlic turns white.

2 Tip in the spinach, and cook, stirring, for about 3 minutes until it wilts. Season well with salt and black pepper. Remove from the heat, stir through the raisins and pine nuts, and leave to cool. Add the ricotta and beaten egg, and stir well.

3 Lay 2 sheets of filo pastry one on top of the other in the cake tin, letting them hang over the edge on two sides. Next, lay 2 more sheets of filo at right angles to the first layer. Continue in this way until you have used 8 sheets for the base of the pie.

4 Spoon the spinach and ricotta mixture into the pie. Fold in the edges of the pastry, and top the pie with the remaining 4 sheets of filo pastry, tucking them in neatly. Brush all over with the melted butter, and bake in the oven for 20-30 minutes until golden and crisp. Serve warm.

Steak, mushroom, and ale pie

 PREP 15 MINS COOK 1¼ HRS

Special equipment • 1.2-litre (2-pint) pie dish

SERVES 4

1 tbsp olive oil
900g (2lb) braising steak, chopped
   into bite-sized pieces
a few sprigs of fresh rosemary, leaves
   picked and finely chopped
1 Bovril or other beef stock cube
1 tbsp plain flour, plus extra
   for dusting
150ml (5fl oz) pale ale
300ml (10fl oz) hot water
30g (1oz) butter
200g (7oz) chestnut
   mushrooms, quartered
salt and freshly ground black pepper
300g (10oz) ready-made puff pastry
1 egg, lightly beaten, for egg wash

1 Heat the oil in a large frying pan over a medium-high heat. Add the meat, and cook, stirring from time to time, for 4-6 minutes until the meat is browned all over. Add the rosemary, crumble over the stock cube, and sprinkle in the flour. Stir until well combined. Increase the heat to high, and add a little of the ale, stirring all the time. Pour in the remaining ale, and let boil for a couple of minutes. Add the hot water, and boil for a few minutes more. Reduce the heat to low, cover

the pan, and simmer for about 30 minutes, stirring occasionally, so that the meat doesn't catch and burn. If the mixture dries out too much, add a little more hot water.

2 Meanwhile, preheat the oven to 200°C (400°F/Gas 6). Melt the butter in a small frying pan over a medium heat. Add the mushrooms, and sauté for 4-6 minutes until golden. Tip into the meat mixture, and stir through. Season well with salt and black pepper.

3 Spoon the meat filling into the pie dish. On a floured work surface, roll out the pastry so that it is about 5cm (2in) larger all around than the top of the pie dish. Cut out a strip of pastry about 2.5cm (1in) in from the edge to make a collar. Wet the edge of the pie dish with a little water; fit the pastry strip all the way around, and press down firmly.

4 Brush the pastry collar with a little of the egg wash, then top with the pastry lid. Trim away the excess. Using your finger and thumb, pinch together the edges to seal. Brush the top of the pie all over with the egg wash, and make 2 slits in the top with a sharp knife to allow steam to escape. Bake in the oven for 20-30 minutes until the pastry is puffed and golden. Serve hot with creamy mashed potato.

GET THE MOST FROM YOUR ROAST

Recipes for roast meat, poultry, and fish, and how to use the leftovers.

GET THE MOST FROM YOUR ROAST

Cooking one dish one day and enjoying it in different ways in the days to come is a clever way to plan your weekly meals. Not only is it thrifty, it is also a great time-saver. By being a little creative and resourceful in the kitchen, you'll be able to turn your leftovers into something special – from delicious roast meat sandwiches, to simple salads and stir-fries.

plan ahead

If you are planning to cook once and eat for the week, a little planning is required. Buy a larger joint of meat or larger fish than you need, and make sure it is good quality. Think about all the flavours and cuisines that would work with the meat or fish, and buy a few more ingredients accordingly. Think about types of dishes and textures, as you don't want soup every day, but a risotto with leftovers one day, and a pie the next, is fine. Remember that a dish is only as good as its ingredients, so buy everything fresh and seasonal if you can.

Using leftover vegetables What to do with leftover accompaniments.

LEFTOVER		TURN INTO

ROOT VEGETABLES

Store
Put cooked root vegetables in a rigid sealable plastic container, and don't overpack, as they can go soggy. Leave to cool before sealing.

Refrigerator
Will keep well for 1–2 days.

Freezer
Leftover root vegetables don't freeze well unless they have been slightly undercooked. Keep for up to 1 month.

Vegetable bake
Layer vegetables in an ovenproof dish. Mix a 200g carton of Greek yogurt with 1 egg and a handful of grated Cheddar cheese. Season, then stir and pour over the vegetables. Cook in the oven for 30 minutes, or until golden, at 200°C (400°F/Gas 6).

Pasta sauce
Stir chopped vegetables into a simmering tomato sauce, cook until heated through, and toss with chunky pasta shapes.

Frittata
Add chopped vegetables to an omelette. Melt a knob of butter in a small frying pan over a medium heat. Pour 3–4 beaten eggs into the pan, and cook for a minute or two. Tip over the leftover vegetables, sprinkle over some Gruyère cheese, and put in a hot oven until set and golden.

Bolognaise
Stir chopped leftover vegetables into a simmering pan of beef mince and tomato sauce.

See Cook's Notes in recipes to find out where you can use leftover root vegetables.

GREENS

Store
Store in a covered bowl or rigid plastic container. Leave to cool, before covering or sealing.

Refrigerator
Will keep well for 1–2 days. Any longer and it tends to go limp and lose its fresh taste.

Freezer
Leftover greens don't freeze well.

Soup
Add leftover greens to your soup at the end of cooking, just before puréeing.

Cheese on toast
Mix into a Gruyère or Cheddar cheese sauce, pile on top of crusty toasted bread, and cook under a hot grill until melted.

Lamb or chicken casserole
Stir into a lamb or chicken casserole for the last 15 minutes of cooking.

Lasagne
Add to your lasagne, as your layer the ingredients in the dish.

Fish cakes and vegetarian burgers
Finely chop and add to fish cakes or vegetarian burgers before frying.

Alternatively, just **reheat greens** in a little olive oil, and toss in lemon juice and chilli oil. Dig in with some fresh crusty bread.

See Cook's Notes in recipes to find out where you can use leftover greens.

MASH

Store
Spoon leftover mash into a rigid plastic container. The shallower it is, the quicker the mash will cool. When completely cool, seal, and put in the refrigerator.

Refrigerator
Will keep well for 1–2 days. It will go hard if left too long.

Freezer
Keep for up to 1 month. It will go watery if left too long.

Gnocchi
Mix 125g (4½oz) mash with 1 egg. Stir in enough plain flour to stiffen the mixture. Using floured hands, scoop up some mash, and roll into a sausage shape. Repeat until it is all used up. Cut into 2.5cm (1in) pieces, indent with a fork, and sit on a floured baking sheet. Refrigerate for 15 minutes, cook, and serve with a sauce.

Fish cakes
Mix mash with flaked cooked salmon and a handful of leftover peas. Stir in 1 teaspoon of horseradish sauce, and 1 teaspoon of wholegrain mustard. Add one egg to bind, and flatten into cakes with floured hands. Fry in hot sunflower oil until golden.

Bubble and squeak
Mix mash with leftover vegetables, such as cabbage, and fry in 4 tablespoons of hot oil and melted butter, until it becomes golden and crispy. Add flavourings such as Worcestershire sauce, creamed horseradish, or mustard.

See Cook's Notes in recipes to find out where you can use leftover mash.

Using leftover meat and fish What to do with your leftover roast, and some great dish ideas.

LEFTOVER		TURN INTO

CHICKEN

Store
Remove the meat from the carcass. Wrap the meat and carcass separately in cling film, then foil. Refrigerate no longer than 2 hours after it has been cooked. Keep away from uncooked meats. Remove stuffing before storing (store separately in a plastic airtight container). Store leftover gravy in a plastic container.

Refrigerator
Will keep well for 2–3 days; use leftover gravy within 2 days.

Freezer
Keep for up to 3 months.

A variety of recipes, including:

Cardamom chicken curry (see p224).

Chicken and pea filo pie (see p224).

Chicken and sweetcorn soup (see p225).

Chicken salad with carrot and apple relish (see p225).

A **pasta bake** or a fragrant **pilaf**.

LAMB

Store
Remove leftover lamb from the bone. Wrap the lamb tightly in foil, and slice when needed. The bone can be used for stock, but wrap it separately in foil. Keep away from uncooked meats. Refrigerate no longer than 2 hours after it has been cooked.

Refrigerator
Will keep well for 1–3 days.

Freezer
Keep for up to 3 months.

A variety of recipes, including:

Flatbreads topped with lamb and hummus (see p228).

Hot and fiery lamb masala (see p228).

Lamb, tomato, and bean casserole (see p229).

Lamb and potato pie (see p229).

A Moroccan-style **shepherd's pie**.

PORK

Store
Slice and store in a shallow rigid plastic container and seal, or put on a plate and wrap well with cling film. If there is a large amount, pack in smaller quantities. Keep away from uncooked meats. Refrigerate no longer than 2 hours after it has been cooked. Store leftover gravy in a plastic container.

Refrigerator
Will keep well for 1–3 days; use leftover gravy within 2 days.

Freezer
Keep for up to 3 months.

A variety of recipes, including:

Roast pork in pitta bread (see p232).

Pork and yellow split pea soup (see p232).

Pork and spring greens (see p233).

Sweet and sour pork (see p233).

A shredded pork and lemongrass **burger**, or pork, bacon, and spinach **pie**.

FISH

Store
Store in a shallow rigid plastic container and seal, or put on a plate and wrap well with cling film. Store away from uncooked foods. Refrigerate no longer than 2 hours after it has been cooked.

Refrigerator
Will keep well for 1–2 days.

Freezer
Keep for up to 3 months.

A variety of recipes, including:

Baked salmon with salsa verde and cucumber (see p236).

Salmon and prawn fish pie (see p236).

Salmon and roasted tomato pasta (see p237).

Salmon with new potatoes, flageolet beans, and parsley sauce (see p237).

A green **salad** or **fish cakes**.

BEEF

Store
Store small quantities in an airtight container, as it will stay more moist if unsliced. Refrigerate no longer than 2 hours after it has been cooked. The bone can be used for stock, but wrap it separately in foil. Leftover gravy can be stored in a plastic container, but use within 2 days.

Refrigerator
Will keep well for 2–3 days.

Freezer
Keep for up to 3 months.

A variety of recipes, including:

Beef and Stilton pie (see p240).

Thai-style beef salad (see p240).

Beef stroganoff (see p241).

Beef with beetroot and spinach (see p241).

Beef and mushroom **stir-fry** or sliced beef, Gorgonzola cheese, and red onion marmalade **pittas**.

TURKEY

Store
Remove meat from the carcass. Wrap the meat and carcass separately in cling film, then foil. Refrigerate no longer than 2 hours after it has been cooked. Keep away from uncooked meats. Remove stuffing before storing (store separately in a plastic airtight container). Store leftover gravy in a plastic container.

Refrigerator
Will keep well for 2–3 days; use leftover gravy within 2 days.

Freezer
Keep for up to 3 months.

A variety of recipes, including:

Turkey, almond, and cranberry pilaf (see p244).

Turkey and noodles (see p244).

Warm turkey and chickpea salad (see p245).

Spiced turkey and greens stir-fry (see p245).

A **curry**, or turkey, ham and Gruyère cheese **quesadillas**.

EVERYDAY

STEP-BY-STEP

EVERYDAY

Make stock Turn a carcass or meat bones into delicious stock.

Chicken A great kitchen staple to have in your refrigerator or freezer.

1 Add your cooked chicken carcass to a large pan, then add a handful of raw vegetables such as carrot tops, celery cut into chunks, onion pieces and skin, fresh thyme or rosemary stalks, a bay leaf, and a handful of black peppercorns.

2 Pour over enough cold water to cover completely. You will probably need around 2.8 litres (5 pints).

3 Bring to the boil, reduce to a gentle simmer, and cook with the lid half-on for about 1 hour, skimming any scum that comes to the top of the pan, if necessary.

4 Remove the carcass and discard, then pour the liquid through a sieve into a large jug.

Beef Richer and darker than chicken, particularly if you roast the bones.

1 Use either leftover bones from a rib of roast beef, or when buying a joint of beef from the butcher, ask him for a bag of beef bones. Tip the bones into a large roasting tin, add a handful of vegetables such as carrot tops, celery chunks, onion pieces and skin, and season. Roast for 30 minutes.

2 Add the roasted bones and vegetables to a large deep pan with some fresh stalks of thyme, rosemary, or a woody herb of your choice, then pour over enough cold water to cover completely.

3 Bring to the boil, then reduce to a gentle simmer. Cook with the lid half-on for about 1 hour, skimming any skum that comes to the top of the pan, if necessary.

4 Remove the bones and discard, then pour the liquid through a sieve into a large jug.

fish stock

When buying fresh fish, ask your fishmonger for some fish heads. Add these to a large pan, pour over water to cover, season well, throw in some fresh thyme, chopped onion, and chopped fennel. Season, bring to the boil, and simmer for about 15 minutes, skimming any scum that comes to the top. Pass through a fine sieve, twice in case of fine bones, refrigerate, and use within 2 days, or freeze for up to 3 months. Oily fish such as salmon doesn't make a good stock as it is too oily and strong in flavour. Use white fish.

How to store stock

Leave to cool for 30 minutes, then cover and put in the refrigerator. To freeze, pour the cool stock into 600ml (1 pint) zip-lock bags, or rigid plastic containers with lids, and freeze for up to 3 months, or pour into ice cube trays and freeze (transferring to a bag once frozen). If keeping in the refrigerator, use within 2–3 days.

4 ideas for leftovers
Whip up a quick 5-minute snack with your leftover chicken, pork, beef, or salmon.

Sandwiches
Ideal for picnics and packed lunches.

Coronation chicken

Mix shredded **leftover chicken** in a bowl with **mayonnaise** to coat. Add a pinch of **paprika**, and a pinch of **medium curry powder**, and mix well. Add a handful of **raisins**, and season. Spoon into a sliced roll filled with **wild rocket leaves**.

Roast pork and apple

Halve a bread roll, and smother one half with **apple sauce**, top with slices of **leftover pork**, then top with a few slices of **sweet eating apple**. Season, and serve with a chunky piece of **leftover crackling**.

Salads
Freshen up your leftovers with a zingy dressing, and crisp salad ingredients.

Beef, rocket, and radish

Put a couple of handfuls of **wild rocket leaves** on a plate, then top with slices of **leftover beef**. Slice 3–4 **radishes** thinly, and sprinkle these over the beef. Drizzle with a little **balsamic vinegar**, and the juice of ½ an **orange**. Season, and serve immediately.

Salmon and noodle

Put **cooked medium rice noodles** in a bowl. Toss with flaked **leftover salmon**, and a few sliced **spring onions**. Mix together 3 tablespoons of **extra virgin olive oil**, 1 tablespoon **white wine vinegar**, juice of ½ a **lime**, a pinch of **sugar**, a pinch of **chilli flakes**, and season. Drizzle over the salad when ready to serve. Garnish with **fresh basil leaves**.

EVERYDAY

ROAST CHICKEN

 PREP 15 MINS **COOK 1¼ HRS**

SERVES 4, PLUS LEFTOVERS

1.35kg (3lb) whole chicken

50g (1¾oz) butter

1 lemon, quartered

salt and freshly ground black pepper

150ml (5fl oz) hot vegetable stock or water

1 Preheat the oven to 200°C (400°F/Gas 6). Sit the chicken in a roasting tin, then coat evenly all over with the butter – this ensures crisp, evenly golden skin. Stuff the lemon quarters into the body cavity – to help keep the meat moist – and season the chicken all over with salt and black pepper.

2 Roast in the oven for about 1¼ hours until cooked through and golden, basting with the juices at intervals as it cooks (about 3 times in all). To check whether the chicken is cooked, pierce the thickest part of the thigh with a knife. If the juices run clear, it is done; if it is pink or bloody, cook for a little longer. Remove to a large plate, cover with foil, and leave to rest in a warm place for about 15 minutes before carving.

3 To make the gravy, tilt the roasting tin at a slight angle, and skim off any fat. Put the tin on the hob or stovetop, and add the stock or water. Bring to the boil, scraping up any bits from the bottom of the tin with a wooden spoon. Reduce the heat slightly, add more seasoning, if you wish, and simmer for 10 minutes. Pass through a sieve if you wish, or serve as it is with the carved chicken. Serve with roast or sautéed potatoes, and seasonal vegetables.

EVERYDAY

Cardamom chicken curry

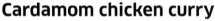

PREP 10 MINS **COOK 35 MINS**

SERVES 4

1 tbsp sunflower oil

1 onion, finely chopped

5cm (2in) piece of fresh root ginger, finely sliced

10 green cardamom pods, lightly crushed

2 tsp onion seeds

2 fresh hot red chillies, deseeded and finely chopped

3 garlic cloves, grated or finely chopped

2 tsp garam masala

350g (12oz) leftover roast chicken, any skin removed, roughly shredded or sliced

salt and freshly ground black pepper

400g can whole peeled plum tomatoes, chopped in can

3 tbsp double cream

2 handfuls of fresh spinach leaves, rinsed

1 Heat the oil in a large pan or deep frying pan over a low heat. Add the onion, and sweat gently for about 5 minutes until soft and translucent. Add the ginger, cardamom, onion seeds, and chilli, and cook for a further 3 minutes, stirring occasionally.

2 Now add the garlic and garam masala, and stir for a few seconds until fragrant, before adding the leftover chicken. Season well with salt and black pepper. Tip in the tomatoes and any juices, and squash with the back of a fork. Fill the tin with hot water, and add this to the pan as well. Bring to the boil, then stir through the cream.

3 Reduce the heat slightly, and simmer gently for 25–30 minutes; if the curry looks too thick, add a little more hot water. Add the spinach at the end of cooking, and stir well until it has wilted. Taste, and season again if needed. Serve hot with fluffy white rice.

VARIATION For a healthier option, use Greek-style yogurt instead of cream.

Chicken and pea filo pie

PREP 20 MINS **COOK 30 MINS**

Special equipment • 18cm (7in) square pie or cake tin

SERVES 6

12 sheets filo pastry

50g (1¾oz) butter, melted, plus extra if needed

350g (12oz) leftover roast chicken, any skin removed, roughly shredded or sliced

250g (9oz) boiled new potatoes, halved

125g (4½oz) frozen peas, thawed

1–2 tbsp mild curry powder

salt and freshly ground black pepper

3–4 tbsp hot vegetable stock

1 Preheat the oven to 200°C (400°F/Gas 6). Lightly brush 6 sheets of the filo with the melted butter. Use them to line the bottom of the pie or cake tin, allowing it to overlap the sides.

2 Toss together the leftover chicken, potatoes, peas, and curry powder, and season well with salt and black pepper. Carefully pour over a little of the stock. Use just enough to wet the mixture and produce a little gravy, but don't add too much because it will soak the pastry.

3 Spoon the chicken filling into the filo pastry shell. Fold the pastry edges in towards the middle, and top the pie with the remaining 6 filo sheets, each brushed with a little melted butter. Tuck the edges of the pastry neatly down at the sides, and make sure that the top is well glazed with melted butter. Bake in the oven for 20–30 minutes until the pastry is cooked and golden. Serve hot.

Chicken and sweetcorn soup

PREP 10 MINS · COOK 30 MINS

Special equipment • blender or food processor

SERVES 4

1 tbsp olive oil
25g (scant 1oz) butter
1 onion, finely chopped
2 x 340g cans sweetcorn
   kernels, drained
350g (12oz) leftover roast
   chicken, any skin removed,
   roughly shredded
3 garlic cloves, grated or
   finely chopped
salt and freshly ground black pepper
1.2 litres (2 pints) hot chicken stock
handful of fresh flat-leaf parsley,
   finely chopped

1 Heat the olive oil and butter in a large pan over a low heat. Add the onion, and sweat gently for about 5 minutes until soft and translucent.

2 Tip 1 can of the drained sweetcorn into the blender or food processor, and pulse a few times until the kernels have turned into a chunky purée. Tip this into the pan with the onion. Stir through the leftover chicken and garlic, and season with salt and black pepper. Increase the heat slightly, and cook for a few minutes.

3 Add the remaining can of drained sweetcorn and the hot stock, and bring to the boil. Reduce the heat slightly, and simmer for 20 minutes. Taste, and season again if needed. Stir through the flat-leaf parsley just before serving.

Chicken salad with carrot and apple relish

PREP 15 MINS

SERVES 4

350g (12oz) leftover roast
   chicken, any skin removed,
   cut into bite-sized pieces
50g (1¾oz) pine nuts, toasted
   (see Cook's Notes)
1 tbsp olive oil
juice of ½ lemon
2 handfuls of fresh spinach
   leaves, rinsed

For the carrot and apple relish
2 carrots
2 sweet red eating apples
2 preserved lemons, finely chopped
small handful of sultanas
salt and freshly ground
   black pepper

1 To make the carrot and apple relish, grate the carrots into a bowl. Quarter and core the apples, and grate into the bowl with the carrot. Add the preserved lemons and sultanas, and mix together. Season with salt and black pepper.

2 Lay the spinach leaves in a large shallow salad bowl or plate, and top with the leftover chicken and toasted pine nuts. When ready to serve, drizzle over the olive oil and lemon juice, and sprinkle with a pinch of salt. Serve with the carrot and apple relish.

COOK'S NOTES

Toast the pine nuts in a small dry frying pan: heat gently for a couple of minutes, tossing frequently, until they turn golden, but watch carefully because they can quickly scorch.

ROAST LEG OF LAMB

 PREP 15 MINS **COOK 1¾ HRS**

SERVES 4, PLUS LEFTOVERS

2kg (4½lb) leg of lamb

4 garlic cloves, peeled but left whole

handful of fresh rosemary sprigs

salt and freshly ground black pepper

600ml (1 pint) hot vegetable stock

1 tsp redcurrant jelly

1 Preheat the oven to 200°C (400°F/Gas 6). Spike the lamb leg evenly all over with the point of a sharp knife, then stuff the garlic cloves and small sprigs of rosemary into the holes. Season the lamb all over with salt and black pepper.

2 Sit the leg of lamb in a roasting tin, and roast in the oven for about 15 minutes, until it begins to brown. Reduce the oven temperature to 180°C (350°F/Gas 4), and continue to roast for a further 1 hour (for rare), basting it with its juices halfway through the cooking time; allow 1½ hours for well done. Remove the lamb to a large plate, cover with foil, and leave to rest in a warm place for 15 minutes while you make the gravy.

3 To make the gravy, tilt the roasting tin at a slight angle, and skim off any fat. Sit the tin over a high heat on the hob or stovetop. Add the stock and redcurrant jelly, and bring to the boil, scraping up any bits from the bottom of the tin with a wooden spoon. Reduce the heat slightly, and simmer, stirring all the time, for 5–8 minutes. Taste, and season if needed. Carve at the table, and serve with roast or creamy mashed potato, fresh mint sauce, and seasonal vegetables.

EVERYDAY

Flatbreads topped with lamb and hummus

PREP 10 MINS   COOK 20 MINS

SERVES 2

1 tbsp olive oil, plus extra
   for drizzling
1 onion, finely chopped
3 garlic cloves, grated or
   finely chopped
250g (9oz) leftover roast
   lamb, shredded
pinch of ground allspice
pinch of ground cinnamon
salt and freshly ground black pepper
2 flatbreads or plain naan
handful of pine nuts, toasted
handful of fresh mint leaves,
   roughly chopped
hummus, to serve

1 Preheat the oven to 200°C (400°F/
Gas 6). Heat the olive oil in a frying
pan over a low heat. Add the onion,
and sweat gently for about 5 minutes
until soft and translucent.

2 Stir in the garlic, and cook for
a few more seconds. Now add the
leftover lamb, and stir through.
Sprinkle over the allspice and
cinnamon, and cook for a few minutes,
stirring now and then. Season with
salt and black pepper.

3 Lay the flatbreads or naan on
a baking tray, and drizzle with a little
olive oil. Spoon over the lamb mixture,
and cook in the oven for about
10 minutes until the lamb is heated
through. Scatter over the pine nuts
and mint leaves, and top each
flatbread or naan with a dollop
of hummus. Serve immediately.

COOK'S NOTES

*If you prefer the lamb minced,
whiz in a blender or food processor
until finely chopped.*

Hot and fiery lamb masala

PREP 15 MINS   COOK 40 MINS

SERVES 4

25g (scant 1oz) ghee, or 1 tbsp
   sunflower oil
1 onion, finely chopped
1 tsp ground cumin
1 tsp ground coriander
2 bay leaves
2 tsp whole black peppercorns,
   lightly crushed
3 tsp mild paprika
1–2 tsp hot chilli powder
3 garlic cloves, grated or
   finely chopped
5cm (2in) piece of fresh root ginger,
   finely sliced
750g jar passata
3 tbsp double cream
75g (2½oz) cashew nuts, ground
300g (10oz) leftover roast lamb,
   roughly shredded or sliced
salt and freshly ground black pepper

1 Heat the ghee or sunflower oil
in a large deep frying pan over a low
heat. Add the onion, and sweat gently
for about 5 minutes until soft and

translucent. Now add the cumin,
coriander, bay leaves, peppercorns,
paprika, and chilli powder, and cook for
a couple of minutes more until fragrant,
stirring the spices into the oil.

2 Tip in the garlic and ginger, and
cook for a few more seconds, stirring,
then pour in the passata, cream, and
nuts. Bring to the boil, reduce the heat
slightly, and add the leftover lamb.
Simmer gently for 25–30 minutes.
Taste, and season with salt and black
pepper. Serve hot with basmati rice.

VARIATION

Stir through some fresh spinach
or 125g (4½oz) of frozen peas,
thawed, for the last 5 minutes
of cooking, if you wish.

COOK'S NOTES

*Ghee is clarified butter that is
used in Indian cooking. You will
find it in specialist Asian stores –
it will give your masala a touch
of authenticity.*

Lamb, tomato, and bean casserole

PREP 15 MINS — COOK 25 MINS

SERVES 4

1 tbsp olive oil

1 onion, finely chopped

8 tomatoes, skinned and quartered

600ml (1 pint) hot vegetable stock

salt and freshly ground black pepper

350g (12oz) leftover roast lamb,
cut into bite-sized pieces

400g can flageolet beans, drained
and rinsed

handful of fresh flat-leaf parsley,
finely chopped

handful of fresh thyme sprigs,
leaves picked

1 Heat the oil in a large pan over
a low heat. Add the onion, and sweat
gently for about 5 minutes until soft
and translucent.

2 Add the tomatoes, and pour in the
stock. Season well with salt and black
pepper. Bring to the boil, then reduce
the heat slightly. Stir in the leftover
lamb and drained flageolet beans, and
simmer gently for about 20 minutes,
topping up with a little hot water
or light stock if the casserole begins
to dry out.

3 Just before serving, stir through
the fresh parsley and thyme, and
serve hot with some fresh crusty
bread, or crisp green salad.

Lamb and potato pie

PREP 20 MINS — COOK 50 MINS

Special equipment • 18cm (7in) round
pie tin

SERVES 4

450g (1lb) potatoes, peeled
and quartered

1 tbsp olive oil

1 onion, finely chopped

handful of fresh rosemary sprigs,
leaves picked and chopped

350g (12oz) leftover roast lamb,
roughly shredded or sliced

salt and freshly ground black pepper

1 tbsp plain flour

300ml (10fl oz) hot vegetable stock

2–3 tsp mint sauce

250g (9oz) shortcrust pastry

1 egg, lightly beaten, for egg wash

1 Preheat the oven to 200°C (400°F/
Gas 6). Cook the potatoes in a pan
of boiling salted water for about
15 minutes, until soft; drain and set
aside. Heat the olive oil in a large pan
over a low heat. Add the onion, and
sweat gently for about 5 minutes until
soft and translucent. Stir through the

rosemary, and add the leftover lamb.
Season well with salt and black pepper.

2 Tip in the flour, and stir through,
then pour in the stock. Keep stirring for
about 10 minutes over a medium heat
until the liquid begins to thicken, then
add the reserved potatoes and stir in
the mint sauce. Simmer for a further
10 minutes. Allow to cool slightly.

3 Divide the pastry into 2 pieces, one
a little larger than the other. Roll out
the larger piece into a large circle on
a floured work surface. Use to line the
pie tin, letting the pastry hang over the
edges. Roll out the other piece to make
the pastry lid for the top of the pie.

4 Spoon the lamb mixture into the
pastry shell, then sit the pastry lid on
top. Using your finger and thumb, pinch
together the edges of the pastry to seal.
Trim away the excess. Brush evenly
with a little egg wash, and bake in the
oven for 40–50 minutes until the pastry
is cooked and golden. Leave to cool in
the tin for at least 15 minutes before
serving. Cut into slices and serve.

ROAST PORK

 PREP 20 MINS COOK 1¾ HRS

SERVES 6, PLUS LEFTOVERS

2kg (4½lb) boneless pork loin, skin scored

4 garlic cloves, grated or finely chopped

handful of black olives, pitted and finely chopped

pinch of dried oregano

sea salt and freshly ground black pepper

olive oil, to coat

1 Preheat the oven to 220°C (425°F/Gas 7). Lay the pork out skin-side down. Mix the garlic, olives, and oregano in a bowl, and season with salt and black pepper. Rub the mixture in a line down the middle of the pork, then roll the pork up tightly and secure with string. Sit the roll in a large roasting tin, cut side down. Rub all over with olive oil, then rub sea salt into the cuts.

2 Roast the pork in the oven for about 20 minutes until the skin is really golden and crispy for perfect crackling. Reduce the oven temperature to 190°C (375°F/Gas 4), and continue to roast for a further 1 hour to 1¼ hours until the pork is cooked through. Remove to a large plate, and leave to rest in a warm place for about 15 minutes.

3 Cut the pork into slices, and serve with gravy, apple sauce, crispy roast potatoes, and seasonal vegetables – and a generous piece of crackling for each portion.

COOK'S NOTES

The butcher will score the skin for you if you ask. For easy carving, remove the crispy crackling in one piece, then slice the meat. Cut up the crackling to serve.

EVERYDAY

Roast pork in pitta bread

PREP 10 MINS COOK 30 MINS

SERVES 2
1 tbsp olive oil
knob of butter
1 onion, finely chopped
50g (1¾oz) fresh breadcrumbs
4 fresh sage leaves, finely chopped
1 egg, lightly beaten
salt and freshly ground black pepper
4 pitta breads
225g (8oz) leftover roast pork,
   thinly sliced
apple sauce, to serve

1 Preheat the oven to 200°C
(400°F/Gas 6). Heat the olive
oil and the butter in a pan over
a low heat. Add the onion, and
sweat gently for about 5 minutes,
until soft and translucent. Stir
through the breadcrumbs and sage,
and cook for a few minutes. Remove
from the heat, and allow to cool.

2 Stir the egg into the cooled
breadcrumb mixture, and season
well with salt and black pepper.
Spoon into a buttered ovenproof
dish, and bake in the oven for about
20 minutes, or until golden brown.

3 Warm the pitta breads in the oven
for a minute or two, or in the toaster,
then slice open the pockets and stuff
with the leftover pork, a spoonful of
breadcrumb and sage stuffing, and
some apple sauce. Serve immediately.

Pork and yellow split pea soup

PREP 15 MINS COOK 55 MINS

SERVES 4
1 tbsp olive oil
knob of butter
1 onion, finely chopped
3 garlic cloves, grated or
   finely chopped
salt and freshly ground black pepper
250g (9oz) dried yellow split peas,
   picked over and rinsed
1.7 litres (3 pints) hot vegetable or
   chicken stock
350g (12oz) leftover roast pork, cut
   into bite-sized pieces
handful of fresh curly parsley,
   finely chopped

1 Heat the olive oil and butter in
a large pan over a low heat. Add the
onion, and sweat gently for about
5 minutes until soft and translucent.
Add the garlic, and cook for a few
seconds. Season with salt and
black pepper.

2 Stir through the split peas, and
pour over the stock. Bring to the boil,
and boil rapidly for about 10 minutes.
Reduce the heat slightly, stir through
the leftover pork, and simmer gently
for 40 minutes, topping up with
a little hot water if the soup gets too
thick. Season well, and stir through
the parsley just before serving.

VARIATION
Add some cubed pancetta or
a few chopped bacon rashers,
if you wish. Add when the
onions have softened, and
cook until golden.

COOK'S NOTES
The split peas will count as one
of your five-a-day portions. Make
sure that you rinse the peas well,
because they can sometimes be
a little gritty.

Pork and spring greens

 PREP 10 MINS COOK 10 MINS

Special equipment • wok

SERVES 4

1 tbsp olive oil

350g (12oz) leftover roast pork, roughly shredded

4 garlic cloves, sliced

2 heads of spring greens, shredded

2 tsp onion seeds

salt and freshly ground black pepper

1 Heat the oil in a wok over a medium-high heat. When the oil is hot, add the leftover pork. Stir-fry for about 5 minutes, moving it around the wok.

2 Add the garlic and greens, and continue to stir-fry over a medium-high heat for about 1 minute, until the greens have just wilted. Add the onion seeds, and stir to combine, then season well with salt and black pepper. Serve immediately, with fluffy rice.

 VARIATION Add a splash of soy sauce at the end of cooking. As it's salty, reduce the seasoning in step 2, if necessary.

COOK'S NOTES

Choose your greens with the seasons – use savoy cabbage, Brussels sprouts, or kale in the winter, and the lighter delicate greens, such as spinach and chard, in the spring and summer.

Sweet and sour pork

PREP 10 MINS COOK 30 MINS

Special equipment • wok

SERVES 4

1 tbsp olive oil

1 onion, peeled and cut into eighths

1 tbsp cornflour

300ml (10fl oz) hot vegetable stock

350g (12oz) leftover roast pork, roughly shredded

200g (7oz) mangetout, halved on the diagonal

For the sweet and sour sauce

2 tbsp tomato purée

2 tbsp light soy sauce

2 tbsp pineapple juice

2 tbsp white wine vinegar

1 tbsp caster sugar

salt and freshly ground black pepper

1 First, make the sweet and sour sauce. In a bowl, mix together the tomato purée, soy sauce, pineapple juice, vinegar, and sugar. Season with salt and black pepper.

2 Heat the oil in a wok over a medium heat. Add the onion, and stir-fry for a few minutes until soft, moving it around the wok so that it doesn't brown. Pour in the sauce, and keep stirring.

3 Mix the cornflour into a paste with 1 tablespoon of water, and add to the sauce along with the stock. Bring to the boil, stirring constantly.

4 Add the leftover pork, reduce the heat to low, and cook for about 15 minutes until the sauce begins to thicken. Add the mangetout for the last 5 minutes of cooking. Taste, and season if needed. Serve immediately with rice or noodles.

BAKED SALMON

PREP 15 MINS · COOK 1¼ HRS

SERVES 4, PLUS LEFTOVERS

3.2–3.6kg (7–8lb) fresh whole salmon, scaled, gutted, and cleaned

125g (4½oz) butter

salt and freshly ground black pepper

handful of fresh flat-leaf parsley, plus extra to garnish

lemon wedges, to serve

1 Preheat the oven to 180°C (350°F/Gas 4). Lay a large piece of foil on a large baking tray (enough to pull up and cover the salmon). Sit the salmon in the middle of the foil, and dot the butter all over it. Season well with salt and black pepper, then scatter the parsley over the fish, stuffing a little in the cavity if you like.

2 Loosely pull together the edges of the foil over the salmon, and seal. Bake in the oven for about 1¼ hours, calculating cooking time at 10 minutes per 450g (1lb), until opaque and cooked through.

3 Unwrap the foil, remove any straggly bits of parsley, and carefully transfer the salmon to a warm plate. Squeeze over the lemon wedges to serve, and garnish with fresh parsley or watercress. Serve with new potatoes and salad, or grilled asparagus.

VARIATION

Salmon is delicious with flavours such as horseradish or beetroot, as they cut wonderfully through the richness. Serve with a spoonful of each on the side, and a watercress salad.

COOK'S NOTES

It's vital that the fish is 100% fresh when you buy it – it should never smell "fishy". Use wild salmon for a special treat.

EVERYDAY

Baked salmon with salsa verde and cucumber

 PREP 15 MINS

SERVES 4

1 cucumber
350g (12oz) leftover baked salmon, sliced or flaked into chunks

For the salsa verde
handful of fresh basil leaves
handful of fresh mint leaves
handful of fresh flat-leaf parsley
2 tbsp white wine vinegar
2 tsp capers, rinsed, gently squeezed dry, and finely chopped
2 garlic cloves, grated or finely chopped
8 anchovies in oil, drained and finely chopped
2 tsp wholegrain mustard
salt and freshly ground black pepper
6 tbsp extra virgin olive oil

1 To make the salsa verde, finely chop all the herbs, and put in a bowl. Drizzle in the vinegar, and stir through. Add the capers, garlic, and anchovies, and stir again. Now add the mustard, and season well with salt and black pepper. Slowly stir in the olive oil. Taste, and adjust the seasoning if needed, adding a little more vinegar or oil as required. Transfer to a serving bowl.

2 Peel the cucumber, slice in half lengthways, and scoop out the seeds using a teaspoon. Dice the flesh, and put in a serving bowl.

3 To serve, arrange the leftover salmon on a platter or 4 serving plates. Spoon the salsa verde over the fish, and place the cucumber on the side.

VARIATION Use raspberry vinegar instead of white wine vinegar – it works wonderfully with salmon.

Salmon and prawn fish pie

 PREP 15 MINS **COOK 35 MINS**

Special equipment • 1.2-litre (2-pint) ovenproof dish

SERVES 2

675g (1½lb) potatoes, peeled and quartered
300ml (10fl oz) milk, plus 2 tbsp extra for mashing potatoes
350g (12oz) leftover baked salmon, flaked into chunks
200g (7oz) cooked, peeled, and deveined prawns
salt and freshly ground black pepper
knob of butter, plus extra for topping
1 tbsp plain flour
1 tbsp wholegrain mustard

1 Preheat the oven to 200°C (400°F/ Gas 6). Cook the potatoes in a pan of boiling salted water for about 15 minutes until soft; drain. Mash well until there are no lumps, then add 2 tablespoons of milk; mash again until smooth. Set aside.

2 Arrange the leftover salmon and prawns in the ovenproof dish so that they are evenly distributed. Season with salt and black pepper, and set aside.

3 Gently melt the butter in a pan over a low heat. Remove from the heat, and stir in the flour with a wooden spoon. Add a little milk and beat until smooth. Return the pan to the heat, and continue adding the milk, a little at a time, stirring constantly, until the sauce has thickened. Whisk to get rid of any lumps, then stir through the mustard.

4 Pour the sauce over the prawns and salmon, and combine. Cover with the mashed potato to make a topping, and dot with extra butter. Bake in the oven for 15–20 minutes until heated through and the topping is crisp and golden.

Cheat... Use a 200g carton of ready-made white or cheese sauce, and stir the mustard into it.

Salmon and roasted tomato pasta

 PREP 15 MINS **COOK 30 MINS**

SERVES 4

12 cherry tomatoes

1 tbsp olive oil

350g (12oz) dried pasta, such
    as penne

350g (12oz) leftover baked salmon,
    flaked into chunks

salt and freshly ground
    black pepper

drizzle of chilli oil

1 Preheat the oven to 200°C
(400°F/Gas 6). Put the cherry
tomatoes in a roasting tin, and
drizzle over the olive oil. Roast
in the oven for 15–20 minutes, until
the tomatoes are beginning to char
slightly and the skins are bursting.

2 Meanwhile, cook the pasta in
a pan of boiling salted water for
about 10 minutes, or until it is
cooked but still has a bit of bite
to it. Drain, and return to the pan
with a little of the cooking water.
Add the leftover salmon and
roast tomatoes, toss together, and
season with salt and black pepper.
Drizzle over a little chilli oil, and
serve immediately.

 VARIATION

Add some wild rocket leaves
or fresh basil leaves when
you combine the salmon
and tomatoes.

Salmon with new potatoes, flageolet beans, and parsley sauce

 PREP 15 MINS **COOK 30 MINS**

SERVES 4

675g (1½lb) new potatoes

knob of butter

1 tbsp plain flour

300ml (10fl oz) milk

150ml (5fl oz) double cream

salt and freshly ground
    black pepper

handful of fresh curly parsley, very
    finely chopped

400g can flageolet beans, drained
    and rinsed

handful of fresh dill, finely chopped

350g (12oz) leftover baked salmon,
    sliced or flaked into chunks

1 Cook the potatoes in a pan of
boiling salted water for 15–20
minutes until soft. Drain, and set
aside to keep warm.

2 Meanwhile, melt the butter
in a pan over a low heat. Remove
from the heat, and stir in the flour
with a wooden spoon. Add a little
of the milk, and beat until smooth.

Return the pan to the heat, and
continue adding the milk, and then
the cream, a little at a time, stirring
constantly. Simmer for 5–8 minutes,
then use a balloon whisk to get rid
of any lumps. Remove from the heat,
season well with salt and black
pepper, and stir through the parsley.

3 Put the beans in a pan, and
gently heat through. Season if you
like, and stir through the dill. Serve
the leftover salmon on a platter or
individual plates with the flageolet
beans and new potatoes on the side,
and the parsley sauce spooned over
the salmon and potatoes.

ROAST RIB OF BEEF

PREP 10 MINS **COOK 1¼ HRS**

SERVES 4, PLUS LEFTOVERS

2.25kg (5lb) rib of beef, bone in (use 2 ribs)

olive oil, to coat

salt and freshly ground black pepper

1–2 tbsp wholegrain mustard

1 Preheat the oven to 200°C (400°F/Gas 6). Rub the beef with olive oil, and season with salt and black pepper.

2 Sit the beef in a roasting tin with the bones on the underside, and rub the mustard over the fatty area. Roast in the oven for about 15 minutes until it begins to brown, then reduce the oven temperature to 180°C (350°F/Gas 4). Roast for a further 1 hour, or until cooked to your liking (see Cook's Notes).

3 Remove the beef from the oven, and leave to rest in a warm place for about 20 minutes. Slice and serve with roast potatoes, Yorkshire pudding, creamed horseradish, and seasonal vegetables of your choice. Remember to save your beef bones for making stock.

VARIATION

If cooking beef off the bone, reduce the cooking time by a couple of minutes per 450g (1lb).

COOK'S NOTES

Always preheat the oven so that it is hot and at the correct temperature before the meat goes in. For beef on the bone: for rare, cook for 10–12 minutes per 450g (1lb) plus 12 minutes; for medium, cook for 12–15 minutes per 450g (1lb) plus 12 minutes; for well done, cook for 18–20 minutes per 450g (1lb) plus 18 minutes.

239

EVERYDAY

Beef and Stilton pie

 PREP 20 MINS COOK 50 MINS

Special equipment • 1.2-litre (2-pint) pie dish

SERVES 2

1 tbsp olive oil
knob of butter
2 onions, roughly chopped
350g (12oz) leftover
   roast beef, sliced
150ml (5fl oz) hot beef stock
salt and freshly ground
   black pepper
125g (4½oz) blue cheese, such
   as Stilton
250g (9oz) ready-made puff pastry
1 egg, lightly beaten,
   for egg wash

1 Preheat the oven to 200°C (400°F/ Gas 6). Heat the oil and the butter in a pan over a low heat. Add the onion, and sweat very gently for 5–8 minutes until soft and translucent.

2 Add the leftover beef, and pour over the stock. Bring to the boil, reduce the heat slightly, and simmer for about 10 minutes. Season with salt and black pepper. Cool slightly, then spoon the mixture into the pie dish, and crumble over the cheese.

3 On a floured work surface, roll out the pastry until it is a little larger than the pie dish. Wet the edge of the dish with a little water. Cut out a strip of pastry about 2.5cm (1in) from the edge to make a collar. Wet the edge of the pie dish with a little water; fit the pastry strip all the way around, and press down firmly. Brush the collar with a little egg wash, and top with the pastry lid. Trim away the excess. Using your finger and thumb, pinch together the edges to seal. Brush all over with egg wash, make a slit in the top, and bake in the oven for 30–40 minutes until golden and puffed. Serve hot.

Thai-style beef salad

 PREP 15 MINS

SERVES 4

350g (12oz) leftover
   roast beef, sliced
2 carrots, cut into fine strips
½ onion, cut into fine strips
125g (4½oz) bamboo shoots
handful of fresh mint leaves
handful of fresh basil leaves
handful of fresh coriander,
   leaves only, plus extra
   to garnish
salt and freshly ground
   black pepper
juice of 1 lime
2–3 tsp caster sugar
1 fresh hot red chilli, deseeded and
   finely chopped
1–2 tbsp Thai fish sauce,
   such as nam pla

1 Put the leftover beef, carrots, onion, bamboo shoots, fresh mint leaves, fresh basil leaves, and coriander in a large bowl, and toss together gently. Season with salt and black pepper.

2 In a small bowl or jug, whisk together the lime juice, sugar, chilli, and fish sauce. Taste, and adjust the seasoning if needed. Pour the dressing over the salad, then garnish with the extra coriander leaves. Serve immediately.

> COOK'S NOTES
>
> Raw onion can be strong — if you prefer a milder flavour, soak the strips of onion in cold water for 10 minutes before using, or use thinly sliced spring onions instead.

Beef stroganoff

PREP 15 MINS **COOK 30 MINS**

Soaking • 30 minutes

SERVES 4

25g (scant 1oz) dried
   porcini mushrooms
1 tbsp olive oil
1 onion, finely chopped
salt and freshly ground black pepper
350g (12oz) leftover roast beef, sliced
   into strips
150–300ml (5–10fl oz) hot
   vegetable stock
300ml (10fl oz) double cream
pinch of chilli flakes

1 Soak the porcini mushrooms
in 300ml (10fl oz) of hot water
for 30 minutes. Heat the olive oil
in a large frying pan over a low heat.
Add the onion, and sweat gently for
about 5 minutes until soft and
translucent. Season well with salt
and black pepper.

2 Drain the mushrooms (reserve the
liquid), and add to the onion with
the leftover beef. Pour the mushroom
soaking liquid through a fine sieve,
and add to the pan with about half
of the stock. Bring to the boil, then
reduce the heat to a simmer.

3 Add the double cream and chilli
flakes, and simmer gently over
a medium-low heat for about
20 minutes, adding more stock
as needed. Check the seasoning,
and serve hot with fluffy white rice
or noodles.

Beef with beetroot and spinach

PREP 15 MINS ♡

SERVES 4

350g (12oz) leftover roast beef, sliced
250g (9oz) fresh spinach
   leaves, rinsed
450g (1lb) ready-cooked beetroot, not
   in vinegar, quartered
3 tbsp extra virgin olive oil
1 tbsp balsamic vinegar
juice of ½ clementine or satsuma
salt and freshly ground black pepper
handful of fresh thyme, leaves picked

1 In a large bowl, gently toss
together the leftover beef, spinach,
and beetroot. In a small bowl or jug,
whisk together the olive oil, balsamic
vinegar, and citrus juice. Season with
salt and black pepper.

2 When ready to serve, drizzle
the dressing over the beef and
beetroot salad, and scatter over
the thyme leaves.

VARIATION

Use freshly squeezed
orange juice if you can't find
clementines or satsumas.

Cheat...

For speed, drizzle with
balsamic vinegar, and
leave out the other
dressing ingredients.

241

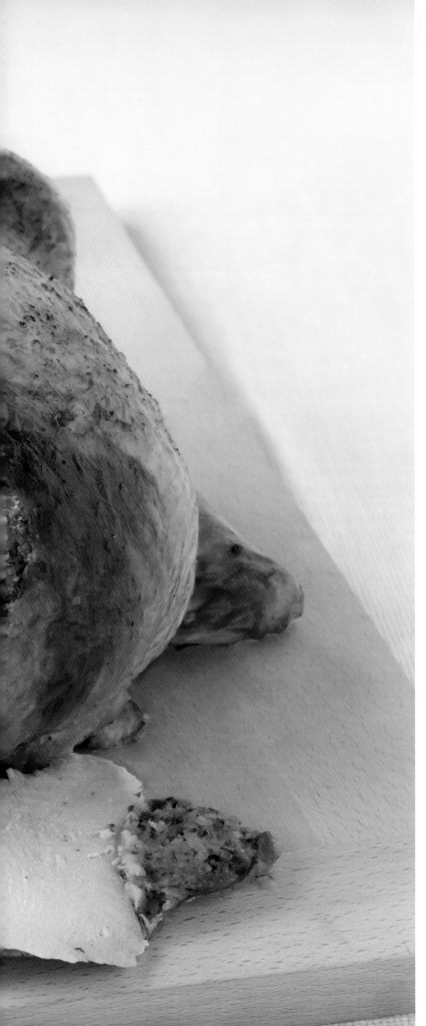

ROAST TURKEY

 PREP 15 MINS **COOK 3¼ HRS**

SERVES 6, PLUS LEFTOVERS

3 onions, 1 finely chopped, 2 peeled
  and quartered

250g (9oz) butter

125g (4½oz) breadcrumbs

handful of fresh flat-leaf parsley, finely chopped

salt and freshly ground black pepper

4kg (9lb) turkey

1 First, make the stuffing. Melt half the butter in a pan over a low heat, add the chopped onion, and sweat gently until soft. Remove from the heat, stir through the breadcrumbs and parsley, season, and set aside to cool. Preheat the oven to 200°C (400°F/Gas 6). Sit the turkey in a large roasting tin, and season, inside and out. Spread the remaining butter over the skin. Stuff the onion quarters into the body cavity, and the stuffing into the neck end. Roast for 20 minutes, then reduce the oven temperature to 190°C (375°F/Gas 5).

2 Cover the turkey loosely with foil, and roast for 20 minutes per 450g (1lb) plus 20 minutes. Baste every hour with juices from the tin. Pierce the bird with a skewer. If the juices run clear, it is ready; if not, cook for a little longer. Remove the foil for the last 10–15 minutes.

3 Remove the turkey from the tin, and put on a large warmed plate. Cover with foil, and leave to rest in a warm place for 15 minutes. Serve slices of turkey with gravy, roast potatoes, cranberry sauce, and seasonal vegetables.

EVERYDAY

Turkey, almond, and cranberry pilaf

PREP 15 MINS   **COOK 30 MINS**

SERVES 4

1 tbsp olive oil

1 onion, finely chopped

3 garlic cloves, grated or
    finely chopped

250g (9oz) basmati rice

900ml (1½ pints) hot vegetable stock

350g (12oz) leftover roast turkey,
    sliced or shredded

salt and freshly ground black pepper

125g (4½oz) flaked almonds, toasted

175g (6oz) dried cranberries

handful of fresh thyme sprigs,
    leaves picked

1 Heat the oil in a large frying pan over a low heat. Add the onion, and sweat gently for about 5 minutes, or until soft and translucent. Add the garlic, and cook, stirring, for a few seconds. Tip in the rice, and stir until the grains are well coated.

2 Pour in the stock, and bring to the boil. Reduce the heat slightly, add the leftover turkey, and stir through. Simmer gently for 20–25 minutes, until the stock has been absorbed and the rice is cooked, topping up with more hot stock as it cooks, if needed. Season well with salt and black pepper.

3 Just before serving, stir through the toasted almonds and cranberries. Sprinkle over the thyme, stir through, and serve hot.

Turkey and noodles

PREP 15 MINS   **COOK 15 MINS**

Special equipment • wok

SERVES 4

1 tbsp sunflower oil

450g (1lb) straight-to-wok
    medium rice noodles

1 bunch of spring onions,
    finely chopped

2 garlic cloves, grated or
    finely chopped

350g (12oz) leftover roast turkey,
    any skin removed, sliced or
    roughly shredded

2 tbsp oyster sauce

2 tbsp Thai fish sauce, such as
    nam pla

1 fresh hot red chilli, deseeded
    and finely chopped

1 tsp sugar

200g (7oz) beansprouts

salt and freshly ground
    black pepper

1 Heat the oil in a wok over a medium-high heat. Add the noodles, and stir-fry for a couple of minutes. Add the spring onions, and toss together. Now add the garlic, and stir-fry for a few seconds more. Remove the mixture from the wok, and set aside.

2 Add the leftover turkey to the wok, and stir-fry over a medium heat for a minute or two, then add the oyster sauce, fish sauce, chilli, and sugar. Cook over a high heat for a few minutes to heat through.

3 Return the noodle mixture to the wok along with the beansprouts, and toss in the sauce until well coated. Taste, and season well with salt and black pepper. Serve immediately.

Warm turkey and chickpea salad

PREP 15 MINS   COOK 10 MINS

SERVES 4

400g can chickpeas, drained
   and rinsed
1 tbsp olive oil
pinch of mild paprika
juice of 1 lemon
salt and freshly ground
   black pepper
350g (12oz) leftover roast
   turkey, sliced or roughly
   shredded
handful of fresh dill,
   finely chopped

1 Put the chickpeas in a pan, and pour over the olive oil, add the paprika and lemon juice, and season well with salt and black pepper. Simmer very gently over a low heat for 5–8 minutes, until the chickpeas have softened slightly and warmed through.

2 To serve, toss the chickpeas with the leftover turkey, taste, and season again if needed. Scatter over the fresh dill, and serve warm with a fresh green salad or some wilted spinach.

VARIATION

You could use canned white beans instead of chickpeas: try cannellini or butter beans.

Spiced turkey and greens stir-fry

PREP 10 MINS   COOK 25 MINS

Special equipment • food processor • wok

SERVES 4

350g (12oz) leftover roast turkey, any
   skin removed, roughly chopped
2 heads of Asian greens such as pak
   choi, trimmed and roughly chopped
1 tbsp sunflower oil
1 onion, finely chopped
5cm (2in) piece of fresh root ginger,
   finely sliced
3 garlic cloves, grated or
   finely chopped
2 green chillies, deseeded and
   finely chopped
1 tbsp dark soy sauce
1 tbsp mirin
handful of fresh basil leaves, torn
salt and freshly ground
   black pepper

1 Put the leftover turkey in the food processor, and process until minced; be careful not to turn it into a paste. Cook the greens in a pan of boiling salted water for about 5 minutes until just wilted. Drain, and set aside.

2 Heat the oil in a wok or large frying pan over a low heat. Add the onion, and sweat gently for about 5 minutes until soft and translucent. Add the ginger, garlic, and chillies, and cook for a further 5 minutes, stirring constantly.

3 Tip in the minced turkey, and stir well to combine. Add the soy sauce and mirin, and stir-fry for 5–8 minutes until the turkey is warmed through. Stir through the reserved greens and the basil, and season with salt and black pepper. Serve immediately.

BATCH AND FREEZE

Some to eat now, and some for the freezer.

BATCH AND FREEZE

Make-ahead dishes for the freezer save you time and effort, meaning you can shop less, cook less, and have meals ready for the oven or microwave – a lifesaver for the busy cook. Batch cooking can simply mean doubling up on your cooking one night and freezing half, or dedicating a day to cooking several quantities for the freezer.

Psst...

Slow defrosting overnight in the refrigerator is not only the safest way to defrost, it is also the best way to retain the food's original flavour and texture. Once food is thawed, warm it through as soon as possible.

Foods you can freeze and what to freeze them in.

FOOD	PACKAGING	STORAGE LIFE	DEFROST AND REHEAT
SOUPS AND STOCKS These are ideal for freezing. Once cooked, leave to cool completely, then pack into 500ml (16fl oz) portions. Don't freeze in over-large portions, as defrosting will take too long.	Pack in sealable freezer bags or rigid sealable plastic containers. The liquid will expand a little, so leave room for this, or spoon stock into ice cube trays and freeze. Once frozen, remove from tray and transfer to a freezer bag and seal. Label.	Soups for up to **3 months** Stocks for up to **6 months**	Thaw overnight in the refrigerator, then reheat in a pan until piping hot, or heat in the microwave on High for a few minutes.
SAUCES AND GRAVIES These are great for freezing and take up little space. If sauces call for the addition of egg yolk or cream omit and add later. Cool completely before freezing.	Freeze in sealable freezer bags or ice cube trays. If using ice cube trays, once frozen, remove from the tray, transfer to a freezer bag, and seal. For thicker sauces, flatten in the bag so storage space is minimal. Leave air space for expansion. Label.	Up to **3 months**	Thaw overnight in the refrigerator, then reheat in a pan until piping hot, or heat in the microwave on High for a few minutes.
STEWS AND CASSEROLES These freeze well and are ideal for batch-cooking. Foods with a very high fat content will go rancid after a couple of months in the freezer, so choose lean cuts of meat. When doubling up recipes, be careful with the seasoning. As a rule of thumb, you will only need to add 1½ times the seasoning. Cool completely before freezing.	Freeze in sealable freezer bags or foil containers, or ladle into rigid sealable plastic containers. Make sure meat is well covered with liquid, otherwise it will dry out. Label.	Up to **3 months**	Thaw overnight in the refrigerator, then reheat in a pan until piping hot, or heat in the microwave on High for a few minutes. Or, reheat in the oven in a casserole at 180°C (350°F/ Gas 4), for about 30 minutes, or until piping hot. Take extra care that the meat is really hot and do not reheat more than once.
PIES AND PASTRIES Baking is the ideal time to batch cook. You can freeze pastry cooked or uncooked. Cool completely before freezing.	**Uncooked** Freeze blocks of pastry layered with wax paper, then wrapped in cling film. Label. **Cooked** Freeze pastry cases and pies wrapped in a double layer of cling film. Label.	**Uncooked** pies and pastry for up to **3 months** **Cooked** pies and pastry cases for up to **6 months**	**Uncooked** tart cases and pastries can be cooked from frozen in the oven at 200°C (400°F/Gas 6), for about 15 minutes. **Cooked** pies and pastry cases should thaw overnight in the refrigerator, then reheat in the oven at 180°C (350°F/Gas 4), for about 30 minutes, or until piping hot.

Portion sizes

Planning If you plan to make more than double or triple batches at a time, think ahead a little, as soups and stews only freeze for up to 3 months, and you don't want too much of one dish.

Amounts When batch-cooking soups, allow about 300ml (10fl oz) per person. Don't freeze portion sizes any larger than 600ml (1 pint).

Sizes It's advisable to freeze sauces in different portion sizes, to suit your requirements, and don't forget to freeze plenty of portions-for-one, for when you are home alone and don't want to cook.

foods that don't freeze well

Cream cheese or **cottage cheese** will separate or become watery, as will **cream**, unless it has been lightly whipped first. **Mayonnaise** and **hollandaise** sauce will also separate when they are defrosted. **Fatty foods** become fattier, and eventually turn rancid, and salad ingredients such as **cucumber**, **lettuce**, **celery**, and **tomatoes** turn to water once defrosted. If you are unsure whether something will freeze, test a small amount first, to avoid any wastage.

5 tips for freezing
Follow these guidelines and there will be no loss of quality of texture, taste, colour, or nutrients.

If freezing large amounts of different foods, use different coloured bags or boxes, use labels, and adopt a colour coding system for yourself so you know what is what.

The coldest part of the freezer is the bottom, so foods will freeze quicker if stored here. Keep this in mind if you want to save on solid containers, and are using an ice cube tray or cookware to freeze food before re-packing into foil, double-wrapped cling film, or bags.

When putting containers of food in the freezer, leave plenty of room around them so they can freeze quicker. Once frozen, they can be removed from the container, packed tightly in foil, double-wrapped cling film, or bags with everything else.

Always be aware that the fresher the food is when it goes in the freezer, the better it will be when it comes out.

Remember to rotate things in the freezer so everything gets used in time. It's first in, first out!

Frozen pre-prepared vegetables stay fresh in space-saving freezerproof plastic bags.

EVERYDAY

249

Freezer packaging The right packaging will protect the food so it keeps for longer.

PLASTIC CONTAINERS
Rigid plastic containers can be used to freeze all foods. Use ones that are durable so they don't become brittle and crack at low temperatures. They are available in all shapes and sizes and are easy to label and reuse.

FOIL
Foil can be used to create your own dish, especially if you have a limited collection of ovenware. Double-line an ovenproof dish with foil, then fill with the food for cooking. Cook as per recipe, leave to cool completely, then put in the freezer. Once frozen, lift out the foil dish and either wrap well in cling film, or put in a large freezer bag, seal, and return to the freezer. Alternatively, fill the foil-lined dish and freeze it uncooked.

ICE CUBE TRAYS
Ideal for freezing small amounts of sauce or stock. Carefully fill with the liquid and freeze when completely cool. Once frozen, transfer the cubes to plastic freezer bags and seal (otherwise the food will get freezer burn). Use this method to freeze leftover red wine, which you can then add to gravies or sauces.

BAGS FOR LIQUID
Line a plastic container with a freezerproof bag, then fill with stock, soup, or sauce, and seal well with wire clips, leaving some room for the contents to expand. Freeze solid, then remove the container and stack the solid bag (labelled).

PLASTIC FREEZER BAGS
Most foods can be stored in polythene freezer bags. They need to be strong, leakproof, and resistant to moisture. Bags with a built-in seal are ideal for all sauces and stews, and blanched vegetables.

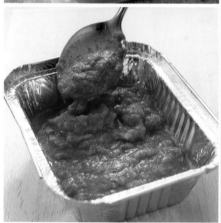

FOIL DISHES
A good choice if freezing foods for a few months. Use heavy-duty aluminium ones; you can cook, freeze, and reheat them in the oven. The foil trays can be recycled, but not the lids, as these are cardboard.

Labelling
Always label and date your food, using a permanent pen, so it won't rub off. Write directly onto the packaging or use labels designed for the freezer (they won't get damp and peel away). If leaving it for other people to reheat, write instructions on the bag or label.

Contents: _Chicken Casserole_

Weight/Portions: _1lb (for 4)_

Packed on: _23/09/08_

Expires on: _23/12/08_

Reheating directions: _120°C_ for _45_ minutes or until done

Psst...
Never re-freeze anything that's already been frozen. There is an increased risk of bacteria multiplying in the thawing process before re-freezing, and the quality of the food will be severely impaired.

3 quick sauces
Batch-freeze these for when you're short on time. You'll be able to make lasagne, curries, and pasta dishes in minutes.

Curry sauce
Use with chicken, prawns, or vegetables. Makes enough sauce for 6–8 servings.

Make
Heat 2 tablespoons of **olive oil** in a large deep-sided frying pan, and add 2 finely chopped **onions**. Cook over a low heat for about 8 minutes, or until soft and translucent. Stir through 2 teaspoons of **ground cumin**, 3 chopped **garlic cloves**, 3 deseeded and finely chopped **fresh medium-hot red chillies**, a grated 5cm (2in) piece of **fresh root ginger**, and cook for a few seconds, then stir in 2 teaspoons each of **garam masala** and **turmeric**, 2 tablespoons of **tomato purée**, and 3 x 400g cans of **chopped tomatoes**. Season well, bring to the boil, and simmer for about 20 minutes. Whiz until smooth with a stick blender, or in a food processor.

Freeze
Leave to cool completely, then transfer to sealable freezer bags in the required portion sizes, label, and freeze.

Reheat
To use, defrost overnight in the refrigerator, then reheat in a pan for 15–20 minutes over a medium-high heat, or in a microwave on High for a few minutes, adding some double cream or yogurt, if you wish.

Cheese sauce
Use with vegetables, bakes, or pasta. Makes enough sauce for 6–8 servings.

Make
Melt 150g (5½oz) of **butter** in a large pan, then remove from the heat and stir in 2 tablespoons of **plain flour** to form a roux. Pour in a little milk, taken from 1.2 litres (2 pints) of **milk**, then put it back on the heat and slowly add the milk, stirring all the time. When all the milk has been added, switch to a balloon whisk and whisk until smooth, over a low heat, for about 5 minutes. Remove from the heat and add 150g (5½oz) of grated **mature Cheddar cheese**, and 2 teaspoons of **Dijon mustard**, and season well.

Freeze
Leave to cool completely, then transfer to sealable freezer bags in the required portion sizes, label, and freeze.

Reheat
To use, defrost overnight in the refrigerator, then reheat in a pan for 10–15 minutes, over a low-medium heat, or in a microwave on High for a few minutes.

Red pepper sauce
Use with pasta, vegetables, or chicken. Makes enough sauce for 6–8 servings.

Make
Roast 6 **red peppers** in the oven at 200°C (400°F/Gas 6) for 15–20 minutes, or until charred and blistered. Leave to cool in a plastic bag (see p59), then peel and chop. Heat 2 tablespoons of **olive oil** in a large deep-sided frying pan and add 2 finely chopped **onions**. Cook over a low heat for about 8 minutes, or until soft and translucent, then add 3 chopped **garlic cloves** and cook for a few seconds. Add the roasted peppers and stir, then pour in 750ml (1¼ pints) of **vegetable stock**, and bring to the boil. Simmer for about 15 minutes, then whiz with a stick blender. Stir through 1 tablespoon of **red pesto**, season well, then whiz again.

Freeze
Leave to cool completely, then transfer to sealable freezer bags in the required portion sizes, label, and freeze.

Reheat
To use, defrost overnight in the refrigerator, then reheat in a pan for 15–20 minutes, over a medium-high heat, or in a microwave on High for a few minutes. Check for seasoning, and add some fresh herbs, if you wish.

Chestnut and bacon soup

   PREP 15 MINS | COOK 30 MINS

Special equipment • blender or food processor

SERVES 8
2 tbsp olive oil
2 onions, finely chopped
250g (9oz) bacon or pancetta, chopped into
   bite-sized pieces
4 garlic cloves, grated or finely chopped
1 tbsp rosemary leaves, finely chopped
salt and freshly ground black pepper
3 x 200g packets ready-cooked chestnuts, chopped
1.2 litres (2 pints) hot chicken stock

1 Heat the oil in a large pan, add the onions, and
cook over a low heat for 5–8 minutes, or until soft
and translucent. Add the bacon or pancetta and
cook for 5 minutes, or until crispy. Stir in the garlic
and rosemary, then season well with salt and
black pepper.

2 Stir in the chestnuts, pour in the stock, and bring
to the boil. Lower the heat and simmer for 15–20
minutes. Using a slotted spoon, remove a couple
of spoonfuls of the bacon and put to one side.
Transfer the rest of the soup to a blender or food
processor and whiz until puréed. Season again
with salt and black pepper if needed, then add
the reserved bacon pieces.

3 Leave to cool completely, then transfer to
a freezerproof container. Make sure the bacon
pieces are covered, seal, and freeze for up to
3 months. To serve, defrost overnight in the
refrigerator, transfer to a pan, and heat until piping
hot. Add a little hot water if the soup is too thick.
Serve with a drizzle of extra virgin olive oil and
fresh crusty bread.

Bean and rosemary soup

PREP 15 MINS | COOK 40 MINS

SERVES 8
2 tbsp olive oil, plus a little extra
   (according to taste)
2 onions, finely chopped
salt and freshly ground black pepper
1 tbsp fresh rosemary leaves, finely chopped
a few sage leaves, finely chopped
4 celery sticks, finely chopped
3 garlic cloves, grated or finely chopped
2 tbsp tomato purée
2 x 400g cans cannellini beans, drained and rinsed
1.2 litres (2 pints) hot chicken stock
2.5kg (5½lb) potatoes, cut into chunky pieces

1 Heat the oil in a large pan, add the onions, and
cook over a low heat for 6–8 minutes, or until soft
and translucent. Season well with salt and black
pepper, then stir in the rosemary, sage, celery,
and garlic, and cook over a very low heat, stirring
occasionally, for 10 minutes.

2 Stir through the tomato purée and beans, add
a little more olive oil if you wish, and cook gently
for 5 minutes. Pour in the stock, bring to the boil,
then add the potatoes and simmer gently for
15 minutes, or until cooked. Taste and season
again with salt and black pepper if needed.

3 Leave the soup to cool completely, then transfer
to a plastic freezerproof container. Seal, and freeze for
up to 3 months. To serve, defrost in the refrigerator
overnight, then transfer to a pan and simmer gently
until piping hot. Add a little hot stock if the soup is
too thick. Serve with fresh crusty bread.

Sweetcorn chowder

PREP 15 MINS | COOK 25 MINS

SERVES 8
2 tbsp olive oil
2 onions, finely chopped
salt and freshly ground black pepper
6–8 medium potatoes, cut into bite-sized pieces
2 x 340g cans sweetcorn, drained
1.4 litres (2½ pints) hot vegetable stock
handful of fresh flat-leaf parsley, finely chopped
4 tbsp double cream (optional), to serve

1 Heat the oil in a large pan, add the onions, and
cook over a low heat for 6–8 minutes, or until soft
and translucent. Season well with salt and black
pepper, then stir in the potatoes and cook over
a low heat for 5 minutes.

2 Mash the sweetcorn a little with the back of
a fork, then add to the pan. Pour in the stock, bring
to the boil, then reduce to a simmer and cook for
15 minutes, or until the potatoes are soft. Stir
through the parsley and season again with salt
and black pepper if needed.

3 Leave to cool completely, then transfer to
a freezerproof container and seal. Freeze for
up to 3 months. To serve, defrost overnight in the
refrigerator, then transfer to a pan and heat until
piping hot. Stir through the cream (if using), and
serve with fresh crusty bread.

Red lentil and tomato soup

PREP 15 MINS · COOK 50 MINS

Special equipment • blender or food processor

SERVES 8

2 tbsp olive oil
2 onions, finely chopped
4 garlic cloves, grated or finely chopped
pinch of chilli flakes
4 carrots, finely chopped
salt and freshly ground black pepper
450g (1lb) red lentils
3 x 400g cans whole tomatoes, chopped in the can
1.4 litres (2½ pints) hot vegetable stock

1 Heat the oil in a large pan, add the onions, and cook over a low heat for 6–8 minutes, or until soft and translucent. Stir through the garlic, chilli, and carrots, season with salt and black pepper, and cook for 2 minutes.

2 Add the lentils, stir, then add the tomatoes and stock. Bring to the boil, then simmer on a very low heat for 35–40 minutes, or until the lentils are soft. Transfer to a blender or food processor and whiz until blended and smooth. Taste, and season with salt and black pepper if needed.

3 Leave to cool completely, then transfer to a freezerproof container, seal, and freeze for up to 3 months. To serve, defrost in the refrigerator overnight, then transfer to a pan and heat until piping hot.

Cauliflower soup

PREP 15 MINS · COOK 40 MINS

Special equipment • blender or food processor

SERVES 8

2 tbsp olive oil
2 onions, finely chopped
salt and freshly ground black pepper
3 garlic cloves, grated or finely chopped
4 celery sticks, finely chopped
2 bay leaves
675g (2lb) potatoes, cut into bite-sized pieces
1.4 litres (2½ pints) hot vegetable stock
2 cauliflowers, trimmed and cut into florets
drizzle of double cream (optional), to serve

1 Heat the oil in large pan, add the onions, and cook over a low heat for 6–8 minutes, or until soft and translucent. Season well with salt and black pepper, then add the garlic, celery, and bay leaves, and cook for 5 minutes, or until the celery begins to soften. Stir in the potatoes and cook for 5 minutes, then pour in the stock, bring to the boil, and cook for 15 minutes, or until the potatoes are nearly soft.

2 Add the cauliflower and cook for 10 minutes, or until it is soft but not watery. Remove the bay leaves and discard, then transfer the soup to a blender or food processor and whiz until smooth. Add a little more hot stock if it seems too thick. Taste, and season with salt and black pepper if needed.

3 Leave to cool completely, then transfer to a freezerproof container, seal, and freeze for up to 3 months. To serve, defrost in the refrigerator overnight, transfer to a pan, and heat until piping hot. Drizzle with double cream (if using), and serve with fresh crusty bread.

Leek and potato soup

PREP 15 MINS · COOK 40 MINS

Special equipment • blender or food processor

SERVES 8

2 tbsp olive oil
2 onions, finely chopped
salt and freshly ground black pepper
3 garlic cloves, grated or finely chopped
6 sage leaves, finely chopped
900g (2lb) leeks, cleaned and finely sliced
1.4 litres (2½ pints) hot vegetable stock
900g (2lb) potatoes, roughly chopped
150ml (5fl oz) double cream, to serve

1 Heat the oil in a large pan, add the onions, and cook over a low heat for 6–8 minutes, or until soft and translucent. Season with salt and black pepper, then stir in the garlic and sage. Add the leeks and stir well, then cook over a low heat for 10 minutes, or until the leeks are starting to soften.

2 Pour in the stock, bring to the boil, then add the potatoes and simmer for 20 minutes, or until soft. Transfer to a blender or food processor and whiz until blended and smooth. Taste, and season with salt and black pepper if needed.

3 Leave to cool completely, then transfer to a freezerproof container, seal, and freeze for up to 3 months. To serve, defrost in the refrigerator overnight, then transfer to a pan, stir in the cream, and heat until piping hot.

EVERYDAY

253

Black bean and coconut soup

PREP 15 MINS · COOK 30 MINS

Special equipment • blender or food processor

SERVES 8

2 tbsp olive oil
2 red onions, finely chopped
2 bay leaves
salt and freshly ground black pepper
4 garlic cloves, grated or finely chopped
2 tsp ground cumin
2 tsp ground coriander
1 tsp chilli powder
2 x 400g cans black beans, drained and rinsed
1.2 litres (2 pints) hot vegetable stock
400ml can coconut milk
flour tortillas, to serve

1 Heat the oil in a large pan, add the onions and bay leaves, and cook over a low heat for 6–8 minutes, or until the onions are soft and translucent. Season well with salt and black pepper. Stir through the garlic, cumin, coriander, and chilli powder and cook for a few seconds.

2 Stir through the black beans, then pour in the stock and coconut milk. Bring to the boil, then reduce to a simmer and cook for 15–20 minutes. Remove the bay leaves and discard, then transfer the rest of the soup to a blender or food processor and pulse ja couple of times so some of the beans are puréed and some remain whole. Add a little more stock if it is too thick. Season again with salt and black pepper.

3 Leave to cool completely, then transfer to a freezerproof container, seal, and freeze for up to 3 months. To serve, defrost in the refrigerator overnight, then transfer to a pan and heat until piping hot. Serve with tortilla triangles.

Ribollita

PREP 20 MINS · COOK 40 MINS

SERVES 8

2 tbsp olive oil
2 onions, finely chopped
salt and freshly ground black pepper
4 garlic cloves, grated or finely chopped
4 carrots, finely chopped
8 tomatoes, skinned and roughly chopped
2 x 400g cans cannellini beans, drained and rinsed
450g (1lb) potatoes, cut into bite-sized pieces
350g (12oz) cavolo nero or curly kale, chopped
1.4 litres (2½ pints) hot vegetable stock
1 tbsp fresh rosemary leaves, finely chopped
½ ciabatta, cut into cubes, to serve
drizzle of olive oil, plus extra to serve
freshly grated Parmesan cheese, to serve

1 Heat the oil in a large pan, add the onions, and cook over a low heat for 6–8 minutes, or until soft and translucent. Season with salt and black pepper, add the garlic and carrots, and cook for 5 minutes.

2 Stir through the tomatoes, beans, potatoes, and cavolo nero or curly kale and cook for 5 minutes. Pour in the stock, add the rosemary, and simmer on a low heat for 15–20 minutes, or until the potatoes are soft. Taste, and season with salt and black pepper.

3 Leave to cool completely, then transfer to a freezerproof container, making sure everything is covered with liquid (add some more stock if needed). Seal and freeze for up to 3 months. To serve, defrost overnight in the refrigerator. Preheat the oven to 200°C (400°F/Gas 6). Place the ciabatta cubes on a baking tray, drizzle with olive oil, and bake in the oven for 10 minutes, or until golden. Meanwhile, transfer the soup to a pan and heat until piping hot. Serve topped with the ciabatta, a drizzle of olive oil, and a sprinkling of Parmesan cheese.

Scotch broth

PREP 20 MINS · COOK 1¾ HRS

SERVES 8

450g (1lb) neck of lamb
salt and freshly ground black pepper
2 tbsp olive oil
1 onion, finely chopped
4 carrots, finely chopped
4 celery sticks, finely chopped
2.3 litres (4 pints) hot light chicken stock
225g (8oz) pearl barley
handful of fresh curly parsley, finely chopped

1 Put the lamb in a large pan, cover with cold water, and season with salt and black pepper. Bring to the boil, then lower the heat and simmer for 30 minutes, or until cooked. Remove with a slotted spoon, leave to cool slightly, then shred and put to one side. Reserve the cooking liquid.

2 Heat the oil in a large pan, add the onion, and cook over a low heat for 5 minutes, or until soft and translucent. Add the carrots and celery, and cook over a very low heat for 10 minutes. Strain the reserved liquid, then add to the pan and pour in the stock. Season with salt and black pepper, then add the pearl barley and lamb. Bring to the boil, then reduce to a simmer and cook over a very low heat for 1 hour, or until the pearl barley is cooked. Top up with hot water if it begins to dry out too much. Stir through the parsley, then taste and season again with salt and black pepper if needed.

3 Leave to cool completely, then transfer to a freezerproof container, making sure the lamb is covered with liquid (add a little cold light chicken stock if it is not). Seal and freeze for up to 3 months. To serve, defrost in the refrigerator overnight, then transfer to a pan and heat until piping hot. Serve with fresh crusty bread.

Spiced butternut squash soup

PREP 20 MINS · COOK 40 MINS

Special equipment • blender or food processor

SERVES 8

2 tbsp olive oil
2 onions, finely chopped
salt and freshly ground black pepper
3 garlic cloves, grated or finely chopped
4 fresh sage leaves, finely chopped
2 fresh medium-hot red chillies, deseeded and finely chopped
pinch of freshly grated nutmeg
1 large butternut squash or 2 small ones, halved, peeled, deseeded, and chopped into small pieces
2 potatoes, peeled and diced
1.4 litres (2½ pints) hot vegetable stock
chilli oil, to serve
grated Gruyère cheese, to serve

1 Heat the oil in a large pan, add the onions, and cook over a low heat for 6–8 minutes, or until soft and translucent. Season with salt and black pepper, then stir through the garlic, sage, chillies, and nutmeg, and cook for a few seconds.

2 Stir in the squash, add the potatoes and stock, and bring to the boil. Reduce to a simmer and cook for 20–30 minutes, or until the squash and potatoes are soft. Transfer to a blender or food processor and whiz until smooth. Season again with salt and black pepper.

3 Leave to cool completely, then transfer to a freezerproof container, seal, and freeze for up to 3 months. To serve, defrost in the refrigerator overnight, transfer to a pan, and heat until piping hot. Serve with a drizzle of chilli oil, and a sprinkling of Gruyère cheese.

Chunky minestrone soup

PREP 25 MINS · COOK 1 HR

SERVES 8

2 tbsp olive oil
2 onions, finely chopped
3 garlic cloves, grated or finely chopped
4 celery sticks, finely chopped
4 carrots, finely chopped
250g (9oz) pancetta, cut into small cubes
handful of fresh flat-leaf parsley, finely chopped
handful of fresh sage leaves, finely chopped
2 tbsp tomato purée
2 x 400g cans chopped tomatoes
2 x 400g cans borlotti beans, drained and rinsed
salt and freshly ground black pepper
2.3 litres (4 pints) hot chicken stock
225g (8oz) fresh or frozen peas
300g (10oz) runner beans, trimmed and cut into 3
300g (10oz) small pasta shapes such as ditalini (or spaghetti, cut into 1cm (½in) pieces), to serve
freshly grated Parmesan cheese, to serve

1 Heat the oil in a large pan, add the onions, and cook over a low heat for 6–8 minutes, or until soft and translucent. Add the garlic, celery, and carrots, and cook over a low heat, stirring occasionally, for 10 minutes, or until soft. Stir in the pancetta and cook for 5 minutes, or until golden.

2 Add the herbs, tomato purée, tomatoes, and beans and stir to combine. Season with salt and black pepper, then pour in the stock. Bring to the boil, cover with a lid, and simmer for 40 minutes. Add the peas and beans for the last 5 minutes of cooking. Taste, and season again, if necessary.

3 Leave to cool completely, then transfer to a freezerproof container, seal, and freeze for up to 3 months. To serve, defrost overnight in the refrigerator, then transfer to a pan. Add the pasta, and simmer until piping hot and the pasta is *al dente*. Top with Parmesan cheese, and serve.

Thick vegetable soup

PREP 15 MINS · COOK 45 MINS

SERVES 8

2 tbsp olive oil
2 onions, finely chopped
salt and freshly ground black pepper
4 garlic cloves, grated or finely chopped
1 tbsp fresh rosemary leaves, finely chopped
4 celery sticks, finely chopped
4 carrots, finely chopped
4 courgettes, finely chopped
2 x 400g cans whole tomatoes, chopped in the can
1.2 litres (2 pints) hot vegetable stock
handful of fresh flat-leaf parsley, finely chopped

1 Heat the oil in a large pan, add the onions, and cook over a low heat for 6–8 minutes, or until soft and translucent. Season with salt and black pepper, then add the garlic, rosemary, celery, and carrots and cook over a low heat, stirring occasionally, for 10 minutes.

2 Add the courgettes and cook for 5 minutes, then stir in the tomatoes, and squash with the back of a fork. Add the stock, bring to the boil, then reduce to a simmer and cook for 20 minutes. Season well with salt and black pepper, then stir through the parsley.

3 Leave to cool completely, then transfer to a freezerproof container, seal, and freeze for up to 3 months. To serve, defrost in the refrigerator overnight, then transfer to a pan and heat until piping hot. Serve with fresh crusty bread.

EVERYDAY

Roasted red pepper soup

PREP 15 MINS **COOK 1 HR**

Cooling • 15 minutes
Special equipment • blender or food processor

SERVES 8
10 red peppers
3 tbsp olive oil
2 onions, finely chopped
3 garlic cloves, grated or finely chopped
pinch of chilli flakes
salt and freshly ground black pepper
2.3 litres (4 pints) hot vegetable stock
large handful of fresh basil leaves, torn, to serve
drizzle of extra virgin olive oil, to serve

1 Preheat the oven to 200°C (400°F/Gas 6).
Sit the peppers in a roasting tin and smother with
1 tablespoon of the oil, using your hands. Roast for
40 minutes, or until soft. Transfer to plastic bags,
knot or seal, and allow to cool for 15 minutes.
Remove the skins and seeds and discard, then
roughly chop the flesh, keeping any juices.

2 Heat the remaining oil in a large heavy-based
pan, add the onions, and cook over a low heat for
5 minutes, or until beginning to soften. Stir through
the garlic and chilli flakes and season with salt
and black pepper. Add the roasted peppers and
juices, pour in the stock, and bring to the boil.
Reduce to a simmer and cook for 15 minutes.
Transfer to a blender or food processor and whiz
until blended and smooth. Season to taste with salt
and black pepper.

3 Leave to cool completely, then transfer to
a freezerproof container, seal, and freeze for
up to 3 months. To serve, defrost overnight in the
refrigerator, then transfer to a pan and heat until
piping hot. Stir through the basil, drizzle with oil,
and serve with fresh crusty bread.

Tomato and chorizo soup

PREP 20 MINS **COOK 40 MINS**

SERVES 8
2 tbsp olive oil
250g (9oz) chorizo, cut into small cubes
2 red onions, finely chopped
4 celery sticks, finely diced
4 carrots, finely diced
3 garlic cloves, grated or finely chopped
salt and freshly ground black pepper
700g jar passata
1.2 litres (2 pints) hot vegetable stock
2 x 400g cans chickpeas, drained and rinsed, and
    drained again
handful of fresh coriander, finely chopped, to serve

1 Heat half the oil in a large heavy-based pan, add
the chorizo, and cook over a medium heat, stirring
occasionally, for 5 minutes, or until beginning to
turn crispy. Remove and put to one side.

2 Heat the remaining oil in the pan, add the onions,
and cook over a low heat for 6–8 minutes, or until
soft and translucent. Stir in the celery, carrots, and
garlic, season with salt and black pepper, then cook
over a low heat, stirring occasionally, for 8 minutes,
or until tender. Add the passata, stock, and
chickpeas, and simmer for 15 minutes. Return the
chorizo to the pan, then taste and season with salt
and black pepper if needed.

3 Leave to cool completely, then transfer to
a freezerproof container, seal, and freeze for
up to 3 months. To serve, defrost overnight in the
refrigerator, then transfer to a pan and heat until
piping hot. Stir through the coriander and serve.

Tomato soup

PREP 15 MINS **COOK 50 MINS**

Special equipment • blender or food processor

SERVES 8
3 tbsp olive oil
3 onions, finely chopped
4 garlic cloves, grated or finely chopped
30 tomatoes, about 1.35kg (3lb), quartered
salt and freshly ground black pepper
2 tsp caster sugar
1 tbsp tomato purée
1.5 litres (2¼ pints) hot vegetable stock
142ml double cream (optional), to serve

1 Heat the oil in a large heavy-based pan, add
the onions, and cook over a low heat for 10 minutes,
stirring so they don't burn. Stir in the garlic and
tomatoes and season with salt and black pepper.
Add the sugar and tomato purée, stir, then leave
to cook over a really low heat for 30 minutes.

2 Pour in the stock, bring to the boil, then lower
the heat and simmer for 10 minutes. Transfer
to a blender or food processor and whiz until
blended and smooth. Taste and season again with
salt and black pepper if needed.

3 Leave to cool completely, then transfer to
a freezerproof container, seal, and freeze for
up to 3 months. To reheat, defrost overnight in the
refrigerator, then transfer to a pan and heat until
piping hot. Stir through the cream (if using), and
serve with fresh crusty bread.

Chilli beef and bean soup

SERVES 8
2 tbsp olive oil
2 onions, finely chopped
salt and freshly ground black pepper
2 red peppers, deseeded and finely chopped
2–3 fresh red chillies, deseeded and finely chopped
550g (1¼lb) braising steak, cut into 2.5cm
    (1in) cubes
1 tbsp plain flour
2.3 litres (4 pints) hot beef stock
2 x 400g cans kidney beans, drained, rinsed, and
    drained again
handful of fresh flat-leaf parsley, finely chopped,
    to serve

1 Heat the oil in a large heavy-based pan, add the onions, and cook on a low heat for 6–8 minutes, or until soft and translucent. Season with salt and black pepper, then stir through the peppers and chillies and cook for 5 minutes. Add the meat and cook, stirring frequently, for 5–10 minutes, or until beginning to brown all over.

2 Sprinkle in the flour, stir well, and cook for 2 minutes. Add the stock, bring to the boil, then cover with a lid and reduce to a simmer. Cook for 1½ hours, or until the meat is tender. Add the kidney beans and cook for 10 minutes more, then season to taste with salt and black pepper.

3 Leave to cool completely, then transfer to a freezerproof container, making sure the meat is covered (add a little more stock if it is not). Seal and freeze for up to 3 months. To serve, defrost the soup overnight in the refrigerator, then transfer to a pan and heat until piping hot. Stir through the parsley and serve.

Split pea and bacon soup

Special equipment • blender or food processor

SERVES 8
2 tbsp olive oil
425g (15oz) bacon or pancetta, chopped into
    bite-sized pieces
2 onions, finely chopped
salt and freshly ground black pepper
4 celery sticks, finely chopped
4 carrots, finely chopped
550g (1¼lb) yellow split peas
1.7 litres (3 pints) hot vegetable stock

1 Heat half the oil in a large heavy-based pan, add the bacon or pancetta, and cook over a medium heat, stirring occasionally, for 5 minutes, or until crispy and golden. Remove with a slotted spoon and put to one side. Heat the remaining oil in the pan, add the onions, and cook over a low heat for 6–8 minutes, or until soft and translucent. Season with salt and black pepper, then add the celery and carrots and cook on a low heat for 5 minutes.

2 Add the peas and stock and bring to the boil slowly. Cover with a lid, reduce to a simmer, and cook for 2 hours, or until the peas are tender. Check occasionally, and top up with hot water if the soup begins to look too thick. Transfer to a blender or food processor and whiz until smooth and blended. Return the bacon or pancetta to the pan, then season with salt and black pepper.

3 Leave to cool completely, then transfer to a freezerproof container, seal, and freeze for up to 3 months. To serve, defrost overnight in the refrigerator, transfer to a pan and heat until piping hot. Serve with fresh crusty bread.

Beef ragù

SERVES 8
4 tbsp olive oil
2 large onions, finely diced
675g (1½lb) lean beef, cut into 1cm (½in) cubes
8 garlic cloves, grated or finely chopped
300ml (10fl oz) red wine
4 x 400g cans chopped tomatoes
2 bay leaves
1 tsp fresh thyme leaves, finely chopped
salt and freshly ground black pepper

1 Heat the oil in a large heavy-based pan, add the onions, and cook on a medium heat, stirring frequently, for 5 minutes, or until soft and translucent. Add the beef and cook, stirring frequently, for 5 minutes, or until no longer pink. Add the garlic and cook for 1 minute, then pour in the wine and allow to simmer and reduce for 5 minutes.

2 Add the tomatoes, bay leaves, and thyme, bring to the boil, then reduce the heat and simmer for 30 minutes, stirring occasionally. Taste and season with salt and black pepper.

3 Leave to cool completely, then remove and discard the bay leaves. Divide the ragù evenly among 4 freezer bags (2 portions per bag), seal, and freeze for up to 6 months.

4 To reheat, defrost overnight in the refrigerator, then transfer to a pan and heat until piping hot. Serve with pasta or creamy mashed potato.

Lamb and aubergine ragù

 PREP 20 MINS **COOK** 35 MINS

SERVES 8

6 tbsp olive oil
2 onions, finely diced
2 medium aubergines, cut into 1cm (½in) cubes
450g (1lb) lean lamb, cut into 1cm (½in) cubes
6 garlic cloves, finely chopped
3 x 400g cans chopped tomatoes
3 bay leaves
1 tbsp dried oregano
handful of fresh flat-leaf parsley, chopped
salt and freshly ground black pepper

1 Heat the oil in a large heavy-based pan, add the onions, and cook over a medium heat, stirring frequently, for 3 minutes. Add the aubergines and cook, stirring frequently, for 5 minutes, or until starting to brown. Add the lamb, combine well, and cook, stirring frequently, for 5 minutes, or until no longer pink.

2 Stir in the garlic and cook for 1 minute. Add the tomatoes, bay leaves, oregano, and parsley, bring to the boil, then reduce the heat and simmer for 20 minutes, stirring occasionally. Taste, and season with salt and black pepper.

3 Leave to cool completely, then remove the bay leaves and discard. Divide the ragù evenly among 4 freezer bags (2 portions per bag), seal, and freeze for up to 3 months. To reheat, defrost overnight in the refrigerator, then transfer to a pan and heat until piping hot. Serve with pasta or rice.

Rich tomato sauce

 PREP 10 MINS **COOK** 30 MINS

SERVES 8

4 tbsp olive oil
4 garlic cloves, finely sliced
4 x 400g cans whole tomatoes, chopped in the can
2 tbsp tomato purée
2 tsp dried oregano
2 bay leaves
salt and freshly ground black pepper
2 heaped tsp green pesto

1 Heat the oil in a large heavy-based pan, add the garlic, and cook over a low heat for a few seconds. Add the tomatoes and tomato purée, bring to the boil, then add the oregano and bay leaves and simmer for 25 minutes, stirring occasionally.

2 Season well with salt and black pepper, cook for 2 minutes, then stir in the pesto and remove from the heat.

3 Leave to cool completely, then remove and discard the bay leaves and discard. Divide the sauce evenly among 4 freezer bags (2 portions per bag), seal, and freeze for up to 6 months.

4 To serve, defrost overnight in the refrigerator or at room temperature for 6 hours, transfer to a pan, and heat until warmed through. Serve with pasta or use to make a lasagne or moussaka.

Spinach sauce

 PREP 15 MINS **COOK** 20 MINS

SERVES 8

4 tbsp olive oil
2 large onions, finely diced
4 garlic cloves, finely sliced
2 red chillies, deseeded and finely chopped
550g (1¼lb) baby spinach leaves, rinsed and roughly chopped
300ml (10fl oz) dry white wine
2 tbsp plain flour
900ml (1½ pints) milk
salt and freshly ground black pepper

1 Heat the oil in a large heavy-based pan, add the onions, and cook over a medium heat, stirring frequently, for 5 minutes, or until soft and translucent. Stir in the garlic and chillies and cook for 2 minutes. Add the spinach and cook for 3 minutes, or until wilted.

2 Add the wine and simmer for 5 minutes, or until reduced by half. Add the flour and combine well. Pour in half the milk, and stir well. Add the rest of the milk a little at a time, stirring constantly, and cook for 5 minutes, or until you have a creamy sauce. Season well with salt and black pepper.

3 Leave to cool completely, then divide among 4 freezer bags (2 portions per bag). Seal and freeze for up to 3 months. To serve, defrost overnight in the refrigerator, transfer to a pan with a little milk, and warm through gently (but do not overcook). Use as a sauce for chicken, fish, or new potatoes, or stir in some grated Cheddar cheese and serve with pasta.

Beef with prunes and pine nuts

SERVES 8
1.1kg (2½lb) lean beef, cut into
  bite-sized pieces
1 tsp freshly ground black pepper
1 tsp cayenne pepper
6 tbsp olive oil
2 large onions, sliced
salt
6 garlic cloves, chopped
125g (4½oz) pine nuts
150g (5½oz) prunes, stoned
150ml (5fl oz) dry sherry
2 tbsp fresh thyme leaves
2 bay leaves
1 tbsp plain flour
900ml (1½ pints) hot beef stock

1 Put the beef in a mixing bowl, add the pepper and cayenne, and mix well. Heat the oil in a large heavy-based pan over a medium heat, add the beef, and cook, stirring frequently, for

5 minutes, or until brown all over. Remove with a slotted spoon and put to one side. Add the onions, season with salt, and cook for 5 minutes or until soft and translucent.

2 Return the meat to the pan, add the garlic, pine nuts, and prunes, and cook for 1 minute. Add the sherry, thyme, and bay leaves, and allow to boil for 5 minutes while the alcohol evaporates. Stir in the flour and add the stock. Combine well, then bring to the boil and simmer for 10 minutes, adding more water if needed.

3 Leave to cool completely, then transfer to a freezerproof container (or 4 freezer bags – 2 portions per bag) making sure meat is well covered, seal, and freeze for up to 3 months. To serve, defrost overnight in the refrigerator, then transfer to a pan and heat over a medium heat for 15–20 minutes, or until piping hot.

EVERYDAY

Beef stew with orange and bay leaves

Special equipment • large cast-iron pan or flameproof casserole

SERVES 8
3 tbsp olive oil
1.35kg (3lb) stewing steak, cut into
  bite-sized pieces
salt and freshly ground black pepper
2 small glasses of dry white wine
3 bay leaves
1.7 litres (3 pints) hot vegetable stock
2 cinnamon sticks
pinch of freshly grated nutmeg
2 x 400g cans chickpeas, drained
  and rinsed
2 oranges, peeled and sliced into rings
handful of fresh coriander, finely
  chopped, to serve

1 Preheat the oven to 180°C (350°F/Gas 4). Heat the oil in a large cast-iron pan or flameproof casserole, add the meat, season with salt and black pepper, and cook over a medium heat, stirring occasionally, for 10 minutes, or until brown on all sides. Carefully add the wine – it will spit – then stir the meat around the pan and allow the liquid to boil for a couple of minutes while the alcohol evaporates.

2 Add the bay leaves, then pour in the stock. Add the cinnamon and nutmeg, and season again with salt and black pepper. Bring to the boil, add the chickpeas, then cover with a lid and put in the oven to cook for 1 hour. Add the oranges and cook for a further 30 minutes.

3 Leave to cool completely, then transfer to a freezerproof container, making sure the meat is well covered. Seal and freeze for up to 3 months. To serve, defrost overnight in the refrigerator, then transfer to a large pan and heat for 15 minutes, or until piping hot. Stir through the coriander and serve with fresh crusty bread.

Beef and parsnip stew

PREP 30 MINS · COOK 1¾ HRS

Special equipment • large cast-iron pan or flameproof casserole

SERVES 8

3 tbsp olive oil

2 onions, finely chopped

handful of fresh thyme leaves

4 garlic cloves, grated or finely chopped

salt and freshly ground black pepper

1.1kg (2½lb) braising steak, cut into bite-sized pieces

4 large carrots, roughly chopped

5 parsnips, roughly chopped

1.4 litres (2½ pints) hot beef stock

knob of butter

400g (14oz) button mushrooms, any large ones halved

1 Preheat the oven to 180°C (350°F/Gas 4). Heat the oil in a large cast-iron pan or flameproof casserole, add the onions, and cook over a low heat for 6–8 minutes, or until soft and translucent. Stir in the thyme and garlic and season well with salt and black pepper. Add the steak and cook, stirring often, for 10 minutes, or until sealed. Add the carrots and parsnips, then pour in the stock. Bring to the boil, then reduce to a simmer, cover with a lid, and put in the oven to cook for 1 hour.

2 Just before the hour is up, melt the butter in a small frying pan, add the mushrooms, and cook, stirring for 5–8 minutes, or until golden. Add to the pan and cook for a further 30 minutes. Top up with hot stock or water if it begins to look dry.

3 Leave to cool completely, then transfer to a freezerproof container, making sure meat is well covered. Seal, and freeze for up to 3 months. To serve, defrost overnight in the refrigerator, then transfer to a large casserole and reheat in an oven preheated to 180°C (350°F/Gas 4) for 30–40 minutes, or until piping hot.

Beef stew with olives

PREP 15 MINS · COOK 1¾ HRS

Special equipment • large cast-iron pan or flameproof casserole

SERVES 8

3 tbsp olive oil

1.6kg (3½lb) stewing steak, cut into bite-sized pieces

4 garlic cloves, finely chopped

2 tsp ground cumin

2 small glasses of dry white wine

2 tbsp white wine vinegar

a few sprigs of fresh rosemary

175g (6oz) black olives, pitted

16 baby onions, peeled

salt and freshly ground black pepper

1.4 litres (2½ pints) hot vegetable stock

1 Preheat the oven to 200°C (400°F/Gas 6). Heat the oil in a large cast-iron pan or flameproof casserole, add the meat, and cook over a medium heat, stirring frequently, for 10 minutes, or until browned all over. Lower the heat and stir in the garlic and cumin. Add the wine and wine vinegar, raise the heat, and allow to boil and reduce for a couple of minutes while the alcohol evaporates.

2 Add the rosemary, olives, and onions, stir, and season with salt and black pepper. Add the stock, and bring to the boil. Cover and cook in the oven for 1½ hours, or until the meat is tender.

3 Leave to cool completely, then transfer to a freezerproof container, making sure meat is well covered. Seal, and freeze for up to 3 months. To serve, defrost overnight in the refrigerator, then transfer to a large pan and heat gently until piping hot. Alternatively, place in an ovenproof dish, cover, and heat through in an oven preheated to 180°C (350°F/Gas 4) for 30 minutes.

Shin of beef with Marsala

PREP 25 MINS · COOK 1½ HRS

Special equipment • large cast-iron pan or flameproof casserole

SERVES 8

1.6kg (3½lb) shin beef, cut into bite-sized pieces

plain flour, to dust

salt and freshly ground black pepper

3 tbsp olive oil

2 red onions, roughly chopped

4 carrots, roughly chopped

300ml (10fl oz) Marsala

200g (7oz) Puy lentils, rinsed and picked over

1.4 litres (2½ pints) hot vegetable stock

2 bay leaves

1 Preheat the oven to 180°C (350°F/Gas 4). Dust the meat with a little flour, then season with salt and black pepper. Heat half the oil in a large cast-iron pan or flameproof casserole, add the meat, and cook over a medium heat, stirring often, for 10 minutes, or until brown on all sides. Remove with a slotted spoon and put to one side.

2 Heat the remaining oil in the pan, add the onions, and cook over a low heat for 6–8 minutes, or until soft and translucent. Stir in the carrots and cook for 5 minutes. Return the meat to the pan, pour in the Marsala, and let it boil for a few minutes while the alcohol evaporates. Stir in the lentils, add the stock, and bring to the boil. Season with salt and black pepper, then add the bay leaves. Cover with a lid and put in the oven to cook for 1½ hours. Check occasionally, and add a little hot water if it looks dry.

3 Leave to cool completely, then transfer to a freezerproof container, making sure the meat is well covered. Seal and freeze for up to 3 months. To serve, defrost overnight in the refrigerator, then transfer to a large pan and cover with a little hot water. Heat very gently for 15–20 minutes, or until piping hot. Serve with fresh crusty bread.

Lamb daube

PREP 25 MINS · COOK 2½ HRS

Marinating • 30 minutes

Special equipment • large cast-iron pan or flameproof casserole

SERVES 8

1.35kg (3lb) lamb (from the shoulder or leg), cut into bite-sized pieces

300ml (10fl oz) red wine

1 star anise

zest of 1 orange, grated

salt and freshly ground black pepper

3 tbsp olive oil

2 onions, finely chopped

400g (14oz) bacon or pancetta, cut into bite-sized pieces

4 celery sticks, finely chopped

4 carrots, finely chopped

4 leeks, cleaned and cut into chunks

1.2 litres (2 pints) hot vegetable stock

2 handfuls of pitted green olives

1 Put the lamb, wine, star anise, and orange zest in a bowl, season well with salt and black pepper, and leave to marinate for 30 minutes (or overnight in the refrigerator).

2 Preheat the oven to 200°C (400°F/Gas 6). Heat half the oil in a large cast-iron pan or flameproof casserole. Remove the meat with a slotted spoon (reserve the marinade) and add to the pan. Cook over a medium heat, stirring often, for 10 minutes or until browned all over. Remove with a slotted spoon and put to one side. Heat the remaining oil in the pan, add the onions, and cook over a low heat for 6–8 minutes, or until soft and translucent. Stir in the bacon or pancetta and cook for 6–10 minutes, or until crispy. Add the celery and carrots and cook over a low heat, adding more oil if needed, for 5 minutes, or until beginning to soften.

3 Stir in the leeks and cook for a couple of minutes, then return the meat to the pan and pour in the marinade and stock. Stir in the olives, bring to the boil, then season with salt and black pepper. Cover with a lid and put in the oven to cook for 30 minutes. Turn the oven down to 150°C (300°F/Gas 2) and cook for a further 1½–2 hours. Check occasionally, and add a little hot water if it looks dry.

4 Leave to cool completely, then transfer to a freezerproof container, making sure the meat is well covered with the sauce. Seal and freeze for up to 3 months. To serve, defrost overnight in the refrigerator, then transfer to a pan and heat slowly for 15–20 minutes, or until piping hot. Alternatively, place in a casserole dish, cover, and reheat in an oven preheated to 180°C (350°F/Gas 4) for 30–40 minutes, or until piping hot. Serve with sautéed potatoes.

Caribbean stew with allspice and ginger

PREP 30 MINS · COOK 30 MINS

Marinating • 30 minutes

Special equipment • blender or food processor • large cast-iron pan or flameproof casserole

SERVES 8

1–2 Scotch Bonnet chillies (according to taste), deseeded

2 tsp allspice

handful of fresh thyme leaves

2 tsp tamarind paste

5cm (2in) piece fresh root ginger, peeled and roughly chopped

salt and freshly ground black pepper

3 tbsp olive oil

4 large chicken breast fillets, skinned and cut into bite-sized pieces

1 tbsp plain flour

1.4 litres (2½ pints) hot chicken stock

4 mixed peppers, deseeded and roughly chopped

5 tomatoes, skinned and roughly chopped

1 Put the chillies, allspice, thyme, tamarind, ginger, and some salt and black pepper in a blender or food processor and whiz to a paste. Add a little of the oil and whiz again. Pour into a plastic bag, add the chicken, and squish together. Leave to marinate for 30 minutes, or overnight in the refrigerator.

2 Heat the remaining oil in a large cast-iron pan or flameproof casserole, add the chicken and marinade, and cook, stirring often, over medium heat for 10 minutes, or until the chicken is golden. Stir in the flour, then add a little of the stock, and stir to scrape up any crispy bits from the bottom of the pan. Pour in the rest of the stock and keep stirring until the flour has blended in.

3 Stir in the peppers and tomatoes and season well with salt and black pepper. Bring to the boil, then reduce to a simmer and cook over a low heat for 30 minutes, or until the sauce has begun to thicken slightly. Taste, and season again if needed.

4 Leave to cool completely, then transfer to a large freezerproof container, making sure the chicken is well covered with sauce. Seal and freeze for up to 3 months. To serve, defrost in the refrigerator overnight, then transfer to a large pan or casserole dish and heat gently for 15–20 minutes, or until piping hot. Alternatively, cover and reheat in an oven preheated to 180°C (350°F/Gas 4) for 30–40 minutes, or until piping hot. Serve with baked sweet potatoes or sweet potato mash.

EVERYDAY

Chilli con carne

PREP 30 MINS · COOK 40 MINS

SERVES 8

6 tbsp olive oil
3 large onions, diced
1.1kg (2½lb) lean minced beef
150ml (5fl oz) dry sherry
8 garlic cloves, chopped
4 green bird's-eye chillies, finely chopped
1 tsp cayenne pepper
1 tsp paprika
2 x 400g cans kidney beans, drained and rinsed
4 bay leaves
3 x 400g cans chopped tomatoes
2 tsp dried oregano
salt and freshly ground black pepper

1 Heat the oil in a large heavy-based pan, add the onions, and cook, stirring frequently, for 5 minutes, or until starting to soften. Add the mince and cook, stirring constantly, for 5 minutes, or until no longer pink. Stir in the sherry and garlic and cook for 1 minute, then add the chillies, cayenne, and paprika, and cook for 5 minutes.

2 Add the kidney beans and bay leaves, cook for 2 minutes, then add the tomatoes and oregano. Bring to the boil, season well with salt and black pepper, and simmer over a low heat for 40 minutes, stirring occasionally.

3 Leave to cool completely, then transfer to a freezerproof container (or 4 freezer bags – 2 portions per bag), seal, and freeze for up to 3 months. To serve, defrost in the refrigerator overnight, then transfer to a pan and heat, stirring frequently, for 15–20 minutes, or until piping hot.

Pork and bean casserole

PREP 20 MINS · COOK 20 MINS

SERVES 8

6 tbsp olive oil
3 large onions, diced
6 celery sticks, diced
1.1kg (2½lb) lean pork, cut into 2cm (¾in) dice
2 tsp paprika
400g can cannellini beans, drained and rinsed
400g can flageolet beans, drained and rinsed
400g can butter beans, drained and rinsed
8 garlic cloves, grated or finely chopped
150ml (5fl oz) dry white wine
300ml (10fl oz) hot vegetable stock
juice of 1 lemon
handful of fresh flat-leaf parsley, chopped
salt and freshly ground black pepper

1 Heat the oil in a large heavy-based pan over a medium heat, add the onions and celery, and cook, stirring frequently, for 5 minutes, or until soft. Add the pork and cook, stirring occasionally, for 5 minutes, or until no longer pink. Stir in the paprika, then add the beans and garlic and cook for 1 minute.

2 Stir in the wine and allow to boil for 3 minutes while the alcohol evaporates. Add the stock, lemon juice, and parsley, season well with salt and black pepper, bring to the boil, lower the heat, and simmer for 20 minutes. Top up with hot water if needed.

3 Leave to cool completely, then transfer to a freezerproof container (or 4 freezer bags – 2 portions per bag), seal, and freeze for up to 3 months. To serve, defrost in the refrigerator overnight, then transfer to a pan and heat for 15–20 minutes, or until piping hot. Alternatively, microwave for 3 minutes on High, then stir and microwave for a further 2 minutes, or until piping hot.

Braised turkey with vegetables

PREP 20 MINS · COOK 20 MINS

SERVES 8

2 tbsp olive oil
knob of butter
4 turkey breast fillets
salt and freshly ground black pepper
2 onions, sliced
2 carrots, sliced
1 fennel bulb, sliced
a few fresh tarragon leaves, roughly chopped
600ml (1 pint) hot chicken stock
handful of fresh flat-leaf parsley, finely chopped, to serve
zest of 1 lemon, grated, to serve

1 Preheat the oven to 180°C (350°F/Gas 4). Heat the oil and butter in a large frying pan, season the turkey well with salt and black pepper, then cook over a medium heat, stirring occasionally, for 10 minutes, or until lightly golden all over. Transfer to a shallow casserole dish.

2 Add the vegetables and tarragon and season well with salt and black pepper. Pour in enough stock so that it comes almost to the top of the dish but doesn't cover the ingredients. Cover with a lid and cook in the oven for 40 minutes, or until the turkey and vegetables are tender.

3 Leave to cool completely, then remove the turkey with a slotted spoon, discard the skin, and slice the meat. Transfer to a freezerproof container, add the sauce and vegetables, and make sure the turkey is well covered – pour in a little cooled stock if it isn't. Seal, and freeze for up to 3 months. To serve, defrost overnight in the refrigerator, then transfer to a large pan and heat gently for 15–20 minutes, or until piping hot. Top with the parsley and lemon zest, and serve with a pinch of black pepper.

Lamb, spinach, and chickpea hotpot

PREP 25 MINS · COOK 20 MINS

SERVES 8

675g (1½lb) lean lamb, cut into 2cm (¾in) dice
2 tbsp plain flour
1 tsp paprika
6 tbsp olive oil
2 large red onions, diced
6 garlic cloves, chopped
2 x 400g cans chickpeas, drained and rinsed
1 small glass of dry white wine
2 x 400g cans chopped tomatoes
salt and freshly ground black pepper
550g (1¼lb) baby leaf spinach

1 Put the lamb, flour, and paprika in a mixing bowl and combine well. Heat the oil in a large heavy-based pan over a medium heat, add the onions, and cook, stirring frequently, for 5 minutes, or until soft and translucent. Add the lamb and cook, stirring occasionally, for 5 minutes, or until evenly browned. Stir in the garlic and chickpeas, and cook for 1 minute.

2 Pour in the wine and allow to boil for 3 minutes while the alcohol evaporates. Add the tomatoes, bring to the boil, then reduce the heat and simmer for 15 minutes. Season well with salt and black pepper, stir in the spinach, and cook for 3 minutes.

3 Leave to cool completely, then transfer to a freezerproof container (or 2 large freezer bags – 4 portions per bag), seal, and freeze for up to 3 months. To serve, defrost overnight in the refrigerator, transfer to a deep baking dish, cover with a lid, and put in an oven preheated to 180°C (350°F/ Gas 4) for 15 minutes. Alternatively, microwave on High for 3 minutes, stir, and microwave for 3 minutes more, or until piping hot.

EVERYDAY

Game stew

PREP 30 MINS · COOK 1 HR

Special equipment • large cast-iron pan

SERVES 8

1.35kg (3lb) (boned weight) mixed game, such as pheasant, venison, and duck, cut into bite-sized pieces
plain flour, to dust
salt and freshly ground black pepper
2 tbsp olive oil
2 tbsp brandy
2 onions, finely chopped
4 garlic cloves, grated or finely chopped
4 celery sticks, finely diced
4 carrots, finely diced
1 bouquet garni
550g (1¼lb) chestnut mushrooms, quartered
2 glasses of dry white wine
1 tbsp redcurrant jelly
1.4 litres (2½ pints) hot chicken stock

1 Preheat the oven to 180°C (350°F/ Gas 4). Dust the meat lightly with a little flour, then season well with salt and black pepper. Heat half the oil in a large cast-iron pan, add the meat, and cook over a medium heat, stirring occasionally, for 6–8 minutes, or until browned on all sides. Remove with a slotted spoon and put to one side.

2 Add the brandy to the pan and stir to deglaze, then add the rest of the oil, if needed, and the onions and cook over a low heat for 6 minutes, or until soft. Stir in the garlic, celery, carrots, and bouquet garni and cook over a low heat, stirring occasionally, for 8 minutes, or until tender.

3 Stir in the mushrooms, then raise the heat, add the wine, and allow to boil for 2 minutes while the alcohol evaporates. Stir in the redcurrant jelly, then pour in the stock. Cover with a lid and put in the oven to cook for 1 hour, or until the meat is tender. Top up with hot water if needed.

4 Leave to cool completely, then transfer to a freezerproof container (or 4 freezer bags – 2 portions per bag), making sure the meat is covered. Seal and freeze for up to 3 months. To serve, defrost in the refrigerator overnight, then transfer to a large pan and heat gently for 15–20 minutes, or until piping hot. Serve with creamy mashed potato.

Beef and celeriac casserole with stout and anchovies

PREP 30 MINS **COOK** 1½ HRS

Special equipment • large cast-iron pan or flameproof casserole

SERVES 8

3 tbsp olive oil
1.1kg (2½lb) stewing steak or
    braising steak, cut into
    bite-sized pieces
2 onions, finely chopped
handful of fresh thyme stalks
8 salted anchovies
1 large celeriac, peeled and cut into
    bite-sized pieces
500ml bottle stout
1.2 litres (2 pints) hot vegetable stock
salt and freshly ground black pepper
5 medium potatoes, cut into
    chunky pieces

1 Preheat the oven to 180°C (350°F/ Gas 4). Heat half the oil in a large cast-iron pan or flameproof casserole, add the meat, and cook over a medium heat, stirring occasionally, for 10 minutes, or until browned all over. Remove with a slotted spoon and put to one side. Heat the remaining oil in the pan, add the onions and thyme, and cook over a low heat for 6-8 minutes, or until soft.

2 Stir in the anchovies, then stir in the celeriac and cook for 5-8 minutes. Add a little of the stout and stir to scrape up all the sticky bits from the bottom of the pan. Add the remaining stout and the stock, season with salt and black pepper, then return the meat to the pan, cover with a lid, and put in the oven for 1 hour.

3 Add the potatoes, together with a little hot water if the casserole looks dry. Cook for a further 30 minutes.

4 Leave to cool completely, then transfer to a freezer-proof container, make sure the meat is well covered with sauce. Seal and freeze for up to 3 months. To serve, defrost in the refrigerator overnight, then transfer to a pan and heat very gently for 15-20 minutes, or until piping hot. Alternatively, put in a casserole dish and reheat in an oven preheated to 180°C (350°F/Gas 4) for 30-40 minutes, or until piping hot.

VARIATION Use 4 carrots, roughly chopped, instead of – or as well as – the celeriac.

Pork with fennel and mustard

PREP 20 MINS **COOK** 20 MINS

SERVES 8

6 tbsp olive oil
2 large onions, sliced
3 fennel bulbs, sliced
1.1kg (2½lb) lean pork, cut into
    bite sized pieces
8 garlic cloves, grated or
    finely chopped
150ml (5fl oz) dry white wine
2 tbsp wholegrain mustard
1 tsp paprika
large handful of fresh flat-leaf
    parsley, chopped
1 tbsp fresh sage leaves, chopped
1 tbsp fresh rosemary
    leaves, chopped
2 tbsp plain flour
900ml (1½ pints) milk
salt and freshly ground black pepper

1 Heat the oil in a large heavy-based pan, add the onions and fennel, and cook for 5 minutes, or until beginning to soften. Add the pork and cook, stirring occasionally, for 5 minutes, or until no longer pink. Add the garlic and cook for 1 minute, then stir in the wine and mustard, raise the heat, and allow to boil for 3 minutes while the alcohol evaporates.

2 Stir in the paprika, parsley, sage, and rosemary, then add the flour and mix well. Add a little of the milk, mix to a smooth paste, then stir in the rest of it. Season well with salt and black pepper and cook for 5 minutes, adding a little more milk if it looks dry.

3 Leave to cool completely, then transfer to a freezerproof container (or 4 freezer bags – 2 portions per bag), seal, and freeze for up to 3 months. To serve, defrost overnight in the refrigerator, then transfer to a casserole dish, cover, and cook in an oven preheated to 180°C (350°F/Gas 4) for 25 minutes, or until piping hot.

Shepherd's pie

PREP 30 MINS | COOK 20 MINS | ❄

SERVES 8

1.1kg (2½lb) floury potatoes
large knob of butter
salt and freshly ground black pepper
6 tbsp olive oil
3 large onions, diced
4 large carrots, diced
1.1kg (2½lb) lamb mince
6 garlic cloves, chopped
2 tsp dried oregano
3 x 400g cans chopped tomatoes
250g (9oz) frozen peas

1 Put the potatoes in a pan of boiling salted water and cook for 15 minutes, or until soft. Drain, then mash well. Add the butter and mash again until creamy. Season with salt and black pepper, then put to one side.

2 Meanwhile, heat the oil in a large heavy-based pan over a medium heat, add the onions and carrots and cook for 5 minutes, or until the onions are starting to soften. Add the lamb and cook, stirring constantly, for 10 minutes, or until no longer pink. Add the garlic and oregano, cook for 1 minute, then stir in the tomatoes and bring to the boil.

3 Add the peas, season well with salt and black pepper, then bring to the boil before lowering the heat. Simmer for 20 minutes, stirring occasionally. Pour a layer of the lamb sauce into 2 large tin-foil dishes, or individual serving dishes, and top with the mashed potato.

4 Leave to cool completely, then cover with lids, seal, and freeze for up to 6 months. To serve, remove the lids and bake from frozen in an oven preheated to 180°C (350°F/Gas 4) for 25 minutes, or until brown on top and piping hot.

EVERYDAY

Coq au vin

PREP 15 MINS | COOK 40 MINS | ❄

SERVES 8

50g (1¾oz) butter
3 tbsp olive oil
2 large onions, diced
10 garlic cloves, chopped
300g (10oz) unsmoked streaky
  bacon, chopped
2 tbsp fresh thyme leaves
750g (1lb 10oz) button mushrooms
salt and freshly ground black pepper
1 litre (1¾ pints) good red wine
1 litre (1¾ pints) hot chicken stock
1.1kg (2½lb) chicken pieces, skinned

1 Heat the butter and oil in a large heavy-based pan over a medium heat, add the onions, and cook for 5 minutes, or until starting to soften. Add the garlic and bacon and cook for 5 minutes, stirring frequently. Add the thyme and mushrooms, season with salt and black pepper, and cook for 2 minutes.

2 Pour in the wine, raise the heat, and allow to boil for 5 minutes while the alcohol evaporates. Pour in the stock, bring to the boil, then add the chicken pieces. Combine well, bring to the boil again, then lower the heat and simmer for 25 minutes.

3 Leave to cool completely, then transfer to a freezerproof container (or 2 large freezer bags – 4 portions per bag), seal, and freeze for up to 3 months. To serve, defrost overnight in the refrigerator, then transfer to a casserole dish, cover, and cook in an oven preheated to 180°C (350°F/Gas 4) for 25 minutes, or until piping hot.

Beef and tomato lasagne

 PREP 30 MINS   COOK 20 MINS

SERVES 8
6 tbsp olive oil

3 large onions, finely diced

675g (1½lb) lean minced beef

6 garlic cloves, chopped

3 tbsp tomato purée

3 x 400g cans chopped tomatoes

2 tsp dried oregano

3 bay leaves

salt and freshly ground black pepper

3 tsp pesto

50g (1¾oz) butter

3 heaped tbsp plain flour

1 litre (1¾ pints) milk

300g (10oz) Cheddar cheese, grated

450g (1lb) lasagne sheets

1 Heat the oil in a large heavy-based pan over a medium heat, add the onions, and cook, stirring occasionally, for 5 minutes, or until starting to soften. Add the beef and cook, stirring constantly, for 5 minutes, or until no longer pink. Add the garlic, cook for 1 minute, then stir in the tomato purée. Add the tomatoes, oregano, and bay leaves, bring gently to the boil, then reduce the heat and simmer for 20 minutes. Season well with salt and black pepper, remove from the heat, then stir through the pesto and put to one side.

2 Melt the butter in a pan over a low heat, add the flour, and stir well. Add a little of the milk, mix well, then add 150ml (5fl oz) more milk, stirring vigorously until smooth. Add the rest of the milk, combine well, then bring to the boil, stirring constantly. Reduce the heat and simmer for 2 minutes to ensure the flour is cooked. Remove from the heat, stir in the Cheddar cheese, then season with salt and black pepper.

3 Pour 1cm (½in) of the beef sauce into the bottom of a large ovenproof freezerproof dish (or 2 medium-sized ones). Cover with a layer of lasagne sheets, then add 1cm (½in) more beef sauce, followed by a small amount of the cheese sauce and a layer of lasagne sheets. Repeat until all the meat sauce has been used up. Make sure you have enough cheese sauce for an even 5mm (¼in) layer on the top.

4 Leave to cool completely, then double-wrap in cling film and freeze for up to 3 months. To serve, remove the cling film and place in an oven preheated to 180°C (350°F/Gas 4) for 35–40 minutes, or until brown on top and piping hot.

Chicken and cornmeal cobbler

 PREP 20 MINS   COOK 1¾ HRS

Special equipment • large shallow cast-iron pan or flameproof casserole • 4cm (1½in) cutter

SERVES 8
2 tbsp olive oil

6 skinless boneless chicken breasts, cut into bite-sized pieces

salt and freshly ground black pepper

2 red onions, finely sliced

4 celery stalks, roughly chopped

2 glasses of red wine

5 carrots, roughly chopped

900ml (1½ pints) hot vegetable stock

150g (5½oz) plain flour, plus a little extra to dust

150g (5½oz) cornmeal

50g (1¾oz) butter

handful of fresh flat-leaf parsley, finely chopped

splash of milk

1 egg yolk, lightly beaten

1 Heat half the oil in a large shallow cast-iron pan or flameproof casserole, season the chicken with salt and black pepper, then cook over medium heat, turning occasionally, for 10 minutes, or until lightly golden all over. Remove with a slotted spoon and put to one side.

2 Preheat the oven to 180°C (350°F/Gas 4). Heat the remaining oil in the pan, then add the onions and cook over low heat for 6–8 minutes, or until soft. Add the celery and cook for 5 minutes, or until soft. Pour in the wine, raise the heat, and allow to boil for a couple of minutes while the alcohol evaporates. Add the carrots, return the chicken to the pan, then season well with salt and black pepper. Pour in the stock and cook, uncovered, over a low heat, stirring occasionally, for 1 hour, or until all the ingredients are tender. Top up with a little hot water if it begins to look dry.

3 Meanwhile, put the flour, cornmeal, and a pinch of salt in a large mixing bowl. Add the butter and rub it in with your fingertips until you have a breadcrumb texture. Stir through parsley, then add the milk a little at a time until the dough comes together. Form into a ball and put in the refrigerator to rest for 20 minutes. Flatten the chilled dough out on a floured surface, then roll it out with a rolling pin. Cut out about 18 rounds using the cutter, then add to the casserole, brushing them with egg yolk, before you put the pan into the oven for 30 minutes to cook the cobbler rounds.

4 Leave to cool completely, then double-wrap in cling film, making sure the meat is covered, and freeze for up to 3 months. To serve, defrost overnight in the refrigerator. Preheat oven to 180°C (350°F/Gas 4), and cook for 30–40 minutes until piping hot, covering it with foil if the top browns too much.

 VARIATION
Add 2 teaspoons of creamed horseradish to the cornmeal topping, or the same amount of wholegrain mustard.

EVERYDAY

Melanzane alla parmigiana

PREP 20 MINS · COOK 20 MINS

Special equipment • large ovenproof freezerproof dish

SERVES 8
6 tbsp olive oil
8 garlic cloves, finely sliced
4 x 400g cans chopped tomatoes
2 tbsp tomato purée
2 tsp dried oregano
1 tsp fresh thyme leaves
salt and freshly ground black pepper
3 large aubergines, cut into 1cm (½in) slices
300g (10oz) Parmesan cheese, grated
400g (14oz) mozzarella, torn into pieces

1 Heat 4 tablespoons of the oil in a large heavy-based pan over a low heat, add the garlic, and cook for 30 seconds. Add the chopped tomatoes, tomato purée, oregano, and thyme and bring to the boil. Season with salt and black pepper, then remove from the heat.

2 Put the aubergine slices in a bowl and brush with the rest of the oil. Heat a non-stick frying pan over a medium heat, then cook the aubergines in batches on each side for 3 minutes, or until golden brown. When each piece is done, remove with a slotted spoon and place on a plate.

3 Pour a 1cm (½in) layer of tomato sauce in the bottom of a large ovenproof freezerproof dish (or 2 medium-sized ones) and cover with aubergine slices. Sprinkle with a handful of Parmesan cheese, then repeat the process until all of the ingredients are used up (you should get 3–4 layers), making sure there is a 1cm (½in) layer of tomato sauce at the top. Cover with the mozzarella.

4 Leave to cool completely, then double-wrap with cling film and freeze for up to 3 months. To serve, defrost overnight in the refrigerator, then reheat in an oven preheated to 180°C (350°F/Gas 4) for 25 minutes, or until browning on top and piping hot. Serve with a crisp green salad.

VARIATION Put an extra layer of mozzarella in the middle. Tear it up into pieces as you do the topping.

Vegetarian leek and mushroom lasagne

PREP 25 MINS · COOK 20 MINS

Special equipment • large ovenproof freezerproof dish

SERVES 8
6 tbsp olive oil
4 large leeks, cut into 5mm (¼in) slices
550g (1¼lb) chestnut mushrooms, sliced
250g (9oz) chestnut mushrooms, grated
2–3 red chillies, deseeded and finely chopped
6 garlic cloves, chopped
150ml (5fl oz) dry white wine
small handful of fresh thyme leaves
2 tbsp plain flour
900ml (1½ pints) milk
350g (12oz) Cheddar cheese, grated
6 tomatoes, roughly chopped
salt and freshly ground black pepper
450g (1lb) lasagne sheets
2 tomatoes, sliced, for serving

1 Heat the oil in a large heavy-based pan, add the leeks, and cook over a low heat, stirring frequently, for 5 minutes, or until starting to soften. Stir in the mushrooms and cook, stirring frequently, for 5 minutes, or until they release their juices. Add the chillies and garlic, and cook for 1 minute. Pour in the wine, raise the heat, and boil for 3 minutes while the alcohol evaporates.

2 Stir in the thyme, then add the flour and mix well. Add a little of the milk, mix well, then add the rest of the milk and cook for 5 minutes, stirring frequently. Add almost all the cheese (reserve some for the topping), remove from the heat, and combine well. Add the tomatoes and season well with salt and black pepper.

3 Put a 1cm (½in) layer of the mixture in the bottom of a large ovenproof freezerproof dish, then cover evenly with a layer of the lasagne sheets. Pour in another layer of sauce and cover with lasagne. Repeat the process until all the sauce is used up – you need to finish with a layer of sauce. Top with the remaining cheese and the sliced tomatoes.

4 Leave to cool completely, then double-wrap the dish in cling film and freeze for up to 3 months. To serve, remove the cling film, top with tomato slices, and place the dish straight from the freezer in an oven preheated to 180°C (350°F/Gas 4) for 30–40 minutes, or until browning on top and piping hot.

STORECUPBOARD

Meal solutions using dried, tinned, bottled, and frozen foods.

STORECUPBOARD

All you need is a well-stocked larder to form the basis of a good meal. It's the bones of your cooking and will transform any dish. With a few added fresh ingredients, mealtimes needn't be a chore. And when shopping is not on the agenda it means there is always something in the cupboard to make a quick supper with.

Storecupboard essentials A list of dry and preserved goods, to always have to hand for last-minute meals.

EVERYDAY

HERBS, SPICES	PASTA, RICE, NOODLES	PULSES, GRAINS, NUTS, FRUITS	OILS, CONDIMENTS, SAUCES	JARS, CANS, AND POWDERS

HERBS, SPICES

PAPRIKA
Best for pork and chicken dishes.
Store for 6 months.

DRIED HERBS
Oregano, thyme, mixed dried herbs, and bay leaves.
Best for chicken, lamb, and fish dishes, stews, and casseroles.
Store for 6 months.

GROUND CORIANDER AND SEEDS
Best for curries.
Store for 6 months.

GROUND CHILLI AND CHILLI FLAKES
Best for adding spice and heat to Indian, Thai, and Mediterranean dishes.
Store for 6 months.

GROUND CUMIN AND SEEDS
Best for adding to a lamb stew or marinade.
Store for 6 months.

GROUND CINNAMON AND STICKS
Best for chicken and lamb stews.
Store for 6 months.

CURRY POWDER
Best for chicken, lamb, and beef.
Store for 6 months.

CAYENNE PEPPER
Best for chicken and meat dishes.
Store for 6 months.

PASTA, RICE, NOODLES

PASTA
For a variety of shapes and sizes, and sauce pairings, see p158.
Best for sauces and bakes.
Store for 1 year.

RICE
Basmati, brown, long grain, risotto (arborio or carnaroli), and paella..
Best for pilaf, kedgeree, salads, and serving as an accompaniment to meat and fish.
Store for 6 months.

NOODLES
Rice and egg noodles, available in a selection of types and thicknesses. You can buy straight-to-wok noodles, that require no cooking, just heating through.
Best for Asian-style dishes, soups, salads, or stir-fries.
Store for 6 months.

PULSES, GRAINS, NUTS, FRUITS

PULSES
Canned and dried Puy lentils, red lentils, green lentils, and yellow split peas. A selection of canned and dried chickpeas, flageolet beans, kidney beans, butter beans, and cannellini beans.
Best for stews, salads, bakes, casseroles, dips, and soups.
Store for 1 year.

GRAINS
Farro, pearl barley, couscous, bulgur wheat, and polenta.
Best for salads and hot pots.
Store for 1 year.

NUTS AND SEEDS
A selection of whole peanuts, walnuts, and cashew nuts, chopped and ground almonds, pine nuts, and dried whole chestnuts.
Sesame seeds, sunflower seeds, and pumpkin seeds.
Best for toppings, and in salads and stir-fries.
Store for 6 months.

DRIED FRUIT
A selection of sultanas and raisins, dates, figs, and apricots.
Best for salads and stews.
Store for 6 months.

OILS, CONDIMENTS, SAUCES

OILS
Olive, extra virgin olive, sunflower, groundnut, and sesame oil.
Best for salads, dressings, marinades, stir-fries, shallow frying, and baking.
Store for 6 months.

VINEGARS
Red wine, white wine, rice wine, balsamic, and sherry vinegar.
Best for salads, dressings, and marinades.
Store for 1 year.

MUSTARDS
English, Dijon, and wholegrain.
Best for cooking and dressing.
Store for 1 year.

PESTO AND PASTES
Harissa, tomato paste, and Thai curry paste.
Best for curries, stirring into casseroles, or pesto for adding to pasta.
Store for 6 months.

SAUCES
Soy sauce, Worcestershire sauce, fish sauce, and oyster sauce.
Best for stir-fries, stews, and casseroles.
Store for 1 year.

SALT AND PEPPER
Sea salt and whole peppercorns. For the best flavour, grind black peppercorns in a peppermill rather than buying them ground.
Best for seasoning hot and cold food.
Store for 1 year.

JARS, CANS, AND POWDERS

OLIVES AND CAPERS
Black and green olives, and small jarred salted capers.
Best for pasta, salads, and dips.
Store for 1 year.

TOMATOES
Tinned whole, and chopped. Jarred sun-dried tomatoes.
Best for stews, casseroles, and pasta sauces.
Store for 1 year.

SWEETCORN
Best for soups or stews.
Store for 1 year.

TUNA AND SALMON
Tuna and salmon, canned, in oil or brine.
Best for pasta, salads, fish cakes, and bakes.
Store for 1 year.

ANCHOVIES
Jarred or canned in olive oil or salt.
Best for pasta, salads, casseroles, and stews.
Store for 1 year.

COCONUT MILK
Best for Thai curries.
Store for 1 year.

POWDERED STOCK (BOUILLON)
Chicken, beef, or vegetable.
Best for gravies, sauces, soups, and stews.
Store for 1 year.

Fridge and freezer staples
Keep both well-stocked with these must-haves.

FRIDGE

FREEZER

BUTTER AND HARD CHEESE
Butter enriches all hot dishes, but you can use olive oil for a healthy alternative. Cheese adds instant protein to a quick dish.
Best for sauces, bakes, baking, and sandwiches.
Store for 1 month (or until its use-by date), or freeze for up to 3 months.

MILK
Semi-skimmed is the most popular, as it contains half the fat content of whole.
Best for sauces, batters, and puddings.
Store for 7 days (or until its use-by date), or freeze for 1 month.

EGGS
Keep them in the refrigerator, unless you plan to use them within a couple of days of purchase.
Best for omelettes, salads, and sandwiches.
Store for 3 weeks (or until their use-by date).

VEGETABLES
You can buy quite a few vegetables pre-frozen, but peas and broad beans are the only vegetables that withstand the process without it impairing their flavour. They make a great standby.
Best for instant soups, adding to fish or meat pies, casseroles, or as a meal accompaniment.
Store for 6 months.

MEAT
Minced beef, and lamb or pork sausages.
Best for chillies and ragùs, or sausage hot dogs or sandwiches.
Store for 6 months.

FISH AND SEAFOOD
Fish fillets (such as haddock, pollack, and salmon) and prawns (shell on or off).
Best for fish pie and barbecues.
Store for 3 months.

storecupboard versus fresh
Frozen food can sometimes be more nutritious than fresh, particularly when fresh vegetables are out of season and have clocked up hundreds of air miles to reach your supermarket. Vegetables for the freezer are frozen soon after being picked, so the nutrient loss is minimal (provided you don't cook them for too long).

Canned foods are without doubt the ultimate in convenience food, and are an economical source of nutrients, needing no preparation at all. They are, however, often canned with lots of added sugar or salt, so check the label before you buy.

5 easy storecupboard meals
Use storecupboard staples to make a complete meal if fresh foods are not available, or if you have not had time to shop.

1 Tuna and rice salad
Mix 150g (5½oz) of cooked and cooled **basmati rice** with a 200g **can of tuna**, drained, and a 400g **can of cannellini beans**, drained. Stir through 1 tablespoon of **olive oil**, and 1 tablespoon of **white wine vinegar**, and toss together with a pinch of **chilli flakes**. Season, and serve on its own, or as part of a salad.

2 Sicilian-style spaghetti
Whiz a handful of **sun-dried tomatoes** in a food processor with a little **olive oil** and a handful of **pine nuts**, until chopped. Heat 1 tablespoon of olive oil in a pan, add the tomato mixture, and cook for a few seconds, then stir in 6 **salted anchovies**, and cook until they begin to disintegrate. Stir in a handful of **sultanas**, and 1 tablespoon of **capers**. Toss with 175g (6oz) of hot cooked **spaghetti**.

3 Salmon stir-fry
Heat 1 tablespoon of **sesame oil** in a frying pan or wok, and add 200g (7oz) of straight-to-wok **medium rice noodles**. Toss, then add a splash of **soy sauce** and **Thai fish sauce**, and a **can of salmon**, drained and flaked, and cook for a few minutes. Season, add a handful of chopped **roasted peanuts**, and serve.

4 Lentil stew
Cook 125g (4½oz) of **puy lentils** in 900ml (1½ pints) of hot **chicken stock** and a pinch of **ground cumin**, for about 30 minutes, or until cooked and softened. Add a 400g **can of chickpeas**, drained, and season. Simmer gently for 10 minutes, and add a splash of **chilli oil** to taste.

5 Couscous salad
Tip 150g (5½oz) of **couscous** into a bowl, and pour over hot **vegetable stock** to cover, so it just sits on the top. Leave for 5 minutes then season, and fluff up with a fork. Combine 2 tablespoons of **extra virgin olive oil** with 1 tablespoon of **Dijon mustard** and a pinch of **paprika**, and add to the couscous. Stir in a handful of **sun-dried tomatoes**, chopped, 1 teaspoon of **capers**, and a handful of **mixed pitted olives**, halved. Serve with salad and hot pitta bread.

EVERYDAY

Wild rice with sun-dried tomatoes and cashew nuts. For recipe, see page 276.

EVERYDAY

Lebanese-style lentils

 PREP 10 MINS **COOK 40 MINS**

SERVES 4
1 tbsp olive oil
1 onion, finely chopped
1 tsp cumin seeds
1 tsp ground cinnamon
1 tsp ground allspice
salt and freshly ground black pepper
350g (12oz) dried Puy lentils or lentilles vertes, picked over and rinsed well
1.2 litres (2 pints) hot vegetable stock
100g (3½oz) pine nuts
25g (scant 1oz) dried apricots, roughly chopped

1 Heat the oil in a heavy large deep-sided frying pan over a low heat. Add the onion, and sweat gently for about 5 minutes until soft and translucent. Stir through the cumin seeds, cinnamon, and allspice, and season well with salt and black pepper.

2 Add the lentils, and stir through until thoroughly mixed. Pour over the hot stock. Bring to the boil, then reduce the heat to low. Simmer gently for 30–40 minutes until the lentils are soft but not mushy. Keep an eye on the pan, and top up with more hot water if the lentils begin to dry out too much.

3 Meanwhile, toast the pine nuts in a small dry frying pan over a low heat for about 5 minutes until they begin to turn golden; watch carefully, as they can scorch very quickly. Tip the pine nuts into the lentils along with the apricots. Taste, and season again if needed. Serve hot.

VARIATION Use pistachio nuts or almonds instead of pine nuts.

COOK'S NOTES
Always rinse dried lentils thoroughly before using. They can be muddy and gritty.

Noodle broth with dried mushrooms

 PREP 10 MINS **COOK 20 MINS**

Soaking • 20 minutes

SERVES 4
25g (scant 1oz) packet mixed dried mushrooms (shiitake, oyster, porcini), rinsed
1 tbsp sesame oil or sunflower oil
5cm (2in) piece of fresh root ginger, finely sliced into strips
2 x 150g packets of straight-to-wok thick or medium udon noodles
1.2 litres (2 pints) hot vegetable stock
2 tbsp light soy sauce
2 tbsp Thai fish sauce, such as nam pla
salt and freshly ground black pepper
splash of chilli oil, to taste

1 Put the dried mushrooms in a bowl, and cover with about 300ml (10fl oz) boiling water. Leave to soak for 20–30 minutes.

2 Heat the oil in a large shallow pan over a low heat. Add the ginger, and cook for 2–3 minutes until fragrant. Tip in the noodles, and stir for a couple of minutes more to break them up. Pour in the hot stock, soy sauce, and fish sauce, and bring to the boil.

3 Meanwhile, strain the mushrooms through a sieve (reserving the liquid). Add the mushrooms to the pan, and reduce the heat to low. Strain the reserved soaking liquid through a fine sieve to remove any grit, and pour the strained liquid into the pan. Simmer gently for 20–30 minutes.

4 Taste, and season with salt and black pepper. Add the chilli oil to taste, and serve hot.

VARIATION Sprinkle in a teaspoon of toasted sesame seeds, if you like.

COOK'S NOTES
The flavours of this soup develop more if it is made a few hours ahead, then simply reheated to serve.

Pearl barley and borlotti bean one-pot

PREP 10 MINS **COOK 1 HR**

SERVES 4

1 tbsp olive oil
1 onion, finely chopped
1 small glass of red wine
175g (6oz) pearl barley
400g can borlotti beans, drained
    and rinsed
400g can whole peeled plum
    tomatoes, chopped in can
1.2 litres (2 pints) hot vegetable stock
salt and freshly ground black pepper
chilli oil, to serve (optional)

1 Heat the oil in a large heavy pan over a low heat. Add the onion and a pinch of salt, and sweat gently for 5 minutes until soft and translucent. Increase the heat, pour in the wine, and simmer for about 5 minutes.

2 Reduce the heat to low, add the pearl barley, and stir well until it has soaked up all the liquid. Tip in the borlotti beans, tomatoes, and hot stock. Bring to the boil again, and keep boiling for a further 5 minutes.

3 Reduce the heat to low once again, season well with salt and black pepper, and gently simmer for 25–40 minutes until the pearl barley is cooked and all the stock has been absorbed. If the mixture starts to dry out, add a little hot water.

4 Drizzle over a splash of chilli oil (if using), and serve hot, either on its own or with some fresh crusty bread.

VARIATION

This is delicious cooked with farro instead of pearl barley. You can find farro in health food stores or the special-selection aisle of supermarkets.

EVERYDAY

Thai green curry

PREP 10 MINS **COOK 30 MINS**

SERVES 4

1 tbsp sunflower or vegetable oil
1 onion, finely diced
1–2 tbsp Thai green curry paste
    (depending on how hot you like it)
400ml (14fl oz) coconut milk
2 tbsp Thai fish sauce, such as nam pla
1–2 tsp palm sugar or demerara sugar
2–3 kaffir lime leaves (optional)
salt and freshly ground black pepper
220g can bamboo shoots, drained
200g packet frozen ready-cooked
    small prawns, defrosted

1 Heat the oil in a large deep frying pan or wok over a low-medium heat. Add the onion, and sauté for about 5 minutes until soft and translucent. Stir through the curry paste, and cook for a further 2–3 minutes until fragrant.

2 Pour in the coconut milk, then fill the can with water, and add this to the pan or wok. Bring to the boil, reduce the heat slightly, and add the fish sauce, sugar, and lime leaves (if using). Season with salt and black pepper.

3 Simmer over a low heat for about 15 minutes, then stir through the bamboo shoots and prawns. Cook for about 10 minutes until the prawns are warmed through. Taste, and adjust the seasoning if needed. Serve hot.

VARIATION

Swap the prawns for chicken or tofu if you prefer.

COOK'S NOTES

A delicious Thai curry requires an authentic curry paste as its base. Unless you are going to make your own, try to buy a good-quality one that has been made in Thailand.

Aduki bean stew

PREP 10 MINS · COOK 30 MINS

SERVES 4

1 tbsp olive oil
1 onion, finely chopped
salt
2 garlic cloves, grated or
    finely chopped
½–1 tsp cayenne pepper (depending
    on how hot you like it)
400g can aduki beans, drained
    and rinsed
400g can whole peeled plum
    tomatoes, chopped in can
500ml (16fl oz) hot vegetable stock
about 12 black olives, pitted

1 Heat the olive oil in a pan over a low heat. Add the onion and a pinch of salt, and sweat gently for about 5 minutes until soft and translucent. Add the garlic and cayenne, and stir through.

2 Tip in the aduki beans and tomatoes, including any juices, and pour over the stock. Bring to the boil, then reduce the heat to low.

3 Simmer gently for 15–20 minutes, stirring through the olives for the last 5 minutes of cooking. If the stew dries out too much, top up with a little hot water. Serve with a crisp salad, new potatoes, or rice.

VARIATION

This is delicious with a couple of chopped preserved lemons stirred through. Halve them, scoop out and discard the flesh, and chop the remainder, then add to the stew with the olives.

Mixed bean medley

PREP 10 MINS · COOK 40 MINS

SERVES 4

1 tbsp olive oil
1 onion, finely chopped
salt
2 garlic cloves, grated or
    finely chopped
125g (4½oz) bacon lardons or
    pancetta cubes
pinch of chilli flakes
2 tsp dried oregano
400g can mixed beans, drained
    and rinsed
300ml (10fl oz) pale ale
900ml (1½ pints) hot vegetable stock

1 Heat the oil in a large heavy deep-sided frying pan over a low heat. Add the onion and a pinch of salt, and sweat gently for about 5 minutes. Stir through the garlic, and cook for about 30 seconds more without colouring.

2 Increase the heat slightly, and add the bacon or pancetta. Cook for about 5 minutes until it begins to turn golden. Sprinkle over the chilli flakes and oregano, and tip in the beans. Stir through.

3 Pour in the ale, bring to the boil, and cook over a high heat for a good 5 minutes. Add the stock, reduce the heat slightly, and simmer gently for 20–25 minutes, stirring occasionally, until the mixture thickens. Serve hot with fresh crusty bread to mop up the flavoursome gravy.

VARIATION

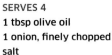

Use any combination of your favourite cooked beans or pulses.

COOK'S NOTES

If the mixture begins to dry out a little, add some water – but don't add too much because it will dilute the taste.

EVERYDAY

EVERYDAY

Hot and sour coconut broth

PREP 10 MINS | COOK 30 MINS

SERVES 4
1.4 litres (2½ pints) hot chicken stock
400ml (14fl oz) coconut milk
4 tbsp Thai fish sauce, such as nam pla
1 tbsp light soy sauce
2–3 tsp tom yum paste
2 tsp palm sugar or demerara sugar
2 kaffir lime leaves (optional)
25g (scant 1oz) mixed dried
   mushrooms (such as shiitake,
   oyster, and porcini)
salt

1 Bring the chicken stock to the boil in a large pan. Add the coconut milk, and continue boiling for about 5 minutes.

2 Reduce the heat to a simmer, then add the fish sauce, soy sauce, tom yum paste, sugar, lime leaves (if using), and mushrooms. Continue to simmer gently over a low heat for about 20 minutes until the mushrooms are soft.

3 Taste, and season with salt if needed, or add a little more sugar, fish sauce, or soy sauce. Serve hot in small serving bowls.

Curried sweetcorn fritters

PREP 10 MINS | COOK 30 MINS

SERVES 4
125g (4½oz) plain flour
salt and freshly ground black pepper
2 eggs
300ml (10fl oz) milk
2 tsp medium curry powder
50g (2oz) semolina
425g can sweetcorn
   kernels, drained
60–90ml (2–3fl oz) vegetable oil
   for frying

1 Sift the flour into a bowl with a pinch of salt. Make a small well in the centre, and break the eggs into it, then pour in a little of the milk. Using a wooden spoon, stir the egg, incorporating the flour little by little, and adding the remaining milk as you go.

2 Switch to a hand whisk, and beat until there are no lumps. Add the curry powder, semolina, and sweetcorn, and season well with salt and black pepper. Stir until everything is well combined.

3 To cook the fritters, heat ½–1 tablespoon of vegetable oil in a non-stick frying pan over a medium heat. Carefully drop in a large tablespoon of the batter. Cook two fritters at a time if the pan is big enough, but do not overcrowd. Shallow-fry for about 2 minutes until the bottom is golden and crisp. Flip over using a spatula or egg slice, and cook on the other side for another 2 minutes. You will need to stir the batter each time before using, and add more oil to the pan as you go.

4 Drain the fritters briefly on kitchen paper, and serve piping hot from the pan either on their own or with a salad.

VARIATION
Switch the curry powder for ground cumin, or use cayenne pepper or paprika.

COOK'S NOTES
The batter for these is best used straight away, and the fritters are best eaten instantly.

Wild rice with sun-dried tomatoes and cashew nuts

PREP 10 MINS · **COOK 30 MINS** · ♡

Soaking • 15 minutes

SERVES 4–6

50g (1¾oz) sun-dried tomatoes
    (about 12)
1 tbsp olive oil
1 onion, finely chopped
salt and freshly ground black pepper
350g packet long-grain and
    wild rice
1 tsp ground turmeric
1.2 litres (2 pints) hot vegetable stock
125g (4½oz) cashew nuts

1 Put the sun-dried tomatoes in a bowl. Just cover with hot water, and leave to soak for about 15 minutes. Drain, roughly chop, and set aside.

2 Meanwhile, heat the oil in a large heavy shallow pan over a low heat. Add the onion and a pinch of salt, and sweat gently for about 5 minutes until soft and translucent. Stir through the rice and turmeric until the grains are well-coated and everything is combined.

3 Pour in the stock, and increase the heat a little. Season with some more salt and some black pepper. Cook for about 5 minutes, allowing the mixture to come to the boil, then stir through. Reduce the heat slightly, and simmer gently for 20–30 minutes until all the stock has been absorbed and the rice is cooked. If the rice is drying out too much while cooking, add a little more hot vegetable stock or hot water.

4 Stir through the chopped sun-dried tomatoes, then toast the cashew nuts in a dry frying pan over a low heat for 5 minutes until lightly golden. Add to the rice mixture, and stir through. Taste, and adjust the seasoning if needed. Serve hot.

VARIATION

Vary the type of nuts to your preference and, if you use sun-dried tomatoes stored in oil, add a little of the oil for extra taste.

Chickpea curry with cardamom

PREP 10 MINS · **COOK 30 MINS** · ♡ · ❄

SERVES 4

1 tbsp vegetable oil
1 onion, finely chopped
salt and freshly ground black pepper
1 tsp cumin seeds
1 tsp ground turmeric
1 tsp ground coriander
6 green cardamom pods,
    lightly crushed
400g can chickpeas, drained
    and rinsed
400g can whole peeled plum
    tomatoes, chopped in can
1–2 tsp garam masala
1 tsp extra hot chilli powder (more
    if you like it hot)

1 Heat the oil in a large heavy pan over a low heat. Add the onion and a pinch of salt, and sweat gently for about 5 minutes until soft and translucent. Stir in the cumin seeds, turmeric, coriander, and cardamom, and continue cooking for about 5 minutes until fragrant.

2 Add the chickpeas to the pan, and stir through well, crushing them slightly with the back of a wooden spoon. Tip in the tomatoes, including any juices, then fill the can with water and add this also. Sprinkle in the garam masala and chilli powder, and bring to the boil.

3 Reduce the heat to low, and simmer gently for about 20 minutes, until the sauce begins to thicken slightly. Season with salt and black pepper. Serve hot with naan bread and basmati rice.

Tuna and white beans with olives

PREP 10 MINS

SERVES 4

400g can butterbeans, drained
  and rinsed
400g can cannellini beans, drained
  and rinsed
2 x 200g cans tuna in olive
  oil, drained
2 tbsp white wine vinegar
salt and freshly ground black pepper
1 tsp wholegrain mustard
½ tsp mild paprika
about 12 black olives, pitted
  and halved
2 tsp capers in vinegar, drained

1 Tip the beans into a large bowl along with the tuna. Add the vinegar, taste, and season well with salt and black pepper.

2 Add the remaining ingredients, and stir through thoroughly. Taste, and season again if needed. Serve immediately, or put in the refrigerator for a couple of hours until needed. If making ahead, bring back to room temperature before serving.

VARIATION

Use flageolet beans instead of butterbeans, if you prefer – these have a much softer texture.

Tomato bulgur wheat with capers and olives

PREP 15 MINS **COOK 15 MINS**

SERVES 4

350g (12oz) bulgur wheat
salt and freshly ground black pepper
150–300ml (5–10fl oz) tomato juice
3 tsp capers in vinegar, drained
12 black olives, pitted and halved
12 green olives, pitted and halved

1 Tip the bulgur wheat into a large bowl, then pour over enough boiling water just to cover – about 300ml (10fl oz). Leave to stand for about 15 minutes.

2 Season generously with salt and black pepper, and stir well with a fork to fluff up the grains. Add the tomato juice, a little at a time, until the bulgur

has absorbed all the juice. Leave to stand for a few minutes between each addition – the bulgur will absorb quite a lot of moisture.

3 Now add the capers and olives, taste, and season again if needed. Serve with a crisp green salad and some warm pitta bread.

COOK'S NOTES

Capers are an invaluable store-cupboard ingredient because they perk up so many dishes. Once you have opened a jar of them, however, make sure that you keep it in the refrigerator.

Vegetarian moussaka

PREP 15 MINS · COOK 30 MINS

SERVES 4

1 tbsp olive oil
1 onion, finely chopped
salt and freshly ground black pepper
1 tsp dried mint
3 tsp dried oregano
400g can aduki beans, drained
   and rinsed
700g jar passata
100g (3½oz) pine nuts
250ml (9fl oz) Greek-style yogurt
1 egg

1 Preheat the oven to 200°C (400°F/Gas 6). Heat the oil in a pan over a low heat. Add the onion and a pinch of salt, and sweat gently for about 5 minutes until soft. Sprinkle over the dried mint and 1 teaspoon of the dried oregano, and stir through.

2 Add the aduki beans, passata, and pine nuts, and bring to the boil. Reduce the heat to low, and simmer gently for 15–20 minutes until thickened. Season well with salt and black pepper.

3 Spoon the bean mixture into an ovenproof dish. Mix together the yogurt, egg, and remaining 2 teaspoons of dried oregano. Spoon evenly over the top of the bean mixture. Bake in the oven for 15–20 minutes, until the top is golden, puffed, and set. Serve hot with a crisp green salad.

Couscous stuffing with harissa and walnuts

PREP 15 MINS · COOK 15 MINS

SERVES 4

225g (8oz) couscous
300ml (10fl oz) hot vegetable stock
salt and freshly ground black pepper
2 tsp harissa paste
handful of raisins
50g (1¾oz) walnuts, halved
4 preserved lemons

1 Tip the couscous into a bowl, pour over the stock, and leave to stand for 10 minutes. Stir with a fork to fluff up the grains.

2 Season well with salt and black pepper, then stir through the harissa, raisins, and walnuts. Halve the preserved lemons, scoop out and discard the flesh, and chop the remainder. Stir into the couscous.

COOK'S NOTES

Use as a stuffing for turkey, chicken, or oily fish, such as mackerel. Harissa is fairly hot. If you don't want any heat, substitute with the same quantity of tomato purée.

STORECUPBOARD

Fried polenta with tomato sauce

SERVES 2

3–4 tbsp olive oil
1 onion, finely chopped
salt and freshly ground black pepper
1 tsp dried oregano
1 tsp chilli flakes
400g can whole peeled plum
   tomatoes, chopped in can
500g packet ready-made polenta,
   cut into slices 5mm (¼in) thick

1 Heat 1 tablespoon of the olive oil
in a large heavy deep-sided frying
pan over a low heat. Add the onion
and a pinch of salt, and sweat gently
for about 5 minutes until soft.

2 Sprinkle in the oregano and
chilli flakes, then tip in the tomatoes,
including any juices. Simmer gently
for about 20 minutes. Season with
salt and black pepper.

3 Meanwhile, heat a tablespoon
of oil in a large non-stick frying
pan over a high heat. Cooking in
batches, fry the polenta slices for
about 5 minutes on each side until
crisp and golden. Remove from the
pan with a spatula or fish slice, drain
on kitchen paper, and keep warm.
Repeat until all the polenta has
been cooked.

4 To serve, divide the warm crispy
polenta among 2 serving plates, and
top with the spicy tomato sauce.
Serve with a wild rocket salad.

COOK'S NOTES

This dish could be served as
a starter for 4 people. Make
the sauce ahead, to save time.

EVERYDAY

Storecupboard pasta

SERVES 4

350g (12oz) penne or other dried
   pasta of your choice
1 tbsp olive oil
3 tsp salted capers, rinsed and gently
   squeezed dry
handful of black olives, pitted
6 sun-dried tomatoes in oil, chopped
   (reserve a little of the oil, optional)
salt and freshly ground black pepper

1 Cook the pasta in a pan of boiling
salted water for 8–10 minutes, or
according to the packet instructions,
until *al dente*. Drain, and return to the
pan with a little of the cooking water.

2 Meanwhile, in another pan,
heat the olive oil over a low heat.
Add the capers, olives, and sun-dried
tomatoes, and cook gently for about
5 minutes, squashing them slightly
with the back of a fork.

3 Tip the mixture over the cooked
pasta, and toss through until evenly
mixed. Add a little of the reserved oil
from the sun-dried tomatoes (if using).
Season well with salt and black
pepper, and serve immediately.

279

Bean burgers

Special equipment • food processor

SERVES 4-6

400g can aduki beans, drained
    and rinsed
400g can chickpeas, drained
    and rinsed
1 onion, roughly chopped
6 salted anchovies in olive oil, drained
1 tbsp wholegrain mustard
salt and freshly ground black pepper
2 eggs
2-3 tbsp plain flour, plus extra
    for dusting
2-3 tbsp vegetable or sunflower oil,
    for frying

1 Put the drained beans and chickpeas in a food processor, and pulse several times until the beans are broken up.

2 Add the onion, anchovies, and mustard, and season well with salt and black pepper. Pulse again a few times. You want the mixture to be well combined, but not sloppy. Now add the eggs, and pulse again until combined.

Add the flour (just enough to bind the burgers), and pulse until incorporated.

3 Heat 1 tablespoon of oil in a large non-stick frying pan over a medium heat. Once the oil is hot, spoon out a portion of the bean mixture (it makes 6 burgers) and, using lots of flour on your hands, form into a flattened burger before adding to the pan. Fry undisturbed for 2-3 minutes on each side until firm and golden. Cook in batches of 2 or 3 burgers at a time, forming the burgers as you go and adding more oil when needed. Serve hot, sandwiched in a bun with crisp lettuce and tomato ketchup.

COOK'S NOTES

Do use the pulse button on the food processor – this gives you more control in achieving the consistency you want. Although the mixture is fairly wet to work with, you will need the 2 eggs for binding. If you prefer some texture, just don't blend the beans as much.

Pasta in brodo

SERVES 4

1.7 litres (3 pints) good-quality
    chicken stock
2 x 250g packets dried stuffed
    tortellini with the filling of
    your choice
salt and freshly ground black pepper

1 Pour the stock into a large pan, and bring to a vigorous boil. Reduce the heat slightly to a rolling boil, and add the pasta.

2 Cook for about 10 minutes, or according to the packet instructions, until the pasta is just soft. Turn off the heat, taste the stock, and season with salt and black pepper if needed.

3 To serve, ladle the broth into 4 warm bowls, dividing the tortellini evenly among them, and serve with fresh crusty bread.

VARIATION
Sprinkle with freshly chopped flat-leaf parsley, or fresh herb of your choice, if you have some.

COOK'S NOTES

If using fresh filled pasta, just follow the cooking guidelines on the packet, again cooking in the stock instead of water. You'll find dried filled pasta in large supermarkets or Italian delicatessens.

EVERYDAY

Lentil dumplings with chilli and cumin

 PREP 15 MINS · COOK 20 MINS

Special equipment · blender or food processor

SERVES 2

125g (4½oz) dried red lentils, rinsed and picked

salt and freshly ground black pepper

1 onion, roughly chopped

2.5cm (1in) piece of fresh root ginger, roughly chopped

pinch of ground cumin

pinch of chilli flakes

2 tbsp plain flour, plus extra for dusting

2 tbsp vegetable or sunflower oil for frying

120ml (4fl oz) Greek-style yogurt, to serve

2 tsp mint sauce, to serve

1 Put the lentils in a pan. Add 450ml (15fl oz) water and a pinch of salt. Gently cook over a low heat for 10–15 minutes until the lentils are soft but not mushy. Tip the lentils into a sieve to drain off any excess water.

2 Put the onion and ginger in a blender or food processor, and whiz until finely chopped. Spoon in the cooked lentils, add the cumin and chilli, and season with salt and black pepper. Pulse a few times until the mixture begins to form a paste. Sprinkle in the flour, and continue to pulse until the mixture just comes together.

3 Tip some extra flour onto a plate. Scoop up about a tablespoon of the lentil mixture and, with floured hands, lightly form into a ball, then gently roll in the flour until well coated. Repeat until all the mixture has been used.

4 Heat enough vegetable oil for shallow-frying in a large non-stick frying pan over a medium heat. Carefully add the dumplings, cooking a few at a time if the pan is not large enough. Fry for 1–2 minutes on each side until golden. Remove from the pan with a slotted spoon, and drain on kitchen paper. To serve, mix together the yogurt and mint sauce in a small bowl. Serve alongside the warm dumplings with a crisp green salad.

Biryani with cardamom and cinnamon

PREP 15 MINS · COOK 30 MINS

SERVES 4

1 tbsp vegetable oil

1 onion, finely chopped

salt and freshly ground black pepper

6 green cardamom pods, lightly crushed

2 dried bay leaves

1 cinnamon stick, halved

1 tsp black peppercorns, lightly crushed

½–1 tsp chilli powder

a few saffron threads

450ml (15fl oz) hot vegetable stock

450g (1lb) basmati rice

50g (1¾oz) flaked almonds

handful of raisins

1 Heat the oil in a large deep-sided frying pan over a low heat. Add the onion and a pinch of salt, and sweat gently for about 5 minutes until soft and translucent. Stir in the cardamom, bay leaves, cinnamon, peppercorns, and chilli powder, and cook for a further 5 minutes until fragrant.

2 Add the saffron to the hot stock, and stir through. Stir the rice into the onion mixture until the grains are well coated, then pour over the stock. Bring to the boil, reduce the heat slightly, cover, and simmer for 15–20 minutes, stirring occasionally so that the rice doesn't catch. Top up with a little hot water if needed.

3 Lightly toast the almonds in a small dry non-stick frying pan over a low heat for a couple of minutes until starting to turn golden (taking care not to let them burn). Stir the almonds and raisins through the biryani, taste, and season well with salt and black pepper. Serve hot either on its own, or topped with some cooked chicken or prawns.

EVERYDAY

FOOD FOR FRIENDS

MENU PLANNERS

Themed menu ideas, each with a "countdown" plan of action, designed for effortless entertaining, to take you through every step – from prep to plate.

15-MINUTE DINNER

Fish is the perfect choice for speedy cooking, as it requires very little done to it, and can sit
in a warm oven until required, leaving little last-minute cooking. The throw-together fruit dessert
uses a "cheat" shop-bought tart base, and can be assembled just before serving.

Mushrooms in garlic sauce p340

Lemon sole with herbs p78

Mixed berry flan p472

COUNTDOWN

15 MINUTES

- **Main course** Put the fish in the oven to cook (step 2).
- **Dessert** Prepare the fruit for the dessert, and chill.

10 MINUTES
- **Starter** Prepare the garlic mushrooms, and keep warm.

5 MINUTES

- **Main course** Make the dressing for the fish, and put to one side.

SERVE
- Serve the mushrooms.
- Keep the fish warm (in the turned-off oven).
- Remove the fruit from the refrigerator. Add the fruit to the flan base with ice cream just before serving.

DINNER IN 30 MINUTES
INDULGENT MEAL FOR TWO

A really quick and easy colourful menu, using a few indulgent ingredients, such as scallops and ripe juicy figs. All dishes are simple, letting the quality of the ingredients speak for themselves. A perfect menu if cooking for two: halve the quantities, as the original recipes serve 4 people.

Scallops with sweet chilli sauce p347

Seared duck with five-spice and noodles p70

Fresh figs with cassis cream p469

COUNTDOWN

30 MINUTES
- **Dessert** Prepare the figs and the cassis cream, cover, and put in the refrigerator.

20 MINUTES
- **Main course** Rub the duck breasts with the five-spice paste, and start cooking them.

10 MINUTES
- **Starter** Cook the scallops and arrange on warmed serving plates with the lettuce garnish.

SERVE

- Serve the scallops.
- Remove the figs from the refrigerator.
- Combine the noodles and duck, and keep warm.

LOW-FAT

A super-quick fresh menu that is low in fat and calories, but high in flavour. Both the starter and dessert can be prepared ahead of time, and kept in the refrigerator, and you can use ready-cooked salmon for the main dish if you are short on time.

Chilled tomato and red pepper soup p41

Baked salmon with salsa verde and cucumber p236

Oriental fruit salad p472

COUNTDOWN

30 MINUTES

- **Dessert** Prepare the fruit salad, cover, and put in the refrigerator.
- **Starter** Prepare the soup, ladle into serving bowls, and put in the refrigerator to chill.

20 MINUTES

- **Main course** Prepare the salsa verde and cucumber, and put in the refrigerator.
- **Main course** Arrange the cooked salmon on plates. Or, cook salmon fillets wrapped in foil in a medium oven for 20 minutes.

10 MINUTES

- **Main course** Remove the salsa verde and cucumber from the refrigerator, and spoon over the plates of salmon. Cover, until ready to serve.
- **Starter** Prepare the garnish for the soup.

SERVE

- Garnish and serve the soup.
- Remove the fruit salad from the refrigerator.

287

DINNER IN 30 MINUTES continued
VEGETARIAN

This menu can be prepared in a flash. The starter requires no cooking, and can be prepared ahead and left to chill. The main course is a quick and healthy stir-fry: meat could always be served with the stir-fry, if you are cooking for non-vegetarians.

Fresh tomatoes stuffed with fruity couscous p46

Asparagus, broccoli, ginger, and mint stir-fry p92

Apricots with Amaretti biscuits and mascarpone p471

COUNTDOWN

30 MINUTES

- **Starter** Prepare the tomatoes, cover, and put to one side.

20 MINUTES

- **Dessert** Make the dessert and put in the refrigerator to chill.
- **Main course** Prepare the vegetables for the stir-fry.
- **Main course** Start cooking the rice to go with the stir-fry (if required).

10 MINUTES

- **Starter** Plate up the tomatoes for the starter, and garnish, if required.

SERVE

- Serve the tomatoes.
- Stir-fry the vegetables.
- Remove the dessert from the refrigerator.

FISH

Fish can be served twice within a menu. This is easy and quick, as the starter is a no-cook salad, the main course can be left in the oven while you prepare the rest of the meal, and the dessert can be prepared ahead.

Smoked fish, fennel, and mango salad p52

Butterflied sardines stuffed with tomatoes and capers p73

Boozy berries with mint and elderflower cream p464

COUNTDOWN

30 MINUTES

- **Dessert** Prepare the dessert, and put in the refrigerator to chill.

20 MINUTES

- **Main course** Prepare the sardines, and put in the oven to bake.

10 MINUTES

- **Starter** Prepare the smoked fish salad; slice the fennel and prepare the mango.
- **Main course** Prepare a crisp green salad to accompany the main course.

SERVE

- Serve the fish salad.
- Turn off the oven, but leave the sardines in, to keep warm.
- Remove the dessert from the refrigerator.

FOOD FOR FRIENDS

DINNER IN 60 MINUTES
HEALTHY

A healthy menu for entertaining, that's both delicious and quick – it's perfectly acceptable for fish to appear twice on the menu. Not only is it ready to eat in an instant, it's also low in fat and good for you. The exotic dessert can be prepared ahead of time, leaving you free to keep your guests company.

Smoked trout with beetroot, apple, and dill relish p40

Baby courgettes with fish and couscous p387

Middle Eastern oranges p466

COUNTDOWN

60 MINUTES
- **Starter** Prepare step 1 and step 3 of the starter, leaving out the apple. Cover and put in the refrigerator.
- **Dessert** Segment the oranges for the dessert, and put to one side.

45 MINUTES

- Preheat the oven.
- **Main course** Slice the courgettes for the main course (step 1).
- **Dessert** Prepare the dessert, arrange on a platter, and put in the refrigerator to chill.

30 MINUTES

- **Main course** Prepare the fish couscous, cover with foil, and put in the oven.

15 MINUTES

- **Starter** Remove the starter ingredients from the refrigerator, and add the apple to the beetroot.
- **Main course** Prepare a crisp green salad to serve with the main course, if required.

SERVE
- Check on the couscous. If cooked, turn off the oven.
- Serve the starter.
- Remove the dessert from the refrigerator.

FOOD FOR FRIENDS

DECADENT

This is a deceptively easy menu for entertaining. It requires no fiddly techniques, but will still impress your guests. The dessert can be prepared ahead, and the goat's cheese starter takes little time and effort to assemble.

Grilled goat's cheese with honey p335

Pork fillet stuffed with olives and jalapeño peppers, wrapped in bacon p67

Caramel banana tart p494

COUNTDOWN

60 MINUTES

- **Dessert** Prepare the tart up to the end of step 2.
- **Main course** Prepare the pork fillet (step 1), and put in the oven.

45 MINUTES

- **Starter** Prepare the starter up to the end of step 1.

30 MINUTES

- **Main course** Check on the pork in the oven and prepare the serving suggestion: a spinach and tomato salad.

15 MINUTES

- **Starter** Place the cheese for the starter on the toast, and complete the recipe. Put to one side.

SERVE

- Put the tart in the oven.
- Serve the starter.
- Remove the pork from the oven and allow it to rest, before slicing and serving.

DINNER IN 60 MINUTES continued
SPICY

A simple menu with lots of authentic Thai-style flavours. The easy and refreshing no-cook dessert is perfect to round off the meal, and the bite-sized starter can be made ahead, leaving you time to concentrate on the main course.

FOOD FOR FRIENDS

Thai fish cakes p361

Pad Thai p381

Lychees with ginger and star anise p473

COUNTDOWN

60 MINUTES

- **Dessert** Prepare the lychee dessert, cover, and chill.

45 MINUTES

- **Starter** Make the mixture for the fish cakes, and shape into patties. Put in the refrigerator to firm up (step 1).

30 MINUTES

- **Main course** Prepare the ingredients for the Pad Thai, and put to one side.
- **Starter** Fry the fish cakes and keep warm, covered, in a warm oven.

15 MINUTES

- **Main course** Soak the noodles for the Pad Thai, and complete steps 2 and 3. Transfer to serving bowls, and keep warm.

SERVE

- Garnish the fish cakes, and serve.
- Remove the dessert from the refrigerator to bring to room temperature.

MEDITERRANEAN-STYLE

This is packed with a mix of cuisines from the Mediterranean that compliment each other.
The main course is easy to execute, and quick to cook, as the meat is bashed thin. The traditional,
indulgent dessert is the perfect treat to round of the meal.

Prawns with garlic and chilli p334

Beef escalopes with anchovies, capers, and olives p64

Orange and chocolate tiramisu p462

COUNTDOWN

60 MINUTES

- **Dessert** Prepare the tiramisu, cover, and chill.
- **Starter** Marinate the prawns in the chilli and garlic mixture, cover, and put in the refrigerator.

45 MINUTES

- **Main course** Bash the steaks for the escalopes, mix the anchovy paste and smother over the meat, cover, and put to one side.

30 MINUTES

- **Main course** Prepare the rocket salad for the main course.

15 MINUTES

- **Starter** Cook the prawns for the starter.

SERVE

- Serve the prawns.
- Start cooking the escalopes.
- When ready to serve, remove the tiramisu from the refrigerator.

GET AHEAD
SPRING

A delicious menu, with all the flavours of spring: lamb is at its best, and the asparagus season has just started. The frittata can be made ahead and served cold, as can the lemon tart, which is perfect for serving after the rich lamb, which will sit in the oven, needing little attention.

Asparagus frittata on crostini p321

Roast leg of lamb p226

Lemon tart p492

COUNTDOWN

DAY BEFORE

- **Starter** Prepare the frittata, cool, cover, and chill.
- **Dessert** Make the lemon tart, cover, and chill.

2 HOURS

- **Main course** Spike the lamb with the rosemary and garlic and put it in the hot oven (step 2).

1 HOUR

- **Starter** Toast the crostini for the starter and put to one side.
- **Dessert** Remove the tart from the refrigerator.
- **Main course** Cook spring greens or carrots and new potatoes as accompaniments, and keep warm.

SERVE

- Cut the frittata and assemble the crostini.
- Remove the lamb from the oven, and let it rest while you serve the starter.

SUMMER

This is an easy menu, ideal for serving four or more people al fresco. All three dishes can be made the day before. The main dish is much lighter than most meat dishes, and can be served alongside a fresh green salad.

Aubergine and Taleggio arancini p354

Sausage and tomato pie p203

Dark chocolate and lemon mousse p473

COUNTDOWN

DAY BEFORE

- **Starter** Prepare the arancini, cover, and chill.
- **Dessert** Make the desserts, cover, and chill.
- **Main course** Make the pastry for the pie, and chill (step 1).

2 HOURS

- **Main course** Roll the pastry out, and line the tin. Chill. Make up the sausagemeat mixture (step 2).

1 HOUR

- **Main course** Assemble the pie and put in the oven to bake (step 3).
- **Main course** Prepare a salad to accompany the pie.

SERVE

- Arrange the arancini on serving plates, and garnish.
- Check on the tart.

GET AHEAD continued
AUTUMN

This simple, seasonal menu is perfect for making ahead, as the flavours develop on reheating. Using ingredients that are in season means you get the best quality produce, at the best prices, and a better flavour to your finished dish.

Leek and potato soup p253

Beef, fennel, and mushroom hotpot p381

Sticky pecan pie p489

COUNTDOWN

DAY BEFORE

- **Main course** Make the hotpot. Cool, cover, and chill.
- **Dessert** Make the pastry case for the dessert (step 1), and chill.
- **Starter** Make the soup. Chill.

2 HOURS

- **Dessert** Prepare the pecan mixture for the pie.

1 HOUR

- **Main course** Put the hotpot in the oven to warm through. Top up with hot water if too dry.
- **Dessert** Fill the pastry case with the pecan mixture and bake in the oven.

SERVE

- Reheat the soup until piping hot, and serve with bread.
- Check on the hotpot.
- Check on the pie.

WINTER

Ribollita just gets better the longer ahead it's made, so it's perfect for a comforting winter menu. The dessert can be assembled in advance, and the casserole can sit simmering away in the oven while you entertain your guests.

Ribollita p254

Pork and bean casserole p262

Apple streusel cake p514

COUNTDOWN
DAY
BEFORE

- **Starter** Make the ribollita, and chill.
- **Dessert** While the ribollita is simmering, prepare the filling for the cake (step 1). Chill.

2
HOURS

- **Dessert** Assemble the cake (first half of step 2), wrap in cling film, and chill.
- **Main course** Prepare the casserole, and put in the oven to cook.

1
HOUR

- **Starter** Remove the ribollita from the refrigerator, and bring it to a gentle simmer.

SERVE

- Put the cake in the oven to cook while you serve the starter and main course.

FOOD FOR FRIENDS

297

PARTY FOOD
CANAPÉS

For a drinks party, a generous selection of meat and vegetarian food is needed, and it should be easy to eat with your hands, presented in bite-sized portions, or on sticks. This menu meets both criteria. Lots of the dishes can conviently be made ahead of time.

FOOD FOR FRIENDS

Roast pumpkin and ricotta crostini p314

Roast sweet potato and chilli tortilla p345

COUNTDOWN

4 HOURS

- Make the **prawn and chicken empanadas**, leave to cool, and put in a sealable container.

3 HOURS

- Make the **sweet potato and chilli tortilla**, chill, and cut up into bite-sized pieces. Cover and put to one side.
- Toast the bread, ready for the **crostini**.

1 HOUR

- Roast the pumpkin and prepare the ricotta mixture for the **crostini**. Assemble, plate up, and cover.
- Cook the **lamb**, then skewer it and keep warm until needed.
- Make the **smoked chicken with basil mayonnaise**.

30 MINUTES

- Cook the **scallops**, then skewer with the Parma ham, and plate up.
- Make the **cucumber rounds**, and top with the mayonnaise. Plate up.

SERVE

- Garnish all the dishes, if you like.
- Put some aïoli or mayonnaise in a small dish to accompany the empanadas.
- Uncover dishes, and serve.

Scallops skewered with Parma ham p327

Prawn and chicken empanadas p347

Smoked chicken with basil mayonnaise on cucumber rounds p320

Skewered lemon, rosemary, and dukkah lamb p357

PARTY FOOD continued
BUFFET

This buffet menu is colourful, and has a range of flavours and textures. You should serve around six different dishes for variety. Most of them can be prepared ahead, relieving last-minute pressure, and they won't spoil if left out on the table for a while.

Halloumi with garlic, chilli, and coriander p341

Sliced beef and rocket salad with green olive and raisin salsa p41

COUNTDOWN

4 HOURS
- Make the pastry for the **tartlets** (if making your own), chill in the refrigerator. Line the pastry cases and chill.
- Cook the potato for the **tartlets** (step 2), and chill.
- Make the **dip**, cover, and chill.

3 HOURS
- Bake the pastry cases blind, then fill and bake (step 3-4).
- Make the dried fruit chutney for the **chorizo**.

1 HOUR
- Make the **bulgur wheat** dish, cover, and chill.

30 MINUTES
- Make the salsa for the **beef and rocket salad**, cover, and chill.
- Fry the **halloumi** with the garlic, chilli and coriander, and arrange on plates.
- Prepare the **chorizo** and plate up with the chutney.

SERVE
- Plate up the **beef and rocket salad** with the salsa, remove the **dip** from the refrigerator, and place all other dishes in serving bowls or plates. Garnish.

Yogurt, aubergine, and pine nut dip p323

Chorizo with dried fruit chutney p342

Tomato bulgur wheat with capers and olives p277

Gruyère cheese, potato, and thyme tartlets p213

AL FRESCO
PICNIC

A tasty mix of traditional foods – pork pie is the ultimate picnic food, and it can be packed whole or ready-sliced, as can the panini. Sweet muffins are an easy sweet dish to pack and eat. Half of the food can be prepared the day before and kept chilled.

Spiced pork and chicken pie p210

Crayfish and crisp lettuce panini with herbed mayonnaise p319

COUNTDOWN

DAY BEFORE

- Make the **spiced pork and chicken pie**, leave to cool, then pack in a sealed container.
- Bake the **blueberry muffins**, leave to cool, and pack in a sealed container.

2 HOURS

- Prepare the **hummus**, cover and leave in the refrigerator.

1 HOUR

- Make the **chicken with aduki beans and herbs**, put in a sealable container, and leave in the refrigerator.

30 MINUTES

- Prepare the **crayfish paninis**, wrap individually in greaseproof paper, and tie with string.
- Prepare the **Caesar salad**, and pack loosely in a sealable container (so you don't crush the salad leaves).

PACKING

- Remove the chicken salad from the refrigerator, and transfer the hummus to a sealable container.
- Pack forks, knives, napkins, and drinks.

Hummus p323

Caesar salad p47

Chicken with aduki beans and herbs p53

Blueberry muffins p520

AL FRESCO continued
VEGETARIAN PICNIC

This picnic has plenty of food that can be made ahead for convenience. The dishes are all easy to pack, and won't spoil in hot weather. Even though it is vegetarian, it won't disappoint the meat eaters, as there is a wholesome pie and some meaty lentils.

Lebanese-style lentils p272

Tomato, red onion, and mozzarella salad p48

FOOD FOR FRIENDS

COUNTDOWN

DAY BEFORE

- Make the **cheese and onion pie**, leave to cool, and put in a sealable container.
- Make the **banana, date, and walnut loaf**, leave to cool, and put in a sealable container.

2 HOURS

- Prepare the **potato and paprika omelette**, leave to cool, slice into portions, and put into a sealable container.

1 HOUR

- Prepare the **lentils**, cover, and leave to sit in a bowl while you prepare the **chickpeas**. Cover both dishes, and leave to sit so the flavours have time to develop.

30 MINUTES

- Stir the **lentils** and the **chickpeas**, and pack in sealable containers.

PACKING

- Make the **tomato and mozzarella salad** last, and pack in a sealable container.
- Pre-slice the **pie** and **loaf** if required, or pack a knife. Pack plenty of napkins and drinks.

Potato and paprika omelette p332

Chickpeas in olive oil and lemon p342

Cheese and onion pie p205

Banana, date, and walnut loaf p518

AL FRESCO continued
BARBECUE

This selection of dishes combines the bold and gutsy flavours of spicy meat, with two delicately flavoured seafood dishes. The potato dish can be prepared ahead, and will be delicious served alongside the other dishes. The lamb koftas can be prepared ahead and are easy to serve and eat.

FOOD FOR FRIENDS

Wasabi beef and pak choi p443

Marinated sweet and hot tuna steaks p448

COUNTDOWN

60 MINUTES

- Light the barbecue. Prepare the **patatas bravas**, then put in the oven.
- Mix up the lamb mixture for the **lamb koftas**, cover, and chill.
- Prepare the **beef** (step 1). If using wooden skewers for the lamb, soak them in cold water.

45 MINUTES
- Marinate the **tuna steaks** (step 1) and **pork tenderloin** (step 1), and put both in the refrigerator.
- Make the dressing for the **squid and rocket salad**, and put to one side.
- Make up the **lamb koftas**.

30 MINUTES

- Put the marinated **beef** and **pork** on the barbecue, and the **lamb koftas**. Cook until ready, and keep warm on a wire rack above the barbecue.
- Check on the **patatas bravas**, remove and cover, if ready, or turn the oven off and keep warm.

15 MINUTES
- Put the **tuna** and the **squid** on the barbecue, along with the pak choi for the beef dish, and cook until charred.

SERVE
- Toss the rocket salad with the dressing, and add the squid.
- Warm some pitta breads on the barbecue for serving with the koftas. Plate up all the meat and fish, and the potatoes.

Chargrilled squid and rocket salad p434

Chilli-slashed pork tenderloin p444

Lamb koftas p448

Patatas bravas p332

AL FRESCO continued
VEGETARIAN BARBECUE

Lots of exciting flavours and textures are needed for a no-meat barbecue: crunchy salads and meaty vegetables, such as aubergines and mushrooms, create a satisfying and healthy al freso meal.
Pop some sweetcorn and vegetable skewers on the grill, too, if you like (see p433).

Potato and leek croquettes p358

Courgettes stuffed with sultanas, red onion, and pine nuts p91

COUNTDOWN

60 MINUTES
- Light the barbecue. Make the **potato croquettes** and put in the refrigerator to firm up.
- Prepare the **lentil, broad bean, and feta salad**, and put to one side, covered, to let the flavours develop.

45 MINUTES
- Prepare the **mushrooms with bread, tomatoes, and feta**, cover, and put to one side.

30 MINUTES
- Cook the **potato croquettes**, then sit on a wire rack above the barbecue to keep warm.
- Prepare the **carrot and shredded cabbage with peanuts**, cover, and put to one side.

15 MINUTES
- Put the prepared **aubergines** on the barbecue, and cook until charred.
- Put the **courgettes** on the barbecue and cook until charred, or cook in the oven (step 3).

SERVE
- Transfer all the salads to serving bowls.
- Plate the courgettes, aubergines, and croquettes onto platters.

Carrot and shredded cabbage with peanuts p50

Lentil, broad bean, and feta salad p40

Chargrilled aubergine with spiced tomato sauce p454

Grilled mushrooms with bread, tomatoes, and feta p455

NO-FUSS FINGER FOOD AND DIPS

Easy food for casual gatherings – no forks required.

NO-FUSS FINGER FOOD AND DIPS

A little planning is the key to an effortless party, along with great food, plenty of drinks, and happy guests. Individual bites that can be eaten without plates and cutlery are ideal party food, and can be served with drinks at an informal party, or before the main meal at a more formal sit down one. Decide what type of party you are having and you're halfway there.

5 instant storecupboard nibbles
Perfect for unexpected guests.

BREADSTICKS
Let guests help themselves to plain, cheese, or sesame-coated sticks. Fill up decorative glasses with them, and offer a selection of ready-bought dips. Or, wrap them with Parma ham and serve with a plate of mozzarella drizzled with a fruity extra virgin olive oil.

TORTILLA CHIPS
These are great for dipping or topping. Serve a variety of plain and spicy chips. Top with pieces of chicken and sliced peppers from a jar. Or, top with a spoonful of finely chopped tomatoes and capers, and a drizzle of soured cream.

MELBA TOAST
Top these crisp bites with a simple ready-made paté and a caper berry, or a meat pâté and a teaspoon of fruity chutney. For a sweeter bite, cover with cream cheese, and top with a slice of exotic fruit such as kiwi, mango, or papaya.

NUTS AND SEEDS
A bowl of mixed nuts are a good standby drinks accompaniment. Better still, pan-fry a selection of nuts with a little sugar, and sprinkle with toasted sesame seeds; or, toast some sunflower and pumpkin seeds with a sprinkling of soy sauce or tamari.

RICE PAPER
Soak in water for 20 seconds, fill with matchstick vegetables and spring onions, or cooked prawns and fresh root ginger, and roll into cones. Tie into rolls with chives, for a smart finish.

Fuss-free entertaining

Keep it simple. It will make life easier if food is loosely themed, so – for example – a Middle Eastern or Mediterranean theme. It can simplify shopping, and will avoid too many competing flavours.

Budget. Have a rough idea of how much you want to spend, and write a shopping list. The more choice you offer, the more costly it will be.

Seasons. In summer, all items can be cold, but in winter it is preferable to have at least 2 or 3 hot items on the menu.

Variety. Choose a good variety of ingredients, from meat and fish, to vegetables and herbs. Always include 3–4 vegetarian dishes.

Prepare. Make up as much as you can the day before (dips, for instance), and keep in the refrigerator, or even earlier, and freeze. Assemble at the last minute.

Skewer it
Little flavoursome bites on sticks are perfect easy-to-eat finger food. The combinations are endless – here are some ideas to get you started.

Sausage and squash A great combination that can be made ahead, and served hot or cold. Roast a tray of chipolata sausages, halved, with a peeled, deseeded, and cubed butternut squash. Toss with olive oil, freshly ground black pepper, and a sprinkling of chilli flakes (if you wish), and cook in the oven at 200°C (400°F/Gas 6) for about 30 minutes, until cooked through. Thread onto skewers.

Melon and feta cheese An updated version of the classic cheese and pineapple combination. Chop watermelon flesh into small bite-sized pieces, and skewer with good-quality salty feta cheese cubes.

Spiced prawns Toss a handful of raw shelled prawns with olive oil, salt and freshly ground black pepper, and a pinch of cayenne pepper. Pan-fry in a little hot oil until pink, then skewer onto lemongrass stalks or wooden skewers.

Seared tuna and lime Cut a raw tuna steak into bite-sized pieces, and toss with olive oil and freshly ground black pepper. Sear briefly on a hot ridged cast-iron grill pan for 1 minute, then skewer with segmented pieces of lime.

Skewered bites of Sausage and squash, Melon and feta cheese, Spiced prawns, and Seared tuna and lime.

4 instant bases Use vegetables for a no-effort quick canapé.

Chicory

These bitter leaves are fabulous scoops for homemade dips, or can be filled with a **ready-made dip** or **hummus** for convenience. Red chicory is also available, so mix and match for plenty of colour. These bases won't wilt quickly, so can be prepared a couple of hours ahead.

Cucumber

Slices of cucumber make the simplest of bases, and can be used for a variety of toppings, such as **ready-made tzatziki** and a **mint leaf** for garnish. Slice a few hours ahead, and top at the last minute.

Radicchio

These bitter leaves make excellent cups to fill and serve as substantial finger food. Fill with a mixture of **couscous, raisins**, and **toasted pine nuts** or try filling with strong-flavoured **blue cheese**, tossed with **diced apple** and **walnuts**. If filling with a food that isn't too wet, they can be prepared a couple of hours ahead.

Baby peppers

These are sweet peppers, great halved and filled with a **strong cheese**, crumbled **feta cheese**, or a **ready-made dip** sprinkled with black pepper. They stay crisp for a long time, so prepare the night before, keep in a plastic bag in the refrigerator, then fill at the last minute.

servings per person

Most recipes in this chapter serve **8** people. If you want to increase recipe yield, simply double the quantities, although do watch the herbs and spices as these only need to be increased by half.

If serving finger foods and dips as a substitute for a main course, allow **8–12** pieces per person.

If serving finger foods and dips as canapés, allow **4–6** canapés per person, per hour. So the longer the party, the more canapés needed.

It's always better to have too much than too little. Many canapés will keep for the next day.

Mayonnaise It's easier than you think, and a great base for dips. Eggs should be at room temperature before you start.

1 Add 2 egg yolks to a glass bowl with a pinch of salt, 1 teaspoon of English mustard, and 2 teaspoons of white wine vinegar. In a jug, measure out 200ml (7fl oz) of light olive oil. Using a balloon whisk, whisk the egg yolk, slowly adding drops of olive oil. Continue adding the oil, a drop at a time, whisking all the time.

2 The mixture will begin to thicken and emulsify. Continue adding the oil, a little quicker now, whisking until all the oil has been added. Don't add the oil too quickly, as the mixture will curdle. (If this does happen, add an egg yolk to a clean bowl, then add the curdled mixture slowly and whisk until it emulsifies again.)

3 When the mayonnaise has thickened and all the oil has been incorporated, taste, and add a little more vinegar and salt and black pepper, if needed. If it is too thick, dilute with a little warm water. Serve with cold cooked meats, fish, or eggs.

FOOD FOR FRIENDS

313

Roast pumpkin and ricotta crostini

 PREP 20 MINS **COOK 50 MINS**

SERVES 16
500g (1lb 2oz) pumpkin, peeled, deseeded, and cut into chunks
2 tbsp olive oil
2 garlic cloves, crushed
grated zest and juice of 1 lemon
2 sprigs of fresh rosemary, leaves picked and chopped
200g (7oz) ricotta cheese
4 sprigs of fresh lemon-scented thyme, leaves picked

For the crostini
2 tbsp olive oil
16 slices of crusty baguette
salt and freshly ground black pepper
1 garlic clove, peeled but left whole

1 Preheat the oven to 200°C (400°F/ Gas 6). To make the crostini, pour the olive oil over the bottom of a baking tray, then gently press the bread into the oil on both sides. Season with salt and black pepper. Bake for 13–15 minutes until golden brown. Remove from the oven, and lightly rub each slice with the garlic. Set the crostini aside on a wire rack to cool, but do not turn off the oven.

2 Put the pumpkin on a baking tray, and toss with the olive oil, garlic, lemon zest, and rosemary. Season with salt and black pepper, then roast for about 35 minutes until tender and golden. Leave to cool slightly.

3 In a bowl, combine the ricotta, thyme, and a little lemon juice. Spoon a little of the ricotta mixture onto each of the crostini, and top with roasted pumpkin, squeezing it a little with your fingers as you go. Arrange on a large serving dish or platter, and serve.

 VARIATION Try a little good-quality balsamic vinegar drizzled over the pumpkin just before roasting, for a sweet-and-sour flavour.

COOK'S NOTES
Use ordinary fresh thyme leaves if you can't find the lemon-scented variety.

Cannellini and dill crostini

 PREP 20 MINS **COOK 15 MINS**

Special equipment • blender or food processor

SERVES 16
400g can cannellini beans, drained
1 tbsp fresh dill, chopped
3 anchovy fillets in olive oil, drained
2 small fresh medium-hot red chillies, deseeded and finely chopped
2 spring onions, thinly sliced
2 tbsp olive oil, to drizzle
85g (3oz) black olives, pitted and finely chopped

For the crostini
2 tbsp olive oil
16 slices of crusty baguette
salt and freshly ground black pepper
1 garlic clove, peeled but left whole

1 Preheat the oven to 200°C (400°F/ Gas 6). To make the crostini, pour the olive oil over the bottom of a baking tray, then gently press the bread into the oil on both sides. Season with salt and black pepper. Bake for 13–15 minutes until golden brown. Remove from the oven, and lightly rub each slice with the garlic. Set the crostini aside on a wire rack to cool.

2 Put the cannellini beans, dill, anchovies, chillies, and spring onions in a blender or food processor, and purée until smooth. Season with salt and black pepper, and transfer to a bowl. To serve, spoon over the crostini, drizzle with the olive oil, and sprinkle with the chopped black olives.

 VARIATION Serve the cannellini topping with your favourite grilled fish and roasted vine-ripened cherry tomatoes.

COOK'S NOTES
Canned cannellini beans make a great storecupboard standby. It takes no effort at all to turn them into a topping for crostini, a dip for crudités, or an antipasto platter.

Baba ganoush

PREP 15 MINS | COOK 45 MINS

Special equipment • blender or food processor • barbecue grill or ridged cast-iron grill pan

SERVES 4
2 large aubergines
4 garlic cloves, crushed
small handful of fresh oregano, leaves picked (optional)
grated zest and juice of 1 lemon
90ml (3fl oz) olive oil
150g (5½oz) pine nuts, toasted and chopped
125ml (4fl oz) Greek-style yogurt
salt and freshly ground black pepper

1 Heat the grill of a barbecue or a ridged cast-iron grill pan until very hot. Add the aubergines, and grill, turning every so often, for 30–45 minutes until the skin is charred and blistered all over; it will become quite black. Remove from the heat, and leave to cool a little before peeling away the skin and roughly chopping the flesh.

2 Put the chopped aubergine, garlic, oregano (if using), lemon zest and juice, and oil in a blender or food processor, and blend to a chunky spread. Transfer to a bowl, and add the pine nuts and yogurt. Season with salt and black pepper, and mix well.

3 Serve with torn chunks of sourdough bread, or toasted slices of baguette.

COOK'S NOTES
You could always roast the aubergines in the oven at 200°C (400°F/Gas 6) for about 30 minutes.

Oysters with chilli and lime mayonnaise

PREP 15 MINS

Special equipment • oyster knife

SERVES 6–8
24 fresh live oysters in their shells
1 tbsp fresh dill, chopped
2 spring onions, thinly sliced diagonally
rock salt, to serve

For the chilli and lime mayonnaise
2 small fresh hot red chillies, deseeded, if you prefer
1 garlic clove, grated or finely chopped
salt and freshly ground black pepper
1 egg yolk
175ml (6fl oz) light olive oil
juice of 1 lime

1 To make the chilli and lime mayonnaise, using a mortar and pestle, pound the chillies, garlic, and a good pinch of salt to a paste. Spoon the paste into a large bowl, then add the egg yolk. Stir thoroughly with a wooden spoon or whisk until smooth. (Sit a folded tea towel under the bowl to stop it from moving around too much.)

2 Gradually add the oil, drop by drop, whisking continuously, ensuring that it is absorbed completely before making the next addition. Once the mixture starts to thicken, add the oil in a slow, thin drizzle. When a third of the oil has been combined, start adding the lime juice a little at a time. Keep adding and whisking until everything is well incorporated. Season with black pepper, cover with cling film, and chill until needed.

3 To prepare the oysters, discard any that have opened or do not close tightly straight away when tapped on the work surface. Use an oyster knife, and hold the oysters over a bowl as you open them. Carefully shuck the oysters one by one, catching any liquid in the bowl and transferring the opened oysters in their shells and their liquid to the refrigerator as you go.

4 Put a layer of rock salt on a platter – this is to keep the oysters level. Arrange the open oysters in their shells on top of the salt, and spoon over the chilled oyster liquid. Spoon a little chilli and lime mayonnaise over the top of each oyster, and serve immediately.

Artichoke and fennel dip

PREP 15 MINS

Special equipment • blender or food processor

SERVES 8

400g can artichoke hearts, drained
  and rinsed
400g (14oz) fennel bulb(s), trimmed
  and chopped
2 tbsp tahini
juice of 1 lemon
1 garlic clove, chopped
1 tbsp olive oil
salt and freshly ground black pepper

1 Put all the ingredients in a blender
or food processor, and whiz or blend
until smooth and creamy. Season
with salt and black pepper.

2 Serve with some grilled Turkish
bread, toasted pitta bread, or ciabatta,
Alternatively, spoon it over a fresh
tomato and parsley salad.

> **COOK'S NOTES**
>
> Tahini is a ground sesame
> seed paste – you'll find it in
> large supermarkets or health
> food stores. It has a rich, nutty
> flavour, and is used throughout
> the Middle East.

Mushroom and mascarpone dip

PREP 15 MINS   COOK 45 MINS

Special equipment • blender or
food processor

SERVES 8

1kg (2¼lb) small to medium
  chestnut mushrooms, quartered
4 tbsp olive oil
1 garlic clove, crushed whole
  with the back of a knife or
  with your hand
grated zest and juice of 1 lemon
2 salted anchovies in oil, drained
  and chopped
salt and freshly ground
  black pepper
small handful of fresh flat-leaf
  parsley, plus extra to garnish
240ml (8fl oz) mascarpone cheese
  or soured cream
drizzle of extra virgin olive
  oil (optional)
pinch of paprika

1 Preheat the oven to 200°C
(400°F/Gas 6). Arrange the
mushrooms on a baking tray lined
with baking parchment, and toss
with the olive oil, garlic, lemon zest
and juice, and anchovies. Season
with salt and black pepper. Roast
for 35–45 minutes until tender and
golden. Set aside to cool.

2 Transfer the cooled mushroom
mixture to a blender or food
processor. Add the handful of parsley,
and whiz or blend to a chunky purée.

3 Put the mushroom purée in
a serving bowl with the mascarpone
cheese, and stir through gently.
Season well, stir again, and sprinkle
with the extra parsley leaves. Drizzle
with a little extra virgin olive oil (if
using), and sprinkle with the paprika.
Serve with thickly cut slices of
grilled or toasted ciabatta.

> **COOK'S NOTES**
>
> This makes a great topping for
> bruschetta. Simply toast some
> slices of ciabatta, rub with
> a peeled garlic clove, and top with
> the dip. Drizzle with a little extra
> virgin olive oil, and serve with
> a rocket and Parmesan salad.

Dill and broad bean dip

PREP 30 MINS COOK 45 MINS

Special equipment • blender or food processor

SERVES 8
750g (1lb 10oz) fresh broad beans
3 tbsp olive oil
1 small onion, finely chopped
salt and freshly ground black pepper
400g can cannellini beans, drained
1 tbsp fresh dill, chopped
2 spring onions, thinly sliced
  on the diagonal

1 Remove the broad beans from their pods, and slip off the skins. Set aside.

2 Heat the oil in a heavy pan over a low heat. Add the onion, and gently sweat for about 5 minutes until soft and translucent.

3 Tip in the broad beans, and cook for 10–15 minutes, stirring occasionally. Add 500ml (16fl oz) water, season with salt and black pepper, and part-cover the pan with a lid. Bring to a gentle simmer, and continue cooking for 25 minutes, mashing the beans a little during this time. Drain, and allow to cool.

4 Put the cooled broad bean mixture in a blender or food processor. Add the drained cannellini beans, dill, and spring onions, and blend to a chunky purée. Season with salt and black pepper. Transfer to a serving bowl, and serve with fresh crusty bread.

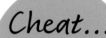

Cheat...
Use frozen broad beans instead of fresh. Leave them to defrost first, then slip off their skins.

COOK'S NOTES

This is good picnic food, served on bruschetta or flatbread with hard-boiled eggs.

Rocket, ricotta cheese, and black olive dip

PREP 15 MINS

Special equipment • blender or food processor

SERVES 4
100g (3½oz) wild rocket leaves
2 garlic cloves, crushed
100g (3½oz) black olives, pitted
grated zest and juice of 1 lemon
90ml (3fl oz) olive oil
250g (9oz) ricotta cheese
freshly ground black pepper

1 Put the wild rocket leaves, garlic, olives, lemon zest and juice, and oil in a blender or food processor, and whiz or blend until smooth.

2 Transfer the rocket and olive mixture to a bowl, add the ricotta cheese, and season with black pepper. Mix well.

3 Serve with torn chunks of warm sourdough bread, thick toasted slices of baguette, or grilled flatbread.

VARIATION

This makes a great pasta sauce – simply stir through hot drained pasta cooked until *al dente*.

COOK'S NOTES

Use good-quality dry black olives with plenty of flavour, and make sure the rocket is very fresh. Buy it loose if possible, as bagged leaves go rotten much quicker.

Roast pumpkin, chilli, and ginger dip

 PREP 20 MINS COOK 45 MINS

Special equipment • blender or food processor

SERVES 8

1kg (2¼lb) pumpkin or butternut
  squash, peeled and cut
  into chunks
4 tbsp olive oil
4 garlic cloves, crushed whole
  with the back of a knife
1 tbsp grated or finely chopped
  fresh root ginger
salt and freshly ground
  black pepper
1 fresh medium-hot long red chilli,
  deseeded and thinly sliced
4 sprigs of fresh flat-leaf parsley,
  leaves only (reserve some
  for garnish)
grated zest and juice of 1 lemon
150ml (5fl oz) Greek-style yogurt
drizzle of extra virgin olive
  oil (optional)
pinch of paprika
slices of grilled sourdough bread,
  to serve
grilled pancetta or prosciutto,
  crumbled, to serve

1 Preheat the oven to 200°C (400°F/ Gas 6). Put the pumpkin on a baking tray, and toss with the olive oil, garlic, and ginger. Season with salt and black pepper. Roast for about 30 minutes until tender and golden. Set aside.

2 Transfer the cooled pumpkin to a blender or food processor, and add the chilli, parsley (reserving a little to garnish), and lemon zest and juice. Blend to a chunky purée. Season with salt and black pepper.

3 Put the pumpkin purée and the yogurt in a bowl, and mix thoroughly. Season if needed, then spoon into a serving bowl. Top with a drizzle of extra virgin olive oil (if using). Garnish with the reserved parsley and a sprinkle of paprika, and serve on grilled sourdough bread, with grilled pancetta or prosciutto over the top.

COOK'S NOTES

This dip is good with grilled or roasted meat. To make it extra hot, simply add another long chilli.

Red pepper and walnut dip

 PREP 20 MINS COOK 30 MINS

Special equipment • blender or food processor

SERVES 8

90ml (3fl oz) olive oil
1 onion, sliced
4 red peppers, deseeded and sliced
2 garlic cloves, crushed
125g (4½oz) toasted walnuts, chopped
grated zest and juice of 1 lemon

1 Heat the oil in a heavy frying pan over a low heat. Add the onion, and gently sweat for about 5 minutes until soft and translucent.

2 Tip in the peppers, and cook for about 30 minutes until soft, stirring regularly. Stir through the garlic, and cook a further 30 seconds, or until the garlic has turned white.

3 Transfer the pepper mixture to a blender or food processor. Add the walnuts and lemon zest and juice, and blend to a chunky purée. Serve with warm pitta breads or crudités such as carrot or cucumber batons for dipping.

 VARIATION

Use macadamia nuts instead of walnuts. You may also like to add about 125ml (4fl oz) Greek-style yogurt and chopped coriander leaves, stirring through the mixture at the end.

COOK'S NOTES

To toast the walnuts, spread them out in a single layer on a baking tray. Toast in a preheated 180°C (350°F/Gas 4) oven for 8–10 minutes, checking frequently to make sure they do not burn.

Prawn, avocado, and watercress sandwich

 PREP 30 MINS COOK 5 MINS

SERVES 4

1 tbsp olive oil

24 raw small prawns, peeled and deveined

1 tbsp finely chopped fresh root ginger

1 small fresh hot red chilli, finely chopped

1 garlic clove, chopped

1 ripe avocado

1 cucumber, thinly sliced

a few sprigs of fresh mint, leaves picked and roughly torn

1 tbsp finely chopped dill

1 tbsp capers, chopped, rinsed, and drained

½ small red onion, finely chopped

250ml (8fl oz) soured cream

juice of 1 lime

8 thick slices wholegrain or granary bread

4 handfuls of watercress

1 Heat the oil in a frying pan over a medium-high heat, and pan-fry the prawns, ginger, and chilli for 3–5 minutes until the prawns turn completely pink and opaque. Add the garlic, and stir through for 30 seconds or so. Set aside to cool, then roughly chop.

2 Halve, stone, and peel the avocado. Dice the flesh, and put in a bowl. Add the cucumber, mint, dill, capers, onion, soured cream, and lime juice. Tip in the chopped prawns, and gently stir through, being careful not to mash the avocado.

3 Spread the mixture evenly over 4 slices of the bread. Arrange the watercress on top so that it will come out over the sides of the sandwich. Cover with the other slices of bread to make 4 sandwiches, and serve.

Crayfish and crisp lettuce panini with herbed mayonnaise

 PREP 15 MINS

SERVES 4

1kg (2¼lb) cooked crayfish tails

4 Italian-style crusty bread rolls

1 oakleaf or other butter lettuce, leaves separated

2 fresh peaches, stoned and sliced

For the herbed mayonnaise

120ml (4fl oz) mayonnaise

juice of 1 lime

small handful of fresh coriander, chopped

small handful of fresh mint leaves, chopped

small handful of fresh chives, chopped

1 anchovy fillet in olive oil, drained and chopped

freshly ground black pepper

1 Remove all the meat from the crayfish tails, being careful not to break it up too much. Tear into four even portions, and set aside.

2 To make the herbed mayonnaise, combine the mayonnaise, lime juice, herbs, and anchovy in a bowl. Season with black pepper, and stir through.

3 Slice the rolls in half, but without cutting all the way through. Open up, and spread with the herbed mayonnaise. Arrange some of the leaves over the mayonnaise, then put the crayfish on top of the leaves. Arrange slices of the peaches between the crayfish, then spoon over a little more of the mayonnaise. Close up the rolls, and serve immediately.

VARIATION

Use peeled and deveined cooked prawns in place of the crayfish.

COOK'S NOTES

Instead of sandwiching this combination in bread rolls, serve as a salad with chopped spring onion or Spanish onion over the top. Or add avocado slices and orange segments. You could even try adding steamed asparagus and halved cherry tomatoes.

Smoked trout, fennel, and mascarpone crostini

 PREP 25 MINS **COOK 15 MINS**

SERVES 4

2 tbsp olive oil
4 thick slices crusty sourdough bread
salt and freshly ground black pepper
1 garlic clove, peeled but left whole
2 smoked trout, about
   300g (10oz) each
150g (5oz) fennel bulb, trimmed,
   halved, and thinly sliced
125ml (4fl oz) mascarpone cheese
30g (1oz) flaked almonds, toasted
juice of ½ lemon
sprigs of fresh chervil, to garnish
1 lemon, cut into wedges, to serve

1 Preheat the oven to 200°C (400°F/Gas 6). Pour the olive oil onto a baking tray, then gently press the bread into the oil on both sides. Season with salt and black pepper. Bake in the oven for 12–15 minutes until golden brown. Remove from the oven, and lightly rub each slice with the garlic. Set aside on a wire rack to keep the crostini crisp.

2 Meanwhile, remove the skin from the smoked trout, and gently remove the flesh from the bones in big chunks.

3 Put the trout, fennel, mascarpone, flaked almonds, and lemon juice in a bowl. Season with black pepper, and gently mix through.

4 To serve, arrange the trout mixture over the crostini, season with some more pepper, and garnish with the chervil. Serve immediately, with lemon wedges for squeezing over.

COOK'S NOTES

To toast the almonds, spread out over the bottom of a small dry frying pan. Toast over a medium heat for a few minutes until golden, stirring frequently to prevent them scorching.

Smoked chicken with basil mayonnaise on cucumber rounds

 PREP 20 MINS

SERVES 6–8

1 smoked chicken breast, about
   250g (9oz)
3 tbsp mayonnaise
1 tbsp ready-made pesto
freshly ground black pepper
2 cucumbers, about 300g (10oz),
   cut into 5mm (¼in) thick slices

1 Remove the skin from the chicken. Slice across the breast into thin slices, and finely chop into small cubes. In a bowl, combine the chicken, mayonnaise, and pesto. Season with black pepper, and mix well.

2 Spoon a good teaspoon of the smoked chicken mixture onto a slice of cucumber, and arrange on platters ready to serve.

Salt cod and red pepper dip

 PREP 25 MINS **COOK 1 HR**

Special equipment • blender or food processor

SERVES 12

2 red peppers
2 garlic cloves, peeled
1 small red onion, finely chopped
4 tbsp olive oil
salt and freshly ground black pepper
2 tbsp Spanish onion, finely chopped
400g can plum tomatoes, chopped
500g (1lb 2oz) salt cod
2 tbsp fresh marjoram, finely chopped
2 tbsp fresh dill, finely chopped
handful of fresh basil leaves, finely chopped
handful of fresh flat-leaf parsley, finely chopped
juice of 1 lemon

1 Preheat the oven to 200°C (400°F/Gas 6). Slice the tops off the peppers, and remove the seeds and membrane. Put a garlic clove and half of the chopped red onion in the cavity of each pepper. Sit the peppers on an oven tray lined with baking parchment. Drizzle with 1 tablespoon of the olive oil, and season with salt and black pepper. Roast in the oven for about 1 hour. Remove from the oven, and set aside to cool.

2 While the peppers are roasting, heat the remaining 3 tablespoons of olive oil in a heavy frying pan over a low heat. Add the remaining onion, and sweat for about 5 minutes until soft. Tip in the chopped tomatoes, including any juices, and cook for a further 10 minutes, stirring from time to time. Season with salt and black pepper.

3 Meanwhile, slice the skin off the salt cod, and flake the flesh into chunks. Add to the tomato sauce after the 10 minutes' cooking time, and cook gently for a further 10 minutes. Set aside to cool.

4 Put the cooled peppers (with garlic and onion) in a blender or food processor with the cooled tomato and cod mixture. Purée until smooth. Transfer to a serving bowl, and season with salt and black pepper. Add the herbs and lemon juice, and stir to blend well. Serve with crostini, broken pieces of toasted bread, or grilled Turkish bread.

Asparagus frittata on crostini

 PREP 20 MINS **COOK 20 MINS**

SERVES 4

4 tbsp olive oil
4 thick slices crusty sourdough bread
salt and freshly ground black pepper
1 garlic clove, peeled but left whole
8 fresh asparagus spears, trimmed
2 tbsp onion, finely chopped
4 eggs
125ml (4fl oz) double cream
60g (2oz) Parmesan cheese, freshly grated
1 handful of fresh flat-leaf parsley, to garnish

1 Preheat the oven to 200°C (400°F/Gas 6). Pour 2 tablespoons of the oil onto a baking tray, then gently press the bread into the oil on both sides. Season with salt and black pepper. Bake in the oven for 12–15 minutes until golden brown. Remove from the oven, and lightly rub each slice of bread with the garlic. Set aside on a wire rack to keep the crostini crisp.

2 Meanwhile, blanch the asparagus spears in lightly salted boiling water for 2–4 minutes. Drain, refresh in cold water, and drain again. Place on a board, and cut each spear in half lengthways. Heat the remaining oil in a heavy frying pan over a low heat, and cook the onion for about 5 minutes until soft and translucent. Add the halved asparagus spears, and cook further for 2 minutes. Preheat the grill to its highest setting.

3 In a bowl, whisk together the eggs, cream, and Parmesan. Season with salt and black pepper, and pour the mixture over the asparagus and onion mixture in the pan. As the bottom is cooking, tilt the pan so the uncooked egg mixture from the top spills over under the frittata. Continue cooking for 3–5 minutes until almost set. To finish off, place the pan under the grill, and grill until the top of the frittata is golden brown. To serve, tear the frittata into 4 rough pieces, and sit on top of the crostini. Scatter with parsley, and serve immediately.

FOOD FOR FRIENDS

Mini beef burgers on pizza bases with chilli and beetroot salad

  PREP 30 MINS · COOK 15 MINS

SERVES 8

1 double packet of pizza dough mix
  (2 x 145g sachets)
400g jar good-quality
  tomato sauce

For the burgers
500g (1lb 2oz) beef mince
100g (3½oz) Parmesan cheese,
  freshly grated
50g (1¾oz) fresh breadcrumbs
3 tbsp olive oil
1 garlic clove, crushed
2 tbsp finely chopped Spanish onion
¼ tsp pimentón (Spanish
  smoked paprika)
2 eggs
2 tbsp fresh flat-leaf parsley, chopped
4 sprigs of fresh thyme, leaves picked
salt and freshly ground black pepper

For the chilli and beetroot salad
350g (12oz) raw beetroot, peeled
  and grated
1 small fresh red chilli, deseeded and
  finely chopped
1 tbsp olive oil
juice of ½ lemon

1 Make the dough, according to the packet instructions. Knead on a floured work surface for about 5 minutes until smooth. Place in an oiled bowl, and cover with a clean tea towel. Leave in a warm place until doubled in size.

2 Meanwhile, put all the ingredients for the burgers in a bowl, and season with salt and black pepper. Mix together well by hand. With damp hands, form the mixture into balls about the size of small walnuts – 36–40 balls. Sit on a large baking sheet lined with baking parchment, and press down with your thumb to flatten a little. Chill to firm, while the dough is rising.

3 Preheat the oven to 200°C (400°F/ Gas 6). Once the dough has doubled in size, remove from the bowl, and knead lightly on a floured work surface. Roll out to about 5-6mm (¼in) thick. Using a biscuit cutter, cut into 4-5cm (1¾-2in) discs, and place on a large baking sheet lined with baking parchment.

4 Transfer the trays of pizza bases and burgers to the oven. Bake for 10-15 minutes until the bases are golden and the burgers are cooked through. Warm through the tomato sauce. Put all the ingredients for the salad in a bowl, and stir through. To serve, spoon a little of the tomato sauce onto the pizza bases, then top with the burgers. Garnish with the beetroot salad, and serve immediately.

Mini chicken burgers with tomato and chilli sauce

  PREP 30 MINS · COOK 30 MINS

Chilling · 1 hour
Special equipment · food processor

SERVES 12

800g (1¾lb) skinless chicken breast
  fillets, chopped into chunks
1 tbsp fresh flat-leaf parsley,
  finely chopped
1 tsp fresh sage leaves, finely sliced
1 garlic clove, finely chopped
100g (3½oz) dates, chopped
50g (1¾oz) hazelnuts, roughly chopped
2 tsp Middle Eastern spice
  mix (dukkah – see p352)
2 eggs
2 tbsp olive oil, plus extra
  for brushing
75g (3oz) fresh breadcrumbs
salt and freshly ground black pepper
400g jar good-quality tomato sauce
handful of basil leaves, torn
1 fresh hot red chilli, finely
  chopped (optional)
12 thick slices baguette
1 garlic clove, peeled but left whole
2 yellow peppers, grilled, deseeded,
  and sliced
2 red peppers, grilled, deseeded,
  and sliced

1 Mince the chicken in a food processor for 10-15 seconds; be careful not to blend into a paste. Transfer to a bowl, and add the herbs, garlic, dates, hazelnuts, dukkah, eggs, olive oil, and breadcrumbs. Mix together thoroughly, and season with salt and black pepper. Cover with cling film, and chill for about 1 hour.

2 Preheat the grill to low. Form the chilled chicken mixture into 12 burger-style portions, then brush the burgers with a little extra oil. Grill the chicken burgers for 6-8 minutes on each side until cooked through. Set aside for 15 minutes in a warm place.

3 Warm through the tomato sauce, with the basil leaves, adding fresh chilli if you like. Lightly brush the baguette slices with olive oil, and toast on both sides under the grill. Lightly rub each slice with the garlic clove. To serve, arrange the bread on a platter. Pile a combination of the yellow and red peppers, then a chicken burger, on top of each slice. Spoon over a little sauce, and serve.

Hummus

PREP 10 MINS

Special equipment • blender or food processor

SERVES 8-10
400g can chickpeas, drained and rinsed
2 garlic cloves, crushed
juice of 1 lemon, plus extra if needed
2-3 tbsp tahini
pinch of paprika
2-3 tbsp olive oil
salt

1 Put all the ingredients except the olive oil in a blender or food processor. Blend to a smooth purée.

2 With the motor running, gradually add the oil, a little at a time, until the hummus reaches your preferred consistency. Taste, and season with salt, adding some extra lemon juice if you like. Blend again. Serve as a dip with some warmed pitta bread.

Yogurt, aubergine, and pine nut dip

PREP 15 MINS **COOK 40 MINS**

Special equipment • blender or food processor

SERVES 8-10
1 large aubergine
1 tbsp olive oil
2-3 tbsp tahini
2 garlic cloves, grated or crushed
juice of 1 lemon, plus extra if needed
pinch of ground cumin
salt and freshly ground black pepper

1 Preheat the oven to 200°C (400°F/ Gas 6). Pierce the aubergine a few times all over with a knife. Next, using your hands, rub the aubergine with the olive oil. Roast in the oven for 30-40 minutes until beginning to char.

2 When the aubergine is cool enough to handle, peel off the skin, and put the roasted flesh in a blender or food processor. Add the tahini, garlic, lemon juice, and cumin, and blend to a purée.

3 Taste, and season with salt and black pepper, adding more lemon juice if needed. Blend again briefly. Spoon into a bowl or serving dish, and serve with pitta breads.

COOK'S NOTES

Make this dip ahead, and leave it in the refrigerator overnight. Remember to allow enough time for it to come to room temperature before serving.

Bruschetta with tomato and basil

PREP 10 MINS

MAKES 8

6 ripe tomatoes, roughly diced
handful of fresh basil leaves,
    roughly torn
4 tbsp extra virgin olive oil
salt and freshly ground black pepper
1 loaf ciabatta
3 garlic cloves, peeled but left whole

1 Put the tomatoes, basil, and olive oil in a bowl. Season really well with salt and black pepper. Set aside to allow the flavours to develop.

2 Preheat the grill to its highest setting. Slice the ciabatta horizontally lengthways, then cut each piece into quarters so that you have 8 pieces of bread in total. Toast both sides until golden.

3 Immediately rub each piece of toasted bread with the garlic. Spoon over the tomato and basil mixture, and serve immediately.

COOK'S NOTES

The longer you can leave the tomatoes sitting in the oil and basil, the better. Peel and deseed the tomatoes, if you wish.

Mini chicken tikka tortillas with yogurt, cucumber, and mint dip

PREP 20 MINS

SERVES 8-10

245g packet plain-flavoured
    corn chips
125–250ml (4½–9fl oz) mango chutney
350g (12oz) cooked chicken tikka
    pieces, chopped into small pieces
fresh coriander, to garnish

For the yogurt, cucumber, and mint dip
200ml (7fl oz) Greek-style yogurt
½ cucumber, peeled, halved,
    and deseeded
1 bunch of fresh mint, leaves picked
salt and freshly ground black pepper

1 To make the dip, tip the yogurt into a bowl. Finely dice the cucumber, and add to the yogurt with the mint leaves. Season well with salt and black pepper. Taste, and season more if needed.

2 Tip the corn chips onto a clean surface, and spread out in a single layer. Add a teaspoon of mango chutney to each one.

3 Add some chicken pieces to each corn chip. Spoon on about a teaspoon of the dip, and garnish with coriander. Serve immediately.

Quail's eggs with celery salt

  PREP 10 MINS COOK 15 MINS

Special equipment • food processor

SERVES 4

2 celery sticks, finely chopped
12 quail's eggs, hard-boiled
and peeled (or buy
ready-prepared ones)
salt

1 Preheat the oven to 200°C (400°F/ Gas 6). To make the celery salt, spread out the celery over a baking sheet, and sprinkle a couple of pinches of salt over it. Stir around a little, then roast in the oven for 5–8 minutes, until crisp and dry. Tip the celery into a food processor, and whiz until fine.

2 To boil the eggs (if they are not ready-prepared), place them in a pan of gently boiling water, then simmer for 2½ minutes. Drain, and rinse in cold water until cool. Carefully peel away the egg shells. Sit the quail's eggs on a serving plate, and sprinkle with a little salt. Transfer the celery salt to a small bowl, or on a plate, and serve alongside the eggs for dipping.

Cheat...
You can buy ready-made celery salt, but it's a bit of fun making your own and it tastes so much fresher.

COOK'S NOTES
Serve a bowl of mayonnaise alongside the eggs as well, with some fresh crusty bread.

FOOD FOR FRIENDS

Garlic and chilli prawn and squid skewers

  PREP 20 MINS COOK 10 MINS

Marinating • 30 minutes
Special equipment • cocktail sticks or mini wooden skewers

SERVES 6

12 large raw prawns, peeled
and deveined
6 baby squid, cleaned and
halved lengthways
2 fresh medium-hot red chillies,
deseeded and finely sliced
3 garlic cloves, grated or
finely chopped
1 tbsp olive oil
small handful of fresh flat-leaf
parsley leaves
2.5cm (1in) piece of fresh root
ginger, grated
salt and freshly ground black pepper

1 Put all the ingredients in a bowl, and season with salt and black pepper. Leave to marinate in the refrigerator for at least 30 minutes, or overnight if you have time.

2 Soak 6 cocktail sticks or mini wooden skewers in cold water

for 30 minutes before using, and preheat the grill to its highest setting.

3 Thread a prawn, a piece of squid, a second prawn, and another piece of squid, onto each of the cocktail sticks or mini skewers. Sit the skewers on a baking tray, and grill each side for about 2 minutes. Serve hot with some Yogurt, cucumber, and mint dip (see p324).

Cheat...
You could use the leftovers in a salad, or a fish pie.

COOK'S NOTES
Use some of the leftover marinade to brush over the prawns while they're cooking.

FOOD FOR FRIENDS

Sesame prawn toasts

PREP 15 MINS   COOK 10 MINS

Special equipment • blender or food processor

SERVES 4

300g (10oz) peeled and deveined cooked prawns
2 garlic cloves, peeled but left whole
small handful of fresh coriander
1 fresh hot red chilli, deseeded and finely chopped
juice of 1 lime
salt and freshly ground black pepper
4 slices white bread
125g (4½oz) sesame seeds

1 Preheat the grill to its highest setting. Blend or process the prawns, garlic, coriander, chilli, and lime juice to a paste. Season well with salt and black pepper, and blend again briefly.

2 Lightly toast the bread, then spoon the prawn mixture evenly over one side of each of the toasts. Spread to cover completely, pressing the mixture down firmly.

3 Now lightly oil a baking sheet, and tip over the sesame seeds in an even layer. Sit the toasts, prawn-side down, on the seeds, and press so that the seeds stick and coat the mixture. Carefully flip the toasts over, and cut into triangles.

4 Slide the baking sheet under the hot grill, and cook the toasts for a few minutes until the sesame seeds begin to turn golden. Keep a careful eye on them, as they can burn very quickly. Serve immediately.

Potato skins with spicy tomato sauce

PREP 10 MINS   COOK 25 MINS

SERVES 8-10

4 large baking potatoes
1-2 tbsp olive oil
salt and freshly ground black pepper
6 ripe tomatoes, roughly chopped
pinch of cayenne pepper
small handful of fresh flat-leaf parsley, finely chopped
150ml (5fl oz) soured cream

1 Sit the potatoes in the microwave, and cook on full power for 3-4 minutes until softened. (Alternatively, rub the potatoes with a little olive oil, and bake in a preheated 200°C (400°F/Gas 6) oven for about 1 hour until soft when pierced with a knife.) Set aside until cool enough to handle.

2 Preheat the oven to 200°C (400°F/Gas 6). Once the potatoes are cool,

quarter each one, and scoop out the flesh, leaving a thin layer of flesh in the skin to make a shell. Sit the skins hollow-side up on a baking sheet, and drizzle over the olive oil. Sprinkle over a pinch of salt.

3 Mix together the tomatoes, cayenne, and parsley, and season with salt and black pepper. Spoon a little of the mixture into each potato skin. Bake in the oven for 15-20 minutes until the skins are golden and crispy. Top each of the potato skins with some soured cream and serve on a large plate.

COOK'S NOTES

To sour your own cream, add a squeeze of lemon juice to some single cream, and leave to sit for 10 minutes before using.

Scallops skewered with Parma ham

PREP 10 MINS **COOK 8 MINS**

Special equipment • skewers

SERVES 8
8 fresh scallops, halved
1 tbsp olive oil
juice of 1 lemon
salt and freshly ground black pepper
8 slices Parma ham, halved

1 If using wooden skewers, soak them in cold water for 30 minutes. Preheat the oven to 190°C (375°F/Gas 5). Mix the scallops with the oil and lemon juice, and season with salt and black pepper.

2 Wrap each scallop half in a piece of Parma ham, then thread onto metal or wooden skewers. You'll probably need 2 scallop halves on each skewer, depending on how big they are.

3 Lay the skewers on a baking sheet, and roast in the oven for 5–8 minutes until the ham starts to crisp. Serve hot with a wild rocket leaf garnish.

COOK'S NOTES

If serving non-meat eaters, omit the Parma ham and cook the scallops for a few minutes less.

Mini topped rye breads

PREP 15 MINS

SERVES 8-10
8 thin slices rye bread
    or pumpernickel
125g (4½oz) Dolcelatte cheese, cubed
300g (10oz) packet ready-cooked
    beetroot (not in vinegar),
    finely diced
2-3 tbsp creamed horseradish

1 Cut the rye bread into small squares – about 6 squares per slice, depending on how big the slices are.

2 Top each bread square with a fine slice of Dolcelatte cheese, a teaspoonful of diced beetroot, and a tiny amount of creamed horseradish. Arrange on platters, and serve.

For a quick alternative, replace the Dolcelatte cheese with hummus.

TAPAS-STYLE

Spanish-inspired food for sharing
– plate after plate.

TAPAS-STYLE

Tapas is a style of eating rather than a particular dish. It's a way of life in Spain, where appetizing hot or cold bites are eaten with drinks. There are robust rustic dishes, such as grilled chorizo, and simple platters of jamon (Spanish ham), olives, and cheese. The most typical of all is the delicious Spanish omelette, the tortilla, which nearly always makes an appearance when tapas is served.

What is tapas?

Tapas derives from the word "tapar", which means "to cover" – traditionally, small bites of food, such as a piece of toasted bread with a slice of ham on top, would be balanced on top of a glass of wine or sherry. Simple traditional tapas such as olives, cheeses, and meats are still served all over Spain in bars as an accompaniment to an apéritif before lunch or dinner. There are no standard tapas to serve together, just plenty of small bowls, with a good range of fresh flavours. If making tapas for quite a few people, serve them all on one platter, along with a choice of two dishes of meat, fish, vegetables, and egg and cheese.

A selection of tapas in traditional Spanish-style clay bowls.

The Spanish platter A selection of good meats, cheeses, and pickles makes for perfect tapas.

COOKED MEATS

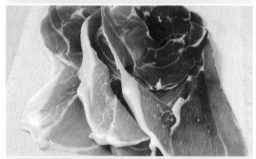

JAMON SERRANO (SPANISH HAM) is a delicious, sweet dry-cured ham that is served raw and sliced paper-thin. It has a deep rich texture, due to the traditional curing methods.

JAMON IBERICO is another cured ham, highly prized, and expensive. It comes from the Iberico pig that is native to Spain.

CHORIZO There are lots of varieties of chorizo, the spicy pork sausage of Spain. It can be smoked, unsmoked, fresh, or cured. Its unique taste is spiced with aromatic flavours, and usually features garlic and paprika. Cured chorizo can be served raw, sliced alongside cheese and olives. Fresh chorizo is often cubed and cooked.

CHEESE

MANCHEGO is the most widely known and widely available Spanish cheese. This salty cheese is made from milk from the Manchego sheep and can be soft or hard, depending on how long it has had to ripen. There are two types: the artisanal (farmhouse) type which is made with unpasteurized milk, and the commercial type made with pasteurized milk. They are both available either semi-cured or cured. It is perfect served alone with a chunk of bread, with a glass of fino or manzanilla sherry, or with quince paste or honey.

You can serve **Parmesan cheese** as an alternative, but keep in mind it's stronger and saltier, so you'll need less.

OLIVES AND PICKLES

MANZANILLA OLIVES are the most popular choice for tapas. They are large, green, sweet Spanish olives that are often stuffed with anchovies or flavoured with lemon, thyme, or oregano. They are the simplest tapas dish. Serve them in a small bowl, with cocktail sticks for serving.

PICKLED CAPERS Jars of pickled capers, and whole caper berries with their stalks on, are a popular tapas accompaniment.

PICKLED ANCHOVIES White anchovies are served in little bowls, either marinated in a little white wine vinegar and a sprinkling of freshly chopped parsley, or teamed with strips of roasted red pepper, and served with cocktail sticks, or on top of sliced bread or toast, sprinkled with paprika.

STEP-BY-STEP

The ultimate Spanish omelette A simple tortilla made with potatoes, onions, and eggs.

1 Peel and slice 5 medium potatoes, about 5mm (¼in) thick. Put about 300ml (10fl oz) of olive oil in a deep-sided ovenproof frying pan (preferably non-stick), add the potatoes, and cook at a gentle simmer for about 15 minutes, or until the potatoes are soft when you poke them with a sharp knife. Remove the potatoes with a slotted spoon and put them in a large bowl to cool.

2 Halve, peel, and quarter 3 medium onions, and slice so you have crescent moon shapes. Tip most of the oil out of the pan (you can sieve and re-use), and add the onions and a pinch of salt. Cook over a low heat until soft and beginning to caramelize. Add to the potatoes and leave to cool.

3 Whisk 5 eggs with a fork, then pour into the cooled potato and onion mixture, season with sea salt and freshly ground black pepper, and combine gently so all the potatoes get coated, trying not to break them up too much. Preheat the oven to 200°C (400°F/Gas 6). Heat 1 tablespoon of the olive oil in the frying pan until hot, then carefully slide the mixture in, spreading it evenly so it covers the base of the pan. Reduce the heat to low-medium and cook for 6–10 minutes, or until almost set.

4 Put in the oven, and cook for a further 10 minutes, or until set and golden. Alternatively, cook one side, then invert onto a plate and add back to the pan to cook the other side. Remove from the pan, leave to cool and completely set, then slice into wedges. Serve warm or cold.

The Spanish kitchen

The essentials

Olive oil is a staple in the Spanish kitchen, and is used liberally in cooking, or used to drizzle over tapas dishes such as roasted peppers or marinated artichokes. It can be served in a bowl, with rustic bread for dipping.

Garlic is essential in Spanish cooking and is added in generous quantities to many dishes. Use for aioli (garlic mayonnaise), or garlic prawns.

Onions are used extensively in Spanish cooking. Choose the mild, sweet, yellow-skinned ones to make the Spanish omelette (see left).

The spice rack

Paprika (pimento) is the best-known spice of Spanish cooking. The highest-quality paprika comes from the western La Vera region, and is oak-smoked to give it its distinctive smoked flavour. It is made from ground chilli peppers, and comes as hot (*picante*) or sweet (*dulce*) paprika. It imparts a wonderful colour and depth of flavour to dishes, particularly pork and chicken, and is used for many tapas dishes, or simply added as garnish.

Saffron is a sweet, yellow, expensive spice, and should be used sparingly – not only because of its cost, but because it can have an overpowering taste if overused. Its strands are traditionally used in paella, chicken dishes, and can also be added to courgette salads.

Cinnamon is used throughout Spain to flavour meat and vegetable dishes. It comes as a bark, or ground to a fragrant aromatic powder. Add the bark to rice dishes whilst cooking, or add the powder to chicken dishes.

Nutmeg is another aromatic spice often used in Spanish cooking. Use it sparingly and freshly ground into potato dishes, meat stews, or sweet dishes such as custards.

Paprika is a key ingredient in Spanish cooking.

FOOD FOR FRIENDS

Patatas bravas

 PREP 15 MINS COOK 1 HR

SERVES 4

6 tbsp olive oil
700g (1lb 9oz) white potatoes, peeled
    and cut into 2cm (¾in) cubes
2 onions, finely chopped
1 tsp chilli flakes
2 tbsp dry sherry
zest of 1 lemon
4 garlic cloves, grated
    or finely chopped
200g can chopped tomatoes
handful of fresh flat-leaf
    parsley, chopped
salt and freshly ground black pepper

1 Preheat the oven to 200°C (400°F/
Gas 6). Heat half the oil in a non-
stick frying pan, add the potatoes,
and cook, turning frequently, over
a medium-low heat for 20 minutes,
or until starting to brown. Add
the onions and cook for a further
5 minutes.

2 Add the chilli, sherry, lemon
zest, and garlic and allow to reduce
for 2 minutes before adding the
tomatoes and parsley. Season with
salt and black pepper, combine well,
and cook over a medium heat for
10 minutes, stirring occasionally.

3 Add the remaining oil, place the
whole lot in a shallow baking dish,
and cook in the oven for 30 minutes,
or until cooked. Serve hot with a
selection of tapas dishes.

Cheat...
You can leave out the
oven cooking, and just
cook them on the hob
instead. The oven
cooking intensifies
the flavour.

Potato and paprika omelette

PREP 10 MINS COOK 55 MINS

SERVES 4

250ml (9fl oz) olive oil
500g (1lb 2oz) potatoes, peeled
    and cut into 1cm (½in) slices
3 onions, finely sliced
2 tsp paprika
6 eggs
salt and freshly ground black pepper

1 Heat the oil in a 25cm (10in) wide
5cm (2in) deep non-stick frying pan
and add the potatoes. Cook over
a very low heat for 15-20 minutes,
or until beginning to soften but not
brown. Carefully remove from the
oil with a slotted spoon and place
in a mixing bowl.

2 Add the onions and a pinch of salt
to the pan with a little oil, and cook
slowly for 10-15 minutes, or until
beginning to soften but not brown.
Remove from the oil with a slotted
spoon and add to the potatoes with the
paprika. Allow to cool for 15 minutes.
Discard all but 2 tablespoons of the
oil, and return the pan to the heat.

3 Meanwhile, break the eggs into
a mixing bowl and beat with a fork.
Season well with salt and black pepper,
then combine with the cold potatoes
and onion, and pour the mixture into
the frying pan. Cook over a low heat
for 15-20 minutes, or until set, then
put under a hot grill or in a hot oven
until the top turns golden. Leave to
rest for 5 minutes, then carefully
transfer to a serving plate. Slice and
serve hot, or cold.

COOK'S NOTES

To remove the omelette from the
pan, ensure it's not stuck to
the sides or the bottom, then place
a large plate over the top and hold
it firmly in place while quickly
turning the pan upside-down.

Mini pork meatballs in spiced tomato sauce

PREP 30 MINS COOK 20 MINS

SERVES 4

300g (10oz) minced pork
1 small onion, finely chopped
1 tsp capers, finely chopped
2 tsp black olives, finely chopped
1 tbsp plain flour
1 egg, lightly beaten
salt and freshly ground black pepper
4 tbsp olive oil
400g can chopped tomatoes
2 garlic cloves, grated
   or finely chopped
1 tsp paprika

1 Preheat the oven to 200°C (400°F/ Gas 6). Put the minced pork, onion, capers, olives, and flour in a mixing bowl, add the egg, and season with salt and black pepper. Mix thoroughly, using your hands, then form into 12–15 2cm (¾in) balls.

2 Heat the oil in a frying pan and fry the meatballs for 8–10 minutes, or until golden brown. Transfer to a baking dish and put to one side.

3 Meanwhile, put the tomatoes, garlic, and paprika in a pan, season with salt and black pepper, then cook over a medium heat for 10 minutes, stirring occasionally. Pour the tomato sauce over the meatballs and bake in the oven for 20 minutes. Serve hot.

Stuffed mushrooms

PREP 20 MINS COOK 15 MINS

SERVES 4

12 medium field mushrooms
3 tbsp olive oil
3 tbsp fresh breadcrumbs
1 onion, finely chopped
2 garlic cloves, crushed
1 fresh red chilli, deseeded
   and finely chopped
handful of fresh flat-leaf
   parsley, chopped
150g (5½oz) minced pork
3 fresh tomatoes, finely chopped

1 Remove the stalks from the mushrooms and discard, then brush the mushrooms with the oil.

2 Put the rest of the ingredients in a mixing bowl and combine well with your hands to form a rough paste. Stuff the cup of each mushroom with a 1cm (½in) layer of the paste.

3 Grill the mushrooms under a medium grill for 12–15 minutes, or until golden brown and the mince is cooked. Serve with a drizzle of olive oil and some fresh crusty bread.

Marinated anchovies, salted almonds, and olives

PREP 15 MINS

Marinating • 1 hour

SERVES 4

For the olives
250g (9oz) mixed green and black olives, unstoned
2 garlic cloves, finely sliced
zest of 1 orange
2 fresh red chillies, deseeded and very finely chopped
1 tsp cracked black pepper
3 tbsp extra virgin olive oil

For the anchovies
150g (5½oz) anchovies in oil
2 garlic cloves, finely sliced
small handful of dill, finely chopped
1 tsp white wine vinegar
freshly ground black pepper

For the almonds
125g (4½oz) unskinned almonds
1 tsp sea salt

1 Put the olives in a small bowl with the garlic, orange zest, chillies, and peppercorns. Drizzle over the oil, give the olives a stir, then leave to marinate in the refrigerator for 1 hour.

2 Meanwhile, put the anchovies and their oil in a small serving bowl. Add the garlic, dill, and vinegar, season with black pepper, then stir to combine. Leave to marinate for at least 30 minutes.

3 While the olives and anchovies are marinating, put the almonds in a small frying pan and heat gently. Sprinkle over the salt, toss to coat, then cook, stirring frequently, for 5 minutes, or until lightly toasted.

4 Transfer the almonds, olives, and anchovies to individual small serving bowls, or one serving dish, and serve at room temperature with drinks.

Prawns with garlic and chilli

PREP 5 MINS **COOK 10 MINS**

SERVES 4
4 tbsp olive oil
6 garlic cloves, grated or finely chopped
1 tsp chilli flakes
1 tbsp dry sherry
250g (9oz) raw shelled prawns
salt and freshly ground black pepper

1 Heat the oil in a frying pan over a medium heat, add the garlic and chilli, and cook gently for 2 minutes.

2 Add the sherry and prawns, turn up the heat, and cook, stirring occasionally, for 5 minutes, or until the juices have reduced by half. Season with salt and black pepper and serve with fresh crusty bread and a crisp salad.

COOK'S NOTES
You can use shell-on prawns if you prefer for this dish – do provide a finger bowl and napkins, though!

Grilled goat's cheese with honey

  PREP 10 MINS | COOK 5 MINS

SERVES 4

2 tbsp runny honey

2 tbsp dry sherry

300g (10oz) fresh goat's cheese, cut into 1cm (½in) rounds

1 French stick, cut into 12 1cm- (½in-) thick slices and toasted

2 tbsp dried oregano

1 Put the honey and sherry in a small pan and stir over a low heat until the honey has completely dissolved.

2 Place a round of cheese on each piece of toast, and pour a little of the honey and sherry mixture on top. Sprinkle over the oregano and grill under a medium grill for 5 minutes, or until starting to brown. Serve immediately with a crisp salad.

COOK'S NOTES

Drizzle with a little more honey to serve, if you wish. There are numerous varieties of honey available – try heather or orange blossom honey.

FOOD FOR FRIENDS

Chorizo with peppers

  PREP 10 MINS | COOK 10 MINS

SERVES 4

2 tbsp olive oil

2 red peppers, deseeded and cut into 2cm (¾in) squares

2 green peppers, deseeded and cut into 2cm (¾in) squares

3 garlic cloves, crushed

300g (10oz) chorizo cut into 2cm (¾in) cubes

2 tbsp dry sherry

1 tsp dried oregano

salt and freshly ground black pepper

1 Heat the oil in a frying pan, add the peppers, and cook over a medium heat, stirring occasionally, for 5 minutes. Add the garlic, chorizo, and sherry, and cook for 5 minutes more.

2 Sprinkle over the oregano, season with salt and black pepper, and serve.

COOK'S NOTES

This is delicious served with slices of rustic ciabatta. Choose the fully dried raw chorizo for this dish, as it requires cooking.

Feta-stuffed peppers

SERVES 4

150g (5½oz) feta cheese
3 garlic cloves, crushed
1 tbsp fresh flat-leaf parsley,
 finely chopped
1 tsp freshly ground black pepper
12 piquillo peppers
4 tbsp olive oil

1 Preheat the oven to 200°C (400°F/
Gas 6). Put the feta, garlic, parsley,
and black pepper in a mixing
bowl and mash together with the
back of a fork to form a smooth paste.

2 Cut the stalk end off the peppers
and discard. Carefully deseed the
peppers, then stuff with the feta
mixture. Brush with oil, then pack
tightly into a small baking dish.
Spoon over the remaining oil and
bake in the oven for 20 minutes,
or until the peppers are soft. Serve
hot with fresh crusty bread.

COOK'S NOTES

*If you can't get fresh piquillo
peppers, use some from a jar.
Drain well before use.*

Mushrooms on toast with Manchego cheese

SERVES 4

2 tbsp olive oil
200g (7oz) closed-cup mushrooms,
 roughly chopped
salt
3 garlic cloves, grated
 or finely chopped
1 tsp paprika
3 tbsp dry sherry
1 tsp freshly ground black pepper
handful of fresh flat-leaf parsley,
 finely chopped
8 slices of soda bread, toasted
100g (3½oz) Manchego cheese, cut
 into shavings with a potato peeler

1 Preheat the oven to 200°C (400°F/
Gas 6). Heat the oil in a frying pan,
add the mushrooms and a pinch of

salt, and cook over a medium heat for
5 minutes, or until the mushrooms
start to release their juices.

2 Add the garlic and paprika and
cook for a further minute. Add the
sherry and black pepper, then raise
the heat and allow to boil until the
liquid has reduced by three-quarters.
Stir in the parsley and remove from
the heat.

3 Lay the toast out on a baking tray,
then carefully spoon the mushroom
mixture on top. Sprinkle liberally with
the Manchego and cook in the oven
for 2 minutes, or until the cheese has
melted. Serve hot with a crisp salad.

Ham with pears

PREP 10 MINS **COOK 15 MINS**

SERVES 4

100ml (3½fl oz) dry sherry
250ml (9fl oz) water
100g (3½oz) white sugar
3 ripe Conference pears, peeled
 and cut into quarters
150g (5½oz) thinly sliced Serrano
 or Parma ham
chilli oil or mint yogurt, to serve

1 Put the sherry, water, and sugar in a pan and bring to the boil. Add the pears, return to the boil, and simmer gently for 15 minutes, or until they are beginning to soften. Turn off the heat and allow to cool for 30 minutes.

2 Wrap each piece of pear in a piece of ham. Arrange on a serving plate and serve drizzled with chilli oil, or mint yogurt.

Grilled sardines on toast

PREP 10 MINS **COOK 10 MINS**

SERVES 4

8 fresh sardines, cleaned, gutted,
 and filleted
4 tbsp olive oil
3 garlic cloves, finely sliced
1 fresh green chilli, deseeded
 and finely chopped
juice of 1 lemon
1 tsp fennel seeds, crushed
2 tbsp fresh flat-leaf parsley,
 finely chopped
salt and freshly ground black pepper
ciabatta, sliced and toasted, to serve

1 Brush the sardines with a little of the oil and cook under a medium grill for 3 minutes on each side. Remove, and allow to cool.

2 Meanwhile, put all the remaining ingredients in a mixing bowl and combine well. Add the sardines, then leave to marinate for 20 minutes, if you have time. Serve on the warm toasted ciabatta.

Spinach with pine nuts and raisins

SERVES 4

1 tbsp olive oil
3 tbsp raisins
3 tbsp pine nuts
3 tbsp dry sherry
200g (7oz) fresh spinach, rinsed
    and roughly chopped
1 tsp paprika
salt and freshly ground black pepper

1 Put the oil, raisins, and pine nuts in a shallow frying pan over a medium heat. When the raisins and pine nuts start to sizzle, cook for 2 minutes, moving them all the time. Carefully add the sherry and cook until the liquid has reduced by half.

2 Add the spinach and paprika and cook, stirring constantly, for 5 minutes, or until the spinach has wilted. Season with salt and black pepper and serve hot or cold.

VARIATION
If you haven't got sherry, use some dessert wine or white wine or a splash of white wine vinegar for sharpness. Use brocolli instead of spinach.

Battered fish with lemon mayonnaise

Special equipment • food processor

SERVES 4

1 egg, plus 1 egg yolk
juice and zest of 1 lemon
250ml (9fl oz) olive oil
salt and freshly ground black pepper
125g (4½oz) plain flour
1 tsp bicarbonate of soda
1 tsp paprika
150ml (5½fl oz) cold fizzy water
250ml (9fl oz) olive oil, for frying
300g (10oz) white fish, such as
    haddock, cut into 1cm (½in) strips

1 To make the mayonnaise, put the egg, egg yolk, lemon juice, and zest in a food processor and blend until a light yellow colour. Reduce the speed and slowly add the oil, a little at a time, until you have a smooth creamy emulsion. Season with salt and black pepper, transfer to a serving dish, and place in the refrigerator.

2 Put the flour, bicarbonate of soda, paprika, and fizzy water in a mixing bowl, season with salt and black pepper, then whisk until smooth. Meanwhile, put the oil for frying in a deep-sided frying pan and set over a high heat until it reaches 200°C (400°F). To test, pop a small cube of bread in the fat. If it sizzles, the fat is ready to use.

3 Put the fish in the batter one piece at a time and coat well. Remove any excess and carefully place in the hot oil. Cook, turning occasionally, for 2–3 minutes, or until the fish pieces are a rich golden brown. Make sure they don't stick together. Remove with a slotted spoon and place on sheets of kitchen paper to remove any excess fat. Sprinkle with a little salt and serve hot with the lemon mayonnaise.

VARIATION
Use beer instead of fizzy water in the batter. It will give a crisp rich dark batter.

Cheat...
Mix the juice of 1 lemon with 2 large tablespoons of ready-made mayonnaise, instead of making your own.

Sweetcorn fritters

PREP 10 MINS **COOK 15 MINS**

Chilling • 15 minutes

SERVES 4
125g (4½oz) plain flour
2 tbsp cold fizzy water
1 tsp baking powder
340g can sweetcorn, drained
1 tsp cayenne pepper
salt and freshly ground black pepper
3 tbsp olive oil

1 Put the flour, fizzy water, and baking powder in a bowl and mix well with a whisk to form a smooth batter. Add the sweetcorn and cayenne, season well with salt and black pepper, and stir to combine. Chill in the refrigerator for 15 minutes.

2 Heat the oil in a shallow frying pan over a high heat. Stir the batter mixture, then carefully place a spoonful of the mixture into the pan - it should spread out to be 7.5–10cm (3–4in) across. Add 2–3 spoonfuls more, depending on the size of your pan, and cook in batches for 3 minutes on each side, or until golden brown. Remove with a slotted spoon and place on kitchen paper to remove any excess oil. Serve with aïoli and a crisp green salad.

COOK'S NOTES
The fritters will be crispier if the mixture is cold when it goes into the pan. Use fresh corn, sliced off the cob, if you can.

FOOD FOR FRIENDS

Baby Gem lettuce with blue cheese and beetroot

PREP 15 MINS

Special equipment • food processor

SERVES 4
150g (5½oz) blue cheese, such as
   Roquefort or Gorgonzola
1 tsp paprika
3 tbsp natural yogurt
1 tbsp fresh mint leaves
salt and freshly ground black pepper
1 Baby Gem lettuce
3 beetroots, cooked and sliced

1 Put half the cheese, the paprika, yogurt, and mint in a food processor and whiz to a creamy paste. Crumble in the rest of the cheese and season with salt and black pepper.

2 Break up the lettuce into leaves, creating at least eight "boats", place a couple of slices of beetroot in each, then fill each one with a heaped teaspoon of the cheese mixture. Serve with fresh crusty bread and chorizo.

VARIATION
Instead of Baby Gem, use chicory leaves or radicchio – they are bitter, but work well with blue cheese.

Mushrooms in garlic sauce

PREP 10 MINS | COOK 15 MINS

SERVES 4

4 tbsp olive oil
400g (14oz) chestnut
　mushrooms, halved
4 garlic cloves, finely sliced
2 red chillies, deseeded and
　finely sliced
4 tbsp dry sherry
1 chicken stock cube
freshly ground black pepper

1 Heat the oil in a frying pan, add the mushrooms, garlic, and chillies, and fry for 2 minutes over a low heat. Add the sherry, crumble in the stock cube, and season with black pepper. Cook over a medium heat for 10 minutes, or until the mushrooms have released their juices.

2 Cook for 3 minutes more, or until the juices have reduced by half, then serve with some fresh crusty bread.

Fried calamari

PREP 15 MINS | COOK 10 MINS

SERVES 4

2 eggs
2 tbsp cold fizzy water
150g (5½oz) plain flour
1 tsp chilli flakes
1 tsp salt
500g (1lb 2oz) small squid,
　gutted, cleaned, and cut into
　1cm (½in) rings
250ml (9fl oz) vegetable oil
　or sunflower oil
lemon wedges, to serve

1 Break the eggs into a bowl, add the fizzy water, and beat well with a hand whisk. Put the flour, chilli flakes, and salt on a plate and mix well. Dip each piece of squid into the egg mixture and then into the flour, making sure they are evenly coated, then put to one side.

2 Heat the oil in a deep frying pan over a high heat until hot, then carefully add the squid, one piece at a time. Do not overfill the pan. Cook in batches for 2–3 minutes, or until golden brown. Remove with a slotted spoon and place on kitchen paper to remove any excess oil. Serve with a squeeze of lemon.

COOK'S NOTES

Do use small squid, as it tends to be much more tender than the larger ones, and buy it fresh.

Tomato, bean, and courgette stew

PREP 10 MINS • COOK 20 MINS

SERVES 4

3 tbsp olive oil

1 large onion, finely chopped

2 courgettes, chopped into chunky pieces

3 garlic cloves, finely sliced

400g can borlotti beans, drained and rinsed

3 fresh tomatoes, diced

1 tsp paprika

1 tsp dried oregano

salt and freshly ground black pepper

chilli oil, to serve (optional)

1 Heat the oil in a deep-sided frying pan, add the onion, and cook over a medium heat for 3 minutes. Add the courgettes and cook for a further 5 minutes, stirring constantly.

2 Add the garlic and beans, cook for 1 minute, then add the tomatoes, paprika, and oregano. Cook for 10 minutes, stirring occasionally, then season with salt and black pepper. Drizzle with chilli oil (if using), and serve with some fresh crusty bread.

FOOD FOR FRIENDS

Halloumi with garlic, chilli, and coriander

PREP 10 MINS • COOK 15 MINS

SERVES 4

3 tbsp olive oil

2 red chillies, deseeded and finely sliced

4 garlic cloves, finely sliced

250g (9oz) halloumi cheese, cut into 5mm (¼in) slices

handful of fresh coriander, chopped

salt and freshly ground black pepper

1 Heat the oil in a shallow frying pan, add the chillies, and cook over a medium heat for 2 minutes. Add the garlic, cook for 1 minute, then remove from the heat. Using a slotted spoon, transfer the garlic and chilli to a plate and put to one side.

2 Return the frying pan to the heat (there's no need to clean it), and carefully add the halloumi. Fry for 3 minutes on each side, or until golden brown. Add the coriander, and the chilli and garlic mixture, and season well with salt and black pepper. Toss together and cook for a further 2 minutes. Serve with fresh crusty bread or a tomato salad.

COOK'S NOTES

Because halloumi cheese doesn't melt, it is great for cooking on a barbecue or cast-iron grill pan.

Chickpeas in olive oil and lemon

   PREP 10 MINS   COOK 5 MINS

SERVES 4

3 tbsp olive oil
2 garlic cloves, finely sliced
400g can chickpeas, drained
    and rinsed
juice of ½ lemon
zest of 1 lemon
handful of fresh flat-leaf
    parsley, chopped
salt and freshly ground black pepper
extra virgin olive oil or chilli oil,
    to serve

1 Heat the oil in a frying pan, add the garlic and chickpeas, and cook for 2 minutes. Add the lemon juice, zest, and parsley, then cook over a medium heat for 2 more minutes.

2 Remove from the heat and season well with salt and black pepper. Serve hot or cold, with a generous splash of extra virgin olive oil or chilli oil.

VARIATION
Use dried chickpeas if time permits. Soak them the night before, then drain and simmer for 1–1½ hours, until soft.

Chorizo with dried fruit chutney

PREP 10 MINS   COOK 30 MINS

SERVES 4

50g (1¾oz) dried apricots
50g (1¾oz) raisins
1 tbsp olive oil
1 onion, finely chopped
300g (10oz) chorizo, cut into
    chunky pieces
3 tbsp dry sherry
50g (1¾oz) walnuts
freshly ground black pepper

1 Preheat the oven to 200°C (400°F/ Gas 6). Put the dried fruit in a bowl, cover with a little hot water, and leave to soak for 10 minutes. Meanwhile, heat the oil in a frying pan, add the onion, and cook over a medium heat for 5 minutes, or until soft and translucent. Add the chorizo and cook for a further 5 minutes, stirring occasionally.

2 Drain the fruit and add to the pan with the sherry and walnuts. Raise the heat and cook for a few minutes until the alcohol evaporates. Season with black pepper, combine well, then transfer to a small baking dish. Cover with foil and bake for 15 minutes. Serve with fresh crusty bread and salad.

Marinated squid salad

Marinating • 30 minutes

SERVES 4
300g (10oz) small squid, gutted
  and cleaned
7 tbsp olive oil
salt and freshly ground black pepper
2 tbsp white wine vinegar
3 garlic cloves, crushed
1 tsp paprika
handful of fresh flat-leaf parsley,
  finely chopped

1 Cut the squid into pieces – a mixture of strips and rings – and brush with a little of the oil and season well.

2 Heat 1 tablespoon of the oil in a frying pan, add the squid, and cook over a medium heat, stirring constantly, for 2–3 minutes, or until the squid is cooked. Remove from the heat and transfer to a serving bowl.

3 Mix the remaining oil with the vinegar, garlic, paprika, and parsley, then season with salt and black pepper. Pour over the squid, combine well, and leave to marinate for at least 30 minutes. Serve with fresh crusty bread and a green salad.

FOOD FOR FRIENDS

Sweet balsamic onions

SERVES 4
3 tbsp olive oil
400g (14oz) baby onions, peeled
  and left whole
3 garlic cloves, finely sliced
3 tbsp balsamic vinegar
salt and freshly ground black pepper
drizzle of olive oil or chilli oil, to serve

1 Preheat the oven to 180°C (350°F/ Gas 4). Heat the oil in a deep-sided frying pan, add the onions, and cook over a low heat, stirring frequently, for 15 minutes, or until evenly brown.

2 Transfer the onions to a small baking dish, packing them in tightly. Sprinkle with the garlic, and spoon over the balsamic vinegar. Season well with salt and a little black pepper and bake for 20 minutes, stirring every 5 minutes. Serve hot or cold with a good drizzle of olive oil or chilli oil and some fresh crusty bread and cheese.

VARIATION Sprinkle in some fresh thyme leaves, and finely chopped rosemary instead of the garlic.

COOK'S NOTES
The onions can be prepared well in advance and will keep under oil for weeks in the refrigerator.

343

Skewered swordfish with caperberries

PREP 15 MINS | COOK 10 MINS

Special equipment • skewers or cocktail sticks

SERVES 4

450g (1lb) swordfish steaks, cut into bite sized peices
salt and freshly ground black pepper
3 tbsp olive oil
1 tbsp white wine vinegar
2 tbsp caperberries
2 garlic cloves, finely sliced
splash of chilli oil, to serve

1 If using wooden skewers, soak them in cold water for 30 minutes before using. Preheat the oven to 200°C (400°F/Gas 6). Thread three pieces of swordfish onto each of 12–15 short skewers or cocktail sticks. Place in a baking dish and season with salt and black pepper.

2 Mix the oil, vinegar, caperberries, and garlic in a small bowl, crushing half the caperberries with the back of a fork. Pour evenly over the swordfish and bake for 10 minutes. Serve with a splash of chilli oil and fresh crusty bread.

Lamb with lemon and olives

PREP 25 MINS | COOK 20 MINS

SERVES 4

3 tbsp olive oil
1 onion, finely chopped
500g (1lb 2oz) lean lamb, cut into bite-sized pieces
6 garlic cloves, finely sliced
1 lemon, cut into eighths
1 tsp chopped fresh rosemary leaves
handful of fresh flat-leaf parsley, chopped
1 tsp paprika
3 tbsp green olives
salt and freshly ground black pepper

1 Preheat the oven to 200°C (400°F/Gas 6). Heat the oil in a frying pan, add the onion, and cook over a medium heat for 5 minutes, or until it is beginning to soften. Add the lamb and cook, stirring occasionally, for 5 minutes, or until no longer pink. Add the garlic and lemon and cook for 1 minute, then add the rest of the ingredients and cook for a further 2 minutes, stirring well.

2 Transfer the mixture to a small baking dish, packing it in tightly. Add 2 tablespoons of water, mix well, then bake for 20 minutes.

3 Remove from the oven and allow to rest for 10 minutes before serving with fresh crusty bread and a crisp green salad.

Roast sweet potato and chilli tortilla

 PREP 15 MINS COOK 45 MINS

SERVES 4–6

550g (1¼lb) sweet potatoes, peeled
   and cut into 2cm (¾in) cubes
1 tsp chilli flakes
5 tbsp olive oil
2 onions, finely chopped
6 eggs
salt and freshly ground black pepper

1 Preheat the oven to 200°C (400°F/
Gas 6). Put the sweet potatoes in
a non-stick baking tray, add the chilli
flakes and 2 tablespoons of the oil,
and mix well. Roast for 30 minutes,
or until browning, turning occasionally.

2 Meanwhile, put the remaining oil
in a deep-sided frying pan, add the
onions, and fry over a medium heat
for 5 minutes, or until soft and
translucent. Add the sweet potato,
combine well, and leave to cool.

3 Break the eggs into a mixing bowl,
season with salt and black pepper,
and beat well with a fork. Pour
onto the potato and onion mixture,
combine well, and pour the mixture
into a pan and cook over a low heat
for 10 minutes, or until beginning
to set. Transfer the pan to the oven,
and cook for a further 10 minutes, or
until the top is golden. Turn out onto
a plate, and serve with a mixed salad.

> **COOK'S NOTES**
>
> If your frying-pan handle is plastic
> or wooden, wrap it with a double
> layer of foil before putting it in
> the oven. To turn the tortilla out,
> make sure it is not stuck to the
> sides and bottom of the pan, place
> a plate over the frying pan, and
> carefully and quickly turn it over.

FOOD FOR FRIENDS

Chicken with cinnamon and peppers

 PREP 25 MINS COOK 20 MINS

SERVES 4

450g (1lb) boneless skinless
   chicken breasts, cut into
   4cm (1½in) cubes
1 tsp paprika
1 tsp ground cinnamon powder
4 tbsp olive oil
1 red pepper, deseeded and cut
   into strips
1 green pepper, deseeded and
   cut into strips
1 onion, sliced
3 garlic cloves, finely sliced
150ml (5½fl oz) hot chicken stock
splash of chilli oil, to serve

1 Preheat the oven to 200°C (400°F/
Gas 6). Put the chicken in a mixing
bowl and rub all over with the paprika
and cinnamon, then set to one side.

2 Meanwhile, heat the oil in
a frying pan, add the peppers and
onion, and cook over a medium heat
for 5 minutes, or until they start to
soften. Add the chicken and cook,
stirring constantly, for 5 minutes,
or until the chicken is no longer pink.
Add the garlic and cook for 1 minute,
then add the chicken stock and
combine well.

3 Transfer to a baking dish and bake
for 20 minutes. Serve with a generous
splash of chilli oil.

Mini pork kebabs

 PREP 15 MINS **COOK 10 MINS**

Marinating • 30 minutes
Special equipment • skewers

SERVES 4

550g (1¼lb) lean pork, cut into
   2cm (¾in) cubes
6 garlic cloves, crushed
1 tsp chilli flakes
1 tsp ground fennel seeds
1 tsp paprika
juice and zest of 1 lemon
3 tbsp fresh flat-leaf parsley,
   finely chopped
1 tbsp dry sherry
2 tbsp olive oil
salt and freshly ground black pepper

1 If using wooden skewers, soak them in cold water for 30 minutes before using. Put all the ingredients in a mixing bowl, combine well, then leave to marinate for at least 30 minutes.

2 Thread the pork onto the small skewers or cocktail sticks and cook in a hot frying pan or griddle pan for 10 minutes, turning frequently. Leave to rest for 10 minutes, then serve with a mixed salad.

Chicken wings with garlic

 PREP 20 MINS **COOK 30 MINS**

Marinating • 20 minutes

SERVES 4

12 chicken wings
2 tbsp lemon juice
2 tsp paprika
3 tbsp olive oil
6 garlic cloves, finely sliced
4 tbsp dry sherry
salt and freshly ground black pepper

1 Pierce the chicken wings all over with the tip of a sharp knife, then put them in a mixing bowl with the lemon juice and paprika and leave to marinate for 20 minutes.

2 Heat the oil in a deep-sided non-stick frying pan, add the chicken wings, and cook over a medium heat, turning frequently, for 10 minutes, or until brown all over.

3 Reduce the heat, add the garlic and sherry, then season well with salt and black pepper. Combine well and cook for 5 minutes, then cover with a lid and cook over a low heat for 15 minutes, turning occasionally. Serve with a crisp green salad.

Prawn and chicken empanadas

 PREP 35 MINS   COOK 30 MINS

Special equipment • food processor
• 10cm (4in) round biscuit cutter

MAKES 10–12
100g (3½oz) butter
juice of 1 lemon
225g (8oz) plain flour
salt and freshly ground black pepper
125g (4½oz) skinless chicken breast
125g (4½oz) cooked prawns, peeled
2 tbsp olive oil
1 onion, finely chopped
3 tbsp dry sherry
3 garlic cloves, crushed
1 tbsp tomato purée
1 tsp cayenne pepper
1 tbsp fresh flat-leaf parsley,
   finely chopped
250ml (9fl oz) sunflower oil

1 Melt the butter in a small pan, then add the lemon juice and 100ml (3½fl oz) water. Add the flour and salt, and stir well to make a paste. Knead well on a floured work surface and put in the refrigerator.

2 Meanwhile, mince the chicken and the prawns separately in a food processor. Heat the oil in a frying pan, add the onion, and cook over a medium heat for 5 minutes. Add the chicken and cook for a further 5 minutes, stirring occasionally. Add the sherry, garlic, prawns, tomato purée, cayenne, and parsley, and season well with salt and black pepper. Mix well and cook for 10 minutes, then allow to cool for 5 minutes.

3 Meanwhile, on a floured work surface, roll out the cooled pastry 5mm (¼in) thick. Using the biscuit cutter, cut out 10–12 rounds of pastry. Place 1 tablespoon of the chicken and prawn mixture in the middle of each and fold in half. Wet the edges a little with some cold water, then crimp together with your fingers.

4 Heat the oil in a deep-sided frying pan until hot, then fry the empanadas in batches over a medium heat, turning them occasionally, for 3–5 minutes, or until golden brown. Serve with aïoli and a crisp green salad.

Scallops with sweet chilli sauce

 PREP 10 MINS   COOK 5 MINS

Marinating • 30 minutes

SERVES 4
4 garlic cloves, grated
3 fresh mild-medium red
   chillies, deseeded and
   finely chopped
3 tbsp dry sherry
1 tsp caster sugar
2 tbsp olive oil, plus a little extra,
   for frying
12 large scallops

1 Put the garlic, chillies, sherry, and sugar in a bowl and mix well until the sugar dissolves. Add the oil and scallops, toss together, then leave to marinate for at least 30 minutes.

2 Transfer the scallops to a plate, using a slotted spoon. Reserve the marinade. Heat a little olive oil in a non-stick frying pan and cook the scallops over a high heat for 1 minute on each side. Remove from the pan and pour in the marinade. Cook over a high heat for 3 minutes, then pour over the scallops. Serve with a crisp green salad.

SIMPLE STARTERS

Little bites with big flavour
– almost in an instant!

SIMPLE STARTERS

For some, the starter is the best part of the meal, and it's not uncommon to choose a selection of starters for a whole meal rather than the traditional three courses, as they are often a lot lighter. Starters are served to stimulate the taste buds, but they should also be visually appealing and delicious. Often, the occasion will determine the choice of starter, whether it's dinner for friends, or a romantic night in. Either way, preparation is fundamental to a relaxed meal.

Menu planning Choose the right starter for the main course.

Choosing the main course first will make it easier to decide on a suitable starter. Remember, the starter is simply to whet the appetite in preparation for the rest of the meal.

The starter shouldn't be too heavy, and should balance and complement the main course.

Consider using not only different ingredients for the starter and main, but also different cooking methods, as you don't want, for instance, pan-fried food twice. Think about colour and texture; serve a crisp and fresh starter if the main course is rich and creamy.

Don't mix up cuisines when menu planning. For example, if serving a Mediterranean-style main course, don't opt for a highly-spiced starter.

If time is of the essence, choose a starter that can be made ahead.

3 five-minute starters Incredibly quick and easy starters to suit any occasion.

Mediterranean salad A simple dish that relies on good-quality ingredients.

Greek mezze A tapas-style combination of textures and flavours.

Trout pâté Look for freshly smoked, rather than vacuum-packed, trout.

Place a handful of **wild rocket leaves** on a serving dish, and top with **sun-blush tomatoes**. Coat some **asparagus** with **olive oil** and cook on a hot ridged cast-iron grill pan until charred. Add to the tomatoes and rocket. Sit slices of **Parma ham** on an oiled baking sheet and cook in a hot oven for a few minutes until they begin to curl and crisp. Halve an **avocado**, stone, peel and fan out on the dish. Top with the crispy Parma ham, then drizzle over a mix of olive oil, **lemon juice**, **chilli flakes**, and season.

Serve 2 ready-made **stuffed vine leaves** with a generous spoonful of ready-made **hummus**, sprinkled with paprika. Warm 1 **pitta bread** on a hot ridged cast-iron grill pan, slice, and add to the plate. Grate a couple of **carrots**, and mix with a handful of **raisins** and a handful of **fresh mint leaves**. Stir in a drizzle of **extra virgin olive oil** and a drizzle of **white wine vinegar**. Serve with the vine leaves, hummus, and warm pitta bread.

Whiz a couple of **smoked trout fillets** with some **Greek yogurt** and a spoonful of **cream cheese**, taste, then add a little **lemon juice**, a teaspoon of **creamed horseradish**, and a handful of **fresh dill** and whiz again. Add plenty of **freshly ground black pepper**, and spoon into individual ramekins. Top with a sprig of fresh dill, and serve with ready-made **Melba toast**.

Simple bruschetta toppings
All these toppings can be prepared ahead – so all you need to do is toast the bread, and serve.

Courgette and saffron
The saffron brings a Spanish flavour to the dish.

Dice a **courgette** into even pieces then add to a frying pan with a little **olive oil**. Cook for a couple of minutes, then add a pinch of **saffron threads** and a squeeze of **lemon juice**. Cook until the courgettes begin to turn golden. Season, and use to top sliced and toasted ciabatta. Garnish with **fresh basil leaves**.

Chicken liver pâté
A rich and delicious French-style pâté.

Cook 3 pieces of **chicken liver** in a pan with a knob of melted **butter**. Cook until sealed, being careful not to overcook or the liver will turn grey. Add 2 finely chopped **garlic cloves** and cook for about 30 seconds more. Pierce the liver with a knife and if there is no trace of blood it is cooked. Add to a food processor along with a handful of small **capers**, rinsed, and whiz until chopped to your liking – either smooth or rough. Slice and toast some ciabatta then top with some pâté and serve.

Roasted mixed pepper
Rub garlic over the bruschetta, if you have time.

Deseed a couple of **red** and **yellow peppers**, slice into strips, then add to a frying pan with a little **olive oil**. Season, and cook until the peppers begin to soften. Raise the heat, add a drop of **balsamic vinegar**, and cook for a couple more minutes. Use to top sliced and toasted ciabatta. Garnish with **fresh basil leaves**.

Olive and chilli
A rustic version of tapenade. Top with salami for meat-eaters.

Finely chop a handful of **black** and **green pitted olives**. Add them to a frying pan with a little **olive oil**. Cook for a couple of minutes, then add a pinch of **chilli flakes** and season. Stir to combine and cook for a few minutes more, then use to top sliced and toasted ciabatta. Garnish with **wild rocket leaves**.

Simple garnish ideas

Fried sage leaves These look and taste wonderful. Choose large fresh sage leaves, and try to leave a little stalk intact. Wash, dry well with kitchen paper, and dip into a bowl of seasoned beaten egg until covered. Fry in a drizzle of hot olive oil on both sides, until golden. Use to garnish salads, pâtés, or soups.

Diced tomato To peel a tomato, mark it with a little cross at its base. Sit in boiling water for 10 seconds then transfer to cold. Peel away the skin, then halve and scoop out the seeds. Chop the flesh into neat pieces. Use to garnish soups, both hot and cold, or sprinkle over fish or prawns.

Citrus fruits Use lemons, limes, oranges, or grapefruits. Always use a sharp knife, and wash the fruit first. Slice into wedges or wheels, then twist, or zest using a fine grater, or cut into spirals by pulling the zester all the way around the citrus fruit. Keep in iced water until needed. Use to garnish fish dishes, salads, or pâtés.

Psst...

Lots of starters lend themselves to upsizing to a main course. Double the quantities of the starter, such as the Seared tuna with black sesame seed crust (p354), or Anchovy, olive, and basil tarts (p359), and serve with a salad, or downsize and serve as canapés with drinks.

Seared tuna with black sesame seed crust. For recipe, see p354.

FOOD FOR FRIENDS

Marinated beef with red pepper aïoli

PREP 20 MINS **COOK 5 MINS**

Marinating • 1 hour

Special equipment • ridged cast-iron grill pan or grill

SERVES 4–6

1kg (2¼lb) Scotch beef fillet, cut into 12 thin slices
3 tbsp wholegrain mustard
1 garlic clove, grated or finely chopped
2 small fresh medium-hot red chillies, deseeded and finely chopped
4 tbsp olive oil
3 sprigs of fresh rosemary, leaves picked

For the red pepper aïoli
250ml (9fl oz) mayonnaise
1 red pepper, roasted or grilled, peeled, deseeded, and roughly chopped
2 garlic cloves, crushed
2 sprigs of fresh oregano, leaves picked
juice of 1 lime
salt and freshly ground black pepper

1 Lay the beef slices in a shallow glass or ceramic dish. Mix together the mustard, garlic, chillies, olive oil, and rosemary in a small bowl or jug, and brush all over the meat. Cover with cling film, and leave to marinate in the refrigerator for at least 1 hour, or preferably overnight.

2 Heat a ridged cast-iron grill pan or grill until hot. Grill the steaks for about 2 minutes on each side or until the meat is cooked to your liking, brushing lightly with the marinade as it cooks. Set aside in a warm place to rest for 10 minutes.

3 To make the red pepper aïoli, blend or process the mayonnaise, red pepper, garlic, oregano, and lime juice until smooth. Season with salt and black pepper. Serve the beef slices with the aïoli in individual serving bowls.

COOK'S NOTES

For finger food, slice the beef into 24 strips, and thread the meat onto skewers. Remember to soak wooden or bamboo skewers in cold water for at least 30 minutes before using, so that they don't catch and burn.

Chickpea fritters

PREP 25 MINS **COOK 15 MINS**

SERVES 4

400g can chickpeas, drained
100g (3½oz) plain flour
2 tbsp fresh flat-leaf parsley, chopped
1 tbsp fresh mint leaves, chopped
1 garlic clove, crushed
¼ onion, finely chopped
2 carrots, grated
3 eggs
1 tsp dukkah (see Cook's Notes)
grated zest of 1 small lemon
salt and freshly ground black pepper
500ml (16fl oz) olive oil, for frying
½ bunch of watercress, to garnish
10 cherry tomatoes, halved
4 balls bocconcini (baby mozzarella) cheese, roughly torn
1 tbsp olive oil
juice of ½ lemon
small handful of fresh chives, cut into 2cm (¾in) lengths

1 To make the chickpea fritters, put the chickpeas, flour, parsley, mint, garlic, onion, carrot, eggs, dukkah, and lemon zest in a bowl. Season with salt and black pepper. Stir through gently until the batter is well mixed.

2 Pour the olive oil into a wide heavy frying pan over a medium-high heat. When the oil is hot, carefully spoon in the chickpea batter to make 4 large fritters. Be careful not to overcrowd the pan, and cook in batches if necessary. Fry the fritters for 4–5 minutes on each side until golden. Remove from the pan, and drain on kitchen paper.

3 To serve, put the cherry tomatoes in a bowl with the bocconcini, extra 1 tablespoon of olive oil, lemon juice, and chives. Toss gently. Arrange a chickpea fritter in the centre of each of 4 serving plates. Spoon the cherry tomato and bocconcini salsa over the top. Garnish each serving with a little of the watercress, and serve immediately.

VARIATION

Make the fritters smaller by dropping a tablespoon of batter at a time into the oil, and serve as finger food with some hummus.

COOK'S NOTES

Dukkah is an Egyptian spice mixture made up of ground toasted nuts and seeds, and usually includes sesame, coriander, and cumin seeds, as well as hazelnuts. Look out for it at Middle Eastern supermarkets and gourmet food shops.

Stuffed aubergine rolls with salsa

PREP 20 MINS COOK 20 MINS

Special equipment • cocktail sticks

SERVES 4
1 large aubergine
125g (4½oz) toasted
    fresh breadcrumbs
1 tbsp fresh flat-leaf parsley, chopped
1 garlic clove, crushed
2 tbsp freshly grated
    Parmesan cheese
2 eggs, lightly beaten
175g (6oz) plain flour
120ml (4fl oz) olive oil
250g (9oz) ricotta cheese
1 tbsp ready-made pesto

For the tomato salsa
3 tomatoes, finely chopped
small handful of fresh
    flat-leaf parsley
1 tbsp olive oil
salt and freshly ground black pepper

1 Cut the aubergine lengthways into 8 even slices, about 5mm (¼in) thick. Put the aubergine slices in a colander, rinse well, and drain. Pat dry with kitchen paper. Put the breadcrumbs, parsley, garlic, and Parmesan cheese in a large flat dish, and season with salt and black pepper. Mix thoroughly until well combined. Put the lightly beaten eggs in another flat dish, and

the flour in a third. Dip the aubergine slices first in the flour, then in the egg, and finally in the breadcrumbs, ensuring that they are evenly coated.

2 Heat the olive oil in 2 large heavy frying pans over a medium heat, using half of the oil in each one. Divide the aubergine slices among the 2 pans, and shallow-fry for 2–4 minutes on each side until golden. Alternatively, cook in 2 batches. Drain on a baking tray lined with kitchen paper, and keep warm.

3 Meanwhile, put the ricotta cheese and pesto in a bowl, and lightly mix together with a fork. To make the tomato salsa, put the tomato, parsley, and olive oil in a separate bowl. Season with salt and black pepper, and stir through gently.

4 To serve, put a tablespoon of the ricotta mixture towards the end of each of the aubergine slices. Roll and secure with a cocktail stick. Place 2 rolls in the centre of each of 4 serving plates, and pile the tomato salsa over the top.

Prawn and courgette balls with caper cream

PREP 30 MINS COOK 20 MINS

Marinating • 1 hour

SERVES 6–8
550g (1¼lb) raw prawns, peeled,
    deveined, and finely chopped
250g (9oz) courgette, grated
1 garlic clove, crushed
2 tbsp fresh flat-leaf parsley,
    finely chopped
grated zest and juice of 1 small lemon
2 eggs
salt and freshly ground black pepper
250ml (9fl oz) soured cream
1 tbsp capers, rinsed, gently squeezed
    dry, and chopped
1 tbsp fresh dill, finely chopped
500ml (16fl oz) olive oil, for frying

1 In a bowl, combine the prawns, courgette, garlic, parsley, lemon zest and juice, and eggs. Season with salt and black pepper. Mix well by hand. Cover with cling film, and marinate in the refrigerator for 1 hour. Meanwhile, put the soured cream, capers, and dill in a separate bowl, and season with black pepper. Stir through until just combined, cover with cling film, and chill until needed.

2 Pour the oil into a wide heavy frying pan over a medium-high heat. Spoon a little of the prawn mixture into the palm of your hand, and roll into a small ball about the size of a walnut. Continue until all the mixture has been used; you will end up with about 36 balls.

3 When the oil is hot, gently drop the balls into the oil using a spoon. Fry for 4–5 minutes, turning gently, or until golden brown all over. Do not overcrowd the pan – cook in batches if necessary. Remove from the pan using a slotted spoon, and drain on kitchen paper.

4 Serve the prawn and courgette balls on individual plates, with individual bowls of caper cream.

COOK'S NOTES

To prepare the courgettes, grate them on the large holes of a cheese grater.

FOOD FOR FRIENDS

Aubergine and Taleggio arancini

PREP 25 MINS COOK 35 MINS

SERVES 6–8

1 aubergine, finely diced
90ml (3fl oz) olive oil
1.2 litres (2 pints) chicken or
    vegetable stock
75g (2½oz) butter, plus an extra knob
1 onion, finely chopped
1 celery stick, finely chopped
2 garlic cloves, grated or
    finely chopped
300g (10oz) Arborio rice
handful of fresh flat-leaf parsley,
    finely chopped
1 tbsp fresh thyme leaves
juice of 1 small lemon
100g (3½oz) Grana Padano cheese,
    freshly grated
salt and freshly ground black pepper
300g (10oz) Taleggio cheese, cut into
    bite-sized pieces
60g (2oz) plain flour
2 eggs, lightly beaten
100g (3½oz) fine dried breadcrumbs
light olive oil, for deep-frying

1 In a heavy frying pan over a
medium heat, fry the aubergine in
half of the olive oil for a few minutes
until golden brown. Season with salt,
and leave to cool on kitchen paper.

2 Keep the stock on a gentle simmer
in a large pan. Heat the remaining oil
and the butter in a heavy pan over
a medium heat. Add the onion and
celery, and sweat until the onion is
soft. Stir in the garlic, and cook for
30 seconds without colouring. Tip in
the rice, stirring until the grains are
well coated. Add a ladleful of simmering
stock, and keep stirring until absorbed.
Keep adding stock in this way for about
20 minutes. Remove from the heat, and
add the parsley, thyme, lemon juice,
and Grana Padano. Mix well. Season
with salt and black pepper, and spread
over a flat tray to cool completely.

3 Wet your hands, take a little of the
rice about the size of a walnut, and
roll into a ball. Push a small piece of
Taleggio and a portion of aubergine
into the centre and cover with rice.
Continue this way until all the rice has
been used. Spread the flour over a flat
tray, and roll the rice balls around in it
until well covered with flour. Dip each
ball into the beaten egg, and coat in
the breadcrumbs.

4 Heat enough oil for deep-frying over
a medium-high heat. Cook in batches,
and deep-fry the rice balls for 10–15
minutes, until golden brown. Serve hot.

Seared tuna with a black sesame seed crust

PREP 10 MINS COOK 40 SECS

Marinating • 1 hour

SERVES 4

4 tbsp olive oil, plus extra for searing
1 garlic clove, grated or
    finely chopped
1 small fresh hot red chilli,
    finely chopped
2 tbsp black sesame seeds, plus extra
    for sprinkling (optional)
salt
2 yellowfin tuna steaks, about 300g
    (10oz) each, halved lengthways
2 radishes
juice of 1 lemon
½ bunch of fresh chives, chopped into
    5cm (2in) lengths

1 Put the oil, garlic, chilli, sesame
seeds, and a sprinkle of salt on a large
flat tray or dish. Mix well. Rinse the
tuna steaks, and pat dry with kitchen
paper. Carefully press the steaks into
the sesame seed mixture so that it
sticks and coats the fish. Turn the
steaks over, and coat the other side.
Leave to marinate in the refrigerator
for at least 1 hour.

2 Meanwhile, cut the radishes into
fine matchsticks, and put them in
a small bowl with half of the lemon
juice (to prevent them browning).

3 Heat a little extra oil in a frying
pan over a high heat. When the oil
is hot, sear each tuna steak for about
20 seconds on each side. Leave to rest
for 5 minutes.

4 To serve, put a seared tuna
steak on each of 4 serving plates,
and drizzle with the remaining
lemon juice. Drain the radish
matchsticks, and scatter over the
top. Sprinkle with the chives and
a few extra sesame seeds (if using),
and serve immediately.

COOK'S NOTES

*You could double the quantities
and serve this as a main course
with a salad of fresh orange
segments, thinly sliced cucumber,
and sprigs of fresh dill or mint,
as well as the radish.*

Skewered lemon and herb chicken

PREP 10 MINS | COOK 15 MINS

Marinating • 1 hour
Special equipment • 12 skewers
• charcoal grill or barbecue

SERVES 4
2 skinless chicken breast fillets, about 250g (9oz) each
1 garlic clove, grated or finely chopped
1 tbsp fresh root ginger, finely chopped
1 small fresh hot red chilli, deseeded and finely chopped
1 tsp finely chopped rosemary, finely chopped, plus extra for garnish
4 sprigs of fresh thyme, leaves picked and finely chopped, plus extra for garnish
grated zest and juice of 1 lemon
4 tbsp olive oil
salt and freshly ground black pepper
2 large mangoes
juice of 1 lime

1 Soak the 12 bamboo or wooden skewers in cold water for 1 hour. Put the chicken, garlic, ginger, chilli, rosemary, thyme leaves, lemon juice, and olive oil in a bowl. Season with salt and black pepper, and leave to marinate in the refrigerator for at least 1 hour.

2 Halve and peel the mangoes, slicing as close to either side of the stone as possible. Thinly slice the flesh lengthways. Put the mango slices in a bowl, add the lime juice, and season with salt and black pepper. Stir gently to mix well, and set aside.

3 Heat a grill or barbecue until medium-hot, and brush the grill with oil. Thread the pieces of chicken evenly onto the skewers. Grill, turning occasionally, for about 15 minutes until the chicken is golden and cooked through. Brush lightly with the marinade while the meat is cooking. Leave for 15 minutes, and keep warm.

4 To serve, divide the skewers evenly among 4 serving plates, pile the mango on top, and scatter over some extra rosemary and thyme to garnish.

COOK'S NOTES

If you have a rosemary bush, break off 12 long thin branches, strip them of most of the leaves, and use the branches as skewers.

Spicy chicken balls with chilli and ginger sauce

PREP 20 MINS | COOK 30 MINS

Special equipment • food processor

SERVES 8
50g (2½oz) dried apricots
1 tbsp honey
3 tbsp brandy
4 skinless chicken breast fillets, about 200g (7oz) each, coarsely chopped
50g (1¾oz) macadamia nuts, chopped
60g (2oz) cooked and cooled rice
2 garlic cloves, grated or finely chopped
2 tbsp fresh sage leaves, finely chopped
1 tbsp fresh basil leaves, finely chopped
1 tbsp fresh flat-leaf parsley, finely chopped
2 small fresh hot red chillies, deseeded and chopped
1 egg
salt and freshly ground black pepper
light olive oil, for deep-frying
watercress, to serve

Chilli and ginger sauce
juice of 4 limes
2 small fresh hot red chillies, deseeded and chopped
2 tbsp olive oil
1 tbsp finely chopped fresh root ginger
1 spring onion, finely sliced

1 Put the apricots, honey, and brandy in a small pan. Simmer for about 15 minutes until the apricots soften and the liquid has been absorbed. Leave to cool.

2 Mince the chicken in a food processor for 15–20 seconds; be careful not to turn it into a paste. Transfer to a bowl, and add cooled apricots, nuts, rice, garlic, herbs, chillies, and egg. Season with salt and black pepper, and mix well. Using wet hands, form into walnut-sized balls; you should end up with 36–40.

3 Heat enough oil for deep-frying over a medium-high heat. Cooking in batches, deep-fry the balls for about 15 minutes, until golden brown. Drain on kitchen paper, and keep warm.

4 To make the sauce, put all the sauce ingredients in a bowl, and mix well. Arrange the spicy chicken balls on a platter, pour over the sauce, and scatter some watercress over the top. Serve immediately.

Baby chicken, leek, and mushroom pies

PREP 15 MINS COOK 50 MINS

Special equipment • biscuit cutter

SERVES 4
2 tbsp olive oil
50g (1¾oz) butter
1 small carrot, finely chopped
1 celery stick, finely chopped
1 leek, white part only,
　finely chopped
1 garlic clove, grated or
　finely chopped
200g (7oz) chestnut mushrooms, diced
500g (1lb 2oz) skinless chicken breast
　fillet, diced
1 tbsp fresh thyme leaves, chopped
grated zest of 1 lemon
½ glass of dry white wine
250ml (9fl oz) double cream
salt and freshly ground black pepper
3 sheets ready-rolled puff pastry
2 eggs, lightly beaten, for egg wash
mixed green leaves and herbs, to serve
tomato relish, to serve

1 Heat the oil and butter in a frying pan over a low heat. Add the carrot and celery, and gently sweat for about 5 minutes until soft. Add the leek and

sweat for a few minutes more until softened. Stir in the garlic, and cook for 30 seconds before adding the mushrooms. Cook, stirring now and then, for another 5 minutes.

2 Increase the heat slightly, and add the chicken, thyme, lemon zest, and white wine. Cook, stirring occasionally, for 15–20 minutes. Pour in the cream, and season with salt and black pepper. Continue to cook for about 5 minutes until thickened slightly. Leave to cool.

3 Preheat the oven to 200°C (400°F/ Gas 6). Lightly oil a 24-hole mini muffin tin. Using a biscuit cutter, cut 24.6cm (2½in) circles from the puff pastry. Use to line the holes in the prepared muffin tin. Spoon the chicken mixture into the pastry shells. Now cut 24.5cm (2in) circles from the puff pastry, and use to cover each of the chicken pies. Gently press the edges together to seal. Brush the tops with the egg wash, and bake for 15–20 minutes, until golden brown. Serve hot with a salad of mixed leaves and a dollop of tomato relish.

Chargrilled asparagus and pancetta

PREP 15 MINS COOK 5 MINS

Special equipment • ridged cast-iron grill pan or griddle

SERVES 4
12 fresh asparagus spears, trimmed
24 thin slices pancetta
1 small radicchio, torn into
　bite-sized pieces
1 butter lettuce, torn into
　bite-sized pieces
100g (3½oz) rocket leaves
200g (7oz) cherry tomatoes
100g (3½oz) Parmesan cheese,
　freshly shaved

For the dressing
1 garlic clove, crushed
4 tbsp olive oil
1 tbsp balsamic vinegar
1 tbsp freshly squeezed orange juice
1 tsp Dijon mustard
salt and freshly ground black pepper

1 Blanch the asparagus spears in a pan of boiling water for

2–3 minutes. Drain, and immediately refresh the asparagus in a bowl of cold water. When the spears are cool enough to handle, drain again.

2 Heat a ridged cast-iron grill pan or griddle until hot. Wrap 2 slices of the pancetta around each asparagus spear. Grill the asparagus spears for about 3–4 minutes until beginning to char, turning once halfway during the cooking time. Set aside.

3 To make the dressing, whisk together the garlic, oil, balsamic vinegar, orange juice, and mustard in a small bowl. Season with salt and black pepper, and whisk again.

4 Toss together the salad leaves, tomatoes, and dressing in a bowl, and divide among 4 serving plates or bowls. Top each serving with 3 of the asparagus and pancetta spears, and sprinkle the Parmesan shards over the top. Serve immediately.

Skewered lemon, rosemary, and dukkah lamb

  PREP 10 MINS **COOK 15 MINS**

Marinating • 1 hour

Special equipment • 12 wooden skewers • charcoal grill, barbecue, or ridged cast-iron grill pan

SERVES 4

1kg (2¼lb) lamb fillet, cut into bite-sized pieces
1 garlic clove, grated or finely chopped
1 tsp finely chopped rosemary leaves, plus extra for garnish
1 tbsp dukkah, plus extra for garnish
grated zest and juice of 1 lemon
4 tbsp olive oil
salt and freshly ground black pepper
200g (7oz) cherry tomatoes, halved
115g (4oz) kalamata olives, pitted
20g (¾oz) fresh flat-leaf parsley
100g (3½oz) feta cheese
extra virgin olive oil for drizzling
4 lemon wedges, to serve

1 Soak the skewers, or some rosemary branches in cold water for at least 30 minutes before using. Combine the lamb, garlic, rosemary, dukkah, lemon zest and juice, and olive oil in a bowl. Stir through until the lamb is well coated, and season with salt and black pepper. Leave to marinate in the refrigerator for at least 1 hour.

2 Heat a charcoal grill or barbecue, or a ridged cast-iron grill pan, until medium-hot. Brush the grill or pan lightly with a little oil. Divide the marinated lamb evenly among the skewers, and thread the pieces of lamb onto each one. Grill, turning occasionally, for 10–15 minutes until browned all over and cooked to your liking. Brush lightly with the marinade while the meat is cooking. Set aside in a warm place for 15 minutes to rest.

3 Toss together the tomatoes, olives, and parsley, and divide among 4 serving plates. Top each serving with 3 lamb skewers, crumble over the feta, and drizzle with a little extra virgin olive oil. Sprinkle a little extra dukkah over the top, and serve with lemon wedges for squeezing over.

> **COOK'S NOTES**
>
> Dukkah seasoning is an Egyptian/ North African spice mix of toasted nuts, seeds, and spices. A couscous salad with grilled aubergine slices makes an ideal accompaniment.

Pork and fennel sausages with fresh tomato salsa

  PREP 10 MINS **COOK 15 MINS**

Marinating • 1 hour

SERVES 4

4 Italian-style fresh pork and fennel sausages
3 tbsp olive oil
2 garlic cloves, grated or finely chopped
4 sprigs of fresh dill
salt and freshly ground black pepper
4 thick slices Italian-style crusty sourdough bread, to serve

For the tomato salsa
4 ripe tomatoes, deseeded and diced
115g (4oz) kalamata olives, pitted and diced
large handful of fresh basil leaves, torn
2 tbsp extra virgin olive oil

1 Put the sausages in a shallow glass or ceramic dish. Add the olive oil, garlic, and dill, and season with a little salt and black pepper. Stir the sausages around so that they are well coated. Cover with cling film, and leave to marinate in the refrigerator for at least 1 hour.

2 Meanwhile, to make the salsa, combine all the ingredients in a bowl, and mix well. Season with salt and black pepper.

3 Heat a grill or barbecue, or a heavy frying pan, until hot. Grill the sausages for 10–15 minutes until cooked through, turning halfway during cooking to brown both sides.

4 Divide the sausages between 4 serving plates, and serve on a piece of toasted ciabatta, with the tomato salsa spooned over. Serve immediately.

 VARIATION Try fresh chicken and chive sausages instead of pork ones.

> **COOK'S NOTES**
>
> If you want a more casual serving option, twist chipolata sausages in the middle, marinate and grill as above (they will take slightly less time to cook), and pile onto a platter with the salsa in a bowl on the side. Alternatively, pile the chipolatas and salsa onto bruschetta drizzled with olive oil and freshly ground pepper, and top with wild rocket leaves.

Croque Monsieur with prosciutto and Gorgonzola

PREP 10 MINS COOK 15 MINS

SERVES 4

8 slices white sourdough bread
2 tbsp unsalted butter
8 thin slices prosciutto
200g (7oz) Gorgonzola cheese,
    thinly sliced
2 tbsp olive oil
4 eggs

1 Butter each of the bread slices on one side. Place 4 of the bread slices buttered side down on the work surface, and divide the prosciutto and cheese evenly among them, arranging them neatly on top of each slice. Cover with the remaining slices of bread, buttered side up, to make a sandwich.

2 Heat a lightly oiled large heavy frying pan over a medium heat. When hot, carefully arrange the sandwiches in the pan. Cook for about 5 minutes on each side until the bread is golden brown and the cheese has melted. Set aside to keep warm.

3 Wipe out the pan, and heat the olive oil until medium-hot. Break each egg into the pan separately, and fry the eggs until done to your preference. Slide a fried egg on top of each toasted sandwich, and serve immediately.

  VARIATION
You could use ham and Gruyère, or a similar soft melting cheese such as Emmental. Or add wholegrain mustard or mayonnaise, if you like.

COOK'S NOTES
For a lighter version, toast the sandwiches using a dry sandwich press, and poach the eggs instead of frying them.

Potato and leek croquettes

PREP 20 MINS COOK 30 MINS

Chilling • 1 hour

SERVES 4

1 leek, white part only,
    finely chopped
1 tbsp olive oil
1 garlic clove, grated or
    finely chopped
500g (1lb 2oz) floury potatoes such as
    Maris Piper or King Edward, peeled
    and cut into chunks
3 eggs
60g (2oz) Parmesan cheese,
    freshly grated
2 tbsp fresh flat-leaf parsley, chopped
salt and freshly ground black pepper
60g (2oz) plain flour
150g (5½oz) fine breadcrumbs
light olive oil for deep-frying

1 In a frying pan over a low heat, gently sweat the leek in the oil for about 5 minutes until soft. Add the garlic, and cook for 30 seconds more without colouring. Set aside to cool.

2 Boil the potatoes in a large pan of salted water for 15–20 minutes until tender; drain. Return to the pan, and mash until very smooth. Add the leek and garlic mixture, 1 of the eggs, Parmesan, and parsley. Season with salt and black pepper. Stir thoroughly. Chill for at least 1 hour to firm.

3 Spread the flour over a flat tray, and lightly beat the remaining 2 eggs in a shallow bowl. Put the breadcrumbs on a separate plate. Using wet hands, roll the chilled mixture into 12 balls each about the size of a golf ball, then form into oval shapes. Gently roll the croquettes in the flour until well coated, then dip each one in the beaten egg, and lastly coat in the breadcrumbs.

4 Heat enough oil for deep-frying over a medium-high heat. Cooking in batches, deep-fry the croquettes for 10–15 minutes until golden brown. Serve hot.

COOK'S NOTES
Be careful how you handle the croquettes because they can be fragile. The colder they are when you form them, the better.

Courgette and pea mini tortillas

SERVES 10
3 courgettes, about 500g
  (1lb 2oz), grated
50g (1¾oz) baby spinach leaves
grated zest and juice of 1 lemon
250g (9oz) frozen peas, thawed
50g (1¾oz) toasted pine nuts
salt and freshly ground black pepper
10 wheat tortillas, halved
2 tbsp reduced-fat mayonnaise
mangetout (snow pea) sprouts and
  pea shoots

1 In a large bowl, mix together the courgettes, spinach, lemon zest and juice, peas, and pine nuts. Season with salt and black pepper.

2 Heat a dry frying pan over a high heat. Add the tortilla halves, 2 at a time, and toast for about 15 seconds on each side. As you cook, set aside the tortilla halves under a clean tea towel to keep warm.

3 Lay one of the tortilla halves flat on a chopping board, and brush lightly with the mayonnaise. Take some of the filling, and place in the centre. Arrange some of the mangetout sprouts and pea shoots on top, so that they stick out at one end, then gently roll up the mini tortilla. Repeat this process until you have made 20 mini tortillas in all.

4 To serve, arrange the mini tortillas on individual serving plates, allowing 2 per person.

COOK'S NOTES

For a change, fill the tortillas with prosciutto or roasted pumpkin instead of courgettes and peas, and serve with a little soured cream or minted Greek-style yogurt. Just add some freshly chopped mint and a little freshly squeezed orange juice to the yogurt, and stir together.

FOOD FOR FRIENDS

Anchovy, olive, and basil tarts

Chilling • 1 hour
Special equipment • 4-hole muffin tin

SERVES 4
1 sheet ready-rolled puff pastry
  (preferably made with butter)
2 eggs
175ml (6fl oz) cream
2 tbsp freshly grated
  Parmesan cheese
salt and freshly ground black pepper
4 anchovy fillets in olive oil, drained
4 balls bocconcini (baby mozzarella)
  cheese, torn
8 kalamata olives, pitted
8 cherry tomatoes, halved
8 fresh basil leaves or small sprigs

1 Preheat the oven to 200°C (400°F/Gas 6). Lightly brush or spray a 4-hole 125ml (4fl oz) muffin tin.

2 On a lightly floured work surface, cut the pastry into 4 squares. Use to line the holes in the prepared muffin tin, pushing the pastry down gently into the corners. Refrigerate for 1 hour until well chilled.

3 Combine the eggs, cream, and Parmesan in a bowl, and season with salt and black pepper. Mix well.

4 Place an anchovy in each of the prepared puff pastry cases, along with a bocconcini, 2 olives, and 4 cherry tomato halves. Spoon the egg and cream mixture into the cases, and top each one with a basil leaf or sprig. Grind over a little black pepper. Bake the tarts in the oven for 25–30 minutes until golden on top. Serve warm, garnished with a fresh basil leaf or sprig.

359

Crab salad with grapefruit and coriander

PREP 10 MINS

SERVES 4
350g (12oz) cooked fresh or canned
    white crabmeat, drained
handful of baby salad leaves
handful of fresh coriander
2 pink grapefruits, peeled, segmented,
    and any pith removed

For the dressing
3 tbsp olive oil
1 tbsp white wine vinegar
pinch of sugar
salt and freshly ground black pepper

1 In a small bowl or jug, whisk together the dressing ingredients. Season with salt and black pepper.

2 Mix the crabmeat with a drizzle of the dressing. Divide the salad leaves and half of the coriander leaves among 4 serving plates, and scatter over the grapefruit segments.

3 When ready to serve, drizzle the salad with the remaining dressing. Divide the crabmeat among the plates, spooning it neatly on top of the leaves. Scatter over the remaining coriander, and serve immediately.

VARIATION Add a pinch of chilli flakes or a deseeded and chopped fresh chilli to the dressing.

COOK'S NOTES
Try to use fresh crabmeat, but drained canned crabmeat will also do. For a professional look, tightly pack the crabmeat for each serving in a small straight-sided pastry or biscuit cutter, then carefully slide out to top the leaves.

Smoked salmon and cream cheese roulades

PREP 30 MINS

SERVES 4
200g (7oz) cream cheese
2 tbsp creamed horseradish
juice of 1 lemon
salt and freshly ground black pepper
300g (10oz) smoked salmon
4 slices of finely sliced rye bread
lemon wedges, to serve
handful of salad leaves, to serve

1 Mix together the cream cheese, horseradish, and lemon juice, then season well with a pinch of salt and plenty of black pepper.

2 Cut the smoked salmon into rectangles about 30cm (12in) wide, then lay out on greaseproof paper. Spoon the cream cheese mixture onto the salmon, and spread evenly all over the surface.

3 Starting from a short end, roll up the salmon as tightly as you can. Next, roll the greaseproof paper around it, twisting the edges of the paper tightly so that you have a sausage shape.

Repeat until all the salmon has been used. Chill for 15–30 minutes to firm.

4 When ready to serve, cut the rye bread into small squares, remove the paper from the salmon and slice the roulade into small rolls. Sit a salmon roll on top of each square of bread, and serve 3–4 per person with a lemon wedge and some salad leaves.

VARIATION Add some finely chopped fresh chives to the cream cheese mixture.

COOK'S NOTES
You could make the salmon roulades ahead, wrap in cling film, and freeze for up to 1 month. When ready to use, defrost for about 1 hour at room temperature, before slicing and serving.

FOOD FOR FRIENDS

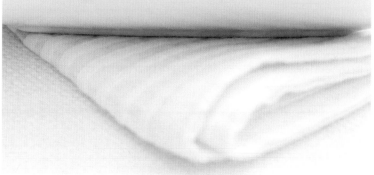

Thai fish cakes

PREP 15 MINS   COOK 15 MINS

Special equipment • food processor

SERVES 4

300g (10oz) peeled and deveined cooked prawns

3 garlic cloves, peeled but left whole

small handful of fresh coriander

2 fresh hot red chillies, deseeded

splash of Thai fish sauce, such as nam pla

splash of dark soy sauce

small handful of fresh basil leaves

juice of 2 limes

1 egg

salt and freshly ground black pepper

3–4 tbsp vegetable or sunflower oil

sweet chilli sauce, to serve

wild rocket leaves, to serve

1 Put all the ingredients except the egg and oil in a food processor, and whiz into a rough paste. Add the egg and plenty of salt and black pepper, and whiz again.

2 Heat a little of the oil in a frying pan over a medium-high heat. Scoop a tablespoon of the mixture, then carefully slide it into the pan and flatten slightly; it should be about 2cm (¾in) thick. Repeat until all the mixture has been used. Shallow-fry for a minute or two on each side until golden. You may need to cook in batches, adding more oil as needed. Drain the fish cakes on a plate lined with kitchen paper.

3 Serve hot with a drizzle of sweet chilli sauce and some wild rocket leaves.

COOK'S NOTES

Use Thai basil, which has a spicy, delicate flavour, instead of regular basil, if you can find it. It has a sweeter taste than regular basil.

Chicken satay

PREP 15 MINS   COOK 10 MINS

Special equipment • 8 wooden skewers

SERVES 4

300g (10oz) skinless chicken breast or thigh fillet, sliced into strips

1 tbsp groundnut (peanut) oil

1 tbsp light soy sauce

1 tsp Thai fish sauce, such as nam pla

3 garlic cloves, crushed

1 tsp red chilli paste

juice of 1 lemon

salt and freshly ground black pepper

For the satay sauce

3 tbsp crunchy peanut butter

juice of 1 lime

200ml (7fl oz) coconut milk

½ tsp medium chilli powder

splash of Thai fish sauce, such as nam pla

1 Soak the wooden skewers in cold water for 30 minutes before using. Put the chicken, groundnut oil, soy sauce, fish sauce, garlic, chilli paste, and lemon juice in a bowl. Season with salt and black pepper, and mix well. Leave to marinate in the refrigerator while you make the satay sauce.

2 Combine the peanut butter, lime juice, coconut milk, and chilli powder in a heavy pan over a low heat.

Simmer gently, stirring occasionally, for about 10 minutes until the sauce begins to thicken and the coconut milk releases its fragrance. Add a little more water if it is too thick, and add a splash of fish sauce, to taste. Remove from the heat, and keep warm until needed.

3 Preheat the grill to high. Divide the chicken strips into 8 equal portions, and thread onto the soaked skewers in loops. Grill for 3–5 minutes on each side until cooked through and golden brown. Serve hot with a little crispy lettuce and a bowl of the satay sauce for dipping.

Cheat...
Instead of making your own satay sauce, use a ready-made one.

COOK'S NOTES

To get ahead, the chicken could be skewered the night before and left in the refrigerator (covered). The sauce can be made ahead of time, too.

Vegetable tempura with chilli dipping sauce

PREP 15 MINS **COOK 15 MINS**

Special equipment • wok

SERVES 4

2 aubergines, sliced into thin rounds
2–3 courgettes, cut into batons
2 red peppers, deseeded and roughly chopped
500ml (16fl oz) vegetable or sunflower oil for frying
75g (2½oz) plain flour
1 tbsp cornflour
200ml (7fl oz) iced water

For the chilli dipping sauce
2 tbsp rice wine vinegar
2 tbsp light soy sauce
1 tbsp olive oil
1 tbsp caster sugar
1 garlic clove, grated or finely chopped
2 fresh hot red chillies, deseeded and finely chopped
salt and freshly ground black pepper

1 First, make the dipping sauce. Whisk together all the ingredients, and season well with salt and black pepper.

2 Once you have all the vegetables prepared, pour the oil into the wok, and heat until very hot.

3 Meanwhile, make the batter. Whisk together the flour, cornflour, and iced water. Do not overbeat; it doesn't matter if the batter is a little lumpy.

4 Drop a little of the batter into the oil, to test whether the oil is hot enough – it should sizzle straight away and become crisp. Dip the vegetable pieces one by one into the batter, and shake away the excess. Carefully add to the oil, a few at a time, and fry for 2–3 minutes until golden and crispy. Remove with a slotted spoon, and keep warm on a plate lined with kitchen paper until all the vegetable pieces are cooked. Serve immediately with the chilli dipping sauce.

COOK'S NOTES

For a perfectly crisp tempura coating, the oil needs to be very hot and the batter light, so don't overwhisk the batter or crowd the wok.

Salt and pepper prawns

PREP 10 MINS **COOK 10 MINS**

SERVES 4

2 tbsp cornflour
1 tbsp sea salt
1 tbsp cracked black pepper
16 raw king prawns, peeled and deveined
4 tbsp vegetable oil
3 fresh hot red chillies, deseeded and finely sliced
3 garlic cloves, grated or finely chopped
6 spring onions, cut into 5cm (2in) pieces, then halved lengthways
splash of dark soy sauce, to serve

1 In a bowl, mix together the cornflour, salt, and cracked black pepper. Add the prawns, and toss until well combined. Set aside.

2 Heat 1 tablespoon of the oil in a frying pan over a medium heat. Add the chilli, garlic, and spring onions, and stir-fry for 3–5 minutes. Remove from the heat, and cover with a lid to keep warm while you cook the prawns.

3 Heat the remaining oil in a separate frying pan over a high heat. Add the prawns, and cook for 3–5 minutes, tossing them gently until they are completely pink.

4 Remove the prawns from the pan with a slotted spoon, and divide among 4 serving plates. Top with the chilli and spring onion mixture, and serve immediately with a splash of soy sauce.

Minced crab balls

PREP 10 MINS **COOK 15 MINS**

Special equipment • food processor

SERVES 4

2 x 170g cans white crabmeat,
   drained, or use fresh
1 fresh medium-hot red
   chilli, deseeded
2 garlic cloves, peeled
handful of fresh coriander
grated zest and juice of 1 lemon
1 tsp Thai fish sauce, such as nam pla
2 eggs, lightly beaten
salt and freshly ground black pepper
125g (4½oz) fine fresh breadcrumbs
3 tbsp vegetable oil for shallow-frying
dark soy sauce, to serve
sweet chilli sauce, to serve

1 Put the crabmeat, chilli, garlic,
coriander, lemon zest and juice, and
fish sauce in a food processor. Whiz
until a rough paste forms, then add
the beaten egg and plenty of salt
and black pepper. Whiz again.

2 Scoop the mixture up using your
hands, and roll into 2.5cm (1in) balls.
Tip the breadcrumbs onto a plate,
and roll the crab balls in them until
well covered.

3 Heat a little of the oil in a frying
pan over a medium heat. Add a few
of the balls at a time to the pan,
to cook in batches. Shallow-fry for
about 5 minutes until golden all over,
moving the balls around the pan so
that they brown evenly, topping up
with more oil as needed. Drain on
kitchen paper. Serve hot with soy
sauce and sweet chilli sauce
for dipping.

Smoked mackerel pâté

PREP 5 MINS

Special equipment • blender or
food processor

SERVES 4

3–4 smoked mackerel fillets, about
   300g (10oz), skinned
300g (10oz) cream cheese
juice of 1–2 lemons
freshly ground black pepper
1–2 tbsp Greek-style yogurt
thinly sliced and toasted brown bread
1 lemon, cut into wedges

1 Using your hands, break up
the mackerel into chunks, and
add to a blender or food processor.
Whiz until broken up completely.

2 Spoon in the cream cheese,
and whiz again until a smooth
paste forms. Add the lemon juice,
a little at a time, whizzing between
each addition. Taste as you go,
adding more lemon as required.

Season with plenty of black pepper,
and whiz again.

3 Add the yogurt, and blend
again until the pâté is completely
smooth. Spoon into a serving dish
or 4 individual ramekins. Serve
with thinly sliced and toasted
brown bread and the lemon
wedges for squeezing over.

 VARIATION Add a pinch of cayenne pepper
to give the pâté a lift.

COOK'S NOTES

Make a day ahead, and keep
covered in the refrigerator until
ready to serve. You don't have to
add the yogurt, but it dilutes
the richness a little and makes
the pâté creamy.

Asparagus with lemony dressing

PREP 5 MINS | COOK 6 MINS

SERVES 4
1 bunch of fresh asparagus, about
   350g (12oz), trimmed
handful of wild rocket leaves

For the lemony dressing
6 tbsp olive oil
2–3 tbsp freshly squeezed lemon juice
pinch of caster sugar
1 tsp mayonnaise
salt and freshly ground black pepper

1 First, make the dressing. Put the olive oil and lemon juice in a jug or small bowl, and whisk until combined. Add the sugar and mayonnaise, and whisk well. Season with salt and black pepper.

2 Cook the asparagus in boiling salted water for 2–3 minutes, or until tender.

3 To serve, sit the asparagus on the rocket leaves, and dress liberally with the dressing. Serve immediately.

COOK'S NOTES

You will need to give the dressing a final whisk just before serving. For a lower-fat version, omit the mayonnaise.

Curried eggs

PREP 5 MINS | COOK 6 MINS

SERVES 4
6 eggs
2 tbsp mayonnaise
1–2 tsp medium-hot curry powder
½ tsp cayenne pepper
salt and freshly ground black pepper

1 Cook the eggs in a pan of boiling water for about 6 minutes, or until hard-boiled. Remove from the pan, and leave to cool, then peel away the shell.

2 Halve the eggs lengthways, and carefully remove the yolk using a teaspoon. Put the egg yolks in a bowl, and mix together with the mayonnaise, curry powder, and cayenne. Season well with salt and black pepper.

3 Now spoon the devilled egg mixture back into each egg white, dividing the mixture evenly among the halves.

4 Serve with some crispy lettuce leaves, Parma ham and a further pinch of cayenne pepper, if you wish.

Cheat...
Hard boiled eggs can be cooked a day ahead. Keep in the refrigerator until ready to use.

COOK'S NOTES

Do not overcook the eggs – 6 minutes maximum – otherwise they will have a black ring around the yolk.

Smoked salmon with mustard and dill dressing

SERVES 4
350g (12oz) good-quality
   smoked salmon
1 lemon, halved
½ cucumber, finely chopped
crusty brown bread, sliced, to serve

For the mustard and dill dressing
90ml (3fl oz) extra virgin olive oil
3 tbsp white wine vinegar
1 tsp wholegrain mustard
1 tsp runny honey
salt and freshly ground black pepper
handful of fresh dill, finely chopped

1 Divide the salmon among 4 serving plates, and squeeze over a little lemon juice.

2 To make the dressing, put the olive oil, vinegar, mustard, and honey in a jug or small bowl. Whisk together until well combined, then season with salt and black pepper. Sprinkle in half of the dill, and whisk again. Taste, and adjust seasoning as needed.

3 Toss the cucumber along with the remaining dill, then spoon the cucumber and dill onto the plates. When ready to serve, drizzle over the dressing, and serve with the brown bread.

Avocado with roasted cherry tomatoes and a paprika dressing

SERVES 4
350g (12oz) cherry tomatoes
1 tbsp olive oil
handful of fresh thyme sprigs,
   leaves picked
salt and freshly ground black pepper
2 ripe avocados
handful of wild rocket leaves

For the paprika dressing
90ml (3fl oz) olive oil
3 tbsp white wine vinegar or
   cider vinegar
1 tsp paprika
pinch of caster sugar
½ tsp mayonnaise

1 Preheat the oven to 200°C (400°F/ Gas 6). Sit the cherry tomatoes in a roasting tin, and toss with the olive oil. Sprinkle over the thyme, and season with salt and black pepper. Roast in the oven for 12–15 minutes until the tomatoes begin to burst and char very slightly.

2 Whisk together the dressing ingredients, and season well with salt and black pepper.

3 Halve the avocados. Carefully remove the stones, then peel away the skin. Slice each of the avocado halves lengthways without cutting all the way through, then fan the avocado.

4 To serve, put an avocado fan on each of 4 serving plates with the rocket and roasted tomatoes, and spoon over the dressing. Serve immediately.

365

Smoked trout with chilli and lime dressing

PREP
10
MINS

SERVES 4

350g (12oz) hot- or cold-smoked trout
large handful of salad leaves
1 bunch of spring onions, finely sliced
4 radishes, finely sliced

For the chilli and lime dressing
2 tbsp rice wine vinegar
2 tsp light soy sauce
splash of sesame oil
½–1 tsp caster sugar
2 fresh medium-hot red chillies,
   deseeded and finely chopped
juice of 1–2 limes

1 Whisk together the dressing ingredients, tasting as you go. Add all of the lime juice, if needed, or use less if the dressing is becoming too sour.

2 Divide the smoked trout among 4 serving plates, then toss together the salad leaves, spring onions, and radishes.

3 When ready to serve, lightly toss the salad with the some of the dressing, and drizzle the remainder over the trout. Serve immediately.

COOK'S NOTES

Prepare the dressing a day ahead, and leave in the refrigerator in a screw-top jar until needed. You could sprinkle over a pinch of toasted sesame seeds for extra texture, if you wish.

Butterflied mackerel with sweet potato and beetroot pickle

PREP
15
MINS

COOK
15
MINS

SERVES 4

2 sweet potatoes, peeled and diced
4 mackerel, about 100g (3½oz)
   each, butterflied
4 medium-to-large ready-cooked
   unpickled beetroots, diced
1 small onion, finely chopped
1–2 tsp onion seeds
juice of 1 orange

1 Cook the sweet potato in a pan of boiling salted water for 3–5 minutes until just beginning to soften; do not overcook. Drain, and allow to cool.

2 Preheat the grill to high. Sit the mackerel on an oiled baking tray, and grill for 3–4 minutes on each side until cooked through.

3 Meanwhile, to make the pickle, gently mix together the potato and beetroot, then stir through the onion and onion seeds. Squeeze over the orange juice, and stir until everything is coated.

4 Serve the mackerel hot, with a little of the sweet potato and beetroot pickle, or serve the pickle separately in a dish for everyone to help themselves.

COOK'S NOTES

Butterflied means that the mackerel has had its back bone removed and has been flattened. Ask your fishmonger to do this for you, or buy it ready-prepared.

Mushroom and ricotta pies with red pepper pesto

PREP 25 MINS · COOK 45 MINS

Special equipment • blender or food processor

SERVES 4

120ml (4fl oz) olive oil
300g (10oz) button
  mushrooms, halved
1 leek, white part only, finely sliced
2 sheets ready-rolled puff pastry
  (preferably made with butter),
  thawed if frozen
200g (7oz) ricotta cheese
1 egg yolk, lightly beaten

For the red pepper pesto
2 tbsp olive oil
1 onion, sliced
2 red peppers, sliced
2 garlic cloves, crushed
zest and juice of 1 small lemon
salt and freshly ground black pepper

1 Preheat the oven to 200°C (400°F/Gas 6), and line a baking tray with baking parchment. To make the red pepper pesto, heat the oil in a heavy frying pan over a low heat. Add the onion, and sweat gently for a few minutes until soft and translucent. Tip in the peppers, and sweat for a further 10–15 minutes until soft. Transfer the onion mixture to a blender or food processor. Add the garlic and lemon zest and juice, and blend to a chunky

purée. Season with salt and black pepper and set aside.

2 Heat another 3 tablespoons of the oil in a clean large heavy frying pan over a medium heat. Add the mushrooms and leeks, and sauté, stirring, for 5 minutes until the mushrooms have browned. Set aside.

3 Cut each pastry sheet into 4 squares. Using a sharp knife, cut diagonal slashes across the surface of 4 of the pastry squares, being careful not to slice all the way through. Spread the ricotta over the surface of the uncut pastry squares, leaving a 1cm (½in) border of pastry all around the edges. Spoon the mushroom and leek mixture evenly over the ricotta, then lay the slit pastry squares evenly over the top of the mushrooms. Pinch and twist together the corners of the pies, and brush the tops with the egg yolk.

4 Sit the pies on top of the prepared baking tray, and bake in the oven for about 25 minutes until golden brown. Serve with the red pepper pesto, and a leafy green salad.

COOK'S NOTES

The pies are slightly open on the edges, allowing steam to escape so that they don't become soggy.

Crisp sweet potato with courgette and chive mascarpone

PREP 15 MINS · COOK 25 MINS

SERVES 4

600g (1lb 5oz) sweet potato, peeled
  and sliced into 8 even discs
2 tbsp olive oil, plus extra
  for drizzling
salt and freshly ground black pepper
1 courgette, about 150g (5½oz)
juice of ½ lemon
150g (5½oz) mascarpone
1 tbsp finely chopped chives, plus
  extra 8 chive stalks, to garnish

1 Preheat the oven to 200°C (400°F/Gas 6). Put the sweet potato in a bowl. Add the 2 tablespoons of olive oil, and season with salt and black pepper. Toss until the sweet potato is well coated. Transfer to a baking tray, and roast for about 25 minutes until golden brown and tender when pierced with a wooden skewer. Set aside to cool.

2 Trim both ends off the courgette, then shave into thin slices. Put in

a bowl with the lemon juice, and season with salt and black pepper. Toss gently to coat thoroughly.

3 Put the mascarpone in a separate bowl, add the chopped chives, and stir through.

4 To serve, put a disc of sweet potato in the centre of each of 4 serving plates. Divide the courgette evenly among each serving, and use to top the sweet potato discs. Place another disc on top, then spoon over the chive mascarpone. Arrange 2 stalks of the extra chives on top of each serving, and drizzle with a little olive oil. Serve immediately.

COOK'S NOTES

This could be served as finger food, by cutting the sweet potato disks into halves or quarters before baking, then topping each piece with courgette and chive mascarpone.

BIG-POT GATHERINGS

Fabulous food in one pot – effortless entertaining.

BIG-POT GATHERINGS

Cooking for larger numbers than usual can sometimes be daunting, but if you keep the food to one pot, it makes life (and the washing up) a lot easier. This informal way of entertaining lends itself to informal eating, when standing up and digging in with a fork is just as acceptable as everyone sitting and being served straight from the pot.

Psst...

Buy mixed stew packs from the butcher, and freeze until needed, or – if freezer space permits – think about buying half a lamb or pig, jointed.

One-pot cooking pots Choose the best pot for the job.

POT		BEST FOR
	**TAGINE** A tagine is a North African cooking pot, and the type of dish it produces goes by the same name. It is a shallow dish with a conical top, and is used in Moroccan cooking. Made of terracotta, tagines can be used in the oven, or on the hob (with a heat diffuser). The cone-shaped lid collects the steam, so the food stays really moist. The bottom doubles up as a serving dish.	Meat, vegetable, and fish curries, and slow-cooked stews.
	**PAELLA PAN** This is a thin flat frying pan, about 4cm (1½in) deep, with two loop handles. It is traditionally made from carbon steel, which responds quickly to heat, but needs to be cared for, as it can easily turn rusty after use, if not dried properly. The size of a paella pan can vary from 46cm (18in) wide, if cooking for about 8, up to as large as 132cm (52in), if cooking for a couple of hundred.	The traditional Spanish rice dish, "paella", where a thin layer of rice is cooked with added herbs and spices, such as saffron, and a mixture of seafood and meat (chicken and rabbit). Paella is traditionally cooked outdoors for large crowds of people.
	**CASSEROLE** This is a large heavy deep pan, used in the oven or on the hob. A cast-iron pan with a tight-fitting lid is the best choice, as it will distribute heat evenly. Casserole pans keep food moist, and are perfect for slow cooking.	Meat or vegetable casseroles and stews that have plenty of liquid in (usually stock). They are ideal for oven-to-table cooking, and perfect for cooking for large numbers, as once in the oven they can be left, and casseroles don't often require accompaniments.
	WOK These pans are used in Asian cooking, and are designed for quick, high-heat cooking. They are often made from carbon steel, which needs to be looked after to last. They are bowl-shaped, with sloping sides: this creates a hot spot at the base, where all the cooking is done. Food can sit at the sides and be brought down to the base to be cooked super-fast. Wok cooking requires food to be constantly moved around.	Stir-fries and Asian curries, using tender slices of meat, seafood, or vegetables. If all ingredients are prepped beforehand, wok cooking is ideal for large numbers, as it can be pan-to-plate in an instant.

Get ahead

When cooking for large numbers, prep needs to be kept to a minimum. Many big-pot recipes require lots of onions: use a food processor and the pulse button to chop them, then store them in a sealed plastic container in the refrigerator for a couple of days until needed. You can do the same with garlic.

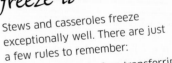

freeze it

Stews and casseroles freeze exceptionally well. There are just a few rules to remember:

Cool completely before transferring to a rigid plastic container or freezer bag.

Freeze as soon as possible after cooling.

Make sure meat is well covered with sauce or gravy, so it remains tender and doesn't suffer freezer burn (see pp248–251).

The best meat cuts for big-pot cooking These undervalued
and good-value cuts of meat are perfect for long, slow cooking.

MEAT		BEST FOR
	**STEWING STEAK** This is the generic term for tougher cuts of meat that require stewing or slow cooking. The best kind of stewing steak is chuck steak, which has the most flavour, and is the most tender. Shin is often served as stewing steak. For more flavour, the meat can be marinated first, or browned and sealed before liquid is added.	Stews and casseroles, or meat curries that require a long, slow cooking time. Add plenty of complementing spices and herbs, such as mustards and horseradish, or fresh rosemary and bay leaves. The quality of the finished dish will depend on the quality of the meat.
	**PORK BELLY** This is an extremely cheap but succulent cut of meat, making it ideal if you're catering for large numbers. It's full of flavour because it's full of fat (which can easily be removed after cooking. Buy in a flat slab, allowing about 150g (5½oz) per person, with or without the bones, or buy in ready-cut slices. The skin that covers the belly can be scored and rubbed with salt to produce crackling: cook high until crisp, then slow and long until the meat is meltingly tender.	Stews and casseroles, slow-roasting flat, or stuffing and rolling to roast. Add lots of flavour, such as garlic and fennel, or apples. Asian flavours, such as star anise and soy sauce, also work well.
	LAMB NECK The neck is composed of three different parts, the best end, the middle end, and the scrag end. The best end is, as the name suggests, the most tender and expensive part, and can be used for roasting as it is near the shoulder and fairly lean. The middle end is a lot fattier and extremely tasty when slow-cooked. The scrag end (the bit nearest to the head) is the cheapest cut, and tends to be bony, but is delicious slow cooked.	Stews, casseroles, and tagines, especially if feeding large numbers. It needs to be cooked long and slow, and needs good punchy flavours to cut through the fat, such as fresh hot green chillies, harissa, or redcurrant jelly. Team it with fresh green vegetables such as cabbage or beans.
	**MINCED BEEF** Like stewing steak, this is a generic term used for beef that has been minced and could be a variety of cuts, so best to ask your butcher. Some minced beef comes from the neck, which can be fatty but is inexpensive, otherwise it will probably be chuck steak, which is a little leaner. Neck mince will go a long way, but is best slowly simmered in a sauce, such as a ragù to tenderize the meat. Chuck mince can be used for frying and foods such as burgers and meatballs.	Casseroles and pies. Ground mince is such a versatile meat and because of its cost, it is an ideal choice for big-pot gatherings. As well as being cheap, tasty, and easy to cook with, it takes on other flavours well, such as Mexican, Italian, or Middle Eastern.

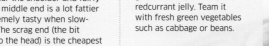

reheat and eat
Stews and casseroles are perfect for reheating; in fact they often taste better when left to sit, or served up the next day. They are ideal if family eating is staggered: the pot can sit in the oven for a few hours, happily stewing away, then be served up when required. It won't be spoilt if reheated for 2–3 minutes in the microwave on High.

Choosing big-pot fish

• **Monkfish** is firm and has no bones, so is ideal for big-pot dishes. Try a Provençal fish stew of tomatoes, olives, and oregano, adding pieces of monkfish for the last 15–20 minutes of cooking.

• **Prawns** are better served without their shells when cooking large quantities. Add them to the pan – to a jambalaya, for instance – at the end of the cooking time, so they are juicy and flavoursome.

• **White fish** such as haddock or cod, or cheaper alternatives such as pollack or coley, need very little cooking. Large chunky pieces can be added to the pan at the final stage of cooking, or wrapped in bacon and baked or steamed on top of spiced rice and spinach.

• **Salmon** is an easy option for big-pot cooking. It can be added to a Thai-style curry, or baked with soy and lemon, and piled high with spiced chunky noodles.

Chicken and prawn paella.
For recipe, see p375.

FOOD FOR FRIENDS

Chicken, aubergine, and tomato tagine

 PREP 30 MINS COOK 25 MINS

SERVES 8
3–4 tbsp olive oil
8 chicken pieces (thighs and breasts)
salt and freshly ground black pepper
2 aubergines, cut into bite-sized cubes
1 tsp ground cinnamon
2 onions, finely grated
3 fresh hot red chillies, deseeded
    and finely chopped
2 tsp ground cumin
2 bay leaves
1.8kg (4lb) tomatoes

1 tbsp tomato purée
4 preserved lemons, halved
    and pith discarded
handful of fresh coriander,
    finely chopped

1 Heat 1 tablespoon of oil in a large wide heavy-based pan, season the chicken with salt and black pepper, and add to the pan. Cook for 8 minutes, or until golden, stirring occasionally, then remove, and put to one side. Toss the aubergines in the cinnamon and add to the pan with 1 tablespoon of oil. Cook over a medium

heat, stirring occasionally, for 10 minutes, or until golden. Add more oil if needed. Remove, and put to one side.

2 Add 1 tablespoon of oil to the pan, then add the onions, chillies, cumin, and bay leaves. Season well with salt and black pepper and cook over a low heat for 5 minutes. Return the chicken and aubergine to the pan along with the tomatoes and tomato purée. Cover with a lid and simmer over a low heat for 25 minutes, topping up with hot water if it starts to look too dry.

3 Stir through the preserved lemons and coriander, and serve with plenty of fluffy couscous and some harissa on the side.

372

Beef and orange daube

PREP 30 MINS **COOK** 2 HRS ❄

Special equipment • large cast-iron pan

SERVES 8
4 tbsp olive oil
1.1kg (2½lb) stewing steak, such as chuck steak or silverside, cut into bite-sized pieces
1 tbsp plain flour
salt and freshly ground black pepper
1 bay leaf
50g (1¾oz) butter
3 large onions, finely sliced
zest and juice of 2 oranges
12 salted anchovies, finely chopped
300ml (10fl oz) red wine
550g (1¼lb) chestnut mushrooms, quartered
1.2 litres (2 pints) hot vegetable stock
handful of fresh thyme, finely chopped

1 Preheat the oven to 150°C (300°F/Gas 2). Heat 2 tablespoons of the oil in a large cast-iron pan, toss the meat in the flour, season well with salt and black pepper, then add to the hot oil with the bay leaf and stir. Cook, stirring occasionally, for 8–10 minutes, or until the meat is no longer pink, then add the butter and cook for 5 minutes, or until the meat is golden. Remove with a slotted spoon and put to one side.

2 Add the remaining oil to the pan, then add the onions and cook over a low heat for 6–8 minutes, or until soft. Add the orange zest, raise the heat a little, then add the orange juice and stir to loosen all the sticky bits from the bottom of the pan.

3 Stir in the anchovies, then add the wine and simmer over a high heat for 2 minutes. Stir in the mushrooms, add the stock and thyme, and season with salt and black pepper. Return the steak to the pan, cover with a lid, then put in the oven to cook for 2 hours, or until the meat is meltingly tender.

Prawn makhani

PREP 20 MINS **COOK** 40 MINS

Special equipment • food processor

SERVES 8
700g (1lb 9oz) (shelled weight) uncooked prawns
salt and freshly ground black pepper
6 garlic cloves, grated or finely chopped
15cm (6in) piece of fresh root ginger, peeled and grated, or finely chopped
3 tbsp vegetable oil
200ml (7fl oz) thick natural yogurt
2–3 tsp medium-hot chilli powder
2 cinnamon sticks, broken into pieces
4 fresh medium-hot red chillies, deseeded and finely chopped
6 cardamom pods, crushed
700g (1lb 9oz) tomatoes
125g (4½oz) cashew nuts, ground, plus a handful, roughly chopped, to garnish
2–3 tsp ground fenugreek
200ml (7fl oz) double cream

1 Season the prawns with salt and black pepper and toss with half the garlic, half the ginger, 1 teaspoon of the oil, the yogurt, and chilli powder. Heat a large deep-sided frying pan, then add the prawns with as much of the yogurt coating as you can, and cook over a high heat, tossing them all the time, for 5–8 minutes, or until no longer pink. Remove and set aside.

2 Heat the remaining oil in the pan, add the rest of the ginger and garlic, the cinnamon, chillies, and cardamom pods, and cook over a low heat, stirring occasionally, for 2 minutes. Add the tomatoes and cook for 10 minutes, or until they start to reduce. Cover with a little hot water and simmer for a further 10 minutes, or until puréed.

3 Push the tomato mixture through a sieve into a food processor and whiz until smooth. Return to the pan, then stir through the ground cashew nuts and fenugreek and simmer for 10 minutes, adding a little hot water if the sauce starts to look too thick. Add the prawns along with the cream, stir, taste, and season, if needed. Cook for 5 minutes, then garnish with the chopped cashew nuts and serve with rice.

COOK'S NOTES

Fenugreek is the key spice in a makhani. If you can find dried fenugreek leaves, use a handful of these, crushed, instead of the ground fenugreek.

Pork goulash

PREP 25 MINS · COOK 1 HR

Special equipment • large cast-iron pan

SERVES 8

1.1kg (2½lb) stewing pork, cut into bite-sized pieces
1 tbsp plain flour
2 tsp paprika
2 tsp caraway seeds, crushed
salt and freshly ground black pepper
2 tbsp olive oil
1 tbsp cider vinegar
2 tbsp tomato purée
1.2 litres (2 pints) hot vegetable stock
6 tomatoes, skinned and roughly chopped
1 onion, sliced into rings
handful of fresh curly parsley, finely chopped

1 Toss the meat with the flour, paprika, and caraway seeds and season well with salt and black pepper. Heat the oil in a large cast-iron pan, then add the meat and cook over a high heat, stirring occasionally, for 8–10 minutes, or until it begins to brown. Add the vinegar and stir well for a couple of minutes, scraping up all the sticky bits from the bottom of the pan.

2 Add the tomato purée, followed by the stock, and bring to the boil. Reduce to a simmer, put a lid on, and cook gently for 1 hour. Check occasionally, and top up with boiling water if the goulash begins to dry out too much – it should be fairly thick, though.

3 Stir through the tomatoes, taste, and season again if needed, then top with the onion rings and parsley and serve with rice.

Gado gado

PREP 20 MINS · COOK 20 MINS

Special equipment • food processor

SERVES 8

4 corn on the cob
salt
350g (12oz) green beans, trimmed
550g (1¼lb) potatoes, unpeeled
450g (1lb) roasted peanuts
4 garlic cloves
3 fresh hot red chillies, deseeded
salt and freshly ground black pepper
2 tsp demerara sugar
juice of 1 lime
4 carrots, finely sliced
200g (7oz) beansprouts
half a cucumber, chopped into bite-sized pieces
6 eggs, hard-boiled, shelled, and quartered
handful of fresh coriander, chopped

1 Cook the corn on the cob in a pan of boiling salted water for 6–8 minutes, or until soft. Add the green beans for the last 5 minutes of cooking. Drain, slice the corn on the cob into chunky rings, and place in a large shallow serving bowl. Meanwhile, cook the potatoes in a pan of boiling salted water for 15 minutes, or until just beginning to soften. Drain and put to one side to cool, then slice and add to the sweetcorn and beans.

2 Put the peanuts, garlic, and chillies in a food processor and whiz until finely ground. Season with salt and black pepper. Add a little water and whiz again to make a paste. Add the sugar and lime juice and whiz again, adding more water, if needed – the paste should be smooth but not too runny.

3 Add the carrots, beansprouts, and cucumber to the cooked vegetables, then pour over the sauce and toss together. Top with the hard-boiled eggs and coriander, and serve.

Chicken and prawn paella

PREP 15 MINS   COOK 50 MINS

SERVES 8

8 chicken thighs, skinned
1.7 litres (3 pints) hot vegetable stock
2 tbsp olive oil
4 red peppers, deseeded
   and cut into strips
700g (1lb 9oz) uncooked
   shelled prawns
salt and freshly ground black pepper
2 x 400g cans chopped tomatoes
450g (1lb) paella rice or basmati rice
400g (14oz) green beans, trimmed
a few strands of saffron
pinch of cayenne pepper
pinch of paprika
handful of fresh flat-leaf parsley,
   finely chopped

1 Put the chicken thighs in a large pan, add 600ml (1 pint) of the stock, cover with a lid, and cook over a low-medium heat for 15–20 minutes, or until the chicken is nearly cooked. Remove with a slotted spoon and reserve the stock.

2 Meanwhile, heat the oil in a paella pan or large frying pan, add the peppers, and cook for 2 minutes. Add the prawns, season with salt and black pepper, then cook over a medium heat, stirring occasionally, for 10 minutes or until the prawns are cooked and pink. Remove the prawns and peppers with a slotted spoon and put to one side.

3 Add the tomatoes to the pan, then the rice, and the reserved cooking stock and stir. Season again, then add another 600ml (1 pint) of the stock, and the chicken. Simmer gently for 20–30 minutes, or until the rice is cooked, adding the remaining stock as you need it. Add the beans for the last 10 minutes of cooking along with the saffron, cayenne, and paprika. Return the peppers and prawns to the pan, heat through, then sprinkle over the parsley and serve.

Cheat...
You can buy ready-mixed paella spices. Add with the rice in place of the saffron, cayenne, and paprika.

COOK'S NOTES

It's traditional in Spain to mix meat and fish. If you're not a fan, choose one to cook with and increase the quantities.

375

FOOD FOR FRIENDS

Mixed fish stew with croutons

PREP 15 MINS COOK 30 MINS

SERVES 8

2.25kg (5lb) mixed fish and shellfish, such as haddock, monkfish, plaice, and shelled uncooked prawns
3 tbsp olive oil
4 garlic cloves, grated or finely chopped
2 tbsp tomato purée
1 onion, finely chopped
8 tomatoes, skinned and chopped
1 tsp fennel seeds
a few strands of saffron

pinch of paprika
1.2 litres (2 pints) light fish stock
salt and freshly ground black pepper
1 French stick
125g (4½oz) Gruyère cheese, grated
handful of fresh flat-leaf parsley, finely chopped, to garnish

1 Wash the fish, then cut it into chunky bite-sized pieces and put to one side. Put the oil in a large wide pan, add the garlic, tomato purée, and onion, and cook over a very low heat for 5-8 minutes, or until the onion begins to soften.

2 Add the tomato, fennel seeds, saffron, and paprika, pour in the stock, and season with salt and black pepper. Bring to the boil, then reduce to a simmer and cook for 10 minutes. Add the fish and shellfish and simmer for a further 10 minutes, or until the fish is cooked.

3 Slice the bread on the diagonal and toast. Serve the soup with the toasted croutons, sprinkle over the cheese, and garnish with parsley.

COOK'S NOTES

A rouille (spicy garlicky mayonnaise sauce) is often served with fish soups and stews. You can buy it ready-made in jars. Spread it on the toasted croutons, sprinkle with the Gruyère cheese, and add to the top of the stew.

Spiced sausage cassoulet

PREP 30 MINS | COOK 2 HRS

Special equipment • large heavy-based pan

SERVES 8

4 tbsp olive oil
2 large onions, sliced
4 celery sticks, chopped
2 large potatoes, cut into 2cm
   (¾in) dice
24 pork chipolata sausages
200g (7oz) bacon lardons
6 garlic cloves, chopped
2 x 400g cans haricot beans, drained
   and rinsed
1 tbsp tomato purée
3 tsp paprika
2 tsp dried thyme
2 tsp dried oregano
1 tsp freshly ground black pepper
300ml (10fl oz) dry white wine
600ml (1 pint) hot vegetable stock
125g (4½oz) fresh breadcrumbs
handful of fresh flat-leaf
   parsley, chopped
50g (1¾oz) butter

1 Preheat the oven to 150°C (300°F/Gas 2). Heat the oil in a large heavy-based pan, add the onions, celery, and potatoes, and cook for 5 minutes, or until starting to soften. Add the sausages and lardons and cook for a further 5 minutes, or until starting to brown.

2 Add the garlic and cook for 1 minute, then add the haricot beans, tomato purée, paprika, thyme, oregano, and pepper. Combine well, then add the wine. Bring to the boil and simmer for 2 minutes, then add the stock and 300ml (10fl oz) of hot water. Bring to the boil, simmer for 10 minutes, then remove from the heat.

3 Mix the breadcrumbs with the parsley and cover the top of the dish with them. Dot with knobs of the butter, cover with a lid, and bake for 1½ hours. Remove the lid and cook for a further 30 minutes. Serve with a crisp green salad.

Mushroom risotto

PREP 15 MINS | COOK 25 MINS

SERVES 8

6 tbsp olive oil
2 onions, finely chopped
50g (1¾oz) butter
250g (9oz) chestnut mushrooms,
   roughly chopped
250g (9oz) chestnut mushrooms,
   roughly grated
6 garlic cloves, grated or
   finely chopped
3 fresh medium-hot red chillies,
   deseeded and finely sliced
550g (1¼lb) Arborio rice
750ml (1¼ pints) hot mushroom or
   chicken stock
2 tsp freshly ground black pepper
large handful of fresh flat-leaf
   parsley, finely chopped
125g (4½oz) Parmesan cheese, grated

1 Heat the oil in a large cast-iron pan or other heavy based pan, add the onions, and cook over a medium heat for 5 minutes, or until soft and translucent. Add the butter, mushrooms, garlic, and chillies, combine well, and cook for a further 5 minutes, stirring constantly.

2 Add the rice and stir well, then add 300ml (10fl oz) of the stock and cook over a low heat, stirring occasionally, until the stock has been absorbed by the rice. Add more stock 150ml (5fl oz) at a time – allowing each addition to be absorbed before adding the next – until the rice is cooked.

3 Add the pepper, parsley, and half the Parmesan cheese, stir through, and serve with more Parmesan cheese on top.

VARIATION Omit the mushrooms and add 6 sliced courgettes or 1½ bunches of asparagus, chopped, with the onion.

Seafood risotto

PREP 20 MINS   COOK 30 MINS

SERVES 8

2-3 tbsp olive oil
450g (1lb) shelled uncooked prawns
salt and freshly ground black pepper
450g (1lb) mixed white fish, such as
    monkfish, sea bass, and haddock,
    cut into bite-sized pieces
16 scallops (with or without roe,
    depending on preference), cleaned
2 knobs of butter
2 onions, finely chopped
4 garlic cloves, grated or
    finely chopped
2 litres (3½ pints) hot vegetable
    stock, or light fish stock
675g (1½lb) risotto rice
2 large glasses of white wine
6 tomatoes, skinned and
    finely chopped

large handful of fresh flat-leaf
    parsley, finely chopped
handful of fresh dill, finely chopped
lemon wedges, to serve

1 Heat 1 tablespoon of the oil
in a frying pan, add the prawns
and a pinch of salt and black
pepper, and cook over a medium
to high heat for a couple of minutes,
or until they turn pink. Remove
and put to one side. Add the fish,
and a little more oil, if needed, and
cook over a medium heat for a couple
of minutes, or until the fish is opaque
and cooked. Remove and put to
one side.

2 Season the scallops with salt and
black pepper, add to the pan with
a little more oil, if needed, and cook
for 2 minutes on each side, or until

opaque. Remove and put to one side.
Add a knob of butter to the pan,
followed by the onion, and cook
over a low heat for 5-8 minutes,
or until soft and translucent. Stir
through the garlic and cook for
a few seconds. Meanwhile, put the
hot stock in a large pan and keep
on a low simmer.

3 Add the rice to the frying pan
and stir well so it soaks up all the
buttery juices. Season with salt
and black pepper, then pour in
the wine and raise the heat a little.
Allow to boil for a few seconds
while the alcohol evaporates. Start
adding the stock a ladleful at a time,
stirring until it has been absorbed
before adding more. Continue like
this until the rice is cooked but
still has a bit of bite to it – about

20 minutes. You may have some
stock left over or you may need
a little more.

4 Stir through the tomatoes, return
the seafood and fish to the pan, then
stir in the herbs and remaining
butter. Taste and season with salt
and black pepper if needed, then
serve with lemon wedges.

COOK'S NOTES

*Adding a little butter at the end
gives a really creamy risotto, but
you can leave it out if you're
counting the calories.*

378

Provençal lamb

PREP 25 MINS · **COOK 2½ HRS**

Special equipment • large cast-iron pan

SERVES 8

4 tbsp olive oil

4 onions, cut into eighths

1.1kg (2½lb) lamb (from the leg), cut into bite-sized pieces

2 tsp paprika

6 garlic cloves, chopped

6 tbsp black olives

2 tbsp capers

4 tsp dried oregano

2 tsp dried thyme

6 tbsp fino sherry

salt and freshly ground black pepper

4 x 400g cans chopped tomatoes

1 Preheat the oven to 150°C (300°F/ Gas 2). Heat the oil in a large cast-iron pan over a medium heat, add the onions, and cook for 5 minutes, or until starting to soften. Add the lamb and paprika and cook, turning frequently, for 8–10 minutes, or until the lamb is no longer pink.

2 Add the garlic, olives, capers, oregano, thyme, and sherry, and cook for 3 minutes. Season well with salt and black pepper, add the tomatoes, stir well, and bring to the boil. Cover the pan with a well-fitting lid and transfer to the oven to cook for 2½ hours. Serve with a roughly mashed herby potatoes and olive oil.

Malaysian-style chicken with noodles

PREP 15 MINS · **COOK 1 HR**

Special equipment • food processor • wok

SERVES 8

8 large chicken pieces (breasts, legs, and thighs), about 1.1kg (2½lb) in weight, or 1 large chicken, jointed

salt and freshly ground black pepper

5 fresh hot red chillies, deseeded

2 tbsp medium-hot curry powder

2 tsp turmeric

2 tsp ground cumin

6 garlic cloves, grated or finely chopped

8 shallots, finely chopped

3 tbsp vegetable oil or sunflower oil

2 x 400g cans coconut milk

2 tsp sugar

6 tomatoes, skinned and chopped

1 red onion, finely chopped

handful of fresh coriander leaves, chopped, plus extra to garnish

600ml (1 pint) chicken stock

450g (1lb) thick egg noodles

1 tbsp vegetable oil, to fry

1 Season the chicken well with salt and black pepper and put to one side. Put the chillies, curry powder, turmeric, cumin, garlic, shallots, and oil in a food processor, and whiz to a smooth paste.

2 Heat a large heavy-based pan, add the paste, and cook over a medium heat for 5 minutes, stirring frequently. Add the chicken pieces skin side down and cook for 10 minutes, or until evenly browned. Turn halfway through cooking.

3 Shake the cans of coconut milk and add to the pan along with the sugar. Season well with salt and black pepper, bring to the boil, then reduce the heat and allow to simmer for 20 minutes, or until the coconut mixture has reduced down. Add the tomatoes and onion and cook for 10 minutes more, then stir through the coriander. Cover and leave to stand while you prepare the noodles.

4 Put the stock in a large pan of hot water and bring to the boil. Add the noodles and cook for 8 minutes, or until almost cooked but not too soft. Drain well. Heat the oil in a wok or deep frying pan, add the noodles, and cook for 3 minutes. Season well with salt and black pepper, then toss together well and transfer to a large shallow platter. Spoon over the chicken, garnish with the remaining coriander, and serve.

Pork belly with onions and potatoes

PREP 25 MINS
COOK 1½ HRS

SERVES 6-8

1kg (2¼lb) piece of pork belly
1 tsp sea salt
6 tbsp olive oil
3 large onions, cut into eighths
4 large potatoes, cut into wedges
250g (9oz) button chestnut
  mushrooms, halved
300ml (10fl oz) white wine
4 garlic cloves, chopped
1 heaped tbsp fresh thyme
600ml (1 pint) light vegetable stock
1 tsp freshly ground black pepper

1 Preheat the oven to 220°C (425°F/Gas 7). Score the skin of the pork belly deeply, then rub the salt and 2 tablespoons of the oil into it. Transfer to a baking tray and place in the oven for 20 minutes, or until the skin has crisped up. Remove from the oven and reduce the temperature to 170°C (340°F/Gas 3½).

2 Heat the remaining oil in a large frying pan, add the onions and potatoes, and cook for 10 minutes, stirring constantly. Add the mushrooms and cook for 5 minutes. Add the wine and cook for 2 minutes. Transfer the mixture to a large baking dish, add the garlic, thyme, stock, and pepper, and combine well. Nestle the pork in the mixture, ensuring the crackling is not covered, and roast in the oven for 1½ hours.

3 Allow to rest for 10 minutes, then cut the pork up with scissors, and serve with steamed broccoli.

FOOD FOR FRIENDS

Pad Thai

  PREP 15 MINS · COOK 15 MINS

Special equipment • wok

SERVES 8

550g (1¼lb) medium or thick
   rice noodles
3 tbsp sunflower oil
4 eggs, lightly beaten
1 tsp shrimp paste (optional)
4 fresh hot red chillies, deseeded and
   finely chopped
6 chicken breast fillets, skinned and
   cut into 5mm (¼in) slices
2 bunches spring onions,
   finely chopped
splash of Thai fish sauce, such
   as nam pla
juice of 2 limes
2 tbsp demerara sugar
salt and freshly ground black pepper
300g (10oz) unsalted peanuts
handful of fresh coriander,
   finely chopped
lime wedges, to serve

1 Put the noodles in a large bowl, cover with boiling water, and leave for 8 minutes, or until soft. Drain and put to one side. Meanwhile, put 1 tablespoon of the oil in a large wok over a high heat and swirl around the pan. Add the beaten egg and whisk it around the wok for about a minute, or until it begins to set – don't let it set completely – then spoon it out and put to one side.

2 Add the remaining oil to the pan, then add the shrimp paste (if using), and chillies and stir. With the heat still high, add the chicken and stir vigorously for 5 minutes, or until it is no longer pink. Stir through the spring onions, fish sauce, lime juice, and sugar and toss together well. Cook for a few minutes until the sugar has dissolved, then season well with salt and black pepper. Return the egg to the pan.

3 Add the noodles to the pan and toss together to coat with the sauce, then add half the peanuts and half the coriander and toss again. Transfer to a large shallow serving bowl and scatter over the rest of the peanuts and coriander. Garnish with lime wedges and serve.

Beef, fennel, and mushroom hotpot

   PREP 40 MINS · COOK 1¾ HRS · ❄

Special equipment • large cast-iron pan

SERVES 8

1.1kg (2½lb) stewing beef, cut into
   bite-sized pieces
salt and freshly ground black pepper
1 tbsp plain flour
2 tsp mild paprika
3 tbsp olive oil
2 onions, finely sliced
3 fennel bulbs, trimmed and
   cut into eighths
150ml (5fl oz) dry white wine
1.2 litres (2 pints) hot beef stock
   or vegetable stock
knob of butter
450g (1lb) chestnut
   mushrooms, quartered
pinch of dried oregano

1 Preheat the oven to 180°C (350°F/ Gas 4). Season the meat well with salt and black pepper, then place in a mixing bowl and toss with the flour and paprika so the pieces are evenly coated.

2 Heat half the olive oil in a large cast-iron pan, add the meat, and cook over a medium heat, stirring frequently, for 8–10 minutes, or until evenly browned. Remove with a slotted spoon and put to one side.

3 Heat the remaining oil in the pan, add the onion, and cook for 6–8 minutes, or until soft. Season well with salt and black pepper, then add the fennel and cook, stirring occasionally, for 6 minutes, or until beginning to soften slightly. Add the wine, raise the heat, and simmer for a couple of minutes until the alcohol evaporates. Return the meat to the pan, pour in the stock, then bring to the boil. Cover with a lid and put in the oven for 1 hour.

4 When the hour is up, melt the butter in a frying pan, add the mushrooms and oregano, and cook, stirring occasionally, for 5 minutes, or until soft. Stir into the beef and fennel and cook for a further 30 minutes. Serve with boiled potatoes.

Pork with rice and tomatoes

PREP 30 MINS | COOK 1 HR

SERVES 6-8
6 tbsp olive oil
3 onions, diced
1.1kg (2½lb) lean pork, cut into
   5cm (2in) chunks
6 garlic cloves, grated or
   finely chopped
handful of fresh flat-leaf
   parsley, chopped
1 tbsp fresh thyme
1 tbsp fresh sage leaves, chopped
2 tsp paprika
150ml (5fl oz) dry white wine
550g (1¼lb) long-grain rice
4 x 400g cans chopped tomatoes
salt and freshly ground
   black pepper

1 Preheat the oven to 150°C (300°F/ Gas 2). Heat the oil in a large heavy-based pan, add the onions, and cook over a medium heat for 5 minutes, or until starting to soften. Add the pork and cook, stirring occasionally, for 5 minutes, or until no longer pink. Add the garlic, parsley, thyme, sage, and paprika and combine well, then add the wine and cook for 5 minutes. Add the rice and tomatoes, stir to combine, then season well with salt and black pepper.

2 Cover with a lid and cook in the oven for 1 hour. Stir occasionally and add a little hot water if it starts to dry out. Remove from the oven and allow to stand for 10 minutes with the lid on before serving.

Baked turkey rolls filled with chestnuts and mushrooms

PREP 20 MINS | COOK 40 MINS

Special equipment • food processor

SERVES 6-8
1.1kg (2½lb) turkey breast fillets,
   cut into 7.5cm (3in) strips
salt and freshly ground black pepper
200g (7oz) ready-cooked chestnuts
8 garlic cloves, grated or
   finely chopped
large handful of fresh flat-leaf
   parsley, finely chopped
125g (4½oz) dried apricots
550g (1¼lb) chestnut mushrooms
1 tsp dried thyme
6 tbsp olive oil

1 Preheat the oven to 180°C (350°F/ Gas 4). Season the turkey strips with a little salt and black pepper and put to one side. Meanwhile, put the chestnuts, garlic, and parsley in a food processor and whiz for 10 seconds.

Add the apricots and mushrooms and whiz for a further 5 seconds. Add the thyme and 3 tablespoons of the oil and whiz for 5 seconds, or until you have a chunky paste. Season well with salt and black pepper.

2 Place 1 tablespoon of the mixture on each turkey strip and carefully roll it up. Place the rolls join-down in a baking dish, making sure they are quite tightly packed. Drizzle over the remaining olive oil, cover with foil, and bake in the oven for 30 minutes. Remove the foil and cook for a further 10 minutes, or until brown. Serve with a crisp green salad.

FOOD FOR FRIENDS

Lancashire hotpot

 PREP 25 MINS **COOK** 2 HRS

SERVES 8

2 tbsp olive oil
8 large lamb chops, each about
   200g (7oz) in weight
900g (2lb) potatoes, cut into
   5mm (¼in) slices
salt and freshly ground black pepper
4 onions, sliced
8 salted anchovies, finely chopped
600ml (1 pint) hot vegetable stock
knob of butter

1 Preheat the oven to 180°C (350°F/ Gas 4). Heat a drizzle of the oil in a large frying pan, add the lamb chops, and cook over a medium heat for a couple of minutes on each side until lightly browned. You might need to do this in two batches if your pan is not that big.

2 Put a layer of the potatoes in the bottom of a 2.3-litre (4-pint) flameproof dish, lay the chops on top, and season well with salt and black pepper. Heat the remaining oil in the frying pan, add the onions, and cook over a low heat, stirring frequently, for 10 minutes, or

until beginning to soften. Stir in the anchovies. Spoon a layer of the onion mixture on top of the chops, then add the rest of the potatoes and the onion mixture in layers, finishing with one of potato.

3 Pour in enough of the stock to come nearly up to the top of the potatoes. Dot the potatoes with butter, cover the dish tightly with foil, then put in the oven to cook for 2 hours, or until the potatoes are meltingly soft and the stock has been absorbed. Remove the foil for the last 20 minutes of cooking. Serve with pickled red cabbage.

VARIATION

Fry 4 lamb's kidneys with the chops and add to the dish.

COOK'S NOTES

The anchovies add richness. Don't worry if you're not a fan – they'll melt away during cooking and you won't be able to taste them.

Tomatoes stuffed with okra and rice

PREP 30 MINS • COOK 1 HR

SERVES 6-8

- 8 large ripe (but not too ripe) beef tomatoes
- 6 tbsp olive oil
- 2 large onions, finely chopped
- 550g (1¼ lb) okra, chopped
- 6 garlic cloves, grated or finely chopped
- 4 tbsp tomato purée
- juice of 2 lemons
- 50g (1¾ oz) pine nuts
- 250g (9oz) long-grain rice
- 1 tsp freshly ground black pepper
- 300ml (10fl oz) hot vegetable stock
- large handful of fresh flat-leaf parsley, finely chopped
- 1 tbsp fresh thyme
- 1 tsp caraway seeds (optional)

1 Carefully cut around the top of each tomato to make a hole 5cm (2in) across. Using a teaspoon, remove the insides, ensuring you leave a wall at least 1cm (½in) thick. Discard the insides and put the tomato shells to one side.

2 Heat 3 tablespoons of the oil in a large frying pan, add the onions, and cook over a medium heat for 5 minutes or until starting to soften. Add the okra and cook for 3 minutes, stirring frequently. Add the garlic, tomato purée, lemon juice, pine nuts, and rice. Season with the black pepper, then stir to combine and add the stock.

3 Cook for 10-15 minutes, or until the liquid starts to dry up. Stir through the parsley and thyme and remove from the heat. Preheat the oven to 150°C (300°F/Gas 2).

4 Stuff the tomatoes carefully and evenly with the rice mixture. Sit them in a deep-sided baking dish, packing them in fairly tightly. Pour over the rest of the olive oil, sprinkle with the caraway seeds (if using), and cover with foil. Put in the oven to bake for 1 hour. Serve with fresh crusty bread and a green salad.

Pork meatballs with tomatoes

PREP 30 MINS • COOK 1 HR

Chilling • 20 minutes

SERVES 6-8

- 3 large onions, finely diced
- 1kg (2¼ lb) lean minced pork
- handful of fresh flat-leaf parsley, finely chopped
- 2 tsp cayenne pepper
- 2 tsp dried thyme
- 2 eggs
- 3 tbsp plain flour
- salt and freshly ground black pepper
- 12 large beef tomatoes
- 6 tbsp olive oil
- 2 tbsp dried oregano

1 Put the onions, minced pork, parsley, cayenne, thyme, eggs, and flour in a mixing bowl, season well with salt and black pepper, then mix together with your hands for 5 minutes or until

you have a chunky paste. Chill in the refrigerator for 20 minutes to firm the mixture up a little. Meanwhile, preheat the oven to 180°C (350°F/Gas 4).

2 Take handfuls of the mixture and roll into balls about 5cm (2in) across – you should get around 24 in all. Place them on a large non-stick baking tray. Cut the tomatoes in half and place them skin-side down among the meatballs, so each meatball is in-between tomatoes and vice versa. Drizzle over the oil, sprinkle with the oregano, then cover the tray with silver foil.

3 Cook in the oven for 30 minutes, then remove the foil and cook for another 30 minutes, or until nicely browned. Serve with fresh crusty bread and green salad.

Courgette, herb, and lemon tagine

 PREP 25 MINS COOK 40 MINS

SERVES 8
2 tbsp olive oil
2 red onions, finely chopped
salt and freshly ground black pepper
4 garlic cloves, grated or finely chopped
pinch of fennel seeds
pinch of ground cinnamon
2-3 tsp harissa (depending on taste)
4 preserved lemons, halved, pith
    removed, and halved again
2 x 400g cans whole
    tomatoes, chopped
1 head broccoli, broken into florets

6 courgettes, sliced
juice of 1 lemon
handful of fresh dill, finely chopped
400g (14oz) couscous
handful of fresh flat-leaf parsley,
    finely chopped
harissa and lemon wedges,
    to serve

1 Heat half the oil in a large heavy-based pan, add the onions, and cook over a low heat for 8 minutes, or until soft and translucent. Season well with salt and black pepper. Stir through the garlic, fennel seeds, cinnamon, harissa, and preserved lemons.

2 Add the tomatoes and stir well, crushing them with the back of a wooden spoon. Bring to the boil, then reduce to a simmer and cook over a low heat for 30-40 minutes. If the sauce starts to dry out, top up with a little hot water.

3 Cook the broccoli in a pan of boiling salted water for 3-5 minutes or until tender, then drain and refresh in cold water. Drain again and put to one side. Heat the remaining oil in the frying pan, add the courgettes, and season with salt and black pepper. Cook over a low heat, stirring frequently, for 5 minutes, or until they start to colour a little. Add a squeeze of lemon and stir through the dill.

4 Meanwhile, put the couscous in a large bowl and pour over enough boiling water just to cover – it should just sit on top. Leave for 10 minutes, then fluff up with a fork and season well with salt and black pepper. Add the broccoli and courgettes to the sauce and stir through the parsley. Serve with the couscous, lemon wedges, and a spoonful of harissa.

FOOD FOR FRIENDS

Spicy lamb with baby potatoes

 PREP 25 MINS COOK 1½ HRS

SERVES 6-8

675g (1½lb) lean lamb,
   cut into 2cm (¾in) cubes
3 tsp paprika
1 tsp cayenne pepper
zest of 2 lemons
10 tbsp olive oil
3 onions, finely diced
1.1kg (2½lb) small potatoes,
   such as Anya

large handful of fresh flat-leaf
   parsley, finely chopped
6 garlic cloves, grated or
   finely chopped
2 tbsp fresh thyme, finely chopped
1 tbsp fresh rosemary leaves,
   finely chopped
6 preserved lemons, quartered
   and pith removed
salt and freshly ground black pepper

1 Preheat the oven to 150°C (300°F/ Gas 2). Put the lamb, paprika, cayenne,

and lemon zest in a mixing bowl, combine well, then put to one side. Heat 4 tablespoons of the oil in a large casserole, add the onions, and cook over a medium heat for 3 minutes. Add the lamb and cook, stirring frequently, for 5 minutes, or until no longer pink.

2 Add the potatoes and cook for 2 minutes, then add the parsley, garlic, thyme, rosemary, preserved lemons, and the rest of the olive oil.

Combine well, season with salt and black pepper, and cover with a lid. Place in the oven and cook, stirring frequently, for 1½ hours.

Baby courgettes with fish and couscous

PREP 20 MINS **COOK** 25 MINS

Special equipment • ridged cast-iron grill pan

SERVES 6–8

8 tbsp olive oil

600g (1lb 5oz) baby courgettes, halved lengthways

juice and zest of 2 limes

3 tbsp tomato purée

1 tsp five-spice powder

1 tsp cayenne pepper

2 tsp paprika

1 tsp freshly ground black pepper

large handful of fresh flat-leaf parsley, finely chopped

4 garlic cloves, grated or finely chopped

550g (1¼lb) white fish, such as haddock, cut into chunky bite-sized pieces

450ml (15fl oz) hot vegetable stock

450g (1lb) couscous

1 Preheat the oven to 150°C (300°F/Gas 2). Put 2 tablespoons of the oil in a bowl, add the courgettes, and mix well until evenly coated. Fry in a hot grill pan for 2 minutes on each side, then put to one side. You may need to do this in batches.

2 Add the rest of the oil to the bowl, together with the lime juice and zest, tomato purée, five-spice powder, cayenne, paprika, black pepper, parsley, and garlic. Mix well, then add the fish, stock, couscous, and courgettes and combine carefully.

3 Transfer to a flameproof dish and cover with foil. Cook in the oven for 20 minutes, then stir well, and serve.

Beef and leek couscous

PREP 25 MINS **COOK** 30 MINS

SERVES 6–8

8 tbsp olive oil

6 leeks, finely sliced

675g (1½lb) minced beef

2 medium-hot fresh red chillies, deseeded and finely chopped

2 tsp paprika

6 garlic cloves, sliced

150ml (5fl oz) dry white wine

450ml (15fl oz) hot beef stock

handful of fresh flat-leaf parsley, finely chopped

450g (1lb) couscous

1 Preheat the oven to 150°C (300°F/Gas 2). Heat the oil in a large heavy-based pan, add the leeks, and cook over a medium heat for 5 minutes. Add the mince and cook, stirring occasionally, for 10 minutes, or until no longer pink.

2 Stir in the chillies, paprika, and garlic and cook for 2 minutes. Pour in the wine and cook for 3 minutes, then add the stock and parsley and combine well. Stir in the couscous, then cover with a lid and cook in the oven for 15 minutes. Stir well and serve.

FOOD FOR FRIENDS

Bulgur wheat with prawns, okra, and dill

PREP 15 MINS · COOK 30 MINS

SERVES 8

400g (14oz) bulgur wheat
8 tbsp olive oil
2 large onions, finely diced
400g (14oz) okra, trimmed
6 garlic cloves, grated or
   finely chopped
675g (1½lb) (shelled weight)
   uncooked prawns
1 glass of dry white wine
large handful of fresh
   dill, chopped
salt and freshly ground
   black pepper

1 Preheat the oven to 150°C (300°F/Gas 2). Put the bulgur wheat in a bowl, and pour in enough boiling water to cover. Cover with a tea towel, leave for 5 minutes, then stir.

2 Meanwhile, heat the oil in a large heavy-based pan, add the onions, and cook over a medium heat for 5 minutes, or until starting to soften. Add the okra and cook for 2 minutes, then add the garlic and prawns and cook, stirring frequently, for 5 minutes, or until the prawns have turned pink.

3 Stir in the wine and dill and cook for 5 minutes, then stir in the bulgur. Transfer to an ovenproof dish, cover with foil, and season with salt and black pepper. Cook in the oven for 20 minutes, stirring occasionally. Serve with a mixed salad.

Spicy pork with chickpeas and tomatoes

PREP 15 MINS · COOK 25 MINS

SERVES 6-8

8 tbsp olive oil
2 large onions, finely sliced
675g (1½lb) minced pork
6 garlic cloves, finely sliced
juice of 2 lemons
2 tsp cayenne pepper
2 x 400g cans chickpeas, drained
   and rinsed
large handful of fresh flat-leaf
   parsley, finely chopped
6 large tomatoes, chopped

1 Heat the oil in a large heavy-based pan, add the onions, and cook over a medium heat for 5 minutes, or until starting to soften. Add the mince and cook, stirring frequently, for 5 minutes, or until no longer pink.

2 Stir in the garlic, lemon juice, and cayenne, and cook for 1 minute. Add the chickpeas and parsley, stir well, then cook for 5 minutes. Add the tomatoes, combine well, then simmer for 15 minutes, stirring occasionally. Serve with a crisp green salad and fresh crusty bread.

Venison, shallot, and chestnut hotpot

PREP 30 MINS • COOK 2 HRS

Special equipment • large cast-iron pan

SERVES 8
1 tbsp plain flour
handful of fresh thyme leaves
salt and freshly ground black pepper
1.1kg (2½lb) boned leg or shoulder of venison, cut into bite-sized pieces
knob of butter
3 tbsp olive oil
250g (9oz) bacon lardons or pancetta, cubed
250g (9oz) shallots, peeled and left whole
2 glasses of red wine
50g (1¾oz) dried mushrooms, such as shiitake, oyster, or porcini, soaked in 300ml (10fl oz) warm water for 20 minutes
250g pack ready-cooked chestnuts
1 litre (1¾ pints) hot vegetable stock
3 fresh rosemary stalks

1 Preheat the oven to 150°C (300°F/ Gas 2). Put the flour, thyme, and some salt and black pepper in a mixing bowl, add the venison, and toss well to coat. Heat the butter with 2 tablespoons of the oil in a large cast-iron pan, add the venison, and cook over a medium heat, stirring frequently, for 6–8 minutes, or until it is beginning to colour a little. Remove with a slotted spoon and put to one side. Add the lardons or pancetta to the pan and stir for 5 minutes, or until brown and crispy. Remove with a slotted spoon and put to one side.

2 Add the remaining oil to the pan, then add the shallots and cook over a low-medium heat for 8 minutes, or until they are turning golden. Return all the meat to the pan, season with black pepper, then add the wine and allow to boil for 2 minutes while you scrape up all the crispy bits from the bottom of the pan.

3 Drain the mushrooms (reserving the liquid) and stir into the pan. Strain the liquid and add to the pan. Stir through the chestnuts, pour in the stock, then add the rosemary. Cover with a lid and put in the oven to cook for 2 hours, or until the meat is tender. Top up with hot water if necessary.

VARIATION
Use stewing beef instead of venison.

COOK'S NOTES

Venison is lower in fat than any other red meat. Buy it in the winter months, when it is in season.

FOOD FOR FRIENDS

Special fried rice with shrimps and chicken

PREP 15 MINS COOK 40 MINS

Cooling • 30 minutes–1 hour, or overnight
Special equipment • wok

SERVES 8
900g (2lb) basmati rice
salt and freshly ground black pepper
5 tbsp sunflower oil
450g (1lb) (shelled weight) uncooked
   shrimps or prawns, chopped
4 large skinless chicken fillets, cut
   into 2.5cm (1in) strips
425g (15oz) pancetta, cubed
225g (8oz) white mushrooms, diced
7.5cm (3in) piece of fresh root ginger,
   peeled and finely sliced
225g (8oz) frozen peas, defrosted
4 eggs, lightly beaten
2 tbsp dark soy sauce

2 tbsp mirin
bunch of spring onions, finely sliced
small handful of fresh flat-leaf
   parsley, finely chopped

1 Rinse the rice well, then place in
a large pan, cover with boiling water,
and add a pinch of salt. Cover with
a lid, bring to the boil, and cook for
15–20 minutes, or until done. Drain
well and put to one side to cool
completely for 30 minutes–1 hour.

2 Meanwhile, heat 1 tablespoon of
the oil in a wok over a high heat, add
the shrimps or prawns, season with
salt and black pepper, and cook for
10 minutes, or until pink. Remove
with a slotted spoon and put to one
side. Heat another tablespoon of the

oil in the wok, add the chicken, season
with salt and black pepper, and stir-
fry for 10 minutes, or until no longer
pink. Remove with a slotted spoon
and put to one side.

3 Heat another tablespoon of the
oil in the wok, add the pancetta, and
cook over a medium-high heat for
6–8 minutes, or until crispy and
golden. Remove with a slotted spoon
and put to one side. Wipe the wok
out with kitchen paper, then heat
another tablespoon of the oil in it.
Add the mushrooms and ginger, and
stir-fry for 5 minutes, or until the
mushrooms start to soften. Add
the peas for the last minute or two.
Remove with a slotted spoon and
put to one side.

4 Heat the remaining oil in the wok,
then pour in the eggs and cook gently,
stirring them around the pan, for
1 minute. Take care not to overcook
them. Add the rice and stir well, then
stir in the shrimps or prawns, the
chicken, pancetta, mushrooms, and
peas. Add the soy sauce and mirin
and cook for 5 minutes, stirring all
the time. Transfer to a large shallow
serving dish, top with the spring onions
and parsley, and serve.

COOK'S NOTES

The rice needs to be completely cold
before you add it to the wok. Ideally,
cook it the day before and chill in
the refrigerator until required.

Spicy pork with caraway seeds and cabbage

PREP 10 MINS   COOK 2½ HRS

Special equipment • food processor

SERVES 8
handful of fresh thyme leaves
4 garlic cloves, finely chopped
2 tbsp olive oil
2 tsp chilli flakes
2.25kg (5lb) piece pork belly,
   skin scored
2 tsp salt
500ml (16fl oz) dry cider
1 Savoy cabbage, halved, cored,
   and shredded
knob of butter
1 tsp caraway seeds
freshly ground black pepper

1 Preheat the oven to 220°C (425°F/Gas 7). Put the thyme, garlic, oil, and chilli flakes in a food processor and whiz to a paste, then rub this all over the flesh of the pork (but not the skin). Sit the pork in

a roasting tin, skin side up, and rub with the salt, getting it into all the cracks. Cook in the oven for 30 minutes or until the skin is golden.

2 Turn the oven down to 180°C (350°F/Gas 4). Pour the cider around the pork, then cover with foil, securing it around the edges of the tin, and cook for 2 hours.

3 Just before the 2 hours are up, put the cabbage in a pan of boiling salted water, and cook for 4–6 minutes or until soft. Drain, then toss with the butter, caraway seeds, and a pinch of black pepper. Transfer to a large shallow serving bowl.

4 Slice or cut the pork into bite-sized pieces and arrange on top of the cabbage along with the juices. Serve with a spoonful of chilli jelly on the side and some fresh crusty bread.

Hot and spicy lamb with broad beans

PREP 30 MINS   COOK 2 HRS

Marinating • 30 minutes
Special equipment • large cast-iron pan

SERVES 8
1.1kg (2½lb) lamb (from the leg),
   cut into bite-sized pieces
2 tbsp olive oil
4 garlic cloves, grated or
   finely chopped
1–2 tbsp harissa (according to taste)
1 tbsp fresh rosemary leaves,
   finely chopped
6 salted anchovy fillets,
   finely chopped
3 tbsp Worcestershire sauce
1 tbsp fresh thyme leaves, finely
   chopped, plus a few extra
   to garnish
juice of 1 lemon
salt and freshly ground black pepper
2 onions, finely chopped
450g (1lb) fresh broad beans or
   frozen broad beans, defrosted
900g (2lb) potatoes, peeled and cut
   into bite-sized pieces
1.2 litres (2 pints) hot vegetable stock

1 Put the lamb in a mixing bowl, add the oil, garlic, harissa, rosemary, anchovies, Worcestershire sauce, thyme, and lemon juice, and mix well. Season with salt and black pepper, then transfer to a plastic bag and squish together well. Leave to marinate for 30 minutes (or overnight in the refrigerator).

2 Preheat the oven to 200°C (400°F/Gas 6). Transfer the mixture to a large cast-iron pan and cook over a medium-high heat, turning occasionally, for 10 minutes, or until the lamb is brown on all sides. Add the onions and cook for 5 minutes.

3 Stir through the broad beans and potatoes, pour in the stock, and bring to the boil. Cover with a lid and put in the oven to cook for 2 hours, or until the lamb is tender. If it starts to look dry, top up with hot water. Season well with salt and black pepper, and serve garnished with a few thyme leaves.

FOOD FOR FRIENDS

Creole-style beef and barley

PREP 30 MINS COOK 2 HRS

Special equipment • large cast-iron pan or flameproof casserole

SERVES 8

1.1kg (2½lb) chuck steak, cut
   into bite-sized pieces
1 tbsp plain flour
salt and freshly ground black pepper
3 tbsp olive oil
2 onions, finely chopped
6 celery sticks, trimmed
   and finely chopped
3 green peppers, deseeded
   and finely chopped
2 tbsp red wine
2 tsp cayenne pepper
2 tsp ground coriander
2 tsp ground cumin
250g (9oz) pearl barley
1.2 litres (2 pints) hot vegetable stock

1 Preheat the oven to 150°C (300°F/ Gas 2). Toss the meat in the flour and season well with salt and black pepper. Heat 2 tablespoons of the oil in a large cast-iron pan or flameproof casserole, add the meat, and cook over a medium heat, stirring frequently, for 8 minutes, or until lightly browned all over. Remove with a slotted spoon and put to one side.

2 Heat the remaining oil in the pan or the flameproof casserole, add the onions, celery, and peppers, and cook over a low heat for 10 minutes, or until completely soft and almost mushy. Add the wine, then raise the heat and allow to boil for a couple of minutes while the alcohol evaporates.

3 Stir through the spices, then season well with salt and black pepper. Return the meat to the pan or the flameproof casserole and add the pearl barley. Pour in the stock, bring to the boil, then cover with a lid and put in the oven for 2 hours. Give it a stir halfway through cooking and add a little hot water if it starts to look dry. Stir through the parsley and serve with fresh crusty bread.

VARIATION
Add 200g (7oz) cooked and sliced fresh corn on the cob at the end of cooking.

Cheat...
Use 2–3 teaspoons ready-mixed Creole spices in place of the cayenne, coriander, and cumin.

Pork Normandy

PREP 30 MINS COOK 1 HR

Special equipment • large cast-iron pan

SERVES 8

2 tbsp olive oil
knob of butter
1.35kg (3lb) lean pork, cut into
   bite-sized pieces
2 onions, finely chopped
2 tbsp Dijon mustard
4 garlic cloves, grated or
   finely chopped
6 celery sticks, finely chopped
6 carrots, finely chopped
1 tbsp fresh rosemary leaves,
   finely chopped
3 Bramley apples, peeled and
   roughly chopped
300ml (10fl oz) dry cider
450ml (15fl oz) double cream
300ml (10fl oz) hot light chicken stock
1 tsp black peppercorns

1 Preheat the oven to 180°C (350°F/ Gas 4). Heat the oil and butter in a large cast-iron pan, add the pork, and cook over a medium heat for 6–8 minutes, or until golden brown on all sides. Remove with a slotted spoon and put to one side.

2 Add the onions and cook over a low heat for 5 minutes, or until starting to soften. Stir in the mustard, add the garlic, celery, carrots, and rosemary, and cook over a low heat, stirring often, for 10 minutes, or until tender. Add the apples and cook for 5 minutes.

3 Pour in the cider, then raise the heat and boil for a couple of minutes while the alcohol evaporates. Return the pork to the pan and pour in the cream and stock. Stir in the peppercorns, bring to the boil, then cover with a lid and put in the oven to cook for 1 hour, or until the sauce has reduced and the pork is tender. Serve with fluffy rice, or creamy mashed potato.

Singapore noodles with shrimps and pork

PREP 15 MINS   COOK 30 MINS

Marinating • 30 minutes
Special equipment • wok

SERVES 8
2 x 450g (1lb) pork tenderloin, cut into 2.5cm (1in) strips
6 tbsp Thai fish sauce, such as nam pla
1 tbsp dark soy sauce
1 tbsp rice wine vinegar
2 tsp five-spice powder
450g (1lb) thin rice vermicelli
3 tbsp vegetable oil or sunflower oil
3 garlic cloves, grated or finely chopped
1 tsp ground coriander
500g (1lb 2oz) mixed exotic

mushrooms, such as porcini, enoki, and oyster mushrooms, roughly chopped, or chestnut mushrooms, sliced
425g (15oz) (shelled weight) shrimps or prawns, chopped
3 onions, finely chopped
4 fresh medium-hot red chillies, deseeded and finely sliced
salt and freshly ground black pepper
300g (10oz) beansprouts
bunch of spring onions, chopped
handful of fresh coriander, chopped

1 Put the pork in a mixing bowl, add the fish sauce, soy sauce, rice wine vinegar, and five-spice powder and leave to marinate for 30 minutes,

(or overnight in the refrigerator). Meanwhile, put the vermicelli in a bowl, cover with boiling water, and leave for 6 minutes or until soft. Drain, rinse, then drain again and put to one side.

2 Heat 1 tablespoon of the oil in a wok, swirling it around well to coat the surface, then add the pork and cook furiously over a high heat for 6–8 minutes, or until beginning to turn golden and crisp. Remove with a slotted spoon and put to one side. Heat another tablespoon of the oil in the wok, then add the garlic and ground coriander and stir. Add the mushrooms and cook for a couple of minutes, then add the shrimps or prawns and stir-fry over a high heat for 5–8 minutes, or until

pink. Remove with a slotted spoon and put to one side.

3 Heat the remaining oil in the pan, then add the onions and chillies and stir-fry for 1 minute. Add the vermicelli, season with salt and black pepper, then stir in the beansprouts. Return the pork and the shrimp or prawn mixture to the wok and stir well. Remove from the heat, top with the spring onions and coriander, and serve.

COOK'S NOTES

When cooking food in a wok, have all the ingredients prepared in advance, so you can work fast.

Fish with tomatoes, potatoes, and onions

PREP 30 MINS • COOK 15 MINS

SERVES 8
3 tbsp olive oil
5 large potatoes, cut into
   bite-sized pieces
salt and freshly ground black pepper
4 garlic cloves, grated
   or finely chopped
handful of fresh flat-leaf parsley,
   finely chopped
550g (1¼lb) cherry tomatoes, halved
2 glasses of dry white wine
675g (1½lb) mixed firm-flesh fish,
   such as red mullet, haddock, and
   sea bass, cut into bite-sized pieces
16 anchovy fillets in oil, drained

1 Heat the oil in a large shallow heavy-based pan, add the potatoes, and season well with salt and black pepper. Cook over a medium heat, stirring frequently, for 10–15 minutes, or until beginning to turn golden

brown. Lower the heat, then stir through the garlic and parsley and cook for a few seconds before adding the tomatoes.

2 Cook for 6–8 minutes, or until the tomatoes begin to split, then raise the heat, add the wine, and allow to boil for a couple of minutes while the alcohol evaporates. Turn the heat to low, add the fish and the anchovies, cover, and cook for 10–15 minutes, or until the fish is tender. Transfer to a large shallow serving dish and serve with a crisp dressed salad and fresh crusty bread.

Chinese-style pork belly

PREP 30 MINS • COOK 2¾ HRS

Special equipment • large cast-iron pan

SERVES 8
1–2 tbsp olive oil
1.8kg (4lb) pork belly, cut into strips
2 onions, finely chopped
salt and freshly ground black pepper
200ml (7fl oz) dry sherry
splash of rice wine vinegar
juice of 2 oranges
3 star anise
10cm (4in) piece fresh root ginger,
   peeled and finely sliced
pinch of five-spice powder
1.2 litres (2 pints) hot vegetable stock,
   or chicken stock
splash of dark soy sauce
450g (1lb) thick egg noodles
knob of butter
handful of fresh flat-leaf parsley,
   finely chopped

1 Heat 1 tablespoon of the oil in a large cast-iron pan, add the pork, and cook over a high heat for 3–5 minutes on each side, or until golden. Remove with a slotted spoon and put to one side. You may need to do this in batches.

2 Heat the remaining oil in the pan (if needed), add the onions, and cook over a low heat for 5–8 minutes, or until soft and translucent. Season with salt and black pepper. Raise the heat, add the sherry and rice wine vinegar, and allow to boil for 5 minutes until the alcohol evaporates.

3 Add the orange juice, star anise, ginger, five-spice powder, stock, and soy sauce and stir well. Return the meat to the pan, bring to the boil, then cover with a lid and put in the oven to cook for 2½ hours. Check occasionally and add a little hot water if it is looking dry.

4 Remove the meat from the pan with a slotted spoon and cut off any excess fat. Chop into bite-sized pieces and return to the pot. Cover with a lid while you cook the noodles. Add the noodles to a pan of boiling salted water and cook for 8–10 minutes, or until soft. Drain well, then transfer to a shallow serving bowl. Dot with the butter, sprinkle with the parsley, and serve with the belly pork.

Pork and clam cataplana

 PREP 20 MINS COOK 30 MINS

Marinating • 30 minutes

SERVES 8

900g (2lb) lean pork
   (leg or tenderloin), cut into
   bite-sized pieces
1 glass of dry sherry
4 garlic cloves, grated
   or finely chopped
2 tsp paprika
2 tsp chilli flakes
salt and freshly ground black pepper
4 tbsp olive oil
300g (10oz) chorizo, diced
2 tbsp tomato purée
3 garlic cloves, grated
2 onions, grated

2 bay leaves
2 glasses of dry white wine
2kg (4½lb) clams, cleaned and
   any open ones discarded
handful of fresh flat-leaf parsley,
   finely chopped

1 Put the pork in a mixing bowl with the sherry, garlic, paprika, and chilli flakes. Season with salt and black pepper and put to one side to marinate for 30 minutes, or overnight in the refrigerator.

2 Heat 1 tablespoon of the oil in a large frying pan, add the chorizo, and cook over a medium heat, stirring often, for 5 minutes, or until starting to crisp. Remove with a slotted spoon and put to one side. Heat another tablespoon of the oil in the pan, add the pork and marinade, and cook for 8–10 minutes, or until the meat is golden on all sides. Remove with a slotted spoon and put to one side.

3 Heat the remaining oil in the pan, add the tomato purée, garlic, onions, and bay leaves and stir well. Leave to simmer over a very low heat for 10 minutes, or until the onion is soft and translucent. Season well with salt and black pepper.

4 Add the wine, raise the heat, and allow to boil for a few minutes until the alcohol evaporates. Add the clams and cook for about 4–5 minutes until the shells open. Discard any that do not. Return the pork and chorizo to the pan, warm through, then transfer to a large shallow serving dish. Sprinkle with the parsley and serve.

COOK'S NOTES

Don't eat any clams that haven't opened during cooking. They are inedible.

FOOD FOR FRIENDS

Turkey and mushroom stew with dumplings

PREP 30 MINS · COOK 1 HR

Soaking • 30 minutes
Special equipment • large cast-iron pan

SERVES 8
50g dried porcini
knob of butter
2 tbsp olive oil
1.35kg (3lb) turkey breast fillet, cut
   into bite-sized pieces
2 onions, finely chopped
4 garlic cloves, grated or finely chopped
2 bay leaves
a few sprigs of fresh rosemary,
   roughly chopped
salt and freshly ground black pepper
6 carrots, cut into chunky pieces
6 celery sticks, cut into chunky pieces
2 tbsp plain flour
200ml (7fl oz) dry sherry
1.2 litres (2 pints) hot chicken stock
handful of fresh flat-leaf parsley,
   finely chopped, optional

For the dumplings
225g (8oz) self-raising flour
125g (4½oz) shredded suet
1 tbsp dried oregano

1 Put the porcini in a bowl, cover with 300ml (10fl oz) hot water, then set to one side to soak for 30 minutes. Preheat the oven to 200°C (400°F/Gas 6). Heat the butter and half the oil in a large cast-iron pan, add the turkey, and cook over a medium heat, turning the pieces frequently, for 5–8 minutes, or until golden all over. Remove with a slotted spoon and put to one side.

2 Heat the remaining oil in the pan, add the onions, and cook for 6–8 minutes, or until soft and translucent. Stir in the garlic, bay leaves, and rosemary, season with salt and black pepper, then add the carrots and celery and cook for 5 minutes. Stir

through the flour and cook for 2 minutes, or until combined with the vegetables.

3 Raise the heat, add the sherry, and allow to boil for a few minutes, stirring continually, until the alcohol evaporates, then pour in the stock. Drain the porcini (reserving the liquid) and add to the pan. Strain the soaking liquid, then add this as well. Return the turkey to the pan, cover with a lid, and put in the oven to cook for 1 hour.

4 Meanwhile, make the dumplings. Put the flour, suet, and oregano in a mixing bowl with a pinch of salt, then add enough cold water, about 150ml (5fl oz), a little at a time, until the mixture forms a dough. Flour your hands and form into 16 dumplings. Add these to the cooking pot for the last 30 minutes of cooking. To serve, sprinkle over the parsley (if using).

Cheat...
You can prepare the dumpling mix a few hours ahead of time and keep it in the refrigerator until ready to cook.

COOK'S NOTES

You can use any kind of poultry for this dish – try chicken thighs, on the bone, or pork. Remember to remove the bay leaves before serving.

Crispy beef and vegetables

PREP 15 MINS | COOK 30 MINS

Special equipment • wok

SERVES 8

3 tbsp cornflour

3 eggs

salt and freshly ground black pepper

3–4 tbsp vegetable oil

1.1kg (2½lb) beef topside, cut
into thin strips

bunch of spring onions, sliced
in four lengthways

3 fresh red chillies, finely shredded

3 garlic cloves, finely sliced

400g (14oz) sugarsnap
peas, shredded

4 pak choi

3 tbsp dark soy sauce

3 tbsp Chinese cooking wine

4 tsp sugar

1 Put the cornflour and eggs in
a mixing bowl, season with salt
and black pepper, and mix together
well. Heat 1 tablespoon of the oil in
a wok, dip the beef into the cornflour
mixture, coat well, then add to the wok
a few pieces at a time. Add more oil, if

you need to. Cook for 2 minutes, or
until crispy and golden. Remove with
a slotted spoon and put to one side.

2 Wipe out the wok with kitchen
paper and heat 1 tablespoon of
the oil in it. Add the spring onions,
chillies, and garlic and cook for a few
seconds, stirring all the time. Add
the sugarsnap peas and pak choi and
stir-fry for 2–3 minutes. Add the soy
sauce, Chinese cooking wine, and sugar
and cook until the sugar has dissolved
and the alcohol has evaporated. Return
the meat to the pan, toss together well,
then serve with rice.

VARIATION Use uncooked shelled
prawns instead of the beef.
Cook them in exactly the
same way.

> **COOK'S NOTES**
> You can omit the sugar, if you
> like. It's not essential, and the
> dish will still taste great.

Lebanese meatballs

PREP 30 MINS | COOK 1 HR | ❄

Special equipment • large cast-iron pan
or flameproof casserole

SERVES 8

675g (1½lb) lean lamb mince

2 onions, roughly chopped

4 garlic cloves, grated or finely chopped

handful of fresh coriander,
finely chopped

handful of fresh flat-leaf parsley,
finely chopped

2 tsp paprika

juice and zest of 1 lemon

2 tbsp tomato purée

4 tbsp pine nuts

3 eggs

6 tbsp plain flour

salt and freshly ground black pepper

8 tbsp olive oil

6 medium potatoes, cut into 2cm
(¾in) pieces

2 red peppers, deseeded and sliced

2 yellow peppers, deseeded
and sliced

3 x 400g cans chopped tomatoes

2 tsp fennel seeds, crushed

1 Preheat the oven to 150°C (300°F/
Gas 2). Put the mince, onions, garlic,
coriander, parsley, paprika, lemon

juice and zest, tomato purée, pine
nuts, eggs, and flour in a mixing bowl
and season well with salt and black
pepper. Mix well, then mash with
your hands to form a chunky paste.
Carefully spoon in a spoonful of the
mixture, and roughly shape into a ball.
Repeat with the rest of the mixture –
you should get 32 meatballs in all.

2 Heat 3 tablespoons of the oil
in a large large cast-iron pan or
flameproof casserole. Cook the
meatballs in batches for 10 minutes
each, turning them several times during
cooking to ensure they brown all over.
As each batch is cooked, remove with
a slotted spoon, and put to one side.

3 When all the meatballs are cooked,
add the potatoes and peppers to the
pan, and cook over a high heat, turning
frequently, for 10 minutes, or until
starting to become golden brown. Add
the tomatoes and fennel seeds, stir well
to combine, then season with plenty
of salt and black pepper. Return the
meatballs to the pan and stir well to
coat with the sauce. Add the remaining
oil, cover with a lid, and put in the oven
for 1 hour. Serve hot from the pan with
fresh crusty bread and a green salad.

Prawn dhansak

 PREP 15 MINS   COOK 30 MINS

SERVES 8

350g (12oz) red lentils
salt and freshly ground
   black pepper
2 tbsp vegetable oil or
   1 tbsp ghee
6 cardamom pods, crushed
3 tsp mustard seeds
2 tsp medium chilli powder
2 tsp turmeric
2 tsp ground cinnamon
2 onions, finely chopped
10cm (4in) piece fresh root ginger,
   peeled and finely chopped
4 garlic cloves, grated
   or finely chopped

3-4 green chillies, deseeded and
   finely sliced
675g (1½lb) (shelled weight)
   uncooked king prawns
1 fresh pineapple, peeled and cut
   into bite-sized pieces
8 tomatoes, skinned and
   roughly chopped
handful of fresh coriander,
   finely chopped

1 Put the lentils in a large heavy-based pan, season well with salt and black pepper, then pour in enough cold water to cover. Bring to the boil, then reduce to a simmer and cook for 20 minutes, or until soft. Top up with hot water if they begin to dry out. Drain and put to one side.

2 Meanwhile, heat a tablespoon of the oil or ½ tablespoon of the ghee in a large heavy-based frying pan, add the dried spices, and cook, stirring all the time, for 2 minutes, or until the seeds pop. Stir in the onions, ginger, garlic, and chillies, and cook for 5 minutes, or until soft and fragrant.

3 Add the remaining oil or ghee to the pan, then add the prawns. Raise the heat and cook, stirring occasionally, for 6-8 minutes, or until pink and cooked. Stir through the pineapple, add the lentils and tomatoes and a little hot water so the mixture is slightly sloppy,

and simmer for 5 minutes. Season again with salt and black pepper, stir through the coriander, and serve.

COOK'S NOTES

Increase the number of chillies according to how hot you want it to be. The four green chillies here will give you a moderately hot dhansak.

Prawn saganaki

SERVES 8

3 tbsp olive oil
2 onions, finely chopped
4 garlic cloves, grated or
   finely chopped
3 x 400g cans whole
   tomatoes, chopped
2 large glasses of dry white wine
1 tsp sugar
salt and freshly ground black pepper
675g (1½lb) (shelled weight)
   uncooked king prawns
250g (9oz) feta cheese
handful of fresh thyme leaves

1 Heat half the oil in a large frying pan, add the onions, and cook over a low heat for 8 minutes, or until soft and translucent. Stir through the garlic and cook for a few seconds more, then add the tomatoes and their juices, the wine and sugar and season with salt and black pepper. Bring to the boil, squashing the tomatoes with the back of fork, then reduce to a simmer. Cook gently over a low heat, stirring occasionally, for 30 minutes, or until the sauce has thickened.

2 Meanwhile, heat the remaining oil in a large frying pan, add the prawns, season with salt and black pepper, and cook, stirring occasionally, for 5–10 minutes, or until pink. Remove with a slotted spoon and put to one side. Preheat the grill to hot.

3 Stir the prawns into the sauce, remove from the heat, and crumble over the feta cheese. Pop under the grill to melt and turn golden brown, then sprinkle over the thyme leaves. Serve with a crisp salad and fresh crusty bread.

Paneer and sweet pepper curry

SERVES 8

4 tbsp ghee or vegetable oil
2 x 250g packets paneer, cubed
10cm (4in) piece fresh root ginger,
   peeled and sliced
3 medium-hot fresh red chillies,
   deseeded and finely chopped
2 tbsp dried curry leaves, crushed
2 tsp cumin seeds
4 tsp garam masala
2 tsp turmeric
8 red peppers, deseeded and sliced
8 tomatoes, skinned and
   roughly chopped
salt and freshly ground black pepper
bunch of fresh coriander,
   finely chopped

1 Heat half the ghee or oil in a large wide pan, add the paneer, and cook over a medium-high heat for 5–8 minutes, or until golden all over. Keep turning the pieces so they don't get too brown. Remove with a slotted spoon and put to one side.

2 Heat the remaining oil or ghee in the pan, add the ginger, chillies, curry leaves, cumin, garam masala, and turmeric, stir well to coat with the oil or ghee, then add the peppers and cook over a low heat for 10 minutes, or until beginning to soften.

3 Add the tomatoes and cook for 10 minutes. Return the paneer to the pan, season with salt and black pepper, then simmer gently for 10–15 minutes. Stir through the coriander, and serve with rice, chapati, or naan bread.

ALL-IN-ONE ROASTS

All your meat and vegetables, in one tray.

ALL-IN-ONE ROASTS

Having a whole meal in one roasting tin couldn't be easier. Put meat or fish of your choice in the tin, add your favourite vegetables, roast, and you have a whole meal for the family. It's a great way of cooking mid-week, when you don't want to use lots of cookware, and makes for minimum-effort Sunday lunches.

Easy meat roasts

These meats are simple to prepare, and simple to cook.

CHOOSE		USE
	**BEEF** **Fillet**, also known as **tenderloin**, is a delicious cut that has little visible fat. The muscle tissue does little work, so the meat is very tender. Choose beef that has a good bright colour.	Sear before roasting, and stuff with a fruity stuffing, such as prunes, or wrap in bacon, if liked. Team with quick-cook vegetables, such as cherry tomatoes, onions, red pepper, or cubes of squash. Try adding a splash of Worcestershire sauce, or rubbing cracked black pepper into the skin before cooking.
	**PORK** Pork chops are delicious used in an all-in-one roast. Choose **thick chops** with the bone attached for the juiciest meat, and a layer of fat around the edge. Snip this with a pair of scissors to produce some crackling. Don't overcook: the flesh should be golden and firm, but springy to the touch.	Rub with olive oil before roasting, and season well. Roast with chopped apples, red onions, apricots, sage leaves, maple syrup, or cider. Or try flavours such as fennel, rosemary, garlic, or celeriac. Sit the chops on top of mixed root vegetables for a really easy roast.
	**LAMB** Lamb **chops** are great for all-in-one roasts, as they are tender enough to cook fast, and have lots of flavour. Buy them with a layer of fat, as it will provide extra juices and flavour. **Loin chops** are cheaper than **chump**, which are meatier.	Add to a tin of butternut squash or sweet potato. Mix with fresh thyme, rosemary, or bay leaves, or splash with soy or Worcestershire sauce. They are good with mustard or redcurrant jelly, and delicious with cumin, coriander, cinnamon, allspice, or paprika.
	**POULTRY** Chicken is incredibly versatile. Use the **breast** or **thigh**, both with bone in, for all-in-one roasts. As with duck, buy a whole one, and ask for it to be jointed. Roast with the skin on, otherwise it will dry out. It can always be removed afterwards. Sear first if preferred, or add straight to the roasting tin. Don't overcook chicken, or it will become dry.	It can cope with many different flavours, from hot chillies, to simple lemon and thyme. Be more adventurous with spices such as saffron, nutmeg, or cinnamon, or try it with coconut, lemongrass, and ginger.

Easy fish roasts

Meaty fish is simple to cook, delicious, and healthy.

CHOOSE		USE
	**SALMON** Salmon is easy and versatile, and perfect for an all-in-one roast, as its firm texture can stand up to fast roasting. Choose either the popular **fillet**, making sure it is quite thick, or the **steak**, which is cut across the main body of the fish, leaving the back bone intact.	It will happily take on a variety of strong flavours, such as lime, lemongrass, sesame oil, ginger, chilli, and soy, or mustards, garlic, or honey. Or it can be cooked simply, sitting on top of spring vegetables, with fresh herbs such as parsley and tarragon.
img_MONKFISH	**MONKFISH** Monkfish has a meaty texture and delicious sweet taste, and its lack of bones makes roasting the perfect cooking method. Only the tail is eaten (although you can sometimes buy the cheeks from the fishmonger) and these come in **fillets**. Before using, remove the transparent membrane that covers the fish.	Because of its non-intrusive flavour it can take on quite strong flavours such as Indian and Thai spices, or salty foods such as bacon, pancetta, or chorizo. Or, team with garlic and lemon, rosemary or thyme, saffron, or fennel seeds.
	**MACKEREL** **Whole** roasted mackerel are easy to cook and handle. No turning is required once they are in the tin – they just need scoring and seasoning. You get a lot for your money with mackerel, and they make such an easy supper dish. Allow 1 or 2 per person, depending on the size of the fish, and cook as soon as you can after buying.	As it is an oily fish, team it with flavours that will cut through the fattiness, such as flavoured vinegars, sherry, oranges, or lemons. Or, cook it with aromatic spices such as coriander seeds, sweet or smoked paprika, and cayenne pepper.
img_HALIBUT	**HALIBUT** Halibut is a really meaty white fish that is mild flavoured and extremely versatile. It is usually bought as **steaks**, either bone in or out, or as **fillets** which are large so require cutting up into portions. It can be quick-roasted in a hot oven, and lends itself to lots of quick cooking accompaniments, such as tomatoes, green beans, courgettes, or peppers.	It has a clean, delicate taste, so doesn't want complicating with too many flavours. Fresh herbs such as parsley, tarragon, or dill, or a little olive oil and lemon juice, will bring out its natural flavour. For a little more punch, try an anchovy or caper dressing, or tomato salsa.

4 storecupboard glazes
Grab something from the storecupboard that will add instant flavour to your roast.

Cranberry
Cranberry sauce can be brushed on a variety of meats before roasting. Great with turkey, ham, beef, and chicken.

Mix with bruised **rosemary leaves** and **port** to glaze beef. Mix with a splash of **soy sauce** and crushed **juniper berries** to glaze venison. Mix with **brown sugar** and **allspice** to glaze ham. Mix with **orange juice** and grated **fresh root ginger** to glaze chicken legs.

Honey
Sweet honey has a natural affinity with pork, but is also tasty with chicken and duck.

Mix with **apricot jam** to glaze pork chops or ribs. Mix with **mustard**, grated **nutmeg**, **allspice**, and crushed **cloves** to glaze ham. Mix with **soy sauce** and grated **fresh root ginger** to glaze chicken legs. Add a splash of **rum** for Jamaican flavour. Add a squeeze of **lime** and grated **fresh root ginger** to glaze duck legs. Mix with **pineapple juice** and **chilli** to glaze chicken wings.

Mustard
Grainy mustards aren't as hot as other mustards and go well with lots of meats.

Mix with **soy sauce** to glaze duck or spare ribs. Mix with **cranberry sauce** to glaze chicken. Mix with a splash of **balsamic vinegar** to glaze beef. Mix with a splash of **whisky** to glaze pork. Mix with **orange juice** to glaze ham.

Chilli sauce
Chilli sauce or sweet chilli sauce adds sweet and tangy kick to meat and oily fish.

Use to glaze chicken, pork, lamb, beef, duck, mackerel, and salmon. Mix with a pinch of **cayenne pepper** or **paprika** to glaze pork ribs. Mix with a squeeze of **lemon** or **lime** to glaze chicken and mackerel. Mix with **balsamic vinegar** to glaze lamb. Mix with **honey** and grated **fresh root ginger** to glaze pork ribs.

Psst...
Use a heavy stainless steel roasting tin, as it conducts the heat well and won't buckle. Non-stick ones are easy to clean, but you might miss out on some of the caramelized meat juices that make great sauces and gravies.

FOOD FOR FRIENDS

A simple sausage supper
Sausages are a cheap alternative to using cuts of meat, but can make a succulent and delicious roast, especially now they are available in so many varieties, from simple pork to rich venison, or even wild boar. Experiment with flavoured and spiced ones, such as tomato and rosemary, or even vegetarian versions. Brush them with any of the glazes, and add easy-cook vegetables to the roasting tin, such as peppers, courgettes, new potatoes, red onions, or squash.

Prepare tricky vegetables Master how to peel, slice, or clean vegetables for roasting.

Shallots Peeling shallots, part of the onion family, can be fiddly and hard on the eyes.

First of all, **blanch** the shallots in boiling water, just for a few seconds (as you don't want them to cook), **drain** and **rinse** in cold water, then **drain** again. The skins should now **peel** away effortlessly and without tears.

Butternut squash These can be extremely large and quite tough to deal with.

A large knife is required to **cut the squash in half** lengthways. Do this on a sturdy chopping board. Then, **trim the top and base** and **scoop out the seeds**. Using a swivel peeler, **peel** away the skin, then either **slice** into chunky half-moon shapes or **cut up** into large cubes.

Leeks Leeks need washing before using, as the leaves often contain grit and soil.

Trim the leek by topping and tailing it, then **remove** any thick outer leaves. Make a **slit lengthways** down the leek, being careful not to go right through then, holding the leaves apart, **rinse** under cold water.

Fennel A bulbous vegetable, with a sweet aniseed flavour that pairs well with fish and pork.

Cut the stalks away from the top of the bulb (**keep the fronds** for garnish, and the stalks for stock). **Trim the base** and **remove any tough outer leaves**. **Slice** as required, **quarter** lengthways for roasting, or **finely shred** if serving raw.

Celeriac This ugly root looks impenetrable, but its velvety flesh is worth the effort.

Celeriac requires a large knife, as it can be quite tough. **Slice off** the top and the base, then work your way around, **slicing away the rough outer skin**. Try to **use it straight away**, as the flesh will quickly go brown. To prevent this, rub with a lemon as you go. Cut in half, then half again, then **chop into cubes**.

more veg prep tips

Whether you are slicing, dicing, or chopping, use the right tools for the job. A sharp chef's knife and a swivel peeler are essential.

Do lots of vegetable prep in one go, then bag it up for the refrigerator if using the next day, or freeze it.

The food processor can always be used for shredding; it's ideal for courgettes or carrots.

Salting aubergines before using reduces their bitterness.

Always wash Swiss chard and spinach thoroughly, as the leaves tend to be gritty, and it will spoil a dish.

When preparing cauliflower, cut up the florets, but don't discard the green leaves, as these are extremely tasty.

When cooking broad beans, remove them from their pods and cook them very briefly, for about 30 seconds, then drain and peel away the thicker outer skin. The bright green bean inside is delicious and soft.

Make the perfect gravy
A delicious sauce for roast meat, made straight from the roasting tin.

1 Once the meat has been removed from the tin, tilt the tin and spoon away the fat, leaving a small amount with the remaining cooking juices.

2 Sit the roasting tin over a medium heat, then add a glass of dry white wine and stir to loosen and scrape up all the bits from the bottom of the tin.

3 Pour in 600ml (1 pint) of hot stock, still stirring and scraping the bottom of the tin. It will begin to come clean.

4 Let the gravy bubble and reduce for a few minutes, allowing the alcohol to evaporate and the sauce to thicken, then season with salt and freshly ground black pepper.

5 Sit a conical sieve in a large heatproof jug, then strain the gravy through the sieve. You can repeat this again, if you wish.

Psst...
Save all vegetable trimmings and peelings, and add them to the tin while making the sauce, then strain. Or, save them for the stockpot. It will add flavour.

4 gravies
More easy sauces to accompany your meat.

White wine gravy
Melt a knob of **butter** in a pan over a low heat, remove from the heat and stir in 1 tablespoon of **plain flour**. Mix to a roux, then return to the heat and slowly pour in a little **hot chicken stock**, taken from 250ml (9fl oz) hot stock, then add a glass of **dry white wine** and simmer for a few minutes. Add the rest of the stock and 2 tablespoons of **double cream**, and cook for a few more minutes. Season, and add a squeeze of **lemon juice** or some chopped **fresh tarragon**. Serve with chicken.

Red wine gravy
After cooking roast beef, remove the meat then skim away the fat, leaving a small amount for flavour. Add 1 tablespoon of **plain flour** and stir, then add a glass of **red wine** and throw in a sprig of **fresh rosemary**. Keep stirring, scraping up the bits from the bottom of the tin, then add a little **hot vegetable** or **chicken stock** and continue stirring and adding, until it thickens, allowing it to boil a little to reduce. Season well, and serve as it is, or strain first.

Beef gravy
Melt a knob of **butter** in a pan, then add a few pieces of **bacon** and cook until golden brown. Stir in a teaspoon of **tomato purée**, then remove from the heat and add a tablespoon of **plain flour**. Add a little **hot beef stock**, taken from 500ml (16fl oz), then put back over the heat, and continue stirring and adding until it reaches the required consistency. Cook for a few minutes to thicken, and add a little **port** at the end of cooking, if you wish. Season, strain, and serve with beef.

Chicken gravy
After cooking roast chicken, remove the meat from the tin, then skim away the fat, leaving a small amount for flavour. Sit the tin over the heat, then add 500ml (16fl oz) of **hot chicken stock**, stirring to loosen bits from the bottom of the tin. Add a few **fresh thyme** stalks and season. Allow it to cook for a few minutes, then strain and serve with chicken.

FOOD FOR FRIENDS

Lamb cutlets with butternut squash, beans, and mint

PREP 15 MINS COOK 30 MINS

SERVES 4

2 tbsp olive oil

pinch of five-spice powder

pinch of cayenne pepper

salt and freshly ground black pepper

8 lamb cutlets

1 butternut squash, peeled, halved, deseeded, and roughly chopped

10 cherry tomatoes

125g (4½oz) fine green beans, trimmed

handful of fresh mint leaves, roughly chopped

1 Preheat the oven to 200°C (400°F/ Gas 6). Put half the oil with the five-spice powder and cayenne pepper in a small bowl with some salt and black pepper and mix together well. Brush half over the lamb cutlets and place them in a roasting tin. Mix the remainder with the squash, and add to the tin. Place in the oven to cook for 20–30 minutes, or until the lamb is cooked to your liking and the squash is golden.

2 Meanwhile, put the tomatoes and green beans in a bowl and toss with the remaining olive oil. Add to the

roasting tin for the last 10 minutes of cooking. They should just char slightly. Sprinkle with the chopped mint leaves, and serve.

VARIATION

If you're on a budget, use lamb chops instead. Trim away any fat before cooking.

Duck with apple and rosemary potatoes

PREP 20 MINS COOK 1 HR

SERVES 4

4 large duck legs
salt and freshly ground black pepper
550g (1¼lb) baby new potatoes, large
   ones halved
3 red-skinned apples, halved, cored,
   and roughly chopped
few stalks of fresh rosemary
drizzle of olive oil
1 Savoy cabbage, halved and leaves
   roughly chopped
pinch of chilli flakes (optional)

1 Rub the duck legs generously with salt and black pepper. Put to one side for 30 minutes, if you have the time – it will help crispen up the skin. Otherwise, cook straight away. Preheat the oven to 200°C (400°F/Gas 6).

2 Heat a large frying pan, add the duck, and cook for 8–10 minutes, or until golden all over. Using a slotted spoon, transfer the duck to a large roasting tin. Add the potatoes and apples, scatter over the rosemary, drizzle with the oil, season, then combine well using your hands. Place in the oven and cook until the duck is

crispy and the potatoes are golden, for about 40 minutes–1 hour. You may need to turn the potatoes halfway through cooking.

3 Meanwhile, put the cabbage in a pan of boiling salted water and cook for 4–5 minutes, or until it is cooked but still has a bit of bite to it. Drain and keep warm. Add to the roasting tin for the last 10 minutes of cooking, tucking it in and around the duck. Sprinkle with chilli flakes (if using). Transfer to a serving dish and serve with redcurrant jelly.

VARIATION

Use some chunky pre-cooked leeks if you're not a fan of cabbage.

COOK'S NOTES

Duck legs respond well to long, slow cooking, but if you prefer to use breasts (they are sometimes more readily available and are leaner), score the skin before cooking so it becomes crispy, and halve the roasting time.

Chicken with lemon and olives

PREP 15 MINS COOK 1 HR ♡

Marinating • 30 minutes

SERVES 4

4 large chicken thighs with skin on
salt and freshly ground black pepper
juice of 1 lemon
drizzle of olive oil
few sprigs of fresh thyme,
   stalks removed
1 large fennel bulb, roughly chopped
handful of green olives, pitted
1 large glass of dry white wine

1 Season the chicken thighs generously with salt and black pepper. Drizzle over the lemon juice and olive oil, scatter over the thyme leaves, then transfer to a large bowl or plastic bag and leave to marinate for 30 minutes. Preheat the oven to 200°C (400°F/Gas 6).

2 Using a slotted spoon, transfer the chicken to a small roasting tin and add the fennel – they should fit snugly. Season well, then put in the oven for 20 minutes.

3 Add the olives and wine, being careful that it does not spit. Return the tin to the oven and cook for a further 20 minutes, then turn the oven down to 180°C (350°F/Gas 4), cover the tin with foil, and cook for another 20 minutes, so the alcohol evaporates but the chicken remains moist. Check if the chicken is cooked by piercing one of the plumpest thighs with the tip of a sharp knife – if the juices run clear, it's cooked. Serve with creamy mashed potato.

Cheat...

Coat the chicken with 3–4 teaspoons of ready-made tapenade before roasting, and omit the olives.

407

Rosemary and chilli sausages with new potatoes

PREP 15 MINS   COOK 40 MINS

SERVES 4

8-12 good-quality pork sausages
2 red onions, peeled and cut
  into eighths
pinch of chilli flakes
handful of rosemary stalks
1.1kg (2½lb) new potatoes, large
  ones halved
salt and freshly ground black pepper
1 tbsp olive oil

1 Preheat the oven to 200°C (400°F/ Gas 6). Put the sausages in a roasting tin along with the onion, sprinkle over the chilli flakes and rosemary, then add the new potatoes. Season well with salt and black pepper, then drizzle over the oil and combine everything together well.

2 Put in the oven to roast for 30-40 minutes, or until the sausages are golden all over and cooked through. Turn the sausages and potatoes halfway through cooking.

VARIATION

Add 1 tablespoon of wholegrain mustard to the mix before cooking.

COOK'S NOTES

Use good-quality sausages that have a high percentage of meat in them.

Pork chops with apple and baby onions

PREP 15 MINS   COOK 35 MINS

Special equipment • food processor

SERVES 4

2 slices white bread
handful of sage leaves
1 small onion, roughly chopped
salt and freshly ground
  black pepper
4 pork loin chops, each about 2cm
  (¾in) thick and 125g (4½oz)
  in weight
12 baby onions or shallots, peeled
  and large ones halved
3 cooking apples, peeled and
  roughly chopped
2 tbsp demerara sugar
drizzle of olive oil
handful of rosemary stalks

1 Preheat the oven to 200°C (400°F/ Gas 6). Put the bread, sage, and onion in a food processor and whiz until you have a crumb mixture. Spread out on a baking tray and put in the oven for 5 minutes, or until golden. Return to the food processor and whiz again until finely ground. Season well with salt and black pepper.

2 Sit the chops in a roasting tin and add the baby onions. Add the apples, and sprinkle them with the sugar, then drizzle over a little olive oil. Add the rosemary, then sprinkle over a pinch of salt, some black pepper, and the golden breadcrumb mixture.

3 Put in the oven to roast for 30-35 minutes, or until the meat is cooked through and the onions are beginning to brown. Turn the chops halfway through cooking. Serve with some new potatoes or mashed potato.

VARIATION

Add some new potatoes to the tin along with the apple and onions. But make sure the tin is big enough so it all roasts rather than steams.

COOK'S NOTES

If the pork is ready before everything else, take it out and keep warm – you don't want it to overcook or it will become dry.

Poussins glazed with honey and wrapped in bacon

PREP 20 MINS **COOK 1 HR**

SERVES 4

4 poussins
2 onions, peeled and roughly chopped
2 tbsp clear honey
12 slices streaky bacon or pancetta
6 leeks, trimmed, rinsed, and chopped
    into chunky 5cm (2in) pieces
1 tbsp olive oil
salt and freshly ground black pepper

1 Preheat the oven to 200°C (400°F/ Gas 6). Wipe the poussins thoroughly with kitchen paper, then stuff with the onions. Brush all over with the honey, then cover the breast of each poussin with 3 slices of the bacon or pancetta. Sit in a large roasting tin.

2 Toss the leeks with the oil, then add to the tin, tucking them in around the birds. Season with salt and black pepper, then put in the oven to roast for 45 minutes –1 hour, or until the poussins are cooked. To test, pierce them with the tip of a sharp knife – if the juices run clear, they are ready. If the bacon begins to blacken, cover the poussins with foil.

3 Remove the birds from the tin and keep warm. Using a slotted spoon, transfer the leeks to a serving dish and keep warm. Place the tin on the unlit hob and tilt to one side. Skim away any fat, then pour in a little hot water and set over a high heat. Bring to the boil, scraping up any crispy bits from the base of the tin, then simmer for a few minutes. Pour into a gravy boat or jug and serve with the poussins, leeks, and some creamy mashed potato.

FOOD FOR FRIENDS

Peppered beef with roasted beetroot and balsamic vinegar

PREP 15 MINS | COOK 1 HR

SERVES 4

1.1kg (2½lb) fillet of beef
1–2 tbsp cracked black pepper
2–3 tbsp olive oil
500g (1lb 2oz) ready-cooked whole
  beetroot (not in vinegar)
1 tbsp good-quality balsamic
  vinegar
6 sweet potatoes, peeled
  and quartered
salt
handful of fresh thyme stalks

1 Preheat the oven to 190°C (375°F/ Gas 5). Roll the beef in the pepper, covering it all over. Put 1 tablespoon of the oil in a roasting tin and set the tin over a high heat. When very hot, add the beef, and cook for 5–6 minutes, or until lightly browned on all sides.

2 Toss the beetroot with the balsamic vinegar and add to the tin. Toss the sweet potatoes with the remaining oil and add to the tin. Season with a pinch of salt, sprinkle with the thyme, and put in the oven to cook

for about 20 minutes if you like your beef rare, 40 minutes for medium, and 50 minutes for well done.

3 Remove the beef and keep warm while it rests. If the sweet potatoes are not ready, continue cooking until they are golden and beginning to char around the edges. Slice the beef and serve with the beetroot, sweet potatoes, and a little creamed horseradish on the side.

VARIATION

Use green peppercorns, if you can find them. They are unripened black ones and taste just as spicy but with a subtly different flavour.

COOK'S NOTES

Crack the back peppercorns in a mortar and pestle, or use a rolling pin.

Roast lamb with cherry tomatoes and new potatoes

  PREP 15 MINS | **COOK 1½ HRS**

SERVES 4
1 tbsp olive oil
900g (2lb) butterflied leg of lamb
1.1kg (2½lb) baby new potatoes
salt and freshly ground black pepper
handful of fresh thyme stalks
12-16 cherry tomatoes on the vine
1-2 tsp redcurrant jelly

1 Preheat the oven to 190°C (375°F/Gas 5). Pour half the oil into a large roasting tin and set over a high heat. When very hot, add the lamb, and cook for 4-6 minutes, or until browned, then turn and brown the other side for 4-6 minutes.

2 Toss the new potatoes with the remaining oil and add to the tin. Season well with salt and black pepper, add the thyme, and put into the oven to cook for 45 minutes, if you like your lamb rare, 1 hour for

medium, and 1¼ hours for well done. Add the tomatoes for the last 15 minutes of cooking. Remove the lamb and keep warm while it rests. Meanwhile, make the gravy.

3 Using a slotted spoon, transfer the potatoes and tomatoes to a serving dish and keep warm. Place the tin on the unlit hob and tilt to one side. Skim away any fat, then add the redcurrant jelly and set over a high heat. Stir well, adding a little boiling water until the gravy reaches the required consistency. Allow to boil, then reduce to a simmer and cook for a couple of minutes. Slice the lamb and serve with the potatoes, tomatoes, gravy, and some mint sauce or jelly on the side.

VARIATION

Add green beans to the tin along with the tomatoes. Blanch them beforehand in some boiling water for 3 minutes.

Roast pork with bacon and chicory

  PREP 10 MINS | **COOK 2 HRS**

SERVES 4
1.8kg (4lb) loin of pork or boneless rolled shoulder
½ tbsp olive oil
1 tbsp salt
400g (14oz) shallots, peeled and large ones halved
150ml (5fl oz) dry cider
4 heads chicory, trimmed
12 slices streaky bacon

1 Preheat the oven to 240°C (475°F/Gas 9). Rub the pork all over with the oil, then smother with the salt. Put in the oven to cook for 15-20 minutes, or until the skin is crispy. Remove the tin from the oven and turn the oven down to 180°C (350°F/Gas 4).

2 Lift the pork up, place the shallots underneath, then sit the pork down on top of them. Drizzle over the

cider and return to the oven to cook for 1¾ hours (see Cook's Notes). Meanwhile, wrap the chicory evenly in the bacon and add to the tin for the last 40 minutes of cooking.

3 Remove the pork and keep warm while it rests for at least 20 minutes. Carve the roast and serve with chicory, and potatoes of your choice, and some apple sauce on the side.

COOK'S NOTES

To calculate the exact cooking time for the pork, allow 25 minutes per 450g (1lb), plus an extra 20 minutes. That's 2 hours in all for a 1.8kg (4lb) roast.

Roast monkfish with peppers

PREP 15 MINS · COOK 30 MINS

SERVES 4

675g (1½lb) monkfish (one or two pieces), membrane removed
4 red peppers, halved, deseeded, and sliced into batons
1 tbsp olive oil
½ tsp mild paprika
12 slices streaky bacon or pancetta

1 Preheat the oven to 200°C (400°F/ Gas 6). Toss the monkfish and peppers with the olive oil, then sprinkle over the paprika. Wrap the fish with the bacon or pancetta so it's covered entirely, then place in a roasting tin with the peppers.

2 Cook for 20–30 minutes, or until the bacon is crispy and the fish is cooked. Remove from the oven and keep warm while the fish rests for 10 minutes. Slice the fish and serve with the peppers and a wild rocket salad.

VARIATION
Add a handful of cherry tomatoes to the roasting tin along with the peppers.

Cheat...
Use 3–4 ready-roasted peppers from a jar. Simply slice and serve with the cooked fish and salad.

Fish with courgettes, aubergines, and tomatoes

PREP 15 MINS · COOK 35 MINS

SERVES 4

675g (1½lb) white fish loins, such as haddock or pollack, skinned and cut into chunky pieces
2 tbsp olive oil
1 tsp fennel seeds, crushed
zest of 1 lemon
salt and freshly ground black pepper
4 small to medium courgettes, sliced
2 aubergines, cut into bite-sized pieces
12 cherry tomatoes
handful of fresh dill, finely chopped
lemon wedges, to serve

1 Preheat the oven to 200°C (400°F/ Gas 6). Toss the fish with half the oil, half the fennel seeds, and half the lemon zest. Season well with salt and black pepper, then cover and set to one side.

2 Meanwhile, put the courgettes and aubergines in a roasting tin with the remaining oil, fennel seeds, and lemon zest and toss together well. Season with salt and black pepper, then put in the oven to roast for 20 minutes, or until the vegetables are beginning to soften.

3 Add the fish and the tomatoes, and cook for a further 15 minutes, or until the fish is cooked through. Sprinkle over the dill and serve with the lemon wedges and some fresh crusty bread.

Marmalade-glazed gammon with new potatoes and chicory

PREP 15 MINS **COOK 1¾ HRS**

SERVES 4-6

1.8kg (4lb) unsmoked gammon joint with no bone

500ml (16fl oz) dry cider

2 bay leaves

3 tbsp marmalade

1 tbsp brown sugar

1.1kg (2½lb) new potatoes, large ones halved

1 tbsp olive oil

zest of 1 orange

salt and freshly ground black pepper

4 heads chicory, trimmed and quartered lengthways

1 Sit the gammon in a large pan, add the cider and bay leaves, then top up with enough hot water to cover the joint, if needed. Put the lid on, bring to the boil, then reduce to a simmer and cook for 40 minutes. Preheat the oven to 180°C (350°F/Gas 4).

2 Remove the gammon from the pan and carefully peel away the outer skin, leaving a layer of fat. Put the marmalade in a pan and heat gently over a low heat until runny. Brush the gammon liberally with the marmalade, then sprinkle over the sugar.

3 Sit the gammon in a roasting tin. Toss the potatoes with the oil and orange zest, season well with salt and black pepper, then add to the tin. Put in the oven to roast for 50 minutes–1 hour (see Cook's Notes). Add the chicory for the last 20 minutes of cooking, tossing it in some of the juices.

4 Remove the gammon from the tin and keep warm while it rests for at least 15 minutes. Slice and serve with the potatoes and chicory.

VARIATION

Use maple syrup or honey instead of marmalade.

COOK'S NOTES

To calculate the cooking time for the gammon, allow 20 minutes per 450g (1lb), plus another 20 minutes. That's 1¾ hours in all for a 1.8kg (4lb) joint. To double-check, pierce it with a knife a few minutes before the end of cooking – if it goes in easily, the gammon is done.

Mackerel roasted with harissa and lime

PREP 10 MINS **COOK 30 MINS**

SERVES 4

4 mackerel (or 8 if small), gutted
  and washed
3–4 tsp harissa paste
1½ tbsp olive oil
2 limes, quartered
1.1kg (2½lb) baby new potatoes,
  large ones halved
handful of fresh coriander,
  finely chopped

1 Preheat the oven to 200°C (400°F/ Gas 6). Lay the mackerel in a roasting tin, then mix the harissa paste and half the oil together. Drizzle the harissa mixture over the fish, making sure the fish are covered inside and out. Add the limes to the tin, then toss the potatoes with the remaining oil and add them to the tin, too.

2 Roast in the oven for 20–30 minutes, or until the potatoes are cooked through – the fish will be cooked by then as well. Scatter with the fresh coriander, and serve with a crisp green salad.

FOOD FOR FRIENDS

Salmon with mushrooms and pak choi

SERVES 4

1 tbsp olive oil

1 tbsp dark soy sauce

½ tbsp mirin (Japanese rice wine)

5cm (2in) piece of fresh root ginger,
   peeled and finely chopped

2 garlic cloves, grated or
   finely chopped

salt and freshly ground black pepper

4 salmon fillets, each about 150g
   (5½oz) in weight

2 pak choi, quartered lengthways

200g (7oz) chestnut mushrooms,
   large ones halved

1 Preheat the oven to 200°C (400°F/
Gas 6). Put the olive oil, soy sauce,
mirin, ginger, and garlic in a bowl and
mix together well. Season with salt
and black pepper.

2 Put the salmon fillets, pak choi,
and mushrooms in a roasting tin,
then drizzle over the oil mixture
and combine well. Put into the oven
to roast for 20–25 minutes, or until
the salmon is cooked through. Serve
with rice.

COOK'S NOTES

*If you can't find mirin, a sweet
Japanese cooking wine, use dry
sherry or omit altogether.*

Jamaican-style fish with sweet potatoes

SERVES 4

1 tsp allspice

1 tsp paprika

5cm (2in) piece of fresh root ginger,
   peeled and finely sliced

2 fresh hot red chillies, deseeded
   and finely chopped

1 tbsp olive oil

salt and freshly ground
   black pepper

4 fillets of white fish, such
   as haddock or sustainable cod,
   each about 200g (7oz) in weight

4 sweet potatoes, peeled and cut into
   bite-sized pieces

handful of fresh coriander,
   finely chopped

1 Preheat the oven to 190°C (375°F/
Gas 5). Mix the allspice, paprika,
ginger, and chillies with the olive oil.
Add a pinch of salt and lots of black
pepper. Smother the fish with most
of the spice mixture. Put to one side.
Toss the sweet potatoes with the
remaining spice mixture and place
in a roasting tin. Put in the oven to
roast for 15 minutes.

2 Add the fish to the roasting tin
and roast for 15 minutes, or until the
potatoes are cooked – the fish will be
cooked by then as well. Sprinkle with
coriander and serve.

FOOD FOR FRIENDS

Lamb with roasted peppers

 PREP 15 MINS COOK 30 MINS

SERVES 4

4 large lamb chump chops,
  or 8 small ones
2 red peppers, deseeded and
  roughly chopped
2 green peppers, deseeded and
  roughly chopped
1 tbsp olive oil
salt and freshly ground black pepper
knob of butter
1 onion, finely chopped
125g (4½oz) chestnut mushrooms,
  finely chopped
small handful of fresh flat-leaf
  parsley, finely chopped

1 Preheat the oven to 200°C (400°F/ Gas 6). Sit the chops in a roasting tin and cut a pocket in each one. Toss the peppers with the oil, season well with salt and black pepper, then add to the tin.

2 Melt the butter in a pan over a low heat, add the onion, and cook for 5 minutes, or until soft and translucent. Add the mushrooms and cook for a further 5 minutes, or until the mushrooms have broken down. Stir through the parsley, season with salt and black pepper, then spoon the mixture into the pocket of each lamb chop. If there's some left over, scatter it over the top.

3 Put in the oven to cook for 20–30 minutes, or longer if you like your meat well done. Toss with the peppers and serve with small cubed roasted potatoes and a spoonful of chilli or mint jelly.

Pork tenderloin roasted with cider and lentils

 PREP 15 MINS COOK 2 HRS

SERVES 4

4 onions, peeled and cut into eighths
4 garlic cloves, grated or
  finely chopped
225g (8oz) Puy lentils, rinsed and any
  stones removed
500ml (16fl oz) dry cider
handful of fresh flat-leaf parsley,
  finely chopped
salt and freshly ground black pepper
450g (1lb) pork tenderloin
drizzle of chilli oil (optional)

1 Preheat the oven to 180°C (350°F/ Gas 4). Put the onions and garlic in a medium-sized roasting tin and add the lentils and half the cider. Stir in the parsley and season well with salt and black pepper.

2 Slash the pork four times diagonally, then sit it on top of the lentils. Drizzle over the chilli oil (if using), then put in the oven to cook. After an hour, top up with the remaining cider and cook for a further hour. If the meat is browning too much, cover with foil. If the lentils start to look dry, add a little hot water.

3 Remove the meat from the tin and keep warm while it rests for 15 minutes. Slice and serve with the lentils.

COOK'S NOTES

If you want to speed up the cooking, use a 400g can of brown lentils instead of the dried. Drain them well and use only half the quantity of cider. The time in the oven should be reduced to 45 minutes, or until the pork is cooked through.

Beef stuffed with prunes and cashew nuts

 PREP 20 MINS **COOK 2 HRS**

Special equipment • food processor

SERVES 6

125g (4½oz) ready-to-eat prunes,
   roughly chopped
125g (4½oz) cashew nuts
handful of fresh flat-leaf parsley
3 garlic cloves, peeled
salt and freshly ground
   black pepper
1.35kg (3lb) silverside of beef
drizzle of chilli oil or olive oil
400g (14oz) shallots, peeled

1 Preheat the oven to 220°C (425°F/ Gas 7). Put the prunes, cashew nuts, parsley, and garlic in a food processor and pulse a few times until well chopped (but not too finely chopped). Season with salt and black pepper.

2 Place the beef on a work surface and make a cut about 2cm (¾in) in from the right-hand side. Slice down nearly to the bottom, stopping about 2cm (¾in) from it, then slice across into the beef, stopping just before you reach the end. Then slice up almost to the top and finally across almost to the opposite end. Roll the meat out and spread with the prune mixture. Now, carefully roll the beef back up, sit it with the cut side down, and tie securely with a string. Transfer to a roasting tin and season.

3 Drizzle over the chilli oil, or olive oil and add the shallots to the tin. Put in the oven to roast for 15–20 minutes, or until browned, then turn the oven down to 180°C (350°F/Gas 4) and roast for 1 hour if you like your beef rare, 1¼ hours for medium, or 1¾ hours for well done. To test if the meat is cooked to your liking, pierce it with the tip of a sharp knife – if it's still bloody, it's rare. If the juices run clear, it's medium to well done.

4 Remove the roast from the oven and keep it warm while it rests for 15 minutes. Carve, then serve with some creamy mashed potato and green vegetable, such as broccoli.

COOK'S NOTES

You could always ask your butcher to cut the beef for you. Also ask for some butchers' string to tie it up with. If not, you can use ordinary string. There should be enough roast beef left over for sandwiches the next day.

Lamb with red onions

PREP
20
MINS

COOK
2
HRS

SERVES 4

8 red onions, peeled and quartered

3 tbsp olive oil

900g (2lb) potatoes, peeled
    and quartered

salt and freshly ground black pepper

2 tbsp mint sauce

900g (2lb) lamb fillet

1 tbsp balsamic vinegar

1 Preheat the oven to 180°C
(350°F/Gas 4). Put the onions in
a large roasting tin and toss with
1 tablespoon of the oil. Add the
potatoes, toss with the onions,
then season well with salt and
black pepper.

2 Mix the remaining oil with the mint
sauce and use to coat the lamb. Add
the fillet to the roasting tin, drizzle
over the balsamic vinegar, and put in
the oven to roast for 1½–2 hours.

3 Remove the lamb and keep warm
while it rests for 15 minutes. Slice
and serve with the red onion and
potato mixture.

VARIATION

Look out for flavoured balsamic
vinegars. An apple balsamic
vinegar would go well with the
lamb – always use a good-
quality thick one.

Chicken with garlic and spiced celeriac

PREP
25
MINS

COOK
45
MINS

SERVES 4

8 chicken thighs with skin on

salt and freshly ground black pepper

2 tbsp olive oil

4 whole garlic bulbs with skin on,
    tops sliced off

4 large potatoes, peeled and chopped
    into bite-sized cubes

1 large celeriac or 2 small ones,
    peeled and chopped into
    bite-sized pieces

1–2 tsp mild curry powder

1 Preheat the oven to 200°C (400°F/
Gas 6). Season the chicken well with
salt and black pepper. Put half the oil
in a large roasting tin and heat on the
hob over a high heat. When very
hot, add the chicken pieces skin side
down, and cook for 5–8 minutes, or
until browned all over, then remove
the tin from the heat.

2 Add the garlic and toss with the
oil. Toss the potatoes and celeriac
with the remaining oil and curry
powder, season well with salt and
black pepper, and add to the tin.

3 Put in the oven to roast for
45 minutes, or until the chicken
and potatoes are cooked and golden.
Give the potatoes and celeriac
a turn halfway through, then
keep an eye on them to check they
don't burn. Serve with wilted spinach.

COOK'S NOTES

*Be careful when heating the oil,
as it will spit a lot when the
chicken is added. You could use
sunflower oil if you prefer.*

Pork with potatoes and mushrooms in wine

PREP 20 MINS | COOK 1¾ HRS

SERVES 6

1.35kg (3lb) boneless shoulder
   of pork, skin scored
sea salt
1kg (2¼lb) potatoes, peeled and
   halved, or large ones quartered
1 tbsp olive oil
a few stalks of fresh rosemary
360ml (12fl oz) dry white wine
250g (9oz) button mushrooms
300ml (10fl oz) hot vegetable stock

1 Preheat the oven to 220°C (425°F/
Gas 7). Sit the pork in a large roasting
tin and rub with sea salt, getting it
into all the cuts. Toss the potatoes
with the oil, season with salt, then
add to the tin along with the
rosemary. Put in the oven to roast for
20 minutes, or until the skin is crispy.

2 Meanwhile, heat the wine in
a pan over a low heat until warm,
then spoon over the meat. Add the
mushrooms, pour in the stock, then
turn the oven down to 180°C (350°F/
Gas 4) and cook for 1 hour.

3 Turn the oven down to 150°C
(300°F/Gas 2) and cook for another
30 minutes, or until the potatoes are
meltingly soft and the liquid has almost
disappeared. Remove from the oven
and keep warm while the pork rests
for 15 minutes. Slice the pork and
serve with the potatoes, mushrooms,
and some fresh crusty bread.

COOK'S NOTES

*Ask the butcher to score the pork
for you. But if you decide to do
it yourself, use a Stanley knife,
or your sharpest kitchen knife
to make cuts about 5mm (¼in)
apart. Go with the grain so the
pork will be easier to slice.*

FOOD FOR FRIENDS

Rack of lamb with flageolet beans and herbs

 PREP 15 MINS **COOK 40 MINS**

SERVES 4

1 rack of lamb with 8 cutlets
½ tbsp olive oil
a few rosemary sprigs, leaves
   finely chopped
salt and freshly ground black pepper
150ml (5fl oz) hot vegetable stock
1 tsp redcurrant jelly
400g can flageolet beans, drained
handful of fresh mint leaves,
   finely chopped

1 Preheat the oven to 200°C (400°F/Gas 6). Smother the lamb with the oil, sprinkle over the rosemary, and season well with salt and black pepper. Sit the rack in a roasting tin and put in the oven to roast for 40 minutes, or longer if you like your meat well done.

2 Remove the lamb from the tin and keep warm (covered with foil) while you prepare the beans. Sit the roasting tin on the hob over a medium to high heat, add the stock, and bring to the boil. Reduce to a simmer, stir in the redcurrant jelly until dissolved, then stir through the flageolet beans and simmer gently for 5 minutes. Remove from the heat and stir through the mint.

3 Slice the rack into 8 cutlets and serve with the beans and some minted new potatoes.

VARIATION
Use cannellini beans or broad beans instead of the flageolet, if you like.

Glazed fillet of beef roasted with potatoes and olives

 PREP 15 MINS COOK 2 HRS

SERVES 6

8 large potatoes, peeled and cut into
   small cubes
2 tbsp olive oil
salt and freshly ground black pepper
2 tbsp redcurrant jelly
1.8kg (4lb) fillet of beef
handful of black olives, pitted

1 Preheat the oven to 200°C (400°F/Gas 6). Put the potatoes in a large roasting tin with 1 tablespoon of the oil, toss together, then season well with salt and black pepper. Put in the oven to roast while you prepare the beef.

2 Put the redcurrant jelly in a pan and heat over a low heat for 5 minutes or until runny, then brush all over the beef and season well with salt and black pepper. Heat the remaining oil in a frying pan and sear the beef over a high heat for a few minutes until browned all over.

3 Turn the oven down to 180°C (350°F/Gas 4). Add the meat to the roasting tin and cook for 1¼ hours if you like your beef rare, 1¾ hours for medium, and 2 hours for well done. Add the olives for the last 10 minutes of cooking, stirring them into the potatoes.

4 Remove the beef, and keep warm while it rests for at least 15 minutes. Leave the potatoes in a little longer if they are not ready. Slice the beef and serve with the potatoes and some fresh watercress.

Perfect creamy mash

 PREP 15 MINS | COOK 25 MINS

SERVES 4

900g (2lb) floury potatoes, peeled and halved or, if large, quartered
salt and freshly ground black pepper
2-3 tbsp warm milk (more if needed)
25g (scant 1oz) butter

1 Put the potatoes in a large pan of salted water, bring to the boil, and cook on a medium heat for about 20 minutes, or until soft when pierced with the tip of a sharp knife. Drain well, then return to the pan, replace the lid, and leave on the warm but unlit hob for 5 minutes, to allow them to dry out a little.

2 Mash well until there are no lumps, then add the milk and mash again. If the potatoes are still a little dry, add some more milk and mash once more.

3 Beat in the butter with a wooden spoon and season well with salt and black pepper. Do not overbeat the potatoes otherwise they will become gluey. You want them fluffy and lump-free.

VARIATION
Jazz up your mashed potato with some finely chopped herbs such as parsley or thyme, a teaspoon of wholegrain mustard, or a handful of grated Cheddar cheese.

Perfect Yorkshire puddings

 PREP 20 MINS | COOK 30 MINS

Resting • 30 minutes
Special equipment • deep six-hole bun tin

SERVES 6

125g (4½oz) plain flour
salt
2 eggs
300ml (10fl oz) milk
1-2 tbsp sunflower oil or corn oil

1 Preheat the oven to 220°C (425°F/Gas 7). Sift the flour into a mixing bowl, add a pinch of salt, and combine. Make a well in the middle, then put the eggs and a little of the milk in it. Using a wooden spoon, stir the egg mixture, incorporating the flour a little at a time as you go and gradually adding half the remaining milk. When all the flour has been mixed in, add the remaining milk, and whisk with a balloon whisk to ensure there are no lumps. Transfer to a jug, and put in the refrigerator to rest for 30 minutes.

2 When the batter is nearly ready to use, add a little of the oil to each hole of the bun tin and put in the oven for 5 minutes, or until smoking hot. Carefully remove, give the batter a final stir, then divide evenly among the holes. Put in the oven to cook for 20-30 minutes, or until risen and golden.

COOK'S NOTES

Make sure the oil is really hot when you add the batter – this will ensure the puddings rise.

Crispy roast potatoes

 PREP 25 MINS | COOK 40 MINS

SERVES 4

900g (2lb) floury potatoes, such as Maris Piper, peeled and quartered
sea salt
1 tbsp plain flour
4 tbsp olive oil

1 Preheat the oven to 220°C (425°F/Gas 7). Put the potatoes in a pan of salted water, bring to the boil, then cook over a medium heat for 10-15 minutes, or until the potatoes are nearly cooked. Drain well, then return to the pan.

2 Put the lid back on the pan and sit it on the unlit hob for 5 minutes for the potatoes to dry out. Add the flour, put the lid on, and shake the pan up and down a few times.

3 Put the oil in a large roasting tin and pop it in the oven until really hot. Remove from the oven and carefully add the potatoes one by one, turning each potato in the hot oil. Season with sea salt and return to the oven to roast for 30-40 minutes, or until the potatoes are golden and crispy. Turn them halfway through cooking.

VARIATION
Use goose or duck fat instead of olive oil or, for a healthy option, rapeseed oil.

FOOD FOR FRIENDS

Apple sauce

PREP 10 MINS **COOK 10 MINS** ❄

SERVES 4

450g (1lb) cooking apples, peeled, cored,
   and quartered
2–3 tbsp sugar (depending on the tartness
   of the apples)

1 Put the apples in a pan, sprinkle over
1 tablespoon of water, then add the sugar. Cover
and cook on a low heat for 10 minutes, or until
the apples have begun to break down.

2 Stir with a wooden spoon until the sauce reaches
your preferred consistency – either a smooth purée
or more chunky. Taste and add more sugar, if
required. Serve warm or cold with roast pork.

COOK'S NOTES

When cool, transfer to a plastic
freezerproof container, and freeze
for up to 1 month. Defrost
thoroughly before use.

Cranberry sauce

PREP 5 MINS **COOK 20 MINS**

SERVES 4

225g (8oz) fresh cranberries or frozen
   cranberries, thawed
4 tbsp port or red wine
75g (2½oz) sugar

1 Put the cranberries in a wide pan and pour over
the port or red wine. Bring to the boil, then cover
and simmer gently for 10–15 minutes, or until they
start to soften and pop. Squash with the back of
a spoon to your desired consistency.

2 Stir in the sugar a little at a time, tasting as you
go, until it has dissolved and the sauce is the right
flavour. Serve with roast turkey or chicken.

VARIATION
Use water or fresh orange
juice instead of the alcohol.

Mint sauce

PREP 10 MINS

SERVES 4

handful of fresh mint leaves,
   finely chopped
1–2 tsp sugar
1 tbsp white wine vinegar

1 Put the mint in a serving bowl and add the sugar
and vinegar. Set aside to infuse for 10 minutes.

2 Stir well to make sure the sugar has dissolved,
then taste and adjust the seasoning, adding more
sugar or vinegar, if needed. Serve with lamb.

VARIATION
Use raspberry vinegar instead
of white wine vinegar.

FOOD FOR FRIENDS

Dauphinois potatoes

PREP 20 MINS **COOK** 1¾ HRS

SERVES 4

900g (2lb) waxy potatoes, peeled and cut into slices
  3mm (⅛in) thick
300ml (10fl oz) double cream
300ml (10fl oz) milk
salt and freshly ground black pepper
3 garlic cloves, grated or
  finely chopped

1 Preheat the oven to 180°C (350°F/Gas 4). Put the potatoes, cream, and milk in a large pan, and season with salt and black pepper. Bring to the boil, then cover and simmer for 10–15 minutes, or until the potatoes are beginning to soften.

2 Using a slotted spoon, transfer the potatoes to a shallow 2.3-litre (4-pint) ovenproof dish. Sprinkle over the garlic and season well with salt and black pepper. Strain the cream and milk mixture, then pour over the potatoes. Cover the dish with foil, then put in the oven to cook for 1 hour. Remove the foil and cook for a further 30 minutes, or until the top has begun to turn golden.

> ### COOK'S NOTES
>
> Sit the dish on a baking tray in case of any spills, or line the bottom of your oven with foil. This dish can easily spill when it starts boiling.

Chunky potato wedges

PREP 10 MINS **COOK** 40 MINS

SERVES 4–6

900g (2lb) all-purpose potatoes,
  such as Maris Piper, skins on,
  washed, quartered lengthways and,
  if large, sliced again lengthways
2 tbsp olive oil
sea salt

1 Preheat the oven to 200°C (400°F/Gas 6). Put the potatoes in a large roasting tin, add the olive oil, and combine well with your hands.

2 Sprinkle with plenty of sea salt, and put in the oven to roast for 40 minutes, or until they are crispy and golden.

VARIATION

Add a pinch of hot paprika to the potatoes before you pop them in the oven.

Potatoes boulangère

PREP 25 MINS **COOK** 50 MINS

SERVES 4–6

50g (1¾oz) butter
6 onions, sliced
900g (2lb) all-purpose potatoes,
  such as Maris Piper, cut into
  5mm (¼in) slices
3 garlic cloves, sliced
750ml (1¼ pints) hot vegetable or chicken stock
salt and freshly ground black pepper

1 Preheat the oven to 200°C (400°F/Gas 6). Melt the butter in a large pan, add the onions, and cook, stirring often, for 10 minutes, or until soft and translucent. Add the potatoes, garlic, and stock, and season with salt and black pepper. Stir well, then cover and simmer for 5–6 minutes, or until the potatoes start to soften but still have a bit of bite to them.

2 Transfer the mixture to a shallow 2.3-litre (4-pint) ovenproof dish and cook for 40–50 minutes, or until the potatoes are tender and most of the stock has been absorbed. Serve with roast beef.

Sweet and sour cabbage

PREP 15 MINS   COOK 1¼ HRS

SERVES 4
1 tbsp olive oil
1 large red cabbage, outer
    leaves removed, halved,
    and finely shredded
2 red-skinned eating apples, cut into
    bite-sized pieces
5cm (2in) piece of fresh root ginger, peeled
    and finely sliced
200ml (7fl oz) balsamic vinegar
2 tbsp soft brown sugar
salt and freshly ground black pepper

1 Put the oil in a large heavy-based pan, add the cabbage, apple, and ginger and cook on a low heat for 10 minutes, or until they have begun to soften and reduce down.

2 Add the balsamic vinegar and sugar, bring to the boil, then cover and simmer for 40 minutes–1 hour, or until the cabbage is soft. Stir occasionally so it doesn't stick. Season well with salt and black pepper and serve with roast pork or pork chops.

VARIATION
Add a handful of sultanas to the cabbage along with the balsamic vinegar.

Quick and easy gravy

PREP 5 MINS   COOK 15 MINS

SERVES 4
500ml (16fl oz) chicken, beef,
    or vegetable stock
1 tbsp plain flour
salt and freshly ground black pepper

1 Put a roasting tin you've just roasted some meat in on the unlit hob and tilt so the fat settles on top of the meat juices. Spoon off almost all the fat, then add the stock and turn on the heat to high. Bring to the boil, stirring and scraping off all the crusty bits that are stuck to the base of the tin as you go, then reduce to a simmer.

2 Mix the flour and a tiny amount of water to a smooth paste, then stir into the tin, using a balloon whisk to avoid any lumps. Cook gently, stirring all the time, for 5 minutes, then taste and season with salt and black pepper, if needed. Strain through a sieve and serve in a warmed jug or gravy boat.

Fruity sausagemeat stuffing

PREP 20 MINS   COOK 40 MINS

SERVES 4
8 good-quality sausages
25g (scant 1oz) butter
1 onion, finely chopped
salt and freshly ground black pepper
handful of fresh flat-leaf parsley, finely chopped
125g (4½oz) dried fruit, such as apricots, prunes,
    or cranberries, finely chopped
1 egg, lightly beaten

1 Preheat the oven to 200°C (400°F/Gas 6). Slice the sausages down each side, remove the skins, and discard. Put the sausagemeat in a mixing bowl and chop with the back of a fork, then put to one side.

2 Meanwhile, melt half the butter in a pan, add the onion, and cook on a low heat for 5 minutes, or until soft and translucent. Allow to cool for a few minutes, then add to the sausagemeat and season well with salt and black pepper. Stir in the parsley and dried fruit, then add the egg and bind together.

3 Roll into balls and sit in a shallow roasting tin. Dot with the remaining butter, and put in the oven to cook for 30–40 minutes, or until the sausagemeat is cooked. If it is browning too much, cover with foil. Serve alongside your favourite meat.

FOOD FOR FRIENDS

Marrow and tomato gratin

 PREP 20 MINS COOK 50 MINS

SERVES 4

2 tbsp olive oil
1 onion, finely chopped
1 marrow, about 900g (2lb) peeled,
    deseeded, and cut into cubes
450g (1lb) tomatoes, finely chopped
3 garlic cloves, grated or
    finely chopped
handful of fresh flat-leaf parsley, finely chopped
salt and freshly ground black pepper
3 tbsp fresh breadcrumbs
50g (1¾oz) Parmesan cheese, grated

1 Preheat the oven to 200°C (400°F/Gas 6).
Heat the oil in a large pan, add the onion, and cook
over a low heat for 5 minutes, or until soft and
translucent. Add the marrow and cook for a further
5 minutes, then add the tomatoes and garlic and
cook over a low heat for 10 minutes, or until the
tomatoes start to break down. Stir through the
parsley, and season well with salt and black pepper.

2 Spoon the mixture into one large gratin dish or
four small ones. Sprinkle over the breadcrumbs and
Parmesan cheese and put in the oven for 20–30
minutes, or until the top is crisp and golden. Serve
with chicken.

Peas and pancetta

 PREP 10 MINS COOK 30 MINS

SERVES 4

1 tbsp olive oil
1 onion, finely chopped
225g (8oz) pancetta, cubed
2 garlic cloves, grated or
    finely chopped
a few fresh rosemary stalks, leaves finely chopped
small glass of dry white wine
225g (8oz) frozen peas, thawed
salt and freshly ground black pepper

1 Heat the oil in a large frying pan, add the onion,
and cook over a low heat for 5 minutes, or until
soft and translucent. Turn up the heat, add the
pancetta, and cook for a further 5–8 minutes, or until
the pancetta is golden. Turn the heat down, add the
garlic and rosemary, and stir for a few seconds.

2 Turn the heat back up, add the wine, and allow
to boil for 5 minutes. Stir in the peas, and simmer
for 10 minutes. Taste and season well with salt and
black pepper. Serve with lamb.

VARIATION
Stir in a handful of finely
chopped fresh mint leaves
just before serving.

Roasted squash with sage and onion

 PREP 15 MINS COOK 40 MINS

SERVES 4

1 butternut squash, peeled, halved lengthways,
    seeds removed, and cut into wedges
2 red onions, peeled and cut
    into eighths
handful of fresh sage leaves,
    finely chopped
pinch of chilli flakes (optional)
salt and freshly ground black pepper
1–2 tbsp olive oil

1 Preheat the oven to 200°C (400°F/Gas 6). Put
the squash, onions, sage, and chilli flakes (if using),
in a large roasting tin and season well with salt and
black pepper. Add the oil and combine all the
ingredients with your hands.

2 Put in the oven to roast for 30–40 minutes, or
until the squash is cooked and golden. Serve with
roast chicken or pork.

COOK'S NOTES

You can prepare the squash
a day ahead of time. Place it
in a sealed plastic bag in the
refrigerator until ready to roast.

FOOD FOR FRIENDS

Caramelized carrots

PREP 10 MINS | COOK 25 MINS

SERVES 4

1.1kg (2½lb) carrots, scrubbed or peeled, trimmed, and cut lengthways and then in half to make chunky batons
50g (1¾oz) butter
sprinkling of demerara sugar
handful of fresh flat-leaf parsley, finely chopped, optional

1 Boil the carrots in a pan of salted water for 10-15 minutes, or until nearly cooked, then drain.

2 Return to the pan with the butter, sugar, and parsley, and cook over a medium heat, stirring now and again, for 10 minutes, or until the carrots start to caramelize. Sprinkle with parsley (if using). Serve with roast chicken or beef.

Squash with chestnuts and cranberries

PREP 15 MINS | COOK 35 MINS

SERVES 4

1–2 tbsp olive oil
knob of butter
pinch of allspice
pinch of cinnamon
1 butternut squash, peeled, halved, deseeded, and cut into bite-sized pieces
salt and freshly ground black pepper
200g packet ready-cooked chestnuts
50g (1¾oz) fresh cranberries or frozen cranberries, thawed

1 Preheat the oven to 200°C (400°F/Gas 6). Heat the oil and butter in a large frying pan, add the allspice, cinnamon, and squash, season well with salt and black pepper, and cook over a low-medium heat, stirring occasionally, for 15 minutes, or until the squash begins to soften a little. Add a little more oil, if needed.

2 Add the chestnuts and stir so they are coated with the oil. Cook over a low heat for 5-10 minutes, then add the cranberries and cook for 5 minutes more.

3 Taste, and season again, if needed, adding a little sugar if the cranberries are too tart (cook until the sugar has dissolved). Serve with roast chicken or turkey.

Green beans with toasted hazelnuts

PREP 5 MINS | COOK 5 MINS

SERVES 4

250g (9oz) fine green beans, trimmed
salt
25g (scant 1oz) butter
75g (2½oz) hazelnuts, roughly chopped and toasted

1 Put the beans in a pan of salted water and boil for 5-6 minutes, or until they are cooked but still have a bit of bite to them. Drain, then refresh under cold water so they stop cooking and retain their colour.

2 Transfer to a serving dish, top with the butter and toasted hazelnuts, and serve with roast chicken or lamb.

> **COOK'S NOTES**
>
> To toast the hazelnuts, fry them (without any fat) in a small pan on a medium heat for 5 minutes, stirring frequently, until evenly toasted. Alternatively, place on a baking tray and roast in an oven preheated to 200°C (400°F/Gas 6).

BARBECUE

Fuss-free sizzling food for outdoor eating.

BARBECUE

The smoky scent of barbecued food is a pleasure we all enjoy. All you need is good food, a fierce grill, and sunshine. Choose your barbecue to suit your needs; coals can take time to heat up, whereas gas barbecues can be used in an instant. Preparing ahead is essential, so you have time to be attentive at the grill, and avoid food spoilage in the heat. Above all, it's about enjoying simply cooked food.

Psst...

When marinating fish, meat, or vegetables, it is a good idea to prepare everything ahead, even the night before, and put it all in large plastic bags. It saves on space in the refrigerator, and you can squish the contents around so they get evenly covered.

Best meat to barbecue
Crowd-pleasing meats that contain enough fat to withstand fierce heat.

MEAT		COOKING TIME
	**BEEF STEAKS** Choose tender portions, such as rib-eye or T-bone, which have a layer of fat and marbling for good flavour. The steaks should be even thickness, about 2.5cm (1in). Add a little marinade of oil and lemon juice for extra flavour, then season with salt and freshly ground black pepper just before you cook them.	Cook over a high heat – about 8 minutes in total for rare, about 12 minutes for medium, and about 16 minutes for well done. Always rest the meat before serving.
	**LAMB CHOPS** They benefit from quick cooking and high heat and, as lamb is a relatively fatty meat, it's perfect for the barbecue. Trim away excess fat, however, as it may make the fire flame. Chops should be about 2.5cm (1in) thick. Marinate with olive oil, garlic, rosemary, salt, and freshly ground black pepper before cooking.	Cook over a medium-high heat – medium rare for about 5 minutes each side, longer if your prefer (but don't overcook).
	**PORK CHOPS** Choose thick pork loin chops, and marinate in a flavoured oil for at least 30 minutes before cooking. Sear the chops first each side for about one minute. **Pork ribs** are also excellent for the barbecue, either cooked as a whole rack, or individually. Cook them in the oven first for about 30 minutes, so you can be sure they're cooked through.	Cook over a medium heat for 4–5 minutes each side after searing. Cook ribs over a high heat for about 15 minutes after cooking in the oven.
	**CHICKEN** Poultry requires a little patience on the barbecue, and can be a tricky meat to get right. Never cook high and fast, as the skin will appear charred and cooked, but the inside won't be. Choice cuts are **wings**, **legs**, and **thighs** with bone in. Marinate in a flavoured oil and roast in the oven first for 20 minutes, slash the flesh, then add to the barbecue.	Cook over a medium heat for 5–10 minutes. Move to the edges of the grill to cook through over a gentler heat for 15–20 minutes, turning frequently.
	SAUSAGES These were made for the barbecue and, if cooked correctly, can be succulent and juicy. The key is to cook low and slow otherwise, as with chicken, the skin will burn and appear cooked, but the inside won't be. Choose sausages with high meat content, and cook until a uniform colour throughout.	Cook over a low heat for 15–20 minutes in total, turning frequently.

Best fish and seafood to barbecue
These are all meaty-fleshed, ideal for cooking on a grill.

FISH AND SEAFOOD		COOKING TIME
	**SARDINES** This oily fish is perfect for the barbecue. Make sure it is very fresh (the smaller ones have more flavour). They can be gutted or left whole. Rub with oil, and sprinkle with sea salt. You can also skewer sardines, from mouth to tail. Cook until the skin turns golden brown. Serve with a squeeze of lemon.	Cook over a high heat for 2–3 minutes each side, depending on size.
	MONKFISH A superb meaty fish for the barbecue. Either cook the tail fillets whole, or cut into equal chunks and skewer. Marinate in olive oil, lemon, salt, and freshly ground black pepper.	Cook over a medium-hot heat for 8–10 minutes. Turn and baste frequently.
	**PRAWNS** Choose large uncooked prawns with the shell on, otherwise they will turn rubbery. You can still marinate them, as some flavour will penetrate the shell. Try olive oil, lemon, chilli, salt, and freshly ground black pepper. Sit them on the barbecue, or skewer them for easy turning.	Cook over a high heat for about 2 minutes each side.
	SQUID Responds well to quick cooking and high heat. Baby squid is more tender than large squid: buy it ready-prepared, flatten the body, score, and keep the tentacles whole. Mix with olive oil, lemon, salt, and freshly ground black pepper. Cook on the grill until it begins to curl up.	Cook over a high heat for about 5 minutes in total.
	**SALMON** If cooking fillets or steaks, make sure they are firm and chunky, so they hold together. Rub with olive oil, salt, and freshly ground black pepper, and add straight to the barbecue, or cube and skewer for kebabs. If cooking whole, drizzle with oil, season, wrap in foil, and put on the barbecue.	Whole: Cook over a high heat for 10–15 minutes in total. Fillet and steak: Cook for about 3 minutes each side.
	**TUNA** Use good-quality and very fresh tuna. Use pieces about 2.5cm (1in) thick. Coat with a mixture of olive oil, salt, and freshly ground black pepper, and add to the barbecue. This lean fish dries out quickly if overcooked, becoming chewy and tasteless, so it's best served quite rare, or just seared.	Cook over a high heat for 3–4 minutes each side. To sear, cook over a very high heat for 1–2 minutes each side.

Best vegetables to barbecue

A selection that need minimum preparation.

VEGETABLE		COOKING TIME
 **PEPPERS** Cook whole or cut into chunks: red, yellow, or orange are the sweetest, but green teams well with meats such as lamb. Rub in a little olive oil, salt, and freshly ground black pepper, and cook until lightly charred. If cooking whole, remove, put in a plastic bag to cool, then remove skin and deseed. If cooking chunks, deseed first.		Cook whole peppers over a high heat for 10-15 minutes, turning every 5 minutes. Cook pieces alone, or skewered with other ingredients, for about 5 minutes.
 **SWEETCORN** Barbecued sweetcorn is deliciously sweet and succulent. For a nutty caramelized flavour, de-husk, coat in olive oil, season with salt and freshly ground black pepper, and sit on the barbecue whole or cut into chunks. Serve with butter. Or, cook whole in the husk: this will protect the corn and steam it.		Cook over a high heat for about 20 minutes.
 **AUBERGINES** Slice lengthways into slices about 1cm (½in) thick, or slice into 2.5cm (1in) rounds. Either way, coat liberally with olive oil, season well with salt and freshly ground black pepper, and sit on the barbecue until charred and crispy, with soft sweet flesh.		Cook aubergine rounds over a high heat for about 5 minutes each side, and slices about 5 minutes in total.
 **COURGETTES** They become sweet and flavoursome on the barbecue. Slice lengthways into slices about 5mm (¼in) thick, coat in olive oil, lemon, garlic, salt, and freshly ground black pepper. Add to the barbecue and cook until golden and tender. Alternatively, slice into chunks, and thread onto skewers.		Cook over a medium-high heat for about 5 minutes in total, turning once. They release themselves from the barbecue rack when they're ready.
 **FENNEL** Once trimmed (keeping the fronds to cook with fish), quarter the fennel and remove the core. Coat in olive oil, lemon, salt, and freshly ground black pepper, and add to the barbecue. If you have time, soften the fennel first by cooking it for 2 minutes in boiling salted water.		Cook over a medium-high heat for about 10 minutes in total. Turn regularly.

3 quick marinades to add flavour and tenderize.

For meat: Szechuan pepper

This will give meat a deep spicy flavour. Mix together 2 tablespoons of **dark soy sauce**, 1 tablespoon of **Worcestershire sauce**, a splash of **mirin**, 1-2 teaspoons of **Szechuan peppercorns**, and a pinch each of grated **fresh root ginger** and grated **garlic**. Loosen with some **olive oil**, then use to coat beef or chicken. Leave to marinate overnight, then add some **salt** and **freshly ground black pepper** before adding to the barbecue.

For fish: Lime and coriander

This is fresh and zesty, and is ideal for oily or non-oily fish. Mix together the juice of 2 **limes**, 3 tablespoons of **olive oil**, 2 chopped **limes**, and a bunch of fresh **coriander**, finely chopped. Season well with **salt** and **freshly ground black pepper**. Coat the fish, then add to the barbecue. Don't leave to marinate too long, or the lime juice will start to cook the fish.

For vegetables: Chilli and lemon

This will give vegetables a hot and zingy flavour. Mix together 4 tablespoons of **olive oil**, the juice of 2-3 **lemons**, and add 2-3 sliced **fresh hot red chillies**, a pinch of **sugar**, and some **salt** and **freshly ground black pepper**. Coat the vegetables with the marinade before adding to the barbecue.

Barbecue preparation techniques
These two preparation methods, perfect for meat and fish, help flavours to penetrate, and speed up the cooking process.

Spatchcock
Flattening the bird ensures even cooking.

1 Lay a whole chicken, or other small poultry, on a board, breast-side down, and legs away from you. Using a knife or poultry shears, cut down either side of the backbone from tail to head.

2 Turn the chicken over, and press it firmly with the heel of your hand, to crush the breastbone. Once flattened, use a sharp knife to cut slits into the legs and thighs to ensure even cooking.

Scoring
This helps the marinade and seasoning penetrate the meat.

1 Make shallow incisions in one direction across the meat, about 1cm (½in) apart, using a sharp knife.

2 Cut shallow incisions n the other direction to form a criss-cross pattern. This helps ensure even cooking. Rub in your chosen marinade or flavourings, and leave to marinate for 1 hour, or overnight.

Skewer it
An ideal way to cook on the barbecue. Try vegetable skewers, too (see "The vegetarian barbecue" opposite). If using wooden skewers, always soak them in water for 30 minutes before cooking, or they will burn.

Meat kebab
This is a good way to make meat go a long way.

All meats can be threaded onto a skewer. Cut the meat into equal-sized pieces, so it cooks evenly, and thread tightly. Marinate meat before threading, and skewer just meat (such as lamb in a lemon and cumin marinade, beef in a wasabi marinade or chicken in a piri piri marinade), or mix meat with vegetables, making sure they are cut the same size as the meat. Good combinations: lamb and aubergine; pork and pineapple.

Fish kebab
Fish cooks through quickly on the grill, so these are super-speedy.

Choose firm, meaty fish, such as monkfish, as it will hold together better while it's cooking. Cut into equal-sized pieces and marinate before threading. Choose one fish, and cook with a quick-cooking vegetable such as cherry tomatoes, red onions, or courgettes, or make a mixed fish kebab, choosing fish that will cook through at the same time, such as swordfish and tuna. Prawns (with or without shell on) and scallops also skewer well.

Fruit kebab
A refreshing alternative to fruit salad. Try using lemongrass as skewers.

Choose firm, chunky fruit that will hold together. Fruits such as pineapple, apple, and banana work well, and can be brushed with a mix of fruit juice, rum, and brown sugar so they caramelize on the grill. They don't need much cooking, and are best cooked on a clean barbecue, so they don't pick up meat or fish flavours. They could always be cooked first, and kept warm in the oven.

3 prepare-ahead salads
Barbecues always need salads, to accompany the meat and fish, and freshen the palate. These can be prepared ahead and left in the refrigerator for a couple of hours until ready to serve.

Tomato pasta salad
Simple, fresh, and super-quick if you have leftover pasta.

Cook 250g (9oz) **farfalle** in a pan of boiling salted water until *al dente*. Drain, and return to the pan. Make a cross at the bottom of 5 **tomatoes**, sit them in a bowl of boiling water for 30 seconds, transfer to a bowl of cold water, and remove the skin. Roughly chop, and add to the pasta with a handful of **fresh flat-leaf parsley**, finely chopped, a handful of **fresh basil leaves**, torn, and 2 grated **garlic cloves**. Season with **salt** and **freshly ground black pepper**, and toss with some **extra virgin olive oil**.

Moroccan couscous salad
An ideal partner for kebabs, chicken, and lamb.

Put 250g (9oz) **couscous** in a large bowl with enough **hot vegetable stock** to just cover. Leave for 5 minutes, then fluff up with a fork. Cook 2 chopped **courgettes** in a little **olive oil** until golden, then add to the **couscous** with a good pinch of **paprika**, the juice of 2 **lemons**, a handful of **fresh flat-leaf parsley**, finely chopped, and a handful of chopped **olives**. Season well with **salt** and **freshly ground black pepper**, and stir to combine.

Curried rice salad
Perfect with barbecued lamb, and fish kebabs.

Put 175g (6oz) **cold cooked rice** in a large bowl with ½ a **red cabbage**, shredded, 1 teaspoon of **medium curry powder**, ½ teaspoon of **cayenne pepper**, 3 tablespoons of **mixed dried fruit**, a handful of **radishes**, chopped, the juice of ½ a **lemon**, 4 tablespoons of **extra virgin olive oil**, and a handful of **fresh flat-leaf parsley**, finely chopped. Season well with **salt** and **freshly ground black pepper**, and stir to combine.

The vegetarian barbecue
Delicious ideas for non-meat eaters.

Make vegetable skewers using a combination of vegetables (see p431, and the method opposite), adding a non-melting cheese such as **halloumi** or **paneer**. If you want to be more adventerous, coat them with yogurt and tikka paste, and add some ripe figs.

Marinate vegetables with punchy flavours: mix with fresh herbs such as mint, dill, coriander, basil, or thyme, with extra virgin olive oil, lemon juice and zest, lime, or orange. Experiment with flavours: try squash with lime and cinnamon, or courgettes with lemon and allspice.

Cook sweet potatoes in foil, then top with spicy tomato and avocado salsa and sour cream, or slice squash (skin on) into rounds, and cook coated in a chilli oil.

Large mushrooms are ideal for the barbecue. Remove the stem, and coat with a spicy teriyaki marinade. Cook until golden, then serve sliced with hot grilled pitta bread, and a dollop of hummus.

Make spicy chilli mushroom burgers, or cheesy Glamorgan sausages, and serve in rolls with home-made coleslaw.

Grill feta cheese parcels and cubes of squash, and serve with balsamic grilled tomatoes and shallots.

A selection of vegetables on the barbecue: broccoli, aubergine, red peppers, and onions make a tasty accompaniment, dressed with oil and vinegar, and seasoned.

Chargrilled swordfish with fennel, tomato, and herb salad

PREP 20 MINS · COOK 6 MINS

Marinating • 1 hour

SERVES 4

1 small fresh hot red chilli, deseeded and finely chopped
1 tbsp small capers, rinsed, gently squeezed dry, and chopped
2 tbsp olive oil, plus extra for brushing
juice of 1 lemon, plus extra lemon wedges, to serve
4 swordfish steaks, about 250g (9oz) each
salt and freshly ground black pepper

For the fennel, tomato, and herb salad
1 fennel bulb, thinly sliced
250g (9oz) cherry tomatoes, halved
2 small fresh red chillies, deseeded and thinly sliced lengthways
½ bunch of fresh chives, snipped into 2.5cm (1in) lengths
large handful of fresh flat-leaf parsley, roughly chopped
4 sprigs of fresh dill, chopped
2 tbsp olive oil
juice of ½ lemon
1 garlic clove, crushed

1 Mix together the chilli, capers, olive oil, and lemon juice in a wide shallow bowl. Add the swordfish steaks, and season with salt and black pepper. Rub the mixture over the steaks, and allow to marinate in the refrigerator for about 1 hour.

2 Heat the barbecue or charcoal grill until hot, and brush lightly with oil. Cook the fish for 2–3 minutes on each side, turning gently. Brush the cooked sides with the excess marinade. Remove from the heat, and divide among 4 warm serving plates.

3 Put the salad ingredients in a serving bowl, toss gently, and serve with the fish for people to help themselves. Serve with lemon wedges for squeezing over.

VARIATION

Omit the capers from the marinade, and scatter some warmed black olives over the fish just before serving.

Chargrilled squid and rocket salad

PREP 15 MINS · COOK 2 MINS

SERVES 4

600g (1lb 5oz) whole squid (choose small young squid, rather than one large one)
4 tbsp olive oil
2 small fresh hot red chillies, deseeded and finely chopped
1 garlic clove, crushed
grated zest and juice of 1 lemon, plus extra lemon wedges, to serve
salt and freshly ground black pepper

For the rocket salad
100g (3½oz) rocket leaves
large handful of fresh flat-leaf parsley, roughly chopped
2 tbsp olive oil
juice of ½ lemon

1 Clean the squid by grabbing the head and tentacles together in one hand, and pulling them out of the body. Cut the head from the tentacles and discard, making sure that the tentacles remain attached as one. Cut or pull out the small beak from inside the tentacles. Pull out and discard the strip of transparent cartilage from inside the body, and rinse the body (the thin outer skin should peel away) and tentacles thoroughly. Pat dry with kitchen paper.

2 Put the tentacles and bodies (tubes and wings attached) in a bowl with the olive oil, chillies, garlic, and lemon zest and juice. Season with salt and black pepper.

3 Heat the barbecue or charcoal grill until hot. Grill the squid bodies and tentacles over a high heat for 1–2 minutes, turning halfway through cooking, until lightly charred on all sides. Remove to a chopping board. Cut the tentacle clusters in half crossways, and put in a bowl. Slice the tubes into 3mm (⅛in) rings, slicing through the wings as you go, and put in the bowl with the tentacles.

4 Add all of the salad ingredients to the bowl with the squid, and toss through gently. Serve immediately with lemon wedges.

VARIATION

This is also delicious with an Asian-style dressing and herbs. Add beanshoots and chopped fresh root ginger, and a little more deseeded and chopped fresh chilli.

Stuffed sardines with crushed potatoes

 PREP 15 MINS **COOK 25 MINS**

SERVES 4
600g (1lb 5oz) new potatoes
4 tbsp extra virgin olive oil
salt and freshly ground black pepper
2 tbsp fresh flat-leaf parsley, finely chopped
16 fresh sardine fillets

For the hazelnut stuffing
3 tbsp olive oil
1 garlic clove, crushed
50g (1¾oz) hazelnuts, finely chopped
30g (1oz) fresh white breadcrumbs
2 tbsp fresh flat-leaf parsley, finely chopped

1 To make the crushed potatoes, put the potatoes in a large pan, and cover with cold water. Bring to the boil, and cook for 15–20 minutes until tender; drain. Arrange the potatoes on a flat tray and, with the flat side of a potato masher, crush slightly. Drizzle with the olive oil, and season with salt and black pepper. Sprinkle with the parsley. Set aside to keep warm.

2 To prepare the stuffing, heat the oil in a frying pan over a low heat. Add the garlic, and cook for 30 seconds. Add the hazelnuts, breadcrumbs, and parsley, and cook for about 5 minutes until the breadcrumbs are golden brown. Season with salt and black pepper.

3 Heat the barbecue or charcoal grill until hot. Rinse the sardine fillets, and pat dry with kitchen paper. Season with salt and black pepper. Brush the grill with a little oil, and arrange half of the fillets skin-side down on top. (It is best to cook the sardines in 2 batches because they cook very quickly.) Grill over a high heat for about 1 minute on each side. By the time you have placed the last fillet on the grill, the first one should be ready to turn. Remove to a plate, and keep warm while you grill the remaining fillets.

4 To serve, divide half of the sardine fillets among 4 serving plates. Spoon a little of the hazelnut stuffing on top of each fillet, and cover with the remaining fillets. Put the potatoes into a serving bowl for your guests to help themselves. Serve immediately with crisp fresh salad leaves.

VARIATION
Use walnuts or pine nuts instead of hazelnuts.

Chargrilled chicken with tarragon mayonnaise

PREP 20 MINS **COOK 30 MINS**

Marinating • 1 hour

SERVES 4

4 large chicken breasts, skin on
4 tbsp olive oil
grated zest and juice of 1 lemon
salt and freshly ground black pepper

For the tarragon mayonnaise
large handful of fresh tarragon, leaves
   picked and chopped
1 garlic clove, sliced
1 egg yolk
185ml (6fl oz) light olive oil
juice of ½ lemon

1 Put the chicken breasts, olive oil, and lemon zest and juice in a bowl. Season with salt and black pepper, and rub the marinade into the meat. Allow to marinate in the refrigerator for about 1 hour.

2 To make the mayonnaise, using a mortar and pestle, pound the tarragon, garlic, and a pinch of salt into a paste. Transfer to a larger bowl, add the egg yolk, and stir thoroughly with a wooden spoon or balloon whisk until smooth. Keep whisking, and add the oil, a drop at a time, making sure that it is absorbed completely. Once the mixture starts to thicken, add the oil in a slow, thin drizzle. When a third of the oil has been used, start adding the lemon juice, a little at a time. Continue adding the remaining oil, whisking, until well incorporated. Season with black pepper, and set aside.

3 Preheat the oven to 200°C (400°F/ Gas 6). Heat the grill of a barbecue or charcoal grill until hot. Grill the chicken over a medium heat for about 10 minutes until charred on both sides. Transfer to a baking tray, and roast in the oven for 15–20 minutes until cooked through. Set aside to cool.

4 Discard the skin from the cooled chicken, and shred the meat lengthways with your fingers. Put in a bowl, add the tarragon mayonnaise, and mix well. Transfer to a serving dish, and serve with torn Cos leaves drizzled with a little lemon juice and extra virgin olive oil.

COOK'S NOTES

Any leftover chicken can be used in sandwiches with sliced avocado and mixed salad leaves.

436

Chicken and chilli burgers

PREP 10 MINS · **COOK** 20 MINS

Chilling · 30 minutes
Special equipment · food processor

SERVES 4

1 onion, peeled and quartered
4 skinless chicken breast fillets
2 garlic cloves, peeled and halved
2 fresh hot red chillies, deseeded
handful of fresh coriander,
    finely chopped
salt and freshly ground black pepper
1 tbsp plain flour
1 egg

1 Put the onion, chicken, garlic, chillies, and coriander in a food processor. Season with salt and pepper, and pulse until combined – be careful not to turn into a paste. Tip the mixture out into a bowl, and mix in the flour and egg.

2 Using your hands, scoop a small handful of the mixture, roll, then flatten into a burger. Repeat until all the mixture has been used. Chill for 30 minutes to firm up.

3 Heat the barbecue or charcoal grill until hot. Grill the burgers over a medium heat for 8–10 minutes on each side until golden and cooked through. Serve with lemon mayonnaise and fresh tomato slices.

> **COOK'S NOTES**
>
> To freeze, layer the burgers between sheets of greaseproof paper, wrap in a plastic freezer bag, and seal. Freeze for up to 3 months.

Mixed fish kebabs

PREP 15 MINS · **COOK** 10 MINS

Special equipment · skewers

SERVES 4

150g (5½oz) monkfish fillets,
    cut into cubes
150g (5½oz) salmon steaks or fillets,
    cut into cubes
150g (5½oz) tuna steaks,
    cut into cubes
grated zest and juice of 1 lime
2 garlic cloves, grated or
    finely chopped
handful of fresh coriander,
    finely chopped
5cm (2in) piece of fresh root ginger,
    finely chopped
splash of olive oil
salt and freshly ground black pepper

1 If using wooden or bamboo skewers, soak in cold water for at least 30 minutes first. Put all the ingredients in a large bowl, and season with salt and black pepper. Using your hands, carefully combine everything until well mixed. Keep in the refrigerator until needed.

2 Heat the barbecue or charcoal grill until hot. Thread the fish chunks onto the skewers in alternating pieces. Grill over a high heat for about 3 minutes on each side, turning only once during cooking. Serve hot.

Chargrilled Sicilian sausages with lentil salad

PREP 15 MINS **COOK 1¼ HRS**

Marinating • 1 hour
Special equipment • metal skewers

SERVES 8

16 Sicilian pork and fennel sausages
   (left in one continuous length)
4 tbsp olive oil
large handful of fresh flat-leaf
   parsley, finely chopped
large handful of fresh mint leaves,
   finely sliced
6 fresh basil leaves, finely sliced
3 sprigs of fresh rosemary,
   leaves picked

For the lentil salad

2 tbsp olive oil, plus 3 extra
   for dressing
1 small onion, finely chopped
300g (10oz) brown lentils, picked
   over, rinsed, and soaked in cold
   water overnight

175ml (6fl oz) chicken stock or water
1 carrot, finely diced
2 celery sticks, peeled and
   finely diced
1 spring onion, finely
   sliced diagonally
2 small fresh hot red chillies,
   deseeded and finely chopped
large handful of fresh flat-leaf parsley
handful of fresh chervil leaves
juice of ½ lemon
salt and freshly ground
   black pepper

1 Form the sausages into one
continuous round. Pierce 2 metal
skewers at right angles through the
sausage coil to hold it in place. Brush
both sides with the oil, then put the
coil in a large shallow dish. Sprinkle
with all the herbs, covering the
sausage both underneath and over
the top. Allow to marinate in the
refrigerator for about 1 hour.

2 To prepare the lentil salad, heat the
2 tablespoons of olive oil in a heavy
pan over a low heat. Add the onion,
and sweat gently for a few minutes
until soft and translucent. Drain and
rinse the lentils, and add to the pan.
Gently cook, stirring, for 2 minutes.
Pour in the stock or water, and bring
to the boil. Reduce the heat slightly,
and gently simmer for about 35
minutes until the liquid has been
absorbed. Allow to cool.

3 Meanwhile, heat the barbecue
or charcoal grill until hot. Grill the
sausage coil over a medium heat for
30–35 minutes, turning once during
cooking and lightly brushing with the
herb and oil marinade. Remove to
a plate, and keep warm.

4 Put the cooled lentils in a shallow
serving dish, and add the carrot,
celery, spring onion, chillies, parsley,

and chervil. In a small bowl or jug,
whisk together the extra 3 tablespoons
of olive oil and the lemon juice to
make a dressing. Pour over the
lentil salad, and stir thoroughly. To
serve, put the sausage coil on a large
round platter, remove the skewers,
and separate the links with kitchen
scissors or a sharp knife. Serve at the
table with the lentil salad, so that
everyone can help themselves.

COOK'S NOTES

You can find Sicilian-style
pork and fennel sausages at
any good Italian delicatessen.

Crispy duck char sui

PREP 15 MINS — COOK 45 MINS

SERVES 4

4 duck thigh and leg joints, small
 incisions made all over with a knife
3 garlic cloves, grated or
 finely chopped
3 tbsp light soy sauce
3 tbsp rice wine
1 tbsp hoisin sauce
2 tbsp clear honey
2 tsp five-spice powder
salt and freshly ground black pepper

1 Preheat the oven to 200°C
(400°F/Gas 6). Put everything in
a large bowl, and season with salt
and black pepper. Mix together so
that the duck is well coated. Wrap
the coated duck pieces in foil, and
roast in the oven for 30 minutes.

2 Preheat the barbecue or charcoal
grill until hot. Carefully unwrap
the foil, and sit the duck on the hot
barbecue or grill skin-side down. Grill
over a high heat, turning frequently,
for 10–15 minutes until golden and
crisp. Remove to a plate, and leave
to rest in a warm place for about
10 minutes. Cut the duck into slices,
and serve with a crisp green salad.

Macadamia-stuffed chicken drumsticks

PREP 20 MINS — COOK 40 MINS

Marinating • 1 hour

SERVES 4

12 chicken drumsticks
4 tbsp olive oil
1 tsp dukkah (see p357), plus extra,
 to serve
3 sprigs of fresh rosemary, leaves
 picked, plus extra, to serve
salt and freshly ground black pepper
lemon wedges, to serve

For the stuffing
2 tbsp olive oil
1 small onion, finely chopped
1 garlic clove, crushed
1 tsp dukkah
6 dates, deseeded and chopped
2 thick bacon rashers, finely chopped
125g (4½oz) macadamia nuts, chopped
2 tbsp fresh flat-leaf parsley,
 finely sliced

1 To make the stuffing, heat the
olive oil in a frying pan over a low
heat. Add the onion, and gently sweat
for a few minutes until soft and
translucent. Add the garlic, dukkah,
dates, and bacon, and cook for
a further 2 minutes. Add the chopped
nuts, and cook, stirring constantly, for
a further 2 minutes. Remove from the
heat, and stir through the parsley. Set
aside to cool.

2 To stuff the chicken, rinse the
drumsticks, and pat dry with kitchen
paper. Carefully loosen and pull back
the skin from each drumstick. Make
a cut lengthways into the meaty part
of each one, and spoon a little of
the stuffing into the pocket. Press the
side of the pocket together with your
fingers, and pull back the skin firmly
over the cut. Sit the drumsticks in
a shallow dish.

3 Mix together the olive oil,
dukkah, and 3 sprigs of rosemary.
Season with salt and black pepper.
Pour the mixture over the drumsticks,
turning them over and around to coat
well. Leave to marinate in the
refrigerator for 1 hour.

4 Heat the barbecue or charcoal
grill until hot. Grill the drumsticks
over a medium heat, turning
occasionally, for about 30 minutes,
until cooked through. Baste with the
marinade while cooking. Serve piled
high on a serving dish, sprinkled with
extra dukkha and rosemary leaves,
and lemon wedges for squeezing over.

> ### COOK'S NOTES
> If you think the drumsticks need
> more cooking, transfer to a baking
> tray, and roast in a preheated
> 180°C (350°F/Gas 4) oven until
> cooked through. You could also
> stuff chicken breasts in this way.

FOOD FOR FRIENDS

FOOD FOR FRIENDS

Lamb fillet with tomato and basil salad

PREP 15 MINS **COOK 20 MINS**

Marinating • 1 hour

SERVES 8

2kg (4½lb) lamb fillet

120ml (4fl oz) olive oil

3 garlic cloves, grated or finely chopped

4 tbsp fresh flat-leaf parsley, finely chopped, plus extra to garnish

3 sprigs of fresh rosemary, leaves picked

pinch of dried chilli flakes

salt and freshly ground black pepper

extra virgin olive oil, for drizzling

For the tomato and basil salad

4 ripe plum tomatoes, cut into quarters lengthways

500g (1lb 2oz) cherry tomatoes on the vine, separated but still with their stems

250g (9oz) yellow bell or cherry tomatoes, halved

1 bunch of fresh basil leaves, about 30g (1oz)

1 garlic clove, crushed

1 small red onion, thinly sliced into discs

3 tbsp extra virgin olive oil

1 Trim the lamb of any fat. Mix together the olive oil, garlic, parsley, rosemary, and chilli flakes in a large bowl, and season with salt and black pepper. Add the lamb, massaging the marinade into the meat. Allow to marinate in the refrigerator for at least 1 hour.

2 Heat the barbecue or charcoal grill until hot. Grill the lamb over a medium heat for 8–10 minutes on each side for medium-rare, or until cooked to your liking. Remove to a plate, cover with foil, and leave to rest in a warm place for 20 minutes.

3 To make the salad, put all the ingredients in a bowl, season with salt and black pepper, and toss gently. When ready to serve, slice the lamb diagonally, and arrange on a serving platter. Scatter with the parsley leaves and a drizzle of extra virgin olive oil, and serve accompanied by the salad.

VARIATION
Add some pesto to the tomato and basil salad, mix through, and serve with a little creamy fresh ricotta cheese spooned over the top and freshly grated Parmesan cheese.

COOK'S NOTES

The lamb could sit marinating in the refrigerator overnight, and the salad can be made ahead, too.

440

Chargrilled lamb cutlets and aubergine with red cabbage slaw

PREP 25 MINS **COOK 10 MINS**

SERVES 4

1 aubergine, about 300g (10oz), thinly
   sliced lengthways
salt, for sprinkling
12 lamb cutlets, trimmed of any fat
2 tbsp olive oil
salt and freshly ground black pepper

For the red cabbage slaw
½ small red cabbage
100g (3½oz) green beans, trimmed,
   blanched, and thinly sliced
   diagonally
1 small cucumber, thinly sliced or
   shaved lengthways
1 spring onion, thinly
   sliced diagonally
1 small red onion, thinly sliced
   into discs
2 celery sticks, peeled and thinly
   sliced diagonally
60g (2oz) hazelnuts, chopped
2 tbsp extra virgin olive oil
1 tsp balsamic vinegar

1 Put the aubergine slices in
a colander, and sprinkle with salt.
Leave to drain for 20 minutes, rinse,
and pat dry with kitchen paper.

2 Heat the barbecue or charcoal
grill until hot. Brush the lamb cutlets
with olive oil, and season with salt
and black pepper. Brush the aubergine
slices with a little olive oil, and season
with black pepper. Grill the lamb over
a medium heat for 3–5 minutes on
each side until cooked to your liking.
At the same time, grill the aubergine
over a high heat for about 3 minutes
on each side until golden. Remove
both the lamb and aubergine to
a plate, and leave to rest in a warm
place for 10 minutes.

3 Meanwhile, finely slice or shred
the red cabbage. Put the cabbage
in a bowl, and add the remaining
slaw ingredients. Season with salt
and black pepper, toss gently, and
serve with the lamb cutlets
and chargrilled aubergine.

Use pine nuts instead of
hazelnuts in the slaw.

Pepper steak with parsley and almond pesto

PREP 15 MINS **COOK 6 MINS**

Marinating • 1 hour
Special equipment • blender or food
processor

SERVES 6

1kg (2¼lb) beef fillet, cut into
   12 thin slices
1 tbsp black peppercorns
1 tbsp green peppercorns
1 tbsp pink peppercorns
salt and freshly ground black pepper
3 tbsp olive oil
1 tbsp seeded Dijon mustard

For the parsley and almond pesto
125g (4½oz) blanched
   almonds, toasted
1 garlic clove, chopped
2 large handfuls of fresh
   flat-leaf parsley
2 large handfuls of baby
   spinach leaves
grated zest and juice of 1 lemon
120ml (4fl oz) olive oil

1 Put the beef fillet slices in a large
shallow dish. Using a mortar and
pestle, pound the black, green, and
pink peppercorns with a little salt
until coarsely ground. Transfer to
a small bowl, add the olive oil and

mustard, and mix together. Brush
the marinade all over the meat, and
allow to marinate in the refrigerator
for at least 1 hour.

2 Meanwhile, to make the parsley
and almond pesto, put the almonds,
garlic, parsley, spinach, lemon zest,
and juice in a blender or food
processor, and season with salt and
black pepper. Whiz briefly. Keep the
motor running, and gradually add
the oil, little by little, until thick and
smooth – if you like a thicker pesto,
you may not need to use all the oil.
Set aside in a bowl, and cover with
cling film.

3 Heat the barbecue or charcoal grill
until hot. Grill the steaks over a high
heat for about 2 minutes on each side,
or until cooked to your liking, brushing
lightly with the marinade while
cooking. Remove to a plate, cover
with foil, and leave to rest in a warm
place for 10 minutes.

4 To serve, put the steaks on
individual plates, and top with
a spoonful of the parsley and almond
pesto. Serve with thick slices of lightly
oiled grilled sourdough bread.

Fillet steaks with horseradish cream

 PREP 10 MINS COOK 10 MINS

SERVES 4
4 beef fillet or rib-eye steaks, about 300g (10oz) each
2 tbsp olive oil
1 garlic clove, crushed
salt and freshly ground black pepper

For the horseradish cream
250ml (8fl oz) mascarpone cheese
1 tbsp freshly grated horseradish
juice of ½ lemon
1 tsp vincotto or good-quality thick balsamic vinegar

1 Heat the barbecue or charcoal grill until hot. Put the steaks in a large shallow dish. Add the oil and garlic, and season with salt black and pepper. Mix well.

2 Grill the steaks over a high heat for 5 minutes on each side, or until cooked to your liking, brushing lightly with the oil mixture while cooking. Remove to a warm plate, cover with foil, and leave to rest in a warm place for 10 minutes.

3 To make the horseradish cream, put the mascarpone cheese in a bowl, and stir in the horseradish, lemon juice, and vincotto or balsamic vinegar. Season with a little black pepper. Divide the steaks between 4 serving plates, and serve with a dollop of the horseradish cream.

Pork kebabs with chilli mango salad

 PREP 20 MINS COOK 10 MINS

Marinating • 1 hour
Special equipment • 12 wooden skewers

SERVES 4
2 pork fillets, about 250g (9oz) each
1 garlic clove, crushed
2 small fresh hot red chillies, deseeded and finely chopped
1 tbsp fresh root ginger, finely chopped
4 tbsp olive oil
salt and freshly ground black pepper

For the chilli mango salad
2 large mangoes (see Cook's Notes)
grated zest and juice of 1 lime
1 small fresh hot red chilli, finely sliced

1 Soak the skewers in cold water for 30 minutes. Using a sharp knife, remove any sinew from the pork. Cut each fillet in half lengthways, then cut each half across the grain into bite-sized pieces.

2 To make the marinade, mix together the garlic, chillies, ginger, and olive oil in a shallow dish. Add the pork, and turn to coat in the marinade. Season with salt and black pepper, and allow to marinate in the refrigerator for 1 hour.

3 Heat the barbecue or charcoal grill until hot. Thread the pieces of pork evenly onto the soaked skewers, and brush the grill with a little oil. Grill the pork kebabs over a low heat for about 10 minutes until cooked to your liking, brushing lightly with a little of the marinade while they are cooking. Remove the kebabs to a plate, cover with foil, and leave to rest in a warm place for 15 minutes.

4 To make the chilli mango salad, peel the mangoes and cut in half (as close as possible to the stone as you can). Cut each half lengthways into thin slices. Put the mango slices in a bowl, add the lime zest and juice, and the chilli, and season with black pepper. Stir gently to mix. Arrange 3 kebabs in the centre of each of 4 serving plates, on top of the chilli mango salad.

COOK'S NOTES

Look for mangoes that are not too ripe (preferably on the green side) for this salad. They should be firm and slightly tart.

Wasabi beef and pak choi

PREP 10 MINS | COOK 10 MINS

SERVES 4

2 tbsp olive oil

2 tsp wasabi paste

4 sirloin steaks, about 200g (7oz) each

200g (7oz) pak choi, cut lengthways into 8 pieces

5 garlic cloves, grated or finely chopped

1 tbsp dark soy sauce

salt and freshly ground black pepper

1 Heat the barbecue or charcoal grill until hot. Mix together 1 tablespoon of the olive oil and the wasabi paste. Use to coat the sirloin steaks, ensuring a thin, even covering.

2 Sit the steaks on the barbecue and grill fiercely over a high heat for 3 minutes on each side. Remove to a plate, and leave to rest in a warm place for 5 minutes.

3 Meanwhile, toss the pak choi in the remaining olive oil with the garlic and soy sauce. Grill for 2–3 minutes, or until charred and just wilted. To serve, cut the steak into 1cm (½in) slices, season, and serve with the pak choi.

FOOD FOR FRIENDS

Marinated pork tenderloin in soy and rice vinegar

PREP 10 MINS COOK 20 MINS

Marinating • 30 minutes

SERVES 4

1 pork tenderloin, about 450g (1lb)

3 garlic cloves, grated
   or finely chopped

5cm (2in) piece of fresh root ginger,
   finely chopped

5 spring onions, finely sliced

2 tbsp olive oil

4 tbsp dark soy sauce

4 tbsp rice vinegar

1 tbsp clear honey

salt and freshly ground black pepper

1 Score the pork all over in a crisscross pattern about 1cm (½in) deep, and sit in a bowl or ceramic dish. Mix together the remaining ingredients, and season with salt and black pepper. Smother this liberally all over the pork, and allow to marinate in the refrigerator for about 30 minutes.

2 Heat the barbecue or charcoal grill until it is hot and any flames have died away. Sit the whole tenderloin on the barbecue, and grill over a medium heat for 20 minutes, turning frequently. Remove to a plate, and leave to rest in a warm place for 10 minutes.

3 To serve, cut the tenderloin into 5mm (¼in) slices, and serve with an Oriental-style salad.

Chilli-slashed pork tenderloin

PREP 10 MINS COOK 20 MINS

SERVES 4

1 pork tenderloin, about 450g (1lb)

3 fresh hot red chillies, finely chopped

4 garlic cloves, grated
   or finely chopped

1 medium onion, very finely diced

2 tbsp olive oil

salt and freshly ground black pepper

1 Heat the barbecue or charcoal grill until it is hot and any flames have died away. Make diagonal slashes halfway through the pork at 3cm (1¼in) intervals. Mix together the remaining ingredients, and season with salt and black pepper. Smother this liberally all over the pork, ensuring that some of the mixture gets into the slashed openings.

2 Sit the whole tenderloin on the barbecue, and grill over a medium heat for 20 minutes, turning carefully and frequently. Remove to a plate, and leave to rest in a warm place for 10 minutes.

3 To serve, cut the tenderloin on the opposite diagonal to the slashes into 1cm (½in) slices. Serve with a refreshing coleslaw.

Lamb fillet basted with anchovy paste

PREP 15 MINS · COOK 40 MINS

Marinating • 30 minutes
Special equipment • blender or food processor

SERVES 4
1 whole lamb neck fillet,
    about 675g (1½lb)
1 onion, peeled and quartered
150g jar salted anchovies
    in oil, drained
2 tbsp capers in vinegar, drained
3 tbsp olive oil

1 Score the lamb fillet in a crisscross pattern about 1cm (½in) deep. Put the remaining ingredients in a blender or food processor, and whiz to a fine paste. Liberally spread the paste all over the lamb, making sure that it makes its way into the scores. Allow to marinate in the refrigerator for about 30 minutes.

2 Heat the barbecue or charcoal grill until it is hot and any flames have died away. Sit the lamb fillet on the barbecue, and grill over a low heat for 40 minutes, turning frequently. Remove to a plate, and leave to rest in a warm place for 10 minutes.

3 To serve, cut into 1cm (½in) slices, and serve with warm pitta bread, hummus, and salad leaves.

COOK'S NOTES

Use best end of neck lamb fillet, or tenderloin – you will find this cut in your butchers. To halve the cooking time, butterfly the fillet by cutting it in half (but not all the way through) and opening it out before marinating.

FOOD FOR FRIENDS

445

BARBECUE

FOOD FOR FRIENDS

Stuffed fillet steak with chilli and parsley butter

 PREP 20 MINS COOK 6 MINS

SERVES 4

4 sirloin steaks, about 225g (8oz) each, cut to a minimum 2.5cm (1in) thick

125g (4½oz) cream cheese

salt and freshly ground black pepper

For the chilli and parsley butter

75g (2½oz) salted butter

1 tsp chilli flakes

2 tbsp fresh flat-leaf parsley, finely chopped

1 To make the chilli and parsley butter, mix together all the ingredients in a bowl until well combined. Form into a sausage shape, and place on a piece of greaseproof paper. Roll up into a tube, twist each end of the paper, and chill for 30 minutes while you prepare and cook the steak.

2 Heat the barbecue or charcoal grill until hot. Take each fillet steak and, using a thin pointed knife (a boning knife is perfect), pierce the side and move the knife from side to side to create a cavity, trying not to increase the size of the opening too much. Using your fingers, push a portion of the cream cheese into each opening. Do not overstuff.

3 Season the steaks and grill them on the barbecue over a high heat for 3 minutes on each side, turning only once. Remove to a plate, and leave to rest in a warm place for 5 minutes. Serve on a bed of baby spinach leaves with a knob of the chilli and parsley butter on top.

446

Texan rack of ribs

  PREP 15 MINS · COOK 1¼ HRS

Marinating • 1 hour

Special equipment • blender or food processor

SERVES 4–6

4 racks of pork ribs, about 25cm (10in) long
2 lemons, sliced
2 onions
4 tbsp olive oil
4 tbsp tomato ketchup
4 tbsp Worcestershire sauce
1 tbsp English mustard
1 tsp chilli powder
1 tbsp clear honey
2 tbsp fresh thyme leaves
1 tsp salt
2 tsp freshly ground black pepper

1 Put the ribs in a large pan of salted water with the lemon slices. Bring to the boil, reduce the heat to low, and simmer gently for 40 minutes to tenderize the meat.

2 Meanwhile, put the remaining ingredients in a blender or food processor, and blend to a smooth sauce.

3 When the ribs are cooked, remove from the pan with a slotted spoon, and drain thoroughly in a colander. Spread the sauce over the drained ribs, and leave to cool. Marinate in the refrigerator for at least 1 hour.

4 Heat the barbecue or charcoal grill until hot. Sit the whole rib racks on the barbecue, and grill over a medium heat for 30 minutes, turning frequently and basting with any leftover sauce. Remove to a plate, and allow to rest in a warm place for 5 minutes. To serve, slice the racks into ribs, and serve warm and sticky with a crunchy salad and plenty of napkins.

Hot beef and chilli burgers

 PREP 20 MINS · COOK 10 MINS

SERVES 4

400g (14oz) lean beef mince
2 onions, diced
2 garlic cloves, chopped
2 fresh hot red chillies, deseeded and finely chopped
½ tsp salt
½ tsp cayenne pepper
½ tsp freshly ground black pepper
handful of fresh flat-leaf parsley, finely chopped

1 Put all the ingredients in a mixing bowl. Using your hands, mix together really well until the texture is thick and paste-like. Form into 8 patties about 4cm (1¾in) thick, and chill until needed.

2 Heat the barbecue or charcoal grill until hot. Cook the beef patties over a medium heat for 5 minutes on each side until nicely browned and cooked through, turning only once during cooking.

3 Serve hot, sandwiched in a burger bun with fresh tomato slices and crispy lettuce.

VARIATION
Try using lamb mince instead of beef mince, and add finely chopped fresh mint leaves when you add the parsley.

COOK'S NOTES
This is a great mixture to prepare ahead. Prepare the meat paste in a bowl, cover, and leave in the refrigerator for up to 2 days.

Lamb koftas

PREP 15 MINS   COOK 15 MINS

Chilling • 1 hour

Special equipment • blender or food processor • stainless-steel or wooden skewers

SERVES 4–6

1 red onion, peeled and quartered

2 garlic cloves, grated or finely chopped

1 fresh medium-hot red chilli, deseeded and chopped

1 tsp fresh flat-leaf parsley, finely chopped

1 tsp fresh coriander, finely chopped

1 tsp fresh mint leaves, finely chopped

1 tsp mild paprika

grated zest of 1 lemon

salt and freshly ground black pepper

700g (1½lb) lean lamb mince

1 Put the onion, garlic, chilli, parsley, coriander, mint, paprika, and lemon zest in a blender or food processor. Season with salt and black pepper, and whiz to a paste. Add the lamb mince, and whiz again until a coarse paste forms. Transfer the mixture to a bowl, and chill for 1 hour until firm.

2 Shape the mixture into 12 sausages, and carefully push each long sausage of meat onto a stainless-steel or pre-soaked wooden skewer to form the koftas. Return to the refrigerator until firm.

3 Meanwhile, heat the barbecue or charcoal grill until hot. Lay the skewers on the hot barbecue, and grill over a medium heat for 15 minutes, turning occasionally, until evenly browned and cooked through. Serve hot with a crunchy salad and hummus.

Marinated sweet and hot tuna steaks

PREP 10 MINS   COOK 5 MINS

Marinating • 30 minutes

SERVES 4

4 fresh tuna steaks, about 200g (7oz) each

For the marinade

2 tbsp dark soy sauce

2 tbsp olive oil

juice of 2 limes

2 garlic cloves, grated or finely chopped

2.5cm (1in) piece of fresh root ginger, finely chopped

2 tbsp dark muscovado sugar

1 tsp cayenne pepper

salt and freshly ground black pepper

1 Put all of the marinade ingredients in a bowl. Season with salt and black pepper, and mix together well. Put the tuna steaks in a plastic freezer bag, tip in the marinade, and seal, making sure that the tuna is well coated. Allow to marinate in the refrigerator for 30 minutes.

2 Heat the barbecue or charcoal grill until hot. Grill the tuna steaks over a high heat for 2 minutes on each side, turning once during cooking. Remove to a plate, and leave to rest in a warm place for 2 minutes. Serve with a fresh green salad.

Spatchcock chicken with lemon, oregano, and paprika

  PREP 20 MINS **COOK 50 MINS**

Marinating • 1 hour

SERVES 4-6

1-2 tsp olive oil
grated zest of 1 lemon, plus juice of 2
1 tsp paprika
½ tsp salt
1 tsp freshly ground black pepper
1 whole spatchcock chicken (you can
   ask your butcher to do this)
1 tbsp dried oregano

1 Put the oil, lemon zest and juice,
paprika, salt, and black pepper
in a bowl or shallow dish, and mix

together well. Add the chicken,
making sure it is well coated in
the marinade. Allow to marinate
in the refrigerator for 1 hour. (Put
the chicken and its marinade in
a plastic freezer bag for better
coverage if you like.)

2 Heat the barbecue or charcoal
grill until hot. Sprinkle the oregano
liberally all over the chicken, and
grill over a low heat for 40-50
minutes until golden and cooked
through, turning frequently. Remove
to a plate, and leave to rest in a
warm place for 15 minutes.

Cheat...
Cook on the barbecue on a
high heat for 15 minutes,
then put in a preheated
200°C (400°F/Gas 6)
oven for 20
minutes.

COOK'S NOTES

To spatchcock a chicken yourself, sit
the chicken breast-side down on a
clean work surface. Using poultry
shears or a good pair of kitchen
scissors, cut along the centre
back of the chicken, running from
thigh to wing on each side and
removing the backbone, from tail
to neck. Open up the chicken,
and flatten by pushing down hard
on the breastbone (see p432).
Secure in position with metal
skewers running from thigh to
opposite wing.

449

Sausage and herb balls

PREP 15 MINS   **COOK** 15 MINS

Chilling • 30 minutes
Special equipment • food processor

SERVES 4
1 onion, quartered
small handful of fresh mint leaves
handful of fresh flat-leaf parsley
handful of fresh basil
1 tsp dried oregano
salt and freshly ground black pepper
400g (14oz) good-quality
    sausagemeat or fresh pork
    sausages, skinned
plain flour, to dust

1 Put the onion, mint, parsley, basil, and oregano in a food processor, and blend to a rough paste. Season well with salt and black pepper.

2 Add the sausagemeat, and whiz again until combined. Using your hands, roll the mixture into 12 balls, each about 4cm (1½in) across. Dust with a little flour to prevent them sticking. Chill for 30 minutes to firm.

3 Heat the barbecue or charcoal grill until hot. Grill the sausage and herb balls over a medium heat, turning occasionally, for 12–15 minutes until evenly browned and cooked through. Serve hot with fresh crusty bread and a spicy or garlic mayonnaise.

Cheat...
Use ready-spiced sausages, and omit the herbs.

COOK'S NOTES
Tip out lots of flour for dusting before rolling the sausagemeat out, so you don't have to put your hands back in the bag!

Pork loin chop marinated in mustard and herbs

PREP 10 MINS COOK 12 MINS

Marinating • 2 hours

SERVES 4

4 large pork loin chops, trimmed of fat

For the marinade
50ml (2fl oz) sweet cider
4 tsp olive oil
4 tsp wholegrain mustard
1 tbsp tomato purée
2 tsp English mustard
2 tbsp fresh thyme leaves
1 tbsp fresh sage leaves, chopped
2 tbsp fresh mint leaves, finely chopped
1 tbsp dried oregano
½ tsp salt
1 tsp freshly ground black pepper

1 Put all the ingredients for the marinade in a small bowl, and mix together well.

2 Using a sharp knife, deeply score the pork chops. Put in a plastic freezer bag, and tip in the marinade. Combine well, being careful not to pierce the bag. Seal, and allow to marinate in the refrigerator for at least 2 hours.

3 Heat the barbecue or charcoal grill until hot. Grill the pork chops over a high heat for 10–12 minutes, turning occasionally and basting with any leftover marinade. Remove to a plate, and leave to rest in a warm place for 5 minutes. Serve with a potato salad.

Jerk white fish

PREP 10 MINS COOK 5 MINS

Marinating • 2 hours
Special equipment • blender or food processor

SERVES 4

700g (1½lb) meaty white fish fillets, such as monkfish or grouper
lime wedges, to serve

For the jerk seasoning
6 garlic cloves
4 fresh Scotch Bonnet chillies
2 small onions, peeled and quartered
2 tbsp fresh thyme leaves
3 tbsp muscovado sugar
2 tsp ground allspice
1 tsp ground cinnamon
½ tsp ground nutmeg
1 tsp freshly ground black pepper
½ tsp salt

1 Blend or process all the ingredients for the jerk seasoning to a smooth, wet paste. Put the fish in a plastic freezer bag, tip in the jerk seasoning, and seal, making sure that the fish is well coated. Allow to marinate in the refrigerator for at least 2 hours, or preferably overnight.

2 Heat the barbecue or charcoal grill until hot. Grill the fish over a low heat for 3–5 minutes on each side until nicely browned and just cooked through. Be careful not to overcook; the residual heat will continue cooking the fish after it has been taken off the barbecue.

3 Cut the fish fillets into chunky slices, and serve immediately with lime wedges for squeezing over, fresh crusty bread, and a crunchy salad.

Teriyaki chicken

PREP 15 MINS **COOK** 20 MINS

Marinating • 20 minutes

SERVES 4
4 chicken breast fillets, skin on

For the marinade
3 tbsp rice wine vinegar
5 tbsp light soy sauce
5 tsp mirin or dry sherry
3 tbsp sugar
5cm (2in) piece of fresh root
ginger, grated

1 To make the marinade, mix together all the ingredients in a bowl until the sugar has dissolved.

2 Using a sharp pointed knife or skewer, pierce the chicken all over. Add to the bowl with the marinade, ensuring that the chicken is completely covered. Marinate in the refrigerator for 20 minutes.

3 Heat the barbecue or charcoal grill until hot. Remove the chicken from the marinade (reserve the marinade), and put on the barbecue, skin-side down. Grill for 15–20 minutes over a medium heat, turning occasionally, until browned all over. Remove to a plate, and leave to rest in a warm place for a few minutes while preparing the teriyaki sauce.

4 Put the reserved marinade in a small heavy pan. Bring to the boil, and continue boiling until it thickens. Cut the chicken breasts into slices, and serve with the hot teriyaki sauce poured over the top.

Beef satay

PREP 10 MINS **COOK** 5 MINS

Marinating • 1 hour

Special equipment • food processor or blender • metal or wooden skewers

SERVES 4
900g (2lb) beef tenderloin (eye fillet), cut into 2.5cm (1in chunks)
3 tbsp crunchy peanut butter

For the marinade
1 onion, quartered
5cm (2in) piece of fresh root ginger
3 garlic cloves, roughly chopped
2 fresh hot red chillies, deseeded
2 tbsp tomato ketchup
2 tbsp light soy sauce
1 tbsp groundnut (peanut) oil
juice of 2 limes
3 tbsp soft brown sugar

1 If using wooden or bamboo skewers, soak in cold water for at least 30 minutes before using. Put all the ingredients for the marinade in a blender or a food processor, and blend until smooth. Put the beef chunks in a plastic freezer bag. Tip in the marinade, squish together, and seal. Leave to marinate in the refrigerator for at least 1 hour.

2 Thread the beef onto metal or wooden skewers, allowing about 5 pieces on each skewer and reserving the marinade. Set aside while you make the peanut sauce.

3 Tip the marinade into a small pan, and bring to the boil. Add the peanut butter, and continue cooking over a medium-high heat, stirring constantly, until the mixture thickens into a sauce. Keep warm.

4 Heat the barbecue or charcoal grill until hot. Grill the beef skewers over a high heat for 5 minutes, turning frequently. Leave to rest for a few minutes, then serve with the warm peanut sauce for dipping.

Piadine with roasted pumpkin, rocket, and dill ricotta

  PREP 20 MINS **COOK 1 HR**

SERVES 8

2 x 7g sachets active dry yeast
1 tsp salt
600g (1lb 5oz) plain flour
2 tbsp olive oil, plus extra
    for brushing

For the filling
1kg (2¼lb) pumpkin, peeled,
    deseeded, and cut into chunks
90ml (3fl oz) olive oil
4 garlic cloves, peeled and crushed
4 fresh sage leaves, finely sliced
salt and freshly ground black pepper
500g (1lb 2oz) ricotta cheese
2 tbsp finely chopped Spanish onion
2 sprigs of fresh dill, finely chopped
2 handfuls of wild rocket leaves

1 To make the piadine, combine 500ml (16fl oz) of water with the yeast and salt in a small bowl, and stir until dissolved. Put the flour in a large bowl, make a well in the centre, and add the yeast mixture and oil. Mix with your hands until well combined. Knead the dough on a floured work surface for about 10 minutes until smooth and elastic. Form into a ball, place in a clean oiled bowl, and cover with a tea towel. Leave in a warm place to double in size; it should take about 1 hour.

2 Meanwhile, preheat the oven to 200°C (400°F/Gas 6). Put the pumpkin on a baking tray, and toss with the olive oil, garlic, and sage. Season with salt and black pepper, and roast in the oven for about 40 minutes until tender and golden. Set aside to cool slightly. In a bowl, combine the ricotta, onion, and dill, and season with a little salt and black pepper. Set aside.

3 Heat the barbecue or charcoal grill until hot. Remove the dough from the bowl, shape into a thick sausage on a floured work surface, and cut into 8 portions. Form the dough into oval shapes, then flatten with the palm of your hand. Roll up and down into long oval shapes about 5mm (¼in) thick. Brush both sides of the piadine with a little olive oil, and grill over a high heat for 1–2 minutes on each side until cooked. They cook quickly, so keep an eye on them.

4 As the piadine come off the grill, spread a little of the ricotta mixture evenly over the top of each one. Put some roasted pumpkin and rocket on one half of each piadina, fold the other half over the top, and serve immediately.

Chargrilled pepper and leek couscous

   PREP 15 MINS **COOK 15 MINS** ♥

SERVES 4

200g (7oz) couscous
250ml (9fl oz) boiling water
1 tbsp soft butter
4 red peppers
75ml (2½fl oz) olive oil
salt and freshly ground black pepper
1 leek, white part only, sliced into
    5mm (¼in) discs
2 garlic cloves, crushed
grated zest and juice of 1 lemon
4 tbsp fresh flat-leaf parsley, chopped
2 tbsp mint leaves, chopped

1 Put the couscous in a large bowl. Add the boiling water and the butter, and stir to combine. Cover the bowl with cling film, and set aside for 5–10 minutes. Using a fork, separate and fluff up the grains. Set aside.

2 Heat the barbecue or charcoal grill until hot. Cut off and discard the tops of the peppers, then cut the peppers in half lengthways. Remove all the seeds. Put the peppers in a shallow dish, add 3 tablespoons of the oil, and season with salt and black pepper. Mix until the peppers are well coated in the oil. Grill the peppers over a high heat for about 10 minutes until they are charred all over and softened. Allow to cool a little. Peel off the skin, and reserve the pepper halves.

3 Heat the remaining 2 tablespoons of olive oil in a frying pan over a low heat. Add the leeks, and sweat gently, stirring occasionally, for about 5 minutes. Tip in the garlic, and cook for a further 30 seconds. Remove from the heat.

4 To finish, cut or tear the pepper halves into strips, and put in the bowl with the couscous. Add the leek and garlic mixture, lemon zest and juice, parsley, and mint. Stir through well, and serve.

> ### COOK'S NOTES
> This dish would make a great partner with either grilled chicken or grilled fish.

Chargrilled asparagus and Gorgonzola

PREP **20** MINS COOK **10** MINS

SERVES 4

16 fresh asparagus spears,
 trimmed
4 tbsp extra virgin olive oil
150g (5½oz) Gorgonzola cheese
freshly ground black pepper

1 Heat the barbecue or charcoal grill until hot. Cook the asparagus in boiling salted water for 2–3 minutes. Drain, and place straight on the barbecue or grill. Grill over a medium heat for about 5 minutes, brushing the spears with a little of the oil as they are cooking, and turning them as they char.

2 To serve, divide the asparagus among 4 serving plates. Gently slice or crumble the Gorgonzola cheese over the asparagus. Sprinkle with black pepper, and drizzle with the remaining olive oil. Serve immediately.

VARIATION

Add some chargrilled prosciutto or pancetta. These are both very quick to char, so watch closely. You could also serve with some fresh baby spinach leaves or thinly sliced fresh pear.

Chargrilled aubergine with spiced tomato sauce

PREP **15** MINS COOK **20** MINS

SERVES 4

2 large aubergines, cut into slices 1cm
 (½in) thick
4 tbsp olive oil
2 garlic cloves, sliced
½ tsp paprika
salt and freshly ground black pepper
400g can chopped tomatoes

1 Heat the barbecue or charcoal grill until hot. Put the aubergines in a colander, sprinkle with salt, and weigh down with a plate. Leave to drain for 15 minutes, rinse, and pat dry with kitchen paper.

2 Meanwhile, heat 1 tablespoon of the olive oil in a pan over a very low heat. Add the garlic and paprika, and cook gently for a few seconds. Season with salt and black pepper. Stir in the tomatoes, and bring to the boil. Reduce the heat slightly, and simmer gently for 15 minutes.

3 Brush the aubergine slices with the remaining oil, then grill on the barbecue or griddle for 3 minutes on each side until golden. Serve immediately with the sauce drizzled over, or served in a bowl on the side.

Chargrilled vegetables and spinach salad

PREP 30 MINS
COOK 15 MINS

SERVES 4

2 large aubergines
salt and freshly ground black pepper
2 yellow peppers, halved and deseeded
2 red peppers, halved and deseeded
150ml (5fl oz) olive oil
2 sprigs of fresh oregano, leaves picked
300g (10 oz) courgettes, cut into diagonal slices 5mm (¼in) thick
6 fresh asparagus spears, trimmed
4 canned artichoke hearts, cut into wedges
4 handfuls of baby spinach leaves
12 black olives
1 small red onion, sliced into thin discs

For the dressing
3 tbsp olive oil
1 tbsp freshly squeezed lemon juice
1 tbsp chopped fresh dill
2 spring onions, thinly sliced

1 Heat the barbecue or charcoal grill until hot. Cut the aubergines into slices 1cm (½in) thick. Put in a colander, sprinkle with salt, and leave to drain for 15 minutes. Rinse, and pat dry with kitchen paper.

2 Meanwhile, put the peppers in a shallow dish, and add 4 tablespoons of the oil and the oregano. Season with salt and black pepper, and mix until the peppers are well coated in the oil. Grill over a high heat for about 10 minutes until they are charred and cooked. Allow to cool a little, peel, and slice the flesh into strips. Set aside. Brush the aubergine and courgette slices with a little oil, and grill on both sides over a high heat for 2–3 minutes on each side until they are just tender and starting to char. Set aside.

3 Cook the asparagus in boiling salted water for 2–3 minutes. Drain, and place straight on the barbecue or grill. Grill over a medium heat for about 5 minutes or so, brushing the spears with a little of the oil as they are cooking, and turning them as they char. Brush the grill with a little oil, and grill the artichoke hearts at the same time, allowing 2–3 minutes for each side. Allow to cool slightly.

4 Put all the grilled vegetables in a large bowl, and add the spinach leaves, olives, and red onion. To make the dressing, in a small bowl or jug, whisk together all the dressing ingredients, and season with salt and black pepper. Pour over the salad, and toss through gently.

Grilled mushrooms with bread, tomatoes, and feta

PREP 15 MINS
COOK 30 MINS

SERVES 4

500g (1lb 2oz) small to medium brown mushrooms, stems trimmed
grated zest and juice of 1 lemon
150ml (5fl oz) olive oil
salt and freshly ground black pepper
½ ciabatta loaf
2 garlic cloves, crushed
2 anchovies in oil, drained and chopped
1 tbsp fresh thyme leaves
1 tsp fresh rosemary leaves, finely chopped
250g (9oz) cherry tomatoes, halved
100g (3½oz) feta cheese, crumbled
fresh flat-leaf parsley, to garnish
extra virgin olive oil, to drizzle

1 Preheat the oven to 200°C (400°F/ Gas 6), and heat the barbecue or charcoal grill until hot. Put the mushrooms, lemon zest and juice, and half the olive oil in a bowl, and stir to combine. Season with salt and black pepper. Grill the mushrooms on both sides over a high heat for 10-15 minutes. Set aside.

2 Tear the bread into bite-sized pieces, and put on a baking tray. Toss with the garlic, anchovies, thyme, rosemary, remaining olive oil, and lots of black pepper. Spread out over the tray, and bake for about 15 minutes until the bread is golden and crisp.

3 To serve, combine the mushrooms and bread in a bowl, and divide among 4 serving plates. Arrange the tomatoes over the top. Top with the feta cheese, garnish with the parsley, and drizzle over a little extra virgin olive oil. Serve immediately.

NO-COOK DESSERTS

For instant glamour – simple prep-and-serve puds.

NO-COOK DESSERTS

Cooking desserts often causes last-minute panic, because you run out of time, or don't have space in the oven. No-cook desserts provide an instant solution, even more so during the summer when heat isn't desired in the kitchen or on the menu.

Best fruit for no-cook desserts

Use fruit at its freshest, and when it's in season.

fresh, canned, or frozen?

Rub cut **fresh fruit**, such as apples and pears, with lime or lemon juice (fresh or bottled) before using it in desserts. The acid will prevent decay, and stop the cut surfaces going brown. Toss a little juice in a fruit salad, too, to stop any discolouration.

Surprisingly, **canned fruit** contains almost the same nutrients as fresh, so it is a good substitute. Taste is the deciding factor, as nothing compares to eating fresh seasonal fruit. But canned, with its long shelf life and year-round availability, is a useful standby. Make sure it is packed in its own juices, and has no added sugar.

Frozen fruit offer little difference from fresh, nutritionally, as they are often frozen within hours of picking, but the flavour won't be as good. Summer berries are a good fruit to freeze, as their season is short. Freezing allows you to enjoy them all year.

CHOOSE		USE
	BERRIES Choose plump and fragrant fruit, with fresh green leaves. Available in the summer.	Don't pile or overcrowd when storing, as they soon turn mouldy. Delicious with balsamic vinegar, mint, chocolate, or lavender.
	APPLE There are hundreds of varieties to choose from. Press them lightly – they should be firm. At their best in the autumn.	Apples add a crisp texture to fruit salads, and team well with cinnamon and vanilla.
	ORANGE Choose heavy ones, as these will contain the most juice. Available all year round.	Sweet varieties, such as the Valencia, navel, and blood orange (perfect for a granita), team well with cinnamon, cardamom, mint, and basil.
	PINEAPPLE A ripe pineapple should smell sweet, and a leaf near the top should come away easily if pulled. Available all year round.	Pair with exotic fruits for a fruit salad. It has a natural affinity to coconut and mint.
	STONED FRUIT Peaches require peeling, but the skin of apricots and nectarines is more palatable. Choose plump fruit, with a smooth skin. Available in the summer and autumn.	Halve and remove the stone, and serve sprinkled with ready-toasted nuts, or soak in a little liqueur and serve with ice cream. The flesh can also be puréed.
	POMEGRANATE Choose heavy fruit. Available in the autumn.	The jewel-like seeds look impressive sprinkled over fruits, ice creams, and sorbets. Mix juice and seeds with Middle Eastern flavours, such as cinnamon, nutmeg, and mint.

CHOOSE		USE
	MANGO Fresh mango is sweet and tangy. Choose heavy ones with tight, unblemished skin. Available all year round.	Purée the flesh, mix it with Greek yogurt, then freeze for an easy frozen dessert.
	PASSION FRUIT This crinkled-skin fruit has a colourful and scented flesh once opened (see opposite). Available all year round.	You can eat the flesh and the seeds. Toss with an exotic fruit salad, or use the juice as a sauce for ice cream, or to make a jelly with a splash of champagne.
	GRAPES Buy grapes that are still firmly attached to the stem. Available all year round.	Try freezing them individually, and eating them straight from the freezer. Steep in dessert wine, and serve with ice cream or mascarpone.
	BANANA Bananas have a high sugar content compared to other fruits. Available all year round.	They are best eaten when the yellow skin is covered in faint brown speckles. Slice or mash, and serve with grated chocolate.
	PEAR Choose ripe juicy dessert pears, such as Conference, for eating raw. At their best in the autumn.	Serve with chocolate, or spices such as star anise and cinnamon. Rub with lemon juice once cut, to prevent discolouration.
	MELON Watermelon, honeydew, and cantaloupe are the most popular varieties. Available in the summer.	Halve and chop, and serve on its own, or as part of a mixed fruit salad. Once cut, they should be eaten as soon as possible.

STEP-BY-STEP

Prepare fruit How to prepare tricky fruits.

Orange
This technique is the quickest, easiest way to segment an orange, leaving the flesh pith-free.

1 With a sharp knife, slice away the top and bottom of the orange, then work around the fruit, slicing away the skin and pith.

2 Slice between each segment, leaving the thin layer of membrane behind until you have cut out all the segments.

Peach
Removing the skin from peaches and other soft fruit, such as nectarines and plums, is necessary for many desserts and sauces.

1 Starting at the base, make a cut crossways around the middle, just through the skin. Then repeat the cut in the other direction.

2 Place the fruit in a heatproof bowl and pour over boiling water. Remove with a slotted spoon, and – when cool – pull off the skin.

Mango
Cutting halves alongside the fibrous stone and "hedgehogging" the mango is the cleanest way to remove the flesh.

1 Standing the mango on its side, cut down each side of the mango, from stem to base, as close to the stone as you can.

2 Cut a crisscross pattern into the flesh of both pieces, but don't go all the way through. Invert the skin so the mango cubes pop up, then remove with a knife.

Pineapple
Take care when handling the sharp outer skin, and use the sharpest knife you can find as the inner core is tough.

1 Top and tail the pineapple. Stand it on its base, and slice the skin from the top down, all the way around the fruit.

2 Cut it in half lengthways, then slice away the fibrous core that runs through the centre of the fruit.

Pomegranate
This delicious Middle Eastern fruit has a tough skin and requires patience when preparing, but it's worth the effort.

1 Slice off the top of the pomegranate with a sharp knife. Slice into quarters.

2 The seeds are in clusters divided by a thin membrane. Pick out the seeds from each quarter.

Passion fruit
They may look impenetrable, but the pulp, juice, and seeds of this exotic fruit are surprisingly easy to extract.

1 With a sharp knife, cut the fruit in half, across the centre.

2 Using a spoon, scrape around the edge of the passion fruit to release the seeds from the membrane. Scoop out the pulp.

STEP-BY-STEP

FOOD FOR FRIENDS

Fruit fool You can use any soft fruit to whip up this quick and easy dessert.

1 Put 500g (1lb 2oz) of hulled strawberries (reserving a few for garnish) in a food processor, and whiz until puréed. Sieve in a little icing sugar to taste (depending on how sweet you like it).

2 Whip 600ml (1 pint) of double cream using a hand or electric whisk. Be careful not to over-beat, as it will spoil in seconds. It should form soft peaks when lifted from the bowl.

3 Sieve the puréed strawberries if you don't like the seeds, then add half the strawberry mixture to the cream, folding in gently until combined. Taste, and add a little more icing sugar if it is too tart.

4 Spoon some of the strawberry mixture into individual dishes, or one large glass dessert dish, then layer with the strawberry cream (fool) mixture, and continue layering until both mixtures have been used up. Instead of cream, you could use mascarpone or fromage frais.

4 storecupboard essentials With these ingredients on standby, you can jazz up a dessert in an instant.

CHOCOLATE
Any kind of chocolate is a must for the storecupboard, but dark is best. It can be grated, chopped, or curled over so many desserts. Try it sprinkled over a cardamom and chocolate mousse, or stir chunks through vanilla or coffee ice cream.

DRIED FRUITS
The ultimate standby. Choose sweet ready-to-eat fruits such as apricots, plump sultanas, prunes, or sour cherries. They taste great soaked in alcohol, or chopped and mixed into ice cream with a splash of rum. Serve with mascarpone, fromage frais, or Greek yogurt for an instant dessert.

NUTS
Buy ready-toasted nuts, such as hazelnuts, pre-chopped or whole. Mix a variety of nuts, if liked, or buy them pre-mixed. Scatter over ice cream desserts, sundaes, or fruits, or mix into Greek yoghurt with some runny honey.

SPICES
Cinnamon, nutmeg, and star anise all add an exotic touch to fruit salads, or sprinkled over ice cream. Soak in orange juice, and use in trifles or chocolate mousses.

STEP-BY-STEP

Cheesecake Add your own fruit and flavours to this simple basic recipe.

1 To make the base, put 250g (9oz) of digestive biscuits in a food processor and whiz until crumbled, or place in a plastic bag and bash with a rolling pin until crushed. Melt 140g (5oz) of butter and stir in the biscuit crumbs. Spoon into a 20cm (8in) round, loose-bottomed flan tin, and spread the biscuit mixture evenly and firmly into the base.

2 Put 3 teaspoons of powdered gelatine into a glass bowl, with the juice of 3–4 lemons, depending on how sharp you like your cheesecake. Stir in 1 teaspoon of water, and sit the bowl over a pan of simmering water. Stir until the gelatine dissolves. Add 50g (1¾oz) of caster sugar, and continue stirring until the sugar dissolves.

3 Make the topping by lightly whisking 400ml (14fl oz) of double cream, then adding 225g (8oz) of mascarpone, and 250g (9oz) of cream cheese. Add a couple of drops of vanilla extract, then pour in the gelatine mixture. Stir well to combine.

4 Carefully pour the mixture over the biscuit base, and smooth the top. Put in the refrigerator, and leave to set for about 2 hours, or overnight if you prefer. Make sure it is completely set before releasing it from the tin. Put on a serving plate or cake stand, and decorate with berries of your choice. Dust with icing sugar to serve.

Fridge and freezer essentials

Frozen yogurts make a healthy alternative to ice cream. Serve shop-bought, or make your own by blending fresh or frozen berries with Greek yogurt, and putting in the freezer until frozen.

Mascarpone and cream cheese are known as the principle ingredients of cheesecake, but can be used for all manner of instant no-cook desserts. Combine with fresh sliced fruit and honey, or a selection of storecupboard ingredients from p460.

Greek yogurt and fromage frais can be served as low fat alternatives to cream. Freshen with a few drops of elderflower cordial or fruit purée, or use instead of cream in the fool recipe on p460.

FOOD FOR FRIENDS

Orange and chocolate tiramisu

PREP 20 MINS

Chilling • 4 hours
Special equipment • electric hand whisk

SERVES 8
20–24 sponge fingers
200ml (7fl oz) orange juice
2 tbsp Grand Marnier or Cointreau
2 large eggs, separated
25g (scant 1oz) icing sugar, sifted
500g (1lb 2oz) mascarpone
finely grated zest of 1 orange
75g (2½oz) orange-flavoured
   chocolate, finely grated

1 Arrange the sponge fingers in the base of a shallow 2-litre (3½-pint) serving dish. Drizzle with the orange juice and Grand Marnier or Cointreau and set aside while the biscuits soak up the liquid.

2 Put the egg yolks and icing sugar in a large bowl and beat with a wooden spoon until smooth and creamy. Beat in the mascarpone until smooth. Put the egg whites in a mixing bowl and whisk with an electric hand whisk until soft peaks form. Fold into the mascarpone mixture, along with the orange zest.

3 Pour the mixture over the sponge fingers and smooth the top. Cover and chill for at least 4 hours or overnight. To serve, decorate with the grated chocolate.

VARIATION For a more traditional version of tiramisu, use coffee and brandy instead of the orange juice and Grand Marnier.

Cheat...
Dust with cocoa powder instead of grating the chocolate.

Meringue and mango mess

PREP 15 MINS

Chilling • 1 hour
Special equipment • electric hand whisk

SERVES 4
200ml (7fl oz) double cream or
   whipping cream
200g (7oz) Greek yogurt
2 tbsp icing sugar, or to taste, sifted
4 ready-bought meringue
   nests, crushed
1 medium mango, peeled and sliced
2 passion fruit
fresh mint leaves, to decorate (optional)

1 Place the cream in a large bowl and whisk lightly with an electric hand whisk until soft peaks form. Gently fold in the Greek yogurt and icing sugar, then fold in the meringue and mango. Divide the mixture between 4 serving glasses.

2 Scoop out the flesh and seeds from the passion fruit, drizzle over each glass, then chill in the refrigerator for an hour. Decorate with mint leaves (if using), and serve.

VARIATION Use 200g (7oz) summer berries, such as raspberries, blackberries, strawberries, and redcurrants, instead of the mango and passion fruit.

COOK'S NOTES
The longer you chill the desserts the softer the meringue will become, so don't refrigerate them for more than an hour if you'd like some crunch.

Blackcurrant jelly with vanilla cream

PREP
15
MINS

Chilling • 4 hours
Special equipment • electric hand whisk

SERVES 4

135g pack blackcurrant jelly
100ml (3½fl oz) double cream or
   whipping cream
¼ tsp vanilla extract
2 tbsp icing sugar, sifted
fresh mint leaves, to decorate
4 small sprigs of blackcurrants,
   to decorate (optional)

1 Chop the jelly into small pieces and place in a measuring jug. Pour over 300ml (10fl oz) boiling water and stir until the jelly has dissolved. Top up to 600ml (1 pint) with cold water or ice-cubes, stirring until the jelly has dissolved. Divide between 4 serving glasses and chill for at least 4 hours or overnight to set.

2 Put the cream, vanilla extract, and icing sugar in a bowl and whisk with an electric hand whisk until soft peaks form. Spoon the cream over the jellies, top each dessert with a mint leaf or two and a sprig of blackcurrants (if using), and serve.

VARIATION

To make an alcoholic version, simply reduce the water to 450ml (15fl oz) in total, and top up to 600ml (1 pint) with crème de cassis.

Cheat...
Top with clotted cream instead of the vanilla cream.

Tropical trifle

PREP
15
MINS

Chilling • 30 minutes
Special equipment • electric hand whisk

SERVES 6

250g (9oz) ready-made ginger
   cake, sliced
100ml (3½fl oz) pineapple juice
250g (9oz) finely chopped
   fresh pineapple
300ml (10fl oz) double cream or
   whipping cream
2–3 tbsp syrup from a jar of
   stem ginger
2 balls stem ginger in syrup,
   finely chopped

1 Line the base of a serving bowl with the slices of ginger cake, then pour over the pineapple juice, and scatter over the pineapple.

2 Put the cream and ginger syrup in a mixing bowl and whisk with an electric hand whisk until soft peaks form. Spoon the mixture over the pineapple, then scatter over the chopped stem ginger. Chill in the refrigerator for 30 minutes, then serve.

VARIATION

Use mango or banana instead of the pineapple, or a mixture of all three.

FOOD FOR FRIENDS

Strawberry and raspberry granita

Freeze • 4 hours
Special equipment • food processor

SERVES 6
125g (4½oz) icing sugar
1 tbsp lemon juice
250g (9oz) raspberries
250g (9oz) strawberries, hulled
single cream, to serve (optional)

1 Put the icing sugar and lemon juice in a food processor with 150ml (5fl oz) boiling water and whiz until the sugar has all dissolved. Add the raspberries and strawberries, and whiz to a purée.

2 Transfer the mixture to a shallow freezerproof plastic container, cover, and place in the freezer for 4 hours. Remove from the freezer every 2 hours and stir with a fork, breaking the mixture up into small pieces. When the mixture has completely broken up into frozen, gravelly pieces, leave in the freezer until ready to serve. It will keep for up to 1 month. Serve straight from the freezer on its own, or with a drizzle of single cream (if using).

> **COOK'S NOTES**
>
> *If you prefer, you can sieve the purée before freezing to remove the seeds.*

Boozy berries with mint and elderflower cream

Chilling • 30 minutes
Special equipment • electric hand whisk

SERVES 4-6
450g (1lb) mixed summer berries, such as strawberries, blackberries, raspberries, and redcurrants
150ml (5fl oz) crème de cassis or sweet dessert wine
200ml (7fl oz) double cream or whipping cream
1 tbsp fresh mint leaves, finely chopped
1-2 tbsp elderflower cordial, depending on taste

1 Put the berries in a shallow serving dish, pour over the cassis or sweet wine, then chill for 30 minutes, or overnight, stirring now and again.

2 Put the cream in a mixing bowl and whisk with an electric hand whisk until soft peaks form. Fold in the mint and elderflower cordial, and serve with the berries.

Lemon and lime syllabub

PREP 15 MINS

Chilling • 30 minutes

SERVES 4
juice of 1 lemon
juice of ½ lime
1 tbsp gin or vodka
4–5 tbsp caster sugar
300ml (10fl oz) double cream
finely grated lemon zest and lime
zest, to decorate (optional)

1 Mix the lemon juice and lime juice in a bowl, add the gin or vodka and sugar, and stir until the sugar starts to dissolve. Pour in the cream and whisk with a balloon whisk until the mixture forms soft peaks.

2 Spoon into 4 serving glasses, then chill in the refrigerator for 30 minutes. Decorate with lemon zest and lime zest (if using), and serve with small thin biscuits or little shortbread rounds.

FOOD FOR FRIENDS

Lime cheesecakes

PREP 10 MINS

Chilling • 4 hours
Special equipment • 4 x 175ml (6fl oz) ramekins or similar • electric hand whisk

SERVES 4
4 biscuits, such as hobnobs
   or digestives
200g (7oz) soft cream cheese,
   at room temperature
200g (7oz) condensed milk
finely grated zest and juice of
   2 limes, plus extra zest to
   decorate (optional)

1 Line the base of each ramekin with a biscuit. Put the cream cheese in a mixing bowl and whisk with an electric hand whisk until smooth, then whisk in the condensed milk until well combined.

2 Add the juice and lime zest and whisk until the mixture becomes smooth, thick, and glossy. Divide among the ramekins and smooth the tops. Chill for at least 4 hours, or overnight. Decorate with the extra lime zest (if using), and serve.

COOK'S NOTES

The biscuit base does soften as it chills, but if you prefer to crumb the biscuit and mix it with a little butter melted in the microwave, this will make a softer base.

FOOD FOR FRIENDS

Middle Eastern oranges

PREP
15
MINS

SERVES 4

4 oranges
1–2 tbsp clear honey
2 tbsp rosewater
good pinch of ground cinnamon
seeds from 1 pomegranate
small handful of chopped
   pistachio nuts (optional)
handful of fresh mint leaves,
   to decorate

1 Slice the top and bottom from each orange and place them on a chopping board. Carefully slice off the skin and pith, leaving as much flesh as possible and following the sides of the orange so you keep the shape of the fruit. Slice the oranges thinly horizontally, discarding any pips as you come across them, then arrange the orange slices on a serving plate. Drizzle with any juice from the chopping board.

2 Drizzle with the honey and rose-water and sprinkle with the cinnamon. Scatter with the pomegranate seeds and pistachio nuts (if using), then decorate with the mint leaves and serve.

Cheat...

Pomegranates can be fiddly to deseed. A 120g pack of pomegranate seeds is a handy shortcut.

Banoffee pie

PREP
15
MINS

Special equipment • electric hand whisk

SERVES 8

20cm ready-made tart case
200g (7oz) ready-made thick caramel
   sauce (such as Dulce de leche)
2–3 ripe bananas
300ml (10fl oz) double cream or
   whipping cream
25g (scant 1oz) dark chocolate

1 Place the tart case on a serving plate. Spoon in the caramel sauce and spread evenly. Slice the bananas and scatter over the top.

2 Put the cream in a bowl and whisk with an electric hand whisk until soft peaks form, then spoon over the bananas. Grate the chocolate over the top and serve.

Melon with vodka, orange, and mint

PREP
15
MINS

Marinating • 15 minutes

SERVES 6-8

1 honeydew melon, cut in quarters
    lengthways, rind and seeds
    removed, and flesh sliced
1 watermelon, cut in half, rind and
    seeds removed, and flesh sliced
1-2 tbsp good-quality vodka
1-2 tbsp fresh orange juice
    without bits
handful of fresh mint leaves,
    roughly torn

1 Arrange the melon slices in a large
flat serving bowl or platter, drizzle
with the vodka and orange juice, then
leave to sit for 15 minutes while the
fruit absorbs the juices.

2 Sprinkle with the mint and serve.

VARIATION
You can use any kind of
melon, but always try and
include watermelon, which
will absorb the vodka.

COOK'S NOTES

Use melons that are only just
ripe – they'll still have a bit
of bite to them.

Knickerbocker glory

PREP
15
MINS

Special equipment • food processor, stick
blender, or electric hand whisk

SERVES 2

200g (7oz) strawberries, hulled
drizzle of strawberry liqueur,
    or other liqueur of your choice
150ml (5fl oz) double cream
2 slices plain sponge cake
6 scoops good-quality vanilla
    ice cream
50g (1¾oz) blanched almonds,
    roughly chopped

1 Roughly slice the strawberries,
reserving 2 whole ones. Put the sliced
ones in a bowl, drizzle with liqueur,
then whiz with a stick blender until
just puréed. Alternatively, use a food
processor and pulse. Whisk the cream
with a hand whisk till soft peaks form.

2 Sit the sponge cake slices neatly
in the base of two tall dessert

glasses, then spoon over 1 tablespoon
strawberry sauce. Add a scoop of
ice cream, followed by a spoonful
of whipped cream. Add another
drizzle of strawberry sauce, then
continue building up in layers,
ending with ice cream at the top.
Sprinkle with nuts and top with
the reserved strawberries.

VARIATION
For an ultra-indulgent
dessert, drizzle over
some warm chocolate
sauce to serve.

COOK'S NOTES

Be careful not to over-whisk the
cream or it will separate. If you're
making the dessert for children,
omit the liqueur.

Vanilla ice cream with coffee drizzle

PREP
10
MINS

VARIATION
Sprinkle with some chopped blanched almonds for added texture.

SERVES 2
6 scoops of good-quality vanilla
   ice cream
2 single or double espressos
pinch of demerara sugar (optional)

1 Remove the ice cream from the freezer and let it soften slightly.

2 Serve 3 scoops of ice cream into two dessert bowls. Sweeten the coffee with sugar (if using), then pour it over the ice cream and serve immediately.

COOK'S NOTES

For an instant mocha dessert, use chocolate ice cream. If you're serving the dessert in a glass dish, be sure it can withstand the heat of the coffee.

Marinated prunes and apricots

PREP
10
MINS

Marinate • several hours

SERVES 4
175g (6oz) ready-to-eat
   prunes, stoned
175g (6oz) ready-to-eat soft
   dried apricots
3 tbsp sweet dessert wine or Marsala
zest of 1 orange
ricotta, to serve

1 Chop the dried fruit into bite-sized pieces, place in a bowl, then drizzle with the dessert wine or Marsala. Leave to marinate for several hours, or overnight, so the fruit softens and absorbs the alcohol.

2 Decorate with orange zest and serve with dollops of ricotta.

VARIATION
Use the dried fruit of your choice, such as golden raisins, cranberries, or delicious sweet cherries.

COOK'S NOTES

Don't use dried fruit that's past its best, as it won't soak up the alcohol.

Grapes marinated in port

 PREP 10 MINS

Marinate • several hours

SERVES 4
1 bunch of seedless red grapes
1 bunch of seedless green grapes
drizzle of good-quality port
vanilla ice cream, to serve

1 Prick the grapes with a knife, then place them in a large shallow serving dish and drizzle with port. Leave to marinate in the refrigerator for several hours or overnight.

2 To serve, bring to room temperature, then spoon into glass dishes and top with a scoop of vanilla ice cream.

 VARIATION
For a lighter dessert, use a drizzle of white port instead.

Fresh figs with cassis cream

 PREP 15 MINS

SERVES 4
12 plump fresh figs
drizzle of crème de cassis
200g tub mascarpone

1 Make a cross in the top of each fig (but don't cut all the way to the bottom), then gently prise it open. Place 3 figs in each of 4 dessert dishes and drizzle with crème de cassis.

2 Mix the mascarpone with a drizzle of cassis and stir gently until lightly marbled. Add a spoonful of mascarpone to each dish and serve.

 VARIATION
You can also serve this dish hot. Sit the figs in an ovenproof dish and drizzle with cassis. Cover with foil and bake in an oven preheated to 190°C (375°F/ Gas 5) fo 15 minutes or until softened and oozing. Serve with cassis cream.

COOK'S NOTES

Cassis is a delicious blackcurrant liqueur that will jazz up many desserts. Keep a bottle in your storecupboard. Serve this dessert when figs are in season and at their best.

Peaches with meringue and raspberry sauce

PREP
15
MINS

Special equipment • stick blender

SERVES 4
175g (6oz) raspberries
4 meringue shells
4 ripe peaches, stoned and roughly
    chopped or sliced
zest of 1 lime, to decorate
single cream, to serve

1 Put the raspberries in a bowl, then whiz with a stick blender. Pass them through a sieve so you have a smooth purée.

2 Break the meringues up with your hands, then scatter the pieces in one large shallow serving dish or 4 individual ones. Top with the peaches, then spoon over the raspberry purée and decorate with lime zest. Serve with a drizzle of cream.

VARIATION

Decorate with lemon zest instead of lime.

Cheat...

Use 2 tablespoons of ready-made raspberry purée. It's a great standby that can jazz up desserts in an instant.

COOK'S NOTES

You can make the raspberry purée up to a day ahead. Keep it in the refrigerator until required.

Dark chocolate and white chocolate mousse

PREP
15
MINS

Setting • 3 hours
Special equipment • electric hand whisk

SERVES 4
125g (4½oz) good-quality
    dark chocolate
125g (4½oz) good-quality
    white chocolate
4 large eggs

1 Break the dark chocolate and the white chocolate up into pieces and place in two separate microwaveproof bowls. Place in the microwave one at a time on Medium for 1–2 minutes or until the chocolate has melted. Stir gently until smooth. If you don't have a microwave, melt the chocolate pieces in a glass bowl over a pan of simmering water.

2 Separate the eggs, adding 2 yolks to each bowl of chocolate, and stirring to combine. Whisk the egg whites with an electric hand whisk until light fluffy peaks form. Fold half into the dark chocolate, stirring for

a couple of minutes until the mixture is well-combined. Fold the other half into the white chocolate, and stir well.

3 Divide the chocolate mixtures among 4 individual glass dishes, spooning them in in layers, and finishing with a dark chocolate top. Place in the refrigerator to set for at least 3 hours, ideally overnight.

COOK'S NOTES

Chocolate is sensitive to heating, especially white chocolate, and can scorch or go grainy – in which case, you've lost it. Check the microwave frequently after about 30 seconds, then keep a constant eye on it. Use large eggs. If you only have small ones, increase the quantity to 6.

Apricots with Amaretti biscuits and mascarpone

**PREP
15
MINS**

SERVES 4
8 Amaretti biscuits
200g tub mascarpone
16 ripe apricots, halved and stoned
handful of blanched almonds, halved

1 Lightly crush the Amaretti biscuits with a rolling pin then divide among 4 individual glass dishes. Lightly whip the mascarpone with a wooden spoon until thickened.

2 Layer the apricots and mascarpone on top of the Amaretti biscuits, finishing with a layer of mascarpone. Sprinkle with the almonds and serve.

Use ripe peaches instead of apricots.

Cheat...
Buy ready-toasted chopped nuts and scatter over the apricots to serve.

Chocolate truffles

**PREP
15
MINS**

Cooling • 30 minutes
Setting • 30 minutes

MAKES 12–14
125g (4½oz) good-quality dark chocolate plus 25g (scant 1oz) good-quality dark chocolate, finely grated
drizzle of Baileys Irish Cream or brandy
25g (scant 1oz) Brazil nuts, finely chopped
50g (1¾oz) dried cherries, chopped

1 Break the whole chocolate into pieces and place in a microwaveproof bowl. Microwave on Medium for 1–2 minutes or until melted, then stir until smooth. Stir in the Baileys or brandy, then add the nuts and cherries.

2 Leave to cool for 30 minutes, then scoop up a generous teaspoonful and form into a ball. Roll in the grated chocolate, then place on greaseproof paper for 30 minutes or until set. Repeat with the rest of the chocolate mixture. Serve as a sweet treat with coffee.

Roll the chocolates in finely chopped toasted almonds or grated white chocolate instead.

471

Oriental fruit salad

PREP 15 MINS

SERVES 4

1 mango, peeled and sliced
1 pineapple, topped, tailed, skin
    removed, and sliced
1 kiwi fruit, skinned and sliced
juice of 1 orange
juice of 1 lime
1 passion fruit, halved
small handful of fresh mint leaves,
    finely chopped

1 Arrange the mango, pineapple, and
kiwi fruit in a shallow serving bowl or
platter. Pour over the orange juice and
lime juice.

2 Scoop out the flesh and seeds
from the passion fruit and spoon over
the fruit. Sprinkle with mint leaves
and serve.

Mixed berry flan

PREP 10 MINS

Freeze • base before filling

SERVES 6

3–4 scoops soft chocolate ice cream
3–4 scoops soft vanilla ice cream
20cm (8in) round plain sponge base
500g (1lb 2oz) mixed summer berries,
    such as raspberries, blackberries,
    strawberries, and redcurrants
drizzle of crème de cassis or other
    liqueur of your choice (optional)

1 Spoon the ice cream onto the
sponge base, then pile on the fruit.

2 Drizzle over the crème de cassis
or other liqueur (if using), and serve.

VARIATION
Use a chocolate sponge base
instead of the plain one.

Dark chocolate and lemon mousse

PREP 15 MINS

Setting • 3 hours
Special equipment • electric hand whisk

SERVES 4
125g (4½oz) good-quality
   dark chocolate
3 tbsp Limoncello liqueur
2 large or 3 small eggs

1 Break the chocolate into pieces and place in a microwaveproof bowl. Microwave on Medium for 1–2 minutes, or until melted, then stir until glossy and smooth. Stir in the Limoncello.

2 Separate the eggs, then place the egg whites in a bowl and whisk with an electric hand whisk until soft peaks form. Add the egg yolks to the chocolate mixture and stir to combine. Fold in the egg whites and beat for a couple of minutes until smooth. Allow to cool.

3 Spoon into 4 glass serving dishes or ramekins and put in the refrigerator to set for at least 3 hours or overnight.

VARIATION
Use brandy instead of Limoncello.

COOK'S NOTES
This contains raw eggs, so is best avoided by children and the elderly.

FOOD FOR FRIENDS

Lychees with ginger and star anise

PREP 10 MINS

Marinating • 30 minutes

SERVES 4
400ml can lychees, drained
   (2 tsp juice reserved)
1 star anise
2 balls stem ginger plus 2 tbsp
   ginger syrup
Greek yogurt, to serve

1 Arrange the lychees and star anise in a glass serving dish. Finely dice the balls of ginger, and scatter over the lychees. Mix the ginger syrup with the reserved lychee juice and drizzle over.

2 Place in the refrigerator for 30 minutes, or longer if you have the time, for the flavours to develop. Serve with dollops of Greek yogurt.

COOK'S NOTES
Star anise has a subtle and fragrant aniseed flavour that goes very well with ginger.

473

FREEZE-AHEAD DESSERTS

Tarts, ice creams, cakes, and treats to make
well ahead of the party.

FREEZE-AHEAD DESSERTS

Making use of the freezer is an economical way of cooking. It saves on time and fuel, and nothing beats having ready-made desserts and puddings to hand for family dinners or unexpected guests. Not only is it convenient, but when home-baking puddings and desserts you can also be assured of the contents, avoiding any hidden ingredients so often found in shop-bought ones.

Psst...

For batch cooking to be efficient, you need to plan ahead. Put a few hours to one side to make a selection of puddings and desserts for the freezer. Use seasonal fruits when they are in abundance, to make desserts, ice creams, pies, and crumbles. Or simply freeze fruit for later use (see p477).

Desserts and puddings Bake, stock the freezer, and defrost when ready to use.

	STORE	DEFROST		STORE	DEFROST
	CAKES **Sponge cake** Freeze unfilled. Double-wrap in cling film then foil. Freeze for up to **3 months**. **Iced sponge cake** Butter icing freezes well. Open-freeze, wrap in foil, and double-wrap in cling film. Freeze for up to **2 months**. **Fruitcake** Double-wrap in cling film and foil. Freeze for up to **3 months**. **Iced fruitcake** Double-wrap in cling film and foil. Freeze for up to **3 months**.	**Sponge cake** Leave in wrapping. **Iced sponge cake** Unwrap before defrosting. Thaw both at room temperature. **Fruitcake** Thaw in the refrigerator. **Iced fruit cake** Unwrap before defrosting. Thaw at room temperature.		**SPONGE PUDDINGS** Wrap in foil, then double-wrap in cling film. Freeze for up to **3 months**.	Remove cling film, top with a round of greaseproof paper, and steam from frozen for about 2 hours, or until heated through.
	CHOCOLATE DESSERTS Prepare chocolate desserts in freezerproof containers. Double-wrap in cling film. Freeze for up to **2 months**.	Thaw in the refrigerator overnight.		**MERINGUES** Freeze in sealable plastic bags, unfilled. Meringues do toughen slightly when frozen. You can freeze egg whites. Freeze for up to **1 month**.	Thaw at room temperature.
	PASTRIES, TARTS, AND PIES **Cooked pastries, tarts, and pies** Custard fillings don't freeze well, but fruit fillings do. Double-wrap in cling film then foil. Freeze for up to **3 months**. **Uncooked pastries, tarts, and pies** Double-wrap your lined tin/rolled out pastry (filled, or unfilled) in cling film then foil. Freeze for **1–2 months**.	**Cooked pastries, tarts, and pies** Thaw at room temperature. **Uncooked pastries, tarts, and pies** Thaw unfilled in refrigerator overnight. Cook filled from frozen at 180°C (350°F/Gas 4) for 20–30 minutes.		**BISCUITS** **Cooked biscuits** Freeze in sealable freezer bags. Freeze for up to **1 month**. **Uncooked dough** Freeze in a ball, or balls, or pre-shape. Double-wrap in cling film. Freeze for up to **1 month**.	**Cooked biscuits** Thaw, and warm in the oven at 190°C (375°F/Gas 5) for about 5 minutes, to crispen up. **Uncooked dough** Thaw, shape, and bake. Bake ready-shaped from frozen at 190°C (375°F/Gas 5), for 5 minutes longer than recipe.
	CRUMBLES Use a freezerproof and ovenproof dish. Prepare fruit and top with crumble mixture. Allow to cool, double-wrap in cling film and foil. Freeze for up to **2 months**.	Cook from frozen at 200°C (400°F/Gas 6), for 30–40 minutes, until golden and cooked through.		**CHEESECAKE** **Uncooked** Open-freeze, then double-wrap in cling film. Don't freeze cooked cheesecake. Freeze for up to **2 months**.	Thaw in the refrigerator overnight.

FOOD FOR FRIENDS

Freeze fruit

Choose

Freeze fruits at their peak, preferably when they're in season.

If fruit or berries are past their best, put them in the blender and whiz until smooth. Sieve, if needed, then pack in plastic sealable containers and freeze, or freeze in ice-cube trays and when frozen transfer to a plastic bag and use as required (see below). Use as a sauce or pie filling.

Watermelons don't freeze well.

Bananas can be frozen in their skins if they have become too overripe for eating. The skins will turn black but the flesh will be excellent to use in puddings and cakes.

Prepare

Always pick through fruit first, discarding any that are bruised, then wash in iced cold water, drain well, and dry thoroughly. Don't leave fruit to soak in water, or it will lose its flavour. Apples, pears, peaches, apricots, and nectarines discolour once sliced, and tend to turn brown while they thaw. To prevent discolouration here are a few tips.

Freeze in a sugar syrup This is just a mix of water and sugar, brought to the boil then left to cool. Slice the fruit into wedges or other desired size, pack into sealable plastic bags or boxes, then pour over the mixture to cover completely, seal, and freeze. Allow about 300ml (10fl oz) of water for every 450g (1lb) of fruit. Apples and pears may need to be soaked in lemon juice first, see below.

Freeze in fruit juice For ease, cut fruit – chopped or sliced apples and pears, for example – can be soaked and packed in fruit juice, such as apple juice, then frozen.

Soak in lemon juice Before freezing cut apples and pears, soak in a mixture of water and lemon juice before packing in sugar syrup or fruit juice. Allow 3 tablespoons of lemon juice for every 150ml (5fl oz) of water.

Steam Steaming the fruit for a few minutes before packing will prevent the fruit from turning brown.

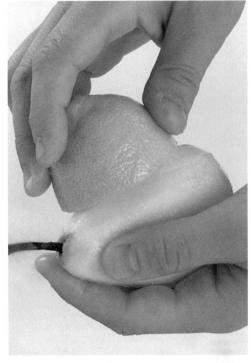

Rubbing cut or peeled fruit with half a lemon prevents the surface turning brown.

STEP-BY-STEP

Freeze soft fruit Freeze fruit when it is at its best, and unblemished.

1 Spread the fruit on a tray covered in greaseproof paper and put in the freezer to open-freeze until frozen.

2 Once frozen, pack into sealable freezer bags (the fruit will now stay separate and not stick together) and put back in the freezer. Freeze for up to 1 year.

freezing tips

A full freezer uses less energy than a half-full or empty one. If you plan to use your freezer a lot, a chest freezer is more efficient than an upright one.

Check the temperature of your freezer: it should be 0°F or lower.

Smaller portions will thaw quicker so don't over-pack batches of cakes.

Never put warm foods into the freezer. Allow to cool completely first.

Defrost puddings and desserts overnight in the refrigerator, if at all possible.

Use natural flavourings in desserts rather than artificial ones, so the flavour will be retained.

STEP-BY-STEP

FOOD FOR FRIENDS

Easy ice cream without a machine

A creamy vanilla ice cream that doesn't require churning.

1 Split two vanilla pods and scrape out the seeds, keeping them for later. Add the pods to a pan with 500ml (16fl oz) double cream, and bring to the boil. Add 75g (2½oz) golden caster sugar, and stir until dissolved.

2 In a bowl, whisk 4 egg yolks until well combined, then strain the warm cream mixture into the eggs, stirring all the time. Add the reserved vanilla seeds, and stir.

3 Pour the ice-cream mixture into a metal loaf tin or plastic tub. Leave to cool completely.

4 Once cool, put into the freezer. When frozen, double-wrap with cling film and freeze for up to 3 months.

Ice cream flavours

Ginger and honey A heavenly combination of soothing flavours, perfect served with a slice of sticky walnut or pecan pie.

Mocha For chocoholics and coffee lovers. Stir chunky or chopped dark chocolate through the ice cream to add texture.

Cherry and Amaretto Sophisticated flavours for the grown-ups. Ideal for entertaining.

Strawberry and elderflower The very essence of summer. Simply whiz up the strawberries with a drizzle of elderflower juice, and serve on a hot day.

Rum and raisin The classic flavours are always a favourite. Enjoy it scooped into a cone or serve along side a piece of home-baked cake.

Mint A simple but refreshing ice cream that requires just a few drops of natural mint extract, add some chocolate chunks also if you wish.

The ice cream should be a smooth consistency, with no ice crystals. Take it out of the freezer for 10 minutes, to soften before serving.

STEP-BY-STEP

Fruit sorbet

Lighter than ice cream: a perfect palate cleanser. You can use any berries.

1 Combine 75g (2½oz) of sugar in a pan with 60ml (2fl oz) water. Simmer gently for 5–10 minutes, until the sugar has dissolved, and the mixture has thickened.

2 Put 1kg (2¼lb) of strawberries in a food processor, and whiz until puréed. (You can pass it through a sieve to remove the seeds, if you wish.) Pour the syrup mixture into the puréed strawberries and stir.

3 Pour the mixture into a freezerproof container, the shallower the better (it will freeze quicker). Leave to cool completely, then put into the freezer.

4 When frozen, remove and stir well to break up any ice crystals, then put back into the freezer. Sorbet is best eaten within a few days, as the fresh fruit taste starts to fade after a while.

Sorbet flavours

Blood orange and Campari An impressive palate cleanser, ideal for entertaining.

Strawberry and balsamic An unusual combination – balsamic vinegar really brings out the intense flavour of the fruit.

Raspberry Use fresh or frozen raspberries for this colourful sorbet, and sieve the seeds before freezing, if you like.

Lemon and lime Tart and refreshing: perfect for a hot summer's day.

Mango This fruit will create smooth-textured sorbet. Serve with other tropical fruit, diced.

Passion fruit You will need at least a dozen passion fruit to make enough sorbet to serve 4. Remove the seeds before freezing.

Serve fruit sorbets on their own, or alongside a freeze-ahead tart made with the same fruit.

FOOD FOR FRIENDS

Mocha pots

PREP 30 MINS

Special equipment • electric hand whisk or mixer • 6 x 150ml (5fl oz) or 8 x 125ml (4fl oz) freezeproof ramekins

MAKES 6-8

150g (5½oz) dark chocolate, broken into pieces, plus a little extra, shaved with a potato peeler, to decorate (optional)

25g (scant 1oz) butter

4 large eggs, at room temperature, separated

salt

75g (2½oz) caster sugar

3 tbsp cold strong coffee

150ml (5fl oz) double cream or whipping cream

cocoa powder, to dust for serving

1 In a bowl set over a pan of simmering water, melt the chocolate with the butter, stirring now and again until smooth. Set aside and leave to cool to room temperature. Meanwhile, place the egg whites with a pinch of salt in a bowl and whisk with an electric hand whisk until stiff peaks form. Whisk in the sugar 1 tablespoon at a time until the mixture is stiff and shiny.

2 Stir the egg yolks into the cooled chocolate mixture one at a time. Fold the egg-white mixture into the chocolate mixture a big spoonful at a time, then stir in the coffee. Spoon the mixture evenly into the ramekins or small cups, leaving room for some whipped cream. Place the cream in a bowl and whisk with an electric hand whisk until soft peaks form. Spoon the cream over the top of the mocha pots, then freeze until solid. Wrap in cling film or foil, and return to the freezer.

3 To serve, defrost overnight in the refrigerator, or for a few hours at room temperature. Dust with cocoa powder and decorate with chocolate shavings (if using).

Cheat...
Use coffee-flavoured chocolate, leaving out the coffee.

Pear and mincemeat pie

PREP 15 MINS **COOK 40 MINS**

SERVES 8-10

400g (14oz) mincemeat

1 tbsp brandy

zest of 1 orange

425g packet puff pastry, rolled out into two sheets 28 x 20cm (11 x 8in)

25g (scant 1oz) ground almonds

1 ripe pear, peeled, cored, and thinly sliced

beaten egg, to glaze

1 In a bowl, mix the mincemeat with the brandy and orange zest. Lay one sheet of pastry on a baking tray, then scatter over the ground almonds, leaving a 2cm (¾in) border around the edges. Spoon the mincemeat mixture over the ground almonds, top with the pear, then brush the border with beaten egg. Carefully

place the second sheet of pastry on top of the first. Press the edges together, pinching the sides with your finger and thumb to decorate them. Make a few slashes on the top with a knife for the steam to escape. Open-freeze on the baking tray until firm, remove then wrap the whole thing in a double layer of cling film or foil, and freeze.

2 To serve, defrost overnight in the refrigerator. Preheat the oven to 200°C (400°F/Gas 6). Carefully transfer the pie to a lightly greased baking tray. Brush the pastry with beaten egg and bake for 30-40 minutes, or until golden brown and cooked through.

VARIATION

Use the zest of a lemon instead of the orange zest.

Almond and peach tart

PREP 20 MINS | COOK 30 MINS

Special equipment • electric hand whisk or mixer • tin 12 x 36cm (5 x 14½in)

SERVES 8

250g (7oz) ready-made
  shortcrust pastry
100g (3½oz) butter, at
  room temperature
100g (3½oz) caster sugar
2 large eggs
100g (3½oz) ground almonds
25g (scant 1oz) plain flour, plus
  extra to dust
4 peaches, halved and stoned
icing sugar, to dust for serving

1 Preheat the oven to 200°C (400°F/ Gas 6). Put a baking tray in the oven to heat up. On a surface lightly dusted with flour, roll out the pastry to a thickness of about 5mm (¼in), then use to line the tin. Trim off the excess pastry with a knife and set the tart case to one side while you make the filling.

2 Place the butter and sugar in a bowl and whisk with an electric hand whisk until creamy, then beat in the eggs. Mix in the ground almonds and flour until well combined, then smooth into the pastry case. Press the peach halves cut-side down into the almond mixture. Sit the tin on the hot baking tray, then bake for 30 minutes or until the almond mixture is golden brown and cooked through. Leave to cool completely, then wrap the tin in cling film and foil, and freeze.

3 To serve, defrost in the refrigerator overnight. Serve cold, or warm through, in an oven preheated to 180°C (350°F/Gas 4) for 20 minutes, or until hot. Dust with icing sugar before serving.

VARIATION

Use other soft fruit such as plums, nectarines, apricots, or summer berries, instead of the peaches.

Apricot meringue roulade

PREP 30 MINS | COOK 20 MINS

Special equipment • electric hand whisk or mixer • Swiss roll tin 32.5 x 23cm (13 x 9in)

SERVES 8

4 large egg whites
salt
225g (8oz) caster sugar
25g (scant 1oz) flaked almonds
icing sugar, to dust
300ml (10fl oz) double cream
400g can apricot halves (240g
  drained weight)
seeds and pulp from 2 passion fruits

1 Preheat the oven to 190°C (375°F/ Gas 5). Line the Swiss roll tin with baking parchment. Place the egg whites in a bowl with a pinch of salt and whisk with an electric hand whisk until soft peaks form. Whisk in the sugar 1 tablespoon at a time until the mixture is stiff and shiny. Spoon into the Swiss roll tin and smooth into the corners. Scatter the flaked almonds over the top, then bake for 15-20 minutes, or until just firm to the touch and golden.

Turn the meringue out on to a sheet of baking parchment dusted with icing sugar, and leave to cool.

2 Meanwhile, place the cream in a bowl and whisk with an electric hand whisk until soft peaks form. Spread the cream over the meringue, then scatter over the apricots and passion fruit seeds. Roll the meringue up, starting from one short end and using the parchment to help you. Wrap tightly in the baking parchment, cover with foil, and freeze.

3 To serve the roulade, unwrap it from the foil and baking parchment, and place on a serving plate. Defrost overnight in the refrigerator, or for a few hours at room temperature. When ready to serve, dust with a little more icing sugar.

VARIATION

Use 250g (9oz) raspberries or blueberries instead of the apricots.

Mini summer puddings

 PREP 30 MINS COOK 10 MINS

Special equipment • 6 pudding basins 200ml (7fl oz)

MAKES 6

about 9 slices white bread, crusts removed

700g (1lb 9oz) mixed summer berries and currants

75g (2½oz) caster sugar, or to taste

icing sugar, to dust (optional)

1 Line the six pudding basins with the bread. You will probably find you need two halves to line the sides, a quarter to fit the base, and – once you have added the fruit – another quarter or two to fit the top. Make sure the basins are well lined – you don't want any gaps or the puddings could collapse when you turn them out.

2 Put the fruit in a pan with the caster sugar and 250ml (8fl oz) water. Bring to the boil, stirring until the sugar dissolves. Simmer gently for 5 minutes, or until the berries start to soften and release their juices. Test for sweetness and add a little more sugar if needed. Spoon some of the juice into the basins so the bread starts to soak it up. Divide the berries among the basins, pushing them down so you can pack in as

many as possible and letting the bread absorb the juice – you do not want any white bread showing when you turn the puddings out. Cover the tops of the berries with the remaining bread, then spoon over the last of the juice until no white bread is visible. Leave to cool. Cover each basin tightly with cling film and freeze.

3 To serve, defrost overnight in the refrigerator or for a few hours at room temperature. Turn out onto

VARIATION

For richer puddings, use brioche instead of bread.

COOK'S NOTES

The exact amount of fruit you need will depend on the size of the berries and currants you use, and how juicy they are, but remember to pack in as many as you can so the puddings do not collapse. Enjoy any leftover berries with some Greek yogurt as the cook's perk.

Sticky toffee puddings

 PREP 20 MINS COOK 25 MINS

Special equipment • blender • electric hand whisk or mixer • 8 pudding basins 200ml (7fl oz)

MAKES 8

200g (7oz) stoned dates (medjool are best)

1 tsp bicarbonate of soda

225g (8oz) self-raising flour

125g (4½oz) butter, at room temperature

175g (6oz) dark or light soft brown sugar

3 large eggs

For the toffee sauce

150g (5½oz) dark or light soft brown sugar

75g (2½oz) butter, cubed

150ml (5fl oz) double cream or whipping cream

salt

single cream, to serve (optional)

1 Preheat the oven to 190°C (375°F/ Gas 5). Butter the eight pudding basins. In a small pan, simmer the dates with the bicarbonate of soda and 200ml (7fl oz) water for 5 minutes until softened. Purée with the cooking liquid in a blender.

2 Sift the flour into a mixing bowl, add the butter, sugar, and eggs, and whisk with an electric hand whisk or mixer until well combined, then mix in the date purée. Pour the mixture into

the pudding basins, then place them on a baking tray. Bake for 20–25 minutes, or until firm to the touch. Meanwhile, make the toffee sauce. Melt the sugar, butter, and cream together in a pan until smooth and combined. Stir in a pinch of salt and allow to boil for a few minutes. Leave the sauce and puddings to cool.

3 Carefully remove the puddings from their tins, using a knife to ease them from the sides. Transfer to a large plastic freezer bag and freeze. Pour the sauce into a small plastic container, cover, and freeze.

4 To serve, defrost the sauce and puddings overnight in the refrigerator. Place the puddings on a baking tray and warm through in an oven preheated to 180°C (350°F/Gas 4) for 15–20 minutes. Warm the sauce in a small pan until gently bubbling. Serve the warm puddings with the hot toffee sauce and some single cream, if you like.

Cheat...

Use a ready-made shop-bought toffee sauce instead, warming it through just before serving.

Blackberry and apple sponge

PREP 20 MINS   COOK 50 MINS

Special equipment • electric hand whisk or mixer • 1.2-litre (2-pint) ovenproof freezerproof dish

SERVES 6

125g (4½oz) butter, at room temperature
125g (4½oz) caster sugar
2 large eggs
175g (6oz) self-raising flour, sifted
2 Bramley apples, peeled, cored, and roughly chopped
250g (9oz) blackberries
2 tbsp caster sugar
icing sugar, to dust (optional)

1 Preheat the oven to 180°C (350°F/ Gas 4). In a bowl, mix the butter and sugar together with an electric hand whisk or mixer until pale and creamy. Beat in the eggs one at a time, adding 1 tablespoon of the flour after each egg. Mix in the remaining flour and set aside. Put the apple and blackberries in the ovenproof freezerproof dish, then stir in the caster sugar along with 2 tablespoons cold water. Spoon the sponge mixture over the top, and smooth the surface.

2 Bake for 50 minutes, or until golden brown and firm to the touch – a skewer inserted into the sponge should come out clean. Leave to cool completely, then wrap in foil, and freeze.

3 To serve, defrost in the refrigerator overnight, then warm through in an oven preheated to 180°C (350°F/ Gas 4) for about 30 minutes, or until hot. Dust with icing sugar (if using), before serving.

VARIATION
Replace 25g (scant 1oz) of the flour with cocoa powder and put the mixture on top of poached pears.

Apple tart

PREP 10 MINS   COOK 25 MINS

Special equipment • 20cm (8in) tart tin • ceramic baking beans

SERVES 6

225g (8oz) ready-made sweet shortcrust pastry
flour, to dust
4 Bramley apples, peeled, cored, and thinly sliced
2–3 tbsp golden caster sugar
knob of butter

1 Preheat the oven to 220°C (425°F/ Gas 7). On a lightly floured surface, roll the pastry out as thinly as you can. Use to line the tart tin, overlapping the edges, then trimming them neatly. Prick the base all over with a fork. Line the case with greaseproof paper and ceramic baking beans, then bake for 10 minutes, or until lightly coloured. Remove the beans and paper, and allow the tart case to cool. Leave the oven on.

2 Arrange the apple slices in the tart case in a neat, overlapping design. Sprinkle with the sugar and dot with the butter. Bake for 10–15 minutes, or until the apples begin to caramelize and the pastry is golden. Leave to cool. Remove from the tin, wrap carefully in cling film and then in foil, and freeze.

3 To serve, defrost overnight in the refrigerator, then serve at room temperature.

COOK'S NOTES

If you would like to serve the tart hot, defrost, then warm in an oven preheated to 190°C (375°F/ Gas 5) for 15–20 minutes.

FOOD FOR FRIENDS

Bread and butter pudding

PREP 10 MINS | COOK 40 MINS

Special equipment • 1.2-litre (2-pint) ovenproof freezerproof dish

SERVES 4–6
20g (¾oz) butter, at
    room temperature
4 thick slices white bread or brioche
4 tbsp thick-cut Seville
    orange marmalade
1 large egg
300ml (10fl oz) whole milk
2 tbsp caster sugar
1 tsp ground ginger

1 Spread the butter over the bread or brioche, then spread with the marmalade. Cut each slice into 4 triangles. Arrange in a lightly buttered ovenproof freezerproof dish. In a jug, lightly beat the egg into the milk, then mix in the sugar and ginger. Pour the mixture over the bread and leave to stand for 30 minutes. Preheat the oven to 180°C (350°F/Gas 4). Bake the pudding for 35–40 minutes, or until set and golden brown. Leave to cool completely, then wrap in foil, and freeze.

2 To serve, defrost in the refrigerator overnight, then warm through in an oven preheated to 180°C (350°F/Gas 4) for 45 minutes, or until puffed up and piping hot.

VARIATION For a more traditional pudding, leave out the marmalade and ginger.

Cherry crumble

PREP 15 MINS | COOK 40 MINS

Special equipment • 2-litre (3½-pint) ovenproof freezerproof dish

SERVES 6
125g (4½oz) butter, cubed
125g (4½oz) plain flour
125g (4½oz) ground almonds
50g (1¾oz) caster sugar

For the filling
550g (1¼lb) stoned cherries
2 tbsp caster sugar
2 tbsp apple juice

1 Preheat the oven to 180°C (350°F/Gas 4). In a bowl, rub the butter into the flour and ground almonds with your fingertips until the mixture resembles rough breadcrumbs. Stir in the caster sugar. Place the cherries in the ovenproof freezerproof dish and scatter over the sugar and apple juice. Sprinkle the crumble mixture over the cherries. Bake for 35–40 minutes, or until golden brown. Allow to cool completely, then wrap in foil, and freeze.

2 To serve, defrost in the refrigerator overnight. Warm through in an oven preheated to 180°C (350°F/Gas 4) for 30 minutes, or until hot and simmering.

VARIATION Instead of cherries, use the same quantity of chopped apples, soft stone fruit, or berries.

Cheat... Stoning cherries can take some time – use three 425g cans cherries when time is short.

Pineapple and syrup upside-down pudding

Special equipment • electric hand whisk or mixer • 1.2-litre (2-pint) ovenproof freezerproof dish

SERVES 4-6
2-3 tbsp golden syrup
400ml can pineapple rings, drained
150g (5½oz) butter
125g (4½oz) golden caster sugar
2 eggs
175g (6oz) self-raising flour, sifted
1-2 tbsp milk

1 Preheat the oven to 180°C (350°F/Gas 4). Grease the ovenproof freezerproof dish. Drizzle in the golden syrup to cover the base, then top with the pineapple rings, and put to one side.

2 Place the butter and sugar in a bowl, then whisk with an electric hand whisk until pale and creamy. Mix in the eggs, one at a time, adding a little of the flour after each one. Fold in the remaining flour, then add the milk a little at a time until the mixture drops easily off the beaters. Pour the mixture over the pineapples and bake in the oven for 40-50 minutes, or until golden brown and springy to the touch. Leave to cool completely in the dish, wrap in cling film and then foil, and freeze.

3 To serve, defrost overnight in the refrigerator. Heat through in an oven preheated to 180°C (350°F/Gas 4) for 30-40 minutes, or until piping hot.

VARIATION Use a sprinkling of brown sugar instead of the syrup, and add a glacé cherry to each pineapple ring.

Chocolate orange profiteroles

SERVES 6
50g (1¾oz) butter
100g (3½oz) plain flour
2 large eggs, lightly beaten

For the chocolate sauce
150g (5½oz) dark chocolate, broken into pieces
300ml (10fl oz) single cream
2 tbsp golden syrup
1 tbsp Grand Marnier

For the filling
500ml (16fl oz) double cream or whipping cream
zest of 1 large orange
2 tbsp Grand Marnier

1 Preheat the oven to 220°C (425°F/Gas 7). Lightly grease two baking sheets. To make the choux pastry, melt the butter with 300ml (10fl oz) water in a pan, then bring to the boil. As soon as the mixture comes to the boil, remove from the heat, and add the flour. Beat hard with a wooden spoon until the mixture is thick and glossy and comes away from the sides of the pan. Gradually beat in the egg a little at a time until the mixture is smooth, thick, and shiny – it should drop easily off the spoon.

2 Spoon the mixture into 12 balls, placing them well spaced apart on the baking sheets. Bake for 10-15 minutes, or until puffed up, then reduce the heat to 190°C (375°F/Gas 5) and bake for a further 20 minutes, or until they are crisp and golden. Remove from the oven and make slits in the sides for the air to escape. Return to the oven for a few minutes so that the centres dry out. Transfer to a wire rack to cool completely.

3 To make the chocolate sauce, melt the chocolate, cream, syrup, and Grand Marnier together in a small pan, whisking until the sauce is smooth and glossy. Leave to cool to room temperature, then transfer to a sealed plastic container and freeze. To make the filling, whisk the cream, orange zest, and Grand Marnier in a bowl until just thicker than soft peaks. Fill the profiteroles with the cream using a piping bag or teaspoon. Wrap in foil, or place in a large plastic food bag, and freeze.

4 To serve, defrost the profiteroles and sauce in the refrigerator overnight. Warm the sauce in a small pan, stirring until smooth. Serve the profiteroles with the hot sauce spooned over.

FOOD FOR FRIENDS

485

Classic treacle tart

PREP 20 MINS   COOK 35 MINS

Special equipment • 20cm (8in) round loose-bottomed tart tin • ceramic baking beans

SERVES 6

225g (8oz) plain flour, plus a little extra to dust
75g (2½oz) cold butter, cubed
salt

For the filling
25g (scant 1oz) butter
3–4 slices of white bread, made into coarse breadcrumbs
3–4 tbsp golden syrup

1 Preheat the oven to 200°C (400°F/Gas 6). Make the pastry by placing the flour and butter in a mixing bowl with a pinch of salt. Using your fingertips, rub the butter into the flour until the mixture resembles breadcrumbs. Add a few drops of iced water, then use your hands to pull the pastry together until it comes away from the edge of the bowl. Transfer to a lightly floured surface and roll into a ball. Flatten slightly, wrap in cling film, and put in the refrigerator to rest for 20 minutes. Try not to handle the pastry too much or it will become tough.

2 Roll the pastry out thinly and use to line the tart tin. Prick the base all over with a fork. Line the case with greaseproof paper, then fill with the baking beans. Bake in the oven for 15 minutes, or until very lightly golden. Remove the beans and paper, then put the tart case back in the oven for a few minutes to crisp up the base. Set aside while you make the filling. Turn the oven down to 190°C (375°F/Gas 5).

3 Place the butter and breadcrumbs in a bowl and mix together with a fork until well combined. Add the syrup and stir until the mixture is smooth but quite stiff. Spoon into the pastry base and level the top. Bake in the oven for 10–15 minutes, or until golden and set. Do not overcook or the filling will become brittle: it should be soft and slightly chewy; the pastry thin and crisp. Leave to cool, then wrap in greaseproof paper followed by cling film, and freeze.

4 To serve, defrost in the refrigerator overnight. Serve at room temperature or warm through in an oven preheated to 180°C (350°F/Gas 4) for 15–25 minutes, or until hot.

VARIATION
Give the tart some extra tang by adding the zest of 1 lemon to the syrup.

Lemon sauce sponge pudding

PREP 10 MINS   COOK 30 MINS

Special equipment • electric hand whisk or mixer • 1.2-litre (2-pint) ovenproof freezerproof dish

SERVES 4

75g (2½oz) butter, at room temperature
175g (6oz) golden caster sugar or caster sugar
zest of 2 lemons
zest of 1 orange
3 eggs, separated
75g (2½oz) plain flour
200ml (7fl oz) milk
juice of 2 lemons
2 tbsp lemon curd

1 Preheat the oven to 180°C (350°F/Gas 4). Place the butter and sugar in a bowl and whisk with an electric hand whisk or mixer until light and creamy. Add the lemon zest, orange zest, and the egg yolks and mix well. Stir in half the flour and half the milk, then repeat to make a batter. Stir in the lemon juice and set aside.

2 In another bowl, whisk the egg whites with an electric hand whisk or mixer until soft peaks form, then carefully stir into the batter. Spoon the lemon curd into the ovenproof freezerproof dish, then pour in the sponge mixture. Sit the dish in a roasting tin half-filled with warm water. Transfer to the oven and bake for 30 minutes, or until golden. Leave to cool completely, wrap in cling film and then foil, and freeze.

3 To serve, defrost in the refrigerator overnight. Warm through in an oven preheated to 180°C (350°F/Gas 4) for 30 minutes, or until piping hot.

VARIATION
For a zesty twist, use orange curd instead of lemon curd.

COOK'S NOTES
To test if the reheated pudding is ready to serve, insert a skewer into the sponge to see if it comes out hot. If the top starts to get too brown before the pudding is ready, cover it with foil.

Chocolate sponge pudding

PREP 15 MINS · COOK 6 MINS · ❄

Special equipment • electric hand whisk or mixer • 900ml (1½-pint) freezerproof microwaveproof pudding basin

SERVES 4
125g (4½oz) butter
125g (4½oz) golden caster sugar
3 eggs
75g (2½oz) plain flour
2 tbsp cocoa powder
25g (scant 1oz) ground almonds
2 tsp baking powder

For the chocolate sauce
50g (1¾oz) butter
125g (4½oz) dark chocolate, broken into pieces
2–3 tbsp double cream or whipping cream

1 Melt the butter in the microwave or in a pan, and put to one side. Place the sugar and eggs in a mixing bowl and whisk with an electric hand whisk or mixer until light and creamy. Sift in the flour and cocoa powder, add the almonds, baking powder, and melted butter, and whisk well to get plenty of air into the mixture.

2 Spoon the mixture into the pudding basin. Cover in cling film and put in the microwave for 5–6 minutes on High. Leave the pudding to cool completely, then double-wrap with cling film, and freeze.

3 Make the chocolate sauce by melting the butter and chocolate together in a pan. Stir in the double cream to thicken. Leave to cool, then transfer to a sealable container, and freeze.

4 To serve, defrost the pudding and sauce in the refrigerator overnight. Reheat the pudding in the microwave on High for 5–6 minutes, or until piping hot. Reheat the sauce in 30-second bursts, stirring, until hot, then pour over the pudding, and serve.

Cheat... Instead of making the chocolate sauce, use a ready-made one. Heat it through just before serving.

FOOD FOR FRIENDS

Chocolate biscuit cake

PREP 10 MINS · ❄

Special equipment • deep 18cm (7in) square tin

SERVES 6
150g (5½oz) butter
250g (9oz) dark chocolate, broken into pieces
2 tbsp golden syrup
450g (1lb) digestive biscuits, crushed
handful of plump golden raisins
handful of unskinned almonds, roughly chopped

1 Lightly grease the square tin. In a small pan, melt the butter, chocolate, and syrup, then remove from the heat and stir in the biscuits, raisins, and almonds. Mix well, then press the mixture into the tin with the back of a spoon. Transfer to the refrigerator to cool completely, then wrap in cling film, and freeze.

2 To serve, defrost in the refrigerator overnight, then slice, and serve.

VARIATION Vary the fruit and nuts to your taste – a handful of chopped cherries and hazelnuts works well, for instance.

COOK'S NOTES
To crush the digestive biscuits, put them in a plastic bag and bash with a rolling pin. Don't break them up too finely though – you want the cake to have plenty of texture.

Classic apple crumble

 PREP 15 MINS COOK 30 MINS ❄

Special equipment • 1.2-litre (2-pint)
ovenproof freezerproof dish

SERVES 4

3 large Bramley apples, peeled, cored,
  and roughly chopped
50–75g (1¾–2½oz) caster sugar
  (depending on the tartness of
  the apples)

For the crumble topping
50g (1¾oz) butter, cubed
125g (4½oz) plain flour
125g (4½oz) golden caster sugar
  or caster sugar

1 Preheat the oven to 190°C (375°F/
Gas 5). Place the apples and sugar
in a pan with a tiny amount of water.
Simmer gently until the apples begin
to break down, but do not let them
get too soft. Spoon into the ovenproof
freezerproof dish.

2 To make the topping, place the
butter and flour in a mixing bowl.
Using your fingertips, rub the butter
into the flour until the mixture
resembles breadcrumbs. Add the

sugar, and rub it in using the same
method. Sprinkle on top of the apple
mixture, then bake for 30 minutes, or
until the topping is a very pale golden
colour. Leave to cool completely, wrap
in cling film and then foil, and freeze.

3 To serve, defrost in the refrigerator
overnight. Warm through in an oven
preheated to 180°C (350°F/Gas 4) for
30 minutes, or until golden brown.

VARIATION
Add a few blackberries or
blueberries to the apples
before you cook them.

Cheat...
A 400g can of stewed apple
and a 250g packet
ready-made crumble
mix are the secret to
an instant-assembly
pudding.

Apple and blackberry brown betty

 PREP 15 MINS COOK 40 MINS ❄

Special equipment • 1.2-litre (2-pint)
ovenproof freezerproof dish

SERVES 4

100g (3½oz) fine breadcrumbs
generous knob of butter,
  at room temperature
zest of 1 lemon
3 Bramley apples, peeled, cored,
  and sliced
150g (5½oz) blackberries
150ml (5½fl oz) fresh orange juice
2–3 tbsp caster sugar (depending
  on the tartness of the fruit)

1 Preheat the oven to 190°C
(375°F/Gas 5). In a bowl, mix the
breadcrumbs with the butter and

lemon zest, and put to one side.
Place the apples in a greased
ovenproof freezerproof dish, then stir
in the blackberries, orange juice, and
enough of the caster sugar to sweeten.
Sprinkle the breadcrumbs on top and
bake for 35–40 minutes, or until
golden. Allow to cool completely,
cover with cling film and then foil,
and freeze.

2 To serve, defrost in the refrigerator
overnight. Warm through in an oven
preheated to 180°C (350°F/Gas 4) for
40 minutes, or until golden brown and
piping hot.

Sticky pecan pie

PREP 15 MINS · **COOK 1 HR**

Special equipment • 20cm (8in) round loose-bottomed tart tin • ceramic baking beans

SERVES 6

½ 500g packet sweet
shortcrust pastry
125g (4½oz) butter
2 tbsp golden syrup
50g (1¾oz) light soft brown sugar
50g (1¾oz) dark soft brown sugar
300g (10oz) pecan nuts, halved
2 eggs, lightly beaten

1 Preheat the oven to 200°C (400°F/ Gas 6). Line the tart tin with the pastry, then transfer to the refrigerator to rest for 10 minutes. Prick the base all over with a fork. Line the case with greaseproof paper and the baking beans, and bake in the oven for 15 minutes, or until very pale golden. Remove the beans and paper and put the case back in the oven for 5 minutes to crisp up the base.

2 Turn the oven down to 160°C (325°F/Gas 3). Melt the butter and syrup in a pan, then remove from the heat and stir in the brown sugars and nuts and allow to cool. Stir in the beaten eggs. Spoon the mixture into

the tart case, spreading it evenly. Bake for 30–40 minutes, or until the pastry case is golden and crispy, but the filling is still slightly soft. Leave to cool completely, double-wrap in cling film, and freeze.

3 To serve, defrost in the refrigerator overnight. Serve either at room temperature or warm through in an oven preheated to 160°C (325°F/ Gas 3) for 30 minutes, or until golden and piping hot.

VARIATION
Brazil nuts or walnuts would work well in place of the pecans.

Cheat...
Mix a 350g jar of ready-made toffee sauce with the pecan nuts. Add to the cooked pastry base and bake for 20–30 minutes.

Pear and cinnamon strudel

PREP 10 MINS · **COOK 40 MINS**

SERVES 4

4 ripe pears, peeled and sliced
2 tsp ground cinnamon
handful of raisins
1–2 tbsp golden caster sugar
15 sheets filo pastry
knob of butter, melted, to brush

1 Line a baking sheet with baking parchment. Place the pear, cinnamon, raisins, and sugar in a bowl, mix well, then put to one side. Brushing the sheets of filo with a little melted butter as you go, layer 3 sheets on the baking sheet, then layer another 3 next to them.

2 Sit another 3 layers of filo pastry on top, placing them with the long edges facing in the other direction. Repeat with another layer of 3 so you have an oblong-shaped base. Spoon the filling down the centre, then fold

over the edges. Top with a final layer of 3 sheets of filo and brush the whole thing with butter. Double-wrap in cling film and freeze.

3 To serve, defrost in the refrigerator overnight. Brush the strudel with more melted butter and bake in an oven preheated to 200°C (400°F/ Gas 6) for 30–40 minutes, or until golden brown.

VARIATION
Use apples instead of pears.

COOK'S NOTES

Check the strudel halfway through cooking, as filo tends to turn golden fairly quickly. Cover with foil if it has.

INDULGENT PUDDINGS

Quick, but still rich and delicious.

Chocolate Amaretti roulade

PREP 30 MINS
COOK 20 MINS

Special equipment • 23 x 33cm (9 x 13in) Swiss roll tin • electric hand whisk

SERVES 8

6 large eggs, separated
150g (5½oz) caster sugar
50g (1¾oz) cocoa powder
icing sugar, to dust
300ml (10fl oz) double cream
    or whipping cream
2–3 tbsp Amaretto or brandy
20 Amaretti biscuits, crushed,
    plus 2 extra
50g (1¾oz) dark chocolate

1 Preheat the oven to 180°C (350°F/ Gas 4). Line the Swiss roll tin with baking parchment. Put the egg yolks and sugar in a large heatproof bowl set over a pan of simmering water, and whisk with an electric hand whisk until very pale, thick, and creamy. This will take about 10 minutes. Remove from the heat. Put the egg whites in a mixing bowl and whisk with an electric hand whisk (and clean beaters) until soft peaks form.

2 Sift the cocoa powder into the egg yolk mixture and very gently fold in along with the egg whites. Pour into the tin and smooth into the corners. Bake for 20 minutes, or until just

firm to the touch. Carefully turn out on to a sheet of baking parchment well dusted with icing sugar. Remove the tin, but leave the top parchment, and allow to cool for 30 minutes.

3 Put the cream in a mixing bowl and whisk with an electric hand whisk until soft peaks form. Peel the top parchment from the sponge, trim the sides to neaten them, then drizzle over the amaretto or brandy. Spread with the cream, scatter with the crushed Amaretti biscuits, then grate over most of the chocolate.

4 Starting from one of the short sides, roll the roulade up, using the parchment to help keep it tightly together. Place on a serving plate with the join underneath. Crumble over the extra biscuits, grate over the remaining chocolate, and dust with a little icing sugar.

VARIATION Mix the cream with 2–3 tablespoons of sweetened chestnut purée instead of the Amaretti biscuits.

Lemon tart

PREP 20 MINS
COOK 55 MINS

Chilling • 30 minutes

Special equipment • 20cm (8in) loose-bottomed tart tin • ceramic baking beans

SERVES 8

125g (4½oz) cold butter, cubed
175g (6oz) plain flour
75g (2½oz) ground almonds
75ml (2½fl oz) juice and zest
    of 2 lemons
75g (2½oz) caster sugar
3 large eggs
175ml (6fl oz) double cream

1 Preheat the oven to 200°C (400°F/ Gas 6). Put the butter and flour in a mixing bowl, and rub together with your fingertips until the mixture resembles breadcrumbs. Alternatively, use a food processor. Stir in the almonds, then stir in enough ice-cold water (about 3 tablespoons) so the mixture comes together to form a dough. Roll the pastry out on a lightly floured surface and use to line the tart tin. Trim off any excess around the edges, then chill for at least 30 minutes.

2 Line the pastry case with baking parchment and fill with ceramic baking beans. Bake for 15 minutes, then remove the paper and beans and return to the oven for a further 5 minutes, or until the pastry is cooked through. Set aside while you make the filling. Turn the oven down to 150°C (300°F/Gas 2).

3 Put the lemon juice and sugar in a mixing bowl, and stir together until the sugar has dissolved. Mix in the eggs and lemon zest. Stir in the cream and pour into the pastry case. Bake for 35 minutes, or until just set – the tart should wobble in the middle slightly when you shake the tin. Leave to cool, then chill until ready to serve. Serve with single cream.

Cheat... Instead of making the pastry case, use a 20cm (8in) ready-made sweet shortcrust pastry base.

Baked chocolate mousse

PREP **20** MINS COOK **1** HR

Special equipment • 23cm (9in) loose-bottomed or springform cake tin • electric hand whisk

SERVES 8–12
250g (9oz) unsalted butter, cubed
350g (12oz) dark chocolate, broken into pieces
250g (9oz) light soft brown sugar
5 large eggs, separated
salt
cocoa powder or icing sugar, to dust

1 Preheat the oven to 180°C (350°F/ Gas 4). Base-line the cake tin with baking parchment. In a heatproof bowl set over a pan of simmering water, melt the butter and chocolate together until smooth and glossy, stirring now and again. Remove from the pan and allow to cool slightly, then stir in the sugar, followed by the egg yolks, one at a time.

2 Put the egg whites in a mixing bowl with a pinch of salt and whisk with an electric hand whisk until soft peaks form. Gradually fold into the chocolate mixture, then pour into the cake tin and smooth the top. Bake for 1 hour, or until the top is firm but the middle still wobbles slightly when you shake the tin. Leave to cool completely in the tin. Remove and dust with cocoa powder or icing sugar before serving. Serve with single cream.

COOK'S NOTES

Be careful not to overcook the mousse or it will turn into a cake. If there's still a wobble when you take it out of the oven, it will be deliciously gooey in the middle.

Espresso crème brûlées

PREP **15** MINS COOK **1** HR

Chilling • overnight

Special equipment • electric hand whisk • 6 x 175ml (6fl oz) ramekins

SERVES 6
5 large egg yolks
125g (4½oz) caster sugar
450ml (15fl oz) double cream
100ml (3½fl oz) full fat milk
3 tbsp strong coffee
1 vanilla pod, split lengthways and seeds scraped out, or ½ tsp vanilla extract

1 Preheat the oven to 160°C (325°F/ Gas 3). Put the egg yolks in a mixing bowl with 3 tablespoons of the sugar, and mix with an electric hand whisk until pale and well combined. Put the cream, milk, coffee, and the vanilla pod and seeds or the vanilla extract in a pan and heat until almost boiling, then stir into the egg yolk mixture. Strain into a jug and pour into the ramekins.

2 Place the ramekins in a deep roasting tin and add enough hot water from the kettle to come halfway up the sides of the ramekins. Cover the tin loosely with foil, then bake for 50 minutes–1 hour, or until just set. The middles of the crème brûlées should wobble slightly when you shake the tin.

3 Remove from the tin, allow to cool, then chill overnight. A few hours before serving, sprinkle the remaining sugar evenly over the tops of the crème brûlées, then place under a very hot grill or blast with a cook's blowtorch until the sugar caramelizes and turns golden brown. Return to the refrigerator until ready to serve.

VARIATION
For simpler crème brûlées, leave out the coffee and use an extra vanilla pod, or ½ a teaspoon more vanilla extract.

Blueberry-ripple cheesecake

PREP 20 MINS **COOK 40 MINS**

Special equipment • 20cm (8in) deep loose-bottomed cake tin • food processor

SERVES 8

125g (4½oz) digestive biscuits
50g (1¾oz) butter
150g (5½oz) blueberries
150g (5½oz) caster sugar,
    plus 3 tbsp extra
400g (14oz) cream cheese
250g (9oz) mascarpone
2 large eggs, plus 1 large egg yolk
½ tsp vanilla extract
2 tbsp plain flour

1 Preheat the oven to 180°C (350°F/ Gas 4). Grease the cake tin. Put the biscuits in a large food bag and crush with a rolling pin. Melt the butter in a pan, then add the biscuit crumbs and stir until well-coated. Press the crumbs into the base of the tin.

2 Put the blueberries and the 3 tablespoons of caster sugar in a food processor and whiz until smooth, then push the mixture through a nylon sieve into a small pan. Bring to the boil, then allow to simmer for

3-5 minutes, or until thickened and jammy. Set aside. Rinse the goblet of the food processor.

3 Put all the remaining ingredients into the food processor and whiz until well combined. Pour the mixture onto the biscuit base and smooth the top. With a teaspoon, carefully drizzle the blueberry mixture over the cream cheese mixture in a swirly pattern. Bake the cheesecake for 40 minutes, or until it has set but still has a slight wobble in the middle when you shake the tin. Leave to cool in the oven for an hour, then cool completely and serve.

Cheat...
Instead of making the blueberry ripple mixture, drizzle with ready-made bluberry compote.

Caramel banana tart

PREP 15 MINS **COOK 35 MINS**

Special equipment • 20cm (8in) tart dish or tin (not loose-bottomed)

SERVES 6

75g (2½oz) butter
150g (5½oz) golden syrup
4 medium bananas, peeled
    and sliced 1cm (½in) thick
200g (7oz) ready-made puff pastry
plain flour, to dust

1 Preheat the oven to 200°C (400°F/ Gas 6). Put the butter and syrup in a small, heavy-based pan and heat until the butter has melted and the mixture is smooth, then allow to boil for 1 minute. Pour into the tart dish or tin. Arrange the banana slices on top of the syrup mixture – this will be the top of the pudding when it's turned out. Place the dish or tin on a baking tray and bake for 10 minutes.

2 Meanwhile, on a lightly floured surface, roll the pastry out into

a round about 23cm (9in) in diameter. It should be about 5mm (¼in) thick. Trim off any excess, if necessary.

3 Carefully remove the tart from the oven and place the pastry circle on top. Use the handle of a small knife to tuck the edge down into the tin, being careful of the hot caramel. Return the tart to the oven and bake for a further 20–25 minutes, or until the pastry is golden brown. Leave to stand for 5–10 minutes, then place a serving plate on top and turn the tart upside-down. Serve with vanilla ice cream.

COOK'S NOTES

The caramel gets very hot. Take care not to touch it when you're topping the bananas with the pastry or turning the pudding out.

Melting-middle chocolate fudge puddings

 PREP 15 MINS **COOK 12 MINS**

Special equipment • 4 x 200ml (7fl oz) pudding basins or ramekins

SERVES 4

100g (3½oz) dark chocolate, chopped
100g (3½oz) butter
150g (5½oz) light soft brown sugar
3 large eggs
½ tsp vanilla extract
50g (1¾oz) plain flour

1 Preheat the oven to 200°C (400°F/ Gas 6). Butter the four pudding basins or ramekins well and place on a baking tray. Put the chocolate and butter in a heatproof bowl set over a pan of hot water and stir until smooth, then set aside to cool slightly for 15 minutes.

2 Mix in the sugar, then the eggs, one at a time, followed by the vanilla extract, and finally the flour. Divide the mixture among the basins or ramekins. Bake for 10–12 minutes,

or until the tops are firm to the touch, but the middles still feel squidgy. Carefully run a knife around the edge of each pudding, then turn out onto serving plates and serve with single cream.

Cheat...
Assemble the puddings the day before, and chill until ready to cook.

COOK'S NOTES

Don't overcook the puddings or the middles will become cakey rather than gooey.

Pavlovas with spiced berries

 PREP 30 MINS **COOK 1½ HRS**

Special equipment • electric hand whisk

SERVES 6

3 large egg whites
salt
200g (7oz) caster sugar
75g (2½oz) icing sugar
1½ tsp ground cinnamon
500g packet mixed frozen
    berries, defrosted
3 tbsp port
½ tsp mixed spice
zest of 1 orange
300ml (10fl oz) double cream
    or whipping cream

1 Preheat the oven to 130°C (250°F/ Gas ½). Line a baking tray with baking parchment. Put the egg whites in a bowl with a pinch of salt and whisk with an electric hand whisk until stiff peaks form. Whisk in half the caster sugar a tablespoonful at a time and continue whisking until the mixture is very stiff and shiny.

2 Sift in the icing sugar, add 1 teaspoon of cinnamon, and fold them in with a large metal spoon. Spoon the mixture onto the baking

tray in 6 heaps, spreading each one out to make a round about 10cm (4in) in diameter. Make a small hollow in the centre of each one. Cook for 1½ hours, or until crisp and easy to peel from the baking parchment. Remove from the oven, and leave to cool on a wire rack for 30 minutes.

3 Meanwhile, put half the berries and any juices from them in a pan with the port, the remaining sugar, the mixed spice, orange zest, and ½ teaspoon of cinnamon and heat until boiling and the sugar has dissolved. Simmer gently for 5 minutes, then stir in the remaining berries and leave to cool.

4 Put the cream in a mixing bowl and whisk with an electric hand whisk until soft peaks form. Place the pavlovas on serving plates and divide the cream among them. Spoon over the spiced berries and serve.

 VARIATION
If preparing this in the summer months, use seasonal fresh berries.

Honeycomb parfait

PREP 20 MINS   COOK 10 MINS   ❄

Freeze • overnight

Special equipment • electric hand whisk
• 20cm (8in) square cake tin

SERVES 12–16

2 tbsp golden syrup

5 tbsp caster sugar

1 tsp bicarbonate of soda

500ml (16fl oz) whipping cream
   or double cream

400g can condensed milk

1 Lightly oil a baking tray with
vegetable oil. Put the syrup and sugar
in a small, heavy-based pan and heat
until smooth, then allow to boil until
the mixture is a dark caramel colour.
Remove from the heat and stir in the
bicarbonate of soda – the mixture will
puff up. Pour the fluffy mixture onto
the oiled baking tray and leave
for 30 minutes or until completely
cool. When cold, break up into
smallish chunks.

2 Put the cream in a mixing bowl
and whisk with an electric hand whisk
until soft peaks form. Whisk in the
condensed milk until well combined.

Stir in the honeycomb chunks, then
line the cake tin with cling film
before pouring the mixture in.
Smooth the mixture into the corners,
cover with cling film, and freeze
overnight until firm.

3 Remove the parfait from the
freezer 15 minutes before you
want to serve it, to allow it to
soften slightly. To serve, scoop
into glass dishes, or slice.

VARIATION

The basic cream mixture
is a good base for all sorts
of flavourings. Try it with
chopped praline, a fruit
coulis, or chocolate chips.

Cheat...
*Instead of making
your own honeycomb,
use 2 chocolate
honeycomb bars.*

Prune and brandy tart

PREP 15 MINS   COOK 1 HR

Special equipment • 20cm (8in) deep
loose-bottomed tart tin • ceramic
baking beans

SERVES 8

150g (5½oz) ready-to-eat prunes (use
   Agen prunes if you can find them)

3 tbsp brandy

250g (9oz) ready-made shortcrust
   pastry (preferably all-butter)

plain flour, to dust

5 large egg yolks

50g (1¾oz) caster sugar

300ml (10fl oz) double cream

½ tsp vanilla extract

generous grating of nutmeg

icing sugar, to dust

1 Preheat the oven to 200°C (400°F/
Gas 6). Soak the prunes in the brandy.
Roll the pastry out on a lightly floured
surface and use to line the tart tin.
Trim off any excess around the edges,
then line the pastry case with baking
parchment and ceramic baking beans.
Bake for 20 minutes, then remove the

parchment and beans and return
to the oven for 5 minutes to dry the
pastry out. Set to one side while you
make the filling. Turn the oven down
to 150°C (300°F/Gas 2).

2 Put the egg yolks and sugar
in a mixing bowl and stir together
until well combined. Heat the
cream, vanilla extract, and nutmeg
in a pan until almost boiling, then
whisk into the egg yolk mixture.
Strain into the pastry case and
scatter over the soaked prunes.
Bake for 40–45 minutes, or until
just set – the tart should wobble
slightly in the centre when you
shake the tin. Remove from the
oven and leave to cool, then chill
until ready to serve. Dust with icing
sugar before serving.

VARIATION

For a simple baked custard
tart leave out the prunes.

Lemon and lime tart

PREP 30 MINS **COOK 45** MINS

Special equipment • electric hand whisk • 20cm (8in) round loose-bottomed flan tin • ceramic baking beans

SERVES 6

125g (4½oz) plain flour
75g (2½oz) icing sugar
salt
75g (2½oz) cold butter, cubed
25g (scant 1oz) cocoa powder
3 eggs
125g (4½oz) golden caster sugar
200ml (7fl oz) double cream
zest and juice of 1 lemon
zest and juice of 1 lime

1 Sift the flour and icing sugar into a mixing bowl with a pinch of salt. Add the butter and cocoa powder, and rub together with your fingertips until the mixture resembles fine breadcrumbs. Add some iced water little by little, about 1-2 tablespoons altogether, and pull the mixture

together until it comes away from the sides of the bowl. Wrap in cling film and place in the refrigerator for 30 minutes.

2 Preheat the oven to 200°C (400°F/Gas 6). Roll the pastry out on a lightly floured surface and use to line the tin. Line with baking parchment, then fill with ceramic baking beans. Bake in the oven for 15 minutes, then remove the beans and paper and set to one side. Turn the oven down to 170°C (325°F/Gas 3).

3 Put the eggs and sugar in a mixing bowl and whisk with an electric hand whisk until pale and creamy. Add the cream, the zest and juice of the lemon and lime, and stir to combine. Pour the mixture into the tart case and smooth the top. Bake for 30-35 minutes or until set. Allow to cool to room temperature, then serve.

Black cherry cheesecake

PREP 30 MINS

Special equipment • 20cm (8in) round springform cake tin

SERVES 6

75g (2½oz) butter
200g (7oz) digestive biscuits, crushed
2 x 250g tubs ricotta cheese
75g (2½oz) golden caster sugar
zest and juice of 4 lemons
142ml carton double cream
11g sachet powdered gelatine
400g can black cherries or morello cherries in juice

1 Grease and line the cake tin. Melt the butter in a pan, add the biscuits, and stir until well coated. Transfer the mixture to the tin, pressing it down firmly with the back of a spoon so that it is level.

2 Mix the ricotta cheese, sugar, and lemon zest together in a bowl. Put the cream in a bowl and whip lightly with a hand whisk until it forms soft peaks. Add to the ricotta mixture and beat with a wooden spoon until well combined.

3 Mix the lemon juice and gelatine in a small heatproof bowl, then sit the bowl over a pan of simmering water and stir until the gelatine dissolves. Add to the ricotta mixture and stir well. Pour the mixture on top of the biscuits, spreading it out evenly. Place in the refrigerator for a couple of hours or until set and firm.

4 Meanwhile, drain the cherries, pouring the juice into a pan. Bring the juice to the boil, then allow to simmer for 10 minutes, or until the juice has reduced by three-quarters. Leave to cool, then pile the cherries on top of the cheesecake, spoon over the sauce, and serve.

COOK'S NOTES

To crush the biscuits, put them in a plastic bag and smash with a rolling pin.

FOOD FOR FRIENDS

Mini chocolate éclairs

PREP 30 MINS · COOK 30 MINS

Special equipment • electric hand whisk • piping bag

MAKES 30
75g (2½oz) butter
125g (4½oz) plain flour
3 eggs
500ml (16fl oz) double cream
  or whipping cream
200g (7oz) dark chocolate

1 Preheat the oven to 200°C (400°F/Gas 6). Melt the butter in a pan with 200ml (7fl oz) cold water, then bring to the boil, remove from the heat, and stir in the flour. Beat with a wooden spoon until well combined.

2 Lightly beat the eggs and add to the flour and butter mixture a little at a time, whisking constantly. Continue whisking until the mixture is smooth and glossy and comes away easily from the sides of the pan. Transfer to a piping bag.

3 Pipe 5cm (2in) lengths of the mixture onto 2 baking trays lined with baking parchment. You should have around 30 in all. Bake for 20 minutes or until golden brown, then remove from the oven and make a slit down the side of each one. Return to the oven for 5 minutes for the insides to cook through. Then remove and leave to cool.

4 Put the cream in a mixing bowl and whisk with an electric hand whisk until soft peaks form. Spoon or pipe into each éclair. Break the chocolate into pieces and place in a heatproof bowl. Sit the bowl over a pan of simmering water and stir until the chocolate is melted and smooth. Spoon over the éclairs and serve.

COOK'S NOTES
You can make the choux buns ahead of time. At the end of step 3, place them in an airtight container and store for up to 2 days.

Raspberry crème brûlées

PREP 10 MINS · COOK 30 MINS

Setting • 2 hours
Special equipment • 6 ramekins • electric hand whisk

MAKES 6
200g (7oz) fresh raspberries
4 large egg yolks
8 tbsp golden caster sugar
560ml (18fl oz) double cream
1 tsp vanilla extract

1 Divide the raspberries among the ramekins. Put the egg yolks and 2 tablespoons of the sugar in a large bowl and whisk with an electric hand whisk until the mixture begins to thicken and becomes pale and creamy.

2 Heat the cream gently in a pan for 5 minutes. Do not let it boil. Remove from the heat, stir in the vanilla extract, and allow to cool for 5 minutes.

3 Slowly add the warm cream to the egg mixture a little at a time, whisking constantly. When it's all in, pour the mixture back into the pan, and cook over a low heat for a couple of minutes, stirring all the time with a wooden spoon until thick. Do not allow to boil. Pour the custard into the ramekins and allow to cool completely. Transfer to the refrigerator to set for a couple of hours or overnight.

4 When ready to serve, sprinkle the tops of the custards evenly with the remaining sugar and place under a hot grill until the sugar bubbles and turns golden brown. Alternatively, use a cook's blowtorch, making sweeping movements with the flame until the sugar starts to caramelize. Allow the topping to harden for 20 minutes before serving.

VARIATION
Use ripe peaches or sweet cherries instead of the raspberries.

COOK'S NOTES
Add the cream to the eggs very slowly otherwise it could curdle and become unusable.

Crêpes with caramelized apples and chocolate

  PREP 15 MINS **COOK 20 MINS**

Special equipment • electric hand whisk

SERVES 4-6
50g (1¾oz) plain flour
salt
1 egg, lightly beaten
150ml (5fl oz) milk
142ml carton double cream
knob of butter
2-3 tbsp golden caster sugar, depending on the sweetness of the apples
4 pink-skinned eating apples, sliced
vegetable oil
125g (4½oz) dark chocolate, grated

1 Sift the flour into a mixing bowl with a pinch of salt and make a well in the centre. Put the egg and a little of the milk in the well. Using a wooden spoon, gradually stir the egg mixture, letting a little of the flour fall in as you go and adding the rest of the milk a little at a time. When it is all incorporated, whisk the mixture with a balloon whisk to remove any lumps. Transfer to the refrigerator to rest for 15 minutes, if you have time.

2 Meanwhile, put the cream in a mixing bowl and whisk until lightly whipped, then set to one side. Put the butter and sugar in a frying pan over a low heat and stir until the sugar has dissolved. Add the apple slices and toss well. Cook for 5-10 minutes, or until caramelized, then put to one side and keep warm.

3 Heat a pancake pan or small frying pan over a high heat. When hot, add a tiny amount of vegetable oil, then swirl it around the pan and pour it into a jug. Add 2 tablespoons of batter to the pan and swirl it around so it covers the base. Loosen the edges of the crêpe with a palette knife and cook for 1 minute, or until golden. Flip the crêpe and cook the other side for a minute or so. Slide onto a warmed plate and repeat until all the mixture has gone.

4 To serve, pile some of the apple mixture and a dollop of cream onto each crêpe, fold, and top with plenty of chocolate shavings.

 VARIATION Serve with sliced bananas and cream instead of the apple. If you're feeling particularly indulgent, you could enjoy the crêpes with ice cream as well.

FOOD FOR FRIENDS

White chocolate and raspberry trifle

 PREP 25 MINS

Chilling • 30 minutes

SERVES 6-8
300g (10oz) Madeira cake or plain sponge cake
700g (1lb 9oz) fresh or frozen raspberries, thawed
2 x 250ml tubs mascarpone
284ml carton double cream
200g (7oz) white chocolate

1 Slice the cake into 2cm (¾in) slices and use to line the base and sides of one large glass serving bowl or 6-8 individual glass dishes. If using fresh raspberries, squash them lightly so they release some of their juices, then spoon half over the sponge cake. If using frozen, drain the fruit (reserving the juice), then spoon half over the cake together with 2 tablespoons of juice. Place in the refrigerator for at least 15 minutes while the sponge soaks up the juices.

2 Meanwhile, put the mascarpone and cream in a mixing bowl and beat with a wooden spoon until well combined. Break three-quarters of the chocolate up into small pieces and place in a small heatproof bowl. Sit the bowl over a pan of simmering water and stir until the chocolate has melted. Spoon half over the raspberries and mix half with the mascarpone and cream.

3 Add the cream mixture and the remaining raspberries to the trifle(s) in layers, ending with a cream topping. Grate over the remaining chocolate. Chill in the refrigerator for 15-30 minutes, then serve.

 VARIATION Use 2 x 400g cans black cherries in syrup. Drain the fruit, reserving the syrup. Spoon 2 tbsp of it over the cake.

COOK'S NOTES

Be careful when melting the white chocolate – don't let any hot water splash on it or it will separate and become unusable.

Crème caramel

PREP 15 MINS **COOK** 1 HR

Special equipment • electric hand whisk • 6 ramekins

SERVES 6
250g (9oz) golden caster sugar
500ml (16fl oz) full-fat milk
1 vanilla pod
3 eggs, plus 3 egg yolks

1 Put half the sugar in a pan with 4 tablespoons of water. Simmer gently, swirling the pan, until you have a rich golden caramel. Divide evenly among the 6 ramekins.

2 Put the milk in a pan. Split the vanilla pod lengthways and add to the pan along with the remaining sugar. Heat gently, but do not allow to boil. Meanwhile, put the whole eggs and the egg yolks in a bowl and whisk with an electric hand whisk until pale and creamy. Slowly add the hot milk, whisking the whole time until the mixture begins to thicken slightly. Remove the vanilla pod.

3 Preheat the oven to 180°C (350°F/Gas 4). Sit the ramekins in a roasting dish, then divide the custard among them and leave to rest for 15 minutes.

4 Pour enough cold water into the roasting tin so that it comes two-thirds of the way up the sides of the ramekins. Carefully transfer the tin to the oven and bake for 45 minutes–1 hour, or until the custards are set. Remove from the oven and leave to cool, then chill in the refrigerator until ready to serve. To serve, turn out onto plates or small bowls, so the caramel sauce streams down over the custard.

Mixed berries with white chocolate sauce

PREP 5 MINS **COOK** 5 MINS

SERVES 4
380g packet frozen mixed berries, such as raspberries, strawberries, blackberries, and redcurrants
125g (4½oz) white chocolate, plus extra to grate (optional)
140ml (4½fl oz) double cream or whipping cream

1 Divide the berries among 4 serving bowls. Break the chocolate into pieces and place in a pan with the cream. Slowly bring almost to the boil, stirring continuously until the chocolate has melted and is well combined.

2 Pour the chocolate mixture over the frozen berries and serve topped with grated white chocolate, if you wish.

COOK'S NOTES
Drizzle in some of your favourite tipple, such as whisky, to the melted chocolate.

Chocolate and buttercream Swiss roll

PREP 25 MINS · **COOK 10 MINS**

Special equipment · electric hand whisk · 20 x 30cm (8 x 12in) Swiss roll tin

SERVES 8

3 large eggs
75g (2½oz) caster sugar
50g (1¾oz) plain flour
25g (scant 1oz) cocoa powder, plus extra to dust
75g (2½oz) butter, at room temperature
125g (4½oz) icing sugar

1 Preheat the oven to 200°C (400°F/ Gas 6). Sit a large heatproof bowl over a pan of simmering water, add the eggs and sugar, and whisk for 5-10 minutes or until the mixture is thick and creamy. Sift in the flour and cocoa powder and fold in gently with a metal spoon.

2 Line the Swiss roll tin with baking parchment, then pour the mixture into the tin and level the top. Bake for 10 minutes, or until the sponge is springy to the touch. Remove from the oven, cover with a damp tea towel, and leave to cool.

3 Turn the sponge out onto a sheet of greaseproof paper dusted with cocoa powder. Put the butter in a mixing bowl and beat with an electric hand whisk until creamy. Whisk in the icing sugar a little at a time, then spread the mixture over the top of the sponge. Using the greaseproof paper to help you, roll the sponge up, starting from one of the short sides. Dust with more cocoa powder, if needed, and serve.

COOK'S NOTES

Swiss roll tends to go quite dry quite quickly, so it's best enjoyed on the day of making.

Baked stem ginger cheesecake

PREP 30 MINS · **COOK 50 MINS**

Special equipment · 20cm (8in) springform cake tin · electric hand whisk

SERVES 6

200g (7oz) digestive biscuits
25g (scant 1oz) butter
4 eggs, at room temperature, separated
175g (6oz) golden caster sugar
150g tub cream cheese, at room temperature
250g tub mascarpone
2 tbsp syrup from a jar of stem ginger
4-5 balls stem ginger, sliced into fine strips
2 tbsp plain flour

1 Preheat the oven to 180°C (350°F/ Gas 4). Grease and line the base of the cake tin with greaseproof paper. Put the digestive biscuits in a plastic bag and crush with a rolling pin. Alternatively, whiz them in a food processor. Melt the butter in a pan, add the biscuits, then stir until well combined. Spoon into the tin and press firmly into the base.

2 Put the eggs yolks and sugar in a mixing bowl and whisk with an electric hand whisk until pale, thick, and creamy. Stir in the cream cheese and mascarpone, then beat with a wooden spoon until smooth. Add the ginger syrup and the sliced ginger and stir well. Sift in the flour and fold in.

3 Put the egg whites in a mixing bowl and whisk with an electric hand whisk until stiff peaks form. Fold into the egg yolk mixture, then spoon over the biscuit base. Bake for 50 minutes, or until golden and almost set - the cheesecake should still wobble slightly. Turn the oven off and leave the cake in there to cool. Remove from the tin and serve.

COOK'S NOTES

Use eggs and cream cheese at room temperature - not straight from the refrigerator. Eggs take longer to whisk when cold.

Chocolate ice cream

PREP 15 MINS

Setting • overnight
Special equipment • electric hand whisk

SERVES 8
125g (4½oz) dark chocolate
50g (1¾oz) milk chocolate
4 egg yolks
4 tbsp golden caster sugar
1.2 litres (2 pints) whipping cream

1 Break the chocolate into pieces and place in a heatproof bowl. Sit the bowl over a pan of simmering water and stir until the chocolate melts. Remove from the heat and allow to cool slightly.

2 Meanwhile, place the egg yolks in a mixing bowl, and whisk with an electric hand whisk for a couple of minutes, or until light and fluffy. Add the sugar a little at a time, whisking constantly until it is well combined. Add the egg mixture to the chocolate a little at a time, whisking until it is all blended.

3 Place the cream in a mixing bowl and whisk with an electric hand whisk until soft peaks form. Fold into the chocolate mixture. Spoon into a freezerproof dish, seal, and place in the freezer overnight to set.

4 Remove the ice cream from the freezer 5–10 minutes before serving so it has a chance to soften slightly.

COOK'S NOTES

This is a great standby dessert. It will keep in the freezer for up to 1 month.

Lemon soufflé pudding

PREP 30 MINS

Setting • 2 hours
Special equipment • 1.2-litre (2-pint) soufflé dish • electric hand whisk

SERVES 6–8
2 tsp powdered gelatine
6 large eggs, separated
125g (4½oz) golden caster sugar
juice and zest of 1 lemon
500ml (16fl oz) double cream
    or whipping cream

1 Soak the gelatine in 3 tablespoons of warm water for 15 minutes, then stir to dissolve. Meanwhile, cut a strip of greaseproof paper 10cm (4in) deep and lightly grease with vegetable oil. Wrap it around the top of the soufflé dish so it stands 2.5cm (1in) higher than the rim of the dish. The oiled side should face inwards. Secure with a paperclip.

2 Put the egg yolks, sugar, and lemon juice in a mixing bowl, and whisk with an electric hand whisk until the mixture is thick and creamy and leaves a trail when the whisks are lifted up. Whisk in the gelatine mixture and leave for 10 minutes, or until it begins to thicken.

3 Meanwhile, place the cream in a mixing bowl and whisk with an electric hand whisk until it forms soft peaks. Fold into the egg yolk mixture. Place the egg whites in a mixing bowl and whisk with an electric hand whisk until stiff peaks form. Fold into the egg yolk mixture along with the lemon zest.

4 Spoon the mixture into the soufflé dish, then transfer to the refrigerator to set for a couple of hours. Remove the paper and serve.

VARIATION
Use a few drops of vanilla extract instead of the lemon zest and juice.

COOK'S NOTES

Make sure you use vegetable oil to grease the paper, as it's tasteless. Olive oil will taint the flavour of the finished pudding.

Peach and nectarine puff pastry tart

 PREP **20** MINS COOK **20** MINS

Cooling • 30 minutes
Special equipment • electric hand whisk

SERVES 8
1 large egg, plus 1 large egg yolk
50g (1¾oz) golden caster sugar
25g (scant 1oz) plain flour
300ml (10fl oz) milk
juice of 1 lemon
375g packet ready-rolled puff pastry
1 egg yolk, beaten, to glaze
4 ripe peaches, halved and stoned
4 ripe nectarines, halved and stoned
handful of icing sugar, to dust

1 Put the egg, egg yolk, sugar, and flour in a mixing bowl and whisk with an electric hand whisk until well combined. Heat the milk in a pan until almost boiling, then slowly whisk into the egg mixture with the lemon juice. Return the mixture to the pan and slowly bring to the boil, stirring continuously. Cook for a couple of minutes, then transfer to a bowl. Sit a piece of greaseproof paper on the surface so the custard doesn't form a skin, then leave to cool.

2 Meanwhile, on a lightly floured surface, roll the pastry out into a 23 x 30cm (9 x 12in) rectangle and place on a lightly oiled baking sheet.

With a knife, score a rectangle on it, leaving a 2cm (¾in) border all round the edge. Press the back of the knife into the border to make horizontal lines – these will ensure the pastry rises. Prick the base of the rectangle with a fork and place in the refrigerator for 20 minutes. Preheat the oven to 200°C (400°F/Gas 6).

3 Brush the border with the beaten egg yolk, then bake for 20 minutes, or until the pastry is cooked and golden. Push the inner rectangle down slightly, then leave to cool for 30 minutes.

4 Spoon in the custard, then top with the fruit, dust with icing sugar, and serve.

VARIATION
Use ripe apricots, when they are in season, as an alternative.

COOK'S NOTES
If the custard thickens too much as it cools, beat it well with a wooden spoon or pass it through a sieve.

Tiramisu bomb

 PREP **20** MINS

Setting • 2 hours
Special equipment • 1.2-litre (2-pint) pudding basin • electric hand whisk

SERVES 8
175g packet sponge fingers
2–3 tbsp brandy
small cup of strong coffee
568ml carton double cream
2 tbsp cocoa powder, plus extra, to dust
2 tbsp icing sugar, plus extra, to dust
300g (10oz) cherries, stoned and halved, or 400g can morello or black cherries, drained and halved, plus 3 whole cherries, to decorate
125g (4½oz) dark chocolate

1 Lightly oil the pudding basin with vegetable oil and line the base with a circle of greaseproof paper. Dip all but five of the sponge fingers into the brandy and then the coffee. Line the bottom of the bowl with halved sponge fingers, then line the sides of the bowl with whole ones. Place them sugar-side out.

2 Put the cream in a mixing bowl and whisk with an electric hand whisk until soft peaks form. Transfer half to another bowl. Stir the cocoa powder and icing sugar into one bowl. Add the cherries to the other.

3 Spoon the mixtures into the basin in alternate layers, then top with the remaining sponge fingers, pressing them down well. Place in the refrigerator for a couple of hours, or overnight.

4 To serve, place a plate on top of the basin and turn the tiramisu upside-down. Remove the basin, then dust with cocoa powder and icing sugar, top with the reserved cherries, and grate over the chocolate.

COOK'S NOTES
It's best to make the bomb the day before you want to serve it and then chill it in the refrigerator before turning it out.

CAKES AND BAKES

Gorgeous baked goodies, made quick and easy.

CAKES AND BAKES

Baking is an enjoyable experience, as long as you remember that it demands accuracy. A few dos and don'ts, a little discipline, and straightforward easy-to-follow recipes are the key to perfect baking. As classic baking recipes can be quite formulaic, you can always be creative with flavourings and fillings.

Basic sponge cake This method will produce feather-light sponge.

1 Preheat the oven to 180°C (350°F/Gas 4). Lightly grease and line 2 x 20cm (8in) sandwich tins (see opposite). Put 225g (8oz) of softened butter in a mixing bowl, with 225g (8oz) of caster sugar, and cream together, using an electric mixer or wooden spoon, until pale and fluffy.

2 Lightly beat 4 room-temperature eggs. Add them slowly, a little at a time, to the butter and sugar mixture, beating well after each addition. Add a tablespoon of sifted flour, taken from 225g (8oz) of self-raising flour, to prevent it from curdling. Continue until all the egg has been added.

3 Using a metal or wooden spoon, fold in the rest of the flour. The mixture should drop off the spoon easily when it's ready. Add a tablespoon of water if the mixture is too thick.

4 Divide the mixture between the two tins, and smooth out evenly. Put in the oven, and bake for about 20 minutes, or until the cakes have risen, are golden, and feel springy if you lightly press the top with your fingertips. Remove, and allow to cool in the tins for 5 minutes before turning out onto a wire rack to cool completely.

Flavour the mixture

Once the basic cake recipe is mastered, you can experiment with different flavours.

Chocolate cake just requires a tablespoon of sieved cocoa powder (pictured above) added with the sifted flour.

Lemon zest or **orange zest** can be added into the creamed butter for a citrus cake, or add both for a St Clement's cake.

Mixed spice or **nutmeg** will spice things up a little, if added with the sifted flour at the end.

Coffee is always a favourite. Add a teaspoon of ground coffee, mixed with hot water, to the creamed butter.

Psst...

If cake batter is left to sit for longer than 10 minutes before it's baked it can curdle and turn frothy, and this won't make for a tasty cake. Always have the oven preheated, and put the prepared mixture straight into the oven.

Line a tin
Turn out your cakes and bakes cleanly and easily.

1 Sit the cake tin on a sheet of greaseproof paper, then draw around the outside of the base with a pencil.

2 Brush the base of the tin with a little vegetable or sunflower oil.

3 Neatly cut the circle out, just inside the pencil line, so the greaseproof paper will fit snugly inside the tin.

Easy toppings
Three simple ways to decorate your cake.

Apricot glaze
Melt 2 tablespoons of **apricot jam** in a pan, over a low heat. This will take 5–10 minutes. While it's still warm, brush liberally and evenly all over the top of the cake with a pastry brush. Leave to cool, and fill with buttercream and apricot jam.

White chocolate drizzle
Place a handful of broken **white chocolate** in a bowl with a **knob of butter**. Sit the bowl over a pan of gently simmering water, and stir the chocolate until it has melted. Heat 3 tablespoons of **double cream** until warm, and stir into the chocolate mixture until glossy. Spread or drizzle the mixture over the top of a cake filled with fresh summer fruit, such as strawberries and raspberries (see Easy fillings).

Mascarpone swirl
Mix 3 tablespoons of **mascarpone** with 2–3 teaspoons of sieved **icing sugar**. Beat with a wooden spoon until it becomes a spreadable consistency. Add a drizzle of **Limoncello** (Italian lemon liqueur), and stir to combine. Taste, and adjust the levels of Limoncello or icing sugar as desired. Spread the mixture over the top of a cake filled with lemon curd.

Easy fillings
Transform a basic cake into an indulgent treat.

Buttercream
Beat together 125g (4½oz) of **softened butter** with 75g (2½oz) of sieved **icing sugar** (you may need a little more or less, adjust according to taste). Add a drop or two of **vanilla extract**, and beat until smooth. If it is too stiff, it will be difficult to spread. Add other flavours to the buttercream, such as maple syrup, almond essence, amaretto, or espresso and chocolate for a mocha filling.

Summer fruits
Add a couple of handfuls of **raspberries (or summer berries of your choice)** to a pan, and sprinkle over a handful of **caster sugar**. Simmer gently for about 5 minutes. Transfer to a bowl and, when cold, put in the refrigerator. Spoon over the bottom half of the cake, with a layer of **fresh raspberries (or summer berries of your choice)**, then cover with the top layer of sponge, dust with sieved icing sugar, and some white chocolate drizzle.

Chestnut cream
Whisk 4–5 tablespoons of **double cream** until it forms soft peaks (be careful not to over-whisk). Spoon in 1–2 tablespoons of ready-made **sweetened chestnut purée**, and stir until lightly marbled. Taste, and add more purée if needed, or sweeten with a little sieved **icing sugar**. Spread over the bottom half of the cake, and sandwich both halves together. Dust with sieved icing sugar and cocoa powder.

Basic biscuit dough A simple mixture for vanilla biscuits.

1 Measure out 125g (4½oz) butter, 175g (6oz) soft brown sugar, and 350g (12oz) self-raising flour, allowing the butter to come to room temperature before you begin. Preheat the oven to 180°C (350°F/Gas 4).

2 In a bowl, mix the butter with the sugar. Add 1 egg, and mix until combined. Add the flour, and 2 teaspoons of vanilla extract, and combine until the mixture forms a dough. Line 2 baking sheets with greaseproof paper.

3 Roll the dough into balls the size of walnuts, and place on the baking sheets, then flatten with your fingers.

4 Bake in batches for 12-15 minutes, until golden, then remove from the oven and transfer to a wire rack to cool completely.

Flavour the mixture

Transform your basic biscuit dough with these delicious flavours.

Hazelnuts and chocolate Add 1-2 teaspoons of cocoa powder to the flour, and a handful of chopped hazelnuts (pictured) to the finished mixture.

Ginger Add 1-2 teaspoons of ground ginger to the flour.

Cinnamon Add a pinch of ground cinnamon to the flour.

Lemon Add lemon juice instead of vanilla extract to the mixture, for zesty biscuits.

Almond and orange Add 2-3 teaspoons of ground almonds to the finished mixture, with the zest and juice of half an orange.

Cranberry and white chocolate Mix a handful of finely chopped white chocolate pieces, and a handful of dried cranberries into the finished mixture.

Psst...

Make sure you always leave a generous space between pieces of dough on the baking tray, because they'll rise and spread slightly as they cook.

Baking ingredients What to choose, and how to use.

INGREDIENT	CHOOSE	USE
**BUTTER**	Both **salted** or **unsalted butter** can be used for baking. It's all down to taste preference, and whether you are reducing the salt in your diet. The amount of salt in salted butter varies, so check the label. Salted butter will keep for longer if you keep it in a butter dish out of the refrigerator.	Salted or unsalted, for cakes and bakes. Use softened butter (at room temperature). This means plenty of air will be held by the fat as you mix, making your cake or bake lighter.
**SUGAR**	**Caster sugar** is finer than **granulated**. Choose **unrefined sugar** (golden caster sugar) if you can, as it is more natural than **white refined sugar**, that has been processed and stripped of its molasses. Unrefined sugar will add a slight caramel flavour to your baking. **"Brown" sugar** does not mean that it is unrefined, it is simply white refined sugar with the molasses added back to it.	Caster sugar, unrefined if possible, for cakes and bakes.
**BAKING POWDER**	This is a raising agent used in baking. It is a mixture of bicarbonate of soda and cream of tartar, a natural raising soda, and is different to **baking soda** or **bicarbonate of soda**, as they don't contain cream of tartar. The two cannot be interchanged. Check the sell-by date of baking powder, as it won't be effective if used when it's old.	Cakes and biscuits. If a recipe calls for self-raising flour and you haven't got any, add baking powder to plain flour (4 teaspoons per 225g (8oz)).
**FLOUR**	**Plain flour** and **self-raising flour** are quite low in gluten, unlike strong bread flour. There are many flours that are suitable for a wheat-free or gluten-free diet, such as **rice flour**, **chestnut flour**, and **potato flour**. If using, consult specialist recipes as they are not interchangeable with plain flour.	Plain flour or self-raising flour, sifted, for cakes and bakes. Don't over-beat once flour has been added, as the gluten will strengthen and you'll get a tough texture. This is why recipes call for flour to be folded in.
EGGS	Choose **large organic** and/or **free-range hens eggs**, as they will improve the flavour and quality of your finished cake.	Use at room temperature. If they are used cold from the refrigerator, they cool the butter down and the mixture can curdle.

Psst...

If you are switching your tins from square to round, go up 2.5cm (1in) in size. If your recipe calls for a round 18cm (7in) tin, you can use a 20cm (8in) square tin. And if switching the other way, from round to square, go down 2.5cm (1in).

Tools of the trade

Cake tins should be rigid and sturdy, so they don't buckle in the heat of the oven. A selection of sizes and shapes is useful. For making a 4-egg sponge cake, you will need 2 x 20cm (8in) sandwich tins. Loose-bottomed cake tins are great – they make turning the cake out a lot easier. A springform cake tin is useful for larger cakes, or more fragile ones such as a baked cheesecake.

Baking sheets should be rigid and sturdy, so they don't buckle in the heat. Have a selection with and without lips.

Biscuit cutters often come in sets, so you have a variety of size and shapes. Metal ones are the best, and you can get straight-sided or fluted.

A wire rack is necessary for cooling all cakes and bakes. Choose a large one if you plan to do batch baking.

Ceramic baking beans are ideal for baking pastry blind, because they are heavy and can be used repeatedly. Take care though, as they get extremely hot. As an alternative, dried beans or rice can be used.

golden rules of baking

Measure with care Always measure everything accurately, and stick to either metric or imperial (never switch between the two). Weigh out ingredients before you start baking.

Resist opening the oven door Don't be tempted to open the oven door whilst baking, at least for the first half of the cooking time. If you do need to peep, leave it as long as possible. Always set the oven temperature correctly, according to the recipe. Cakes and biscuits don't need a particularly hot oven. If using a fan oven, adjust accordingly, or switch the fan off if you can.

Vanilla sponge

PREP 15 MINS · **COOK** 30 MINS

Freeze • before filling

Special equipment • electric hand whisk • 18cm (7in) round cake tin

SERVES 4-6

2 eggs, lightly beaten
75g (2½oz) caster sugar
a few drops of vanilla extract
75g (2½oz) self-raising flour
50g (1¾oz) butter, at
    room temperature
125g (4½oz) icing sugar
2 tbsp lemon curd

1 Preheat the oven to 180°C (350°F/ Gas 4). Put the eggs and sugar in a mixing bowl, and whisk with an electric hand whisk for 5 minutes, or until pale and creamy. Add a few drops of the vanilla extract.

2 Sift in the flour, a little at a time, folding each batch in gently before adding more. Pour the mixture into the lightly greased cake tin. Bake in the oven for 30 minutes, or until lightly golden. To test, pierce the centre of the cake with a skewer - if it comes out clean, the cake is cooked. Remove from the oven, and leave to cool in the tin for 10-15 minutes, then loosen the edges with a knife and leave to cool completely.

3 Meanwhile, put the butter in a mixing bowl and beat with a wooden spoon for a few minutes until creamy. Sift in the icing sugar, beat well, then add a few drops of vanilla extract and beat again. Remove the cake from the tin and slice in half horizontally. Cover the bottom half with the buttercream and the top half with the lemon curd. Sandwich together and serve.

Madeira cake

PREP 15 MINS · **COOK** 1½ HRS

Special equipment • electric hand whisk • 18cm (7in) round cake tin

SERVES 4-6

150g (5½oz) butter, at
    room temperature
150g (5½oz) caster sugar
3 eggs, lightly whisked
225g (8oz) self-raising flour
juice of 1 lemon

1 Preheat the oven to 180°C (350°F/ Gas 4). Put the butter and sugar in a mixing bowl and beat with an electric hand whisk for 5 minutes, or until pale and creamy.

2 Whisking all the time, add the eggs a little at a time, along with a little of the flour to stop the mixture curdling. Stir in the lemon juice, then fold in the rest of the flour. Spoon the mixture into the lightly greased cake tin.

3 Bake for 1-1½ hours, or unti cooked through. To test, pierce the centre of the cake with a skewer - if it comes out clean, the cake is cooked. Remove from the oven and leave to cool for 10 minutes in the tin, then run a knife around the edge to loosen. Leave to cool completely, then turn out onto a plate and serve.

Cheat...
Instead of waiting for the butter to come to room temperature, use ready-softened butter from a tub.

Chocolate chip cookies

PREP 10 MINS · COOK 30 MINS

Special equipment • electric hand whisk or mixer

MAKES ABOUT 30
200g (7oz) butter, at
    room temperature
300g (10oz) caster sugar
1 large egg
1 tsp vanilla extract
300g (10oz) self-raising flour
150g (5½oz) dark- or
    milk-chocolate chips

1 Preheat the oven to 180°C (350°F/ Gas 4). Line two baking trays with baking parchment. In a bowl, beat the butter and sugar together with an electric hand whisk until creamy, then mix in the egg and vanilla extract until completely combined.

2 Beat in the flour until the mixture forms a soft dough, then mix in the

chocolate chips. Roll the dough into about 30 balls, each the size of a walnut, and place on the baking trays, leaving space around each one for it to spread. Flatten them slightly, then bake in two batches for 15 minutes, or until golden. Carefully transfer to a wire rack to cool completely.

VARIATION

Make double chocolate chip cookies by replacing 25g (scant 1oz) of the flour with cocoa powder.

COOK'S NOTES

Don't worry if the golden cookies are still a little soft when you take them out of the oven – they will firm up as they cool, to become deliciously chewy.

Rich chocolate biscuits

PREP 15 MINS · COOK 20 MINS

Special equipment • electric hand whisk or mixer

MAKES 16
100g (3½oz) butter, at
    room temperature
50g (1¾oz) caster sugar
125g (4½oz) plain flour
25g (scant 1oz) cocoa powder
melted dark or milk chocolate,
    to drizzle (optional)

1 Preheat the oven to 180°C (350°F/ Gas 4). Line two baking trays with baking parchment. In a bowl, mix the butter and sugar together with an electric hand whisk until pale and creamy. Sift in the flour and cocoa powder, and beat until the mixture comes together to form a dough. You may need to bring it together with your hands at the end.

2 Roll the dough into 16 balls, each about the size of a walnut, and sit on the baking trays. Press the middle of each one with your thumb to flatten it, or use a fork, which will decorate it at the same time. Bake for 20 minutes, then transfer to a wire rack to cool completely. Drizzle over the melted chocolate (if using), and allow to set before serving.

COOK'S NOTES

Buy a good-quality cocoa powder and chocolate (if using) – it will make all the difference.

Raspberry, lemon, and almond bake

PREP 20 MINS · **COOK 40 MINS**

Special equipment • 20cm (8in) square loose-bottomed cake tin

SERVES 8

125g (4½oz) plain flour
1 tsp baking powder
75g (2½oz) ground almonds
150g (5½oz) butter, cubed
200g (7oz) caster sugar
juice of 1 lemon (about 3 tbsp)
1 tsp vanilla extract
2 large eggs
200g (7oz) fresh raspberries
icing sugar, to dust (optional)

1 Preheat the oven to 180°C (350°F/ Gas 4). Line the base and sides of the cake tin with baking parchment. Sift the flour into a bowl, add the baking powder and ground almonds, and mix well. In a pan, melt the butter, sugar, and lemon juice together, stirring until well combined.

2 Stir this syrupy mixture into the dry ingredients, then mix in the vanilla extract and the eggs, one at a time, until the mixture is smooth and well combined. Pour into the tin, then scatter the raspberries over the top. Bake for 35–40 minutes, or until golden and a skewer inserted into the cake comes out clean.

3 Cool in the tin for 10 minutes, then turn out and cool completely on a wire rack. Dust with icing sugar before serving (if using). To serve, cut into rectangles.

VARIATION This cake also works well with blueberries, or a mix of soft berries instead of the raspberries.

Berry friands

PREP 15 MINS · **COOK 35 MINS**

Special equipment • electric hand whisk • 6-cup muffin tin

MAKES 6

100g (3½oz) icing sugar
45g (1½oz) plain flour
75g (2½oz) ground almonds
3 large egg whites
75g (2½oz) unsalted butter, melted
150g (5½oz) mixed fresh berries,
   such as blueberries and raspberries

1 Preheat the oven to 180°C (350°F/ Gas 4). Sift the icing sugar and flour into a bowl, then stir in the ground almonds. In another bowl, whisk the egg whites with an electric hand whisk until they form soft peaks.

2 Gently fold the flour mixture and the melted butter into the egg whites to make a smooth batter. Spoon the batter into the muffin tin (lined with muffin cases if it isn't non-stick), then

scatter over the berries, pressing them down slightly into the batter so they all fit in. Bake for 30–35 minutes, or until golden brown and risen. Leave to cool in the tin.

VARIATION Use chopped stoned fruit such as apricots, peaches, or plums instead of the berries, but make sure they are really ripe and juicy.

Chocolate cake with chocolate fudge icing

PREP 20 MINS · COOK 40 MINS

Special equipment • 2 x 20cm (8in) round sandwich tins • electric hand whisk or mixer

SERVES 8–12

200g (7oz) self-raising flour
25g (scant 1oz) cocoa powder
4 large eggs
225g (8oz) caster sugar
225g (8oz) butter, at room temperature
1 tsp vanilla extract
1 tsp baking powder

For the chocolate fudge icing
45g (1½oz) cocoa powder
150g (5½oz) icing sugar
45g (1½oz) butter, melted
3 tbsp milk, plus a little extra to slacken the mixture

1 Preheat the oven to 180°C (350°F/ Gas 4). Grease the 2 sandwich tins, then line with baking parchment. Sift the flour and cocoa powder into a large bowl, and add all the other cake ingredients. Mix together with an electric whisk for a few minutes until well combined. Whisk in 2 tablespoons of warm water from the kettle so the mixture is soft enough to drop easily off the whisk beaters. Divide evenly between the sandwich tins, and smooth the tops.

2 Bake for 35–40 minutes, or until risen and firm to the touch, then leave to cool in the tins for 5 minutes before turning out to cool on wire racks.

3 Meanwhile, make the icing. Sift the cocoa powder and icing sugar into a bowl, add the butter and milk, and mix with an electric hand whisk until smooth and well combined. Add a little extra milk if the mixture is too thick – you need to be able to spread it easily. Spread over the tops of the two cooled cakes, then sandwich together.

> *COOK'S NOTES*
>
> The cakes are cooked when they start to shrink away from the edge of the tin.

Apple streusel cake

PREP 20 MINS • COOK 1¼ HRS

Special equipment • 20cm (8in) round loose-bottomed or springform cake tin • electric hand whisk

SERVES 8

125g (4½oz) plain flour
125g (4½oz) butter, at
  room temperature
125g (4½oz) caster sugar
1 tsp ground cinnamon
2 large eggs, lightly beaten
½ tsp vanilla extract
1 Bramley apple, peeled, cored,
  and cut into chunks
50g (1¾oz) sultanas

For the streusel topping
75g (2½oz) butter, cubed
100g (3½oz) plain flour
25g (scant 1oz) ground almonds
50g (1¾oz) caster sugar or light
  soft brown sugar
1 tsp ground cinnamon

1 Preheat the oven to 180°C (350°F/ Gas 4). Lightly grease and base-line the cake tin with baking parchment. Sift the flour into a bowl, add the butter, sugar, cinnamon, eggs, and vanilla extract, and mix with an electric hand whisk until pale, creamy, and well combined. Spoon the mixture into the tin and level the top. Scatter with the apple and sultanas.

2 In another bowl, rub the cubed butter for the topping into the flour with your fingertips until the mixture resembles breadcrumbs. Stir in the ground almonds, sugar, and cinnamon. Scatter over the fruit in the tin and level the top, pressing down slightly. Bake for 1¼ hours, or until a skewer inserted into the cake comes out clean with no trace of uncooked cake mixture (it will probably be a bit damp from the fruit, though). Leave to cool in the tin for 20 minutes and serve warm, or leave to cool completely.

Cheat...
Use ready-made crumble mixture, but add some ground cinnamon for extra flavour.

COOK'S NOTES

This cake also works well as a warm pudding served with custard, ice cream, or cream.

Pecan, coffee, and maple cake

PREP 15 MINS • COOK 40 MINS

Special equipment • 2 x 18cm (7in) round sandwich tins • electric hand whisk

SERVES 8

225g (8oz) self-raising flour
175g (6oz) caster sugar
175g (6oz) butter, at
  room temperature
3 large eggs
2 tbsp espresso, or strong coffee
75g (2½oz) pecans, chopped

For the icing
50g (1¾oz) butter
1 tbsp maple syrup
200g (7oz) icing sugar
2 tbsp espresso, or strong coffee
  made with water
20 pecan halves or 50g (1¾oz)
  chopped pecans, to decorate

1 Preheat the oven to 180°C (350°F/ Gas 4). Lightly grease the 2 sandwich tins and base-line with baking parchment. Sift the flour into a large bowl. Add the sugar, butter, eggs, and coffee, and mix with an electric hand whisk until well combined. The mixture should drop easily off the beaters when they are gently tapped on the edge of the bowl. Add a little extra coffee if it seems too thick. Stir in the pecans, divide the mixture between the tins, and level the tops.

2 Bake for 35–40 minutes, or until risen, firm to the touch, and slightly shrunken from the side of the tins. Leave to cool for 5 minutes in the tins, then transfer to a wire rack to cool completely.

3 Meanwhile, make the icing. Melt the butter and maple syrup together in a small pan. Sift the icing sugar into a bowl, add the butter and syrup mixture along with the coffee and mix with an electric hand whisk for a few minutes until thick, smooth, and a creamy coffee colour. Spread over the tops of the two cooled cakes, then sandwich together. Decorate around the edge of the top with pecans.

VARIATION
This works well with walnuts instead of pecans.

Coconut and lime cake

PREP 20 MINS · COOK 1¼ HRS

Special equipment • 18cm (7in) round deep tin • electric hand whisk or mixer

SERVES 8
225g (8oz) self-raising flour
225g (8oz) caster sugar
225g (8oz) butter, at
    room temperature
4 large eggs
50g (1¾oz) desiccated coconut
zest of 1 lime
2 tbsp lime juice

For the icing
100g (3½oz) icing sugar
zest of 1 lime
2 tbsp lime juice
300g (10oz) cream cheese,
    at room temperature
15g (½oz) toasted desiccated coconut,
    to decorate

1 Preheat the oven to 180°C (350°F/ Gas 4). Lightly grease the tin and base-line with baking parchment. Sift the flour into a large bowl, add the caster sugar, butter, and eggs and mix with an electric hand whisk until well combined. Whisk in the coconut, lime zest, and lime juice. Spoon into the tin and level the top. Bake for 1–1¼ hours, or until risen and firm to the touch. Leave to cool for 5 minutes in the tin, then cool completely on a wire rack. Carefully divide the cake into three equal layers using a serrated knife.

2 To make the icing, sift the icing sugar into a bowl, add the lime zest, lime juice, and cream cheese, and whisk with an electric hand whisk until the mixture starts to thicken. Taste to make sure it is sweet enough. Add more icing sugar if it isn't. Spread over the three layers of the cake, then sandwich them together. Scatter the toasted coconut over the top to decorate.

VARIATION Cut the cake into two rather than three layers. Spread the icing more thickly, to use it up.

> **COOK'S NOTES**
> Toast the desiccated coconut in a small non-stick frying pan. There is no need for any fat, as it is already very oily, but this means it can burn easily and stick to the bottom of the pan, so shake the pan gently over the heat until the coconut is golden brown.

Orange and pistachio cake

PREP 15 MINS · COOK 40 MINS

Special equipment • electric hand whisk • 20cm (8in) round springform cake tin

SERVES 6
175g (6oz) butter, at
    room temperature
175g (6oz) caster sugar
2 eggs
175g (6oz) self-raising flour
175g (6oz) Greek yogurt
75g (2½oz) pistachio nuts,
    finely chopped
75g (2½oz) blanched almonds,
    finely chopped
zest and juice of 1 orange
zest and juice of 1 lemon
1 tsp baking powder
mascarpone, to serve

1 Preheat the oven to 180°C (350°F/ Gas 4). Lightly grease the cake tin and base-line with baking parchment. Put the butter and sugar in a mixing bowl and whisk with an electric hand whisk for 5 minutes, or until pale and creamy. Whisking all the time, add the eggs one at a time, along with a little of the flour to stop the mixture curdling.

2 Add the yogurt, pistachio nuts, almonds, orange and lemon zest and juice, and mix well to form a smooth batter. Sift in the remaining flour and the baking powder and carefully fold in. Pour the mixture into the tin.

3 Bake in the oven for 40 minutes, or until a skewer inserted into the centre of the cake comes out clean. Remove from the oven and leave to cool in the tin for 10 minutes, then release the sides and leave to cool completely. Slice and serve with spoonfuls of mascarpone.

VARIATION Sift icing sugar over the top of the cake before serving.

Toffee apple tray bake

PREP 20 MINS · COOK 45 MINS

Special equipment • electric hand whisk or mixer • 22 x 30cm (8¾ x 12in) tin

MAKES 18 SQUARES
350g (12oz) Bramley apples, peeled, cored, and thinly sliced
squeeze of lemon juice
350g (12oz) self-raising flour
2 tsp baking powder
350g (12oz) light soft brown sugar
4 large eggs, lightly beaten
225g (8oz) butter, melted
1 tbsp caster sugar

For the toffee sauce
100g (3½oz) butter
100g (3½oz) light soft brown sugar
1 tbsp lemon juice
salt
crème fraîche, to serve (optional)

1 Preheat the oven to 180°C (350°F/Gas 4). Line the base and sides of the tin with baking parchment. Put the apple slices in a bowl and toss with the lemon juice to stop them turning brown while you make the cake mixture.

2 Sift the flour into a large mixing bowl, add the baking powder and brown sugar, and stir well. Mix in the eggs and the melted butter to make a smooth batter. Pour into the tin and smooth the top. Arrange the apple slices in three or four long lines along the top of the mixture and sprinkle with the caster sugar. Bake for 45 minutes, or until the cake is firm to the touch and a skewer inserted into the middle comes out clean.

3 Meanwhile, make the sauce by melting the butter, sugar, and lemon juice in a pan with a pinch of salt, whisking with an electric hand whisk until the mixture is thick, melted, and smooth. Leave to cool slightly. Pour the sauce over the cake while it is still in the tin, gently brushing the sauce all over the top of the cake. Serve warm or cold with a spoonful of crème fraîche, if you like.

Cheat...
Use a ready-made toffee sauce instead of making your own.

White chocolate and macadamia nut blondies

PREP 25 MINS · COOK 20 MINS

Special equipment • 22 x 30cm (8¾ x 12in) tin

MAKES 24
300g (10oz) white chocolate, chopped
175g (6oz) butter, cubed
300g (10oz) caster sugar
4 large eggs
225g (8oz) plain flour
100g (3½oz) macadamia nuts, roughly chopped

1 Preheat the oven to 200°C (400°F/Gas 6). Line the base and sides of the tin with baking parchment. In a bowl set over a pan of simmering water, melt the chocolate and butter together, stirring now and again until smooth. Remove, and leave to cool for about 20 minutes.

2 Once the chocolate has melted, mix in the sugar (the mixture may well become thick and grainy, but the eggs will loosen the mixture). Using a balloon whisk, stir in the eggs one at a time, making sure each is well mixed in before you add the next. Sift in the flour, fold it in, and then stir in the nuts. Pour the mixture into the tin and gently spread it out into the corners. Bake for 20 minutes, or until just firm to the touch on top but still soft underneath. Leave to cool completely in the tin, then cut into 24 squares, or rectangles for bigger blondies.

VARIATION
Add some dried chopped cranberries for added colour and texture.

COOK'S NOTES
When melting the chocolate, be careful that no water splashes into it – it will ruin the chocolate.

Chocolate and hazelnut brownies

  PREP 25 MINS | **COOK 15 MINS**

Special equipment • 23 x 30cm
(9 x 12in) tin

MAKES 24
300g (10oz) dark chocolate (at least
   50 per cent cocoa solids, or higher
   for more bitter brownies), chopped
175g (6oz) butter, cubed
300g (10oz) caster sugar
4 large eggs
200g (7oz) plain flour
25g (scant 1oz) cocoa powder
100g (3½oz) blanched hazelnuts,
   toasted and roughly chopped

1 Preheat the oven to 200°C (400°F/
Gas 6). Line the base and sides of
the tin with baking parchment. In
a bowl set over a pan of simmering
water, melt the chocolate and butter
together, stirring now and again, until
smooth. Remove, and leave to cool.

2 Once the chocolate has melted,
mix in the sugar and then the eggs,
one at a time, making sure each is
well combined before you add the
next. Sift in the flour and cocoa
powder, then fold in gently before
stirring in the chopped nuts – the

mixture should be thick and glossy.
Pour into the prepared tin and spread
gently so the mixture fills the corners,
then smooth the top.

3 Bake for 12–15 minutes, or
until just firm to the touch on top
and still soft underneath. Leave to
cool completely in the tin, then cut
into 24 squares, or rectangles for
bigger brownies.

 VARIATION
Chopped walnuts or pecans
work well in place of hazelnuts.
Or leave the nuts out altogether
if you have an allergy.

COOK'S NOTES

*Never overcook brownies or you
will end up with chocolate cake.
It is time to take them from the
oven when they are just firm to
the touch on top but still gooey
in the centre. They will firm up
as they cool.*

Strawberry and cream Victoria sandwich

   PREP 20 MINS | **COOK 25 MINS** | ❄

Special equipment • 2 x 20cm (8in)
sandwich tins • electric hand whisk

SERVES 8
225g (8oz) butter, at
   room temperature
225g (8oz) caster sugar
4 large eggs, lightly beaten
225g (8oz) self-raising flour

For the strawberry and cream filling
100ml (3½oz) double cream
175g (6oz) strawberries, hulled
   and sliced
icing sugar, to dust

1 Preheat the oven to 180°C (350°F/
Gas 4). Line the bases of the sandwich
tins with baking parchment. In a bowl,
mix the butter and sugar with an
electric hand whisk until light and
creamy. Whisk in the eggs a little at
a time, adding in a little of the flour

if the mixture looks as if it is going
to curdle. Sift in the remaining flour
and fold in gently with a large metal
spoon. Divide the mixture between
the tins and bake for 25 minutes,
or until risen and firm to the
touch. Leave to cool in the tins
for 5 minutes, then transfer to
a wire rack to cool completely.

2 To make the filling, place the cream
in a bowl and whisk with an electric
hand whisk until soft peaks form.
Spread over one of the cakes, then
top with strawberries. Place the other
cake on top, then dust thickly with
icing sugar.

 VARIATION
For a more intense strawberry
flavour, spread a layer of
strawberry jam on the top of
first cake before you cover it
with cream.

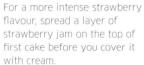 **FOOD FOR FRIENDS**

Cherry and almond cake

PREP 20 MINS **COOK 1¾ HRS**

Special equipment • electric hand whisk or mixer • 20cm (8in) round, deep, loose-bottomed or springform cake tin

SERVES 8-10

150g (5½oz) butter, at
   room temperature
150g (5½oz) caster sugar
2 large eggs, lightly beaten
250g (9oz) self-raising flour, sifted
1 tsp baking powder
150g (5½oz) ground almonds
1 tsp vanilla extract
75ml (2½fl oz) whole milk
400g (14oz) pitted cherries
25g (scant 1oz) whole blanched
   almonds, chopped (lengthways
   looks pretty)

1 Preheat the oven to 180°C (350°F/ Gas 4). Lightly grease the cake tin and line the base with baking parchment. In a bowl, beat together the butter and sugar with an electric hand whisk until pale and creamy. Beat in the eggs one at a time, adding a tablespoon of the flour before adding the second egg.

2 Mix in the remaining flour, baking powder, ground almonds, and vanilla extract. Stir in the milk – the mixture should drop easily off the beaters

of the whisk. Mix in half the cherries, then spoon the mixture into the tin and smooth the top. Scatter the remaining cherries over the top, followed by the chopped almonds.

3 Bake for 1 hour 30 minutes–1 hour 45 minutes, or until golden and firm to the touch. The exact cooking time will depend on how juicy the cherries are. To test, insert a skewer into the cake – if there is uncooked mixture on it, put the cake back into the oven for another 5 minutes and test again. If the surface of the cake starts to brown too much before it is fully cooked, cover with foil. When cooked, leave to cool in the tin for 5 minutes, then transfer to a wire rack to cool completely before serving.

Cheat...
If you can't get hold of fresh cherries, use a 425g can or jar of cherries, but make sure you drain them well.

Banana, date, and walnut loaf

PREP 20 MINS **COOK 1¼ HRS** ❄

Special equipment • electric hand whisk • 18 x 9cm (7 x 3½in) 2lb loaf tin

SERVES 8-10

100g (3½oz) butter, at
   room temperature
100g (3½oz) caster sugar
2 large eggs
225g (8oz) self-raising flour, sifted
2 bananas, about 300g (10oz)
   in total, unpeeled
100g (3½oz) stoned dates
   (medjool are best), chopped
50g (1¾oz) walnut pieces,
   roughly chopped
1 tsp baking powder

1 Preheat the oven to 180°C (350°F/ Gas 4). Line the loaf tin with baking parchment. In a bowl, beat the butter and sugar with an electric hand whisk until pale, light, and fluffy. Add the eggs one at a time, beating well as

you do so, and adding a tablespoon of the flour after each one. This will stop the mixture curdling.

2 Peel and mash the bananas in a small bowl with a fork, then stir into the loaf mixture, along with the chopped dates and walnuts. Fold in the remaining flour and the baking powder, then spoon the mixture into the tin. Smooth the top, pressing well into the corners. Bake for 1 hour–1 hour 15 minutes, or until risen and firm to the touch. If the top of the cake starts to brown too much before it is fully cooked, cover with foil. Leave to cool in the tin, then cut into slices.

COOK'S NOTES

For maximum sweetness, use really ripe bananas with brown speckled skins.

Light fruitcake

Special equipment • electric hand whisk or mixer • deep 20cm (8in) round tin

SERVES 8–12
175g (6oz) butter, at
    room temperature
175g (6oz) light soft brown sugar
3 large eggs
250g (9oz) self-raising flour, sifted
2–3 tbsp milk
300g (10oz) mixed dried fruit
    (use a luxury mix if possible)

1 Preheat the oven to 180°C (350°F/Gas 4). Line the base and sides of the tin with baking parchment. In a bowl, beat the butter and sugar together with an electric hand whisk until pale and creamy, then beat in the eggs, one at a time, adding a little of the flour after each one. Stir in the rest of the flour and the milk – the mixture should drop easily off the beaters. Add the dried fruit and mix until well combined.

2 Spoon the mixture into the tin, level the top, and bake for 1 hour 30 minutes–1 hour 45 minutes, or until firm to the touch and a skewer inserted into the middle of the cake comes out clean. Leave in the tin to cool completely.

Lemon, lime, and poppy seed cake

Special equipment • electric hand whisk • 18 x 9cm (7 x 3½in) 2lb loaf tin

SERVES 8–10
175g (6oz) butter, at
    room temperature
175g (6oz) caster sugar
3 large eggs, lightly beaten
zest of 1 lemon
zest of 1 lime
2 tbsp lemon juice
175g (6oz) self-raising flour
2 tbsp poppy seeds
1 tbsp lime juice
100g (3½oz) icing sugar

1 Preheat the oven to 180°C (350°F/Gas 4). Line the base and sides of the loaf tin with baking parchment. In a large bowl, beat the butter and caster sugar together with an electric hand whisk until light and fluffy. Beat in the eggs a little at a time, then gently fold in the lemon and lime zest, together with 1 tablespoon of the lemon juice. Sift in the flour, then fold in with the poppy seeds.

2 Transfer to the tin and smooth the top. Bake for 1 hour, or until risen, golden, and firm to the touch. Leave to cool in the tin for 5 minutes, then remove and leave to cool completely on a wire rack.

3 Meanwhile, mix the remaining lemon juice with the lime juice in a bowl. Sift in the icing sugar and combine to make a runny glacé icing. Place a piece of baking parchment under the wire rack to catch the drips, then spoon the icing over the cake, letting it drizzle down the sides. Leave to set before serving.

COOK'S NOTES

If you don't like poppy seed, use the same amount of chopped pine nuts instead.

Blueberry muffins

PREP 15 MINS · COOK 20 MINS

Special equipment • 12-cup muffin tin

MAKES 12
50g (1¾oz) butter
250g (9oz) self-raising flour
1 tsp baking powder
75g (2½oz) caster sugar
finely grated zest of
    1 lemon (optional)
salt
250g (9oz) plain yogurt
2 large eggs, lightly beaten
250g (9oz) blueberries

1 Preheat the oven to 200°C (400°F/ Gas 6). Line a muffin tin with muffin cases. Melt the butter in a small pan, then leave to cool. Sift the flour into a large bowl, mix in the baking powder, sugar, lemon zest (if using), and a pinch of salt, then make a well in the centre.

2 Mix the yogurt, eggs, and cooled melted butter together in a large jug, then pour into the dry ingredients, along with the blueberries. Mix until just combined, but don't over-mix or the muffins will be heavy. Don't worry if there are a few lumps left in the mixture.

3 Spoon evenly into the muffin cases and bake for 20 minutes, or until risen and golden. Cool in the tin for 5 minutes, then serve warm or leave to cool.

 VARIATION Use raspberries in place of blueberries, or orange zest instead of the lemon.

COOK'S NOTES
The muffins are best eaten warm, soon after making, or on the day they're made.

Spiced honey cake

PREP 10 MINS · COOK 35 MINS

Special equipment • 9 x 18cm (3½ x 7in) 2lb loaf tin

SERVES 8
125g (4½oz) self-raising flour
2 tsp mixed spice
1 tsp ground cinnamon
1 tsp ground ginger
½ tsp bicarbonate of soda
100g (3½oz) clear honey
60g (2oz) butter
60g (2oz) dark or light soft
    brown sugar
1 large egg
120ml (4fl oz) whole milk

1 Preheat the oven to 180°C (350°F/ Gas 4). Line the base and sides of a loaf tin with baking parchment. Sift the flour, spices, and bicarbonate of soda into a bowl. Melt the honey, butter, and sugar together in a pan until smooth and combined. Mix into the flour, then stir in the egg and milk until the mixture is well combined. Don't worry if it looks very runny – this is how it should look.

2 Pour into the tin and bake for 30–35 minutes, or until risen and firm to the touch. Leave to cool completely in the tin before serving.

 VARIATION Use a flavoured honey, or substitute the honey with golden syrup.

COOK'S NOTES
You can keep the cake for a few days, or even up to a week, in an airtight container – the flavour will mature and the texture will become stickier.

Spiced carrot and orange cake

PREP 20 MINS · **COOK 30 MINS**

Special equipment • 20cm (8in) square cake tin • electric hand whisk or mixer

MAKES 16 SQUARES
175g (6oz) self-raising flour
1 tsp ground cinnamon
1 tsp mixed spice
½ tsp bicarbonate of soda
100g (3½oz) light or dark soft brown sugar
150ml (5fl oz) sunflower oil or light olive oil
2 large eggs
75g (2½oz) golden syrup
125g (4½oz) carrots, trimmed and coarsely grated
zest of 1 orange

For the icing
75g (2½oz) icing sugar
100g (3½oz) cream cheese, at room temperature
1-2 tbsp orange juice
zest of 1 orange, plus extra to decorate (optional)

1 Preheat the oven to 180°C (350°F/Gas 4). Line the base and sides of a square cake tin with baking parchment. In a large bowl, mix together the flour, spices, bicarbonate of soda, and sugar. In another bowl, mix the oil, eggs, and syrup together, then combine with the dry ingredients. Stir in the carrot and orange zest, transfer to the tin and level the top. Bake for 30 minutes, or until firm to the touch. Leave to cool in the tin for 5 minutes, then cool completely on a wire rack.

2 For the icing, sift the icing sugar into a bowl, add the cream cheese, orange juice, and orange zest and whisk with an electric hand whisk until the mixture becomes thick and spreadable. When the cake is cool, spread the icing over the top. Decorate with extra orange zest (if using), and cut into 16 squares, to serve.

VARIATION Add 50g (1¾oz) chopped walnuts to the cake mixture and scatter more over the icing instead of the orange zest.

Sticky date flapjacks

PREP 25 MINS · **COOK 40 MINS**

Special equipment • 20cm (8in) square cake tin • blender

MAKES 16
200g (7oz) stoned dates (medjool are best), chopped
½ tsp bicarbonate of soda
200g (7oz) butter
200g (7oz) light soft brown sugar
2 tbsp golden syrup
300g (10oz) rolled oats

1 Preheat the oven to 160°C (325°F/Gas 3). Line a square cake tin with baking parchment. Place the dates and bicarbonate of soda in a pan with enough water to cover, simmer for 5 minutes, then drain, reserving the liquid. Whiz to a purée in a blender with 3 tablespoons cooking liquid, then set aside.

2 Melt the butter, sugar, and syrup together in a large pan, stirring until the mixture forms a smooth sauce (you might need to give it a quick whisk to bring it together). Stir in the oats, then press half the mixture into the base of the tin.

3 Spread the date purée over the top of the oats, then spoon the remaining oat mixture over the top, gently easing it over the dates. Bake for 40 minutes, or until golden brown. Leave to cool in the tin for 10 minutes, then mark into 16 squares. Leave to cool completely in the tin before serving.

VARIATION  For plain flapjacks, leave out the dates.

Tropical angel cake

PREP 15 MINS · COOK 30 MINS

Special equipment • electric hand whisk or mixer • 1.2 x 1.5-litre (2 x 2¾-pints) savarin ring mould

SERVES 6–8
4 large egg whites
½ tsp cream of tartar
150g (5½oz) caster sugar
50g (1¾oz) plain flour
10g (¼oz) cornflour
25g (scant 1oz) desiccated coconut

For the topping
200g (7oz) Greek yogurt
200g (7oz) mixed peeled and chopped tropical fruit, such as pineapple and mango
seeds and pulp from 2 passion fruits
lime zest, to decorate

1 Preheat the oven to 190°C (375°F/ Gas 5). Put the egg whites, cream of tartar, and 1 tablespoon of cold water in a large mixing bowl and whisk with an electric whisk or mixer until the mixture forms stiff peaks. Whisk in the sugar 1 tablespoon at a time until the mixture is stiff and shiny.

2 Sift in the flour and cornflour and gently fold in with the coconut until well combined. Carefully spoon into the tin and smooth the top, pressing down gently so there are no air spaces left. Bake for 15 minutes, then reduce the oven temperature to 180°C (350°F/Gas 4) and bake for a further 15 minutes, until the mixture is firm to the touch and golden brown.

3 Place the tin upside-down on a wire rack and leave until completely cold, then carefully ease the cake out of the tin with a round-bladed knife or small metal spatula and place on a serving plate.

4 To make the topping, beat the yogurt lightly so it is smooth and creamy, then spoon into the centre of the cake. Top with the fruit, then drizzle over the passion fruit seeds. Finish by scattering over the lime zest.

Cheat... Use shop-bought ready-prepared fruit, or well-drained fruit from cans.

Apricot crumble shortbread

PREP 20 MINS · COOK 1¼ HRS

Chilling • 1 hour
Special equipment • electric hand whisk • 12.5 x 35.5cm (5¼ x 14¼in) tin

MAKES 10 BARS OR 20 SQUARES
200g (7oz) butter, at room temperature
100g (3½oz) caster sugar
200g (7oz) plain flour
100g (3½oz) cornflour
400g can apricots in natural juice, drained and roughly chopped

For the topping
75g (2½oz) butter, cubed
150g (5½oz) plain flour
75g (2½oz) demerara sugar or caster sugar

1 Cream the butter and sugar together in a bowl with an electric hand whisk until pale and creamy. Sift in the flour and cornflour and combine so that the mix comes together to form a dough. (You'll probably need to use your hands to bring it together at the end.) Knead the dough lightly until smooth, then push evenly into the base of the tin, lined with baking parchment, and smooth the top. Chill in the refrigerator for at least an hour or until firm.

2 Preheat the oven to 180°C (350°F/ Gas 4). Make the topping by rubbing the butter into the flour in a bowl with your fingertips until the mixture resembles breadcrumbs. Stir in the sugar. Scatter the apricots evenly over the chilled base, then top with the buttery crumb mixture, pressing down quite firmly. Bake for 1¼ hours, or until a skewer inserted into the centre comes out clean with no uncooked mixture on it (it might be a bit damp from the fruit, though). Leave to cool in the tin. When cold, remove from the tin and cut into 10 bars or 20 squares.

VARIATION Use plums instead of apricots.

COOK'S NOTES
You can make the topping in the food processor – use the pulse button so the mixture isn't overworked.

Ginger biscuits

Special equipment • electric hand whisk or mixer

MAKES ABOUT 35
225g (8oz) butter, at
  room temperature
175g (6oz) light or dark soft
  brown sugar
1 tbsp syrup from a jar of stem ginger
1 large egg
350g (12oz) self-raising flour
1 heaped tbsp ground ginger
3 balls of stem ginger in syrup,
  drained and finely chopped

1 Preheat the oven to 190°C (375°F/Gas 5). Line two baking trays with baking parchment. In a bowl, mix the butter, sugar, and syrup together with an electric hand whisk or mixer until creamy. Mix in the egg until combined, then work in the flour, ground ginger, and stem ginger until the mixture comes together to form a soft dough.

2 Roll the dough into about 35 balls, each the size of a walnut, and place on the baking trays. Flatten them with your fingers, then bake in two batches for 12–15 minutes, or until golden brown. Carefully transfer to a wire rack and leave to cool completely.

 VARIATION Leave out the stem ginger and syrup and use a tablespoon of golden syrup or black treacle instead.

COOK'S NOTES
The biscuits will firm up as they cool, so don't worry if they're still a little soft when you take them out of the oven.

Shortbread wedges

Chilling • 1 hour
Special equipment • 18cm (7in) round cake tin • electric hand whisk or mixer

MAKES 8 WEDGES
100g (3½oz) butter, at
  room temperature
50g (1¾oz) caster sugar, plus a little
  extra to dust
100g (3½oz) plain flour
50g (1¾oz) cornflour

1 Preheat the oven to 160°C (325°F/Gas 3). Lightly grease the cake tin. In a bowl, cream the butter and sugar together with an electric hand whisk or mixer until pale and creamy. Sift in the flour and cornflour and beat until the mixture forms a stiff dough. Knead lightly to bring it together, then push the dough into the tin and smooth it down. Prick with a fork, then mark into 8 wedges. Chill the dough for at least an hour, or until firm.

2 Bake for 40 minutes, or until pale golden and firm to the touch. While the shortbread is still warm, mark the wedges again, dust with a little caster sugar, and leave to cool completely in the tin. When cold, cut into wedges.

 VARIATION To make individual biscuits rather than wedges, cook the dough in small rounds on a baking tray.

COOK'S NOTES
Use good-quality butter – it will give the shortbread the best flavour.

523

Vanilla cupcakes

PREP 25 MINS · **COOK** 20 MINS

Special equipment • electric hand whisk or mixer • 12-cup patty tin

MAKES 12

125g (4½oz) butter, at
    room temperature
125g (4½oz) caster sugar
2 large eggs
125g (4½oz) self-raising flour, sifted
1 tsp vanilla extract
1 tbsp milk, if necessary

For the icing
100g (3½oz) icing sugar
15g (½oz) cocoa powder (optional)
100g (3½oz) butter, at
    room temperature
few drops of vanilla extract
25g (scant 1oz) milk or dark
    chocolate, shaved with a vegetable
    peeler (optional)

1 Preheat the oven to 190°C (375°F/Gas 5). Line the patty tin with parchment cupcake cases. Place the butter and sugar in a bowl, and whisk with an electric hand whisk or mixer until pale and fluffy. Beat

in the eggs one at a time, adding a little of the flour after you add each one. Add the vanilla extract and then the rest of the flour, and mix until smooth and combined – the mixture should drop easily off the beaters. If it doesn't, stir in the milk. Divide the mixture among the parchment cases using two teaspoons. Bake for 20 minutes, or until risen, golden, and firm to the touch. Transfer the cupcakes to a wire rack to cool.

2 To make the icing, sift the icing sugar and cocoa powder (if using), into a bowl, add the butter and the vanilla extract, and whisk with an electric hand whisk until the mixture is light and fluffy. Ice the cupcakes, giving the top of each one a swirly design. Scatter over the chocolate shavings, if using.

VARIATION

For lemon cupcakes, add the zest of ½ lemon to the cake mixture and 1-2 tablespoons lemon juice to the icing. Leave out the cocoa powder.

Swiss roll

PREP 20 MINS · **COOK** 15 MINS

Special equipment • electric hand whisk or mixer • 32.5 x 23cm (13 x 9in) Swiss roll tin

SERVES 8-10

3 large eggs
100g (3½oz) caster sugar, plus
    extra to sprinkle
salt
75g (2½oz) self-raising flour
1 tsp vanilla extract
6 tbsp strawberry jam, raspberry jam,
    lemon curd, or hazelnut spread

1 Preheat the oven to 200°C (400°F/Gas 6). Line the base and sides of the Swiss roll tin with baking parchment. In a large bowl set over a pan of simmering water, whisk the eggs, sugar, and a pinch of salt with an electric hand whisk for 5 minutes, or until very thick and creamy – any of the mixture dripping from the beaters should sit on the surface for a few moments before sinking in.

2 Remove the bowl from the pan and sit it on a work surface. Whisk the mixture for another minute, or two until cool. Sift in the flour, add the vanilla extract, and fold in very gently. Pour into the tin and gently level into the corners. Bake for

12-15 minutes, or until firm to the touch and the cake has shrunk away from the sides of the tin.

3 Sprinkle a large sheet of baking parchment with caster sugar, then turn the cake out upside-down onto it. Leave to cool for 5 minutes, then peel off the parchment the cake was cooked in. If the jam is too thick to spread, warm it in a pan, then spread it over the top of the cake. Make a small indent with the back of a knife along one of the short sides, about 2cm (¾in) in from the edge. With this side facing towards you, start to roll the cake up, using the parchment to keep it tightly rolled and in shape. When the cake is completely rolled up, leave to cool in the parchment. Peel off the parchment and place the cake, joint downwards, on a serving plate. Dust with extra caster sugar, if needed, before serving.

COOK'S NOTES

Swiss rolls are best eaten on the day they are made, as they do not contain added fat to help them keep.

FOOD FOR FRIENDS

Chocolate marble cake

PREP 15 MINS · COOK 1¼ HRS

Special equipment • electric hand whisk or mixer • 18 x 9cm (7 x 3½in) 2lb loaf tin

SERVES 8–10
175g (6oz) self-raising flour
1 tsp baking powder
175g (6oz) butter, at room temperature
175g (6oz) caster sugar
3 large eggs
1 tsp vanilla extract
1–2 tbsp milk
1 tbsp cocoa powder

1 Preheat the oven to 180°C (350°F/ Gas 4). Line a loaf tin with baking parchment. Sift the flour into a large mixing bowl, add the baking powder, butter, sugar, eggs, and vanilla extract and mix together with an electric hand whisk until well combined. Whisk in enough of the milk so that the mixture drops easily off the beaters.

2 Spoon half the mixture into a second bowl and mix in the cocoa powder to make the chocolate part of the cake. Spoon the two mixtures alternately into the tin, then lightly swirl together with a knife or skewer in a figure-of-eight pattern to create the marbled effect.

3 Bake for 1 hour 15 minutes, until risen and firm to the touch. Leave to cool in the tin for 5 minutes, then turn out on to a wire rack to cool completely.

VARIATION
For extra flavour, add the zest of 1 orange.

COOK'S NOTES

The marbled appearance of the cake depends on how carefully you swirl the two mixtures together. Swirl them together thoroughly for a marbled look.

Marmalade and ginger loaf

PREP 15 MINS · COOK 1¼ HRS

Special equipment • electric hand whisk or mixer • 18 x 9cm (7 x 3½in) 2lb loaf tin

SERVES 8–10
225g (8oz) self-raising flour
175g (6oz) butter, at room temperature
175g (6oz) caster sugar
3 large eggs, lightly beaten
1 tsp baking powder
1 tsp ground cinnamon
1 tsp ground ginger
150g (5½oz) thick-cut Seville orange marmalade, plus 2 tbsp extra to brush

1 Preheat the oven to 180°C (350°F/Gas 4). Line the base and sides of a loaf tin with baking parchment. Sift the flour into a large bowl, add the butter, sugar, eggs, baking powder, spices, and marmalade, and mix with an electric hand whisk until well combined.

2 Pour into the tin and smooth the top. Bake for 1 hour 15 minutes, or until risen and firm to the touch. Cover the top of the cake with foil for the last 30 minutes if it starts to brown too quickly. Leave to cool in the tin for 5 minutes. Warm the marmalade in a pan, then brush the top of the cake generously with it. Remove from the tin, and leave to cool completely on a wire rack.

FOOD FOR FRIENDS

Dorling Kindersley would like to thank:

Kate Titford for contributing to the *Cakes and Bakes* chapter.

Guy Mirabella for contributing to the *Simple Starters*,
No-fuss Finger Food and Dips, and *Barbecue* chapters.

Editors Michael Fullalove, Siobhan O'Connor

Nutritionist Fiona Hunter

Designers Miranda Harvey, Mandy Earey

Thanks to Susan Downing for commissioning all of the book's photography,
including selection of photography teams and creation of the style brief.

Art Directors Nicky Collings, Luis Peral-Aranda, Lisa Pettibone, Sue Storey

Prop Stylists Sue Rowlands, Rachel Jukes

Food Stylists Annie Rigg, Fergal Connolly and Aya Nishimura, Cara Hobday,
Jenny White, Jane Lawrie, Penny Stephens

Presentation styling Nicola Powling

Indexer Marie Lorimer

Proofreader Sue Morony

Editor-in-Chief acknowledgments:

A very big thank you to Mary-Clare Jerram at Dorling Kindersley for giving me
the opportunity to be involved, and sharing her enthusiasm and excitement for
my ideas. And a massive thank you to my editor Laura Nickoll, who I have
enjoyed working with so much. She has had such passion for the project,
remained utterly calm throughout, and has been an infallible support.

Also to friends and family, that have tried, tested, suggested, and tasted recipes;
my mum for being a real home cook; my daughters Kim and Lorna for being good
eaters (but I wish they would cook more!); and Jos, my husband, for his invaluable
advice, and for being the most patient human being I've ever met.

Useful information

All the recipes have been tested on a gas ring hob and an electric oven – for a fan oven reduce the temperature by approximately 10°C. If in doubt about how accurate your oven is, it may be wise to invest in an oven thermometer.

Measurements

There are many variables in cooking, from intensity of the heat to type of pan used, so certain recipes may take less time or longer. All recipes have been tested, and the cooking times given are as accurate as possible, but learn to rely on your instincts for doneness, and check as you go.

• Use the measurements stated, especially when baking.
• Use measuring spoons. The recipes refer to a level spoon, unless otherwise stated.
• Use a measuring jug for liquids, and take the measurement looking at it from eye level.
• Never mix metric and imperial.

Conversion charts

LINEAR MEASURES

3mm	(⅛in)	2.5cm	(1in)	10cm	(4in)	20cm	(8in)	30cm	(12in)
5mm	(¼in)	5cm	(2in)	12cm	(5in)	23cm	(9in)	46cm	(18in)
1cm	(½in)	6cm	(2½in)	15cm	(6in)	25cm	(10in)	50cm	(20in)
2cm	(¾in)	7.5cm	(3in)	18cm	(7in)	28cm	(11in)	61cm	(24in)
								77cm	(30in)

WEIGHTS

10g	(¼oz)	85g	(3oz)	250g	(9oz)	750g	(1lb 10oz)	2kg	(4½lb)
15g	(½oz)	100g	(3½oz)	300g	(10oz)	800g	(1¾lb)	2.25kg	(5lb)
20g	(¾oz)	115g	(4oz)	350g	(12oz)	900g	(2lb)	2.5kg	(5½lb)
25g	(scant 1oz)	125g	(4½oz)	400g	(14oz)	1kg	(2¼lb)	2.7kg	(6lb)
30g	(1oz)	140g	(5oz)	450g	(1lb)	1.1kg	(2½lb)	3kg	(6½lb)
45g	(1½oz)	150g	(5½oz)	500g	(1lb 2oz)	1.25kg	(2¾lb)		
50g	(1¾oz)	175g	(6oz)	550g	(1¼lb)	1.35kg	(3lb)		
60g	(2oz)	200g	(7oz)	600g	(1lb 5oz)	1.5kg	(3lb 3oz)		
75g	(2½oz)	225g	(8oz)	675g	(1½lb)	1.8kg	(4lb)		

VOLUME MEASURES

1 tsp		75ml	(2½fl oz)	240ml	(8fl oz)	500ml	(16fl oz)	1.4 litres	(2½ pints)
2 tsp		90ml	(3fl oz)	250ml	(8fl oz)	600ml	(1 pint)	1.5 litres	(2¾ pints)
1 tbsp (which is		100ml	(3½fl oz)	300ml	(10fl oz)	750ml	(1¼ pints)	1.7 litres	(3 pints)
equivalent to 3 tsp)		120ml	(4fl oz)	360ml	(12fl oz)	900ml	(1½ pints)	2 litres	(3½ pints)
2 tbsp		150ml	(5fl oz)	400ml	(14fl oz)	1 litre	(1¾ pints)	3 litres	(5¼ pints)
3 tbsp		200ml	(7fl oz)	450ml	(15fl oz)	1.2 litres	(2 pints)		
4 tbsp or 60ml (2fl oz)									